CHRISTIANITY
IN
WORLD HISTORY

CHRISTIANITY
IN
WORLD HISTORY

The Meeting of the Faiths
of East and West

by

AREND TH. VAN LEEUWEN

Foreword by Dr Hendrik Kraemer

Translated by

H. H. HOSKINS

CHARLES SCRIBNER'S SONS
New York

75,310

Contents

v

CONTENTS   vii

Preface

THE present book was written after a number of years of active missionary service in Indonesia, when a period of enforced furlough gave me the opportunity to rethink my experiences in parts of the Muslim world. The first draft originated from a contribution to the study scheme, 'The Word of God and the Living Faiths of Men,' of what was then the Department of Missionary Studies of the International Missionary Council and the World Council of Churches. It passed through its first test in a series of lectures for the Graduate Course of Ecumenical Studies of the Ecumenical Institute near Geneva.

I want to express my sincere gratitude to the Missionary Council of the Netherlands Reformed Church in whose service this book was written, and particularly to its Secretary, Mr S. C. Count van Randwijck, for his continuous practical and spiritual encouragement. Publication was made possible largely through the efforts of the Rev. Victor Hayward. From the very beginning the Rev. David Paton took a great interest in its theme and was willing to read the manuscript. It was a real pleasure to co-operate with the Rev. H. H. Hoskins over the translation, and with the editor, Miss Barbara Sullivan.

A. TH. VAN LEEUWEN

Foreword

IT is a great pleasure to me to write a foreword to this important book written by my friend, Dr A. Th. van Leeuwen. I do not conceive such a foreword in the vein of a laudatory advertisement, nor as a first attempt at a critical assessment. I only want to give a word of strong and warm commendation, supported by some arguments to indicate the significance of this book.

From time to time the appearance of a book is an 'event'. Dr van Leeuwen's book definitely falls into this category. Whether looked at from the angle of cultural history, cultural philosophy, theology or Christian missions, it fully deserves the description of an 'event'. It starts in the first chapter by making a scholarly and imaginative use of cultural anthropology and the enormous extension of horizons this science has opened up for us in our efforts to understand the character and spread of civilizations over the globe since the appearance of the great revolution, represented by the agricultural/pastoral neolithic civilization. Against this background, in succeeding chapters, the total cultural history of mankind in its representative forms is surveyed and characterized in a masterful way, which makes the book a spiritual and intellectual delight. The two key words around which the sketches of these civilizations move are 'ontocracy' and 'theocracy'. All the great civilizations of the Near East, of the Middle East and the Mediterranean, of India and China, have been 'ontocratic'; that is to say they were founded upon an apprehension of cosmic totality. Dr van Leeuwen explains this fundamental fact in great detail and with a firm grasp of the essential motive forces.

The pivot of the book is contained in Chapters Two and Three, where a theological analysis of the Old and New Testaments concentrates on the crucial point that the Bible is the only place where the ontocratic view is rejected without compromise in the name of theocracy. The only other place, besides Israel, where emancipation from the ontocratic conception of man and world has been realized, is Greece, though here it was on the different basis of the logos in man.

The main aim of the book is, however, to interpret the peculiarly dynamic character of Western civilization and its world-wide explosive effect, particularly in the present revolutionary stage of technocracy, which is creating an unprecedented crisis for all religions,

Christianity included. The great importance of the book lies not so much in the fascinating and often provocative way in which it describes the meaning and spirit of all the great civilizations up to the present time of revolutionary encounter and interpenetration, but in the analysis of Western civilization as a unique phenomenon, in comparison with and contradistinction to the great ontocratic civilizations—a uniqueness which can only be accounted for by the biblical-prophetical and Greek rational strains in it. As far as I know, Dr van Leeuwen's book is the first one in which this has been accomplished so comprehensively and with so much knowledge. The only comparable book is Northrop's *The Meeting of East and West*, but with regard to Western civilization it does not appreciate the significance of the prophetic-biblical view and with regard to Eastern civilization it is too exclusively riveted to China.

Although in the nature of the case Dr van Leeuwen's book occupies itself intensively with the past, its real object is not to afford us an excellent piece of historical writing. Its concern is the present and future of this planetary world, into which the dynamic of Western civilization has brought us, and which confronts the whole world with the question: What is man? This also confronts the Church and Christian missions with the necessity for a total re-examination of the ways in which their calling is expressed. The book fully deserves and, I hope, will evoke scholarly discussion. Still more does it deserve serious consideration and discussion in the world of Church and missions; for although many pages might give the impression of being written by a brilliantly gifted cultural anthropologist and historian, the book is really born out of a passionate devotion to the missionary obligation of the Church and a deep concern for helping to trace new ways for its fulfilment. The last chapter of the book, on Christianity in a planetary world, evidences this concern very plainly. It need cause no amazement that, in comparison with the magnificent, wide divine-human framework in which our present planetary world has been set, the final chapter makes a fragmentary impression. It cannot be otherwise, as we are no spectators of a piece of enacted history, but involved as actors in it. That being so, this unusually important book should not only become a subject for reviews, but the focus of thorough discussion from many sides. I for one, therefore, express the wish for a fuller explanation and motivation from Dr van Leeuwen's pen in the near future of what is *concretely* implied in the well-known ecumenical proposition that the whole Church must bring the whole Gospel to the whole world. Admirable as that expression is, it is in danger of remaining a seductive slogan. I have the same wish with regard to a more explicit spelling out of the meaning and purport of 'secularism' in the biblical perspective, and of what is concretely meant when we say that 'in this age of ours "Christianization" can only mean that peoples become involved in the onward movement of Christian history.' I close by expressing these wishes, because I am confident that Dr van Leeuwen, who here only touches on these points in passing in his final chapter, has abundant ability to shed more light upon them.

H. KRAEMER

One

Christianity and Cultures

THE face of the world in this twentieth century of ours is under-going changes of a revolutionary—one might say of a truly volcanic—character. It seems fairly certain that the period of Western domination is coming to an end. The Asian peoples have won their independence and the process of emancipation in Africa keeps that continent in a state of ferment.

If one thing is crystal clear, however, it is that the end of Western domination does not in the least mean the end of expansion so far as Western civilization is concerned; on the contrary, that would appear to be on the point of achieving conquests greater than any it has made hitherto. Of course, its development in recent times has been attended by enormous dangers.

Ever since the First World War took place Europe has been obsessed by a recurrent mood of defeatism. The various prophecies warning of nihilism round the corner came true in the most frightful way in the frenzied eruption of National Socialism, which took place, we must remember, among a people to whom belonged the very greatest triumphs of Western civilization. In face of that nightmarish horror all 'progress' must stand indicted. However, it remains true that Western civilization has not been halted in its tracks; it marches irresistibly on, careless of the abyss which lies on either side the way. In fact its advance determines the relative positions of power in the world today. Europe has been obliged to surrender her hegemony in favour of the two powers able most freely and fully to exploit the Western technological revolution: the United States and Soviet Russia. By resolutely adapting herself to the demands of Western technocracy Japan has been enabled to grasp at control over the 'Asiatic sphere of interest'. With the Communist revolution in China the signs are the same, although the ideology is different. As for the other nations in Asia they can only hope to keep their newly won independence so long as they do not drop too far behind in the present race for rapid technological advance. If they should fail on that score, their political sovereignty will be just a façade serving to conceal behind it the real dispositions of power in the world.

It would be a very serious mistake therefore to suppose that the thing of primary significance about this age in which we live is simply that the period of 'colonialism' is drawing to a close. No doubt the political emancipation of the African and Asian peoples is the most spectacular and apparently also the most dramatic aspect of the contemporary scene. What is of really crucial importance, however, is that though flying the colours of emancipation, they are joining the ever increasing ranks of those nations which follow the standard of Western civilization. The revolutions which the countries of Asia and Africa are now experiencing are their way of advancing further—on their own initiative and on their own behalf this time—along a path which Western dominance had formerly forced them to tread, whether they would or no. It is not only that their material prospects depend upon the degree of perfection to which they bring their technological development and upon the speed with which they do this; the ideology to which all this is geared and which drives it forward is in large measure of Western origin too. In the period of Western hegemony the necessary conditions were created under which the various nationalistic movements in the Orient were able to grow and are now powerfully constrained to move forward in a particular direction. Even in those cases where typical reactionary tendencies threaten to take control of this nationalism—as sometimes happens—any return to a pre-Western past is simply not feasible; not only would it lead in the end to political isolation and economic suicide, but a nationalism which tried to follow such a path to its logical conclusion would find it intrinsically impossible and have to admit defeat. For him who has once eaten of the tree of Western civilization there can be no turning back; he finds himself caught up in a history from which there is no return and is thrust forward along a devious way, with gorges and precipices on either side, yet leading upwards towards broader prospects and more copious expectations which are to be realized only at the cost of greater and greater exertion and continuously mounting risk.

The period of Western hegemony, now almost over, has been accompanied by the expansion of Christianity on a world scale. One can scarcely deny that the two things have gone together. Naturally the relationship between them is not all that simple; the missionary movement has not been just the handmaid of white imperialism. Accusations to that effect are the outcome of sheer prejudice against Western missions and of a complete misunderstanding of what the motives behind them were. Anybody who takes the trouble to study the missionary history of the last two centuries must be struck at every turn by the very great degree of independence with which the whole missionary enterprise has discharged its calling, often in direct conflict with the clear interests of colonial government and colonial capitalism. That Western missions have also failed in many respects, have raised their voice all too faintly in situations which called for unconditional and prophetic protest and have often been far too unaware of being distracted by political and economic ends is beyond question. It is not to any of these things that I refer, however, when I write about a relationship between Western dominance and the spread of Christianity. That relationship is something more than a reprehensible foible; it arises out of the peculiar character which belongs to Western expansion as such.

In this connection it is helpful to make some comparison with the growth of Islam. This has always brought with it, sooner or later, a transformation according to an Islamic pattern of life in which religious, political, social and cultural influences together formed a self-contained whole. From no point of view could it be said, however, that for the Asian and African peoples the coming of Islam has meant a complete change in their traditional outlook and customary ways of life; and Islamic expansion has never, despite its initial successes, had the outlook, the dynamic or the technical means at its disposal to assume the proportions of a world-wide movement.

The modern expansion of the West, therefore, is a unique phenomenon in world history. Never before has one civilization spread itself over the entire globe. Never before have foreign domination and the penetration of new cultural influences taken so firm a hold upon the life of peoples and so profoundly affected the roots of existence as this process of transculturation among the Asian and African peoples is doing in modern times. For that matter the spread of a 'religion' and the transference of 'non-religious' aspects of a civilization have never in the past been anything like so loosely interconnected as is the case in modern times with the expansion of Christianity and the spread of Western civilization. Whereas multifarious elements of Western civilization have penetrated to the remotest corners of the earth and been enthusiastically accepted there, the success of Christian missions has been relatively small. Churches which in most cases comprise a tiny fraction of the total population have been implanted—and that is all. Non-Western countries which have achieved independence are certainly implementing a programme of Westernization; but, generally speaking, that is coupled with an open aversion to Christianization.

It is at this point, though, that the questions begin to crowd in upon us. Is it not precisely within the bosom of Christianity itself that this divorce—or distinction—between Western civilization and Christian faith has come about? And does it not in fact rest on the presuppositions of Christian thinking? Is not the process of emancipation from religious constraints, which is usually referred to as 'secularization', itself a product of Western Christian civilization, and has it not been set in motion by forces nurtured in the course of Christian history? Are not all the 'non-religious' elements of Western civilization—modern technology, science, democracy, capitalism, socialism, nationalism—which have thrust their way into non-Western countries and been welcomed there, among the fruits of that very civilization which was formed and driven forward by the dynamic spirit of Christianity? Could it be that in modern Western civilization Christianity is 'submerged', that it is coming now to the non-Western nations in the guise of 'secularism' and incognito, so to speak? What else could account for the strange ambition and mysterious ability of the West not only to expand but in so doing to eat away, like an acid, the essentially religious texture of the non-Western patterns of life? How explain otherwise the global perspective of Western expansionism and its universal fertility as the source of a world civilization in the making? Is it not conceivable that Christianity today has entered a phase of its history in which it presents itself no longer in the form of a self-contained *Corpus Christianum*, but in the bifurcated form of a greatly reduced, weakened and divided Church on the one hand and of a victorious 'secularized' civilization on the other? Is it unreasonable to maintain that the peculiar connection between Western expansion and the modern missionary enterprise must be understood as the special kind of relationship which exists between two branches of one and the same tree?

It is at any rate possible to present tentative propositions of this sort in a positive, theological form. Thus Lesslie Newbigin. in some outline notes for a biblical approach to modern history, recently asserted that:

> . . . What is happening now . . . is that the peoples who have no history are being drawn into the history of which the centre is Jesus Christ; and that is the only history. In other words, that which has been static, or at least cyclical, in which the only movement was round and round, life and death, rise and fall—that is being drawn into a movement which is linear and dynamic, which is moving irreversibly and can never be back where it was before. The ferment of change which arises from the impact upon ancient cultures of the Gospel, or at least of that kind of life which has its origin within Christendom, is the force which is giving an irreversible direction to that which was static or merely cyclical. When I say the impact of the Gospel or of that kind of life which has its origin within Christendom, I include technology, western political ideas, Communism—all those things which have come into the eastern world from the West and have their roots in the Christian tradition.[1]

Even if we are not prepared to accept such an ambitious thesis on our own account, that does not absolve us from the duty of finding an answer to the questions which it throws up. There is a good deal of talk nowadays about missionary frustration. By this is meant, of course, the frustration of the Western missionary enterprise; for nobody is going to suggest that the apostolic task of the Church of Jesus Christ, with which the New Testament confronts us, is in danger of being frustrated in our time. What is now in an obvious impasse is that particular form of Christian expansion which, setting out from the West, has during the last two hundred years embraced the world. It is not fortuitous that this impasse and the end of the period of Western dominance have come about together. Those critics who have insisted upon identifying the missionary movement with Western imperialism will say that the explanation stares one in the face. On the missionary side we must not let any specious answers of that sort interfere with sound thinking, but realize that it is all the more urgently demanded of us to think through, with all its implications, the problem which the present period sets before us.

Put in its simplest form, it comes down to asking whether in the independent countries of Asia there is nowadays any place for Western missions. Has the moment perhaps arrived for handing over the task of proclaiming the Gospel to the indigenous Churches, which are the

obvious instruments for the purpose and are unencumbered with the
enormous handicap of a foreign origin—the factor which puts such
great, and indeed almost insuperable, difficulties in the way of Western
missions? Has it not always been the ultimate aim of Western missions
to make themselves superfluous, and may it not be that the moment
has now arrived for putting them quietly to sleep? When the question
is put in that form, there are weighty reasons for answering it in the
negative. One may point to the crushing burden which the relatively
small and weak non-Western Churches are shouldering; one can point
out that in the face of so many hundreds of millions of non-Christians
the responsibility for evangelization is too great and too heavy for
them. The really decisive consideration, however, is the ecumenical
and supra-national nature of the world Church, which now, in the
hey-day of nationalism more than at any other time, cries out for the
most forceful demonstration.

Yet the problem cannot really be dealt with satisfactorily at this
level; time and again the issues will be decided by secondary factors.
The roots of the problem lie deeper. What is at stake here is not
primarily responsibility for evangelizing the non-Christian world any
more than it is the unity of the world Church. That the Western
missionary movement is required to make drastic changes where its
strategy, organization, method and spirit are concerned—that is quite
certain; and one can very well imagine that within the framework of
ecumenical relations between the Churches in Western and non-
Western countries various forms of co-operation will take shape,
wholly or partly new, and answering to the demands which evangelization makes of the world Church in the present era. But even if this
adjustment is made, the hard core of the problem would still not
have been tackled at all; for that is contained within the question of
the meaning, the purpose and the future of Western civilization itself.
The outstanding thing about the period of missionary activity now
behind us is surely not just that in it—and for the first time in history
—the Gospel has been preached 'to the ends of the earth', but that all
this came from the West. We have ventured to suppose that in the
spread of modern Western civilization throughout the world something of the spirit of 'Christianity incognito' is at work. Although
the period of Western domination is ending, the impact of Western
civilization on the non-Western world has only just entered the first
stage. What does that involve for the history of the Church? Along

with the period of Western dominance, the movement of Western missions—at any rate in the form it has assumed during that period— is also approaching its end. Yet is there not in the Western missionary enterprise an essential element which does not stand or fall with the specific form that enterprise has taken over the last two centuries, which may be able to find new channels of advance and may perhaps blossom forth in unexpected ways? In saying this I have in mind both the character of the missions as missions and in particular the fact that they are *Western*. One must of course distinguish the two aspects, although they properly belong together.

> Inasmuch as missions are a God-given task of the Church, they partake of its continuous, permanent character; their responsibility and activities extend beyond individual persons and generations. Apart from superior powers of world history, only human sin can make an untimely end of their labour.[2]

Thus writes van Randwijck in *Some Reflections of a Mission Board Secretary*. Naturally that holds good for every Church; the missionary mandate rests upon every congregation, whether in Boston or in South India. It comes of the very being of the Church that in every part of the world she has an equal part in her Lord's commission to preach the Gospel to the ends of the earth. There is no reason why the congregation of Madras should not bear the same apostolic responsibility towards the American people as, vice versa, the Churches of the United States have regarding the evangelization of India. However, the point at issue here is not the apostolic character of the Church as such but the particular historical calling which the Western Churches and missions have up till now fulfilled. Is their task finished then and must they now, as father to son, transfer their obligation to what we are in the habit of describing as 'the younger Churches'? If we assume for a moment that this is in fact the case, then we have to ask ourselves what then is the specific obligation which is being transferred? It is consequent upon the way that the Western Churches have acquired of looking on the non-Western world as the 'terrain' in which the Gospel of the Kingdom must be proclaimed. That task has not yet been completed; as yet it has hardly even been started on. It can be argued that the evangelization of the world is not due for completion until the Kingdom of God has come. The outlook of Western missions, however, is not shaped exclusively by the eschatological perspective, but in a special way by the historical significance of Western Christianity and Christian civilization. By 'missions' was meant 'going forth into the non-Christian world', which in practice came to the same thing as the 'non-Western' world.

Does not the Church today, throughout the world and in the West as well as the East, find itself situated in a 'non-Christian world'? To confuse the preaching of the Gospel with the spread of Christian civilization is highly dangerous; and it may be a necessary and extremely wholesome corrective to put the matter in these terms as a way of impressing upon the Western Churches that when it comes to the point, they are 'in the mission field' on their home ground, surrounded by non-Christian and anti-Christian forces. Nevertheless one cannot carry such a point of view to its logical conclusion without furthering another sort of confusion, different but no less dangerous. The danger in this case is that history itself may be repudiated or denied. Whilst the Gospel is not the same thing as Christianity, the latter is a necessary consequence of it. Wherever the Gospel is proclaimed there arises—like an atmosphere for the Church to breathe in—the additional element of 'Christianity', which contains within it the first principles of a 'Christian civilization'. Christianity is an historical phenomenon: that is, it accompanies the passage of the Gospel through human history and, like all history, it lies under the judgment—and the patience—of God. It has its ups and downs, its seasons of ebb and flow; it brings forth fruit, sublime fruit, and commits frightful errors and sins; it spreads itself abroad and yet is subject to peculiar geographical limitations.

The history of Western Christian civilization is certainly not to be equated with God's action in human history, but just as certainly it stands in a special relation to the history of the Church and the progress of the Gospel through the world. Whenever Western missions have proclaimed the Gospel in the non-Western world and whenever this has given rise to new Churches, Western Christianity and Christian civilization have made the journey too. This impact of the West goes from strength to strength; it is the dynamic factor behind the 'awakening' of the non-Western world; it supplies the backbone of world history in the present age. If Western missions were to cease completely, that would not absolve the 'younger Churches' from their responsibility to discharge the rôle in history which the Western missions have so far fulfilled; for however unwilling they might be, they would have to shoulder it themselves. A 'younger Church' may be no more than a few decades old; but this does not mean that it is back in the situation found in the 'Acts of the Apostles'; it is living in the twentieth century. That is why all talk of 'older Churches' and 'younger Churches' is misleading in the extreme, because in the movement of Christian history the last are every whit as old as the first—they too have twenty centuries between them and *Annus Domini* —and the first are quite as young as the last in that the issues confronting both are the issues of our time and not of the past, however recent or remote, relatively speaking, that past may be.

A Church can be more or less completely isolated, as is the case with the Church of China now, but that makes no difference, in principle, to the rôle which she is called upon to play. The Communist revolution has its origin in Western history; and the Communist victory in China is the latest phase of the dynamic process set in motion by the impact of the West. The ideological challenge and the decisions which face the Chinese Christians in the political, economic, social and cultural spheres are of universal significance; they put the Chinese Church into the position of having to testify to the authority of her Lord and to do so, vicariously, for the whole Church throughout the world. She can sever completely all her connections with Churches in the West; she can renounce her own origin in the Western missionary movement; she can identify herself as thoroughly as it is possible for a Church to do with the dominant ideology. What she cannot do, however, is to put Chinese history in reverse and get back to the time when China was still untouched by Western civilization in her internal affairs and lived in comparative isolation under the sway of Confucianism.

When Western missions began working in the non-Western world, obviously they were not in the least degree able to foresee what would eventually come of their activity and of the encroachment of Western civilization which went with it. So far as that goes they have worked often enough wholly or partly in the dark and also often without the faintest idea of the size and the repercussions of their enterprise. But the mainspring of all their endeavours and the driving force was a vision which demanded entry into the non-Christian world in order to bring about there a fundamental change. In Western missions the Church has entered for the first time in her history into the dimension of world-wide responsibility; and now at last she sees the entire world, actually and concretely, as one single whole, as the sphere of Christian action and proclamation, as the field in which the Lord will establish the signs of his approaching Kingdom. All this is history; and no part of it can be retracted now. It is impossible in our twentieth century for any people or any Church to fall back on positions held prior to the impact of the West. When one considers the march of history one may be sure that the movement initiated by the Western missionary venture has simply come to the end of the beginning. It is the whole Church—and all her members, collectively, throughout the world—that fulfils her apostolic obligation within the framework of that movement. This is the reason why there can be no question, in fact, of any transfer of responsibility; for there are no 'older' or 'younger' Churches which could possibly stand in a legator-legatee relationship towards one another. It would mean that on principle each Church would stay put on its own doorstep and that its missionary outlook would be restricted within the borders of its own land and people, or at the most within those of a single continent. The idea not only conflicts with the nature of the Church; it also strikes at the very heart of Western missions. The Asian and African Churches bear conjointly with the Western Churches the responsibility for evangelizing Asia and Africa; and what they conjointly set forward is the Western missionary movement. This is something to be distinguished categorically from the other affirmation—unimpeachable in itself—that all Churches, of the East as of the West, are responsible together for the evangelization of the Western countries. For the modern history of Christianity has *not* been in the nature of a movement from Asia and Africa to the West; whilst the history of modern times *is* governed by the impact which Western civilization is making upon the non-Western world.

I. CULTURE AND HISTORY

It has to be admitted that the spread of Western civilization as the predominant factor in current history presents an extremely complex and obstinate phenomenon for cultural analysis. There has not been a single theory of cultural development so far which has succeeded in offering for this unprecedented phenomenon an explanation which really does justice to all its aspects. Here is a dynamic process of a unique and yet of a universal character. Not only would it seem impossible to stand far enough away from it to form an 'objective' judgment, but above all the process itself appears to undermine all the positions which cultural analysis has constructed and to make it difficult in the extreme to establish any new positions on solid ground. We find ourselves no longer in the situation of the Enlightenment in which, two centuries ago, Voltaire worked out his philosophy of history. That was something quite fascinating and attractive in itself, a first attempt to set our own European culture within the context of the cultural history of the human race as a whole, based on such data as were then available regarding other peoples and cultures. Europe was still only on the threshold of colonial expansion and the eve of the Industrial Revolution. The conception of human nature developed by the Enlightenment was static and its outlook on history highly schematic. It took seriously only the history of modern times; everything before that was consigned to superstition, error and darkness. Although anti-religious in tendency its understanding of history was typically apocalyptic, because from the darkness of the past to the light of the present and to that golden age of reason which was about to dawn in the not distant future no historical development was feasible—only an inexplicable transformation from night to day. After Voltaire the philosophy of culture moved off in two directions, both of which are adumbrated in his great work, written in 1756, on the general history of mankind, *Essai sur les moeurs et l'esprit des nations*. Interest in the 'customs' of the various peoples assumed the form, with the Romantic Movement in Germany, of a passionate longing to find new values in foreign cultures. As against the rationalistic idea, Romanticism stressed the great variability of human nature and the wide range of experiences of which it is capable. Though the operative purpose behind this new interest was to construct a picture of the whole human species from its very beginnings, the resulting tendency was towards an empirical approach first and foremost; and thus a foundation was laid for the growth at a later date of scientific ethnography. It was above all Herder's *Ideas on the Philosophy of Mankind, Ideen zur Philosophie der Geschichte der Menschheit* (1784–1791)—that paved the way for cultural anthropology.

In Herder's thought there is to be seen also at work the other tendency, already recognizable in Voltaire's idea of the 'spirit' of the nations. This was the line followed by those philosophers of history in Europe whose thought is markedly teleological in character. Herder conceived of human life as being closely related to its setting in the natural world. In the whole of the universe there is no higher form of development than human life, which constitutes a link between the natural and the spiritual worlds. Human life is itself yet another universe, within which the various races form a breeding-ground, as it were, for the appearance of higher types of human organism. The civilizations of China, India and the primitive cultures are static; at all events, they do not evince the steady cumulative development of historical progress. Europe, because of its peculiar climatic and geographical conditions, is the favoured territory. Only there can human life truly be said to be historical. Just as the human organism is the supreme development within the universe, so is European culture the supreme product and achievement of the historical human organism.

This idea of a progressive purpose in universal history became one of the dominant themes in German idealist philosophy. Nature's plan in history was understood to be the development of rational freedom; and in modern European civilization this was actually being realized. It was Hegel who furnished the most impressive philosophy of history in his dialectical theory of three principal phases in human history. The first, corresponding to the 'thesis', is Asiatic. In this stage, exemplified in the civilizations of China, India and the Near East, the individual is totally subject to the will of the ruler and the state is an absolute monarchy. Thus Asia was the scene of man's infancy, in which nature, and not spirit, was the prevailing influence. The second stage—antithesis—centred in the Mediterranean and is represented by the classical civilization of Greece and Rome. Here, reacting against Asian absolutism and attaining some measure of individual freedom, man came to maturity. Synthesis is reached with the third and final stage, in which Germanic culture triumphs and man becomes aware of his freedom, yet freely assents to 'the submergence of the individual in the universal idea'.[3]

In an address delivered in the year of the French Revolution Schiller declares that the task of universal history is to show how the present came to be what it is; and indeed to this very day no philosophy of history has proved capable of transcending this inherent and regulative principle. Since all philosophizing about history is a peculiar product of Western civilization, its ultimate aim so far has inevitably been to explain the course of history leading to the present condition of Western civilization. In other words it has of necessity always been Europeo-centric; and one might say that constructing philosophies of history is a way by which European civilization has continually reminded itself of both its situation and its direction. I will mention just a few outstanding and diverse examples.

Comte's positivism, although of course it owed nothing to Hegel, was based on a theory of mental activity divided into three stages: the theological, the metaphysical and the positivist or scientific. This theory, especially in the form in which it was elaborated by J. S. Mill and Herbert Spencer, was really the victorious scientific achievement of the nineteenth century expressing itself under the guise of history and, dividing the theological stage on evolutionary lines into the successive phases of fetishism, polytheism and monotheism, was an attempt to justify Christianity from a rationalistic viewpoint as the culmination of religious evolution.

Spengler's *Untergang des Abendlandes* revived Hegel's dialectical concept of history, but actuated now by a romantic impulse combined with the fatalistic outlook of a naturalism governed by the principles of biology. To designate the Asian stage, to which Christianity and the Eastern aspects of European culture were now consigned, Spengler chose the title 'Magical', whilst the Mediterranean stage he called 'Apollonian' and the Germanic 'Faustian'. Hegel's optimism, which conceived of the present stage as the 'veteran age' of full spiritual maturity, was exchanged a century later for a cyclical fatalism which saw in the plight of European civilization, shattered by the First World War, only the phase of senility, with no prospect before it other than that of inescapable doom. Though weighed down under this negative prognostication, as a 'morphology' of cultural history it was no less Europeo-centric, or even Germano-centric, than its great fore-runner had been in the hey-day of German idealism.

Spengler's work was so fantastic and arbitrary that there was every reason for a British historian to make a fresh attempt at projecting a universal history of mankind based on a more reliable scientific foundation. Toynbee's work in ten parts, *A Study of History*, is based on a scheme of twenty-one 'societies', to some extent at least standing towards each other in a parent-child relationship. One principal advantage of this concept is that it marshals the immensely abundant data of cultural history into what for any intelligent reader becomes a comprehensive and intelligible whole; but closer study reveals that although the material is brilliantly handled in detail, with a very fine psychological and historical sense, the scheme does far too much violence to the complex reality and forces it into a naturalistic conception of culture. It becomes clear that the consecutive evolution of Hellenic and Western society has been made to serve as a model for the evolution of all other societies. Therein lies the *vitium originis* of the entire work; for there is probably not a single instance of a non-Western society of which the historical development has run parallel to that of Western society and its predecessor. Even this survey of universal history did not succeed in slipping the reins of Europeo-centric thinking.

For our final example we take Karl Jaspers' philosophy of history, *Vom Ursprung und Ziel der Geschichte*. One of the most interesting features of this abstruse work is its pseudo-theological approach. From beginning to end of the record the formal categories of Christian theology which relate to the unity of the human race are insisted upon; but the content they are given is a very different matter. In place of the universal revelation in Christ as the centre of history, Jaspers puts the *Achsenzeit* as the decisive, pivotal event; and in so doing he makes a very obvious attack on the exclusive claims of Christian dogmatics. In the 'time of axis' (*Achsenzeit*) God has revealed himself historically in various ways and has opened up many ways to himself. It is as if, in the language of universal history, God utters an admonition against the claims of exclusivism.[4] True, this 'time of axis', the period about 500 B.C., is restricted to China, India and the Occident (Israel–Hellas); but in it the foundations are laid of universal history. Examined more closely, however, this axial turn of historical events appears rather in the light of a speculative assumption, entirely overshadowed by a second 'time of axis', the precursor of which is the present age. It is now in fact that world history really begins; and Jaspers expressly says that the current axial period is due exclusively to the course of European history, which constitutes the true 'middle' between the universal origin and the universal end of mankind's history.[5]

Is it then possible to make a *radical* break with the Europeo-centric conception of history? We have seen that in Voltaire already, and then above all in Herder, one can detect two diverging lines, one of which moves in the direction of a philosophy of history which apparently just has to be Europeo-centric. The other line broadens out into the modern science of cultural anthropology; and it is this same science which sets its face, with the greatest determination and on the basis of much painstaking and detailed study of a wide range of cultural data, against such Europeo-centric tendencies. The notion of culture that has become normative for this science is finely expressed in the symbol of 'the tree of culture'. Facing the front page of Kroeber's well-known handbook of anthropology there is a plate depicting the twin trees of Paradise in the fashion of modern science: with the 'tree of life' next door to the 'tree of good and evil', that is, of human culture.

> . . . the course of organic evolution can be portrayed properly as a tree of life, as Darwin has called it, with trunk, limbs, branches, and twigs. The course of development of human culture in history cannot so be described, even metaphorically. There is a constant branching-out, but the branches also grow together again, wholly or partially, all the time. Culture diverges, but it syncretizes and anastomoses too. Life really does nothing but diverge: its occasional convergences are superficial resemblances, not a joining or a reabsorption. A branch on the tree of life may approach another branch; it will normally coalesce with it. The tree of culture, on the contrary, is a ramification of such coalescences, assimilations or acculturations . . . the specific processes of life and the specific processes of culture are drastically different.[6]

The 'tree of culture' metaphor also gives its title to a work by another outstanding American anthropologist, Ralph Linton. This survey of the history of culture was published posthumously; and in the introduction Adelin Linton explains the title by referring to the difference from the tree of biological evolution in terms similar to Kroeber's. In this case it is the tropical banyan tree which serves as the particular paradigm of the 'tree of culture'.[7] It is worth noticing that the tree here chosen as a symbol of general cultural history is that which has played such a prominent part in Indian symbolism and has long been a familiar image for Indology of the structure and evolution of Indian culture and religions.[8] The very choice of this metaphor as a kind of basic apperception regarding the evolution of culture points to a funda-mental naturalism which puts out of court straight away any possible admission that in world history, taken as a whole, Western civilization has a unique part to play.

The conception of culture expressed in the idea of the 'tree' embraces every human culture. That is a postulate of major importance in the science of cultural anthropology, at any rate so far as the extremely influential school represented by the American writers already mentioned is concerned. They hold no brief whatever for the opinion, current among ethnologists with an evolutionary outlook in the nineteenth century and the early decades of the twentieth, that mankind's evolution is in fact unilinear and culminates in Western civilization. If that were so, Western civilization would offer a standard for determining the stage of development reached by the non-Western peoples. In terms of this evolutionary way of thinking, one spoke of 'nature peoples' and 'culture peoples' and therefore applied the idea of 'culture' only to those peoples who by Western standards can be said to have reached a stage of development which admits them to the ranks of the 'civilized nations'. Cultural anthropology now rejects that evolutionary standpoint and starts from a conception of culture which is really identical with the basic mould of human existence. 'Human culture' is therefore a tautology. Since man is a social being, there can be no culture without a society. Conversely, such a thing as a cultureless society is unknown. 'Cultureless peoples' simply do not exist. Culture is defined as 'social heredity' (Linton), as 'the whole of social tradition' (Lowie), as 'that complex whole which includes knowledge, belief, art, morals, customs, and any other capabilities and habits acquired by man as a member of society' (Tylor). In each case the two essential elements, the human and the social, are represented in the definition.[9] Beyond the range of man there are societies, but no cultures. Culture is 'that which the human species has and o-her social species lack.'[10]

The concept 'culture' has been through an interesting process of development. The word itself—in the sense of 'cultivation' or 'nurture' —goes back to (pre-)classical Latin. Its application to human society and history is recent; it seems to have started after the middle of the eighteenth century and then at first only in the German language. The Romance languages—and English with them—continued for a long time to use 'civilization' instead of 'culture' to denote social cultivation, improvement, refinement or progress. The term 'civilization' goes back to the Latin *civis, civilis, civitas, civilitas*, where the root idea is political and urban: the citizen within an organized state, as opposed to the tribal member. The word 'civilization' would seem to be a Romance formation of the Renaissance period, probably French, derived from 'civilisar', meaning 'to achieve or impart refined manners', urbanization and improvement. There is a near parallel in Italian as far back as Dante.[11]

Today both terms still have this meaning of 'betterment' or 'progress towards perfection' in a variety of uses, whether popular or academic. In the eighteenth century they were employed almost always in the singular, with a connotation not restricted to Western peoples. In the course of the nineteenth century, however, there came about a profound change. As Romanticism developed, so interest also grew in the distinctive structure, spirit and unfolding of particular cultures. The rapid strides made by ethnology in adding to our knowledge of non-Western peoples lent considerable support to the idea of a pluralistic diversity of cultures throughout the world.[12] The evolutionary approach fitted this plurality of cultures into a scheme of development from 'nature' to 'culture', whilst the Europeo-centric assessment of Western civilization, in its modern phase, as the final goal of cultural evolution was greatly reinforced by the fact of Western hegemony. It appears that the science of cultural anthropology now advocates a concept which on the one hand recognizes and upholds a great diversity of cultures, but on the other hand is firmly anchored in that older connotation of 'culture' (in the singular) as that which raises human existence above the subhuman level of nature. As for Western culture, so far from being the highest stage in cultural evolution, it is a specimen *inter alia*, a twig of that tree which branches out in a multiplicity of cultures. In the nature of the case there can be no question of precedence or superiority, since all the branches derive from a single trunk.

This kind of interpretation has been compared with that of the modern study of linguistics.[13] When ethnology was still talking in terms of 'nature peoples' and 'cultureless peoples', philology was being forced to recognize that even such peoples possess a language. In studying the structures and immense diversity of languages in the world as a whole, philologists had to acquire a detached viewpoint regarding the structure of languages belonging to their own cultural group. Obviously they were bound in the end to arrive at the question of what language in general—as a phenomenon characteristic of human beings—signifies and what bearing the multiplicity of languages may have on this matter. This comprehensive notion of language in the study of general linguistics is one particular example of the general idea of culture which forms a basis for cultural anthropology.

Thus Kroeber—with Lowie for precedent—is completely in line with this when he asserts that the ideal frame of reference for cultural anthropology must comprise the totality of known culture. Whilst any national or tribal culture may be studied and analysed in isolation

—and indeed must be so for certain purposes—such a culture must to some extent be an artificial unit, when detached in that way for reasons of expediency. The ultimate unit for ethnologists is 'the culture of all humanity at all periods and in all places'.[14] What are we to make, though, of this idea of culture, unless we have a clear understanding of the idea of history—of the history of mankind, which is the special business of the philosophy of history and which, as we have seen, is apparently bound to be Europeo-centric in character? Kroeber himself, in his own work, argued with ever increasing emphasis that cultural phenomena are on the whole more amenable to an historical than to a strictly scientific approach. He based his view on the neo-Kantian distinction between nature, as the subject matter of science, and culture, as being the dimension of human spiritual self-consciousness (*Geist*) and therefore the subject matter of history. Although he rejected an all-or-nothing dichotomy between science and history, he opposed the tendency prevalent among anthropologists and sociologists to regard the method of physics—or more narrowly of nineteenth century physics—as the proper method for all sciences, including those specifically concerned with human culture.

It really is worth remarking, therefore, that cultural anthropologists are examining more thoroughly the basic assumptions of their method and coming more and more to realize that the character of human culture is historical, is something qualitatively different from the essence of nature, which is the proper object of physics and biology. If they press on with examining their fundamentals in this way, they are bound to come up against the major problem, which they have so far been careful to avoid. It just will not do to have an historical approach which refuses to go beyond the recognition of certain facts about cultural phenomena as having an intrinsic significance—when and where they occur, for example, and what their qualitative character really is; for such an approach must take into consideration above all the particular 'when' and 'where', as well as the qualitative reality, of the human subject studying the phenomena in question. Both the philosopher of history and the cultural anthropologist have their particular time and place and their own 'qualitative reality' in Western civilization. If physics and biology—not to mention historical studies— can never be independent of the human subject who knows the phenomena of nature, still more must it be true of cultural anthropology that it can never break free of the particular culture, in this

CHRISTIANITY AND CULTURES

case the Western culture, which produces it. There is no instance of
a tribal culture or of any non-Western civilization being studied by
its own members with the approach adopted by this Western science.
Such an approach only becomes possible when based on a complex
of cultural conditions among which are a universal concept of human
history and an outlook upon the situation, the task and the potentialities
of man, both of which are peculiar to the Western world. By way of
illustration take the example, already cited, of philological science.
Philology has taken a tremendous step forward in getting beyond the
languages of the Western cultural milieu and concentrating on the
question of language as a universal human phenomenon. The Western
languages are nothing more than a branch on the great tree of
languages. Yet would the philosophy of linguistics be able to detach
itself in a similar way from Western culture by presenting Western
philology as an arbitrary specimen of philology in general? Now this
question is one which applies to every aspect of culture. Again and
again it will appear that a set of Western cultural phenomena can be
subsumed under some aspect of culture in general and can be compared
with parallel phenomena in other cultures; but as soon as one brings
into the picture the scientific method, with its presuppositions, and the
human agent who studies and analyses and subjects these phenomena
to intense scrutiny, one is compelled to admit that in Western culture
there is apparently a special creative force and that only within the
context of that culture does this force engender that peculiar approach
which one may look for elsewhere in vain.

The dilemma is strikingly illustrated by Ruth Benedict's *Patterns
of Culture*. This study offers a splendid example of method and approach
in cultural anthropology. What distinguishes that science from its
companions among the social sciences, she argues, is that it takes
seriously the investigation of other societies besides our own. The
crucial weakness of the major social sciences is that instead of studying
mankind they make do with studying one local variation, that is to
say, Western civilization itself. Anthropology deals with culture as a
whole, in the same way that philology deals with languages; these
acquire an identity by selecting over a narrow range from an almots
unlimited number of sounds, and from this process there results an
intelligible unity. So it is with a culture; it comes into being through
a process of selection from the inexhaustible reservoir of cultural traits
or potentialities of human behaviour. For anyone who belongs to

Western civilization it still takes an enormous effort to view his own culture 'objectively', as just one among many configurations. It involves something very much like a 'Copernican revolution' in our outlook. The fourteenth century rebelled passionately against having the earth consigned to a position within the solar system. In Darwin's time men fought with every available weapon to defend the unique status of the human soul. We are quite happy now to admit that the earth's revolving round the sun and the animal ancestry of man have little or no bearing on the uniqueness of our human achievements.

> If we inhabit one chance planet out of a myriad solar systems, so much the greater glory, and if all the ill-assorted human races are linked by evolution with the animal, the provable differences between ourselves and them are the more extreme and the uniqueness of our institutions the more remarkable. But *our* achievements, *our* institutions are unique; they are of a different order from those of lesser races and must be protected at all costs. So that today, whether it is a question of imperialism, or of race prejudice, or of a comparison between Christianity and paganism, we are still preoccupied with the uniqueness, not of the human institutions of the world at large, which no one has ever cared about anyway, but of our own institutions and achievements, our own civilization.[15]

This puts Western civilization in a quite extraordinary position. One is reminded of Herder, who allotted to Europe a place in the universe of cultures analogous to that of man in the whole organic world. Since Copernicus and Darwin have not, in the event, derogated from 'the uniqueness of our human achievements'—this, surely, is what the argument implies—therefore the science of anthropology can in no way prejudice the uniqueness of Western civilization, even though that civilization be but a branch on the tree of culture as man himself is a branch on the tree of organic evolution, and the earth a 'planetary accident' within the universe. In fact the ultimate aim of this anthropologist is, apparently, to arrive at a better understanding of the structure of Western civilization. One of the theoretical factors justifying our study of primitive peoples, she would say, is that facts relating to simpler cultures may throw light on certain specific data which would otherwise remain baffling and intractable. Western civilization, comprising the highest and most complex society known to us, and the material it presents are too intricate and too close to our vision to be seen in proper focus. Therefore the way to an understanding of our own cultural processes which will prove the most economical in the end is a devious one. We have an example of this in the method employed by Darwin. When he found the historical relations of human beings with their immediate forebears in the animal kingdom too involved to deploy as evidence for the fact of biological evolution, he made use instead of the structure of beetles; and the process which in the complex physical organization of the human is obscure, in the case of the simpler situation was made convincingly clear. So too with the study of cultural organizations; the shortest route to an understanding of our own civilization is by way of the study of primitive societies. Cultural anthropology is tied to a point of departure and a concern which are ultimately Europeocentric; and it can no more avoid these than a man can dodge out of range of his own shadow.

There is yet another reason why the anthropologist will always be confronted with Western civilization, even when the object of his study is the most remote of primitive societies. Ruth Benedict observes that Western civilization has spread itself further afield than any other local group so far known to us. But she does not seem to think that any explanation of this fact is required, beyond a reference to 'fortuitous historical circumstances'. Indeed she is anxious to emphasize the fact that the spread of white civilization, extensive though it is, is not an isolated circumstance of history. The Polynesian group has spread from Java to Easter Island, from Hawaii to New Zealand; and the Bantu-speaking tribes spread from the Sahara into southern Africa. 'But in neither case do we regard these peoples as more than an overgrown local variation of the human species.'

Should cultural anthropology be able to provide us with a viewpoint radically different from this? Certainly, the man of today who takes it for granted that his own cultural standards are the equivalent of 'human nature' is just about as provincial in his outlook as an Australian bushman. The fundamental difference, however, is that despite their expansion neither the Australian aborigines nor the Polynesian groups have had the will or the way to spread their culture over the entire world. The expansion of Western civilization is not an 'isolated' historical circumstance, it is true; but it is all the same, both extensively and intensively, and whether viewed in its quantitative or its qualitative aspect, a phenomenon without precedent or parallel in history. Moreover, this civilization has engendered not only the most bizarre forms of race prejudice, religious narcissism, social self-idolization and ultra-primitive narrow-mindedness, but also a universal outlook, a sustained and revolutionary self-criticism, a compulsive quest for radical renewal, an indefatigable thirst for discovery and adventure and that marvellous passion for 'objective' knowledge, which is the motive power of modern science and also impels cultural anthropology to break through every barrier of pride and prejudice and provincial isolation which Western man has erected against other cultures.

Bronislaw Malinowski is outstanding among anthropologists as one whose work was guided by the conviction that any study of non-Western cultures must of necessity involve the analysis of the 'dynamics of cultural change'. In what he wrote during his latter years he strongly advocated the claims of a term coined by Don Fernando Ortiz: namely, 'transculturation'. The processes of cultural change which are working themselves out over the whole contemporary world under the impact of Western civilization are not to be assessed in a one-sided fashion—from the side, that is, of Western civilization—as if all that was happening was an assimilation of non-Western cultures. Nor for that matter can they be properly assessed from the other side as though they involved for the non-Western cultures nothing more than a correction in their development, a partial accommodation. Any serious investigation of cultural change ought to take into account the complete range of factors involved and in particular to allow for the circumstance that Western civilization is itself undergoing a process of rapid cultural transformation. The Western impact on the non-Western world involves a transition in which each side plays an active part and each is merging with the other to realize a new form of civilization. In the present world-wide process of 'transculturation' it is no longer easy to distinguish internal from external factors. The process is one which transforms the existing order of society, the civilization in its social, spiritual and material aspects, and changes it from one type into another. Within the process the two variants are independent evolution, induced by pressures and forces arising spontaneously inside the community, and diffusion, which depends upon contact between different cultures; but in the current process of transformation it becomes increasingly difficult to distinguish the one from the other. That is because cultural change, in the broadest sense of the term a factor always to be found in human civilization, has assumed in both these forms a speed and a scale unparalleled in previous history. Cultural change in Africa today differs only superficially, if at all, from that which is transforming the backward rural countries of Europe into a new type closely akin to the proletarian model found in the industrial areas of the United States and of Europe itself.[16]

Cultural anthropology and sociology are giving more and more prominence to this extremely productive and rewarding insight and its influence within that science is on the increase. However, we are not quite at the heart of the matter yet. Whilst fully recognizing that in this process of transculturation Western and non-Western cultures together are caught up in a giddy current of profound and dynamic change, one is bound at the same time to reckon with the fact that the dynamic element, the initiative, lies with Western civilization, which started the process in the first place and now keeps it going. The transculturation which is taking place within the Western countries today does of course occur in the form of a transition from a rural to an industrial society; yet at a different level and in a far more intensive way the same influence is at work within the heart and centre of the technological revolution itself. I mean here the transition into the atomic age, the consequences of which for the world as a whole it is impossible to calculate, but which Western civilization has nurtured and brought to fruition. For a science which takes as its ideal context the totality of known culture one of its most imperative tasks must surely be to find out precisely which of those forces now operative in Western civilization are most likely to take charge of it—as well as of other cultures—in the continuing process of trans-culturation, with all the confusion which that brings in its train.

2. THE MEETING OF EAST AND WEST

In his book, *East versus West, a Denial of Contrast*, the Indian sociologist, Kodanda Rao, tries his hardest to show that the differences between Western and non-Western culture are not really significant at all. One of the ideas forming the groundwork of this study, which represents a point of view enjoying considerable favour at the present time, is that the difference between East and West comes with the rise of modern civilization. Until about A.D. 1600 'Eastern civilization' was common to both West and East; after that 'Westernization' started, in the West first, but subsequently in the East too, so that the civilizations of the East will in the future be simply 'Western'. There has been a time-lag, but no difference in kind. In so far as there is resistance and conflict, it is not so much between the two civilizations as between cultural traits common to both. In both East and West vegetable oil, kerosene oil, gas and electricity as means of illumination have contested the field; manual labour has competed with machine power, and the animal-drawn vehicle with the railway train and the motor bus; religion has clashed with science, and tradition with innovation. Every new thing is foreign and alien. To the hand-loom weaver of China textiles manufactured in power mills are equally foreign and alien, whether the mills in question happen to be in China, in Japan or in Manchester, whether the capital behind them and the labour inside them be British or Chinese. Western civilization has not been an integrated pattern, which might be accepted or rejected *en bloc*. It has been much more like a medley of technicalities and trades, of ingredients extremely varied and even contradictory in character. In modern times all the values of the West have been turned upside down; but this change is neither uniform nor complete. Monarchies and republics, personal and proletarian dictatorships, exist cheek by jowl; so also do capitalism and Communism, religion and science, nationalism and internationalism, agriculture and industry. These elements of Western civilization are not all linked together; and in the process of diffusion they do not all stick together either.[17]

Not only is there no necessary cohesion between the various elements out of which civilizations are constituted, but one cannot even regard civilizations as social units in themselves. Ninety-nine per cent of people, irrespective of race, play a passive as opposed to a creative rôle; and even the creative section are passive with regard to ninety-nine per cent of their civilization. In fact all human beings, in the East as in the West and without distinction of race or colour, are on the same footing, in the sense that each individual acquires culture by imitating his fellows. Thus the relationship is one between the individual 'creator' and the rest of humanity, and not between one group and another. Everything newly created is exotic until accepted; and then it becomes indigenous. What is a group in relation to one factor is not necessarily a group in relation to all other factors.

Even if we dismiss as unacceptable such an atomistic conception of culture, we are left with a number of very substantial objections to the idea of a contrast between East and West. For one thing, where do the frontiers lie? Russia represents 'to a large extent the Orient for the Occident and the Occident for the Orient' and has been 'a meeting-place of the East and the West by her history and by her nature'.[18] Toynbee contends that Islam has less in common with either Hindu civilization or that of the Far East than it has with the Orthodox Christian and the Western; whilst the gulfs that divide the Hindu and Far Eastern civilizations from our own are possibly not so wide as the gulf dividing them from each other. There again a great deal depends on what plane of civilization one has in mind. Whereas in the economic plane the culture embraces an area co-extensive with the whole habitable and navigable surface of our planet, in the cultural plane itself it is confined to the countries inhabited by Catholic and Protestant peoples in Western Europe, America and the South Seas.[19] The further back we go in European history, the more does the culture-area contract and the coincidence between the political, economic and cultural planes increase.

There are two points of view which contradict each other in a remarkable way. The one sees the unity in Western civilization as arising from its Christian foundations and its common possession of the Greek, the Roman, the Jewish and the Christian heritage. The process of secularization, however, spells the end of this unity; so that the only feature shared by the peoples in the West nowadays would seem to be their race—or rather their white complexion.[20]

Over against this many would say that only the rise of modern civilization has given us anything that might be called specifically 'Western', although as that civilization spreads the epithet 'Western' comes to have less and less meaning. According to this point of view, the essential difference between East and West is that the latter overcame scholasticism, whereas the former did not. It is a matter of fundamental method. Whilst Japan becomes more and more a part of the West, so far as the intellectual mission of mankind is concerned, on the other hand some European nations which prefer argument to experiment are 'orientalized'—that is to say to that extent are rendered static. 'The great intellectual division of mankind is not along geographical or racial lines, but between those who understand and practise the experimental method and those who do not understand and who do not practise it.'[21] The Chinese modernist, Dr Hu Shih, allies himself with this point of view. As he sees it, the difference between East and West begins with the Greeks, who applied themselves to both humane and scientific studies, whereas the Chinese never went beyond historical matters and the humanities. However, this difference did not become strikingly evident until about A.D. 1600 and after with the growth of modern science. Whilst Galileo, Kepler, Boyle, Harvey and Newton worked with the phenomena of nature, their Chinese contemporaries worked with words, books and documentary evidences.[22] Likewise Gandhi refused to admit a contrast on a geographical basis. The peoples of Europe, before they were touched by modern civilization, had much in common with the peoples of the East; and even today those Europeans whom modern civilization has not affected are far better able to mix with Indians than with men moulded by it.[23]

There have been many attempts to construct a synthesis between 'East' and 'West'; but I shall mention only three of major importance. Northrop, in *The Meeting of East and West*, finds the key to the meaning of Western civilization in ancient Greek culture, which broke away from that purely pictorial or aesthetic exoticism which characterizes the civilization of the Orient. The Occident has investigated things in their theoretical element, whilst the Orient has for the most part explored their aesthetic aspect. When one analyses the East and West in order to establish what are their scientific and philosophical foundations, one finds that they are saying not, as Ananda Coomaraswamy has suggested, the same thing nor, as Kipling affirmed, two incompatible things but something different yet complementary in each case. Thus although the two great civilizations differ in a most fundamental and far-reaching way, there can none the less be one world—the world of a single civilization, accepting as its criterion of the good a positivist and theoretically scientific philosophy which conceives of all things—man and nature alike—as comprising the aesthetic component mastered by the Orient and the theorizing component which the Occident has pursued with so much genius.[24]

The Indian philosopher, Radhakrishnan, taking certain Hindu presuppositions as his starting-point, has built up an East-West synthesis and has expressed this in several of his writings.[25] For him the contrast is pre-eminently one between Eastern 'religion' and Western 'thought'. Asia and Europe represent complementary sides of human culture: Asia the spiritual and Europe the intellectual. In the realm of religion India typifies the East. The Semitic spirit falls within a region of twilight between East and West. Greece and Rome enshrine the spirit of the West. There is not a single living religion which has a Western origin. Christianity is an Eastern religion, which through being transplanted to the West has acquired forms characteristic of the Western mind. The difference between the pure and simple teaching of Jesus and the course taken by Christianity in the West illustrates vividly the differences between Eastern and Western attitudes towards religion. The Western mind is rationalistic and ethical, positivist and practical, the Eastern more inclined to inward life and intuitive thinking. The firm insistence on the personality of God in the Christian religion is something inherited from Greek intellectualism. The characteristics of intuitive realization, non-dogmatic toleration and insistence on the non-aggressive virtues and on a universalist ethic mark Jesus out as a typically Eastern seer. On the other hand an emphasis on definite creeds and an absolutist dogmatism, with all its consequences —intolerance, exclusiveness and confusion of piety with patriotism— are the outstanding features of Western Christianity. This intellectual religion of the West has its impressive virtues as well as its defects, just as the intuitive religion of the East has them too. The modern encounter between these two may well pave the way to a strong spiritual unity, if each can learn to appreciate the other, putting aside all chilly criticism and patronizing judgment. Perhaps the time will come—and sooner than many of us expect—when the church, the temple and the mosque will keep open door for all men of goodwill and when the whole human race, though not united by one name, will nevertheless be bound together by one spirit.

Whereas Northrop, the American scientist, searches for a synthesis on a strictly philosophical basis, and whereas the Indian religious thinker, Radhakrishnan, wants to merge East and West together in an all-inclusive synthesis of strongly Hindu tendency, the European political thinker, De Kat Angelino, envisages a harmonious co-operation between East and West within the framework of a philosophy of Western colonial dominance, conceived on the grand scale.[26] What differentiates the East and the West in the first instance is their respective social structures. The Western personality is ubiquitous and everywhere 'itself'; but the Eastern personality is 'topical' (locally confined). In contrast to the dynamic character of the Western *milieu*, that of the East is static. If we compare a peasant in an occidental village with a shopkeeper in an Eastern city, the latter may appear to be more occidental than the former; but the crucial point is that in the present age the occidental village is coming to be the satellite of the big city, whilst in the East on the other hand, the agrarian spirit of the village with its strong sense of the solidarity of the familial group is carried over into the larger agglomerations. The evolution of the modern Occident began through the rise of the republican cities with their extraordinary flair for organization and their creative resources, their adventurous and victorious energy. That development had no parallel in the East; and it was this event which marked the parting of the ways for East and West. The occidental personality is able to move at will from one place to another without any feeling of being uprooted. It moves through the world of abstract ideas as readily as through space. Modern society is captive neither to place nor yet to the present moment; it can envisage the interests of a very remote future. Indeed its outlook towards the future is guided by this capacity in a variety of spheres: production, commerce, education, science, organization, jurisdiction, legislation, hygiene and social services. The freedom of personal manoeuvre, closely bound up with the division of labour which yields a highly fractionized variety of functions, has formed the basis of modern occidental civilization. The Eastern mentality is imprisoned in clan, caste, village, community. Because there is no division of labour and money plays only a very limited rôle, economic life bears a familial stamp. Such a mentality is imprisoned within the moment and lacks any ability to organize for a remote future. With oriental communities, the basis for jurisdiction is provided by a unified corpus of traditions and customs that guarantees the established order, but is of course both local and limited.

There is an arresting likeness between the pattern of Eastern civilization and the Middle Ages in the West. The Occident of today is virtually separated from the Orient by the space of five hundred years—years of painstaking effort and tremendous activity. When we speak of the conflict between East and West therefore, we have to distinguish not only various kinds of antagonism, but the two distinct orders under which they come. The first of these may be categorized as synchronic antithesis. That is to say that the great empires of the past, coming in contact with the peoples they had subjugated, were made aware of a contrast so far as race, religion, morals and so forth were concerned, but only on a parallel plane of cultural development. With modern colonialism there arises a new order of conflict—a 'diachronic antithesis'—resulting from the cultural lag of the Eastern civilizations. Now this conflict engendered by the time factor continues within and cuts right across the life of those oriental nations which have felt the impact of the West. In the colonial relationship between West and East is to be found the great task which history has imposed upon Western and Eastern peoples alike. Through mutual co-operation they are to achieve together a humanitarian and universalistic world culture to which all subsidiary cultures will make a real contribution.

The three types of approach which we have glanced at here have one thing in common. Though starting from very different premisses they all attempt to offer a diagnosis of the great encounter between cultures in the world today. Confronted, however, with the elemental forces at work in the creative and destructive process of transculturation, their ideas of synthesis strike one as being rather speculative and even delusory. It is highly unlikely that the advancing technological revolution will set very much store by the need for a synthesis of the theorizing and the aesthetic conceptions. Hindu religiosity is under fire; and it may well be that a syncretistic mysticism could provide it with a temporary refuge against the assaults of Christian missions and modern secularism alike; but all that has nothing whatever to do with a genuine encounter between East and West, let alone with a possible synthesis. As for colonial dominance, it has indeed constituted a necessary phase of the conflict and has made a very deep impression. It has issued, however, not in harmonious co-operation but in a radical anti-colonialism.

3. ISRAEL, THE WEST AND THE WORLD

We have now in some measure at least reconnoitred the ground which forms the meeting-place between Western and non-Western cultures; and we have uncovered some of the snares and pitfalls which make that ground so very difficult to negotiate. There is no beaten track to follow, and it is most likely impossible to find a central point of vantage from which to survey the ground as a whole. What one can do, however, taking as the starting-point such exploration as has already been done, is to indicate some of the possible lines of advance which any future expeditions ought to pursue.

In the first place the philosophy of history and cultural anthropology are two ways of approach which have a common origin but have drifted much too far apart in these days; and what we badly need now is a fresh confrontation of the one with the other. The philosophy of history can no longer be treated—as it used to be during the nineteenth century—as a Europeo-centric exercise. It must take full account of the complete change in the position and rôle of Western civilization, a change which raises for it problems without parallel, except perhaps for those which the Copernican and Darwinian revolutions presented. There again, cultural anthropology cannot hope to escape the toils of a naturalistic relativism unless it is prepared to pay much more attention to its own origin and roots in Western culture and to its essential character, which is to be an historical science. If only it would remember that its basis is of this specific kind, it would learn how to view the philosophy of history and its problems in a new way.

The second thing is that the universal significance of Western civilization first became apparent when it began to spread over the world in the modern period; but the forces which gave rise to this development had been preparing for several centuries past. The point of view fashionable today which sees the distinctively 'Western' course of events beginning about A.D. 1600 comes down to us from the period of the Enlightenment and its particular way of looking at the history of Europe. Modern Western civilization can be adequately interpreted only when one goes back to the historical springs out of which it arose.

My third point is that if the spread of modern Western civilization over the world is ever to be understood, this can only be done within the total setting of Christian history and the course it has taken. There is such an integral connection between this and the progress everywhere of the modern missionary movement that one is really forced to that conclusion. The popular distinction between a 'Christian' antiquity and Middle Ages and a 'secularized' modern period does not make for a sound approach to history. It cuts at the root of any really adequate conception of the modern West and yields a distorted image of antiquity and the mediaeval world. The legacy of Hellenic culture is, of course, a most important and persisting element in the Christian history of Western civilization and deserves to be treated as such; but every attempt to isolate the Greek tradition or to give it an exclusive importance makes nonsense of Western history.

In his brilliant essay on *Man's Western Quest*, Denis de Rougemont traces the spiritual venture which is the very heart and soul of history in the West to the central and seminal fact of the Incarnation. This is the source of the mysterious dialectics of the West and of the dynamic forces which have shaped its history to a disconcerting pattern of paradoxes. Whatever is peculiar to Western man and typical of him depends ultimately upon a decision that he makes—the decision of faith in the person of Christ, represented at the human level in the person of the Christian.

> *Word,* and not silence; *made flesh* and not concept; *Grace,* instead of merit or spiritual techniques. *Faith,* and not direct knowledge of the divine; *History,* instead of Myth. Recognition of the flesh and hence of matter as realities of our present life. *Paradox, tension, dialectic.* . . . And love of one's neighbor as oneself, corresponding with the love of God, replacing the sacred, and founding the *person.*

No doubt the Christian way is not the sole operative element in Western history, but decisive it has been; and it has remained axial, is so still at this present time. There is no such thing as the 'de-Christianization of the West':

> Europe remains the place where the strongest density of human history is to be observed. . . . Europe has behind her and bears within herself Greco-Latin Antiquity, the Middle Ages, the Renaissance and the Enlightenment, Romanticism, Nationalism and Socialism, and she has entered upon the technical era while retaining the vital marks and the conflicts of all those successive phases. Such historical density is a powerful impulse in the Western Quest.[27]

It must be remarked that in spite of its lucidity, when it ends by pleading for a dialogue between West and East, this essay gets lost in a maze of contradictions. By the close of this century, so the author prognosticates, the West will have acquired leisure enough to turn to religion and to cultural diversions. The East, having mastered technics and dealt with its material poverty, will put a brake on prolification and start to think much more in European terms. The perplexing thing is that just at the moment when the West may be achieving the conditions which make leisure for all practicable, it is spiritually desiccated; whilst the East is so eager to seize hold of our technics that in the process it loses sight of its own values—values of which we all stand in the greatest need. West and East ought therefore to take stock of each other's vision and genius. The dreams of Columbus gave us America, those of the scholar and the alchemist our modern technics. Does the vision of the Eastern sages perhaps proffer salvation, true peace of spirit?[28]

One is obliged to ask whether the author is not, all of a sudden, forgetting his own initial thesis: namely that the very pulse of Western history beats in a decision, the crux of which is the Incarnation. Can the remedy for that spiritual malaise which besets the West as a result of its technocratic achievements lie then elsewhere than in the Christian faith? Is the dialogue really a dialogue between technics and mysticism? Does not the author himself attest that there would be no technics or modern science without the message of the Incarnation? How is it possible to contend on the one hand that modern Western civilization is no less 'Christian' than the Middle Ages and then finally to emasculate the thesis by suggesting that it is Eastern 'religion' which provides a practicable solution to the spiritual needs of the West? Is it in fact true that the East, now that it has adopted Western technocracy as the answer to its material wretchedness, finds itself in a dilemma and threatened with spiritual suicide? Is it not rather the case that the East has involved itself in the circumstances and decisions of Western history and therefore finds itself confronted, willynilly, with the choice to which world history leads, the choice which the future holds for East and West alike: the choice between Christ and antichrist, annihilation and the risen Lord? What an appalling prospect opens before us in the idea of a 'dialogue' between the West, assuaging its thirst at the fountain of Eastern 'religion' (and therefore presumably having taken leave of its own Lord and Saviour) and the East, satiated and giddy with the wine of technocracy, yet empty of all faith in him who is the bread of life. Such a prospect surely exceeds in horror that of Orwell's *Nineteen Eighty-Four*; for over this total desert there hovers the seductive mirage of 'religion'.

Perhaps the final impression made by this otherwise penetrating analysis is blurred because it does not probe deeply enough into the roots of Western history. The present study is based on the conviction that the roots of Western history are to be discovered in the history of the people of Israel as it is recorded and proclaimed in the Bible. That history is unrepeatable; but when we look at Western history against the background of the history of Israel we see there analogies indicative of a genuine kinship. We must first of all therefore—in the next two chapters—try to understand the significance of the Old and New Testaments in their creative relationship to Western history.

Chapter Four outlines the characteristics of that fundamental pattern of life from which the biblical message of creation is such a radical departure. The fifth and sixth chapters give some account of the course of Western history, of the contrast it presents, externally, to its counterparts, and also of those forces which move it from within. Chapter Seven relates how, in our own time, the whole world is being drawn into the current of Western history and so of revolutionary change. The final chapter is an attempt to formulate some at least of the major questions confronting Christianity in the planetary world of tomorrow—and, for that matter, of today.

Two

Israel amid the Nations

I. THE HEBREW MIND AND ITS GENIUS

THE setting for the story of God's dealings with his people and with the nations, as related in the Old Testament, is this world of ours; and so far as place and time are concerned its dimensions, relatively speaking, are narrow enough, forming as it does merely a part of the cultural history of the ancient Near East—and of that only in its later period. The people of Israel did not fall like a bolt from the blue, but emerged and matured within this particular unit of culture. From it derived their high degree of prosperity and power—ephemeral though it was; and the disasters which befell them are inseparably linked with the peoples of the ancient Near East and their history as a whole.

The dramatic spectacle which the Old Testament offers us is of a course of events peculiar and unique, at once human and divine. In that it witnesses to God's covenant with his people, it presents itself as a message without parallel and one which demands to be believed and obeyed. Yet this testimony in narrative guise is at the same time the evidential account of events, directed indeed by the sovereign will of God, but played out in the arena of the 'common history' of nations. That is why the Old Testament offers such stubborn resistance to any one-sided approach which in one way or another misconstrues the divine-human character of the material.

One fruitful way of getting to grips with this peculiar character of the Old Testament is to analyse the special structure of the Hebrew language.[1]

The Hebrew language conceives the 'being' of things and of the world as a whole, not as objective and static, but as something living and active. The way in which it encounters reality is analogous to the encounter between person and person. In that personal situation it sees the deepest and fullest disclosure of reality possible. The 'being' of a person is not commensurable with the 'being' of impersonal objects. That a person 'is' means that he is living, acting, that he presents himself as an 'I'. It is God, primarily, who is fully a person,

46

an 'I'. The verb *hayah*, when it refers to God, expresses his personal, dynamic, active being vis-à-vis his people and his creation. 'Obey my voice, and I will be your God, and you shall be my people,' (Jer. 7:23). This confrontation with a dynamic self-disclosure on God's part determines the Hebrew way of conceiving reality as a changing, moving, affective and dramatic whole, responding to God's call and attesting his mighty acts: 'Hear, O heavens, and give ear, O earth; for the Lord has spoken,' (Is. 1:2).

Just as *hayah* denotes the dynamic and personal character of reality, so the relation to this of the subject who knows is conveyed by the verb *yada'*. In contrast to the Greek verbs for 'know', in the Hebrew *yada'* the aspects of personal experience and encounter are paramount. This strongly volitional element finds its most profound expression when it is God himself who 'knows' his creatures, not merely in the general sense of having a concern (Ps. 50:11), but more especially in regard to his election: 'I know you by name,' (Ex. 33:12). 'You only have I known of all the families of the earth,' (Amos 3:2).

Another key word which conveys very clearly the personal character of Hebrew thinking is *'emeth*. In the Septuagint this is usually rendered by the Greek word for 'truth'—*alētheia*; but the Hebrew connotation is sharply opposed to the Greek concept. The word *'emeth* signifies a reality which is 'solid' (*'amen*), that is, 'trustworthy, valid'. In this sense a person who is *'emeth* is someone who can be trusted. The term is closely related to the word *'emunah*, meaning 'faith'; thus it comes to mean 'faithfulness'. The verb for 'believe' (*he'emin*), derived from the same root, means 'to declare faithful, firm, sure'. To believe God is to say *'amen* to him. God is the God of *'amen* (Is. 65:16).

This conception of truth is closely bound up with the prominent rôle played in Hebrew thinking by 'the word' (*dabhar*). The most penetrating thing that can be said about the word is that it is *'emeth*. Here too there is an obvious and radical difference from Greek modes of thought. The Greek idea of *logos* goes hand in hand with a static conception of reality as the object of theoretical, impersonal knowledge. The logos as the essential, objective order of reality corresponds to an analogous logos in the 'knowing' subject, i.e., to human reason. The Hebrew *dabhar*, on the other hand, is fundamentally dynamic in character. Its character arises from a personal relationship between the one who speaks the word and the one who hears it.

In the Old Testament it is the Word of God in particular which gives this term its constitutive meaning—and that is rooted in the prophetic proclamation. It is noteworthy that the prophets not only 'hear' the Word—they also 'see' it. So comprehensive is the Word that it takes control of each and all of a man's corporeal faculties; yet the primary character of the Word is not lost. The visual remains always secondary to the aural and never becomes a contemplative or mystical apperception of a timeless ideal reality.

How much indeed this is so is evidenced especially by the fact that in the theophanies God himself is never visible, although he is most certainly heard through his Word (Ex. 33:18 ff.). It is in terms of this setting that one has to understand the true character of the 'anthropomorphism' which is said to mark the Old Testament conception of the Godhead. The 'human form' which is there ascribed to God never implies a shape (Greek *morphē*), but invariably relates to the dynamic qualities, faculties and acts in which the person of God is disclosed.

The priority of the word over the visible form and of hearing over sight also has a great deal to do with the special importance which the Hebrew mind attaches to the category of time. An intuitive and spontaneous sense of temporal rhythm is a common enough thing in 'primitive' mentality. In Hebrew thinking the consciousness of time became the medium of a unique historical consciousness. The Old Testament affirms that beneath the surface of the time-rhythm an unrepeatable and irreversible trend moves towards the final consummation of history. The creation story in Genesis 1 both anticipates and epitomizes this theme, in the rhythm of the light, which is called 'day', dispelling the night and leading up to the ultimate fulfilment on the seventh day of the completion of God's works. Thus every Sabbath is a sign and token of the great Sabbath at the end of all time, the 'Day of the Lord'.[2]

This time-rhythm focused upon the final end and purpose also dominates the chapters of Genesis that follow. The titular heading of the fifth chapter runs: 'This is the book of the generations (*toledhoth*, begettings) of Adam.' It is a formula which recurs over and over again.† Indeed the whole Book of Genesis is made up of this 'book of generations'. The word *toledhoth* can also be taken to mean 'history' (Gen. 37:2, Revised Standard Version). The 'history' of the ancestors

† Gen. 6:9; 10:1; 11:10, 27; 25:12, 19; 36:1, 9; 37:2.

has its fulfilment in the begetting of the first-born. This line is carried on 'after the flood' (Gen. 10:1) right up to Abram. The whole life of Abram turns on the one central event of the begetting of the first-born, through whom he will make a great nation (Gen. 12:1), that is, the people of Israel. In its turn the history of that people has its *raison d'être* in the promise of the coming of the first-born, the Messiah. Then too St Matthew's Gospel has a titular opening which is a direct reference to that of Genesis 5: 'the book of the genealogy of Jesus Christ, the son of David, the son of Abram.'[3] In him 'the time is fulfilled' (Mk. 1:15).

The Hebrew has no word for 'eternity', as that is conceived by the Greek mind—the divine sphere exempted from the category of time. In fact Hebrew thought cannot possibly envisage a dimension of eternity which would be timeless. The word *'olam* means 'endless duration'. The assertion that God is *'olam* (Ps. 136; Is. 40:28) points to the endless duration of his covenant. Just as a slave bound to his master for life is called *'ebhedh 'olam*, so does God establish an 'everlasting covenant' (*berith 'olam*) with his people.

2. IS THE OLD TESTAMENT PRIMITIVE?

In the field of the phenomenology of religion it is current practice to talk about the 'primitive' spirit of the Old Testament. That idea is the predominant feature of Pedersen's quite outstanding study of Israel's life and culture.[4] The term 'primitive' in this case is meant to connote a psychic structure governed by the totality of life and the world. It is not altogether clear whether 'the fundamental psychological conception' of the Old Testament, which this scholar labels 'primitive', is anything more than a variety of the general pattern of culture in the ancient Near East. At all events he represents Babylonian and Israelite society as being both, in their original forms, varieties of the general primitive pattern.

This characterization is certainly not wrong, but it is extremely inadequate. A purely phenomenological account does not make contact with the essential nature of the Old Testament at all. It overlooks the fact that right through the Old Testament there runs a clear line of polemic directed against the 'primitive' spirit underlying the ancient civilizations of Western Asia. The very kernel of the Old Testament, theologically speaking, lies just at the point where the book sets itself in radical opposition to those features which are of the essence of the 'primitive' mentality. Therefore one ought not to assign this characteristic to the People of Israel without making careful reservations.

(a) The primitive mentality, in its phenomenologically typical and ideal form, is thoroughly empirical.[5] To even the most primitive belief, however, there is a background of latent 'primitive monism' that wells up spontaneously out of the deepest springs of primitive life and thought. This monism, though dormant as it were, is always there below the surface; and as soon as primitive religion gets mixed with other cultural traditions, it makes itself apparent.

> Pantheists and monists are the heirs of a very ancient tradition; they sustain among ourselves a conception whose original founders, primitive or savage peoples, deserve more respect than they usually receive.[6]

Kraemer gives the term 'primitive' such a broad connotation that it is made out to be the fundamental characteristic of all 'naturalist' religions.[7] Similarly, the Sinologist, de Groot, in his study of the Chinese religions, starts from the basic insight that the three religions of China 'are three branches, growing from a common stem, which has existed from pre-historic times; this stem is the religion of the Universe, its parts and phenomena.'[8]

This primeval monism is thus of the very essence of primitive religion. It is precisely on this point, however, that Israel parts company at the outset with the primitive apprehension of reality. In other 'higher religions' the chaotic empiricism of the primitive stage gives place to a strong belief in a universal order of nature which embraces within a single totality the abundant variety of arbitrary powers. In the case of Israel this development never occurred. Paul Volz, in his stimulating study of this matter, has shown effectively that the God of Israel never shed his demonic character.

> Yahweh became demonic; while conversely, since Yahweh absorbed everything demonic and was himself the mightiest demon of all, the Israelites no longer required any demons.[9]

In this paradoxical fashion—and just because it clung tenaciously to a 'primitive' belief—Israel's psychology broke away from the naturalistic-cum-monistic structure of the primitive mentality in general.

(*b*) When tribal religions are taken up into a broader and higher unit of culture, the vague and nameless multitude of powers develops into a polytheistic system of one kind or another. The classic example of this is the Homeric epoch of Greek religion. At no time in her history did Israel pass through the intermediate phase of polytheism; she, as it were, skipped that particular stage. Yahweh never assumed the features of the gods and Israel's faith arose directly from a dynamistic and animistic foundation.[10] The name 'Yahweh', which is in origin Kenite or Ugaritic, takes us back to an indefinable Power encountered in the lightning and thunder. The term *'elohim* (God) refers to the formless and nameless plurality of primitive forces which make their presence felt in that experience.

(*c*) Magic is an essential element in primitive religion. No primitive religion in fact can succeed in driving magic from its midst or suppressing it without committing suicide.[11] Magic practices were very much a live reality in Israel. That kind of outlook was fully within the capacities of her psychic structure. The Psalms especially are full of a sense of the tremendous menace of magical forces.[12] Sorcerers are among the great host of enemies which the royal psalms in particular denounce; they are, that is to say, among the Gentiles (*goyim*). In the Old Testament then sorceries are much more than just an anti-social or illegitimate activity. The fight against magic is here part of that radical opposition to the Gentiles which forms the backbone of the Old Testament. Practitioners of magic are described as *rasha'*, godless; and their works are 'an abomination to the Lord'. † In this respect the Old Testament opposes to the death an attitude and outlook to which primitive religion is linked by every fibre of its being.

(*d*) There is a close relationship in primitive religion between magical and mythical ways of thought. The philosopher, Ernst Cassirer, even employs the term 'mythical' to characterize primitive thinking generally.[13] The nature of myth is determined by the primitive structure of participation; but in the Old Testament one finds not a mythical participation in the cyclical rhythm of nature, but a participation of quite another kind—namely in the rhythm of history, which begins with God's creative acts and moves purposefully forward in the direction of the final 'Day of the Lord'. This means that the formal

† Deut. 18:9 ff.; Ex. 22:18; Lev 20:27.

structure of participation is preserved in Israelite modes of thought, but the content and function of it are entirely different.

(e) The attitude of participation harbours a profound longing for a still more complete union in which every distinction between subject and object is obliterated and all tensions are overcome. Lévy-Bruhl uses the term 'mystical' to describe the primitive mind generally. In Israel, however, no form of mysticism was able to take root. Viewed over against the personal sovereignty of God, the Creator, the idea of his being fused or identified with his creation is patently absurd. It is this belief which explains the otherwise mysterious fact that Israel remained barren of mystical systems which flourished so abundantly within other highly developed religions.[14]

(f) The next point has to do with Israel's relation to the primitive idea of community. In this respect too the spirit of Israel could quite justifiably be called 'primitive'. Kinship is a major element in the Israelite notion of community.[15] The term ʿam, usually rendered people, originally denoted a sacred community, bound together by a common worship. Here again closer scrutiny reveals the paradoxical character of Israel's 'primitive' spirit. Israel broke away from the religious tradition among primitive peoples which stands for the concept and validity of a universal, cosmic, moral and ritual law, on which the welfare of the group depends. Not until the 'umbilical cord' linking the tribal conception of community with the sacred order of the universe was cut through was Israel born as a 'nation'. When that happened, the term ʿam was transformed from a general sociological category of primitive community life into a unique expression of Israel's election from among the goyim.

(g) 'Primitive' as a general descriptive term for a type of spiritual structure is usually contrasted with the 'modern' mentality; and that can be typified fairly enough as a striving after a 'theoretical control over the world'. Mankind pursues a course between these two poles. As it moves away from the 'primitive' and towards the 'modern' outlook, so the separation between subject and object increases. This is the road between the extremes of embryo and logos, which man travels in 'becoming man'. A thoroughgoing mysticism is his way of attempting to revert to pre-natal, unconscious being. The opposite extreme to that is the complete ascendancy of the logos. The modern mentality moves onward to that goal, to an end which is total secularization. Religion, as it manifests itself in its historical forms, oscillates between these two extremities.[16]

On the way that leads from the primitive to the modern what place is to be accorded to the basic outlook of Israel? The amazing thing is that the anthropological features which according to this analysis are indispensable to the whole process of 'becoming man' are the very factors which Israel repudiated. Not only did she withstand the enticements of mysticism and persistently refuse to admit the claims of the logos upon her; she also refused to keep company with that magical and mythical attitude which, generally speaking, has been the hallmark of religion in its various historical manifestations. On the road which man follows in order to 'become himself' it looks as if there can be no place for Israel at all.

The truth is that Israel's history cannot be comprehended in terms of these general anthropological categories. Rather it is the Old Testament itself which compels us to seek to understand the issues of anthropology and religion in general in the light of the peculiar history of Israel. The people of Israel do not constitute one among many species of mankind. Rather is mankind to be understood in the light of the history of Israel. This way of viewing the question gives rise to the considerations which now follow.

3. ISRAEL IN THE SETTING OF THE ANCIENT NEAR EAST

The culture and religion of Canaan, with which the people of Israel found themselves involved after their entry into the country, formed part of a larger unit of civilization. Where precisely one draws the boundaries of that civilization will depend on how one interprets the evolution of cultures within what Breasted called 'the fertile crescent'. Toynbee postulates a 'Syriac' civilization, embracing not only Israel, but also the Aramaeans, Philistines and Phoenicians. There are grounds for distinguishing on the one hand between a West-Semitic civilization, which included the Arab peoples, and on the other a Babylonian civilization,[17] closely affiliated to the antecedent Sumerians. From as early as the beginning of the third millennium before Christ a Semitic population akin to the Amorites and with a high level of civilization was to be found in Canaan.

The culture of that country was profoundly affected by Egyptian as well as by Babylonian religion. To this was added the influence of Hittite civilization, which reached its zenith during the fourteenth century B.C., when Syria lay under the political domination of the Hittites. Hittite civilization declined as a result of the large-scale migration of peoples at the close of the second millennium and its place was taken, along the coastal plain, by that of the Philistines.

One can sum the matter up by saying that at the time when the Israelites overran the country, Canaanite civilization bore the mark of a variety of cultural influences and that these have left their traces in the social life and legal system of Israel. It is quite obvious in the Old Testament that so far as religion is concerned the predominating influence was Babylonian—a fact which has given rise in the past to some very hasty conclusions. Increasing attention is being given nowadays to the remarkable way in which the Old Testament handles the Babylonian traditions and alters them radically in the process. This has modified our viewpoint; but of course it in no way detracts from the tremendous importance of the Babylonian influences.

When one takes a broad look at the Babylonian religion and its course of development, one cannot but be struck by the presence of an overruling continuity, as prominent here as it is in Egyptian religion—and not only there, but in those of two other great civilizations, China and India. Sumerian-Babylonian religion can be traced back in an uninterrupted line to its sources in the fourth millennium B.C. In the second millennium the various popular religions were fused with the religion of Assyria; and in that process they merged to form a single polytheistic system or superstructure on a Sumerian basis. A continuous current then flows through the second and first millennia. Although in the tremendously syncretistic course of Hellenistic civilization this flowed in another direction, it never lost anything of its original capacity for absorbing and amalgamating with everything that lay in its path.

Archaeological evidence offers abundant proof of the predominantly chthonic character of the old Sumerian religion.[18] But in the course of time this made way for the religious system of Babylon, with the astral phenomena which were its major element. The religion of Marduk was far from being a genuine innovation, in spite of all the cultic and theological reforms that came with it.

Indeed it was introduced—and introduced effectively—because it set forward the primeval chthonic religion under new forms.

It is not at all surprising that we come across these same basic features in the area which formed the immediate environment of Israel. The principal god of the Canaanites, Ba'al, shared his name with a host of local ba'als. Ba'al is the earth-power, manifesting itself in any or every place, in mountain, stream or tree. He is the power of procreation and of vegetation and is at the same time the god of the sun and of the heavens. This duality of function is meant to express, in a primitive way, the all-embracing harmony of the universe, which the cyclical course of terrestrial nature contains within itself. The female aspect of chthonic fertility, represented by deities such as Ba'alah, Astarte, 'Asherah and 'Anath, retained its dynamistic and animistic ethos. These figures can hardly be said to have attained the status of real deities in a polytheistic pantheon. The Canaanite and Phoenician religions were closely inter-related. The chthonic quality of the Phoenician cult was embodied above all in the young god of dying and reviving vegetation, Adonis, a double of the Sumerian god, Tammuz. Again, the religion of the Aramaeans and of Ugarit, which recent excavation has brought to light, do not differ in essentials from this general pattern, although the last-mentioned does exhibit a number of peculiar features.

Thus amid the confusing variety of religions associated with West Asia in ancient times one can detect an under-lying unity and indeed a continuity, which were preserved without interruption for some thousands of years. Diverse though these cults, rites, myths, festivals and deities might be, the inter-relationship which existed between them all brought with it a high degree of reciprocal toleration and a well-nigh unlimited capacity for mutual assimilation, identification and absorption into the larger whole. The most primitive fertility cult devoted to a vaguely conceived chthonic power and the loftiest astrological speculations of Babylonian theology stem from one and the same root. They belong together; for they are the trunk, the branches, the bloom of one basic apperception: the primal and the ultimate identity of all that is, the unity of all the elements of life, human, superhuman and subhuman, in a single and comprehensive totality. That apperception, however refined and elaborated in ritual systems and theological speculations, springs from a primary, spontaneous and unreflecting intuition which may be dormant but is always present, secreted in the deepest recesses of the soul. It is the source of that whole complex of religious traditions and practices in Canaan which in the most literal sense confronted Israel.

4. THE CREATION STORY AND THE BABYLONIAN MYTH

Hardly anyone nowadays would seriously contest the view that the creation story in Genesis 1 contains reminiscences of the Babylonian myth of Marduk's victory over Tiamat. The real interest here lies therefore not in pointing out the dependent connection, but in asking how it is to be interpreted. When we go more deeply into the matter we see that what we have here is a striking example of Israel's attitude towards her religious environment and of the way in which, as she got to know about these mythical traditions, she learned to deal with them. One scholar who has made a thorough investigation of this question is Hermann Gunkel. He tries to track down when and how it was that Israel became familiar with this Babylonian material and took it over, foreign though it was, into her own religious traditions.[19] He finds traces of the Babylonian myth which lies behind Genesis 1 in various other parts of the Old Testament as well, especially in the Book of Job, the Psalms and some of the prophetic texts. In the light of this it seems even more reasonable than it did before to suppose that this piece of mythology persisted as a living tradition for a long time among the common people of Israel. Gunkel's conclusion is that the creation story belongs to an old Israelite tradition which had adopted Babylonian material already in the earliest period after the entry into Canaan and in the form which Canaanite tradition had given it. Then Israel set to work on the material herself, elaborating the form until it served to express Israel's own faith. The prophetic traditions regarding the Creation fitted neatly on to the ancient popular tradition. This was later revised under the priestly code and so emerged in the definitive form we now find in Genesis 1.

However that may be, the Babylonian epic, *Enuma elish*, as we now have it, is not itself the original version of the myth; it is a later redaction of very ancient Sumerian material.[20]

The version of the poem known to us, in which Enlil is imprisoned by Marduk, the god of Babylon—and at the time when this new version appeared, also the chief god of the Babylonian empire— opens with a description of the universe as it was in the beginning.

The primeval chaos consisted of three commingled elements: Apsu, who represents the sweet waters; Tiamat, who represents the sea; and Mummu, who probably represents the clouds and mists. There was nothing but water; and as yet there were no gods. Then amidst this watery chaos there came into existence two gods, Lahmu and Lahamu, begotten by Apsu and born of Tiamat. These two divinities produced the next pair, Anshar and Kishar, respectively the upper (male) and lower (female) halves of the universe. They bring forth Anu, god of the sky, who in his turn begets Nudimmud—another name for Ea or Enki, the god of the sweet waters—who in his original form represents the earth itself. The new deities, Anu and Ea, stand sharply opposed to the forces of chaos and their association with inertia and inactivity. Apsu and Mummu openly turn against the new gods and their new ways. The wise Ea perceives their intention and to thwart it institutes the 'configuration of the universe'. By a sacred spell he casts Apsu into a deep and deadly sleep and erects upon him—that is, upon the sweet waters, now subdued by the magic craft—his own abode: the earth resting upon sweet waters. In this abode Marduk, begotten by Ea, is born. It is Marduk who dominates the scene in the succeeding section of the poem. At the urgent pleading of the other gods he agrees to do battle with Tiamat and her entourage, against whom they are apparently powerless. Armed with the weapons of a god of storm and thunder, he ensnares Tiamat in the meshes of his sturdy net and his arrow pierces her heart. He cuts her body in two and lifts up half of it to form the sky. Marduk then makes his abode on this part of her body, directly opposite to that made by Ea on the body of Apsu, and as a counterpart to it.

The poem finishes with Kingu, Tiamat's second husband and principal bodyguard, being condemned by the assembled gods and executed. Under Ea's direction, mankind is created from his blood. In token of their gratitude the gods build Marduk a city and a temple, with thrones, each mounted on a dais for their assembly. At the first meeting there Marduk is solemnly installed as king.

It is impossible here to give more than a truncated and utterly unpoetic outline of the poem; but it is in fact a magnificent example of cosmogonic thinking. Its full import cannot be grasped within a single dimension. In order to get a clear idea of how this piece of poetic mythology bears on the biblical story of the Creation one has to take a closer look at it in some aspects.

The first thing to note is the fundamental unity of myth and ritual under-lying the whole work. It became in fact the special book of the Babylonian New Year festival, which lasted in all for twelve days of the month Nisan during the spring season. The poem was customarily recited on the third day of the celebrations.

The cosmogonic events which the epic celebrates are rehearsed and represented in the New Year ritual. Such a cosmogony offers a primordial pattern for the whole of existence. The poem extols the enthronement of Marduk as king; and this is identified in the New Year ritual with the enthronement of the Babylonian king himself. The universe is depicted as a state, since vice versa the Babylonian state is identical with the universe. The cosmogonic process whereby the alluvial land emerges from the watery chaos is repeated afresh each year as the Euphrates overflows its banks.

It is worth noticing too that the victory of order and culture over chaos and inertia is made to appear a magical achievement; and yet this magic takes its strength and its effectiveness from precisely that skill which is rooted inextricably in the very primeval chaos it is wrestling to conquer and control. This ambivalence runs right through the cosmogony of the poem.

The cyclical movement which imposes itself on everything is an obvious feature of both the myth and the ritual. All things return, ultimately, to their first beginning. The epic describes how Marduk, when he has conquered the powers of chaos, makes his dwelling upon the upper part of Tiamat, the sky. The name of this heavenly abode is Esagila. It is the prototype of the temple which the gods build in his honour after his accession to the throne: the earthly Esagila, which is itself the prototype of the temple in Babylon where the New Year rites were enacted. This Babylonian temple was also called 'Esagila'. Now the heavenly Esagila is the celestial counterpart of the dwelling-place which Marduk's father, Ea, had earlier erected on the corpse of Apsu—the place, in fact, of Marduk's birth. So it is that having triumphed over chaos he returns to the heavenly image (Esagila) of the place where he had himself been born. Through his triumph he reverts to his nativity. The triumph is heavenly; but it is his earthly birth which it reiterates. Likewise Apsu (sweet waters, earthly power) is 'repeated' in Tiamat (the ocean, heaven); and so too Ea (chthonic power) recurs in Marduk (heavenly order).

In point of fact, nothing really 'happens' in the poem. The order which Marduk builds in overcoming chaos is grounded in chaos, is a product of its constituent elements, realized through its resources of magic and delimited by its destiny. It could not be otherwise; for Marduk is a god, and 'the origin of the gods' is . . . primeval chaos.

Humankind is formed from the blood of Kingu, second husband to Tiamat. Through the veins of men there flows the vital force of the chaos-power—bound by Marduk, condemned and executed by the gods, it is true; yet it is his body which yields in death the very stuff of which men are made. Not only the stuff, but its manipulator too, is chthonic in character. It is Ea, prompted by the ingenuity of Marduk, who forms mankind from Kingu's blood. 'That work was not meet for human understanding': it was the work of a magician's cunning.

Thus the cosmogonic process celebrated here is significant anthropologically. It reflects what was earlier referred to as the process of 'becoming man'. In terms of a cosmogony the myth depicts the human consciousness emerging from its embryonic state and being born. Just as Ea builds his abode upon Apsu, so man builds his conscious activities on the foundations of his embryonic life. Chaos is not really vanquished, but only hypnotized. It sleeps the sleep of death; but it is not annihilated. So is it with the universe, which comes into being out of chaos; so is it also with man, who is a 'micro-cosmos', or better, a 'micro-chaos', the universe in miniature. Ea and Marduk, Tiamat, Kingu and Apsu, the whole cosmogonic process in fact—it is all in man's own self.

The Old Testament contains many a reminiscence and reflection of the cosmogonic struggle as the Babylonian myth envisages it. A common theme in the Babylonian and Ugaritic mythologies, which form the background to this type of material in the Old Testament,[21] is the fight between one of the major gods and an enormous sea-monster which has rebelled against their divine rule. The result of the contest is that the monster, a dragon or serpent, is totally defeated. Now the allusions to this in the Old Testament differ from the original Babylonian and Ugaritic myths in that from the whole richly elaborated mythological drama the Old Testament selects only one special feature: it focuses attention entirely on the combat between a god and the dragon of the deep. The polytheistic setting, the naturalistic import of the myth as representing the cycle of vegetation, the chthonic bonds which the victorious gods impose upon the defeated monster—all these aspects which are an integral part of the original myth—are ignored and discarded. This eclecticism has the effect of turning inside out the purport of the original. What in the myth is ascribed to one or other of the innumerable gods or to several gods at once the Old Testament simply ascribes to Yahweh. He is the one who possess the power and authority to do what in the myth lies with the gods.

In so far as the theme of the original polytheistic myth is reflected in this account or adumbration of a contest between Yahweh and the dragon of chaos, it is proper to speak of an Old Testament mythology. The contest is clearly connected with the creation of heaven and earth.[22] Psalm 74 sings of God's mighty acts in creation: 'Thou didst divide the sea by thy might; thou didst break the heads of dragons on the waters.' This and parallel texts refer to some primeval battle which preceded the creation.† In Ezekiel 32:2–6 (cf. 29:3–5) the theme is even more clearly in evidence. Behind that passage lies the Egyptian theory of kingship, with its notion of the royal functions as an intrinsic part of the natural phenomena of vegetation.[23] The Egyptian idea Ezekiel combines in his own peculiar fashion with Semitic mythology about the dragon of chaos. Thus he deploys mythological themes in order to launch a withering attack on the mythology: ' "Because you said: 'The Nile is mine, and I made it,' therefore, behold, I am against you, and against your streams, and I will make the land of Egypt an utter waste and desolation . . ." ' (Ezek. 29:9). The myth becomes the mouth-piece of God's judgment in history.

In Isaiah 51 the Lord is called upon to awake 'as in days of old', when he cut Rahab in pieces and pierced the dragon. The 'days of old' here certainly refers to the event of creation, although the allusion is in the first place to the Exodus from Egypt (v. 10)—the miracle which is also the pledge of release from the Babylonian captivity, still awaited by Israel (v. 11). That will be like a new creation (vv. 6–8). Psalm 89 presents a similar picture. In the course of a hymn of praise addressed to the God of the chosen people, Israel, the primeval battle of the Lord with Rahab is recalled. Here Rahab, the primeval dragon, has become a pseudonym for Egypt, the arch-enemy of Israel.

In the Book of Job the two chapters (38 and 39) in which Job

† See Is. 51:9 ff.; Job 7:12; 26:12 f.; 38:8 ff.; Ps. 89:10; 104:9; Prov. 8:29; Jer. 5:22.

extols God's power in the works of his creation are followed by a description of the two mythological Nile monsters, the 'behemoth' and the leviathan. There is a further allusion here to the monstrous power of Egypt. Yet the Lord plays with the dragon 'as with a bird', yea, the monster is 'the first of his works' (Job 41:5, 40:20 ff.; cf. Ps. 104:26). In the apocalyptic twenty-seventh chapter of Isaiah we find 'leviathan' used together with the dragon (tannin) as pseudonyms for two great empires. In this case the mythological battle is linked with the final victory of God over his enemies at the last day: then the Lord will lead his scattered people back to the holy mountain of Jerusalem.

What we have here then is a radical demythologization of the material. First a particular feature, the battle with the dragon, is selected. Secondly this battle is attributed to God. In the third place the main outcome of the battle is the historical salvation of Israel. It is most remarkable in this connection that the message of the prophets centres upon God's dealings with and for his people in history, and that in their proclamation creation as an event plays only a subsidiary rôle. The keystone of prophetic witness to the Lord's power is the Exodus from Egypt.[24] When God's acts of creation are spoken of it is always in direct association with Israel's election. There is copious evidence of this, in Deutero–Isaiah especially. † If we assume, as is now generally accepted to be the case, that the doxologies in the Book of Amos (4:13; 5:8; 9:6) are later editorial additions, this is the clearest possible indication that the proclamation as it concerns God's activity in creation is secondary in character. The God of Israel also in the beginning created heaven and earth (Amos 9:3–6). The work of creation is a part of salvation![25]

5. THE CREATION STORY (GENESIS 1:1–2:4a)

Genesis 1 presents us with an ancient tradition, traces of which are discernible in various parts of the Old Testament; but it presents this in a version systematically worked over and edited. The mythological colouring which was still vivid enough in many of the passages cited above—even though they include no more than fragments of a far richer Babylonian-Ugaritic mythology—is very drastically toned down in Genesis 1. The whole narrative here bears the stamp of theological reflection.

Gunkel talks about the 'Yahweh-myth' of the conflict between

† See Is. 40:21–24; 43:1, 15, 21; 44:2, 21, 28; 45:11–13, 18; 51:13; 54:5 (cf. Jer. 27:5; 31:35 f.; 33:25 f.).

God and the dragon of chaos; but when it comes to the stories contained in Genesis 1-11 he explicitly rejects the term 'myth' in favour of 'saga'.[26] As explicitly, Karl Barth[27] takes over the definition of Genesis 1 as saga from Gunkel. He maintains that the expression 'myth of creation' is doubly a contradiction, as regards both the biblical creation-story and myth itself. Genuine myth indeed has never been concerned with the theme of creation. For myth, properly speaking, man, the world and the gods constitute a total reality, self-existent and self-sufficient, without Creator, God or history. And yet, of course, Genesis 1 is no 'history' either, in the accepted sense of the word. It is a saga: that is, a poetic representation, intuitively conceived, of a concrete, unique reality which is both prehistorical and historical, being particularized in time and space. Broadly speaking the Bible contains a mixture of saga and history. The creation story is an exception in that it is pure saga, 'prehistorical history'. It is history, yes—but history of a prophetic and divinatory order.

There is however one aspect of the creation story which the term 'saga' does not adequately describe: and that is the liturgical character of the text. When one remembers the liturgical use made of the Babylonian epic, *Enuma elish*, in the New Year ritual, it would seem reasonable enough to suppose that the biblical creation story had a similar place in the ritual of the New Year festival among the Israelites.[28] Any such inference is put out of court, however, by the fact of an unbridgeable gulf between the spirit of the Babylonian myth and the spirit of Genesis 1. The Babylonian New Year festival is properly seen to be the 'most complete expression of Mesopotamian religiosity,'[29] the purpose of which was to establish that harmony with nature which was indispensable to a fruitful existence for the community. The three main Israelite festivals (Passover, Pentecost and the Feast of Ingathering or of Booths) on the other hand were dominated by the idea of historical commemoration. Their original naturalistic background was radically transformed so that they had become festivals commemorating God's deliverance of Israel from Egypt.† The celebrations at the New Year did not belong in the series of main festivals. Taking place at the seventh new moon, they simply marked the fact that time was divided according to the moon.[30] The liturgical reciting of the text of Genesis 1—so thoroughly anti-mythical and undramatic—was wholly appropriate therefore to this unmythical

† Cf. Ex. 13:8, 9; Deut. 16:3, 12 f.; Lev. 23:43.

festival. God made the sun and the moon to be 'for signs and for seasons and for days and years' (Gen. 1:14). Within this order of things it is the New Year, a straightforward demarcation of time. Creation is a (pre-)historical act. Unlike the cosmogonic myth, creation cannot be re-enacted or dramatized by man; it can only be commemorated and accepted in faith and gratitude.

It is time now to take a look at what is contained in the creation story itself, comparing it first of all with the *Enuma elish*. The Babylonian epic is not only a cosmogonic myth—it is theogonic too. It starts with an account of the primeval chaos, when 'Apsu, the primeval abyss, the origin of the gods, and the mistress Tiamat, the sea, who gave birth to all of them, still mixed up their waters with one another.' Apsu and Tiamat together make up the eternal, theogonic and cosmogonic reality which in the mysterious procreative union of the male with the female element brings forth the totality of being: gods, the world and human kind. Genesis 1, verse 2, refers to this mythical beginning; but the sharp sting of its anti-mythical purpose lies in the fact that it is the second verse, and not the opening one, which does so. The point of contention is expressed in what was originally the title of Genesis 1, although we find it now at the end: '*These* are the generations of the heavens and the earth,' namely, that in the beginning they were created by God. The term 'generations' (*toledhoth*) points forward to the ensuing chapters of Genesis. We have already noted that the word refers to the history of the patriarchs, to the 'begettings' of the first-born son, and that in some places it may be rendered simply as 'history'. One could therefore even say: 'This is the history of heaven and earth.' The acts of creation adumbrate the history of God's dealings with mankind—a history which he will begin with his people.

The opening verse likewise contains a direct attack on the myth. 'In the beginning God created the heavens and the earth.' This would seem to be a plain contradiction of the next verse, which harks back to the opening cosmogonic section of the mythical epic and itself speaks of an entirely different sort of beginning, connecting it with the primeval waters of chaos. Yet whereas according to the myth primeval chaos, in the last analysis, governs everything from start to finish, here it is overcome once for all by God's acts in creation which quite literally leave it behind.

The terminology in verse 2 is very revealing: 'The earth was *tohu* and *bohu*'. The word '*tohu*' is probably an echo of the Babylonian 'Tiamat'; whilst '*bohu*', which is invariably coupled with '*tohu*' in the Old Testament, may be a form of 'Bau', name of the Phoenico-Babylonian goddess of night and primeval mother of man. In the Old Testament these terms signify 'emptiness, worthlessness, vanity'. *Tohu* sometimes has the same meaning as *tehom*—the chaos that lurks beneath the inhabited world (Job 26:7); but chaos is also upon the earth, out beyond the region of men. *Tohu* is therefore also 'the desert, no man's land, the accursed place' (Num. 20:5). Israel's salvation out of this *tohu* is described as an act of creation.

Small wonder then that the Gentiles especially are branded as *tohu* and that this is directly associated with the thought of God's creative acts. Just as God triumphs in these acts over the primeval chaos, so he creates his people by accounting the *goyim*, the Gentiles, as *tohu* and delivering Israel out of their hand. *Tohu* became a technical term for idols and idolmakers as well.

Tohu quite often occurs in composite expressions with '*ephes* or '*aphes*. The Gentiles are reckoned by God to be '*ephes wa-tohu* (Is. 40:17, and so forth). These two words are pretty well synonymous and frequently occur in the same context.† In this context '*ephes* is intended to denote 'nothingness, non-existence'; and it corresponds with the verb '*aphes* which, when it occurs in a similar context, means 'to cease, to come to an end' (cf. Is. 16:4; 29:20; in conjunction with *tohu*, v. 21). Furthermore, the plural form of the term '*ephes* appears in the poetic phrase '*aphse ha-'ares*: the ends of the earth. Several scholars have connected this expression with the Babylonian Apsu, the primeval chaos and ocean, hailed in the opening verses of the epic as 'the origin of the gods'. The Babylonian cosmology which Israel adopted conceives of this primeval ocean as encircling the earth, so that it can truly be said to be 'the ends of the earth'.[31]*

But against the background of that cosmological idea the term takes on a still more profound significance. Generally speaking, the phrase '*aphse ha-'ares*, the ends of the earth, means simply: the Gentiles, the nations (*goyim*); but there is a twofold implication here. First it points to the fact that the Gentiles are spread over the whole earth: and then it also lays bare their 'nothingness'. Thus the expression is

† Cf. Is. 34:12; 41:12, 17, 24, 29; 45:6, 14; 52:4; 54:15; Deut. 32:36.
* Cf. Zech. 9:10 = Ps. 72:8; Prov. 30:4.

always employed in a context where God's creative and saving power is demonstrated by his actions in defeating and driving out the nations, the *'aphse ha-'areṣ*, so that men may know that he rules over Jacob to the ends of the earth. †

The nations (*goyim*) belong to the primeval ocean, the mythical chaos, which their own mythology declares to be 'the origin of the gods', the totality out of which all things arise. *'Ephes* and *tohu* are exactly parallel terms. Whilst the latter refers to *tehom*, Israelite equivalent of the Babylonian primeval ocean, Tiamat, the former directly recalls Apsu, the male partner of Tiamat. Both these terms denote 'nothingness, non-being', and in that sense are frequently applied to the *goyim*. The nations are accounted by God to be *'ephes wa-tohu* (Is. 40:17). The God of Israel, that is to say, condemns the Gentiles on the verdict of their own myths, which extol Apsu and Tiamat as the theogonic, cosmogonic and anthropogonic source of the totality of being.

Creation means that these *'ephes wa-tohu*, this Apsu and this Tiamat, are revealed as 'nothingness' and hurled back into the abyss of 'nothingness'. This is the *creatio ex nihilo*—for philosophy an insoluble problem, but in its biblical setting the uttered promise of salvation, of exodus, in a literal sense 'out of nothing': *ex nihilo*.

It is God's word which creates. The story of creation begins with the proclamation that God said: 'Let there be light'; it begins at the point where God shatters the timeless silence of chaos, at the moment when his word sounds forth. There is a formal similarity between creation by the word of God and various conceptions to be found in other religions of the ancient Near East. It is all the more remarkable therefore that Babylonian-Assyrian religion knows nothing of a creation by the divine word.[32]

The divine word certainly has a cosmogonic function in Egyptian religion; but the 'word' in this case is a physical, spermatic power, representing the mystery of the self-generating universe. In short it belongs to the mythology which is repudiated at the outset in the account of creation.[33]

What then does God's word signify in the creation story? We can hope to understand what it means only when we take that story as an account of primeval prehistory, antecedent to the history of

† Ps. 59; cf. Ps. 2; 72; 22:28; 67:8; 98:3; Is. 52:10; Mic. 5:3; Jer. 16:19 f.; Deut. 33:17; 1 Sam. 2:10.

Israel. The idea of the creative word runs right through the Bible; and the whole book is imbued with it. What the Lord did in the beginning, when he got rid of chaos and created heaven and earth, he does over and over again, when he addresses himself to the patriarchs and to the prophets. God is for ever calling men out of the darkness, out of chaos, out of nothingness and idleness to the light of his creation.

God's creative acts, therefore, do not merely cause things to be; they go far beyond that. God creates by separating, dividing. His word calls the light into being and divides it from the darkness of the mythical primordium. God saw the light that it was good; and thus he 'divides' between good and evil. All mythological cosmogony envisages a continuous struggle between the powers of good and evil—a struggle in which no real victory or real defeat is possible; for both forces have their origin in the selfsame chaos, the womb of all things; both parties have need of each other and without each other could not exist. Their conflict is a part of the unending rhythm of things; it is—to borrow a phrase of Heraclitus—'the father of all things'. Over against all this, creation implies that darkness, chaos and evil are positively rejected, consigned to idleness and nothingness, which is their proper essence. That is not to say that they no longer have any being. This is a point of the utmost importance. The chaos-power described in Genesis 1, verse 2, does not cease to exist, but it is deprived of its mythical energy. It is exposed in all its vanity and is no longer able to be what in the myth it really is: totalitarian.

The darkness is deprived of an independent existence in its own right; it continues to exist only by the favour of God, by the favour, that is to say, of the light which is the first of his works. God called the light day; and thus he creates time. The darkness of the mythical chaos is essentially timeless, the eternal and everfruitful womb into which all things return. The first of God's works in creation is time. Time is neither a mystical intuition nor a philosophical abstraction, but something concrete: day-time. The creation story really does have to do with 'ordinary' days, the seven days of our week; and this—'our' time—is God's time. That, in brief compass, is the good news.

To create is to 'divide'. As the light from the darkness, good from evil, time from mythical eternity, so on the second day of creation that other element of chaos is divided: the waters are separated from the waters. God made 'a firmament in the midst of the waters' (v. 6 ff.). The firmament is the effective sign of God's faithfulness towards his creation; it is his handiwork and it declares his mercy (Ps. 19:1; 150:1; 89:2 ff.). The striking thing that emerges from this is that the spreading out of the firmament is directly connected with the scattering of Israel's enemies (Is. 40:23; 44:24 f.; Ps. 136). It is this firmament that God calls Heaven (v. 8). Thus 'heaven' comes to be far more than just a cosmological notion; it becomes the guarantee of God's faithfulness towards the earth. Just as the light was called day—the good news that man has time to live in—so is the firmament called heaven, in proclamation of the fact that mankind has space to live in too. It is for this reason that the heavens declare God's righteousness (Ps. 50:6; 97:6).

To create is to divide. The creation of the earth, like the creation of heaven, takes place through an act of dividing. Like the day and like the firmament, the earth attests God's everlasting mercy and truthfulness.

That is why, when the Old Testament glories in the creation of the world and tells of how the nether waters have been driven back, it celebrates in one and the same breath the driving back of the enemies of God and of Israel and extols the election of Israel. The exodus through the Red Sea is compared to the third day of creation. †

Looked at from that point of view, the sea too, like the night and the upper ocean, forms part of the creation. The waters bring forth swarms of living creatures (v. 20). It is asserted that 'God created the great *tanninim*' (v. 21) as the first of these sea-creatures. This is a reminiscence of the battle between Yahweh and the dragon of the sea. So complete is God's ascendancy over it that even the primeval dragon is included in his work of creation (Ps. 104:24 f.).

First and foremost, however, it is the earth which is created to 'put forth' vegetation (vv. 11–13); from being a desert, a *tohu wa-bohu*, the earth is changed into fertile land. This again is a creative act belonging to the prehistory of Israel's election. So God brings his people through the desert into a goodly land (Deut. 8:7–10). So too, one day, he will make the wilderness a pool of water (Is. 41:18).

It is beneath this heaven and upon this earth, surrounded by the tokens of his everlasting mercy, that man is made in God's own

† See Ps. 66:5; cf. Ps. 77:15; Is. 17:13; cf. Is. 8:5–10.

image, male and female (v. 26 ff.). The partnership betw_ and man is often described as a partnership between man and wo. 'For your Maker is your husband,' (Is. 54:5 f.). 'As the bridegroom rejoices over the bride, so shall your God rejoice over you.'† All other creatures are created 'according to their kind'; but man is created in God's image, in the partnership of 'I' and 'You', male and female—the sole differentiation which the creation knows within the human race.

Whereas in the other religions of the ancient Near East man is no more than one among the elements of the universe, having the same origin and the same destiny as the rest of the totality of being, in the Old Testament it is exactly the reverse. There the rest of the creation is called, albeit in a subservient rôle, to play its part in that unique history which God initiates with mankind. With the creation of man in God's image, in the partnership of male and female which represents God's partnership with his people, there begins the history of God's covenant, the central feature of the creation. About this centre the whole of nature is ranged. When the Lord speaks to his people, heaven and earth are commanded to give ear (Is. 1:2); and so shall it be when the New Covenant is established (Hos. 2:18; Is. 11:6).

On the seventh day God rests; at rest also is his work of creation, at rest in the partnership now accomplished. Therefore man is to rest upon the seventh day and keep that day holy. It is 'the day of the Lord', crown of the days of that creative labour, foreshadowing too of that final 'day of the Lord', the goal and purpose of all history. 'I will be their God, and they shall be my people,' (Jer. 31:33): in that day it will come true.

6. THE PARADISE STORY AND BABYLONIAN MYTHOLOGY

Between the creation story as edited by the 'Elohist' and the story of Paradise, in which one can detect the hand of the editor known as the 'Yahwist', there is an important point of analogy, in that both narratives present an advanced stage of demythologization. It will be sufficient for our purpose if we limit our concern to certain features of the Paradise story which offer direct evidence of its unique message, as contrasted with the mythological ideas of the ancient Near East.

† See Is. 62:5; cf. Hos. 1:2 ff.; 2:19 f.; 3:1 f.; Jer. 3:1 f., 6 f.; 4:30 etc.; Ezek. 16: 23.

First there is the conception—fundamental to the whole story (Gen. 2:4a–3:24)—of 'Paradise' (to give it its customary name) as the dwelling-place of the first man. Remarkably enough, there is no trace of this in the Sumerian or Babylonian-Assyrian material. It has much to say instead of 'abodes of the gods' and of 'islands of the blessed'.[34] The question of how man may attain immortality—that privilege which the gods claimed for themselves alone—is indeed the principal theme of the Gilgamesh Epic. The knowledge of immortality as revealed by Utnapishti to Gilgamesh is 'a hidden thing and a secret of the gods'.[35] Utnapishti had himself obtained immortality with the help of Ea. The primary concern of the Gilgamesh Epic is with the mystery of life and its resuscitation out of death.[36] Three times there is described a journey through the realm of the dead. Knowledge of the secret of immortality is of a magical nature; the secret is divine, but is one that men may unlock by superhuman skill and insight.[37] Over the waters of death Gilgamesh at last reaches the island of Utnapishti. There Utnapishti explains how it is that he has entered the company of the gods and has obtained everlasting life by telling him the story of the deluge, which he guards as a divine secret. On the way back Gilgamesh goes down to the bottom of the sea and there obtains the plant of everlasting life, the secret of which Utnapishti has divulged to him. Later on during the return journey the hero goes for a bathe. Meanwhile a serpent comes up out of the water, snatches the plant and devours it, 'sloughing its skin on its return' (acquires, that is, the actual power to renew its own life). Thus Gilgamesh loses his last chance to get immortality and returns to Uruk.

The 'thorny plant of wondrous power' is, in fact, the elixir of life; the quest for this magical remedy, in a number of varieties, is a common feature of the religions of the ancient Near East. Another equally common *motif* was that of the serpent which was held to harbour a divine chthonic power and magical insight.[38] For that reason the serpent was regarded as an apotropaeic, protective symbol, a symbol of fertility and an animal of an ominous character. The serpent, coming up out of the ground, signifies the mysterious power of Mother Earth. It makes its abode in the depth of ocean, in the realm of death which is also the source of everlasting life. Gilgamesh calls it 'the earth-lion'. By snatching the plant of everlasting life the serpent obtains the cherished gift of rejuvenation, which Gilgamesh had tried to seize in vain.

The Babylonian epic demonstrates in a dramatic way the inevitability of death. Even a superhuman being like the demi-god Gilgamesh, despite his having passed through the gate of the sun-god and crossed the waters of death, must eventually face the bitter truth: that no one can escape from death. He has to recognize that death is 'the fate of mankind'.[39]

Closely connected with the Gilgamesh Epic is the myth of Adapa.[40] Like Adapa, Gilgamesh can boast of 'wisdom'; he has been initiated into the mystery of life out of death. Both of them fail in their attempt to lay hold of everlasting life. Why? Because the gods 'retain life in their keeping'. The manner in which the gods reserve life to themselves is, however, extremely ambiguous. In the ultimate, Gilgamesh and Adapa are not the obvious victims of a divine decree, but rather of a quirk of fate, a queer concatenation of accident, deceit and error. Is not death really and truly . . . life? And is eternal life itself not . . . death? Where Utnapishti dwells, on the isle beyond the waters of death, and where Anu inhabits the realm of heaven, there is the place both of eternal life and of the hereafter, that is to say, of death. The Gilgamesh Epic and the Adapa myth both declare that eternal life remains the exclusive right of the gods. Yet the heroes of both do at least possess divine wisdom; and this gives them a power which is at any rate partly divine. That it is only partly divine is the cause of man's insatiable hunger and thirst for the food and drink of immortality. Essentially, the tenor of this mythological theme is so tantalizing because it hints at the secret truth that immortality is not completely out of reach. That divine wisdom which the heroes Gilgamesh and Adapa possess is also the privilege of the priest and the magician, in short, of all such as have the knowledge of 'the secret of the great gods'. All science, in the last analysis, is the outcome of magical insight.[41]

All this provides a background to the consideration of the story of Paradise in the Bible, to which we may now turn. Notice first of all how the Paradise narrative treats the mythological conception of 'Eden'. 'Eden' as the mythical garden of God would seem to be a notion familiar enough to the later prophets of the Old Testament. In the story of Paradise, however, there is little more than a faint echo of that mythological conception; for it is reduced to a quasi-concrete, geographical reference to the spot where God planted a garden: 'in Eden, in the east,' (Gen. 2:8). This 'Paradise' is most clearly not a garden of the gods or an isle of immortality beyond the ocean. It is a garden planted for the man whom God has formed from the dust of the earth. The garden here is obviously an archetype of the world, as it is also the centre from which God's blessing is conferred upon the earth as a whole. It is, so to speak, an epitome of the earth itself.

Man is not created within the garden of Eden, but is put there to till and tend it. Thus the service which man renders within the garden anticipates his future task outside it, on earth. In the beginning there was 'no man to till the ground', so that the earth as yet was like a desert (2:5); and at the close of the story man is turned out of the garden 'to till the ground from which he was taken,' (3:23). In the Babylonian epic man is brought forth by the gods for their own ends: in order, that is, to perform those rites and ceremonies without which the gods could not exist. The Paradise story, on the other hand, says that man is created to serve the earth. Man is not of divine or semi-divine origin, but is formed of the dust of the ground. Man ('adham) belongs to the ground ('adhamah) and is appointed to till the ground. It is on this same ground that the garden is planted. Paradise is of the earth, earthy, through and through.

The 'tree of life' is a mythological conception which one comes across among a great number of races.[42] The succession of meanings which it has acquired is of such a wide diversity that one cannot find a common point of reference which would embrace them all. The analogue which comes nearest to suggesting the 'tree of life' of the Paradise story is the wonderful magic plant which is to the fore in the Gilgamesh Epic and the Adapa myth. It goes without saying that the meaning intended in the biblical narrative contrasts sharply with the fundamental viewpoint of Babylonian mythology. The 'tree of life' to which the Bible refers is neither inaccessible nor indeed under an interdict; for God has planted the garden for man and puts him close by the tree of life. There it is in the background of the story: a silent witness to the God who has breathed into man's nostrils the breath of life. Whereas Babylonian mythology is governed by the invincible necessity of death, at the centre of the story of Paradise there is the life that witnesses to the living God.

After the Fall it was the precise opposite: what had been, naturally enough, the gift of life was now corrupted into a magic life-elixir.

The place of life is turned by its corruption into the torment of Tantalus for mortal men. From that place nothing more of good for man can come; it can only put a seal upon his mortality. That is why the Lord sent man forth from the garden of Eden (3:23): away from the mythical bliss which, out of his fear of death, man has projected beyond death's frontier. It is from a mythical 'eternity', from a timeless bliss, that man is driven out. In his inexorable mercy God compels man to enter upon the road of history. To the true eternal life which God gives there is no way back, but only a way ahead.

Truly, eternal life is grounded in the 'fear of the Lord'. In the Book of Proverbs the theme of the 'tree of life', fully demythologized, becomes a symbol of the *Ḥokhmah*, the wisdom that consists in the fear of the Lord. † This is a unique theme in the Old Testament, and one which establishes an immediate connection with the other tree featured in the story of Paradise.

In Sumero-Babylonian mythology there is no parallel to the biblical 'tree of the knowledge of good and evil'; nor is one to be found in any other religion. In the Old Testament the knowledge of good and evil is that perfect and comprehensive knowledge possessed by God and his angels alone (2 Sam. 14:17, 20).[43] That divine knowledge includes the knowledge of good and evil, over which man has no claim to exercise control. Only the Creator, by whose virtue and authority the good creation is made to exist, really *knows* what is good and what is evil. In the Paradise story, therefore, the command not to eat of the tree of the knowledge of good and evil is not intended to trouble or to tempt mankind. The reason for it is self-evident: it is demanded of necessity by the partnership between the good Creator and his good creation.

With the opening of Genesis, chapter 3, there appears the disruptive power which perverts and overturns the nature of things. This is the serpent, who 'was more subtle than any other wild creature that the Lord God had made.' The word ʿ*arum* means crafty, cunning, shrewd, sensible; it suggests insight, keen discernment of some kind, whether in a good or a bad sense. When the serpent is said to be exceedingly ʿ*arum*, this clearly points to a superior, quasi-divine power of discernment which neither men nor animals possess. At the same time, the epithet hints at a misuse of this superior insight. The Hebrew noun *naḥash* (serpent) is almost certainly related to the verb *naḥash*, meaning

† See Prov. 3:18; 11:30; 15:4; 14:27; 10:11; 13:12; 16:22; cf. Ps. 36:7 ff.

to practise divination, to observe or interpret the omens—a widespread custom totally condemned by the prophetic writers (2 Kings 21:6; Deut. 18:10; Lev. 19:26, etc.).

The serpent in the Paradise story represents just this wisdom through the lore of magic and the use of divination. As befits his magician's character, he regards the tree of knowledge as a tree of magical wisdom, within the reach of man and able to make him 'like God' (3:5). The Paradise story does not say that man cannot possibly aspire to magic; it is indeed within his 'power'—but this 'power' betokens death, and this 'freedom' leads to the slavery of sin.

The serpent, as the source of this superior and fatal wisdom, is the first and principal object of God's judgment. In the condemnation of the serpent the story strikes its shrewdest blow at the religions of the *goyim*; for it was their proud boast and most dearly cherished claim that they could afford the mastery over magical lore and wisdom. Thus the whole story is a frontal attack on those religious forces amid which the people of Israel were living in the land of Canaan.

The theme of this story recurs again and again in the Old Testament. In fact it can be taken as a prototype of Israel's history. There is an evident parallelism here. In the one case, man is created, is put into the garden of Eden and finally expelled; in the other, Israel is created, is consequently transferred to Canaan, the 'good land' (Deut. 8:7, 10), and is eventually expelled on account of its disobedience to the word of the Lord (cf. Deut. 8:7–20). Conversely, Israel's history may be taken to epitomize the history of mankind. Israel's election points to the election of mankind, whose destiny it is to live as his partner in the presence of God. Israel must tread the way of exile and be scattered among the nations; and thus she treads the way of man, who was sent forth from the garden of Eden to till the ground from which he was taken (Gen. 3:23).

7. THE BIBLICAL STORY OF THE FLOOD AND THE BABYLONIAN TRADITIONS
CONCERNING THE DELUGE

We have seen that the Paradise narrative goes a very long way towards demythologizing ancient mythological traditions. Side by side with that, however, one finds in the Old Testament traces of this mythology in its original form. The name 'Eden' itself recalls a mythical conception of the 'garden of God' (Is. 51:3; Ezek. 28:13;

31:8, 9) or a 'delightful garden' (Ezek. 36:35; Joel 2:3). The twenty-eighth chapter of Ezekiel associates the king of Tyre with the mountain of the gods and with Eden, the garden of God. The figure of Daniel is probably a reminiscence of a mythical Phoenician hero.[44] Evidently we are moving here among a number of mythical elements which are a far cry from Genesis 2 and 3. In fact the gulf between them reveals just how drastically the mythical features have been modified in the Paradise story. We shall have occasion to come back to this point in dealing with the tower of Babel.

First, however, it is worth paying some attention to the story of the Flood and the Babylonian traditions connected with it. There are a number of differing versions of the deluge story, including a Sumerian and an old Babylonian version, whilst the Atrahasis Epic also concerns itself with the subject. The Hebrew and Babylonian accounts of the deluge most probably derive from a common source of some kind; and that may very well have originated in Babylonia, where the Book of Genesis does indeed locate the home of post-diluvian mankind (Gen. 11:1 ff.), and whence Abram migrated to Palestine (Gen. 11: 27 ff.).[45]

The Babylonian version forms part of the epic which tells of the journey of Gilgamesh in quest of immortality. That is, as a matter of fact, the point of the deluge story which Utnapishti recounts to him. The drift of the story as found in Genesis is the exact opposite of this. Noah is not a hero who has succeeded in pilfering a divine secret from the gods; he is rather 'a righteous man, blameless in his generation'; Noah 'walked with God' (Gen. 6:9). The 'life' which is 'found' by Utnapishti is that mysterious privilege beyond the reach of common mortals: to be like the gods. The life bestowed on Noah and his family is the full, abundant life, embracing the whole earth which is God's creation, the life that flows from the everlasting covenant which the Lord establishes with his creation; it is a life for all men. That is why the Genesis story mounts up to 'the generations of the sons of Noah, Shem, Ham and Japheth'; and 'sons were born to them after the flood,' (Gen. 10: 1). These 'generations' (*toledhoth*) signify the history of mankind.

8. THE TOWER OF BABEL AND THE MOUNTAIN OF THE GODS

The pre-diluvian origin of cities is a familiar idea in Babylonian epic literature. The Gilgamesh Epic would appear to say that Babylon had been rebuilt after the deluge in accordance with the divine, primordial wisdom which the 'exceedingly wise' hero had written down, before the event, at the command of Ea.[46] All reference to such a primordial origin for the cities of Mesopotamia has, however, been rigorously excluded from the account in Genesis 10. There these great cities represent the achievement of post-diluvian men.

The theme of the founding of Babylon is picked up again in Genesis 11:1-9, where it is interpolated between Genesis 10:1-32—the first genealogical section—and Genesis 11:10 ff., which continues the genealogy. The question of literary sources is a complicated one which we cannot go into here.[47] There can be no doubt that the story of the tower of Babel, as it now stands in Genesis 11:1-9, forms a consistent whole; and its meaning is plain enough. The connection with Babel must derive from an ancient tradition, a tradition which is clearly Babylonian in origin and—one would be inclined to think —must be closely related to the tradition preserved by Berossos which tells of the rebuilding of Babylon after the Flood. At all events, the two stories—of the tower of Babel and of the Deluge—are parallel in their extant biblical form; and the latter story does in fact have to do with the resumption of the history of mankind after the Flood.

The tower of Babel story reminds one even more forcibly of the biblical Paradise saga, which is likewise, of course, part of the 'Yahwist' text. Both stories refer to the origin of mankind and to a subsequent migration to a place 'in the east' (Gen. 2:8; 11:2), which in both cases is associated with Mesopotamia (Gen. 2:14; 11:2). The theme of Genesis 11:1-9 echoes, in some respects at least, that of the Paradise narrative: there is the attempt to become like God (Gen. 2:5; 11:4), followed by God's judgment and man's expulsion, with the consequent dispersal of mankind over the face of the earth.†

There is a definite parallelism between Eden (Gen. 2:8) and Shinar (Gen. 11:2) in this respect; one must assume that an ancient mythological tradition lies behind them both. As for the connection of that tradition with Babel, it may well be owed to the idea of Babel as the centre of the earth—an idea fully consonant with the 'primitive' view of the world and one familiar to the Babylonians of antiquity. The name 'Babylon' means *Bab-ili*, that is, 'the gate of the god (Marduk)', the place where heaven and earth meet or touch each other. Babylon is thus the source and centre of all countries,

† See Gen. 3:8, cf. 11:5; 11:6-8, cf. 2: 22-24.

the 'seed of the countries' (zer matati) and 'the navel-string of the countries' (rikis matati).[48] One of the fifty titles of Marduk is 'the Lord of the lofty navel-string'.[49]

Although the city of Babylon was already in existence by the latter part of the third millennium B.C., it was King Hammurabi (c. 1792–1750 B.C.) who made it the centre of a huge empire. Babylon became the centre of the cult of Marduk, which in turn became a religion of sufficient importance to survive the historical decline and eventual downfall of the empire. Eleven centuries after Hammurabi, Nebuchadnezzar II revived the political power of the empire and restored the capital city to its former glory as the renowned metropolis of antiquity (cf. Dan. 4:29 ff.). The story in Genesis probably alludes to the destruction of the city by the Assyrian king, Tukulti-Ninurta I in the year 1227 B.C.: that is to say, during the Mosaic or early Canaanite period of Israel's history. Whatever the historical reference,[50] however, it is scarcely of first importance to us, since it does nothing to illuminate the meaning of the biblical story. Moreover, the saga speaks, not of any 'destruction', but of the fact that the building was 'left off' (Gen. 11:8).

The 'gate of the god (Marduk)', which became the name for the city as a whole, originally denoted the sacred precincts of the temple tower of Marduk, situated in the centre of the city. Almost certainly, the 'tower with its top in the heavens' of the Genesis-saga is this very same temple tower.[51] It was an edifice famous throughout the ancient world. Rising to a height of nearly 300 feet, it was surpassed in size at that time only by the two largest pyramids of Gizeh. The base was square, its length and breadth being equal to the height. This kind of temple tower, the so-called 'ziggurat', can be traced back to the end of the third millennium B.C. and had undoubtedly developed, through a long course of evolution, out of still earlier types.

The ziggurat is what is known as a 'high temple', to be distinguished from another type, the 'low temples', so-called. It had at first taken the form of an artificially raised terrace, not unlike the 'high places' (bamoth) of the Western Semites (cf. 2 Kings 23:8, etc.). From the twenty-first century B.C. onwards the kings of the third dynasty of Ur—Urnammu, Dungi and their successors—started to erect on top of these terraces the earliest, ladder-like temple towers. Both terraces and towers, it seems, represented the primeval hill which when the universe originated was the first feature to emerge from the waters of chaos. The idea is a commonplace also in Egyptian religion, where temples were identified with the primeval hill; and this was reflected in their nomenclature and their architectural lay-out with ramps or steps.[52] In a variant of the *Enuma elish* Epic we read that in the beginning earth was flung on to a rush mat which was floating upon the primeval waters and that in this way a primeval hill was formed. The idea of 'deluge-hills', as they are called, seems to have been a familiar one in ancient Mesopotamia. The temple tower of Babel was known as the 'house of the foundation of heaven and earth' (*e-temen-an-ki*); and a similar name was given to the ziggurat of Nippur: 'string between heaven and earth'. Those names recall the Egyptian conceptions of the primeval hill and the navel of the earth. The names of the city of Babylon itself—'navel of the earth,' 'gate of god (Marduk)'—are taken from the ziggurat in the centre of the city. The earth's navel is its centre and highest point—like that of the prostrate human body—just as it is the string which binds heaven and earth together. The word ziggurat means, literally, 'mountain-peak'. The temple towers were comparable therefore to mountains and were regarded as being the thrones of the gods. Old Sumerian names for the temple towers often represent them to be cosmic mountains. The mountain of the gods is, in fact, the navel of the earth.

The temple towers may originally have had three stories and then later five (after the number of the planets) or seven (being the total of the planets plus the sun and moon). The tower of Babel had seven stories, signifying the seven celestial spheres. The sixth and seventh stories formed a small sanctuary at the top; it was a miniature copy of the big 'low temple' which lay beneath it, alongside the temple tower. The 'low temple', called 'house with the elevated top' (Esagila), was the principal sanctuary of Marduk. It had the familiar division into three parts, common in ancient Babylonia as elsewhere; there was an ante-room, main room (for the worshipper) and *adyton* (housing the image of the god). This tripartite arrangement corresponded to the tripartite structure of the universe: viz. the waters of the nether world (the ante-room contained a large water-basin called 'Apsu'), earth, and heaven. The tower and the 'low temple' were complemented by a third temple outside the walls of the city: the *Bit Akitu* (Festival House). These three together corresponded with the structure of the universe too.

The New Year festival centred upon these three buildings. The ziggurat stood for the primeval mountain to which, on the occasion of their festivals, the celestial beings came down from heaven. At the season of the New Year celebrations, the god left his heavenly abode, descending by way of the heavenly 'porch' on top of the ziggurat to the earthly 'Esagila', the large temple of Marduk next the temple tower. When the god had passed three days in the *Bit Akitu*, the nether world, the procession returned in triumph to 'Esagila', the temple of Marduk, whence it moved on to the ziggurat. It then ascended by the main staircase to the small sanctuary at the top, where the sacred marriage and the edicts of the assembled gods regarding destiny were solemnly ratified. Thus were accomplished both the accession to the throne and the ascension of the god into heaven.

The ziggurat had besides another function.[53] Various classical authors make mention of the 'Tomb of Bel'. This must almost certainly be the ziggurat, which did indeed stand for the 'mountain' as a symbol of the earth, the nether world or place of sunrise. At the same time, the ziggurat as the *cosmic* mountain represented the nether world, the earth and heaven. It was the all-inclusive image of the totality of the universe.

All this makes the meaning of the biblical tower of Babel story perfectly clear. The ziggurat of Babel was the centre of the New Year festival rites which reiterated the primeval victory of Marduk over Tiamat, and in the course of which the *Enuma elish* Epic was recited. The refashioning of the tower of Babel story is part of the fatal attack which the whole account of creation in the Bible (but especially Genesis 1:2) launches against precisely that conception of totality for which the ziggurat—cultic centre of the New Year festival—stands. Careful study of each verse of the biblical saga of the tower shows that it is concerned to refute the whole ziggurat mythology. The cosmic significance of the ziggurat is fully recognized, but at the same time is exposed as a human attempt at self-realization on a superhuman level, a reaching for the stars, a manifest example of the inordinate ambition to take heaven by storm. Babylon, centre of the universe, becomes the centre of confusion, the very point from which mankind is scattered abroad, the place and the sign of God's judgment upon man's attempt to be like God (v. 9).

Genesis 11:1-9 must not be viewed in isolation, but as a saga making part of the prehistory of Israel. Whereas Genesis 10 is concerned with the spread of nations over the earth, the genealogy of Shem in Genesis 11:10 ff. is concerned only with the begetting of the eldest son, leading up to a climax in the appearance on the scene of Abram, who from chapter 12 onwards becomes the principal figure in the drama. The first part of the history of Abram must be weighed against the tower of Babel story to which it is, as it were, the effective reply. Abram is called by God to leave Ur of the Chaldees, cradle of the Sumero-Babylonian religion. As opposed to mankind's attempt to make a name for itself (Gen. 11:4), now it is the Lord who will make of Abram a great nation (Gen. 12:2). God's judgment, seen in the confusion and scattering of the nations, becomes a new beginning of history: the history of his blessing and of his design ultimately to gather the whole earth into the restored unity of his Kingdom.

9. THE TEMPLE AT JERUSALEM AND THE TOWER OF BABEL

Genesis 11 is certainly not the only place in the Old Testament where reference is made to the Babylonian ziggurat. In Exodus 20:24-26 the sacred labour of hewing stones for the (steps up to the) altar is condemned as profanation; and the ritual act of ascending to the altar, because it presents an image of the cosmic mountain, is deplored as an impudent exposure of man's nakedness (Ex. 20:26). Very probably there is another allusion to the ziggurat in the story of Jacob's dream at Bethel (Gen. 28:10 ff.); and in later times an elevated altar was set up at Bethel by King Jeroboam in competition with the Temple at Jerusalem (1 Kings 12:25 ff.).

This really brings us to the heart of the matter; for Israel was acquainted with the idea of the ziggurat, not merely from Babel or through her encounter with the holy places of Canaan, but because it had a position of importance at the very centre of her existence as a nation. In the Jerusalem Temple itself there was, as a matter of fact, a sanctuary resembling the ziggurat: it was the great altar of burnt offerings which stood before the entrance or 'forefront of the house'.[54] The name given to the upper stage of this altar—*har'el*— signified that the altar was intended to represent the 'mountain of God'. Its lowest part, or foundation, bore the same name as the corresponding part of the Babylonian ziggurat: to wit, 'bosom of the earth' (cf. Ezek. 43:12–27)[55]. Thus the ziggurat, which had originally been a sanctuary in its own right—set up, in the case of Babylon, alongside the temple of Marduk—in Jerusalem was actually erected within the Temple, and inside the porch at that.

King Solomon had built the Temple at Jerusalem to Phoenician designs (1 Kings 5 ff.). The construction therefore expressed a symbolism common enough in the ancient Near East, according to which the temple represents the structure of the universe. Like the Babylonian temples, the one at Jerusalem comprised three parts, corresponding of course to the tripartite universe. These were the porch, called 'ulam; the main room or 'Holy Place', called hekhal; and the 'Holy of Holies' or 'oracle', called debhir. These names may very well have been borrowed from Canaan. The function of the temple in pre-Israelite times was basically the same in Canaan as in Mesopotamia (and Egypt). The temple as the abode of the god was called the god's 'house' or 'palace' (hekhal). The deity was thought of as living within the sanctuary, just as the king lived in his palace. In their architectural features, the throne-rooms of Babylonian and Assyrian palaces exactly resemble the sanctuaries of the area. Just as the Babylonian temple contained in its ante-room a large water-basin called 'Apsu', which represented the waters of the nether world, so did the Temple of Solomon have its large bronze 'sea' (1 Kings 7:23 ff.). The twelve oxen upon which this 'sea' was set may at one time have had some connection with the zodiac; for they looked towards the twelve points of the compass (1 Kings 7:25 ff.). The pillars of the Temple porch (1 Kings 7:15 ff.; 2 Chron. 3:15 ff.; Jer. 52:20 ff.) may have represented plants or trees—symbols of the earth's fertility (cf. the pomegranates, 1 Kings 7:18, 20, 42). The lampstand with its seven branches was also symbolic of a plant or tree (cf. Ex. 25:31 ff.); and there is reason to think that a number of chaos-dragons were depicted on its pedestal. In all probability the lampstand was an image of the cosmic tree which was rooted in the deep ocean (tehom) and supported the planets (i.e. the lights of the lampstand) on its branches (cf. Ezek. 31:4 ff.). These and other evidences suggest that the Temple was rich in cosmic symbolism, like the Babylonian and, presumably, the Canaanite temples and their furnishings. The ziggurat-like altar of burnt offerings, therefore, was nothing unusual, but on the contrary was a normal part of the whole symbolism of the Temple.[56]

Yet in reading the account of the building of the Jerusalem Temple one does not get the impression that this cosmic symbolism had an intrinsic significance for the Israelites even remotely comparable to the place which it generally occupied in the religions of antiquity. The very detailed record of the Temple building is marked by an arresting matter-of-factness in tone and style. Not a word is said about elaborate exercises in magic such as were an indispensable prelude to the building of pagan temples. It is even openly admitted that because the undertaking was so holy, Solomon was obliged to seek the help of a foreign artificer in bronze—and, what is more, of a pagan Phoenician—for the work of constructing the sacred pillars and many other bronze appurtenances (1 Kings 7:13). That points to an obvious confusion and ineptitude on the part of Israel which contrast strangely with her consciousness of being a people chosen by God from among all the nations of the world. Israel never made any pretensions to religious or cultural achievement; nor could she, or would she, compete in such matters with the surrounding nations. As immigrant parvenus with a nomadic background, the Israelites were poor, religiously and culturally speaking, and inferior by the standards of the ancient Near Eastern civilizations. Therefore they could hardly do other than behave as newcomers and tiros, submissive before their mentors who possessed so much more wisdom and experience.

Still, this deference went only so far. Beyond a certain point Israel showed herself to be irrepressibly creative in applying her own spirit and outlook to what she had taken over from other peoples and giving it a radically different function. Whilst accepting the general view of the universe, she broke the force of the pagan interpretation of it by envisaging everything as the handiwork of the God of Israel's own history. In the same way she freely adopted the microcosmic symbolism of the pagan temple, whilst draining it of all magical significance as a representation of the divine totality of the universe.

The Temple at Jerusalem was distinguished from its general prototype in one crucial particular: it was the place of which the Lord had said: 'My name shall be there.' What this declaration means is explained by the presence of the Ark of the Covenant in the *debhir*. The Ark stood for the decisive act of God's self-revelation to his people in history: 'I am the Lord your God, who brought you out of the land of Egypt, out of the house of bondage,' (Ex. 20:2). This is his 'Name', for which a house was built in Jerusalem. The content of the *debhir* is likewise revolutionary in its implication: the totality of the universe, so comprehensively delineated in the symbolism of the Temple and its paraphernalia, is demythologized and dedivinized; there is a breach made in its all-inclusive self-sufficiency; it is reduced to being the creation of him whose Name is manifested in history. Thus it was that even in the Temple there was always this one feature persistently reminding Israel of the journey through the wilderness. Time and again the point is made that poles had been fitted into the rings on either side of the Ark, 'to carry the ark by them'; and the imperative rider is added: 'The poles shall remain in the rings of the ark; they shall not be taken from it,' (Ex. 25:14 f.). It had already been so in the days of the tabernacle. When later on the Ark was laid to rest in the *debhir* of the Temple at Jerusalem, the poles, by reason of their great length, served as a reminder of the fact that the Ark had been made to be carried about (1 Kings 8:8). The God of Israel is an 'onward-going' God. He is 'on the move' (2 Sam. 7:4 ff.). He is the God of history.

10. KINGSHIP IN ISRAEL AND IN BABYLON

David's proposal to build a temple for the Lord was closely connected with his own position as king. 'See now, I dwell in a house of cedar, but the ark of God dwells in a tent,' (2 Sam. 7:2). The reaction of the prophet Nathan to David's proposal is to remind him of his own humble past as a shepherd (v. 8). The prophet's deep-rooted objection to the building of a temple should be put alongside Samuel's resistance to the introduction of kingship. Both prophets saw clearly that the longing after a king and after a 'house of cedar' for the Lord which would match with the royal palace sprang from a desire to be 'like all the nations' (1 Sam. 8:5). During the period of the Exodus there had been neither king nor temple.

There is a vehement protest against the pattern of kingship shared by the other religions of the ancient Near East in Ezekiel 28, where the prophet denounces the pride of the king of Tyre.[57] This prophetic denunciation is of a piece with the protest against Babylonian mythology which one encounters in the creation and flood narratives and in the saga of the tower of Babel. Here it is focused on the mythology of kingship.

In a rather different form the theme recurs in the 'lamentation over the king of Tyre' in Ezekiel 28:11–19.[58] The prophet declares that this same king who claims to have his dwelling upon the mountain of the gods is consumed by the fire of those stars amid which he had thought himself able to move. The form and tenor of his protest are not unlike what one finds in the tower of Babel story. They remind one too of the oblique attack on the Eden mythology in the story of Paradise.

Another interesting variation on the theme occurs in Ezekiel 31. The prophecy in this case most likely refers to the mythological notion of the cosmic tree, so closely related to that of the cosmic mountain.[59]

As a final example one might instance Isaiah 14:12–15, a prophecy regarding the destruction of Babel. The assault here is directed against the conception of Babel as the mountain of the gods and against the mythology of kingship linked with it.[60]

These passages make it clear that in the story of the tower of Babel we have a theme which recurs persistently in the prophetic parts of the Old Testament, and more particularly in Ezekiel. The theme is combined—and this is the point of outstanding importance—with a protest against the mythology of kingship. The Old Testament shows itself keenly aware that these two mythological ideas—of the cosmic mountain and of the divine kingship—are interdependent. They are deeply and inextricably embedded in that pattern which constitutes the basis of civilization in the ancient Near East. As H. Frankfort has argued so convincingly in his study of 'kingship and the gods', it was the king's function to preserve a harmonious relationship between society and the universe. Whether he was the very god incarnate—as in Egypt—or the servant of the gods who ruled over the land—as, for example, in Mesopotamia—he was in any event the chief instrument in the integration of society with nature and of concord with the gods.

According to the basic Egyptian conception of kingship the Pharaoh was a god incarnate; and it was he who maintained the cosmic order. His coronation had something of the character of cosmic event, in fact, of the creation of the universe. His throne was a 'copy' of the primeval hill. Since his rule was in itself a reflection of Re, god of the sun, the ideas of creation, sunrise and kingly rule were always being mingled and merged together. At his death the king became one with Osiris, the god of resurrection. The royal tomb was equated with the primeval hill. The king had to die in order to enter the earth and so, as a chthonic god, bring benefits to man. Just as the dead king was identified with Osiris, so Osiris, himself a dead king, represented all kings. In the person of the king—that is to say, in Osiris—there was repeated the ever-recurring mystery of death and resurrection in the cycle of nature.

The mythology of kingship was perhaps less impressive in Mesopotamia than in Egypt. There the king was regarded as a mortal charged with a divine commission; he was the chosen servant of the gods. He maintained the harmony between society and nature simply by watching over the service of the gods and attuning the life of the community to the divine will. Although the king's rôle in the celebration of the New Year festival at Babylon was more modest than that of his Egyptian counterparts, his participation was none the less essential. This was especially the case with the rites of the day of atonement on the fifth day of the festival. The king was then the central figure of a ritual drama in which he was reinvested with the regal insignia in token of the renewed life of nature. On the ninth day of the festival the king guided a triumphal procession to the subterranean temple, *Bit Akitu*, thus representing Marduk's destruction of Tiamat, the power of chaos.

Although Egypt and Mesopotamia held different views as to the nature of the universe and the corresponding function of kingship, fundamentally their conceptions were the same. The royal function was to integrate the powers that govern the universe with the life of society and to maintain that relationship.

We have already shown, with the aid of a number of prophetic texts, that it is precisely this conception against which the Old Testament directly or indirectly takes its stand. Frankfort quite rightly says that as compared with Egyptian and even Mesopotamian kingship, that of Israel lacks sanctity.

> The relation between the Hebrew monarch and his people was as nearly secular as is possible within a society wherein religion is a living force.[61]

Kingship in the Old Testament is caught in a very awkward position between two opposed and apparently irreconcilable points of view. In some of the Psalms the king is treated with very great respect indeed.[62] Other writers, on the other hand, voice the strongest disapprobation. Hosea says point-blank that God will have nothing to do with the kingship: 'They made kings, but not through me. They set up princes, but without my knowledge,' (Hos. 8:4; cf. 7:3; 10:3; 13:10). Between the two extremes of divine approbation and total repudiation the kingship has a fairly stormy passage through the Old Testament.

The Book of Judges already envisages the kingship which was soon to be instituted; and it quite clearly falls into two distinct parts. The first (Chapters 1 to 12) has an unmistakably anti-monarchic bias, whilst the latter part has a frankly pro-monarchic tendency, with its oft-repeated refrain: 'In those days there was no king in Israel; every man did what was right in his own eyes,' (Judg. 17:6; 18:1; 19:1; 21:25). There is then a very evident cleavage running through the Book of Judges. For the tribes of the people of Israel who had come in from the desert it was the time of their first major crisis, when they had their first real encounter with 'the promised land'. The primitive theocracy, run by a rapid succession of military chieftains, largely on the basis of their personal qualities, was simply not suited to cope with the new situation for any length of time; and the demand for a settled, hereditary and central authority grew more and more persistent.

Martin Buber bases his study of 'The Kingship of God'[63] on an examination of the radically theocratic vein running through the whole of the Old Testament. The watchword of Gideon, 'The Lord shall rule over you!' is echoed with equal forthrightness in a number of 'king-sayings' preserved in the Pentateuch (Deut. 33:2 ff.; Num. 23:21). These sayings are unquestionably old; and they embody the primitive admission of Yahweh's kingship which became a permanent factor in the history of Israel. They take us back to the making of the Covenant on Sinai, according to the oldest tradition of all, preserved in Exodus 24. Every aspect of what is meant by the affirmation that 'Yahweh is king' is present here.

Opposition to the introduction of the kingship did not spring from a desire to cling to the Bedouin way of life—even though small groups, such as the Rechabites, did survive, who were prepared to appeal to ancestral custom. No: the key to prophetic hostility lay in the recognition that Yahweh was king. The great crisis which led to the institution of the kingship was the loss of the Ark to the Philistines. It looked very much as if the office of 'judge' would completely disappear; it no longer meant anything in the military or political spheres, and now even its charismatic aspects were gone. In that political and spiritual vacuum men could think of nothing better to do than to look about them: 'Now appoint for us a king . . . like all the nations (*goyim*),' (1 Sam. 8:5, 20).

Therein lay the sting of that particular remedy. In this longing to order her political and religious life in conformity with the *goyim* Israel was playing fast and loose with her own election. What mattered was not that she wanted to have a human *melekh* (king), but that she wanted to have one after the pattern of her neighbours. If Yahweh is *melekh* in his own unique way, which sets him apart from the pagan gods, so then the people of his Covenant ought to set themselves apart by having a *melekh* who will be the instrument of that Covenant. The people had openly declared, however, that such a *melekh* was not what they desired.

It is only right to pause a little at this juncture, at this moment of profound crisis, and to take the full measure of its significance. Israel's entry into the land of Canaan marks the fulfilment of a journey which had led her out of the land of Egypt, out of the house of bondage. She has reached the promised land, where there is freedom for her to build her own way of life. Now answer must be given to the crucial question whether it lies within her to build in some other way than according to the age-old, well tried pattern of the ancient Near East. Here is Israel, raw and resourceless, with nothing to show but the unbelievable conviction that Yahweh, her God, is alone the true God, set down in surroundings overwhelmingly rich in cultural, social, economic, political and religious traditions. It is therefore not surprising —one would say rather it was inevitable—that what had happened previously to all the tribes and nations who had found their way into that *milieu* of ancient culture should now happen to Israel; after a period of conflict, of clinging to the ancestral customs, of instinctive disliking for whatever was new, she is slowly but surely absorbed, outflanked and intoxicated with the superiority of that civilization the portals of which she had presumed to enter. Israel grows civilized; she casts aside her barbaric past and sets up a state—with a monarchy, like all the *goyim*.

Israel gets her own way; but the manner in which she does so has a disconcerting drawback in the nature of this gift which she has wrested from the Lord. She must bear the responsibility, in fact, for this kingship and for all its consequences; it is her own choice, her own invention. For that very reason it now proves to lack just that essential quality which marks it among the other nations, where its source is in myth, where it is bred and proffered of the gods. That divine kingship of the nations reaches back into the primeval ages and is lost in the obscurity of their mythical atmosphere. Israel's kingship comes by the clear light of day, by an historic act of decision, made at a definite time and in a known place—and it is through and through a decision of men. The Lord has no hand in it. The king is one among the people and of like standing with them (1 Sam. 12: 14, 15, 25).

In that radically demythologized form, under that withering condemnation on God's part of the pagan notion of kingship, the king is indeed a divine gift. On that point even those texts which regard the introduction of the human kingship as *ipso facto* a rejection of the kingship of the Lord are perfectly clear. It is the Lord's will, it is his doing, that he is thus rejected. It is he who grants his people a king. Therein lies the paradox: as though through the eye of a needle this novel institution passes into the life of the Israelite nation. Straight is the way that lies before such a king; for he is to walk, not after the way of the kings of all the nations, but after the law of the Lord. At that same moment when Israel, thinking to force the issue and to have her way, seizes the initiative out of God's hands, he is in full control once more, remoulding this act of disobedience and rebellion to serve his own design. The king becomes the anointed of the Lord, a man chosen by him to be prince over his people Israel (1 Sam. 10:1; cf. 12:3).

In this paradox of the kingship is seen the paradox of Israel's history as the chosen people; and that in its turn bears witness to the paradox of the whole history of man on this earth which the Lord has made. The history of the Israelite kingship is the history of creation, of sin, of destruction, of creation 'anew'.

When the Lord makes a beginning with the history of this kingship, his first act is to expel those mythological powers which are the 'origin of the gods' and of the pagan kingship for which they stand, and then to choose his own king making of him a new creation: he 'gives him another heart', and the spirit of God comes mightily upon him (1 Sam. 10:9 f.). Nevertheless, this first king does not keep the commandment of the Lord; he is overwhelmed beneath the powers of magic and darkness which he has himself invoked (1 Sam. 28:6 ff.). The kingship, however, is not completely swept away in the flood of this disaster. Just as through Noah a new start was made with the history of mankind, so in David the history of the kingship is re-created and continued; and as mankind after the Flood lives by virtue of God's covenant with Noah and with every living creature, so the kingship in Israel exists after Saul's downfall by virtue of God's covenant with David and with the people of Israel. Just as the rainbow was always to be the sign of God's everlasting favour towards mankind after the Flood, so now the Lord decrees that 'David my servant may always have a lamp before me in Jerusalem, the city where I have chosen to put my name,' (1 Kings 11:34).

There are two specific tokens of God's promise to keep faith with the kingship in Israel: first the Ark of the Covenant and secondly the continuance of David's line. Solomon, like the Ark, is a sign of God's unending faithfulness towards the kingship. The record of his doings is steeped in a sense of the tremendous tension between God's kingship and the efforts of the Israelite king to be 'like all the nations'. Solomon is famed for his wisdom, which enabled him to discern between good and evil. Such wisdom was a gift of the Lord (1 Kings 3; 4:34); and it was by virtue of that gift that Solomon stood out above all who came before and after him and that, more than in any other episode in the history of the Israelite kingship, the history of his reign can be said with justice to resemble the account of Paradise. With him Israel reaches a condition of *shalom*, of peace and prosperity, not altogether unlike the Paradisal state of blessedness. Chapter 11, however, marks a sudden turn, akin to the unexpected change of tone at the beginning of Genesis 3. Right through the record of Solomon's nobility and wisdom there runs something of that vein of irony which appears from the very outset in Genesis 11: 'Now the whole earth had one language . . . Then they said, "Come, let us build ourselves a city, and a tower with its top in the heavens" . . .' Viewed in that light, the description of Solomon's throne acquires a special overtone. The throne of ivory and gold had six steps. The like of it had not been made in any kingdom (1 Kings 10:20). We know that the throne, like the temple tower and the elevated altar, stood for the cosmic mountain. Now we are told that Solomon has out-Babeled Babel itself.

Solomon's empire was brought down by a revolution—and by a revolution of a unique and most peculiar kind, eloquent of the intensity of the struggle which marked Solomon's reign to vie with the splendour and glamour of the Near Eastern absolutist monarchies. In the whole of Egypt's long history, says Frankfort:

> . . . there is no evidence of any popular uprising . . . there could be competing claims among members of the royal house, . . . The people at large could not and did not interfere . . . all power was vested in the king, who alone maintained an order which was thought of as one coherent whole, established in all essentials at the time of creation.
>
> The power of the king over his subjects did not cease with death, and . . . was experienced not as a tyranny reluctantly endured but as a relationship which established for each subject his function and place in the world.[64]

In Israel an absolute authority of that kind was unthinkable. Even whilst Solomon was still on the throne, opposition to the heavy yoke which he had laid on the people was brewing. In the end the prophet Ahijah fixes upon Jeroboam to be the chosen instrument of God's judgment on Solomon's idolatrous reign and proclaims him prince over the ten tribes of Israel. In a most profound sense, this is a revolution of the Covenant, directed against pagan absolutism. With this as with all such 'covenant revolutions', the real point at issue is the kingship of Yahweh. Therefore these revolutions share to the full in the Lord's promise regarding his people and regarding the kingship which he has chosen; but equally they fall under the full impact of his impending judgment. They are an instrument of his holy will—nothing more nor less; and it is precisely on that score that these revolutions themselves so evidently fail. All that Jeroboam did was to try pitting against the absolutism of the monarchy the absolutism of his revolution. But there is no form of absolutism compatible with the kingship of the Lord. A kingship at the service of his purposes is the only possibility.

The state is in fact an emergency measure,[65] taken by man on his way out of Paradise, the sign of God's manner of election, of choosing, as it were, clean through the facts of human pride and sin. Henceforth David's house and Zion's Temple exist perpetually within the shadow of the northern kingdom of Israel, that sign of humiliation, of schism, of protest and rebellion against tyrants and idolaters. Yet on the other hand Israel cannot dispense with Judah and with Zion; for there it has pleased the Lord to set his name; there rests the Ark of the Covenant; there reigns the house of his chosen servant, David. Though cleft in two, yet still the people of God are one. What does this paradox of mutual dependence in mutual division signify? By it Israel and Judah—that is, the whole people of Israel—are to know that the broken edifice of the kingdom and the state stands on the edge of abysmal ruin and that if it stands, it does so only because God forbears and is patient.

The end of God's forbearance means also the end of the kingship and the state. 'And the Lord said, "I will remove Judah also out of my sight, as I have removed Israel, and I will cast off this city which I have chosen, Jerusalem, and the house of which I said, My name shall be there," ' (2 Kings 23:25 ff.). Such was the end of the road which the people of Israel began to tread when they took to themselves kings 'like all the nations'. The crux of the whole matter is in that phrase: it explains why Israel's political career—the rise, aggrandizement and eventual downfall of the kingship—has a universal and not just a local significance. What befell Israel holds good likewise for 'all the nations' which she so much wanted to be like. The calibre of pagan kingship is here put to the test; the conception of it is weighed in the balance and is found wanting. The Old Testament calls down judgment upon the pagan kingdoms and empires; but God makes an example of his own people. It is upon them that the judgment falls.

Thus God confounds the pride of pagan kingship; yet in so doing he affirms his own. Just as Israel's political history is an object-lesson to the nations in judgment and destruction, so too does it exemplify God's promise to restore and to renew. The house and kingdom of David are destroyed—but not completely and not for ever. God the Creator sets a limit, in time and space, to the untrammelled power of chaos. 'Be broken, you peoples, . . . speak a word, but it will not stand, for God is with us,' (Is. 8:5 ff.). The tree of David's royal line is felled—root and branch? Not so; for there shall come forth a shoot from the stock of Jesse, and a branch shall grow out of his roots. Then shall the Lord of Israel be king over all nations. For out of Zion shall go forth torah (Mic. 4:1 ff.). State and kingship perish; but the kingship of the Lord remains, because he reigns through the Torah.

II. THE TORAH

The Old Testament is witness to the fact that the kingship and the kind of state which goes with it constitute an emergency measure and a temporary one. This was not the case during the period after the Exodus and is not to be so either when God's Kingdom and his reign of peace have come. That is typified in the prophetic visions where the term *melekh* (king) for the coming earthly ruler is never used. They speak rather of a 'ruler' (*moshel*, Mic. 5:2) or employ the unpretentious title of 'regent' or 'prince' (*nasi*', Ezek. 34:24; cf. 27:21; 32:30, etc.). The right ordering of life is not something provided by the state, but is laid down in the Torah. It does not follow that state and kingship, as such, are rejected out of hand. Everything depends on whether they are the right sort of state, the right sort of kingship—whether, that is to say, they are duly founded upon the Torah. The Torah is concerned with the Lord's rule over his people in the here and now—as the shepherd tends his flock, leads them out and in, protects them from danger, escorts them through the lofty and the low places, admonishes, chastens, punishes, brings home the wanderer. The Torah constitutes the real presence of the Lord with his people. Like his Word, his revelation, his Covenant—and in a similar way—the Torah testifies to his holiness and faithfulness.[66]

The word torah as we find it in use among the early prophets means the Word of the Lord, which they themselves actually speak (Is. 8:16, 20); but this word comes to be written down in a book, 'that it may be for the time to come as a witness for ever' (Is. 30:8 f.), so that 'the word' can then be taken to mean a larger compilation of prophetic utterances or of priestly instruction (Is. 1:10; 2:3; Mic. 4:2; Is. 42:4, etc.). The process comes to a halt for a time in Deuteronomy, which is described simply as torah (Deut. 17:18 f.; cf. 2 Kings 22:8, 11; Josh. 8:32). In the event, the whole Pentateuch, as a single corpus, gets the name 'torah of the Lord' or 'torah of Moses' (1 Chron. 16:40; 2 Chron. 23:18).

The heart and substance of the Torah then is *history*; and that is why from the very outset it assumes the narrative form. That the Torah begins with the account of creation is a fact of the utmost significance. Just as God's creative action is to 'divide', to separate, so the Torah separates off the life of Israel from the life of the *goyim*, here and there taking from it a little, but consigning the greater part to the scrap-heap. As God's Word goes forth into chaos, Israel makes her way into the land of Canaan, makes room there for living the life of the Covenant, drives a wedge into the surrounding culture and religion with shattering effect, picking out from them, however, whatever might serve to strengthen her own order of society in accordance with God's holy will. The Torah continues and extends God's creativity towards Israel through her history and her environment.

At the same time we must remember that after the story of creation comes the story of Paradise. The Torah is not only the record of God's creative acts, but also of Israel's pride and downfall. As it turns out, Israel is unequal to the task of living as the Torah requires, she loses heart and falters before it: so that at last it is the Lord himself who causes judgment and destruction to fall upon an order of state and kingship built on sand and rotten to the core. Israel is scattered among the *goyim*. Here there is driven home to us the profound meaning of the paradox that the whole Torah, although in fact it bears very largely upon society in the land of Canaan and on Israel's life there, is none the less the 'Torah of Moses', the Pentateuch, which is entirely concerned with the period of the Exodus and sojourn in the desert. Thus the Torah bears witness of itself that it is a way to be trodden, a path and not a pattern: a prospect in the wilderness, but not the good land: a promise, but not a consummation: a journey out of the house of bondage, but not a dwelling in liberty: a commandment, but not a realization. The Torah is no ultimate solution, gives no final answer. It points above and beyond itself towards the promised land which even Moses may not enter, though he sees it from afar. Yet it is precisely in all this that the Torah is 'perfect, reviving the soul' (Ps. 19:7).

In Canaan the people of Israel experienced a radical change in their way of life, exchanging a half nomadic existence for an agrarian one. What is more, this agrarian order became itself increasingly urbanized under a variety of influences. A critical situation arose, because it seemed likely that Yahweh would come to be regarded as a 'Ba'al', a divine landlord, worshipped side by side with the countless number of indigenous Baalim, each with his local cult enacted on every high hill and under every green tree. It was a danger difficult to contend with, not only because these mysterious chthonic powers were so numerous and so imponderable, but more especially because the belief in Yahweh had, at the outset, no cultus or ritual to set beside theirs. Consequently the expedient adopted by Jeroboam was to establish a central cult of Yahweh-Ba'al—not without assistance from the priests of the Canaanitic high places—and to set up temples, wherever he could, on the high places themselves. The other course—represented by the Temple cult in Jerusalem—was to centre worship exclusively upon Yahweh, who was seated invisible upon his throne between the cherubim and above the Ark of the Covenant. Yet this too was a cult, with an obvious affinity to the pagan cultic practices all around it. The aim of the Deuteronomic reform therefore was not the merely formal one of centring the cult on the Temple of the capital city; it was rather to breathe new life into the proclamation: 'Hear, O Israel: The Lord our God is one Lord' (Deut. 6:4), grounded in the covenant which Yahweh had made with his people. Throughout the Book of Deuteronomy the note of personal, inward commitment to the Lord, 'with all your heart and with all your soul,' takes precedence over the purely outward and visible performance of ritual sacrifice.

The kind of structure which one associates with the Temple as a building is also discernible in the cultic ordinances. The Temple had its three compartments, each in closer proximity than the last to the actual presence of the Lord above the Ark of the Covenant. The overall pattern of the Temple followed the traditional conception current among the other religions; and only within the heart of the sanctuary, within the Holy of Holies itself, did that pattern part company with pagan naturalism in any radical way. So it was with the cult. Israel drew from her environment a good many magical customs and ideas; but these things were made to serve a special purpose in distinguishing the chosen people even more sharply from the other nations. Fundamentally, the purpose of the various tabus is to give expression to the key commandment that Israel is to obey the voice of the Lord and to keep his Covenant.[67]† So too the distinction between what is holy and what is 'common', what is clean and what is unclean, which looms large throughout the Torah, is really a matter of being able to discern what the will of the Lord is. It revolves entirely about this point (Lev. 10:8 ff.). Thus although magic invaded the life of the people of Israel from their religious environment and pervaded the very air they breathed, the Torah purified it, subjecting it to an elemental change.

† See Ex. 19:15; cf. 1 Sam. 21:5 f.; Deut. 24:5; Lev. 15:16 ff.; 22:4.

The cultic and ritual ordinances and tabus which are undoubtedly there in the Torah do not imply any identification with, or syncretistic adaptation of, the religious heritage of other peoples. If these features are incorporated, they are also thoroughly reorientated. Every ordinance is declared to be a commandment of the Lord which he gave to Moses, and of him alone. All are historicized and embedded in the history of the Covenant. Israel is bound by these ordinances simply and solely because it is the Lord who has given the word of command; and when she puts them into practice, she does so purely in obedience to him who led his people forth out of the land of Egypt. In that way these observances and customs are emancipated and rescued from the powers whose ends they serve in the other religions; they are detached from the whole background of religious, social, political and hygienic motives with which they are combined in the pagan heritage.

There is a further aspect of this which deserves particular attention. Although some part of the general religious inheritance is incorporated in the Torah, by far the larger and indeed more weighty part was found to be of no use and was put to one side or even expressly repudiated. The Code of Holiness (Lev. 17–26), a homiletic exposition and expansion of earlier laws, is fiercely hostile in particular towards the pagan powers of death and eros. Thus the practices of witchcraft and of tattooing on behalf of the dead are condemned in the same breath with sacred prostitution (Lev. 19:26 ff.; cf. Deut. 23:18 f.; Ezek. 44:22, etc.). The only fitting status for death and eros—so intimately related to each other—is to be subject to the sovereignty of the Lord. 'I am Yahweh!' Along the same line child sacrifice (Lev. 18:21; 2 Kings 16:3; 17:17; 21:6), castration and contraceptive practices (Deut. 23:1 f.; Is. 56:3 ff.; Gen. 38:9 f.) are unreservedly condemned.

The marital code of the Torah is to be viewed in the same light. The marriage laws of the Israelites reflected in a number of ways the evolution of social attitudes and ideas generally current regarding the place of women. Yet since nothing in the Covenant is of more importance than the solidarity of the people and since the family is the basic constitutive element in that respect, it is above all the family which is preserved in Israel as a stable institution through every crisis and every phase of social change. For the same reason the tribal organization, even though the course of events after the advent of the Davidic Kingdom hastened its decline in the political sphere, still remained important as a basic principle and as an ideal in a theological context. The Covenant made at Sinai was continued and upheld in the confederation of the twelve tribes (Ex. 24:4; 1 Kings 18:31; Is. 49:6; Ezek. 45:8, etc.).

To that extent it is true that, as compared with the legal systems of the highly civilized peoples of the ancient Near East, the Torah perpetuated a fairly primitive nomadic structure of human relationships[68]; and in spite of every development or ramification, of every reinterpretation and accretion of material, it remained firmly rooted in the Mosaic Covenant. Therein lies the fundamental difference between the Torah and the Code of Hammurabi—a difference which is not just a question of differing levels of civilization, but goes far deeper than that. Hammurabi's code is a code of civil law, promulgated by the king. Behind the king lies the divine warranty of Shamash, god of the sun and of justice. As the god in his heavenly wisdom maintains the harmony of the universe, so does the king imitate and represent him on earth in maintaining the harmony of human society. The king has, it is true, a sacred office to discharge; but the legal code which he promulgates is not at all religious in character; it is, quite literally, the king's law, by means of which he rules and administers his empire. The people as such have no part to play in the code whatever. The whole basis of the Torah, on the other hand, is the Covenant; and the Torah's central purpose is the creation of a holy people. In every jot and tittle it is Torah of the Lord, his guidance and his instruction. It admits of no distinction between 'fas' and 'jus', between sacred and profane law. All the ordinances of the Torah, whether cultic, social or political, are the commandment of the Lord. They stand therefore side by side and linked together by that common bond; and to that divine commandment the king is to submit himself just like every other member of the community. The Torah therefore is no legal code, but the record of God's acts and ordinances, of the obedience and disobedience of his people, of the divine mercy and judgment. His holy will brooks no conditions.

If the Torah is not a legal code, neither does it enshrine a social programme; but it does indicate concretely what being a member of the holy people really implies. The course of social development in Canaan modified profoundly the relations of the people of Israel among themselves. The Book of the Covenant spoke to that situation of crisis by demanding justice (*ṣedhagah*) for the poor, the widow, the orphan and the stranger (Ex. 22:21 ff.; 23:6 ff.). The duty to protect widows, the orphaned and the poor was a generally accepted ideal in the East. With Israel the ideal became a central, unconditional and paramount command, firmly grounded in that *ṣedhagah* which God had shown in his election of Israel. Israel saw herself, in relation to the Lord, as being in the position of the neighbour, with all that that implies of solidarity and support. This basic theme of the Torah is fully brought out by the prophets in their tremendous struggle for justice in the face of social pressures, corruption and the pursuit of riches and power. They sound the deepest note of the Torah when they assert that to do justice and to obey God are 'the whole law'. Faithfully they testify, first to the impending judgment of God and then, in the end, to its actual descent upon his hardened and corrupted people. The Torah itself becomes a judgment; and yet it remains the world's light. What Israel failed to attain or to be—a society that lives by the Covenant— the Lord will teach to all the nations. And then out of Zion shall go forth torah (Is. 2:3; Mic. 4:2).

12. ZION AND BABEL

In the eleventh chapter of Genesis there emerges the theme to which even the creation story has been leading up, and which from that point on dominates not only the whole of the Old Testament, but the New Testament as well. Amidst all the confusion and disorder of mankind the line of Shem reaches a climax in the coming of Abram, from whom will spring the people of Israel. The career of Noah is re-enacted, as it were, in these events, although under another form. Noah himself is called out from among mankind to take his departure, to move forward out of chaos and to take up his abode in the Ark, his course set for a new earth. The terms '*adhamah* and 'earth' ('*ereṣ*) are interchangeable. The story of the Deluge links up with the pre- ceding story of creation and also with that of Paradise (Gen. 7:13, 14, 21, 22). Like Adam, Noah is conveyed to the centre of the earth (Mount Ararat here is a parallel to Paradise) and like Adam he returns thence to the '*adhamah*, and his posterity multiply and fill the earth; only this time the accompanying sign is totally different. Whereas Adam was driven out of Paradise, Noah returns from Mount Ararat to earth through the grace of God.

The thematic repetition continues. The ninth chapter of Genesis ends with the growing wickedness of Noah's offspring (cf. Gen. 4); and then comes chapter 10 with the 'generations of the sons of Noah' (cf. Gen. 5). The story of the tower of Babel, which follows at this point, reproduces the story of Paradise, though 'one people' appears in the place of Adam. This story too connects up with the narratives of creation and of the Deluge. Noah's ark carried him upon the Flood to the centre of the new earth, whence he and his posterity were to go forth and cover the earth; likewise Abram is led by God through the chaos which is the world of many races and peoples to the centre of a new mankind—the land of Canaan. It is the creative act of God himself: just as in the beginning he had gathered together the waters and caused the dry land to appear, so now he will make ready a country for his chosen people. One might put it that mankind, which the event of Babel has scattered abroad, does indeed attain to its destiny —that is, to multiply and to fill the earth—but does so through the judgment and mercy of God: to wit, through Abram and him alone. There is no other way for the nations (*goyim*) to be blessed, for them to have their part even yet in the blessing given to Noah, than by means of this one man and of this one 'great people', Israel. Henceforward Israel has this double task: to manifest in her own existence both 'nation' (*goy*) and 'people' (*'am*) and also to represent both these, to live as the paradigm of both: as the 'nation'—that is, as one among the many into which God divided the descendants of the sons of Noah upon the earth: and as the 'people'—the unification in one people of the human race.

This distinction between *'am* (people) and *goyim* (nations) is drawn clearly enough in the course of the Old Testament and its history. Israel alone is *'am*—God's chosen people—and all other peoples are *goyim*. Yet in these chapters of Genesis that terminological distinction simply does not appear—rather, the opposite is the case. All the earth was 'one *'am*' (Gen. 11:6); but the promise is made to Abram that there will come of him 'a great *goy*'. We should have expected just the reverse. It throws a revealing light on the terminology in question; for it is precisely as the one chosen 'people' (*'am*) that Israel represents the oneness of the human race, and it is the *goyim* who are to experience the blessing and to be gathered into the 'great *goy*'. It is now apparent, not only that we are unjustified in regarding Israel's 'particularism' as something set over against her 'universalism' and even opposed to it, but that in so doing we obscure and pervert the obvious meaning of the Old Testament. It is in her 'particular' function and calling—and precisely there—that Israel is truly 'universal'. If God has called this 'particular' people into being, it can only be because of the 'universal' purpose which he has in view.

We are now in a position to probe yet further into the meaning of the tower of Babel story. The city of Babel, as represented by its ziggurat, was the navel of the earth and the centre of the universe. The building of the tower ceases; there it stands like a torso. The myth is shattered; the nations set out on the road of history. Babel, the metropolis, is a standing testimony to the truth that God descends, that God intervenes in history. Babel is still the centre and origin of mankind—specifically, that is, of its confusion. It becomes the instrument of God's design, of what he intends for the whole earth. There is no way back to Babel, just as there can be no returning to Paradise. The Lord directs the nations towards the future, where their destiny lies. If the way back to Babel is closed and the myth broken, the way forward points to Zion. Isaiah and Micah both prophesy that in the latter days the mountain of the Lord's house will be established as the highest of mountains, and all the nations shall flow unto it, and out of Zion shall go forth torah (Is. 2; Mic. 4). Here Zion becomes the counterpart of Babel. Zion is the mountain of the Lord; and the striving of mankind at Babel to build for themselves a city and a tower with its top in the heavens contrasts with the raising of Mount Zion to be the highest of all mountains, which is an act of God. Over against the unnerving fear of mankind 'lest we be scattered abroad' is set the free and joyful resolution of the nations to go up to Zion. On the one hand there is the panic, the confusion, the scattering, and on the other the festive gathering. On the one hand the cry is: 'Come, let us build ourselves a city and a tower with its top in the heavens,' and on the other: 'Come, let us go up to the mountain of the Lord, to the house of the God of Jacob.' On the one hand there is the striving, 'Let us make a name for ourselves,' and on the other the longing to learn the torah that goes forth out of Zion, the city where the Lord has chosen to set his name. On the one hand is confusion and enmity, on the other an eternal peace.

We can now see why the Temple at Jerusalem was modelled on the normal pattern of the ancient temple which represented the mountain of the gods. The Temple at Jerusalem represented the mountain of the Lord. Babel is forsaken; and Zion is the centre of the earth. The myth of the cosmic mountain is demolished, to make room for Zion as the pivot of human history. Here indeed the Old Testament does assume the accents of myth. On Sinai Yahweh is acclaimed as king; and here at Zion is his lasting habitation, here the King reigns in majesty from his throne (Ps. 24; 99; 132; Is. 6). David brings the Ark to Zion and Solomon builds the Temple for the Ark above which Yahweh sits upon the throne between the cherubim. It is from an eschatological viewpoint therefore that we are to understand these events: Yahweh becomes king upon the cosmic mountain. He is king over all the nations of the earth (Ps. 98; 99; 48). Out of Zion he rules victorious over his enemies, over the nations who make war on him and on his chosen congregation (Ps. 74:2); from Zion he smites them and scatters them. Because David and his son have prepared this dwelling-place upon Zion for Yahweh, the King, an eschatological light falls upon their own kingship; it is interpenetrated by the radiant splendour of the everlasting kingship of God (Ps. 2; 110). Zion is the mountain of Yahweh, Jerusalem the city of God; and there are no other cosmic mountains than these (Ps. 87). Here the myth yields up its command of the nations; and Zion as the cosmic mountain is extolled in the very language which the nations employ to honour their gods, their cities and their mountains. Here too the myth is caught up in the liturgy of adoration, when all the nations dance and sing before the King, Yahweh, upon the mountain which is the source of them all. As the cosmic mountain, Zion stands for the whole earth; and Israel as the ʿam of the Lord and as the great goy, has Zion for her dwelling-place because she is to represent all the 'peoples' (ʿammim) or 'nations' (goyim). There Israel fulfils her rôle, during the time between the scattering of mankind from Babel and its being gathered in again to Zion—the representative rôle of being the one ʿam which mankind originally was (Gen. 11: 1, 6).

The language used to denote the nations is also mythical in character. We had occasion earlier on to discuss the term ʾaphse ha-ʾareṣ, literally, 'the ends of the earth', an expression which in the Old Testament signifies the nations of the earth. We noticed that ʾaphse is the plural form of apsu, the primeval ocean. Right through the Old Testament there runs the idea that the salvation of Zion in the midst of the hostile nations round about is in the nature of a new creation. Just as once the waters were gathered together and the earth appeared (Gen. 1:9), and as after the Flood the waters receded from the earth so that Noah's ark came to rest upon the top of Mount Ararat (Gen. 8:4), so again and again must the nations retreat from Zion, the mountain of the Lord (Ps. 2; 46; 48, etc.). The passage through the Red Sea leads directly up to Mount Zion, as Noah's ark, passing over the waters, has landed on Mount Ararat (Ex.15: 1–18).

Now the expression *'aphse ha-'areṣ* is peculiarly ambivalent. As the plural of *apsu*, the term implies that the Gentiles are to be associated with the primeval waters of chaos, with the ocean that surrounds the earth. They are the threat that lurks upon the furthest frontier, which the Lord has indeed deprived of its totalitarian power and confined to 'the seas'; and yet the seas can rage and flood the earth. At the same time however the term explicitly suggests that the Gentiles properly belong to the earth (*'ereṣ*). Admittedly they form 'the ends' of it—literally the boundary-line at which the earth 'leaves off'. But for the Hebrew mind this term 'boundary' has an inclusive implication: it refers to the total content enclosed within the boundary. Thus 'the ends of the earth' fall within the total compass of the dominion of the Lord who reigns as king in Zion (Ps. 72:8). The paradoxical character of the expression *'aphse ha-'areṣ* is rooted in the history of creation and refers to it. Were the Gentiles to be abandoned to their own myth and to their own fate and regarded from the viewpoint of their own religion, they would constitute no part of God's creation; they would stand outside, a total negation. That however is not, and never has been, the case. They are not abandoned to their myth or their fate, but are involved from the outset in God's mighty acts of creation; they belong to the earth which the Lord has rescued out of the primeval ocean; they are 'the ends' towards which God's purpose is directed, the ultimate reason for the work which he has begun on his mountain of Zion, centre of the earth.

The Hebrew synonyms support this analysis. *Qeṣoth ha-'areṣ*, literally, 'the ends or extremities of the earth', has the same inclusive meaning: all the earth (Is. 40:28). Another frequently occurring term is *'iyyim*, coastlands, islands; it is used especially by the Second Isaiah as a straightforward synonym for 'the ends of the earth' and for 'the nations', the 'Gentiles' (Is. 40:15; 41:5; 42:4; 49:1; 51:5). The rendering in the Septuagint is more often than not simply *ethnē*, the Greek word for Gentiles. Thus the term is used as a close parallel with *'aphse ha-'areṣ*; they both have a similar, paradoxical function in that they testify to the creation *ex nihilo*.

The great theme of God's historical activity in the Old Testament is that of gathering and scattering and gathering again. The whole earth was one; they were scattered (Gen. 11); but in the latter days they shall forgather again (Is. 2). This basic theme is then developed rather like a fugue; that is, the theme is reiterated in the history of God's dealings with the people of Israel. Though all mankind upon earth is scattered abroad, its hidden unity remains, preserved in the people which the Lord brings forth out of Abram. The place of Babel is taken by Zion. Israel therefore represents all mankind, in unity and scattering, in pride and sin and fall. God's judgment on his people is his judgment upon all the earth; and when the Lord has mercy on his people and gathers them again, the action adumbrates his blessing which he has promised to bestow on each and every nation. Israel then is the vanguard of the nations; her history is the centre and epitome of all history and the revelation of God's purposes for all mankind. Henceforth the light of Zion falls upon Babel— and the shadow of Babel upon Zion. The land of Israel comes to be known simply as *ha-'areṣ*, just as the people of Israel is called simply *'am* (Lev. 26:42, 12). Israel and the land of Israel represent the whole earth, the whole of mankind. Israel herself is a new creation, and her land the token of a new earth which the Lord will create. For that very reason the life of the whole earth hangs upon the promise that Israel is to return to her land. As the scattering of Israel among all nations is a sign of God's judgment upon all the earth, so also the promise that God will gather them again from among all the nations whither he has scattered them is made on behalf of all mankind. The Lord reveals by Israel, his people, what his purpose is for the whole earth. First he judges Zion, then Babel and the nations (Is. 13 ff.). If Israel is scattered among the nations, so too must they be scattered;† and if the Lord pleases to have compassion upon his people and gather them from among all peoples, so too will he gather all the nations.*

Certainly it is a 'remnant' of Israel which is to return and be gathered again (Is. 10:20 f.; Jer. 23:3; Ezek. 6:8), as in the judgment of the nations it is likewise only a remnant of them that will be left

† See Num. 10:35; Ps. 92:19; Is. 24:1; Jer. 49:32, 36.
* Is. 11:12; Jer. 30:1 ff.; Ezek. 11:17; 29:13; Is. 2; Mic. 4.

(Is. 16:14; Ezek. 29:14 ff.; 36:3 ff.); but this remnant is *pars pro toto*, the first fruits of the coming harvest. Again and again the Lord begins by a remnant to create anew: by means of Noah, Abram, Judah, the house of David, Jerusalem, Emmanuel. In the remnant the Lord proves himself faithful. Upon the remnant the salvation of the whole created order depends.

The idea of Zion as the focal point of God's purpose for the whole earth forms the background also of the New Testament; and the rest of this chapter will deal briefly with that aspect of the question. The New Testament proclaims that Jesus is the king chosen of the Lord. Psalms 2 and 110 have an extremely important place in that proclamation; for the Lord set his king upon Zion, upon his holy mountain. As a child, Jesus comes out of Egypt (Mt. 2:13 ff.), thereby re-enacting the exodus of the people of Israel. We remarked, in discussing Exodus 15:1–18, how the journey through the Red Sea ended up on Mount Zion, just as Noah's ark had come to rest on Mount Ararat. When Jesus was baptized, he went up immediately out of the water, signifying that he is the beginning of the new earth, the new creation, the new mankind. At that moment a voice from heaven says: 'This is my beloved Son, with whom I am well pleased.' Jesus, risen up out of the water, is set as king upon Zion, the mountain of the Lord (Ps. 2). In the 'voice from heaven' (of Mt. 3:17) we have an allusion to the voice of the Lord on Sinai, when he declared his Covenant and gave the ten commandments (Deut. 4:12 f.). Jesus fulfils the Torah. He is king on Zion and thus the fulfilment of Sinai; and from him will go forth torah for all the nations. Satan is referring to the heavenly voice ('This is my beloved son'), when he says: 'If you are the Son of God. . . .' (Mt. 4:3, 6). The second temptation itself reminds Jesus of the connection between the Temple at Jerusalem and the cosmic mountain; but the third temptation refers directly to his kingship on Mount Zion. Jesus has to choose between Babel and Zion, between the kingship which is 'like all the nations' and the kingship of the servant of the Lord, who identifies himself with the hungry people in the wilderness.

The same voice from heaven comes to Jesus again later, when he is transfigured on a high mountain (Mt. 17:1 ff.). Jesus, in the words of Psalm 2, is set as the Lord's king upon Zion, his holy mountain. As Jesus and his disciples were coming down from the mountain, he forbade them to tell anyone of what they had seen until after his resurrection; and then he makes it clear to them that he must suffer. It meant that only through the cross and resurrection—and not before —would they see fulfilled what his transfiguration had anticipated: namely, the Son of man coming in his kingdom (Mt. 16:28 f.; 17:9 ff.). Jesus will be set as king upon Zion, as the crucified and rejected servant of the Lord.

It is of particular significance in this connection that Gethsemane was situated on the slopes of the Mount of Olives (Lk. 22:39; cf. Mt. 26:36). In fact the Mount of Olives has a major rôle in the historical career of Jesus. It is there that Jesus is smitten like the shepherd; but it is also the spot from which he sets off on his journey and entry into Jerusalem as king—an anticipation of his eschatological kingship. According to Luke, it was from the Mount of Olives that Jesus was taken up into heaven; and his eschatological return is likewise to take place on this Mount (Acts 1:9 ff.). We are given a definite impression that the ascension of Jesus from this Mount was preceded by a repetition of the passover meal which had previously taken place before his agony and arrest on the Mount of Olives (Acts 1:4; cf. 1:13). The agony at Gethsemane arose then from the fact that Jesus was tempted to avoid the cross by asking his heavenly Father to grant a triumphant revelation of the Son of Man as the Messianic king—an event which is not to be until the day of his eschatological return.

The Mount had had an apocalyptic significance for Zechariah (Zech. 14); and a like vision is to be found in the book of the prophet Joel (Joel 2:28 ff.). On the day of Pentecost Joel's prophecy is fulfilled. On that day Jerusalem assumes its eschatological rôle as the mountain of the Lord. Yet at this juncture a new element also appears. Jesus, the Risen Lord, sends his disciples forth as witnesses from Jerusalem to the ends of the earth. In the New Testament therefore Zion acquires a new function as the 'centre' of salvation: now it is not only the place of gathering, but also the point of departure for the apostolic mission to all the nations.

The opposition between Babel and Zion continues, it is true. The Revelation to John prophesies of God's judgment upon Babylon; but beyond that a new heaven and a new earth appear, and a New Jerusalem, coming down from heaven. The contrast which Paul envisages between Adam and Christ applies equally to the old and the new Jerusalems: the former city was of the earth, the second is from heaven (cf. 1 Cor. 15:47). It is a consequence of this that the contrast between Zion and Babel is no longer an absolute, but a relative contrast. The earthly Jerusalem, along with Rome, belongs to the first earth which will pass away. Both now represent a stage on the road to the New Jerusalem, which is destined to take their place. Rome can never displace Jerusalem or become a substitute for it; but neither is it necessarily bound to be a reproduction of Babel. What it can be is a stage on the road which the Gospel takes from Jerusalem *en route* for the ends of the earth.

Three

Jews, Greeks and Barbarians

I. ESCHATOLOGY AND HISTORY

THE message of the New Testament is that in Jesus Christ the time is fulfilled (Mk. 1:15). He appears in the fullness of time (Gal. 4:4). In him the Scripture has been fulfilled (Lk. 4:21). Jesus proclaims to the people of Israel that he is the fulfilment of the Torah and the prophets: the Old Testament too is fulfilled in him. Whatever has been said in the foregoing chapter about the course of Israel's history amid the nations might be reiterated step by step with the New Testament in view. Thus Matthew's Gospel begins with 'The book of the genealogy of Jesus Christ, the son of David, the son of Abraham', picking up the theme of 'the generations of the heavens and the earth' (Gen. 2:4) and 'the book of the generations of Adam' (Gen. 5:1). Thus too the Fourth Gospel starts off with an epitome of Genesis 1, when it declares that Jesus Christ is the Word of God through whom all things have been made. In a similar way, the account of creation forms a basis for Paul's message that we have been created in Christ Jesus (Eph. 1:4; 2:10, 15; 3:9; 4:24; Col. 1:15, 23): once we were darkness, living in futility (Eph. 5:8; 4:17; *mataios*=Hebrew *tohu*; cf. Gen. 1:2; Is. 44:9, in the Septuagint), tossed to and fro and carried about with every wind of doctrine (Eph. 4:14; cf. Gen. 1:2: the waters); but now we are light, now we are built on a solid foundation (Eph. 2:20; 3:17; cf. Gen. 1:9).

Jesus is the 'last Adam' (1 Cor. 15:45) and he is also the 'last Noah' (Mt. 24:37). Before Abraham was, he is (Jn. 8:58). In him is consummated the promise made to Abraham for all the families of the earth (Lk. 1:55, 73). He is the last Moses, the last Aaron, the last Joshua (Heb. 1 ff.). He is son of David and greater than Solomon (Mt. 12:42), greater than the Temple (Mt. 12:6), greater than all the prophets (Heb. 1:1 ff.).

What all this means is that Jesus Christ represents, sums up and fulfils in his own person the whole history of the people of Israel. When the people of Israel reject him as their king with the cry: 'We have no king but Caesar!' they set a seal on what they had been doing all along, in choosing a king 'like all the nations' and rejecting the Lord from being king (Jn. 19; 1 Sam. 8). Upon the cross Jerusalem slew her last prophet (Mt. 23:37); and then and there God executed his final judgment upon the Temple—for Jesus is that Temple (Jn. 2:20 f.; Mt. 26:61; 24:2; 27:45 ff.). Just as the people of Israel had been carried off into exile in Babylon and had been scattered among the nations, so Jesus is delivered over into the power of the Roman Empire, his body broken, his disciples scattered (Mt. 26:26, 31).

In this Jesus history itself is consummated, in him all things are brought finally to a head; and after him no new thing can come. He is the Word of creation who is present throughout the whole of the Old Testament; but now the Word becomes flesh, and in him the whole fullness of God dwells, bodily (Jn. 1: 14; Col. 2:9). He is God's last Word. God cannot come closer to his people than in the incarnate Word, Emmanuel, God with us, in whom the Lord visits his people. Here the election of this one people out of all the nations of the earth meets us with a constraining power. It has pleased the Lord to be with his people in his only begotten Son, born of a Jewish mother, circumcised and dedicated in the Temple, preaching to the people of Israel, choosing Jerusalem as the capital of his kingship at the cross, in his resurrection and in the outpouring of his Spirit.

It is a vital mistake to suppose that the New Testament is 'more spiritual' than the Old. Rather, the opposite is true; and the absolute scandalousness of the Gospel in Jewish eyes consists precisely in the claim that in Jesus the spiritual Word has come in the flesh. Yet it is true, of course, that the New Testament goes to the extreme in the other direction. Although, on the one hand, everything is concentred upon this one man in his earthly, bodily life, death and resurrection, on the other hand to the earthly dimension a new dimension is, added. Not only the earth—which from the third verse of Genesis 1 onwards becomes the arena of history—but the heavens too are taken up into the consummation of history. According to Genesis 1, verse 1, they are created together with the earth. The first Deluge merely floods the earth; but when the last Noah shall come on the clouds of heaven, then not only the earth but the heavens will pass away, and there will be a new heaven and a new earth (Mt. 24:30 ff.; Rev. 21:1). The first Adam was of the earth; the last Adam is of heaven (1 Cor. 15:45 ff.). Thus the eschatological prospect of the restoration of Zion and the return of the remnant to the land of Israel broadens out in the New

Testament into the vision of the New Jerusalem coming down out of heaven from God (Rev. 21:10). Seated at the right hand of God, the Christ reigns, not only in the midst of his enemies on earth (Ps. 110), but over all principalities and powers in the heavenly places (Eph. 1:20 ff.).

It is against this background that Jesus' prophecy concerning the destruction and restoration of the Temple is to be understood. When Jesus purifies the Temple and the Jews ask him what sign he has to show, he replies: 'Destroy this temple, and in three days I will raise it up,' (Jn. 2:19). He spoke of 'the temple of his body', which would be destroyed on the cross and restored at the resurrection (v. 21 ff.). That in this he represents and epitomizes the destruction and restoration of the people and the land of Israel is very clear from the inclusion of a verse from Psalm 69, which the disciples apply to the action of Jesus in purifying the Temple: 'For zeal for thy house has consumed me.' That psalm is a cry of extreme distress and desolation; but it ends, like Psalm 22, with a victorious affirmation of God's power and salvation which are to be displayed here on earth, specifically in the restoration of Zion and of the cities of Judah, so that his servants 'shall dwell there and possess it' (Ps. 69:35 f.). Jesus declares that in his resurrection that expectation is to be fulfilled. In the life, death and resurrection of his Son the Lord identifies himself with the life, destruction and restoration of his chosen people and their land. That is how Jeremiah too sees the New Covenant that the Lord will make with the house of Israel and with the house of Judah: the city shall be rebuilt for the Lord, it shall not be uprooted or overthrown any more for ever (Jer. 31:31–40).

The risen Lord is the New Israel. In his ascension into heaven he reigns as king over the heavenly Zion; and when he shall come on the clouds of heaven, the heavenly Zion will descend with him, its temple and its lamp. The new Zion shall be a new Paradise, making manifest what had been the whole import of the Old Testament: that what the Lord has always purposed is the *shalom*, the good life and the true life at peace with him, for the whole earth. The kings of the earth will bring into the New Jerusalem the glory and honour of the nations and on either side of the river of the water of life, which flows through the city, stands the tree of life of which the leaves shall be 'for the healing of the nations' (Rev. 22).

In the outpouring of the Holy Spirit at Pentecost that expectation is fulfilled: and yet it is still lacking, this fulfilment, in almost every particular. True, it was Jerusalem which Jesus had expressly indicated as the place where they were to await the promise of the Father (Acts 1:4); true, there are gathered together men out of every nation (Acts 2:5), and indeed they hear the disciples speaking in their tongues the mighty works of God (Acts 2:11). It is not yet come to pass, however, that the Lord has poured out his Spirit upon all flesh. The three thousand souls who that day were added to the Church (Acts 2:41) are only the first beginning of what the prophet Joel sees the Lord as doing in the last days. They are all Jews who are here gathered into one, even if they are of the Diaspora and dwellers among every nation under heaven. As yet the Gentiles are untouched by the Spirit. Above all, Jerusalem is the old Jerusalem still; as yet the New Jerusalem is in the heavens, where the Lord is. The sun is not yet turned into darkness, nor yet the moon into blood. Clearly, the 'last days' have dawned; but 'the day of the Lord . . . the great and manifest day' is not yet (Acts 2:17, 20). That day has been appointed by the Father, by his own authority; but in these 'last days' Jesus, the Risen Lord, sends out his disciples to be his witnesses 'in Jerusalem and in all Judea and Samaria and to the end of the earth'. It is in the last days that the Gentiles are taken up into the salvation and restoration of Israel. Jesus has said as much in his reply to the disciples: this Gospel of the kingdom will be preached throughout the whole world, as a testimony to all nations: and then the end will come (Mt. 24:14).

In the Acts of the Apostles this testimony to the nations is recorded for us. The book itself, being a part of the New Testament, witnesses to the power of the Risen Lord and to the work of his Spirit. Paul's ministry takes place under the pressing urgency imparted to it by the approaching day of the Lord; and his being called to become the Apostle of the Gentiles corroborates and, as it were, actualizes the sign of the 'last days'. The Acts of the Apostles likewise constitutes the beginning of what is usually called 'the history of the Church and missions'—a history continued, of course, up to this very day. There does not seem to be any definite dividing-line that one can point to between the New Testament itself and what came after it. The Apostles did not succeed in carrying the Gospel 'to the uttermost parts of the earth'; and the close of the ages has not arrived yet. If they were conversant with 'the last days', then so are we. Our history is included within the same eschatological setting that they lived in themselves; and—to put it the other way round—their witness was subject to the same charge and the same promise as is our own.

If we were to pursue this to its logical outcome, we should have to conclude that the Canon really ought to be limited to the four Gospels: that is to say, to such documents as witness to the life, death and resurrection of Jesus. Yet this would only push the problem a stage further back, since the four Gospels are themselves part of that witness which we find described in the Acts of the Apostles. When the early Church closed the Canon, it did so in full awareness of the fact that one thing characterized the Apostles' testimony which was lacking in the testimony of later generations: namely that the Apostles were 'witnesses of the resurrection' (Acts 1:22), and thus had been directly involved in the revelation of the Lord during his earthly life. This first-hand witness was the corner-stone of their testimony; and all that succeeding generations could do was to build upon it.

However, none of this takes away from the fact that the Acts of the Apostles mark the beginning of the history of Church and missions. They are set in the first century of our 'Christian era', within the area of the Hellenistic *oikoumenē*. That is true of the Gospels and of the life of Jesus. Jesus was born in the reign of Caesar Augustus, in a colonial province of the Roman Empire. No wonder then that Christian theologians have attempted, time and again, in dealing with this idea of the 'fullness of time' (Gal. 4:4) in which God sent forth his Son, somehow or other to link it up with or even deduce it from the universal peace which the reign of Augustus conferred upon the Hellenistic *oikoumenē*. All such speculations, however, come to grief on one vital point: that Jesus, and Jesus alone, is the norm and substance of the 'fullness of time'; it is the *close* of the ages, not a particular period of history: it is the fulfilment of Old Testament history in the coming of the kingdom of the Lord—the very opposite and negation of the kingdoms of the nations. Speculations of this sort also suggest a false solution to the question of how the 'fullness of time' is to be related to the historical period in which Jesus lived. The event which had been hailed as the close of the ages nevertheless came to be *Annus Domini*, the inception of our Christian era. The 'last Adam' is also the 'founder' of a Church and the point of departure of a missionary movement; and both of these have their part in mundane history as a whole. Vice versa, that history is itself taken up into the 'last days', when the Gospel is to be proclaimed to the ends of the earth. The

fundamental problem lies just there; the relationship between eschatology and history is at one and the same time a totally eschatological
and a totally historical relationship.

One very widely acclaimed answer to this riddle consists of
representing Jesus as the central point of history. The New Testament
then becomes the successor to the Old, and history moves first from
creation to Jesus and then from Jesus on to the Kingdom of God.
The Trinitarian formula provides an excellent basis for this theory;
the age of the Father (Old Testament) is followed by the coming of
the Son (New Testament), whilst we live now in the age of the
Spirit (Church and missions). This answer, however obvious and
attractive it may appear to be, fails to meet the case, because it distorts
the significance of both Old and New Testaments; it involves a wrong
interpretation of our own history and a confused view of what the
Trinitarian formula means. The New Covenant does not 'follow
upon' the Old Covenant, but fulfils it. Our history is not the sequel
to the New Testament, but is embraced by it. The Kingdom of God,
which Jesus has proclaimed and the Revelation of John displays,
lies not behind but before us. Church and missions do not constitute
a new period, something on a par, as it were, with the preceding
history of Israel and of Jesus and the Apostles, but the outpouring of
the Spirit is the sign of the 'last days'.

The previous chapter has described how the Old Testament
envisages the history of Israel amid the nations. Genesis, chapters 1 to
11, prefigures and anticipates the history of Israel, which begins with
Genesis 12. The people of Israel are not one among many nations,
but a new creation of the Lord's. Israel lives amid the Gentiles,
between Egypt and Babylon. We saw how the story of creation in
Genesis 1 is at the heart of the proclamation of God's victory over the
power of the Gentiles. In the life, society, state and culture of Israel
the Lord the Creator is active in carrying out his purposes. The
religious ideas, the mythology, cult and ritual, the social and legal
traditions, yes, and even the political structure of the Gentile peoples
are incorporated into the life of Israel. The promised land lies right
at the centre of the 'sphere of influence' of the ancient civilizations;
and Israel's history unfolds itself amidst the history of the neighbouring
great powers. In this special situation Israel is called to be a light to
the nations and the salt of the earth: she is to be the paradigm of God's
creation. Just as God's Word has gone forth upon the primeval chaos

and has delimited it, tamed and subdued it, put it to his service, subjected it to his own sovereign action, so will the Lord do with and through his people Israel. In the life of Israel the Lord purposes to make subject to himself and to use for his own ends the way of life, spiritual and material, of the Gentiles—a way of life which is in itself a totalitarian one. His will is to breach the absolutism of the pagan religions, to break them open and so make room for his creative action. We saw how the Lord's purpose with Israel went unfulfilled; but he persists with it through this creative activity of his, continually repeated—a prolonged struggle between his holy will and the stubborn desire of his people to be like all the nations round about them. The Torah is the story of Israel in the wilderness, en route for the promised land. The prophets look towards the future when the Lord will establish his kingship over his people, make an everlasting covenant with them and settle accounts once and for all with the powers of chaos. But it is beyond even Israel to realize God's will and fulfil his purpose. Nevertheless, the Old Testament affords an absolutely unique example of a tenacious struggle, waged over many centuries, between God's creative power and the primeval forces that dominate the life of the Gentiles.

It is a struggle which takes place entirely within the confines of Israel. The Lord has created this people to represent mankind, has chosen this land as centre and pattern of the world. Here he will show what is his purpose for every nation. In this place is the proof to be given, in the sight of the Gentiles, that the good life is possible on earth, the life lived in harmony and peace, in the community of a people, without raising a tower with its top in heaven. Nowhere in the Old Testament, however, is the possibility envisaged that the Gentiles might be able—and might wish—to conform to this pattern or that such a way of life could prevail among the nations. The Gentiles remain on the outer edge, for the most part, like the un-tamable strength of the ocean, or at best like the coastlands and islands on the furthest frontier. The Lord makes use of them to chastise his unruly people; and then at the Last Day they become the object of his final judgment. It is only in a context of eschatological prophecy that the Gentiles come into the picture in another fashion, as the object of God's mercy and grace, even as peoples whom he chooses along with his chosen people. Only at the close of the ages does the Old Testament see the nations also coming up to Zion and submitting themselves to the Torah; but of this as an historical reality, extended through the temporal and spatial dimensions of the Gentiles' own mode of existence, the Old Testament sees no possibility at all.

It would be quite wrong to suppose that with the New Testament that possibility looms upon the horizon of history. In that case the New Covenant would be no more than a means of extending the Old Covenant to include the nations and so of allowing them to repeat in their own way what Israel had done before them. Down the centuries Christian theology has moved between the Scylla and Charybdis of underrating the Old Testament on the one hand and overrating it on the other. To give the Old Testament less than its proper status is to overlook the fact that it is, after all, the Old Testament which Jesus fulfils; and then the age of Israel is reckoned to be superseded by the age of the Church and an opposition is all too easily permitted to arise between the Old Testament God of judgment and wrath and the New Testament message of love and forgiveness. On the other hand, to overvalue the Old Testament amounts to denying that it has in fact now been fulfilled in Jesus. When that happens, the Church is expected to direct various attempts at establishing a Christian order which sets out to reproduce the Torah among the Gentiles.

Jesus talks about the Old Testament as 'the Scriptures'. Luke's Gospel ends with the Risen Lord appearing to his disciples. He 'opened their minds to understand the scriptures': everything written concerning him in the law of Moses, in the Prophets and in the Psalms must be fulfilled; for in the Scriptures is written 'that the Christ should suffer and on the third day rise from the dead, and that repentance and forgiveness of sins should be preached in his name to all nations, beginning from Jerusalem.' The Gospel consists for the Gentiles in the fact that the Scriptures—the Old Testament—have been fulfilled in Jesus. What that means is that there is the Old Testament for the Gentiles, not indeed for them to repeat—that is out of the question, for the Scriptures are unrepeatable—nor yet to fulfil, for that Jesus has done, but in order for them to hear its message, to repent and to receive forgiveness of sins. Jesus declares that all this 'is written in the Scriptures'. The preaching of the Gospel to the Gentiles does not open up any new potentialities, as it were, above and beyond the Old Testament, but is the realization of it in an eschatological sense.

What then is the content of the message? First of all, the crucified Lord is proclaimed among the Gentiles. In his body the Temple has been destroyed. In his person Jesus endures the judgment of God, entailed by the people of Israel's failure to be the salt of the earth. Yet because Israel stands for all the nations, in her failure the Gentiles are compelled also to recognize their own. Faced with the cross they must come to repent and to see that what Israel has failed to achieve they themselves have never even attempted. In the second place, it is the Risen Lord who is proclaimed. By his resurrection Jesus becomes the eternal Temple of the New Jerusalem. The Lord has mercy on his people; a remnant shall return and the city be rebuilt; within the promised land Israel shall dwell in harmony and peace. In this mercy which the Lord shows towards his people the Gentiles may perceive his forgiveness extended to every nation; for the New Jerusalem is to be the centre of a new heaven and a new earth, and into it the nations will bring their honour and their glory. By his resurrection the Risen Lord reveals that in his own person the new Temple is even now raised; by this the Gentiles may know that for them too the new life is already possible. But still it is only the beginning of the 'last days'. The Risen Lord does not remain on earth; he ascends to heaven so that the nations may know that all authority has been given to him, not merely on earth but in heaven too. Whenever and where-ever his Gospel is proclaimed, the ascended Lord is at work through his Spirit among the nations. He is already active therefore in establishing God's kingdom as far as the uttermost parts of the earth and in bringing to pass what the Old Testament had foreshadowed.

What manner of men were they among whom this message that Jesus Christ has fulfilled the Scriptures was proclaimed? The New Testament was written in Greek; and it addressed itself to the *oikoumenē*. At Pentecost Jews from every nation under heaven heard the disciples talking to every man among them in his own language. All the nations enumerated here lay within the sphere of the Hellenistic *oikoumenē*, being either part of it in the fullest sense or else situated on its borders. The New Testament, however, was not written in one of the 'native' languages, let alone in each and all of them. Like a flash of lightning, the Spirit at Pentecost had for a single instant flooded with light the horizon of 'all the nations'. The written Gospels, on the other hand, were restricted to one language, and that the lingua franca of the Hellenistic world. The confines of Israel and of the Hebrew language had to be transcended; and that meant resorting to the Greeks. The Septuagint had no doubt done something to prepare for this, but the New Testament falls into a new, indeed a unique, category. The significance of the New Testament's being written in Greek becomes fully apparent only when we postulate the comparable case of an Old Testament written, not in Hebrew, but in the language of ancient Babylonia. The Septuagint, of course, is simply a translation of the original Hebrew; but putting the Old Testament on record in the Babylonian language would have amounted to a confession on the part of the people of Israel that the Exile was not merely a sign of God's judgment, calling them to repentance so that one day salvation would come and they could return to Zion, but that the Lord had delivered his people into the hands of the Gentiles for the conversion of all the nations. Yet even the Book of Jonah, although it does admittedly contemplate the conversion of Nineveh as a real and historical event, is no more than an edifying story, written in Hebrew.

Jesus is 'greater than Jonah' (Mt. 12:41). The writing of the New Testament in Greek in itself witnesses to the fact that in Jesus the fullness of time has arrived. The Gospel is literally committed to the language of the pagan world. It is not simply that the Greek language does duty in this case as an effective medium of evangelization—like the later translated versions of the Bible for example—but first and foremost that it was the language of the *oikoumenē* and principally, of course, of the Roman Empire (Lk. 2:1). In the New Testament Rome occupies the rôle which in the Old Testament had belonged to Babylon. The name for Rome in the Revelation of John is simply 'great Babylon'; and just as in the Old Testament the judgment of Babylon precedes the return of the people of Israel to Jerusalem and the rebuilding of the holy city, so here the fall of 'great Babylon' is seen as the final judgment heralding the descent of the New Jerusalem. In this way Rome acquires a unique significance as the ultimate adversary of the people of God. In Genesis 11 Babylon is the capital of the entire world, and the Book of Revelation sees 'the great Babylon' as similarly representative of 'the cities of the nations' and as the capital of 'the kings of the earth' (Rev. 16:19; 17:9).

Jesus too views the function of Rome in this apocalyptic light. His birth was preceded by the decree of Caesar Augustus that 'the whole *oikoumenē*' should be enrolled. That decree is directly matched by Jesus' declaration that 'this gospel of the kingdom will be preached throughout the whole *oikoumenē*, as a testimony to all nations; and then the end will come,' (Mt. 24:14). When Jesus says this to his disciples, he is sitting on the Mount of Olives, after leaving the Temple; and his discourse provides an explanation of his prophecy that the Temple will be destroyed down to the very last stone (Mt. 24:1 f.). The setting for this preaching of the Gospel to the whole *oikoumenē* is the beginning of the tribulation, to be followed by 'the desolating sacrilege spoken of by the prophet Daniel, standing in the holy place' (Mt. 24:15). Jesus is here predicting the approaching destruction of Jerusalem by the Romans—the final repetition of what Antiochus Epiphanes had perpetrated in the second century B.C., and Nebuchadnezzar four centuries before that. Rome is the Babylon of the last days. The conflict mounts to its eschatological climax.

Against that apocalyptic background the writing of the New Testament in the Greek language appears in full and striking perspective. It is to the apocalyptic adversary of the Lord that the Gospels are purposely addressed, nay more, into whose hands they are placed. It is in the very language of that ultimate and universal embodiment of pagan pride and unbelief that in the fullness of the time God's final Word must be proclaimed; and thus the written Word follows the pattern laid down by him who was the Word incarnate. Jesus had indeed given himself over likewise into the hands of Pontius Pilate; it is neither accidental nor incidental that in one and the same breath the Apostles' creed mentions the name of the Roman governor together with that of the crucified Lord. The close association of those two names is to be set against the preceding affirmation that Jesus was born of the Virgin Mary. The name of Mary here confirms the fact that Jesus was a Jew, 'the son of David, the son of Abraham' (Mt. 1:1–16), 'born of woman, born under the law' (Gal. 4:4). The name 'Pontius Pilate' here signifies that Jesus is delivered up to the Gentiles. 'Crucified under Pontius Pilate' means that there at the cross the Temple is destroyed once and for all, now that Jesus has borne in his own body the judgment of God. At the cross, the dividing wall of hostility between Israel and the Gentiles has been broken down; and Jesus has reconciled both to God in one body. By his resurrection he raises that eternal Temple in which both Jews and Gentiles, created 'instead of the two one new man' in Jesus, may praise and serve the Lord through the Spirit (Eph. 2). It was 'under Pontius Pilate' that God was in Christ reconciling the world to himself, not counting their trespasses against them (2 Cor. 5:19). That means that the Roman state stands straightaway under the grace of God. The apocalyptic judgment pronounced upon Babylon Jesus has suffered in his own body on the cross; Rome therefore is no longer doomed to be a second Babylon. Once already, in the Old Testament, a pagan state had been the means of bringing salvation and restoration to God's people: that is, in the Second Isaiah where the Achaemenid King Cyrus appears as a servant of the Lord and saviour of the chosen people. Even so, it is to the Jews that the Book of Isaiah conveys this message, not to the Persians. It is written in Hebrew, and neither King Cyrus nor his subjects had any chance of learning for themselves what it was that the God of Israel purposed to do through them. The rôle of Pilate, however, cannot be likened to that of Cyrus. On the contrary Pilate is the one who, as he himself says, 'has power to release Jesus and power to crucify him' and thus bears final responsibility for ordering the crucifixion, which was then carried out by Roman soldiers. Still less can he be said to have followed in the steps of Nebuchadnezzar. He did all he could to effect the release of Jesus and washed his hands in innocency. He stands back, as it were, out of the limelight, his rôle a passive one, himself more a factor than a 'governor'. In the Apostles' creed the ambiguity of his rôle is nicely expressed by the phrase, 'under Pontius Pilate'; and the basic reason for this ambivalence appears from the words of Jesus: 'You would have no power over me unless it had been given you from above; therefore he who delivered me to you has the greater sin,' (Jn. 19:11). It is the people of Israel who deliver up their king, with the cry: 'We have no king but Caesar!' (Jn. 19:15), thus rounding off that historic process which had started with their clamouring for 'a king to govern us like all the nations' (1 Sam. 8:5). The Roman state has indeed no part in that history, but is simply caught up in it, an involuntary participant in the final act. Because the Jewish people choose Caesar in preference to Jesus, the Roman Empire becomes the object of God's reconciling act. 'Under Pontius Pilate' the eschatological shift occurs which brings the pagan *oikoumenē* into an integral relationship with the 'fullness of time'. Unlike its predecessors—Egypt, Assyria, Babylonia and Persia—the Roman Empire is no longer just an instrument of God's purposes, but is now itself subject to the Gospel. Now, at the very heart and centre of her historical existence,

Rome actually finds herself confronted with the message of salvation, which is no longer the exclusive concern of Israel but also her own. What Isaiah had once prophesied concerning Egypt applies now to the Roman people: 'In that day there will be an altar to the Lord in the midst of the land of Egypt, . . . And the Lord will make himself known to the Egyptians; and the Egyptians will know the Lord . . . And the Lord will smite Egypt, smiting and healing, and they will return to the Lord, and he will heed their supplications and heal them . . . In that day Israel will be the third with Egypt and Assyria, a blessing in the midst of the earth, whom the Lord of hosts has blessed, saying, "Blessed be Egypt my people, and Assyria the work of my hands, and Israel my heritage," ' (Is. 19:19 ff.). That prophecy did not materialize so far as Egypt and Assyria were concerned. Their empires had been destroyed, and the Lord did not in fact make himself known to those nations. The New Testament is not in Egyptian or in Assyrian; it is written in Greek. Jesus is born under Augustus, not under the Pharaoh, and crucified under Pontius Pilate, not under Nebuchadnezzar. In the endless succession of conquest-states that dominate the Fertile Crescent it falls to the Roman Empire to have the land of Israel under colonial rule at the very juncture when the 'fullness of time' arrives. Within the Roman *oikoumenē* the good news is first proclaimed: that 'the old has passed away, behold, the new has come,' (2 Cor. 5:17). The sober verdict of 'the old' is that if Rome turns out to be 'like all the nations', repeating the story of earlier empires, well, that is only to be expected. But this fatal necessity has been annulled at the cross; the door is opened into a new mode of existence such as witnesses to the kingship of the Lord.

That this privilege should fall to the lot of the Roman Empire is not an end in itself. The Gospel must be preached 'to the ends of the earth' and 'to all the nations'. For the Apostles the *oikoumenē* comprises the furthest limit conceivable and is for them the same thing as 'the whole world'; nor was there any reason why the 'fullness of time' should not have happened under the Babylonians or the Achaemenids. That in fact it appears with the Romans simply means that what applies equally to all times happened to them because it was 'the close of the ages'. Nevertheless the Roman *oikoumenē* is privileged in being singled out as the place where the Gospel breaks through the frontiers of the people of Israel and comes to the Gentiles. This localization goes along with the election of the land of Israel.

If it had pleased God to choose the people of his covenant in the steppes of Asia and to have them migrate to North West China, then the privilege of the Romans would have belonged instead to the Han empire of China. The place and time of Israel's history were indeed 'arbitrarily chosen': arbitrarily in that the election is the Lord's. The same factor governs the 'accidental' circumstance that the Gospel is not proclaimed everywhere all at once, but starting from Jerusalem makes its way through the *oikoumenē*; and thus too it comes about that Jesus is born and crucified under the Roman imperium and not under some Chinese or Indian régime; thus it is that Greek becomes the language of the New Testament and that Paul's ministry was peculiarly related to the Roman state; and, one might add, the Christian Church has for the same reason had a very particular connection, up to the present time, with those nations which have received the legacy of the *oikoumenē*. Lastly, it is the same 'arbitrary' factor which has made the missionary expansion of Christianity throughout the world go hand in hand with the spread of a civilization closely affiliated to Christian antiquity. None of this was pre-requisite; it is just as likely to have happened otherwise. There is no question here of any *a priori* relation; we can only distinguish, in retrospect, certain specific relations. Nor, since these relations are purely historical, is it legitimate to confine the Gospel within them. The 'fullness of time' is the close of the ages, not a period of history. It concerns all nations and not just one exclusive historico-geographical constellation called Christendom or Christianity.

2. PAUL'S MINISTRY TO GREEKS AND BARBARIANS

It is the ministry of Paul, 'the apostle to the Gentiles', which illustrates most clearly and completely what the proclamation of the Gospel to the Hellenistic *oikoumenē* means. In the preamble to his Letter to the Romans he confesses himself 'under obligation both to Greeks and to barbarians, both to the wise and to the foolish'; for the Gospel is 'the power of God for salvation to every one who has faith, to the Jew first and also to the Greek,' (Rom. 1:14, 16). Here then is a twofold contrast: of Greeks with barbarians and of Jews with Greeks.

Among the Rabbinical writings there is a discourse by Rabbi Jehuda, in which he praises God that he was created neither pagan nor woman nor 'uncivilized'. This is remarkably like the prayer of the Greek philosopher Thales, who expresses his gratitude to the Fate

(Tyche) for three things: that he was born a man and not an animal, a man and not a woman, a Hellene and not a barbarian.[1] The measure of agreement here is as illuminating as the points of difference between them. In their masculine pride Greek philosopher and Jewish Rabbi are at one. A Gentile, however, is something essentially different from a barbarian. The basic meaning of 'civilized', in a Rabbinical context, is 'having knowledge of the Torah, in contradistinction to "the people who know not the Law" (ʿam ha-ʾareṣ). Again, in Hebrew and Aramaic the word barbar is a Greek borrowing and is never synonymous with the idea of goy, Gentile. In Jewish historiography the Babylonians, Medes and Romans are described as 'conquerors of the barbarians'. No Greek would ever describe himself as 'barbarian', any more than a Jew could possibly be styled 'a Gentile'. As the Greeks saw it, the Jews were in origin barbarians, whilst for the Jews the Greeks were part of the Gentile world. But the point of reference in each case is fundamentally different. 'Barbarian' is a racial, ethnical, cultural term, whereas the term goy is rooted categorically in the history of the Lord's redemptive dealings with his chosen people. Notions of racial and cultural distinctiveness play at the most a secondary rôle in this connection.

The Hellenizing process set in motion by Alexander's career of conquest was carried a good deal further by the Seleucids; but when the Seleucid Empire had been absorbed into the Imperium Romanum, the resurgent oriental cultures reacted strongly against Hellenization.[2] During the Seleucid period a great many Jews—in Israel as well as in the Diaspora—learned to speak Greek; and so many of them became 'Hellenes', in the cultural sense in which Isocrates had employed the term: that is to say, they participated in the culture of the Greeks (paideia). As regards physis they were barbarians, but in respect of nomos they were Hellenes. The abundance of Hellenistic-Jewish literature, in the form of original works as well as translations, attests the fact that the Jews of the Diaspora were even more strongly affected by this Hellenizing process. Such literature not only supplied the needs of the Diaspora but served as Jewish propaganda among the Greeks and stimulated to an extraordinary degree that reciprocal assimilative process which turned Jews into Greeks and a good number of Greeks into Jews.

The sharp resistance of the majority of Jews in the motherland to the attempt on the part of Antiochus Epiphanes radically to Hellenize the Jewish people (166 B.C.) set a gulf between 'Hellenism' and 'Judaism',³ whilst, as it turned out, Judaism was able to maintain itself in being, even in the Diaspora. Thus the term 'Hellene' came gradually to be synonymous with 'idolater and heathen'. From the Greek and Hellenistic-Jewish point of view, this amounted to a complete debasement of the term, since it was now no longer referred to the *paideia* (culture) but to the *latreia* (cult); and Hellenism became identified with *eidololatreia* (idolatry). When Christianity had taken a hold on the Greek world, 'Hellene' gradually came to mean 'Gentile'.⁴

It is in the Talmud that the reaction is most bitter and uncompromising. Learning the Greek language is there forbidden; and the study of Greek wisdom is put on a par with the herding of swine. This fanaticism, which was racial and religious as well as political, scorned Greek culture along with Greek idolatry, even though there are in the Talmud traces of a more positive attitude. In contrast to this, Hellenistic Judaism learned to distinguish between the Greek pagan ethos, cult and mythology on the one hand and the language, philosophy and more neutral elements of Greek civilization on the other. These it attempted, eclectically, to assimilate. Philo regarded himself and behaved in every respect as an educated Greek. Not only does one very seldom come across the term 'Gentiles' (*ethnē*) in his writings, but there is nothing there to suggest that he conceives of the Hellene as being a Gentile at all. He was taken up with the cosmopolitan idea of a growing unity between Hellenes and barbarians; and he extolled the Emperor Augustus as a kind of world saviour for Hellene and barbarian alike. It is not always clear whether he regards the Jews in this connection as barbarians or as constituting a third category. The latter is certainly the case when he is indicting Hellenes and barbarians together for their idolatry. The Jewish people and religion were in his view ordained to bring the knowledge of the true God to Hellenes and barbarians, to settle all differences and disputes between them and thus to provide 'the religion for the *oikoumenē*'.

It was whilst this process of assimilation—involving Jews, Greeks and barbarians—was going on that the Gospel made its appearance, bringing into the flow of current opinions and ideas a message which was utterly new.

The Gospel had been preached for the first time to 'the Greeks'—

that is, to the non-Jewish, Greek-speaking inhabitants—by Jewish Christians at Antioch (Acts 11:20). After that, the Acts of the Apostles makes regular mention of the fact that Paul and Barnabas are addressing themselves to 'Jews and Greeks'. By 'Greeks' here is meant that part of the mixed Greek and Jewish population of the province of Asia Minor and the Greek cities of Corinth and Thessalonica who were not Jews—particularly Hellenistic frequenters of the synagogue (Acts 14:1; 18:4; 17:4). As a result of this missionary enterprise, congregations were formed in the Greek-speaking areas, comprising (a few) Jews and (a considerable number of) Greeks. The expression 'Jews and Greeks' in Acts is identical then, in some instances, with 'Jews and Gentiles' (Acts 14:1 f.). Generally, however, the term 'Greeks' means, in the usage current at the time, 'the Greek-speaking, non-Jewish population'.

In his letters (1 Cor.; Gal.; Rom.; Col.) Paul includes the Greeks in the two sets of opposites: Jews and Greeks in the first case, Greeks and barbarians in the second. In the preface to his Letter to the Romans he addresses them as 'Gentiles' (Rom. 1:13, 16), yet at the same time as 'Greek' (Rom. 1:15). That the Jew took precedence over the Greek was always fundamental to his preaching; but in addition he recognized the Greek as being privileged above the barbarian, the 'wise' above the 'foolish'. The first of these distinctions has its roots in Scripture—it is an integral part of the Gospel's very foundations; whereas the second owes its point to Hellenic culture. These are two types of contrast, therefore, pertaining to fundamentally different categories. Still, a certain parallelism is unmistakably present here. As apostle to the Gentiles, Paul regarded the *oikoumenē*—that is, the 'Greeks' in a linguistic and cultural sense—as his field of missionary operation. His 'obligation towards barbarians' in all probability refers to the 'internal proletariat' as well as the 'external' (to use Toynbee's expression); it refers to the 'foolish' and uncivilized, the lowest classes of society, as well as to the Scythians (Col. 3:11), the Germans and the Celts, and also certainly the bulk of the Spaniards, in the non-Hellenized or semi-Hellenized border regions.

In the final section of his Letter to the Romans Paul explains why he has so far been prevented from coming to Rome: it has been his ambition 'to preach the gospel, not where Christ has already been named, lest I build on another man's foundation.' In this way he fulfils Isaiah's prophecy concerning the Servant of the Lord (Rom.

15:20 f.; Is. 52:15). It is precisely this ambition of his which now at last leads him to decide to visit Rome, because he has finished his work in the eastern part of the Mediterranean (Rom. 15:23). Now he hopes to visit the Romans *en passant*, since he has longed for many years to come to them, as soon 'as I go to Spain' (Rom. 15:23 f.).[5] His destination then is Spain; and what he expects of the Romans is 'to be sped on my journey there by you, once I have enjoyed your company a little.' He had already said as much, implicitly, in the opening part of his letter. His apostleship takes in 'all the Gentiles', the Romans included (Rom. 1:5 f.); and he intends to come to them 'in order that I may reap some harvest among you as well as among the rest of the Gentiles,' (v. 13). This is made still clearer by what follows: 'I am under an obligation both to Greeks and to barbarians, both to the wise and to the foolish: so I am eager to preach the gospel to you also who are in Rome,' (v. 14 f.). That would seem to run counter to his dictum about not preaching the Gospel 'where Christ has already been named,' (Rom. 15:20); and it is precisely for that reason that he stresses so repeatedly that Rome is not the object of his journey. It is with 'the rest of the Gentiles' that he is concerned. The conclusion: 'so I am eager to preach the gospel to you also who are in Rome' follows from the premiss about his obligation 'both to Greeks and to barbarians'. In other words, the Romans—who are 'Greeks'—are taken into his journey on the way to 'the barbarians'. We learn from the final chapter who are meant here: the 'rest of the Gentiles' and 'the barbarians' are the inhabitants of Spain. Rome is simply a port of call *en route*.

Within the scheme of salvation in its historical setting therefore the phrase 'to Greeks and to barbarians' is to be put side by side with: 'to the Jew first and also to the Greek' (Rom. 1:16). The preaching of the Gospel comes from the Jews to the Greeks; but its ultimate objective is 'the barbarians, the rest of the Gentiles', as the closing passage in the letter confirms. Paul announces his intention of calling at Rome on his way to Spain, but he adduces a fresh reason for delay: for the present, however, he is going 'to Jerusalem with aid for the saints'. This is a 'service in things material' rendered by the congregations of Macedonia and Achaia and offered in return for the 'things spiritual' of Jerusalem, in which as Gentiles they have come to share (Rom. 15:25 ff.). Thus Paul's projected visit to Jerusalem gives powerful emphasis to the words 'to the Jew first and also to the

Greek'. When he has concluded his visit to Jerusalem—and not before—he will go 'by way of you to Spain' (v. 28). Rome lies on the route from Jerusalem to Spain. The 'Greeks' are a halfway house between Jews and barbarians.

To all this he adds a remarkable conclusion: 'And I know that when I come to you I shall come in the fullness of the blessing of Christ' (v. 29). The term 'fullness' is of central importance in the New Testament and particularly in the letters of Paul; for it takes in every dimension of the fulfilment in Jesus Christ. In Christ all the fullness of God was pleased to dwell (Col. 1:19; 2:9; Eph. 3:16 ff.). The Church is the fullness of Christ who fills all in all, and is attaining to the maturity of his fullness (Eph. 1:20 ff.; 4:7 ff.; Jn. 1:16). Christ has come in the fullness of time (Eph. 1:9 f.; Gal. 4:4; Mk. 1:15). His love is the fullness of the Torah (Rom. 13:10; Mt. 5:17). It all falls into place within the 'mystery' which Paul reveals to the Romans, explaining to them that 'a hardening has come upon part of Israel, until the full number of the Gentiles come in, and so all Israel shall be saved,' (Rom. 11:25 f.). In the service of that eschatological purpose of the Lord Paul now intends to make for Spain; and on the way he will come to Rome 'in the fullness of the blessing of Christ'. We may take this as referring back to and fulfilling the blessing of Abraham, which is to extend to 'all the families of the earth' (Gen. 12:1 ff.), and the kingship of the Lord over 'the earth and the fullness thereof' (Ps. 24). Paul stresses the fact that his apostolic mission is to 'all the Gentiles' (Rom. 1:5): 'from Jerusalem and as far round (*kuklôi*, 'in a circle') as Illyricum I have fulfilled the gospel of Christ,' (Rom. 15:19). Now—and once again from Jerusalem—he is going to carry the Gospel even into Spain, thereby fulfilling the command of Jesus which requires him to be his witness in Jerusalem . . . and to the ends of the earth (Acts 1:8). Spain was indeed, according to the geography of the time, at the ends of the earth.

The Letter to the Romans was sent from Corinth about A.D. 57. At that time Paul was already fully aware that the 'unbelievers in Judea' constituted a danger for him (Rom. 15:31). In his parting counsel to the elders of the church at Ephesus, only a few months after the Letter to the Romans had been despatched, Paul confesses that the Holy Spirit has testified to him, saying 'in every city that imprisonment and afflictions' await him (Acts 20:23). Then he adds: 'But I do not account my life of any value nor as precious to myself, if only I may accomplish (*teleiôsô*: bring to its *telos*, bring about its eschatological end) my course and the ministry which I received from the Lord Jesus, to testify to the gospel of the grace of God,' (Acts 20:24). When he said this, his intention of going to Spain must have been uppermost in his mind. His work in those eastern parts was finished; there they would see his face no more (Acts 20:25; cf. Rom. 15:23). That is why he had appealed to the Roman brethren to pray that he might 'be delivered from the unbelievers in Judea', so that, God willing, he might come to them on his journey through to Spain (Rom. 15:30 ff.).

In all probability Paul did in fact reach Spain and die there, though presumably not as a martyr. There then he finished his course and his ministry in a double sense, the end of his life at the end of the earth. Thirty years later, in A.D. 96, his Spanish journey was known about in Rome. Clement says that Paul, having been:

> . . . seven times in bonds, driven into exile, stoned, appearing as a herald in both the East and the West he won noble fame for his faith; he taught righteousness to the whole world, and after reaching the limits of the West bore witness before the rulers. Then he passed from the world and went to the holy place . . .[6]

This reflects most admirably Paul's ambition to carry the Gospel to the ends of the earth. Spain is 'the last outpost of the West'. Primitive tradition knows nothing about Paul's being put to death in Rome; the legend makes its first appearance between A.D. 160 and 170 in the *Acta Petri*, a Gnostic apocryphal work. It arose out of the desire to find some sanction for the claims to authority of the Roman Church and disregards the fact that for Paul Rome was merely a stage on his route from Jerusalem to the end of the earth.

Paul's journey to Rome was a direct consequence of the 'imprisonment and afflictions' which he was already expecting at the time when he wrote his Letter to the Romans (Acts 20:23). Imprisoned by the Roman authorities at Jerusalem because of an uproar among the Jews, he appealed on the grounds of the Roman citizenship which was his by birth (Acts 22:25 ff.). From then on he had the benefit of Roman protection against the assaults of the Jews (Acts 23:23 ff.). Before Porcius Festus, the governor, and in face of the latter's attempt to have the trial held in Jerusalem, Paul again takes a stand on his citizenship. It is an appeal which Festus is obliged to allow: 'You have appealed to Caesar; to Caesar you shall go,' (Acts 25:9 ff.); but the appeal itself inhibits Paul's release, which King Agrippa would have been willing to effect: 'This man could have been set free if he had not appealed to Caesar,' (Acts 26:32). Paul's imprisonment thus became the means of his reaching Rome, for the express reason of his own appeal to Caesar and in the charge of a centurion of the Augustan Cohort (Acts 27:1). Once in Rome, he was permitted private lodging under military guard; and for two whole years he lived there at his own expense, preaching the Gospel quite openly, without let or hindrance (Acts 28:16, 30). At this point the Acts of the Apostles ends.

Paul's decision to visit Rome, 'in passing,' on his way to Spain becomes all the more pregnant with meaning when seen against this background. His status as a Roman citizen was of fundamental importance for his apostolic ministry. He appealed, not in order to save his own skin, but to oblige the authorities to do their duty and maintain justice. The thesis concerning the ruling authority, which he expounds in his Letter to the Romans, is likewise the ground of his own appeal to his Roman citizenship and to Caesar's tribunal: 'Rulers are not a terror to good conduct, but to bad,' for they are God's servants for their good (Rom. 13:3 f.). His appeal to Caesar therefore goes hand in hand with his preaching to the Gentiles.

To grasp the full significance of this one must turn to the Old Testament. There the closest parallel to Paul's attitude is to be found in Moses' meeting with Pharaoh. Just as the Lord had charged Moses to go to Pharaoh and demand justice and freedom for the people of Israel, so the Lord Jesus charges Paul to bear witness of him at Rome (Acts 23:11). There is, however, a crucial difference. Moses demands freedom for his people to leave Egypt; Paul demands freedom to stay in the Roman Empire and to preach the Gospel throughout the *oikoumenē*. Through a series of miracles, and purely from fear of death, the Pharaoh is ultimately compelled to let the people of Israel go. Moses makes no appeal to any tradition or consciousness of justice on the Egyptians' part. The very possibility of such a thing lies beyond the horizon of the Old Testament. All that is possible is a song of thanksgiving to the Lord for having thrown Pharaoh's chariots and horsemen into the sea (Ex. 15). Egypt is Rahab, the primeval dragon; the Exodus is God's creative act. The same is true of the Babylonian exile. Nowhere is any appeal made to Babylonian law and order; there is only the hope of a new Exodus into the promised land. Paul, on the other hand, desires no Exodus; on the contrary, it is *from* Jerusalem that he comes, carrying the Gospel within the Roman Empire. He really believes it possible that the Roman authorities who are his interrogators will be converted through his preaching (Acts 26:29); and his appeal to Caesar's tribunal was likewise certainly prompted by his ambition to witness to the Lord Jesus before the highest authorities of the empire. Both the Gospels and the Acts of the Apostles show a marked confidence in the ability of the Roman authorities to maintain justice and order and to ensure the freedom necessary for evangelization. In dealing with the Roman rulers Paul conducts himself with the same confidence and resolution that the Old Testament prophets had shown towards the kings of Israel. But now a new element comes in. Paul not only proclaims the will of the Lord, as the prophets had done, but he appeals in the first instance to Roman law—the law by which the rulers are themselves bound. Something really fundamental has changed here since the days of the Old Testament. The Torah has in fact been fulfilled and through Jesus Christ has now come to the Gentiles, as Jeremiah had prophesied: 'But this is the covenant which I will make with the house of Israel after those days, says the Lord: I will put my law within them, and I will write it upon their hearts; and I will be their God, and they shall be my people. And no longer shall each man teach his neighbour . . . for they shall all know me . . . for I will forgive their iniquity and remember their sins no more,' (Jer. 31:31 ff.). In his Letter to the Romans Paul proceeds on the assumption that now, in the fullness of time, this prophecy has been fulfilled, not only in Israel but also among the Gentiles: 'When Gentiles who have not the law do by nature what the law requires, they are a law to themselves, even though they do not have the law. They show that what the law requires is written on their hearts, while their conscience also bears witness . . . on that day when, according to my gospel, God judges the secrets of men by Christ Jesus,' (Rom. 2:14 ff.). His appeal to the Roman law starts therefore from the eschatological fact that the Lord has now laid his law upon the hearts of the Gentiles. This is no theory about some kind of 'natural law', but part and parcel of his testimony. His appeal to Roman justice and to his rights as a citizen does not stand by itself, but is bound up with his witness to the Gospel which he continues to proclaim, even during his trial. Behind his appeal to Caesar there is the higher 'court of appeal', the Lord Jesus himself; behind and above the privilege of the Roman citizen is that of the apostle to the Gentiles. By his appeal he witnesses to the fact that Jesus is now Lord over the pagan world and that the pagan conscience is therefore no longer autonomous or left to its own resources, but is in reality free 'to perform the Torah' which Jesus has fulfilled.

This agrees fully with his thesis that the ruling authority is the servant of God. His terms for 'authority' and 'rulers' (respectively: *exousia* and *archontes*) are the same as are frequently used to designate the heavenly principalities and powers. Paul proclaims, as part of the Gospel, that the God of our Lord Jesus Christ has made him sit at his right hand in the heavenly places, far above all heavenly powers, and he has put all things under his feet and has made him the head over all things for the Church which is his body, the fullness of him who fills all in all (Eph. 1:20 ff.). All this is in fulfilment of Psalm 110. The 'enemies' in that psalm are the *goyim*, the nations. The idea had developed in late Jewish theology, however, that each nation has its own appointed angel—a doctrine found in a specific form in the Septuagint. The statement in Deuteronomy 32:8 to the effect that the Lord fixed the bounds of the peoples 'according to the number of the sons of God'—namely seventy (cf. Ex. 1:5: 'For the Lord's portion is his people, Jacob his allotted heritage,' Deut. 32:9)—is in the Septuagint rendered as: 'according to the number of the angels of God'. The doctrine finds a place in the New Testament, as Psalm 110 is fulfilled in the ascension of the Lord Jesus. The 'enemies' in the midst of whom Jesus rules at the right hand of God are the heavenly powers. The Letter to the Hebrews, taken in its entirety, is to be regarded as an exegesis of Psalm 110, which is fulfilled in the cross and resurrection as well as in the ascension of Jesus; and Hebrews testifies that Jesus sits at the right hand of God, 'having become as much superior to the angels as the name he has obtained is more excellent than theirs'. The angels are all 'ministering spirits sent forth to serve, for the sake of those who are to obtain salvation,' (Heb. 1:5, 14). The same thing is said here—literally, with the same terms—of the angels (*leitourgika*, spirits sent forth to *diakonia*) as in Romans 13 is postulated of the governing authorities and rulers: that they are 'God's servant (*diakonos*) for your good', 'ministers (*leitourgoi*) of God' (Rom. 13:4, 6).[7]

It is important to notice that, where this matter is concerned, Paul passes over in complete silence the fact that both the Roman state and the Roman law rest on the sacred foundation of the state religion, just as he has nothing to say regarding the emperor worship which in his time was already exerting a powerful and growing influence. In another context he simply states that 'although there may be so-called gods in heaven or on earth—as indeed there are many "gods" and many "lords"—yet for us there is one God, the Father, from whom are all things and for whom we exist, and one Lord, Jesus Christ, through whom are all things and through whom we exist,' (1 Cor. 8:5 f.). This is the position he assumes also in the Letter to the Romans; and he declares that in itself the Roman state possesses no sacral power, but derives its authority exclusively from the fact that it has been appointed to the service of the God and Father of Jesus Christ, the ascended Lord—appointed indeed 'for your good', that is, 'for the sake of those who are to obtain salvation'.

That service the Roman state continues to perform during the latter days before the Last Day comes and the Lord returns. In that way it serves to expedite the proclamation of the Gospel throughout the *oikoumenē*, which of course is taking place in the very last days before the end should come. If the barrier between Israel and the nations is now transcended, that is so by virtue of the authority of the ascended Lord who rules over the angels, the heavenly powers to whom the nations are subject, and uses them to further the preaching of the Gospel. It is in this sense that we are to understand the close of Matthew's Gospel: because Jesus has been given all authority in heaven and on earth, his apostles are to go and make disciples of all the nations (Mt. 28:18 ff.).

That it is Jesus to whom this authority has now been given—that is the crucial point of this proclamation. The whole of the Old Testament had already testified to the fact that God possesses such authority. He is the Creator, who has pierced Rahab and has made leviathan his plaything. Egypt and Babylon are the instruments of his hand. But the great eschatological change which provides the proclamation with a content and a direction wholly new is brought about in the crucifixion and resurrection of Jesus. That becomes clear when one compares the attitude of Jesus towards the Roman government with the attitude of Paul.

For that purpose let us take as our starting-point Paul's testimony in his first Letter to the Corinthians. He is making known the wisdom of God, hidden in a 'mystery'—not the wisdom of the rulers of this age, who are destined to pass away. 'None of the rulers of this age understood this; for if they had, they would not have crucified the Lord of glory,' (1 Cor. 2:6 ff.). The word for 'rulers' (*archontes*) is the same as is applied in Romans 13 to the rulers of the state. It has the same dual significance here, for it refers to both the heavenly and the earthly powers. Behind Pontius Pilate there stand the heavenly 'rulers'. When Jesus says to Pilate: 'You would have no power over me unless it had been given you from above,' (Jn. 19:10 f.), he is really saying what Paul also affirms in Romans 13; and the difference between Jesus' attitude and that of Paul is all the more revealing for that very reason. To a large extent Paul identified his own sufferings with those of his Lord. He is quite prepared to die in Jerusalem 'for the name of the Lord Jesus' (Acts 21:13); and in spurning the efforts of the brethren at Caesarea to protect him from a martyr's death he was rejecting the same kind of temptation as the Lord himself had undergone at the hands of Peter (Acts 21:12; cf. Mt. 16:22). He completes in his flesh what is lacking in Christ's afflictions for the sake of his body, that is, the Church (Col. 1:24); he is always carrying in the body the death of Jesus (2 Cor. 1:24); he is a prisoner in the Lord (Eph. 4:1 ff.; cf. 3:13 f.; 6:19 f.).

It is fairly certain that Paul would have suffered the fate of his Lord at Jerusalem—for Festus was no less disposed than his predecessor, Pilate, to 'do the Jews a favour' (Acts 25:9; cf. Mt. 27:15)—if he had not invoked his Roman citizenship. The apostle enjoyed a privilege which Jesus did not have. The appeal to Caesar played a crucial part in both their trials, but with opposite effect in each case. Pilate had eventually handed Jesus over for crucifixion because he was driven to do so by the Jews, who argued that by releasing Jesus he would make himself an accessory to rebellion against Caesar (Jn. 19:12 ff.). The same kind of arguments were urged in the case of Paul (Acts 25:8; 24:5), but this time the Jews were up against his appeal; for he had the protection of his Roman citizenship. Paul's invoking this privilege is in sharp contrast to the obstinate silence of Jesus (Mt. 27:14; Jn. 19:9). Whereas Paul expressly reminds the governor of his obligation to uphold the law (Acts 24:10), Jesus submits at all points to Pilate's authority, which 'has been given him from above' (Jn. 19:11).

Jesus suffers and dies as the king of the Jews; in him Israel's course among the Gentiles is accomplished and he is delivered into the power of Rome, just as Israel was delivered over to Egypt and to Babylon. He must die in expiation for the world. 'Now is the judgment of this world, now shall the ruler (*archon*) of this world be cast out.' At the cross the power of the 'rulers (*archontes*) of this age', who crucify him, is annulled; and by the same token the great eschatological event is ushered in: 'And I, when I am lifted up from the earth, will draw all men to myself.' He said this 'to show by what death he was to die' (Jn. 12:31 f.), at the same time intimating his resurrection and as ension.

Although Paul was ready to die for his Lord, the idea that he either needed or was able to repeat the death of Jesus was to him plain blasphemy (1 Cor. 1:13). It had been the Lord himself who during the night stood by him in the prison and charged him to bear witness also at Rome (Acts 23:11). In Jesus' resurrection the old has passed away and the new has come, yes, even for the 'rulers of this age', who may now learn the good news that the Roman state lies no longer under the tyranny of 'gods' and 'lords' whose day is over, and that Jesus has all authority on earth and in heaven. The enmity between Israel and the Gentiles has been resolved. The eternal Son of David has established his kingship over the entire *oikoumenē*. The Lord stretches forth his mighty sceptre from Zion (Ps. 110). The Gospel is proclaimed from Jerusalem, at Rome and in Spain, to the very ends of the earth; and the blessings of the Torah, now fulfilled, descend upon the Roman state itself. Paul's citizenship becomes a sign of the resurrection and a witness to it; it is created anew through the power of the risen Lord. The Greeks, hitherto alienated from the citizenship (*politeia*) of Israel, have been brought near in his blood (Eph. 2:12); and Roman citizenship (*politeia*: Acts 22:28) acquires thereby a new significance, because it is placed now under the authority of the commonwealth (*politeuma*) that is in 'heaven, and from it we await a Saviour, the Lord Jesus Christ, who will change our lowly body to be like his glorious body, by the power which enables him even to subject all things to himself,' (Phil. 3:20).

That is what Paul's appeal to his Roman citizenship means: Jew and Gentile are reconciled in one body and the reality of this is demonstrated in his person and in his ministry. He possesses a dual *politeia*. We have considered how great a transformation this involves for the Roman state; but what consequences does it have, on the other hand, for the *politeia* of Israel? Men have often wanted to find a world of difference between Jesus and Paul, who is usually accused, in particular, of wanting to Hellenize the Gospel. In so far as the reproach is aimed at Paul's message concerning the crucified and risen Lord it is quite baseless and invariably rests on a gross misunderstanding of what the Gospel means. Still, in one particular Paul did indeed commit himself to a decision which had far-reaching effects on the course of history. It was his decision to invoke his status as a Roman citizen. There is a parallel to this, in a way, in the question of the language of the New Testament. Jesus spoke Aramaic; but his Gospel was written down in Greek. Jesus was a Jew; but Paul combined a Jewish origin with Roman citizenship. Jesus totally repudiated the nationalistic struggle of the Jews against Roman domination; his kingship is not of this world. Paul went further. He deliberately took sides with the Roman state against the aspirations of Jewish nationalism. For Paul the Roman state had an eschatological significance, because it represented 'the world'. We who live two thousand years later, however, look at the Roman state from yet another point of view, that is, a relatively historical and geographical one. In Chapter Five we shall see just how far-reaching the historical consequences of opting for the Roman *oikoumenē* have been. One result was that Christianity became much too closely identified with the political and cultural ethos of the Hellenistic *oikoumenē*; and it followed from this that missionary expansion was in large measure halted by tenacious resistance on the part of all the various anti-Roman and anti-Hellenistic movements and groupings, whether Jewish, heretic Christian, Muslim, Persian or Asian.

It would be in the highest degree absurd, however, to put the blame or the onus for the course taken by history on to the shoulders of Paul. Even if he did, in the political sphere, decide deliberately in favour of the Roman order and Roman ascendancy over the barbarians, all the same he subordinated the Roman power completely to the authority and the judgment of God; and he testifies that any advantage the Greek might have over the barbarian is now at an end. For that matter the New Testament as a whole shakes the Hellenistic conception of the *oikoumenē* to its very foundations. That conception, once purely geographical, had assumed a cultural and political character and had come to replace the ancient idea of the *polis*. The Hellenistic ideal ceased to be the monopoly of a particular nation; it became cosmopolitan and embraced all that was, in the widest sense, 'humane'. Thus the *oikoumenē* came to be identified with the world within which this cosmopolitan culture prevailed, as opposed to the barbarism which persisted on its frontiers. During the period of the Roman Empire the philosophical notion of the Hellenistic *oikoumenē* was fused with the politico-religious order of the Roman imperium, which glorified Caesar in the rôle of saviour (*soter*) and benefactor (*euergetēs*).[8]

It is a feature characteristic of the Septuagint that the term *oikoumenē* —which occurs quite frequently there, particularly in the Psalms and in Isaiah—is nowhere used in this political-cum-cultural sense, though this Greek translation of the Old Testament is otherwise steeped in Hellenistic ideas. *Oikoumenē* in the Septuagint always means the whole earth, as being the arena of God's mighty acts.[9] This meaning is carried over from the Old Testament into the New. The *oikoumenē*— identical, from Augustus' point of view, with the Roman Empire (Lk. 2:1)—is the whole world: that is to say, all the nations (*ethnē*= *goyim*), the totality of the Gentiles to whom the Gospel of the Kingdom must be proclaimed (Mt. 24:14). The devil showed Jesus 'all the kingdoms of the *oikoumenē*' (Lk. 4:5). Here is evidence enough that the biblical perspective reaches far beyond the confines of the Hellenistic world—the more so as in Matthew the term *kosmos* is used (Mt. 4:8). The Hebraic-Aramaic background is discernible in the apocalyptic prophecies regarding the tribulation which is to come upon the whole *oikoumenē* (Hebr. *'olam*; Aram. *'alma*; Rev. 3:10; Lk. 21:26; Acts 11:28; Rev. 12:9; 16:4); whilst the expression 'the *oikoumenē* to come' (Heb. 2:5)—a pure Hebraism—is to the Greeks foolishness.

Paul's enemies regarded his activities as a mighty 'turning upside down' of the Hellenistic *oikoumenē* (Acts 17:6; 19:27; 24:5). He himself used the term only twice, on both occasions when quoting from a psalm. He concluded his speech on the Areopagus with a reference to the day when God would judge the *oikoumenē* in righteousness (Acts 17:31; cf. Ps. 9:8; 96:13; 98:9). In the Letter to the Romans he quotes Psalm 19:6 in evidence of Israel's having heard the Word of God: 'Their voice has gone out to all the earth, and their words to the ends of the *oikoumenē*,'—that is, the voice and the words of God's creation, the heavens, the day and the night, that tell the glory of God (Rom. 10:18). The dimension here is that of God's universal Word of creation and of judgment, and not the limited sphere of a political and cultural order.

The sharp lines of distinction between Jew, Greek and barbarian in the Hellenistic *oikoumenē* were more or less eliminated, as the symbiotic process issued gradually in a single cosmopolitan civilization. But in Paul's preaching something fundamentally different occurs. There Jew and Greek are not merged into one. The 'advantage' of the Jew is fully preserved (Rom. 3:1 ff.); but equally he emphasizes the privilege which the Greek has over the barbarian. He himself is highly conscious of possessing both these privileges (Acts 23:6; 21:39; 22:28). Looking out from Jerusalem, he sees the *oikoumenē* as consisting of all the Gentiles to whom the Gospel must be preached. From Rome he surveys the *oikoumenē* as the world over which Caesar exercises authority as the servant of God. The fulfilled Torah goes forth from Jerusalem to Rome, and the Roman law goes forth from Rome to Jerusalem—and both Torah and law go forth to the barbarian. Still, Paul goes from Jerusalem via Rome to the barbarian, to the end of the earth, proclaiming the Gospel that is a stumbling-block to the Jews and foolishness to the Greeks. At the cross every privilege has been annulled. There can be no question here of Greek and Jew, circumcised and uncircumcised, barbarian, Scythian, slave, free man; but Christ is all, and in all (Col. 3:11; Gal. 3:28).

3. ZION AND ATHENS

When Paul invoked his citizenship, he was testifying to the authority of the risen Lord in a manner which cut clean across the general current and course of things. The Revelation of John, only a few decades later, has no room for such an attitude. It prophesies of God's wrath against 'the great Babylon'. Paul's attitude in the New Testament is not the signal for some transformation of the state under the influence of the Gospel proclamation and of the life and witness of the Church, but the ultimate and final consequence of belief in God's clemency and in the power of his Son: an island, as it were, which is soon to be submerged once more beneath the rising tide of emperor-worship and deification. Neither for Paul himself nor in his exhortations offered to the Church at Rome do the principle and privileges of citizenship take on a broader and more profound significance as a sort of corner-stone for the reformation of government and state. The fact remains, however, that Paul's appeal in its political aspect was of great importance in that by it he administered to the Roman government a powerful reminder of its own proper traditions —traditions which the current process of orientalization was more and more threatening to undermine. His appeal is seen in the most revealing light against the background of the classical legacy of Hellas.

Hellenic culture as reflected in the New Testament is a mere shadow of the past. Paul, preaching in Athens, summarily describes the Greeks as idolaters; and their entire history is dismissed as 'the times of ignorance' which God has decided to overlook, commanding all men everywhere to repent (Acts 17). There is nothing at all to suggest that the Gospel has here penetrated to the very centre of a culture which could not only pride itself on a unique history but, through its encounter with the Christian Church and theology, was to call into being a unique Christian civilization. Whilst Rome appears in Acts and in the Pauline letters to the greatest possible advantage, Athens is exhibited as being in a state of advanced senility.

If Paul had lived five centuries earlier, he might perhaps have expressed himself in much the same vein; but if he had, his preaching would have been untimely in the extreme; for the Greeks of the age of Pericles would have had every right to insist that the apostle who aspired to be 'to the Greeks a Greek' should think them something other than just any old primitive tribe. He would have owed it to himself to take full account of the fact that, just as Israel had found it necessary to set herself over against the civilizations of the Near East, so this city and its culture were likewise fundamentally opposed to them, even though it might be from diametrically contrasted motives. In the New Testament there is no real confrontation of Israel with Hellas. For a trial of strength having the same calibre as the struggle between Israel and Babylon in the Old Testament one must look in the New Testament to that between the Kingship of Jesus Christ and the authority of Caesar. Even this encounter might be represented as in essence the contraposing of the two cities, Zion and Athens, but only if one is prepared to put the centre of Hellas in the same general category as Babylon or imperial Rome. The city which the classical age of Greece had brought into being, however, was never meant to 'o'er-top heaven'. Its *raison d'être* was something quite different.

The idea of the Greek city state is magnificently illustrated by

Plato when he makes the Sophist Protagoras, in the book of that name, describe how, by instituting the *polis*, man raises himself above the primitive level and moves on to a higher stage of development. The *polis* comes into being by a voluntary connection of the citizens, but not without gifts bestowed from above: gifts of wisdom and skill for various cultural attainments, derived from Hephaestus and Athene, are conferred upon it by Prometheus, whilst to them Hermes adds the gift of Zeus, namely, a religious devotion to the numinous powers (*aidôs*) and justice (*dikē*).[10] These divine gifts are for every citizen alike. When Athens was at the zenith of her greatness and prosperity, Pericles—in the speech which Thucydides has preserved for us—eulogized the *polis* as the free community of citizens who bind themselves voluntarily to abide by the law which each and all accept. Only in that way can it fulfil the conditions required for the unhampered growth of all spiritual values, cultural excellence and general welfare. Each citizen has an equal share in the direction and conduct of judicial and political affairs. The *polis* offers a complete contrast, therefore, to the tyrannical systems of the barbarian peoples, who are mere vassals of the state, subjected to an alien will. Aristotle could recognize no *polis* either in the Macedonian Empire of Philip, the father of Alexander the Great, or in the Achaemenid Empire of Darius.[11] It is in the *polis* that man—who according to Aristotle is 'a political being by nature'—first comes into his own and achieves his destiny. But the law, to which all the citizens freely submit, remains the indispensable foundation. It is also an essentially religious one. The *polis* is a cultic community, and its political organization of a sacral character which makes it binding upon every citizen. Zeus is the divine protector of the *polis* (*poliouchos*); Themis (Right) and Dikē (Justice) are his consort and his daughter.

Plato and Aristotle depict the citizen as the completely free man with full command over himself, his own master (*archon*). Though free, he puts himself under the law, as the only means of securing the *polis* against the despotism of the tyrant on the one hand and mob rule on the other. Freedom of this kind can only be made effective under a democratic form of government, since that gives equal rights to every citizen; and that is why equality and freedom are found together among the chief supports of the Greek city state.[12]

It stands to the everlasting credit of the classical age of Hellas that it gave concrete political form to the idea of liberty (*eleutheria*).

That Hellas flourished for all too brief a time detracts not at all from
the value of that idea, any more than the persistence of the Egyptian
and Indian civilizations through thousands of years can be taken to
indicate the worth of the conception of man and the universe under-
lying them. There is a sense in which Hellas can be said to stand
alongside Israel. In the course of their history both attempted a noble
and, of its kind, unique experiment, a brave endeavour to cut loose
from an apparently unavoidable pattern of civilization. Both experiments miscarried within a short time; and in both cases the
failure was dialectical in character: it was owing as much to the
strong as to the weak qualities of both peoples; and if it was inherent
in their mistakes, it was no less so in their successes. Neither Israel nor
Hellas possessed the strength to go on resisting the infiltration and
superior power of the ancient pattern of Near Eastern civilizations,
from which they had tried to break free. Also both peoples fell
victim to an exclusive pride in the unique character of their
undertakings.

The Hellenic attempt to emancipate man and educate him to
complete freedom was only partly successful. We know now—and
today can understand much more clearly than our predecessors did
a century ago—how very deeply Hellas was rooted, even in her
classical age, in the primitive, pre-Homeric religious past. The
rationalizing of the ancient myths, the speculative philosophizing
about the essence of man and of the world, the triumph of anthro-
pomorphic art over the divine powers—these were all part of a
courageous struggle, obstinately maintained, to master and bring
under control the superhuman and subhuman dimensions outside
man as well as within his own soul: and to do this, not with the
help of magic but solely in the strength of the human logos, that
faculty inherent in man which enables him by rational contemplation
to detach himself from himself and from the world, and to elevate
himself above animal instinct and the unconscious being of things.
Hellas was aware all the same that it lived by those very forces which
it was attempting to master. The confederation of city states was
viable only because it was originated and nurtured by the oracle of
Delphi, where the chthonic Pythia watched over the 'navel of the
earth'. High above the city of Athens under a radiant sun, the Acropolis
shouldered the Parthenon, temple of the eternal maiden Athene,
guarding the mystery of endless death and resurrection in the vegetable

world, and the Erechtheum, sanctuary of the chthonic god, Erechtheus, where the serpent kept vigil over the tree of life. Apollo could never rid himself of Dionysus. This ambivalent awareness that in gods and men the divine and the demonic powers are both at work —each other's nearest kin and deadliest enemy—finds its most sublime expression in the tragedies. Yet even in relation to the gods the 'free' citizen was not really free. If it proved possible, sometimes, to put gods and men on a footing of equality, it was none the less realized that what had been netted was only small fry. The leader remained inaccessible and shrouded in mystery. Like men, the gods were themselves at the mercy of the uncontrollable *Moira* (Fate); they too were simply manifestations of the comprehensive reality of being, within which all existence, divine, human and subhuman, is subsumed.

This ultimate powerlessness in face of the elements which men were striving to control proved fatal for the Greek *polis* and its culture. Its downfall came about precisely through the one particular in which Hellas seemed to have been most successful; and the calamity is to be imputed not indeed so much to her failures as to her achievements. The Greeks themselves knew that well enough. There was nothing they feared so much as *hybris*; and at the same time they knew that they owed all their cultural achievements to the good offices of Prometheus, the rebel and stealer of the divine fire. That was why their society always had to be based firmly on that other divine gift of *aidos*, a religious deference towards the gods, upon which *dikē* (justice and righteousness) depended. The *nomos*, the law of the city, was on the one hand based on the free consent of the citizens; it was resolved upon democratically and was a perfect expression of the ideas of liberty and equality. Yet the *nomos* was at the same time absolute, divinely decreed. To observe the *nomos* was to reverence the gods (*nomizein*); and the official cult formed the basis of this observance. The free citizen, though actuated entirely by his own free will, was none the less unconditionally bound by the sacral law of the city state, by means of which the goodwill of the gods, the essential character of the *polis* and the preservation of human life itself were secured. The law was *sotēria*, salvation.[13] That is why Socrates died without protest; for the law was the very essence of the *polis*; it had 'brothers in Hades' and a divine origin. In the fifth century B.C. that divine authority of the city law was finally discarded; so that the *nomos* became a purely human invention. As the Greeks broadened their horizon, its unconditional claims lost their backing and were obliged to give way before the discovery that there were other peoples who had other, and sometimes better, laws. Sophist thought carried this discovery to its ultimate conclusion and represented *nomos* as the product of arbitrary human will, setting it over against the eternal reality of nature (*physis*). This meant that, so far as the idea of liberty is concerned, a final breach had been made in the walls of divine despotism; but it also spelt the end of the authority of the state cult and thus removed the foundation of the *polis*. It was Plato who, in resolving the crisis for Sophism, began that process of change which led to the Hellenistic dissolution. In the death of Socrates Plato saw the state law passing over to the inner world of the individual soul. The Stoic philosophy located true freedom in the discovery by the individual man, within himself and with the aid of his logos, of the cosmic law. The Hellenistic conception was that this law, which man discovers in himself and in the cosmos, was embodied in the person of the divine king, who also represented the law of the state. The *polis* came to be identified with the cosmos—the Greek citizen was cosmopolitan. Thus the classical idea of liberty dug its own grave. The dam which had once sheltered the *polis* against the flood-tides of oriental despotism collapsed under the *hybris* of its builders.

It is self-evident therefore that there could not be in the New Testament any real encounter with classical Hellas. Paul's citizenship is in fact the only thing there which faintly recalls the Greek conception of the *polis*. Whenever the apostle opposes Greek wisdom to the wisdom of God in Jesus Christ, he is directing his polemic against Gnosticism. It says a good deal that the Greek *dēmos*, which is one of the three constitutive elements of the *polis* according to the classical conception, only appears in the debased and caricatured form of a turbulent and anarchical mob (Acts 12:22; 17:5; 19:30 ff.). There is no trace of a democratic council (*boulē*). We have in the magistracy of colonial Philippi only the '*archontes*' or rulers of the '*polis*' (Acts 16:19 ff.; cf. the *politarchai* of Thessalonica, Acts 17:6, 8); and it is against them that Paul appeals to his status as a Roman citizen. Yet as we have already seen, Paul invariably deals with the *archontes* in their capacity as guardians of law and order whom one has an obligation to obey; again in Romans 13 there is nothing to suggest that the *archontes* referred to were elected in any democratic way. The Gospel and Greek democracy remain complete strangers to each other in the New Testament; and there are no grounds for predicting that in the course of Western civilization they might become enthusiastic partners.

The event of decisive importance for world history which the apostle proclaims to the Greeks is that in the cross of Jesus Christ the Temple has been abolished. The Gospel does exactly the opposite of what the Athenians were expecting. Whereas they regarded the message about Jesus and the resurrection as one among the many oriental cults and philosophies which had been making their way into Greece for centuries past (Acts 17:18), what Paul proclaimed was the *end* of all philosophies and cults. God, the Creator, does not dwell in shrines made by man (Acts 17:24). The expression *acheiropoiētos* (not made by the hands) is part of the essential terminology of the New Covenant, whilst *cheiropoiētos* (made by hands) is of the essence of the Old. Just as Jesus, like a true prophet, cleansed the Temple at Jerusalem, prophesying that in his own body he would destroy the Temple made by hands and in three days would build another, not made by hands (Jn. 2:13 ff.; cf. Mk. 14:58; Acts 7:48), so Paul's spirit is stirred within him as he sees the city of Athens full of idols and preaches that in the cross God has destroyed every temple and has raised up the new Temple in the resurrection of Jesus Christ. Similarly in his letters Paul contrasts the circumcision 'made in flesh by hands' (Eph. 2:12) with the circumcision of Christ, not made by hands (Col. 2:11). The Letter to the Hebrews makes the same point: that through the more perfect tabernacle not made with hands, that is, not of this creation, Jesus Christ has entered once for all into the holy place of the New Covenant (Heb. 9:11). For every believer also this is true, that 'if the earthly tent we live in is destroyed, we have a building from God, a house not made with hands, eternal in the heavens,' (2 Cor. 5:1).

Of course, the cross signifies God's judgment on the cult and Temple at Jerusalem, but therein also upon all cults and all temples. The official cult of the classical age of Hellas is lumped together with the contemporary widespread vogue of syncretistic religion under the 'times of ignorance'. The verdict which Paul was here pronouncing on the sacral foundations of the *polis* was much more radical than anything that the keenest strictures of the Sophists could ever have implied. It is true that the Greek sceptics had declared the cult to be a man-made institution, but they had offered no alternative whatever. On the contrary, by breaching the defences of the *polis* they quickly laid it open to the direct onslaught of oriental religiosity. Without realizing it, they signed the death-warrant of the very culture which as the product of human genius they wanted to safeguard and perpetuate. Their criticism sprang more particularly from a concept of man which was untenable apart from the binding sacral obligations provided by the cult and the law of the *polis*. Deprived of these foundations, the classical idea of liberty was left completely in the air; and that was why the more circumspect among Greek thinkers were always extremely careful to insist upon them.

In the decadent condition of the Greek *polis* during the New Testament period it was only to be expected that when approaching the Athenians Paul would confine his direct attack to the question of their religion (*deisidaimonia*, Acts 17:22). In fact, however, the whole New Testament constitutes a many-sided, even if indirect, polemic against the Greek concept of the *polis* and the humanist interpretation of culture underlying it. The Greek ideal of *eleutheria*, that is to say, the total autonomy of man—the quintessential meaning of which was expressed by the Sophist Protagoras when he said that 'Man is the measure of all things'—is precisely what the Bible unmasks as the original sin of the human race. That 'liberty' is now the very bondage from which the world has been set free by its crucified and risen Lord. For the Greek this 'freedom' was a privilege of the citizen; and it was based on the enforced labour of vast masses of slaves. This 'freedom' meant the autarchy of man, who sets himself up as the norm, superior to and contemptuous of the woman: the right and the duty to fulfil one's own individual potentialities, recognizing the neighbour merely as another individual seeking the same end for himself: the self-idolization of the *polis*, holding the barbarian at his proper distance: the loneliness of the logos, which is a microcosm in itself, an image of the universe which is likewise a self-sufficient totality. Upon this freedom the New Testament verdict is that it is the freedom according to the flesh, beneath the tyranny of sin. The freedom of the Covenant is just the opposite of the Greek idea. The experiment failed, so far as Hellas was concerned, not because it rested on *hybris*, but because it sought to realize a kind of freedom which turned out in the end to be the self-enslavement of man.

Nevertheless Hellas did hazard the attempt, unique of its kind, to establish a state grounded in the free and equal choice of every citizen. It is necessary to stress this very heavily indeed, since the attempt itself is not appreciated or valued at its true worth in the New Testament, at any rate not explicitly. That fact cannot be attributed merely to the condition of the Roman Empire which was already well on the way to assuming a pattern of full-blown oriental despotism; it resulted also from the form in which the Gospel was preached, namely, as the message of the 'Kingdom of God'. Not only did Jesus himself apply his parables in a variety of ways to his royal authority and its imminent approach; for the early Church too the exegesis of Psalms 2 and 110—which proclaim the kingship of the Lord on Zion and his reign, seated at the right hand of God, until he shall have put all his enemies under his feet—became of paramount importance. There is an eschatological perspective, beyond the kingship of Christ, which alone sounds a different note. When all things are subjected to him, then the Son will also be subjected to him who puts all things under him, that God may be everything to everyone (1 Cor. 15:28). This would appear to be borne out by the Revelation of John, which refers explicitly to Jesus' eschatological kingship as the kingship of the Lamb (Rev. 22:1). The fact remains that during the 'latter days', for so long as Christ reigns from heaven, the whole stress falls on his power and authority over all heavenly and earthly powers and rulers. In Romans 13 the *archontes* and *exousiai* come under the judgment imposed from above—of an absolute kind—but are not subject to any judgment from below, on the people's part.

This one-sidedness is a dangerous thing, because it means that a situation characteristic of the Old Covenant is reinterpreted and gets carried over into the eschatological conditions of the New Testament, even though in the Old Testament itself it had been from the very outset a matter for reproof in the sharpest terms. I refer here simply to what was argued in the preceding chapter regarding the origins of kingship in Israel. When the people of Israel want to have a king, 'like all the nations', they consider kingship as the only form for a state worth taking seriously. In the Old Testament therefore the term for 'state' is the same as for 'kingdom' (*mamlakhah*); and Israel sees the *goyim* more or less exclusively as nations represented by a divine king. The use of the word *polis* in the Septuagint is manifold; but never does it bear the meaning of 'state'. In almost every case it renders the Hebrew '*ir*, signifying 'a fortified town'. The function of Israelite towns was not to be centres of culture or of civic institutions or of a legal code; and the idea of regarding them as the basic pattern for the state was certainly never contemplated. The town acquired its significance from the fact that it offered protection against enemies. The city *par excellence* is Jerusalem: the city of king David, chosen by him for the natural defences which it afforded— the fortress of Zion, centre of the kingdom; and as it is the city of David and Solomon, there the Temple is set up, where the Ark is, where it has pleased the Lord for his name to dwell. Jerusalem is the city of God; his holy mountain is the joy of all the earth, Mount Zion, the city of the great King. Within her citadels God has shown himself to be a sure defence (Ps. 48). So also the New Jerusalem, coming down from heaven, shall be the city of the King sitting upon his throne (Rev. 22:1).

Likewise in the New Testament the word *polis* nowhere signifies 'the state'. In Romans 13 the talk is of 'governing authorities' and 'rulers'; and existence in its political aspect consists in fulfilling the command to 'honour the emperor' (1 Pet. 3:13 ff.).

Thus whilst the kingship of the Lord Jesus, who is now seated at the right hand of God, has direct political implications—seeing that earthly kings and rulers are subject to his authority—the existence of his chosen people, the Church, on the other hand, nowhere seems to have any political consequences at all. Yet the first Letter of Peter, which urges submission to the emperor, speaks of the Church as 'a royal priesthood, a holy nation, God's own people' (1 Pet. 2:9). In the Hebrew text of Exodus 19:6, from which that is a word for word quotation, it even says: 'a kingdom (*mamlakhah*) of priests'. The Church is the fulfilment of the promise made to Israel. This 'kingdom of priests', as the Book of Exodus conceives it, contrasts sharply with the 'kingdom' which the people of Israel later took to themselves under Saul and David. Through their desire to have a king 'like all the nations', they repudiated their own election as a kingdom of priests. As 'the holy nation' (*goy qadhosh*), Israel had been called to establish a kingdom without an earthly king and to live by the Covenant to which each member of the community had pledged himself by his own free decision. In the New Covenant this is fulfilled; for the Church has come, not to Sinai, but to 'the Jerusalem above', to the Mount Zion and to the city of the living God, the heavenly Jerusalem (Gal. 4:25 f.; Heb. 12:18 ff.). The Church therefore is a 'kingdom of priests, a holy nation' in heaven. 'Our commonwealth is in heaven,' (Phil. 3:20)—the word used here, *politeuma*, is taken directly from the political terminology of the Greeks. It signifies *politeia* as well as *polis*; and so the implied meaning is (constitution of the) city state, citizenship. The heavenly Jerusalem, which is free (Gal. 4:26), is not only the city of the great King but also a state, a *polis*, in which all the members together constitute a free kingdom of priests. In the Old Testament this heavenly *polis* had been hailed from afar as a future *patris* (homeland). The true Israel had lived by faith, looking forward to the *polis* which God was preparing for them. They acknowledged that they were strangers (*xenoi*) and sojourners (*parepidēmoi*) on the earth (Heb. 11:10, 13 ff.). Now that true Israel, together with the Gentiles, who are no longer strangers (*xenoi*) to the covenants of promise but have now become party to the commonwealth (*politeia*) of Israel (Eph. 2:12 f.), has reached the heavenly *polis*. The Church, the Israel of the New Covenant, is now a community of 'aliens and sojourners' on earth; for her *politeuma* is in heaven. What the Diaspora is for the people of Israel the earth is for the Church (1 Pet. 1:1; 2:11).

Just as the heavenly Jerusalem reveals God's judgment upon its earthly counterpart, so too the *politeuma* and the 'kingdom of priests, the holy nation' in heaven, is the very antithesis of earthly kingdoms. The kings of the Gentiles exercise lordship over them; but in the Church the master is as the servant (*diakonos*). As servant, Jesus is among his disciples; and as his Father has appointed a kingdom for him, so does he appoint a kingdom for them, that they may eat and drink at his table in his kingdom, and sit on thrones judging the twelve tribes of Israel (Lk. 22:24 ff.). The good news of the 'kingdom' therefore is not simply the message that Jesus is king; it is at the same time the proclamation of that 'kingdom', that *politeuma*, which his holy people together constitute in heaven. There is the true freedom. 'For you were called to freedom, brethren; only do not use your freedom as an opportunity for the flesh, but through love be servants of one another,' (Gal. 5:13). This calling and commandment reprove both the despotism of earthly kingdoms and the 'freedom' of the Greek *polis*. The Church, though still under subjection to the rulers of this age who are destined to pass away (1 Cor. 2:6; Rom. 13:1), lives now already conformed to the commonwealth of the heavenly *polis*, in which the law of freedom through love and mutual service prevails (Rom. 13:8 ff.); and it is the message of this commonwealth that the Church proclaims among the nations of this world (1 Pet. 2:9).

Now exalted at the right hand of God, Jesus has all authority in heaven and on earth, above all rulers in heaven and on earth. He is the king of kings; but it is in his very ascension that he has received from the Father the promise of the Holy Spirit, who is seen and heard on earth (Acts 2:33). The Lord is the Spirit; and where the Spirit of the Lord is, there is freedom (2 Cor. 3:17). The Spirit is 'the living law' of the commonwealth of the New Covenant, the kingdom of priests who are likewise all prophets (Acts 2:17 ff.; Joel 2:28 ff.). Transformed by the Spirit, the Church—body on earth of the Lord in heaven—carries out here below the work which the Lord continues from above. It is the Lord who makes the rulers of the nations his servants. It is the Church which calls the nations to repentance and renewal in order that they may be transformed according to the law of freedom through love which informs the commonwealth of heaven.

The new heaven and the new earth are as much a transformed *polis* as a transformed kingdom; and the extent to which this is true is evident particularly from the Greek word for the Church, *ekklēsia*. The Letter to the Hebrews, when describing the heavenly *polis*, habitually mentions the *ekklēsia* in conjunction with it: 'You have come . . . to the *polis* of the living God, the heavenly Jerusalem, and to innumerable angels in festal gathering, and to the *ekklēsia* of the first-born who are enrolled in heaven, and to a judge who is God of all,' (Heb. 12:23). Clearly, this description conjures up first and foremost the picture of the New Israel, a kingdom of priests, brought together in the gathering of the whole people (festal gathering: *panēguris*: cf. Hos. 2:11; 9:5; Ezek. 46:11) as cultic community. The word *ekklēsia* also points to this. In the Septuagint it translates the Hebrew *qahal*, the gathering up of the whole people of Israel in the community of the Covenant (Deut. 9:10; 23:2; Neh. 13:1, etc.); in the heavenly Jerusalem it is the New Israel which is brought together, just as the whole people was gathered at Sinai when the Lord concluded his Covenant with Israel (Ex. 24) and as at the consecration of the Temple at Jerusalem Solomon kept the feast, 'and all Israel with him, a great *ekklēsia* (*qahal*) from the entrance of Hamath to the brook of Egypt, before the Lord our God,' (1 Kings 8:65).

Yet these terms point no less definitely in the direction of the Greek *polis*. That too was a sacral community which came together at regular intervals in *panēguris*, in festal gathering, in order to sacrifice to the gods. The Greek *ekklēsia* was the assembly of citizens at which the *dēmos*, the people, ordered their affairs as a 'democracy' (cf. Acts 19:32, 39 f.). The citizens were the *ekklētoi*, those called out and called together by the 'herald' (*kērux*). So it is with the proclamation of the Gospel; the *kērugma* is that which calls together the citizens of the *ekklēsia* in the heavenly *politeuma*.

That explains why the Church figures in Israel as the people of the New Covenant (*qahal*) and among the Greeks as the new *ekklēsia*, the citizenry of the heavenly *polis*. Neither in Israel nor in the pagan world does the Church accept a place and function as one of the host of religious sects and cultic communities; on the contrary, the Church is the holy nation, the kingdom of priests, the assembly of the citizens of the *polis*.

4. CHRISTIANITY AND THE WEST

The eschatological event of the 'fullness of time', which for all nations has now come in Jesus Christ, also turned out to be the beginning of our 'Christian era' and of the history of 'Christianity'. The term *Christianoi* occurs only infrequently in the New Testament. As soon as the Gospel was preached to Greeks for the first time—that was at Antioch—the inhabitants of the city gave the disciples the nickname of *Christianoi* (Acts 11:26) and from then on the term became familiar among the peoples of the *oikoumenē* (cf. Acts 26:28; 1 Pet. 4:16). It was never made use of by the Apostles in preaching the Gospel. The Church is the New Israel, within which Jews and Gentiles are reconciled and united in one body; it is the *ekklēsia* of the heavenly city, not a new religion or cult or sect. Many times in his letters Paul refers to the members of the Church as 'Gentiles'. Terms such as 'Christian' and 'Christianity' are foreign to the Gospel; for they reduce the eschatological acts of God in Jesus Christ to something which conditions and characterizes a particular religious group, dragging the Church, which is the people of God, down to the level of a sociological, cultural and religious phenomenon. To put it in the language of the New Testament: 'Christianity' is a word according to the flesh, not according to the Spirit. It is in fact exactly what orthodox Judaism accused it of being: a halfway house between Jews and Gentiles. 'Christianity' is in every respect a bastard product: something between heaven and earth, between the Old Covenant and the New, between eschatology and history, between Spirit and flesh, between Church and world, between state and sect, between Christ and culture. But that is not the end of the story; for a halfway house of that kind is a solecism, is impossible by its very nature. Just as the twilight can be either the dawning of the day or the harbinger of night, so 'Christianity' is always constrained to choose; it can never stay where it is. For so long as it is still 'Christianity', so long as the salt is still not altogether saltless, it continues to enshrine the mystery of the crucified and risen Lord. It is the Lord himself who in the midst of 'Christianity' bears his cross, is delivered into the hands of sinners and consummates thereby God's act of reconciliation. It is the Lord himself who in the midst of 'Christianity' reigns as the risen and ascended Lord.

Everything expounded in this and in the preceding chapter regarding Israel's history amid the nations and the passage of the Gospel from Jerusalem to the ends of the earth, from the Jew through the Greek to the barbarian, has set its mark on the history of Christianity. That is not to say that it has been repeated there; for the Old and New Testaments are both of them unrepeatable and incomparable. Yet it is certainly the case that both Testaments have their analogies in the history of Christianity.

Paul's ministry to the Greeks, to Rome and finally to Spain bears a definite relation to the rise of Western Christianity. The decline of the West Roman Empire, the transference of Christian antiquity to the barbarians by the Church of Rome, the rise of the West European cities, the struggle between Pope and emperor and the attempts to renovate the Roman Empire, the Renaissance and the Reformation, the emergence of capitalism, the Enlightenment and the secularizing process consequent upon it, the expansion of Western Christianity— through the whole history of Christianity in the West there runs the dynamic of the Gospel's course from the Jew to the Greek, from the Greek to the barbarian. In Byzantine history too that course is discernible, albeit along a very different line of development. Running through this history of Christianity is a recognizable analogy with the history of the Old Testament: Exodus (from Israel); a journey to the promised land during the first three centuries; the period of the kings, namely, the Constantinian era; the processes of paganization and Judaizing, prophetic protest, reformation, disruption of the Constantinian era and reduction of the Church to a synagogue in an alien or inimical world; expansion into the *oikoumenē*. The New Testament supplies analogies too, but they are not so much in the nature of parallels as an unveiling through the course of history of things which the New Testament anticipates and reflects already in their rudimentary form. The Gospel makes its appearance in the Graeco-Roman world; it breaks through the ties of sacral traditions, but at the same time feels the temptation simply to 'Christianize', without destroying them. When the Gospel yields to that temptation, the result is Byzantinism. When, however, the Church succeeds in throwing off such impediments—greatly assisted by the decline of the West Roman Empire—then it recovers something of the freedom of the classical *polis* and with it the greatness and the failings of classical Hellas, but this time minus the tutelage of Greek religion. Nihilism has its outcome in despotism. A democracy turned to anarchy and insurrection of the masses calls out for dictatorship and yet new sacral obligations. A new *oikoumenē* announces its arrival; and this time it encompasses the world.

Four

The Pattern of Non-Western Civilizations

I. THE EURASIAN *OIKOUMENĒ*

IN the two preceding chapters the distinctive features of that cultural *milieu* to which the people of Israel and the early Christian Church itself belonged received the main emphasis. The ancient civilizations of the Near East and the Mediterranean were continued by and merged into the large unit of Hellenistic civilization, which in so great a measure determined the 'Western' trend of Christianity. To the minds of those who lived in it the Hellenistic world was one and the same thing as the *oikoumenē*—literally, 'the inhabited world', but in fact only the 'civilized' world, of which the frontiers were fixed at the furthest outreach of Hellenistic culture. To the west the *oikoumenē* was bounded by the ocean, and men had some vague idea of the Indians and Chinese, living on the outer fringes of Asia. The rest of the world—the dimensions of which they grossly under-estimated—was either wilderness and waste land or was occupied by savages. The existence of transoceanic continents such as Australia and America was of course unsuspected.

This Hellenistic conception was not altogether without foundation. The world of Hellenism is indeed a unit clearly distinguishable, on the one hand from Chinese and Indian civilization and on the other from the African world outside the Mediterranean area. In the centuries immediately before and after Christ men could hardly envisage those roots which in so many ways linked the Hellenistic with a much larger area of civilization spread out over the whole Eurasian continent. Kroeber proposed to extend this ancient concept of *oikoumenē* to include this larger area, and to employ it as a convenient designation for the total area affected by influences traceable to the main high centres of Eurasia, where most new culture up to that time had been produced.[1] For in spite of all regional divergences—and they were profound—there were historical ties which, time and again, welded together the cultures of Asia, Africa and Europe. Already in palaeolithic times the core industries constituted a tri-continental unit; and this was likewise the case in the periods which followed, when microliths and, later, agriculture and domestication spread throughout the continent, to be followed in their turn by bronze technology, urbanization, the alphabet, iron-working and their several concomitants. Some of these achievements penetrated deep into Oceania and equatorial Africa. All higher civilization did first develop within an irregular band or tract stretching from Britain and Morocco roughly to Java and Japan and including, in A.D. 1500, all the more advanced of the Christian, Muslim, Hindu and Buddhist nations. Outside this belt culture was distinctly inferior: in the outer regions of the primitive peoples of the Old World there were no peaks of higher culture—everything was derivative or reduced.[2] This *oikoumenē* of the Old World was separated by an immense gulf from the New World, the hemisphere of the Americas which had, until 1492, a preponderantly autonomous cultural history—dominated likewise by a kind of 'nuclear belt'—with its twin climaxes in Mexico and Peru.

The conception of the Eurasian continent as one unit of civilization is proved right, in the first instance, by the insights afforded by study of its historical development. True, the study of prehistory is still a relatively young science and one often forced by the scarcity of data to some very bold speculations; yet it provides sufficient basis for a rough sketch of the evolution of human culture. If we identify the beginnings of culture with the first break made by humans with their animal condition through the use of tools and of fire for domestic purposes, recent estimates suggest that we must go back at least 600,000 years. In the deposits of the third inter-glacial and last Ice Age (anything, that is, from 30,000 to 150,000 years ago) there have been found skeletal remains of the physical type known as Neanderthal Man. From this type, the 'first man', evolved the 'Aurignacian' type; from *homo sapiens* came the 'second man', that is, our own type. That happened at the close of the last glacial epoch, when immigrants introduced into Europe a new archaeological period, the Upper Palaeolithic, which went along with an enormous expansion or enrichment of culture. Man then became a systematic hunter and food-gatherer.

People of that technological level settled nearly all the regions which are inhabited today. The type is still to be found in the jungles of south-east Asia; and its most interesting representatives are the food-gathering groups of Australian aborigines. In the New World many more food-gathering groups survived until the arrival of Europeans. Indeed mankind has lived by this method of food-gathering and by a hunting economy for all but the last 7,500 years. Certain definite limitations alone made that economy viable: for example, the small size of local groups, restricted accumulation of property, a technology based on continuous migration and a social organization concentrated wholly on kinship relations.[3]

It was the Neolithic period which first brought the advance from a food-gathering to an agricultural type of economy—a transition fraught with such far-reaching consequences that one can justifiably speak of the 'Neolithic revolution'. It seems that the technique of developing domesticated and more productive grains was first in use somewhere east of the Caspian and was then diffused over a wide area from western central Asia. As a result of this great change in the mode of production, which took place some eight thousand years or more ago, agriculture revolutionized thousands of food-gathering communities and introduced new patterns of living. The population vastly increased. Large numbers of people were released from food production for specialized work, which resulted in many inventions. Land suitable for primitive agriculture passed increasingly into the hands of a few wealthy owners who disposed of armed forces and created governmental bureaucracies. The emergence of monetary systems facilitated commerce. New kinds of specialists helped to achieve the 'second Neolithic revolution', with its characteristic pastoralism. Cattle, sheep, goats and pigs were domesticated at some time between 8000 and 6000 B.C., or very soon after, the horse possibly as early as 3000 B.C., the camel and donkey at about the same time and the reindeer by about A.D. 500 in northern Asia.[4]

The type of plant and animal domestication developed in south-west Asia during the Neolithic period formed the basis of all the civilizations of the Old World, excepting those of south-east Asia, Japan and the African continent south of the Sahara. Everywhere else village life still follows the original Neolithic pattern of south-west Asia. However, through a process of migration, made necessary by the rapid growth of population and by soil exhaustion, that pattern was diffused and developed along two divergent lines. According to the demands of the geographical and climatic conditions some groups concentrated on agriculture, whilst other communities, particularly in the Eurasian steppes and the more or less arid parts of south-west Asia and North Africa, went over to a specifically pastoral economy.

It is these pastoral groups which have played such an outstandingly dynamic rôle in the history of Eurasia. Men who live by agriculture are involved in one sort of relation to nature, men who depend for life upon their possession of cattle in quite another sort. It is this latter type of man that Alfred Weber has called 'the third man'— the type which up to our own day has swayed the course of history and seems now at last to have reached a point of universal transition to a new type of human being.[5] A cattle-rearing people is bound to be warlike, always on the alert for abactors. According to Schmidt this way of life, which, he argues, makes it second nature to be counting flocks and herds, accounts for the strongly developed rationality of the 'cattle people', impelling them irresistibly, as it were, to set up a state.[6] These are the typical overlords, in whom the instinct to domineer over the herd also predisposes them to subjugate, domesticate and rule their weaker human neighbours. In consequence of a change of the earth's axial tilt there took place, between 4000 and 3000 B.C., a process of devegetation in northern Asia, and in central Asia a desiccation into steppes, which drove nomadic peoples out of these regions into more southerly parts of Asia. There, when they had poured like a torrent over the agricultural peoples of the Neolithic village pattern, they became the organizers of the civilizations of the Nile and of the Euphrates-Tigris valley. It was also these aristocratic 'cattle cultures' which occupied central Europe, when the forests were gradually replaced by grass lands during the Neolithic and bronze ages. There they subjugated the agricultural communities.

In the second millennium B.C. these peoples once again played a rôle of exceptional and historic importance; for between 1800 and 1500 B.C. they were pressing southward across a line running through the whole Eurasian continent from India to the Balkans. Pretty well all the peoples concerned in this great migration, whose languages all belonged to the Indo-European stock, were known as 'Aryans', after the name of those tribes which invaded India: it is a term which ought always to be applied solely to the cattle peoples, though it is often misused. Epic poetry—a characteristic product of this period— flowered in India, as also in Scandinavia and Ireland. In India it is the culture of the ruling class with which we are familiar through the Vedas; but at the same time there occurred a gradual process of fusion with what had survived of the Indus civilization. In Greece these invasions brought the Minoan civilization to an end and during the Homeric period laid the foundations of Hellenic culture. The Achaemenid Persians derive from these peoples.

The typical cattle culture is based on the mixed dairying and incidental grain-farming economy of the Eurasian steppes. The horse assumed an importance in these cultures for purposes of war and in particular for dragging the war-chariots of the nobility; but within the economy as a whole it was of secondary importance. Typical horse cultures have developed in the Mongolian plateau, east of the steppes. The peoples living there, for whom—next to sheep and camels—the horse was the main pillar of their economy, were of Mongoloid extraction; and they spoke languages of the Turco-Tartar group, though their culture was closely akin to the circumpolar cultures. It was from these regions that already before the second millennium B.C. and as part of the movement south-eastwards of that same mighty *Völkerwanderung* which brought the 'Aryans' into the south and south-west, the ancestors of the Chinese Shang dynasty came as conquerors into north-west China. There they introduced the horse; but it was used with chariots, not as a mount; the earliest use of cavalry would seem to have developed at a later time, at about the middle of the first millennium B.C. It was in the Mongolian plateau that the horse culture became fully developed, the people there being averse to agriculture and addicted, as nomads, to a domestic animal economy. The superiority of their cavalry and the development of specific cavalry tactics gave these peoples, from the end of the third century onwards, the power to exert a constant pressure upon the cattle peoples of the steppes to their west. Some groups such as the Huns penetrated into western Europe, to be followed later by the Avars. The long history of continued migration from the steppes of Asia eventually concluded with the Mongol conquest of Russia in the middle of the thirteenth century A.D. All these invaders, with the exception of the Magyars, have been absorbed into the local populations. So long as they were completely nomadic, the horse peoples came to evince the qualities of the 'overlord' in an extreme form; but, in sharp contrast to the Aryans, they have not proved able, in more settled circumstances, to maintain their own typical culture. The empires they achieved by conquest were generally shortlived. Those which lasted longer, such as the

Liau Empire and, above all, the later Mongol Empire in China, assumed a Chinese pattern and were administered largely by a Chinese bureaucracy. In central and south-west Asia too these peoples have been assimilated to other civilizations. It was Islam which effectively laid hold on the Mongols in central and south-western Asia and later on the Turks. In the case of the Turks, their ability to adapt themselves to a settled civilization was amply demonstrated by the way in which they handled the heritage of Byzantine civilization, above all in their political mastery.

The extremely dynamic rôle which the steppe peoples played in the history of Eurasia was in south-west Asia and North Africa fulfilled in a different direction by the Semites. The chief and decisive factor in their rise to prominence was the progressive desiccation of the Near East and of North Africa after the end of the last glacial advance, believed to have taken place about 10,000 years ago. The villagers retreated to mountain slopes and upland valleys or to river valleys and oases, where they adopted a dual economy, adjusting themselves to both nomadic herding and settled farming. In the course of time some Semitic tribes became exclusively nomadic, whilst in the agricultural areas the south-west Asiatic pattern of village and city life predominated. The Asiatic Semites were exposed to the continuous influence of the neighbouring Mesopotamian and Egyptian civilizations. By 2300 B.C. they had conquered Mesopotamia, where they maintained the pattern of an irrigation culture. These were the progenitors of Hammurabi. Time and again, wave after wave of nomadic and semi-nomadic Semites swept out of the arid regions into the fertile parts of North Africa and of south-west Asia. The people of Israel entered upon their history in this way; and it was in a similar phase of migration and expansion that Islam eventually entered upon the stage of world history.

To a great extent therefore it has proved to be the pastoral peoples who have played the decisive part in the dramatic movements within Eurasian history, right up to the modern period of Western techno-logical expansion in fact; yet they have never of themselves engendered higher civilizations. When they did not—like some waves of horse peoples—appear simply as destroyers, they lighted upon centres of agriculture, the pattern of which they took over or even animated with their peculiar genius and then superseded with their own social structure. Through just such a reciprocity of influences the history of the Eurasian civilizations came to be realized. Through the length and breadth of the Eurasian continent the Neolithic village pattern has always formed the substructure of the higher civilizations. On that Neolithic foundation city life—which is synonymous with what we are accustomed to call 'civilization'—has sprung into being in various parts of the Old World. In the New World there has been a parallel though independent growth.

The earliest civilizations of Eurasia all started, it would seem, independently of one another in the great river valleys. A number of complex but propitious circumstances account for the fact that the first remarkable urbanization happened at four particular centres— beside the Tigris and Euphrates, along the Nile and a little later in the valleys of the Indus and the Hwang Ho. Those circumstances were partly geographical and climatological; but they must also be taken to include the evolution of certain preparatory factors within the agricultural populations already occupying those territories and the fruitful exchange of influences with other immigrating peoples. Other localities received their irrigation techniques from these four centres; and from them the pattern of urbanization likewise spread to ever more distant regions. The first centres of 'civilization' arose probably in Egypt and Mesopotamia during the first half of the fourth millennium B.C.[7] If it is true—as has been suggested above—that immigrants from northern Asia did in fact become the architects of civilization in these valleys, it follows that they must have been the first to acquire and develop there the techniques of irrigation and urban organization. At all events a process of exceedingly rapid change and a vast increase in the previously sparse population marked that initial period. The Indus valley civilization began apparently somewhat later, but here the chronological question is still obscure. At any rate it is a case of city life arising on the foundations of a very old tradition of agricultural existence. As for the Hwang Ho civilization of northern China, that is considerably younger; it almost certainly originated at about the end of the third millennium B.C.

The civilizations which blossomed and spread out from these centres displayed in many respects striking characteristics of their own, which they both preserved and at the same time deepened and enriched in the course of their long history. All the same these civilizations had their roots in a common basic pattern, a pattern closely connected with their origin as irrigation cultures. Karl Wittfogel coined the term 'hydraulic civilizations' with that in mind. He distinguishes two levels of irrigation farming. Small scale irrigation farming he calls 'hydro-agriculture'; whilst he reserves the term 'hydraulic agriculture' exclusively and specifically for that type of large scale, government-directed farming which we encounter for the first time in the four centres of civilization already referred to and later on in a succession of other places.

The hydraulic economy has three paramount distinctive features. Hydraulic agriculture involves one special type of division of labour; it intensifies cultivation and it calls for co-operation on a big scale. Hydraulic farming in general has to meet a double challenge. Its fight against the disastrous consequences of too little water may well involve a fight against the equally disastrous consequences of too much. This struggle on two fronts brings with it a fundamental division of labour: namely, preparatory measures to safeguard the productive use of water and protective measures to safeguard the crops from periodic excessive inundation—both operations being quite distinct from the farming as such. For work of this kind to be managed effectively a web of organization is needed, which covers at any rate the dynamic core of a country's population. Clearly, organization of such range and complexity demands a central leadership uniquely adapted by its very nature for wielding supreme political power. No matter whether its heads were originally war leaders, peace-time chiefs, priests or 'hydraulic officials', the hydraulic administration held a position which gave it, ultimately, complete power over the whole community. Thus the government not only has the monopoly of directing the 'heavy' engineering, but also carries out the mathematical and astrological operations, indispensable to improving hydraulic production, which at the same time bolster up the superior power of the hydraulic leaders. The next step is for the government to embark on further hydraulic projects such as aqueducts, navigable canals and large non-hydraulic constructions: huge defence works, palaces, tombs, temples, roads and capital cities. The masters of hydraulic society were great builders, constructing their palaces and temples in particular in a monumental style. All these undertakings gave the hydraulic state good reason to levy and control whole armies of forced labour; and this centralized managerial power had far-reaching societary consequences. Non-governmental forces competing with the state for the leadership of society were prevented from crystallizing into independent bodies strong enough to counterbalance and gain control of the political machine. The state could have various forms of secular and religious authority at its disposal, but it took every means always to keep the dominant religion integrated with its power system. Since the ruler exercised complete administrative, managerial, judicial, military and fiscal authority, there could be no effective constitutional checks; for even a highly systematized code of law cannot bind the autocratic law-giver otherwise than by the restrictions inherent in any self-imposed norms. The structure of society—its class divisions and proprietary relations—is in the end determined by the bureaucratic pattern of the state, which checks the rise of independent powers within industry and trade and by its fiscal policy forestalls the growth of strong property interests that do not depend on governmental revenues. Such is the pattern which Wittfogel designated by the term 'oriental despotism'.[8]

Naturally, what happened in practice was much more diversified than this scheme would suggest. Every shade of difference is represented in the passage from simple to complex, from compact to loosely composed hydraulic patterns; and it makes an important difference whether one is concerned with core regions or with marginal areas. Nevertheless, Wittfogel quite deliberately chooses the term 'oriental' as the comprehensive term of reference. In between the typical pastoral society, persisting mainly in Inner Asia and the Near East on the one hand, and modern industrial society on the other, he admits in general just three main types of society. Hydraulic society, the pattern of which prevails in all its sub-types, dwarfed all other societies in its dimensions and its institutional diversity. For all that one must see as types of society in their own right, first, the higher agrarian civilizations of Greece and Rome, existing side by side with the self-perpetuating East for almost a thousand years. Yet it is true, even of these ancient societies, that they were eventually orientalized. One type—and only one—has maintained its proper structure: namely, the feudal society which developed in Japan and in Europe. But one can point to radical differences between these two, so that only of European feudal society can it be said that it has become distinctly and radically different from the 'oriental' type of hydraulic society.

A primary characteristic of hydraulic civilizations is their extraordinary staying power. The four civilizations which have developed from the four original centres have all persisted through several millennia. However it is on this score that Egyptian and Mesopotamian civilizations have differed in the course of their history from those of India and China. Only the two latter civilizations have continued to the present time, whereas those of Egypt and Mesopotamia have gone under; yet undoubtedly their fundamental pattern has subsisted without interruption under their Persian, Hellenistic and Islamic successors— a striking proof of the incredible toughness and deep-rooted tenacity of the hydraulic pattern. Still the conquests in that region have been so thorough, and the cultural changes so radical, that one cannot speak of a continuity of ancient civilizations of the Near East. In India and China, on the other hand, there has persisted through all crises and foreign invasions, through every period of blossoming and of decay, of expansion and recession, of order and of chaos, a tradition which, when the very centres of culture were shifted, survived unbroken and remained in its essentials unaffected by the rise of new religious movements or political conflicts.

In order to mark this difference Alfred Weber distinguishes between 'primary' and 'secondary' cultures. From the four most ancient centres of the Old World have come 'primary' cultures; in China and India these have maintained their 'primary' character in uninterrupted continuity, right up to the present period of Western impact. In this connection he does not overlook the remarkable period between the ninth and sixth centuries B.C., when quite independently of one another and yet, notably enough, at the same time there arose in different civilizations religious and philosophical movements destined to become of far-reaching importance. Jaspers has defined this period as a 'time of axis'; but the conclusions he has drawn disregard the radical differences between these various movements.[9] Confucianism, Taoism and Buddhism have played a rôle in Chinese and Indian civilizations which was essentially in harmony with the fundamental cultural pattern of their *milieu*. Zoroastrianism was a mutation of ancient Persian ideas; and it only achieved a universal significance beyond the confines of Persian civilization through the influence it exercised upon Judaism and later on Islam. In contrast both the Jewish prophets and the early Greek philosophers, however radically opposed their presuppositions may have been, represent an absolutely fundamental departure from the ancient traditions of the surrounding peoples.

The continuity of civilization as one finds it in China and India was broken in the Near East, not only by repeated shifts of the cultural centres but also by counter-movements inspired by an essentially different spirit. In this case, the 'primary' cultures of Mesopotamia and Egypt were succeeded by 'secondary' cultures. It is a question of a complex of cultural trends, in some ways so disparate in character that one cannot easily fit them into a scheme. Alfred Weber's analysis, though not altogether satisfactory, does at any rate provide an acceptable survey of the historical succession which took place. He distinguishes between a first stage of secondary cultures (a) antiquity of Western Asia: Jews and Persians; (b) Mediterranean antiquity: Greece, Rome and Christian antiquity, and a second stage (a) the Orient: Byzantium, Russia, Islam; (b) the Occident. Western culture has received an important part of its technological and scientific heritage, in particular, from Mesopotamian civilization; but it cannot be said that Western culture actually sprang from it. Between the two there lies a tumultuous history, marked by interruptions and excisions, by catastrophe and renewal, which have sundered the West by a vast distance from that primary basis which has supported the cultural structure of India and China to the present day.

2. THE ONTOCRATIC PATTERN

It was argued in Chapter Two that there is in the Old Testament a persisting confrontation with the traditions of Mesopotamian civilization. Indeed the Old Testament is to be read as a unique account or documentation of the people of Israel's struggle to preserve their peculiar genius by breaking away from the pattern of a primary civilization. The story of the tower of Babel reflects the radical judgment of Israel's faith upon a conception of totality basic to Babylonian religion and society. The remarkable thing about the story is that this judgment is levelled, in and through the Babylonian story, against a universal idea; for the narrative expressly declares that the whole world was concerned with building the tower and, because of Babel, had become scattered and confused.

This strictly theological thesis is confirmed in an amazing way by the evidences of the history of religions. The notion of the cosmic mountain can be traced back to a very early period, for we find it already on prehistoric monuments[10] and likewise among primitive peoples.[11] This shows that the idea is rooted in very ancient religious insights belonging to the common Eurasian stock. In Indian religion the idea of the cosmic mountain, Meru, acquired an important mythological and ritual function; it is shared also by the Ural-Altaic, Iranian and Germanic peoples.[12] Before we take a closer look at the concept of Indian symbolism in particular we must understand that this concept does not stand by itself but is one specific variant of a basic apperception of the universe. In Chapter Two it was pointed out that the mythological and liturgical ideas centred upon the ziggurat were rooted in basic notions that at a more primitive level appeared everywhere. The story in Genesis 11 enshrines the same criticism as was voiced by the prophets against the heathen habit of prostration 'upon every high hill and under every green tree' (Jer. 2:20; 3:6; 17:1 ff.). These highly sophisticated Babylonian and primitive Canaanitic conceptions form part of a much larger religious heritage, to be met with not only over the whole of south-west Asia, but in a great number of variations throughout the Eurasian continent. The association of 'high hill' with 'green tree' points to a complex of analogous variants of one basic notion. A frequent combination is that of stone and tree, together forming the sacred place representing the power and life of the earth and of the whole universe. We find it in the 'holy centres' throughout east and southeast Asia and even among the primitive aborigines of Australia. From the ancient Indus civilization the tradition passed over into later Hinduism and into Buddhism. Greek religion inherited it in the form of prehistoric and Minoan customs. The Greek *omphalos*, an upright stone, was venerated at Delphi as the tomb of the serpent; it was the navel of the earth, the link between heaven and the middle and nether worlds.

The phallic symbolism which is properly connected with the erect stone also determined the beginnings of Chinese ancestor worship. There is various evidence that the ancestral tablet was originally a phallic symbol and that in fact ancestor worship, intimately linked with the gods of the soil and grain, originated in phallicism, the fertility cult widespread among primitive peoples. In the earliest Chinese script earth was associated with the phallus: and the same token represented the word 'ancestor'.[13]

The phallicist cult of the erect stone, the *linga*, used to be very widely spread throughout south-east Asia. The archaeological evidences lie scattered over Java and Sumatra in the Indonesian archipelago and over Cambodia and Champa (Southern Annam), in countries, that is, which have been strongly affected by Indian culture. In Cambodia the *linga* appears, as a rule, associated with the symbolism of the cosmic mountain. At one time there was a relation between the temple, as representing the cosmic mountain, and the essence of royal power which was venerated in the *linga*. *Linga* and stupa both go back to very ancient ideas which were common currency in India and south-east Asia; both represent the departed ancestor or king as that point in which the totality of the universe is concentrated. Likewise with the ancestor cult of China: what lies deep beneath these ideas is a primeval cult of earth and fertility, which even in prehistoric times had established a close relation between earth and ancestors, identified with the erect stone. The temples were a type of the cosmic mountain, like the royal palaces. The mountain temples of Khmer took the form of a stair-pyramid. At the top the king of heaven, the god Shiva, embodied in the *linga*, occupied his throne, just as the earthly king reigned in his palace. Legend has it that kingship first arose in Champa when Shiva had his *linga* brought down to earth and caused the founder of the dynasty to set it up there. In Cambodia, as well as in Java and Bali, the dead monarch was worshipped in the *linga* stone, erected over the spot where his ashes were deposited. The legend of *lingodbhavamūrti*, which tells how Brahmā and Vishnu together venerated the cosmic *linga* (Shiva), is frequently depicted; here the function of the *linga*, the column that reaches up to the pinnacle of heaven and down into the lowest depths of the nether world, is clearly to represent the totality of the universe.[14]

Like the mountain and the stone, the tree too has cosmic significance. In fact, any 'green tree' which is worshipped represents, in either a ritual or a mythological context, the living cosmos, incessantly regenerating itself.[15] The idea of the cosmic tree, with which the Mesopotamian tradition has already familiarized us, is widespread, more especially as the inverted tree of which the roots stretch up into the heights of heaven and the branches reach out to cover the earth. It is an idea found in Indian, Chinese, Altaic and Germanic mythology; the tree's trunk is the cosmic column, the axis of the universe. Thus the symbolic functions of mountain, stone and tree merge into one another.

In Indian symbolism the apprehension of cosmic totality manifests itself in an enormous variety of facets. The dissemination of Buddhism over the whole of Asia resulted everywhere in a fusing and mixing together of ancient local traditions which can be traced back to prehistoric periods and to the conceptions prevalent in India, which themselves derive through a long process of growth from a primitive substratum. Indian symbolism therefore is the most representative expression of the cosmic pattern that one can meet with in the whole Eurasian continent.

There is a deep-rooted affinity between the Vedic hymn (Rigveda X, 129), which describes the emergence of the universe from the primeval waters, and the Babylonian hymn, *Enuma elish*. It is however the Vedic hymn which concentrates specifically and exclusively on the one primal element; and this became a decisive factor for the later development of Hinduism, including its loftiest philosophical speculations, and also for the trend of Buddhist thinking.

> In the beginning darkness wrapped in darkness prevailed; all was expanse of water without light; that which had been enclosed as seed of life within its covering shell, that One was born by the power of tapas (warmth). (Rigveda X, 129,3.)

This one primordial principle is 'self-begotten' (*svayambhū*); the totality of the universe is self-supporting. As in the Babylonian conception, this is the theo-cosmo-anthropogonic principle that everything has come into being out of primeval chaos. In that 'golden seed' (*hiranyagarbha*) 'all gods were conjoined: in the navel of the Unborn was established The One who is the ground of all worlds,' (Rigveda X, 82). This primordial 'seed' is absolute ruler over all that exists (*Prajāpati*), the unification of the male and female elements; for the 'seed' (*garbha*) is at once the embryo and the mother-womb. As well as being the 'navel' of the world, it is the 'nave' (hub) of the wheel of the universe—(the term '*nābhi*' in Sanskrit has both meanings)—the five-spoked wheel within which all that exists coheres and which rotates for ever (Rigveda I, 164).

This primordial navel or nave, in the centre of the universe, is likewise celebrated as the pillar of the world (*Skambha*), upholding all gods as the tree-trunk supports the branches (Atharvaveda X 7, 38). We have here then a whole complex of like concepts regarding the monistic origin, principle and centre of the cosmos: seed, embryo, womb, navel, nave, trunk—and the related idea of the cosmic tree. In more recent cosmogonic conceptions we often find a combination of various aspects of the primordial germ of life: as the seminal grain from which the cosmic tree arises, as an essence belonging to the animal kingdom (world-egg, or tortoise), and as the navel of a god.[16] The cosmic tree is a lotus which evolves out of the primordial germ or from the navel of the god (Vishnu) lying within the primeval ocean. In later Buddhist mythology this cosmic lotus acquires a predominant rôle. Thus it is related how in the night when the Bodhisattva descended into the womb, a lotus rose from the nether waters up to the heaven of Brahmā (Lalita-vistara 64, 11). This lotus, sprung from the (male) seed which penetrated the mother-womb of the primeval ocean, conjoined within itself the primal two-in-oneness, or duality in unity, of the universe: Agni (the fiery, masculine, active spiritual principle) and Soma (the fluid, feminine, passive, material principle), respectively the upper and lower parts of the cosmos.

This duality in unity is to be seen also in the association of lotus and tree as representations respectively of the lower and upper parts of the universe. The cosmic tree is as often pictured upside down, with its roots in heaven, as it is in the normal position. Various ideas are interwoven here: two kinds of sacred tree have been taken to symbolize the cosmic tree itself, namely, the Ashvattha (ficus religiosa) and the Nyagrodha (banyan, ficus Indica). The former appears early, in fact on clay seals of the Indus civilization, and divine status is attributed to both trees. A peculiarity of the Nyagrodha is that out of its top it produces air-roots; thus it serves to symbolize the cosmic tree in both normal and inverted positions. Both trees are parasitic: that is to say, their seed is deposited in bird-droppings on another tree and there grows until its roots and branches batten upon the 'victim' which is killed off at the trunk. In Indian symbolism this combination of supporting trunk and parasitic tree comes to express the duality in unity of the universe. The cosmic lotus, rising out of the primeval waters, upholds with its stalk or stem the cosmic tree of the upper part of the universe, which with its branches supports and nourishes all that exists. The idea is closely akin to that which is expressed in the Babylonian Epic by the conception of Marduk building the ordered cosmos upon the primeval waters (Apsu).

In this combination—the cosmic lotus, supporting with its trunk or stalk the branches of the cosmic tree—the Indian classification system is depicted in its basic form. The duality-in-unity of lotus and tree, water and fire, female and male, passive and active, matter and spirit, lower and upper parts of the cosmos, governs the entire universe. All that exists, in whatever category of being, whether the religious, social, political, economic, cultic, philosophic, whether the divine and the demonic, the human, superhuman or subhuman spheres, from the highest degree of organic life to the very lowest order of inorganic matter—everything in principle partakes of this duality and to a greater or lesser extent shares both aspects of the totality of existence. Indian speculations in the realms of magic, ritual and philosophy have been deeply pre-occupied with this fundamental duality (*dvandva*) of existence—a duality which is nothing other than the ambivalent manifestation of the primordial One, the immortal germ or navel which is at once the nave and the trunk, rooting down into the darkness of the nether world and stretching up into the highest spiritual spheres.

With this dualistic classification, which is further expressed in the opposition of the right and left halves of the cosmic tree, there goes along another type of classification according to the four points of the compass, in which the trunk divides its branches to give a fourfold division or, with the introduction of a fifth branch running perpendicularly upwards, a division into five parts. If the interjacent points of the compass are then represented, this scheme extends to a series of divisions, as 8–9, 16–17, 32–33, etc.

Now the idea of cosmic totality expressed in the form of the lotus-trunk-branches has its strict analogy in the Indian conception of the cosmic mountain, called Meru. It says somewhere that this central mountain is 'like a tree-trunk of which the branches are the courses of the four winds, and which lies betwixt the vault of heaven and the midst of the ocean. This is the sole pillar, support and stay of the three worlds: and of all mountains it alone is worthy to be mentioned.'[17] The cosmic mountain is identical with the *stambha* or world-pillar and the trunk of the cosmic tree. More particularly, the mountain, Meru, is to be identified with the root of the lotus, and the top of the mountain with the lotus's stalk or stem.

We find this symbolism, displayed in an extensive variety of ways that are analogous expressions of one fundamental theme, in the architecture and artistic or decorative treatment of Indian temples and in Buddhist stupas and pagodas throughout those Asian countries where Buddhism has established itself. One might instance as an especially impressive example the famous stupa Borobodur in central

Java (eighth century A.D.). Although this building represents a Tantric type of Mahāyāna Buddhism, the stupa as such has been the cultic object *par excellence* in Buddhism from the very start, since remains of the deceased Gautama Buddha's ashes were kept inside it. Buddhism re-attached itself in that way to the ancient cult of the dead. It is not really surprising that the stupa-tumulus came to represent the cosmic mountain; for that is just what it had been from the very beginning. The tomb itself is a mountain, the central point where nether world, earth and heaven meet, centre and totality of the universe to which the dead return. We remember that the Babylonian ziggurat was both Marduk's throne and his tomb. In the structure of the stupas of northern India, with their rectangular terraces, one can recognize the stair-pyramid type, known to us from the ancient Near East. The stupa and the ziggurat both derive from a common pattern; and the Borobodur itself is a stair-pyramid, constructed according to the original tripartite scheme. From the foot or base of the building arises a dome-shaped edifice, comprising five rectangular and four rounded terraces topped by a central *dagoba* (reliquary) thrusting upwards like a perpendicular column. The series of reliefs and images of Bodhisattvas and Buddhas makes it clear that this tripartite scheme is meant to express the Buddhist conception of the tripartite universe, in which the human being rises from the nether world of desire to that sphere where the desire is indeed overcome, but the individual is still bound by the earthly form, until finally he can rise into the heavenly sphere of the Buddhas in which all outwardly visible form ceases to be. The pilgrim ascends the stupa by making his way round and round, along successive terraces, meditating upon the reliefs and pictures as he goes. In that way, he describes in person the *mandala*, the series of concentric circles, familiar in Tantric Buddhism, themselves an image of the universe.

A whole line of scholars—among them Paul Mus and Bosch, who have carried out a good deal of pioneering work—have shown from the symbolism of the architecture, reliefs and images how not merely the general design but likewise the minutiae and details of ornamentation express through the powerful impact of a subtle and varied reiteration the selfsame theme of the primordial oneness and manifest plurality of the cosmic totality, in order that the devotee of Buddhism may ascend in meditative contemplation from the external plurality of material existence to the hidden oneness which is the ground of all existence. To pious contemplation the Bodhisattva and the Buddha himself, in his image, are seen to be the microcosmic expression of that macrocosmic totality; the ample posture of the crossed legs, the body and the head, crowned with an apical arrangement of the hair, possess the tripartite stupa form. There is a good deal of evidence to indicate that the Buddha figure evolved from the veneration of the sacred column or trunk representing the centre of the universe.[18] Buddhist tradition has it that as soon as he was born the Bodhisattva set his feet upon the earth, turned to the north, in seven strides reached the pole, and exclaimed: 'I am in the centre of the world; I am at the source of the world,' (Majjhima-nikāya III, 123).[19]

Thus the primitive veneration of the Buddha is to be understood not in terms of images but of symbols: his footsteps, the lotus (his birth), the Bodhi-tree (his enlightenment, *sambodhi*), the wheel (first preaching) and the stupa (his death). All these symbols declare the Buddha to be the concentration point of the cosmic totality and the embodiment of the primordial One from which everything proceeds. It is hardly surprising therefore that from the original preaching of Gautama Buddha there gradually developed Mahāyāna Buddhism. The Buddha 'with the weapon of his metaphysical knowledge (*jñāna*) has felled the cosmic Brahman-tree',[20] that is to say, he has returned to its primordial principle and has identified himself with the imperishable Essence. In venerating the Buddha himself as the cosmic centre, Mahāyāna is simply making explicit what was already there, in embryonic form, in the original meditation on the Buddha's cosmic symbols. Buddhism then, from the very outset as well as in the abundant variety of its later development, becomes the most widespread and the richest manifestation of what we might well call the ontocratic pattern, the dominance of pure Essence.

3. THE ONTOCRATIC STATE

In its oldest form the Buddhist stupa was topped by a sunshade. This with its stick and covering material represented the trunk and leafy roof of the cosmic tree which rises upon the cosmic mountain. It is precisely by reason of this symbolic function that the sunshade or *pajong* has become pre-eminently the emblem of divine and princely dignity.[21] On the reliefs of the Borobodur one often sees Gautama Buddha portrayed underneath a *pajong*; and thereby he is honoured both in his royal authority and in his cosmic totality. Again there are Buddhist reliefs on which there appears an empty throne and above it a tree of which the foliage consists of a number of sunshades. The symbolism of the empty throne was known in ancient Indian iconography, where it represents the cosmic Essence, Brahmā. Early Buddhist iconography, which in its oldest forms goes back to the second century B.C., applied this symbolism to the Buddha. In the Jatakas, the stories about previous incarnations of the Buddha, there is often a throne, consisting of a flat stone set up at the foot of a sacred tree; on it the hero of the legend receives the royal investiture.[22] The flat stone is an altar on which, as early as in prehistoric times, relics and sacred objects were deposited and on which the deity reclined; at the same time it was the place of princely residence. Throne and altar are in fact one and the same. Like the tree, the empty throne has cosmic significance too. In later development the flat stone became a chair and then a throne raised on steps; and sometimes the throne was made to resemble the stair-pyramid, representing the mountain Meru with the cosmic trunk rising above it.

Here then we find a development parallel to that which we can trace in the Near East. The idea of cosmic totality, in primitive Canaanitic religion expressed in the combination of high place and green tree, is in the advanced Babylonian civilization represented by the ziggurat, the steps of which the king ascended as representative of Marduk. Within his palace the king reigned from a throne with seven tiers. Temple, altar and deity possess a structure strictly analogous with palace, throne and king, for the state is the embodiment of the cosmic totality.

It says much that in Indian iconography the theme of the throne-altar was most positively in vogue during the period of the Gupta empire, when the idea of universal royal authority attained its fullest form. The monarchs took the title of *mahārājadhirāja*; and the cosmic horse sacrifice (*ashvamedha*) was their special royal privilege. The title *chakravartin*, which means 'he who motivates the wheel', was borne by the Buddha, who turns the wheel of instruction (*dharma*), as well as by the king, who keeps in motion the wheel of law and order (*dharma*) in society and the state. In erecting stupas, temples and images of the Buddha, the prince caused himself to be venerated at the same time as the 'cosmic centre'. In view of this, the Borobodur in the centre of Java acquires a particular significance as expressing the cosmic foundation of royal authority. It has been pointed out already that in the Shaivite temples of Indonesia the departed prince was venerated in the *linga* or in the image of Shiva identifiable with it. When Buddhism established itself in Java, it was in intimate fusion with Shaivite religion. We may well see Borobodur therefore as symbolizing the universal power wielded by the kingdom of central Java as from the centre of the universe.

There has been an interesting interaction between Indian and Hellenistic symbolism. Hellenistic art influenced Indian iconography, as one can detect in the reliefs depicting a throne with lions. Indian symbolism, on the other hand, made a strong impression on Alexander the Great. After his death his successor had constructed a throne on which Alexander's diadem, sceptre, crown and other regalia were placed and on which daily sacrifice was offered up. There, and in that manner, the commands of the dead prince were received. In India it was a custom, at a still earlier time, whenever the prince himself was absent, to administer the kingdom with the aid of the princely sandals which were exhibited on his throne.[23] This reminds one of the veneration of Buddha's footprints as one of his symbols in early Buddhist iconography (after his birth Gautama Buddha came in seven strides to the centre of the universe).

It need hardly be said that this notion of the divine kingship of the Bodhisattva, which became such a favourite theme in popular tradition and iconography, was fully developed only in later Tantric Buddhism;[24] but still it was something which grew slowly from the original seed and it was a theme with a very long tradition in India. It is in conformity with the general trend of Indian thought that it should be not the person of the king but kingship itself which was treated as divine. The king was the guardian, executor and servant of the Dharma, the cosmic order, which was also the basis of the order of society. It is the priest, the *purohita*, who has knowledge of the Dharma and is for that reason the agent of the royal authority.[25] This dual unity of king and priest has its divine archetype in Agni, the original *purohita*, and Indra, the primordial king. Agni commits the bolt, the sign of sovereignty, into the hands of Indra; and they function together as 'Indrāgni' or 'Agnīndrau' (Aitareya Brāhmana II, 37). Agni, Indra and the other gods and goddesses are, in the last analysis, aspects of the cosmic Essence, That One (Tad Ekam) (Rigveda X 82, 3; I 164, 46). The One is both Agni, the sacerdotium, and Indra, the regnum; likewise Brahman is both *brahmā* and *kshatra*, priestly and royal rule (Shatapatha Brāhmana X 4, 1, 9). In the Divine One the functions of the Brāhmana and of the Kshatriya are fused together.

According to the ancient account of Manu (Manusmriti ch. 7, 1 ff.) the king was created in the beginning from eternal and essential particles of those eight *devas* (deities) who form the group known as the 'guardians of the world' (*lokapâla*) and as such are said to protect the eight main points of the universe.[26] The eight divinities—Sun, Moon, Fire, Wind, Yama, Kubera, Varuna and Indra—stand for the essential characteristics of kingship. The king came to be associated particularly with Vishnu. The first king was crowned by Vishnu, who entered even into his body. Therefore the entire universe bows to the king as a god; therefore also all kings are endowed with Vishnu's greatness on earth (Mahābhārata 12, 59, 127 ff.). The king at his consecration must take the three strides of Vishnu, thereby imitating the god who pervades and subjugates the whole universe. In this ceremony the king aspires to identify himself with Prajāpati, the primordial Essence and Origin of the universe. There are strong reasons for thinking that this view of the king as the divine being, extending his sway over the earth and promoting the welfare of his people, was known already to the prehistoric Indo-Europeans.[27]

It is Chinese civilization which offers us the most impressive example of the growth and durability of an 'ontocratic state' in Asian history. In spite of the peculiar features of this Chinese civilization which distinguish it so radically from the general cast of civilization in India as well as from the two great civilizations centred in the Near East, the basic pattern is recognizably the same. The theory has been put forward that the cult of the earth was introduced into the Yellow River basin in the middle of the second millennium B.C. as a new religious pattern which had originated in Mesopotamia.[28] A supposition of this kind is not merely dubious in the extreme—it is also superfluous. The more obvious course is to think in terms of a common prehistoric Eurasian background out of which civilization developed independently in the four earliest centres. A connection between the ancient ancestor cult and the phallic fertility cults has been pointed out already; and the ancient state cult has its roots in this close association between the ancestors and the earth. Mo tzu, the philosopher, says:

Formerly in the time of the sacred kings of the three dynasties, when they first founded their kingdoms and established their capitals, they selected a site for the principal earth altar of the kingdom, erected the ancestral temple, and chose luxuriant trees to make a sacred grove.[29]

The earth altar was originally an upright stone on top of a mound which rose in tiers and was situated beneath a sacred tree, just as we know it to have been in ancient India and the Near East. The cult of the earth altar was intimately bound up with that of the royal ancestors; for the altar was a symbol of the dynastic authority. Each territorial chief erected an earth mound for the worship of whatever god presided over the feudal domains. Into the mound was incorporated a sod from the imperial earth altar, which the overlord had received at his investiture. In the matured society of the Chou dynasty (from c. 1050 B.C.), the gods of the homestead, village, fief and empire formed a divine hierarchy corresponding to the human hierarchy on which it was superimposed. The imperial earth altar became the square marble altar located within a vast enclosed and square park, just outside the north wall of Peking. On this altar solemn sacrifice was offered by the emperor or his proxy on the day of the summer solstice, when the earth is at the height of its vitality.[30]

With the square altar of earth to the north there corresponded the round altar of heaven, to the south of the city. Just as the round form and the south appertain to heaven, so do the square form and the north pertain to the earth. The modern altar of heaven, constructed in the fifteenth century A.D., comprised three terraces of white marble. The centre stone of the topmost platform was held to be the central point of the universe. A flight of nine steps gave access to each terrace, and these corresponded to the nine sections of heaven and the nine points of the compass. Likewise the marble blocks of the platform were laid in nine concentric circles, and everything else was arranged in multiples of the same number. The 360 pillars in the balustrade signified the number of days in the Chinese lunar year and of degrees in the celestial circle.[31] Upon this altar the imperial sacrifice was offered on the night of the winter solstice, when the benignant influence of heaven reaches its lowest point. On the north side of the upper terrace a large perpendicular tablet, with the inscription, 'Imperial Heaven, Supreme Emperor', stood within a shrine. Between two shrines that contained tablets of the imperial ancestors the emperor, as Son of Heaven, worshipped heaven as the oldest progenitor of his house.

The term *Shang Ti*, meaning 'Heaven', can be traced back to the ancient *Ti*, which was itself current as early as the second millennium B.C. The scribal token used for this term is probably to be taken as representing the burnt offering made to the first ancestor of the royal dynasty; so the word *Ti* would then signify 'deified royal ancestor'. In the Chou period, *Ti* came to be equated with 'Heaven' (*Shang* meaning 'above')—so that the emperor became the 'Son of Heaven'. Later on *Ti* was employed as an imperial title.

Thus was the emperor identified with the cosmic centre, which was also the place of the ancestors. The whole structure of the altars of heaven and earth and of other altars where the imperial sacrifices occurred was meant to indicate the cosmic totality at the centre of which the emperor dwells as the all-commanding axis on which both the order of the universe and that of society and the state depend. In prehistoric times the king probably lived apart, outside his capital, in a cluster of thatch-roofed buildings arranged in the form of a square (like the earth) and grouped round a chamber in which the royal ancestor *Ti* was venerated. His manner of life was regulated throughout the year in the minutest detail to conform with the structure and movement of the universe, within which everything that exists is classified according to its place and function in relation to the whole. As the seasons changed, so the emperor would change his room, his clothing, his food, his intercourse with his wives and so on. Even in the historical period, when the king lived in the heart of his capital, this ancient palace with its thatched roof remained the place where his supernatural powers were fully exercised. In the *Ming T'ang*, the Sacred Hall, at the New Year, he promulgated laws, and there for ten days he would remain. On the first day of every New Moon he 'proclaimed the New Moon' there and held an audience. The emperor was the high priest of the state. From his throne he ruled over the terrestrial universe, conforming himself to the eternal, unalterable and predetermined cosmic laws, to the 'Tao of the universe'. That is why in the Chinese classics we find the imperial government described as 'Tao in the State or Dynasty'.[32] 'The ruler occupies the place of Heaven, the ministers that of the Earth, and the people represent all living beings.' The Chinese state was ontocratic; it was governed by the cosmic totality, represented the absolute dominion of that totality and applied its power to preserve the life and order of nature and society.

Of outstanding historical importance too has been the Iranian conception of sacral kingship. Politically as well as culturally Iran has for the most part occupied a key position in the history of the Eurasian continent. Behind the east Iranian data there lie vestiges of the common Aryan (i.e. Indo-Iranian) heritage, and still further back some evidences of Indo-European origin, now but dimly discernible. The person of the Iranian king was divine in that he was held to be descended from the gods. He was brother to the sun and moon, and therefore his real home was among the stars. He was the Aion incarnate.[33]

The Iranian king is the cosmic ruler, the Lord of the Seven Climes. He represents both the three worlds of the universe and the three classes of society and he reigns over the septempartite earth.[34] Moreover he is *shah i zamân*, the sovereign of the present age. He exercises priestly functions, especially as a fire-priest and in carrying out the great horse sacrifice, which had been a royal privilege since Indo-Iranian times. On the other hand the mythical rites and ceremonies associated with the New Year, in which the king acts as the great dragon killer who after his victory consummates the *hieros gamos*, the sacred marriage, remind one very much of the Mesopotamian traditions.

The Iranian conception of divine kingship has had an exceptionally powerful influence on other civilizations. Two streams, the Indo-Iranian on one side and the Mesopotamian on the other, here conjoined to fertilize, through Iran, the whole of Hellenistic civilization, and then maintain their course through the later Roman Empire, through Byzantine and, eventually, through Islamic civilization. The Slavonic peoples absorbed an essential part of this heritage, and in Western Europe traces of it survive even now. We shall have more to say about this in another connection, but may for the present content ourselves with considering some striking illustrations of this pervasive influence.

The cosmic pattern of the state is clearly reflected in the circular form of the royal residences, as that is to be detected in a number of Median, Parthian, Sassanian and Abbasid cities. The circle was itself divided into four main sectors by streets radiating along the four cardinal points of the compass.[35] At the precise point of intersection the palace was situated. The royal residence was thus an image and representation of the universe, at the centre of which the king occupied his throne, being, as it were, the 'axis and pole of the world' and 'king of the universe'. The splendid Abbasid Empire had such a centre in Baghdad, the 'round city' of Mansur, the greatest urban centre of the Middle Ages, which became the prototype of 'round cities' throughout the Orient; whilst through Arab military and commercial expansion the plan was introduced into the Western world. It is to be found as far west as Denmark in the military centres of the Viking empires.

The Iranian idea of the cosmic throne hall also found its way to the West. Not only in the Persian-Arabian tradition but likewise in those legends which the Crusaders brought back to Europe do we encounter the theme of the revolving throne. The throne of the famous Iranian king, Khusrau Parvéz, moved in a circular course and was surrounded by a planetarium. The king with his vassals and satraps presented a picture of the heavenly hierarchy; he was 'Sun' and thus 'cosmocrator', the astral power which determines all things.[36] One calls to mind in this connection the final scene of the Babylonian Epic, *Enuma elish*, where all the gods enthrone Marduk and swear allegiance to him; Marduk for his part allots to each his special place and function in the astral cosmos. This is the prototype of the enthronement and investiture of the Babylonian kings. Persian ideas derived from this tradition, passed on via the Chaldeans without a break. The ceremonies of the Achaemenid kings included this procession of the throne in a circular movement; and on the tide of Hellenistic influences the idea penetrated to Rome, where inside the imperial palace Nero provided himself with a rotunda which revolved on its own axis day and night, 'just like the world'. Nero was depicted as Apollo Helios in a number of official portraits. The emperor Septimius Severus' image appeared on the façade of his palace between the planetary gods, as lord of the seven celestial spheres.[37] From the Roman emperors this theology of rule descended to the mediaeval autocrats of the West. The Byzantine coronation ceremonies too embraced these Iranian-Hellenistic traditions. The ancient Near East had envisaged the world as a circle or *clipeus* and placed the cosmocrator—the god-king—at its centre; the symbolism appears on Assyrian and Achaemenid monuments; and closely akin to it, with the same solar significance, is the raising of the emperor on a shield. When the Byzantine sun emperor was thus elevated, it meant that he was being proclaimed as the cosmic centre; and it was the same with the elevation of the Persian sun king at the New Year feast.[38]

The pattern of the ontocratic state, the basic pattern of the four earliest centres of Eurasian civilization, persisted without interruption for thousands of years and spread far and wide. Rooted in primordial and primitive ideas, it seems to have possessed an amazing power of survival. It would take us too far afield to describe here and now how a similar pattern evolved among the ancient civilizations of the New World; but though it might in detail take differing forms, we find there the same basic pattern. In fact the themes of the first eleven chapters of Genesis, it would appear, are universal in character. The major theme running right through the Old Testament is that which proclaims the kingship of the Lord and the unremitting struggle against the challenge of the ontocratic state. Fundamentally, the decision which faced the people of Israel was a choice between ontocracy and theocracy.

Now that we have taken stock of some main principles, it is time to add some brief account of a few of those features which, being grounded on this pattern, came to hold a predominant position in Indian and Chinese civilization.

4. INDIAN CIVILIZATION

When it comes to sketching the essential features and main lines of development of Indian civilization, the basic pattern of Indian cosmic symbolism serves as a good starting-point and introduction to the subject. The symbol of the cosmic tree, with its branches reaching along the four points of the compass and upwards, grafted on to the stem of the lotus, its roots rising from the depths of the ocean, illuminates a good many aspects of Indian culture, religion and society. It expresses both the composite character of Indian civilization and its fundamental unity, its rich elaboration in the course of history, but also the fact that in spite of every change it has never cut itself off from its primordial roots.

The unity which Indian civilization has conserved for at least three thousand years has been greatly facilitated by the relatively isolated geographical situation of the continent and by its enormous expanse, which has proved able again and again to absorb the invader.

Within this geographical unity the environmental factors are extremely diverse, and one result of this has been a cultural dichotomy going back to prehistoric times. South and East India belong in many respects to the complex of cultures in south-east Asia. The Indus civilization in the north-west, however, as the primary centre of the Indian continent, developed out of the south-west Asiatic Neolithic base and bears the mark of those same Asiatic cattle peoples who gave impetus to the growth of ancient Sumerian civilization. Even before the discovery of iron this civilization had disintegrated after a gradual decline caused by a change of climate, deforestation and soil exhaustion at about the middle of the third millennium B.C. Its fate was sealed by a succession of barbarian invasions on the part of Indo-European-speaking peoples from the eastern steppes. One of these was the Aryan invasion, so called, which subdued the Himalayan plateau and the Punjab about the middle of the second millennium B.C. and later pressed on from there into the valley of the Ganges. Indian society, as it is known to us in the light of history, emerged from a long process of fusion between the aristocratic pattern of life among these semi-nomadic cattle peoples and the indigenous pattern of agri-cultural and settled village life. Racially speaking the Aryans have gone without trace; but their languages were accepted and survived throughout North India. So far as their cultural and religious influence is concerned, one can only say that the Aryan invasion was merely an episode in the slow evolution of civilization in India. So it would appear. In the long run the basic determinative trends have proved to be those which managed to survive from the pre-Aryan period or have reappeared like an under-current, through a gradual process of fusion and adaptation, finding a way back to the surface. Within what we now characterize as 'Hinduism' a very minor part belongs to specifically Aryan elements.

In every century the pattern which has continued to form the basis of Indian society and civilization is that of the self-supporting village, with its primitive agricultural economy. Each village was in fact a self-governing community, possessing common land for cultivation and pastorage and preserving its status under whatever political domination, whether Hindu, Pathan, Mogul, Maratha, Sikh or British. Only in the latest period of colonial rule did Western influence really encroach on this age-old pattern. Of the major struggles in Indian history none was for the exercise of rights within the village itself but rather for rights over the village community, so as to exact tax or tribute, not to seize the land.[39] Karl Marx has described this never-changing type of social organism:

> The law that regulates the division of labour in the community acts with the irresistible authority of a law of Nature . . . The simplicity of the organization of production in these self-sufficing communities . . . supplies the key to the secret of the unchangeableness of Asiatic societies . . . in such striking contrast with the constant dissolution and refounding of Asiatic States, and the never-ceasing changes of dynasty. The structure of the economic elements of society remains untouched by the storm-clouds of the political sky.[40]

There is an intimate connection between this closed community life of the village and the caste system, which has proved to be a factor of equal importance for the self-perpetuation of Indian society. The very complex caste system which eventually emerged through a long course of evolution came about as the result of a train of complicated factors. The extreme rigidity of the system became apparent from the twelfth century A.D. onwards, when the exigencies of defence against the Muslim pressure began to cause social stagnation. In South and East India many more specialized local groups developed than in the north-west, and the established lines of interaction are far more elaborate there. Organization on the principle of caste of the so-called scheduled classes, below the four main classical divisions, is peculiarly characteristic of the south. The background to this social system is a structure which belongs to the south-east Asiatic tradition. Totemism and exogamy, along with a classificatory system of relationships, appear to have been universal among the Dravidians in earlier times,[41] and one is reminded here of the Polynesian taboo customs. Moreover, as in many other parts of the Eurasian continent, the technical and economic continuity of self-governing village life was strongly conducive to the formation of hereditary occupation groups, tending naturally to endogamy. The caste system flourished like tropical vegetation; and its ready proliferation must convince us of the overwhelming power of primitive trends to impose themselves upon the social pattern introduced by the Aryans, for the growth of this complicated network belongs to a patently non-Vedic tradition and started to make headway only in the post-Vedic period. The process is reflected in the Mahābhārata, the classical epic in process of formation between 500 B.C. and A.D. 400. During that span of time the traditional exogamy of the patrilineal clan system (with some latent matrilineal tendencies) gave place to caste endogamy. Clan relationships implied hypergamy, since the female side is classified as inferior to the male: the clan receiving the women was superior to that which provided them. This inherent quality of the clan, being indicative of status, tended strongly towards endogamy, and the rise of the caste system is to be explained, partly at least, by the gradual prevalence of that endogamous trend.[42]

At the same time this non-Vedic development in the constitutive period found support, remarkably enough, in the classical Aryan division into four main classes. These were the Brahmins, Kshatriyas, Vaishyas and Shūdras, which had a common origin in the primeval man, Purusha, respectively from his mouth, arms, lowers parts of the body and feet (R.V. X 90; Manu I 31; M.Bh. XII 296, 6). These classes were called *varna*, meaning literally 'colour', in reference to the system of mythical classification. This prescribed a function for each of the four according to its colour: white, red, yellow or black. Together they made up the totality of society, represented by the number 'five' (*pañchajanah* means 'the whole people'. *Pañcha* is 'five'). This system runs through and predominates in the whole structure of the Mahābhārata, which tells of the conflict between the two groups of the Bhāratas; it represents the dualism, common among primitive peoples, of both unity and contrast between the two halves of the community. Its archetype is the ambivalent relationship between the upper and nether parts of the universe, between gods and demons, light and darkness and so forth. The epic is in fact a myth; and it voices the basic idea of Indian symbolism, embedded in the image of the cosmic lotus tree. One might sum up the development of the Indian caste system in a metaphor by saying that the classical division into four classes was grafted on to a complicated and changing nexus of caste distinctions with their roots in ancient pre-Aryan traditions. It is because the system emerged out of such deep-rooted and primitive notions and because it maintained itself continuously in a vital association with the authoritative formulas of the sacred books, receiving thus a 'higher sanction', that one can view it without a shadow of misgiving as 'sanātana-dharma', embodying in a permanent form the ontocratic pattern of cosmic totality.

This Indian society, with its ancient village life and emergent caste structure, was however by no means a static one. The south, for which the earliest historical records date from about the first century B.C., was in frequent contact with other civilizations and in the third and second centuries B.C. was already despatching ships to Southern China, Indonesia, Arabia and East Africa. Roman traders and even soldiers in the service of South Indian kings, Jews, Syrian and later Persian Christians, followed still later by Arab traders, maintained a brisk traffic with the West, whilst in the Mongol period trade flourished with China. From South India as its base cultural influence moved outwards to 'Further India' and the Indonesian archipelago, where the cultural and political pattern of South India superseded local primitive traditions.

North-west India, by its geographical lay-out exposed to foreign invasion, was brought into contact with the West by the sixth century B.C., when Darius I annexed the Punjab and Sind to the Achaemenid Empire. It has been suggested that the emergence of the new pattern of bureaucratic organization owed its original impetus to this contact. After the raid by Alexander the Great, the Maurya Empire consequent upon it showed signs of a strong Persian influence. There is extant an authentic document concerning the rule of the founder of the Maurya Empire, Chandragupta, written by Kautilya, his minister of finances. The book is an *arthashāstra* or treatise on matters of economic and political interest, and it contains a remarkable political philosophy, including materials and ideas going back to the first ages of Indian history. It sets forth a complete theory regarding the structure and purpose of the state as an omnipresent and all-inclusive agency to advance human welfare. Here is a well-balanced philosophy of enlightened despotism. The state (*rājya*, kingdom) is grounded in the sovereignty (*aishvarya, svāmitva*) of the divine kingship which exists to promote *dharma*. The idea of *dharma* is probably best understood as the basic Indian term for what we have called 'ontocracy'. The state, under the rule of a beneficent kingship, is the self-manifestation of that total order which pervades the Being of the whole universe in all its ramifications. At the social and political level *dharma* is that uninterrupted preservation of equilibrium, justice, welfare and culture, which is at one with the universal order. The state therefore is an 'analogy' of the universe, an organism within which every part has its function and its place (*sva-dharma*), not only according to its position in society but also having regard to the four periods of life (*varnāshrama*). By the royal authority this organism is protected against anarchy (*matsya-nyāya*: logic of the fish). If there were no ruler to administer punishment on earth, the strong would devour the weak, like the fish of the sea. Punishment (*danda*) is essential to maintain justice; the ruler thereby shields the persons and the property (*mamatva*, *svatva*) of his subjects. In return for his services to his people he receives revenue and has the right—indeed the duty— to tax them. The author rounds off his political philosophy with the doctrine that every state has of necessity its definite sphere of influence (*mandala*). The anarchy (*matsya-nyāya*) in relationships between states which is an inevitable consequence of this can only be neutralized by the undisputed sway of a world sovereign (*sārvabhauma*). Only in a world state can universal peace prevail.

Various modern Indian writers on social and political science, such as B. K. Sarkar[43] and Panikkar,[44] have equated the theory of the omnipotent state as developed in Kautilya's *arthashāstra* with modern *étatisme* and state socialism and with the idea of the *Kulturstaat*. It is tempting to put Kautilya in a category with Machiavelli and those European thinkers after him who have powerfully advocated political 'realism' and extolled the ethos of *Staatraison*. Sarkar protests against the usual tendency of Western Indology to regard the Indian mentality as essentially 'other-worldly' or concentrated upon the spiritual sphere of the soul; and he demonstrates in considerable detail the 'positive' background of Hindu sociology, which turns out to be thoroughly 'secular' in its spirit and outlook. He points to the vast Hindu literature of *shāstras* and *vidyās*—each specializing in one social field or another— which deal with the concerns of society, the economy, law and the state: that is to say, with worldly, material, non-transcendental and non-mystical aspects of life.

It is worth-while taking a closer look at the thesis of this con- temporary Indian thinker. His sociology starts from the presupposition that human life is never governed by religion, which is at all points a glossy superstition arising from the vain effort to comprehend the nature of God, but is governed rather by the desire and ability to live and prosper in response to the thousand and one stimuli of the universe and to exploit the innumerable variety of natural forces (*vishva-shakti*). This desire and this power are the basis of civilization, of *dharma*, and are spiritual by their very nature. What is called 'materialism' has never existed at any epoch of civilization or in any phase of *dharma*.

It has been supposed and believed during the last century that Hindu civilization is essentially non-economic and non-political, . . . and that its sole feature is ultra-asceticism and over-religiosity. . . .

Nothing can be farther from the truth. . . . The literature, fine arts, religious consciousness, industrial life, political organization, educational system, social economy, etc. of the Hindus—all have sought to realize this synthesis and harmony between the eternal antipodes and polarities of the universe: the worldly and other-worldly, the positive and transcendental, the many and the one, culture and faith, science and religion, caste disunions and vedantic oneness, image-worship and the realization of the Infinite (Brahmā).[45]

The thing to notice about this no doubt partly justified protest is that despite its explicitly 'positivist' and even anti-religious attitude, it remains none the less an expression in modern style of the classical Indian way of thinking which starts from the basic apprehension of the undivided Oneness of all that exists. This classical conception comes out clearly in the well-known Hindu scheme which proposes four objects of human endeavour, directed to attaining material prosperity here and now (*abhyudaya*) and the ultimate bliss of self-realization (*nishreyasa*). Of these objects three could be described as 'this-worldly': *kāma* (physical and sexual needs); *dharma* (the achievements required for maintaining social harmony and justice); and *artha* (economic, political and military concerns). They are inextricably bound up, however, with the fourth object: *moksha* (mystical communion with the primordial Essence of the cosmos and man). This unity of mundane with mystical concerns is again reflected in the fourfold scheme of life periods (*āshramas*), whereby the novitiate (*brahmacharya*) and practice of family life (*grhiastha*)—for the continuation of one's line and the preservation of society—are followed at a riper age by the two stages of ascetic retirement and mystical contemplation (*vana-prastha* and *sanyāsin*). It is not surprising therefore that the very same unity of existence which is urged on the 'positivist' side in India is on the other side brought to our attention by thoroughly religious Hindus, when they wish to register a protest against the secularization of modern life and the consequent subordination or negation of the spiritual and religious aspects. For their part they would interpret the classical Indian conception of the state as self-manifestation and up-holder of the eternal *dharma*, as a fundamental religious idea which the modern theory of the secular state repudiates.[46]

Both interpretations are equally right, for each assumes and complements the other. Kautilya's political treatise on the omnipotent state belongs to the category of *arthashāstras* (or *nītishāstras*), expositions of the social, political and economic concerns of man; but these writings deal with one only of the four objects of human life. Besides them there are the *kāmashāstras* and *dharmashāstras* and, finally, the *mokshashāstras*, that is, the literature about man's mystical goal. The whole corpus of this literature is indivisible. Where the 'ontocratic state' is concerned, it makes no sense to make a contradistinction between 'religious' and 'secular'; for the rule of *dharma* is at one and the same time profoundly religious and utterly mundane.

Just because the state evinced this essential unity in its 'secular' and 'religious' functions, no real distinction could be drawn between secular and religious authority. Through every change in the relative position and mutual relationship between the Kshatriya and the Brahmin class, the royal and priestly functions remained closely integrated. The sacredness of kingship and the all-embracing claims of the state kept the priestly class always in a position of dependence. The Brahmins, in their turn, carried out certain indispensable functions in the service of the state: in calendar making and administration, in legislation and all kinds of fiscal responsibilities. In these managerial tasks they maintained their religious authority; but except for the court priest (*purohita*) and a few judges, they ceased to be professional priests. It was by reason of these 'secular' attainments that under Muslim and British colonial rule the Brahmins proved useful as administrative officials.[47]

Indian scholars have rightly observed that such a concept of the state did not allow the emergence of any parallel or independent authority; nor indeed had the individual any rights vis-à-vis the state.[48] The protection that *dharma* afforded was to the community in general and not to the individual; and the people's welfare, which it was the state's duty to protect, bore no relation to the rights of the private individual.[49] The village people led their communal life, scarcely affected by political and administrative unification or the rise and fall of kingdoms and empires, whose main interest was to exact taxes and obtain revenues from the pastoral and cultivated land. The few towns which sprang to life amid an ocean of self-governing villages continued dependent on the economic and political control of the state. Apart from the political and religious centres, even those towns which had a predominantly commercial importance could only support their handicraft industries by meeting the needs of the ruling and priestly classes. Between the autarchy of the village and the centralism of the state there was no room for a bourgeoisie to emerge, independent and powerful enough to challenge the political monopoly of princes and emperors.[50]

The early history of Buddhism is very instructive in this respect. From the Buddhist narrative books one gets a picture of an economy dominated by such institutions as the 'guilds' (shrenis) of peasants, artisans and merchants. These guilds however lacked political power or influence. In the republics of the time of Gautama Buddha the merchants had no place in the assemblies which advised the rulers on public affairs; and they were all governed by the Kshatriya class. Early Buddhist documents have so far yielded no instance of anything having been organized on the lines of a European guild or Hanseatic league.[51] Public works and irrigation were essential to the agrarian system, and that made a centralized bureaucratic organization inevitable. It was, of course, concentrated in the towns. Governmental activity was based in and upon them, so that they were never able to take an independent course or gather such reserves of economic power as might have given birth to social and political forces competing with the monopolist position of the government. Thus the aristocratic republics of the early Buddhist period do not seem to have grown up in opposition to the general trend of monarchical rule.[52]

The great Maurya emperor, Ashoka, who gave Buddhism a favoured position and did much to promote its expansion, has been compared with Constantine the Great. There is certainly a likeness between the positions of Buddhism and Christianity under those two emperors. In both cases a religion of a minority, which for several centuries had been spreading among the people through its own inner strength, was publicly recognized as the dominant ideology. The dignitaries, monks and theologians of the Church in the East Roman Empire upheld and promoted through their attitude and through the doctrines they proclaimed a most intimate connection between the altar and the throne, very much as did the leaders and members of the Buddhist sangha in India. There is a direct analogy between the application of the idea of the divine kingship to the Byzantine Christ and to the Buddha in later Buddhism. We have seen already how the pattern of the ontocratic state, rooted

in ancient Irano-Indian and Mesopotamian traditions, was handed on
through Persia to Byzantium. Against this background of similarities
the profound dissimilarities become all the more strikingly apparent.
The rise of the Maurya Empire followed on the Persian invasion and
the outreach of Hellenism to the borders of India under Alexander
the Great; but those two conquests, the Achaemenid Empire of
Darius I and the Macedonian Empire of Alexander, were separated
by more than two centuries, during which Greek culture had its
rise, reached its prime and began to decline. In face of the Persian
threat, Hellas came to realize that her war of emancipation was the
struggle of 'civil liberty', which had been nurtured by the city-state,
against oriental despotism. Moreover, in the sixth century B.C.,
when Darius was invading the Punjab and Sind, the people of Israel
were conducting their struggle for spiritual and physical survival
against the Babylonian empire. The exile in Babylon laid a foundation
for the Old Testament in its definitive form, as the unique record of
the conflict between the kingship of God and the ontocratic state.
Hellas and Israel were but fleeting episodes, islands destined to be
once more engulfed by the waves of imperial absolutism; but they
remained models which in later centuries inspired dynamic and
revolutionary forces. In the West the Church measured its strength
against the Caesaropapism of the East Roman Empire; and it was
from Rome that the tradition of the Hellenic *polis* came over into
Europe. In India a countermovement of that kind was totally lacking.
Buddhism capitulated 'body and soul' to the monarchic ideology, and
that without one gesture of defiance; and, as we have already
established, its ritual and iconography greatly helped to sanctify
and deify royal autocracy. The ontocratic core of Buddhism simply
became the central focus of the ontocratic state in its religious aspect.
When Buddhism later turned out to be unequal to the challenge of a
resurgent Hinduism and state patronage was withdrawn, the foundations of its position in India gave way.

In her study of the contrast between Indian and Western philosophy
the Indologist, Betty Heimann, finds the antithesis between them
expressed in two maxims; that of the West: 'Man is the measure of
all things,' (Protagoras, c. 500 B.C.), and the Indian maxim: 'This
Atman is the same in the ant, the same in the gnat, the same in the
elephant, the same in these three worlds . . . the same in the whole
universe' (Brhadâranyaka Upanishad I 3, 22, c. 1000 B.C.).[53] It is

certainly not permissible to take the spirit of the Upanishads as a basis for interpreting every aspect and every phase of Indian religion; and it would be even more dangerous to apply the religious side as *the* principle which explains the course taken by Indian civilization and its peculiar features. It is highly questionable whether there is such a thing as the specifically Indian way of thinking; and in any case all attempts at isolating 'an Indian mentality', as a self-contained organism, are bound to lead to untenable conclusions. Still there is in Indian civilization an undeniable and characteristic tendency which has left its mark everywhere. That fundamental trend could be called a *horror individuationis*, an urge to shy away from individualized existence and to seek to be absorbed in that sub-individual or super-individual Oneness in which all individual features are annihilated. This tendency is typically neither religious nor irreligious nor yet anti-religious; it is more fundamental than any distinction between religious and secular concerns; it lies at the roots equally of the most lofty mysticism and most primitive magical pre-occupations and of all scientific, logical and mathematical speculation, however rigorous. The Indian doctrine of *karma* does not represent a specifically religious or mystical approach to reality—rather it expresses this fundamental aversion from individual being. All that exists has emanated from the primeval matter and, in the end, will be absorbed into it again.[54] Gods, demons, men, animals, spiritual and material beings, organic and inorganic matter, all existence has ultimately the same origin and the same end. All things are interrelated and are free, in principle, to assume any alternative form of existence; for every individual form is a transient manifestation of the undifferentiated primordial matter which alone is real and 'true', transcendent and eternal. *Moksha*, or identity with that unchanging and timeless totality, is attained when the continuous process of coming to be and ceasing to be of individual forms is at an end, when nothing persists but that unmoving sea whose waves are for ever stilled.

Although, of course, this basic idea can manifest itself in typically 'religious' phenomena, Indian religious life simply cannot be isolated from the other aspects. The *karma* doctrine is a strictly rational and axiomatic principle, not a whit less scientific than the law of the conservation of energy, which the nineteenth century accepted as the foundation of the modern natural sciences. The various systems of *yoga* are not just 'soteriological precepts'; they rest on a rigorous psychological and epistemological speculative theory and on an experimental technique. The cosmological thesis of a series of infinite universes is no less rational than the cosmological ideas of Hellenic antiquity or of the Middle Ages in Europe. The subtle philosophical analyses of later Buddhism are among the most consistent and carefully thought-out epistemological systems. The fact that Mahāyāna Buddhism threw up a full-blown pantheon in no way conflicts with that, for the same idea that underlay the strictly logical speculations exhibited itself in emotional, ritual and artistic forms. When Indian arithmetic introduced the concept 'nil' as a concept of number, it acquired also a philosophical significance as a concept of the Absolute, the timeless and formless Essence, Nirvana, the complete cessation of all emanation and resorption, all movement. This does not show that Indian mathematics is 'religious', but that in it that basic notion is expressed which can also find expression in religious forms; or to put it the other way round, it shows that the idea of Nirvana is not specifically a religious one, but is a strictly rational and 'scientific' formulation about the essence of reality. Unlike Greek thought and, at a later period, Western rationalism which was nurtured in part at least on fresh sources, Indian rational thinking never could or would break away from the idea of the primordial identity of man with cosmic totality.

This fundamental apperception accounts for the noteworthy absence of historical interest in Indian civilization. For the period which followed the earliest contacts and invasions, Muslim historiography is the first to offer us any direct information of value to the chronologist. It has been pointed out that the only Indian (Kashmiri) historical work that has so far proved satisfactory to Western scholars is the *Rājatarangiṇī*, literally, the 'waves of dynasties'. Its purpose, however, was not to record facts but to lead its readers into the *sāntarasa*, the passive mood of total indifference towards all earthly happenings. The history of individuals, of families and races, is a perpetual process of arrival and departure.[55]

5. CHINESE CIVILIZATION

China, like India, is a self-sufficient continent. Its enormous variety of climate, temperate in the north but semi-tropical in the south, in conjunction with its geographical situation—the predominance of mountainous regions bordered by coastal plains and intersected by three great river valleys—has made this a country well suited to support a dense population with an advanced and complex culture on a more or less autarchic basis. China is almost shut off from the outside world in every direction by natural barriers: by the circumpolar forest to the north, the ocean to the east, and to the south and west by well-nigh impassable mountains. Only in the north-west does the country lie open to the Asiatic steppes; and it was always from that quarter that—with the single exception of the Manchus—foreign invaders penetrated into and conquered China.

It was these periodic invasions by nomads which, from the very beginning, caught up Chinese civilization into the dynamic move-ments of Eurasian history, in so far as that history was determined by the migrations of horse and cattle peoples from northern Asia and their intercourse with the four primary centres of civilization in the Old World. The Chinese sage, Mencius, took the periodic rhythm of these invasions as a starting-point for his theory of a cyclical course of Chinese history, moving round at intervals of approximately five hundred years. Those who conquered China from abroad were gradually absorbed by a culture whose traditions they first adopted and then continued. After an age of confusion, each cycle was rounded off with a hey-day of cultural prosperity and political expansion. The inevitable decay and dissolution that followed in the wake of this efflorescence were the occasion for fresh invasions; and so the next cycle began its course.

A rhythm of this sort is indeed discernible in the history of the ancient Shang dynasty, which began at about the middle of the second millennium B.C. Its origin can be traced to the influx of nomads from the north-west, itself a part of that large scale movement which brought the Aryans to India. Although they did introduce a number of new cultural elements, they are of significance mainly because they enriched the local Neolithic cultures of North China and integrated all these factors in a unified, genuinely 'Chinese' civilization. Even at this early date the art of writing had developed through the patronage and practice of a literate aristocracy—a witness to the respect for education which since that time has been a characteristic of the Chinese at every period of their history. The process of integration was carried further by the Chou dynasty, originally vassals of Shang. Under the leadership of a military aristocracy they tried to establish a highly centralized feudal order. As a reaction to this, there followed in the first half of the second millennium B.C. a period of dissolution and rivalry between a number of warring states. Under the Han dynasty (206 B.C. to A.D. 221), which carried on the abortive absolutism of Shih Huang Ti in a much modified and moderated form, China reached another interlude of prosperity. Danger threatened from the Huns (Hsiung Nu), who were later on to pour into Europe. Not only was this successfully averted, but Chinese imperialism was able to subdue the whole eastern half of Asia; and through the Parthians an extensive silk trade grew up with the Western world. During the four centuries that followed on this first empire, various centrifugal forces were in control. The resemblance between this period of decay and the European 'Dark Ages' is too obvious for words. The Huns conquered the whole of North China in the early part of the fourth century A.D. They had been called in by a Chinese ruler to assist him in a civil war; but just like the Goths who had started off as Roman auxiliaries they finished up by seizing the empire for themselves. The rôle which South China began to assume in this period might be compared to the position of the East Roman Empire, in that, having escaped the Tartar invasions, it kept alive the culture and traditions which had grown to full maturity under the Han empire. The collapse of the north removed the centre of gravity to the south which, from being a colonial territory, quickly became the mainstay of Chinese culture.[56]

All the same there is a clear and essential difference between Chinese and Western history in this respect. Of course, the Roman tradition runs through the whole history of Western Europe; but a recognition of this does not alter the fact that the cultural centre shifted decisively on to the ground of the 'barbarian' peoples, and that this to a great extent determined the currents of power, the dynamic forces, in Western history. In China no comparable break occurred. After the Tartars came fresh hordes of barbarian invaders—this time of Tungusian stock; but they were completely absorbed, so far as language and culture are concerned, into the Chinese heritage. In fact it was owing to these foreign masters that the literary traditions of the Han era were revived and kept in being. Once again China entered upon an age of imperial splendour, under the absolutist rule of the T'ang dynasty (A.D. 618 to 907). Consequently, the north-west provinces, which had always been the breeding-ground for a policy of centralization, lost their position of leadership, became a prey to nomadic invaders and were reduced at last to a wilderness by the devastating fury of the Mongols. The Ming Empire, which forced the Mongols out, was organized after the T'ang model, but never recovered control over North-west or Central Asia. As a result, the continental trade-route was neglected, whilst the south and its sea trade became proportionately more and more important. The sharp contrast between north and south became a prime factor under the Manchus (A.D. 1644 to 1911). These foreign rulers made their base in the north and came up against very stubborn resistance from South China.

China then has had a tumultuous history, marked in its forward movement by a rhythmic alternation of opposites: invasion and absorption, nomadic conquest and indigenous government, centralism and disintegration, imperialistic ambition and isolationist pacifism, cultural efflorescence and decay, the ascendancy now of the north and then of the south. Throughout its long history, however, China has preserved a continuous tradition in culture and politics, which may indeed have been interrupted but has never been destroyed. However eccentric, at times, the swing of the pendulum, it seems always to have been drawn irresistibly back to its proper course. The basic theme is never abandoned, so that Chinese civilization has conserved its 'primary' character and carried it into our twentieth century.

Chinese mythical tradition itself offers to explain this fundamental fact, when it relates how the founder of the first historical dynasty succeeded the five emperors of the golden age. This ruler owed his position to his great skill in regulating the floods which had covered the whole empire, almost to the top of the highest hills. That achievement was, as it were, the keystone of the work of his five predecessors, who had taught the people the crafts and manners of civilization and had established the forms of government, the sacrifices and the rules of right conduct. From the very beginning, flood control and irrigation have been pre-requisites of civilization in the Hwang Ho valley and have remained so through the whole of Chinese history. The emperor had been also 'the first ploughman' and continued to be so in a ceremony repeated each year. The state or the dynasty was identified with 'the gods of the soil and grain'.

The main function and continuing importance of Confucianism consisted in its being, or having become at any rate, that kind of social and political ideology which best answered to the need for a unified state. It supplied the cement for a durable social order. Confucius himself flourished during a period of political and social disintegration, when philosophical thought and the quest for an ethical basis for living were vigorous and widespread to a degree never since paralleled in China. Confucius represented just one of the 'hundred schools of philosophy'. The fact that this period coincided with the classical age of Greece has prompted a good deal of comparison between them; and indeed the circumstances leading in both China and Greece to a restless mood of spiritual activity are comparable. Yet this only serves to underline the contrast between Greece and China which came to diametrically opposed conclusions and practical results, although the premises were in both cases very much the same. In Greece the self-conscious democratic spirit of the competing city states proved victorious in the struggle with Persian despotism; whereas in China a parallel situation of strife and discord between the various groups and states was taken to be a symptom of decadence, of the decay of a past feudal order, so that men sought by every means in their power to restore the harmonious rule of an ideal government, anchored by common consent of every faction and of every school in the unifying imperial dynasty. Confucius directed all his efforts to achieving a return to the ideal pattern of the primeval golden age of the first five emperors, a pattern faithfully pursued by the ancient Chou dynasty, but since fallen into abeyance. Thus the mythical past, together with an idealized version of history, became the absolute standard and model for all order in time to come. That is why the core of his reactionary philosophy was represented in the 'rectification of terms', the restoration of each stone of the ruined social edifice to its proper place. The cement that binds and holds together this ideal order of things is loyalty (*chung*)—the very antithesis of the idea of liberty associated with classical Greece. Such loyalty, displayed in a strict observance of ritual custom, taught that deference which a son owes to his father and kinsmen, the officer to his prince, the prince to his emperor.

The Chou period—object of Confucius' nostalgia—had witnessed the creation of a rigidly stratified society, in which the whole feudal order was made to depend directly on the king. At the same time the system rested on a sharp division between nobility and commons, of whom only the former enjoyed the benefits of literacy and a full education. Next under the nobility came the class of court officials and administrators .The mass of peasantry formed the base of this social pyramid. They were divided up according to the 'eight family system', which meant that every ninth field was worked jointly by the group on behalf of the overlord. They also constituted a reservoir of forced labour, available for various government projects, such as irrigation and flood control, public works and defences. The class of merchants and skilled craftsmen was small and weak and, ranking even below the class of bureaucrats, had no significant function.

It need hardly be said that the design of an ideal social order as proposed by Confucius was a thoroughly aristocratic one. For the nobility the guiding principle was the ideal of the *chün tzü*, the 'gentleman', fully educated and so understanding the true ethos of loyalty and 'the rites'. This raised him above the law and the exactions of the penal code. Law and (what comes to the same thing) a system of penalties can only apply to the common people who have not received the education of a gentleman and can therefore be made to deport themselves properly, according to their station within society as a whole, only by coercive measures. Thus it is not altogether true to say that Confucianism is basically optimistic. It is essentially an aristocratic class–ideology which proceeds on the unquestioned assumption that the nobility are able and willing to discharge the functions which are theirs by nature and upbringing. It is taken to be self-evident and quite beyond dispute, however, that force must be employed to constrain the masses to their appointed place and function within the larger whole. In this respect Confucianism resembles the Aristotelian philosophy, which has always started from the unalterable fact that the masses were destined by nature for slavery and that the norm of what qualifies as 'human' could only apply to the *élite* of free citizens. Such a rigid social dichotomy evidently failed, in both these instances, to offer any lasting solution of political and social problems. In Greece and Rome Stoicism proposed a cosmopolitan philosophy which in principle threw over the distinction between slaves and free men, but at the same time set the *polis* on the path of decline within the unified empire. Confucianism was only able to become the firm basis of the social structure because it passed through a similar process of development.

The theorizing speculations of Confucius might be aimed against the break-up of the ancient feudal order, but they could not hold it back. It led, in the third century B.C., to a crisis and a new orientation which set the stage for the next two thousand years. The decisive impetus came from the north-western Ch'in state, which had already been governed for a considerable time on totalitarian principles. The theories of the strongly anti-Confucian school of the Legists were effectively applied there; and what enhanced their success was the fact that a great part of the population consisted of Hunnish barbarians. The system of the great family and the feudal eight family villages was swept away; and each family was allotted its own place of abode. All power was concentrated in the ruler through his administrative machinery. The state was divided up into districts supervised by officials and all feudal distinctions were abolished. The old ideal of a literate aristocracy with its 'gentleman' ethic was replaced by the rule of penal law, applicable to all subjects equally. A professional military class, sharply distinguished from the civilian bureaucracy, ousted the nobility. Agriculture and warfare were the staple activities of the state. As soon as the Ch'in state had subjugated the whole of China, the great emperor Shih Huang Ti imposed this totalitarian system throughout the country. It has been said of him that he 'combined the administrative and organizing ability of an Augustus Caesar with the megalomania of a Hitler'.[57] The landed gentry were transferred en masse to the imperial centre. All books of history or social science which did not accord with the official ideology were ordered to be burnt. The Chinese script was rigorously standardized. The peasant population was put to forced labour on a tremendous scale to expedite huge public works. The emperor arrogated to himself for the first time the title 'Ti', previously reserved for the legendary heroes of the past.

Although the Ch'in empire turned out to be no more than the tyrannical adventure of one man and immediately after the death of Shih Huang Ti (in 206 B.C.) his totalitarian system was overthrown in a welter of reaction, it had been a radical operation, and one which left ineradicable scars upon society in China. The country was never able to revert to the ancient feudal order. The Han emperors set up a façade of feudalism, but in reality maintained the centralist system. It was to this that the Confucian doctrine owed its advancement from being a minor school of political philosophy to a monopolist position as the sole official ideology. The Han emperors, themselves of peasant stock, enlisted Confucianism in support of a policy which in fact simply sealed the fate of the old feudal order that Confucius had idealized. The Confucian ideal of aristocratic morality was transformed in being grafted on to the principle of a centralized bureaucracy. The nobility of birth and blood bequeathed its ethos to the new ruling class which now only education marked off from the mass of the population.[58] Confucianism carried the day by taking over vital elements of the opposing Legist philosophy. The gulf between nobility and commons was in fact widened by this transmutation; for though entry to the class of bureaucrats was available, in principle, to any commoner able to pass the examinations, education by Confucian standards had now become a wall dividing a privileged *élite* from the mass of the population. On the inside the 'gentleman' ethic prevailed and according to this—theoretically—the whole state was governed. Outside the wall, on the other hand, the stern practicalities of the penal system reigned supreme and the ruling class was actually kept in power on the basis of the Legist philosophy. By means of this fusion of contrasting elements Confucianism became the well-balanced ideology offering the only workable solution to the dilemma of how to run a 'hydraulic' type of society in a reasonably humane way.

Ever since the eighteenth century the Confucian system has been an object of admiration among a rationalist *élite* in modern Europe. The spirit of Confucianism does indeed come close to the modern European outlook, particularly in its highly developed historical consciousness, contrasting sharply with the almost complete absence thereof in Indian civilization. Reverence for an admittedly idealized past was not expended upon primordial myths, but on the contrary was directed in a critical spirit to renovating the present order according to an ideal pattern. The antiquarian labours of the Confucian school, devoted to recovering the lost literature of the feudal period, were inspired by a zealous wish to recreate the image of the golden age as a shining example of morality and a stimulus to current efforts at imitation. To give the ancient traditions their proper status as doctrine it was necessary for the earlier records to be continually rewritten; for not only must the present order tally with the ideal past, but the legendary materials in turn are to be remodelled to fit the image of the ideal order as the contemporary scholar-class conceived it. This historical discipline, handed on from one generation to another in a spirit of rational matter-of-factness and of scepticism with regard to fantastic or extraordinary events, produced a remarkably fine critical sense.

However suggestive of modernity this mental outlook may be, it is part of a cultural complex separated by an enormous gulf from that of modern Western civilization. Max Weber, perhaps more than anyone else, has probed into the underlying reasons for this and has tried to find out what have been the fundamental motives guiding Chinese society along a normative course into the twentieth century, without one substantial break or deviation within the last two thousand years.[59]

This is best illustrated perhaps from the character of the Chinese city. Right from the time of the Shang dynasty, in the latter half of the second millennium B.C., city life has played an important part in Chinese civilization. The Chou aristocracy were concentrated in cities which served as fortified centres of taxation and government. These urban centres, however, never grew into politically independent communities after the style of the Greek *polis* or the mediaeval cities of the West. Rebellion against bureaucratic excesses was frequent enough; but these revolts never materially damaged the system and were never aimed at acquiring political advantage or freedom for the city. Urban populations had nothing of the outlook or attitude which in the West gave rise to the citizenry, the bourgeoisie. That is all the more remarkable in that China certainly had 'guilds' similar to the trade guilds of England. To an even greater extent than was common in the West, these guilds had the power to regulate the economic life of the cities and in many cases had complete jurisdiction over their members; but they did not try their hand at the kind of systematic political strategy that in the West turned the 'township' into an autonomous community for economic, civil and, above all, military purposes.

One considerable difference was that the *polis* in the ancient world was built up on sea trading, whereas China always remained a predominantly continental state, with a self-sufficient economic life based on agrarianism. Nevertheless this in itself need not have inhibited the growth of a distinctively urban civilization. Like the Chinese cities, those of continental Europe in the Middle Ages came into existence because they were founded by princes and feudal overlords to be administrative and fiscal centres. In the West, however, they became the hard core of opposition to princely and feudal power; they schemed to enlarge their privileges and formed military communities well able to offer resistance and to shut their gates at any attempt on the part of feudal lords to violate their rights. The Chinese cities had neither the will nor the technical resources to do that kind of thing.

The reasons for all this are to be looked for in the structure of Chinese society and in the social ideology inseparable from it, which nipped in the bud any prospect of development for those forces that in the West led to the rise of a bourgeoisie. In such a rigidly stratified society the class of merchants and craftsmen were quite unable to acquire an independent status. They were caught, so to speak, between two fires. There was a tremendous downward pressure constantly exerted by the top of the social pyramid upon the base; but the 'base' itself, in developing almost incredible powers of resilience, tenacity and passive resistance, thereby exhausted its stock of those active forces which otherwise might well have become so much dynamite beneath the structure of the pyramid. In other words, we have to look for the 'underlying' causes at the top as well as at the bottom.

The class of officials also occupied a highly privileged position, in an economic sense, which gave them the best opportunities for accumulating property. Thus there emerged a typical form of bureaucratic capitalism, relying on prebendal revenues and land tenure, tied up with the invariably uncertain status of officialdom, obsessed with accumulating the maximum amount of revenue and property in the shortest possible space of time, setting itself against any and every reform that might affect its monopolist position and tending therefore to an ever increasing traditionalism.

Supported by the social order, the enormous authority of the family, with its strictly patriarchal leadership, reigned supreme. Ever since feudalism and the 'great family' system were abolished under Shih Huang Ti, imperial policy has tended generally and persistently to favour 'private property', that is, small scale land tenure by each individual peasant family, as forming the basic unit for taxation by the state. As against the family and its authority, the bureaucratic class and even the state were ultimately in a weak position. This family influence extended to the city, since every inhabitant retained his connection with his family of origin and its land, to which the ancestor sacrifices were taken, so that the city was still attached by its roots, as it were, to the community of the village.

Confucianism has always carefully maintained its exclusive

position as the official ideology of the state and defended it against competing religions. It was no accident that the rise of Taoism and the penetration and spread of Buddhism were both very much accelerated in the period of political disintegration which set in after the Han Empire. When Confucianism was adopted as the official cult and philosophy of the state, it inevitably stirred the forces of popular religiosity to opposition, as did the state religion of the Roman Empire. What is commonly known as 'Taoism' is in fact an extremely complex phenomenon, merging the mystical philosophy of the anti-Confucianist school of Lao Tzu with a bewildering variety of primitive local customs and magical rites which can be traced back to the Neolithic past and were bound up, particularly in South China, with a much broader south-east Asian tradition. When Confucianism became the philosophy of the educated ruling class, the ideas and rites and practices of Taoism served the despised masses as a rudimentary form of self-expression. In that same era of turmoil and confusion Buddhism, which had already begun to penetrate by the Central Asian trade-route, spread with such resounding success that by about A.D. 500 it had obtained a firm foothold among all levels of the population. Having once enjoyed a season of imperial patronage, it was able during the centuries that followed to ensure itself a lasting place in Chinese civilization, in spite of Confucianist antipathy and of determined resistance from the Taoist priesthood. Even the brief but severe persecution of A.D. 845, which took heavy toll of other foreign religions such as Manicheism, Zoroastrianism and Christianity, was unable to stem the tide of Buddhist influence. The very next year it could congratulate itself on enjoying the favour of the new emperor and made a quick recovery.

Notwithstanding all this and the official patronage which a number of T'ang emperors extended towards Taoism and Buddhism, neither of these religions ever acquired political power. At the top of the social pyramid Confucianism remained firmly entrenched as the only feasible concept of government headed by a literate bureaucracy. However much the ruling class might feel the need to resort to them in their ritual and magical aspects, Taoism and Buddhism remained at the bottom, indispensable as a means of satisfying the popular need. In so far as their function has been to uphold the dominant social and political pattern, both religions have proved an effective 'opiate to the people'. Of course, Taoism was potentially a breeding-ground of secret societies and revolutionary movements; and the power of the rival Buddhist priesthood was potentially dangerous. Yet at no time in fact did either religion produce an alternative to the existing pattern of society; on the contrary, they both helped to carry its centralizing tendencies to an extreme pitch. So far as Buddhism is concerned, we have already seen how well its mystical monism was accommodated to the notion of royal absolutism; and we find a similar correspondence in Taoism itself. The idea of Tao, the primordial Oneness of cosmic totality, represents in its mystical aspect the timeless bliss of the self when identified with Tao; but in its political aspect, Tao manifests itself in the emperor as cosmic centre of the social order. Thus the philosophy of Lao Tzu supports a doctrine of the absolute authority of the ruler. The Legist school was strongly influenced by Taoist thought, which lies behind its doctrine of a unified and universal law for the whole of society, under the direction of a totalitarian governor.[60] Their ideal aim was to bring the system to such a degree of perfection that it would work both universally and automatically, without any need for interference on the part of the ruling autocrat. In this condition the people would lead a life of primitive simplicity, without reflection or dispute; when not serving the state as soldiers, they could be engaged in farming. Agrarian 'passivity' and warlike activity were alike inspired directly by the one Tao, pervading the social order and the universe.[61]

In China then the concept of the 'ontocratic' state has been accepted unanimously as an axiomatic principle at every level of the population and by the various philosophies and religions, however diverse. The tensions and conflicts arose because of differences or contrasts in the manner of interpretation and through the clash of rival social groups. There has never been any shortage of philosophers ready to point out that the three religions are three ways to a single goal. The well-known dictum that China 'contains three religions and yet it is only one religion' (han san wei yih) expresses the general intuitive awareness that here are three branches of one and the same tree—'the great tree of Asiatic paganism', which the sinologist, de Groot, has called 'Universism', the worship of the universe in all its aspects and manifestations.[62] It is a tree whose roots thrust back into the Neolithic past of the Eurasian oikoumenē.

The nature of this primary structure and its self-perpetuating continuity must account for the fact that the course it took never permitted the modern concept of science to evolve. Generally speaking Confucianism carefully avoided giving free rein to magical practices, to the various forms of divination and sorcery exploited by the popular religion. Drawn none the less from the same stock and itself nourished upon the same vital sap, it could offer no resistance to these things on principle; and what is more it was as often as not addicted to them, either openly or in secret. In so far as Confucian rationalism contrived to keep a firm footing on such treacherous ground it was modelled on the uniform ideal of traditional learning in the ancient sacred literature, it was backward looking, it was prompted by the desire to belong to the privileged bureaucratic class. The contempt meted out to the popular Taoist priesthood forced their pseudo-scientific speculations down to the lowest reaches of stupidity, and thereby stifled any possible chance of their magico-mystical experiments in alchemy and the medicinal arts, in the search for the elixir of life, opening a door—as was the case in the West—to the discovery of exact scientific principles. True, Chinese civilization has a number of important inventions to its credit; but the direction given to these and the use made of them suffered under the limitations of the social system—further evidence of the fact that systematic technical progress is not achieved through a series of discoveries in themselves, but only when there is present a spirit of a particular kind. The magnetic compass was used originally to determine a favourable location for graves, and later on, in accordance with China's continental orientation, was confined to the purposes of inland navigation. Gunpowder was put into fire-crackers as a pro-tection against evil spirits and it was first put to military uses by the Mongol invaders.[63] Paper, silk and porcelain were typical luxury articles; and because education for literacy was monopolized with such persistent care, the art of printing was restricted to its use by the government, just as knowledge of astronomy was applied only in the service of the state. All this points again to the fact that between the literate bureaucracy and the illiterate peasant masses there neither was nor could be any room in Chinese society for the growth of an independent urban class.

Five

The West and its Counterparts

1. INTRODUCTION

IN this chapter we shall concern ourselves with those developments in history which gave rise to what is called 'Western' civilization. The previous chapter contained some attempt to outline the essential features of the principal civilizations of Asia, from which the history of Western civilization differs in so many of its aspects. Whenever people from within the bosom of Western civilization have had more than a superficial contact with the non-Western world, they have become convinced of profound differences. In the course of Western history the sort of encounter has taken place which has given birth to the idea of an opposition between what have come to be known as 'the West' and 'the East'. However serious the objections which may be offered to this formula, the fact remains that Western civilization has gone its own way and, in so doing, has expressed a definite sense of direction, a choice more or less consciously made.

Chapters Two and Three described how the people of Israel quite deliberately detached themselves from their environment and how, because they came within the orbit of the Hellenic empire, the course of Israel's history—together with that of Christianity as its offspring—was turned in the direction of the West. This new geographical orientation, however, meant parting company with certain cultural developments which tended in an altogether different direction, although there was also a continuous encounter with them. Western civilization has developed through an ever renewed exchange of influences with its counterparts. We must therefore pause a little longer at the most notable milestones on this journey.

2. HELLENES AND BARBARIANS

Minoan civilization, which preceded that of the Hellenes, was probably produced by communities crossing the Mediterranean from North Africa and settling in Crete. Desiccation of the Afro-Asian steppe, which began at the close of the Ice Age, accounts for their desire to emigrate.[1] From the seventeenth century before Christ onwards, this Minoan civilization spread to continental Greece; but it was liquidated when Achaeans and other barbarians burst through from the European hinterland in the latter part of the fifteenth century B.C. These Achaeans were the progenitors of Hellenic civilization itself. Their arrival was connected with a *Völkerwanderung*, reaching its climax at the close of the thirteenth century B.C., in which the Hittite empire in Anatolia was overwhelmed. Toynbee employs the term 'Syriac' to describe a new civilization which arose when Philistines, Phoenicians, Aramaeans and Hebrew nomads entered the Near East from various directions.[2]

Minoan civilization had a number of ties with the Orient. Its closest racial connections were with Asia Minor, whilst the trading connections of Crete were with Egypt, Syria and Mesopotamia. Creto-Mycenaean religion on the Peloponnesus was clearly related to the religions of the ancient East, especially in the vegetation cults for the dying and resurrected deities and for the great mother-goddess.[3] From the beginning of the first millennium B.C. the Phoenicians were chiefly instrumental in taking over oriental ideas; and their colonization of the western and southern coasts of Asia Minor established direct links with the Orient, just as did the colonization of Cyprus where older elements of Phoenician culture fused with Hellenic influences that were flowing in.

These links with the Orient, which had existed from the earliest times, were given fresh impetus in the Hellenic period. Greeks went to Asia and to Egypt as mercenaries, as traders and as physicians-in-ordinary to the Persian kings. Oriental influences affected the Greek sciences of astronomy, mathematics and medicine. Popular beliefs, astrological speculations and astral religion fed upon oriental conceptions. As the members of the oriental pantheon were adopted and given an Hellenic interpretation, the way was eventually made ready for Hellenic syncretism.

One must look partly to Asia for the origins of Hellenic civilization. The Achaeans entered the Peloponnesus during the second millennium B.C. in several waves, the Dorians being the latest. So far as language is concerned, they were of Indo-Germanic origin; but they were gradually assimilated into the indigenous population. When they spread over the Aegean islands and settled there, nothing at that early stage gave promise of a distinctive Hellenic culture. It was during the first millennium B.C. that the decisive turn of events occurred which made the Greeks conscious of their unique cultural destiny. Herodotus has expressed the classic definition of this peculiar Greek consciousness: 'the Greek race was separated of old from the barbarians, as being subtler and more removed from simpleness and folly'.[4] This distinction was displayed above all in four great achievements: in literary form, through the epic poetry of Homer: in a religious form, through the rise of Olympian religion: in a political form, by the creation of the *polis*: and finally, in the creation of Greek philosophy.

In all these respects Greek civilization found its earliest fulfilment in the Ionian region of Asia Minor. The Homeric epic, a product of the 'heroic age', is constructed according to a patriarchal, monogamous system. This reflects an Achaean tradition of northern origin, contrasting sharply with the matrilineal customs of the Aegean or Hittite races.[5] Its aristocratic setting suggests obvious parallels between this literature and other poems in the same *genre*, especially the Edda. The Homeric gods are conquering chieftains, aloof from the cares of agriculture and the indigenous Aegean milieu of chthonic fertility-cults. The migration of Ionians across the sea to the coasts of Anatolia only served to intensify this contrast. The Homeric epic, in its main features, is Ionian. It was Ionia that for many reasons was to lead the forward movement against the agricultural and tribal worship of the gods of the soil, which Herodotus characterized as 'silly nonsense'. From Ionia Homer passed to Hellas, where in the sixth century B.C. Athens became its central home; and from there it spread through the mainland of Greece.[6] It was the Ionians who for the first time became conscious of a complete contrast between the Hellene and the barbarian, in their struggle with the tribes of the Anatolian interior, a struggle as between fully human and subhuman creatures. Whereas the primitive conception of the universe was that of an interplay of innumerable but undefined powers, the Ionians attained the idea of a world ruled by personal beings, superhuman yet manlike in mind and shape. In this way they gave a particular direction to Hellenic civilization. Herodotus tells us that Homer and Hesiod:

> made for the Greeks a genealogy of the gods, and gave them their surnames, and divided the offices and arts among them, and described their forms.[7]

Their social organization too eventually distinguished them from the barbarians. Here again the Ionians blazed the trail, along with the other seafaring Greek settlers on the Anatolian littoral, the Aeolians and the Dorians. For the traditional organization by custom and kingship they substituted the principles of locality and law. A new social unit grew out of the ships' companies: it was the *polis*, a political community of men, irrespective of tribe, held together by the common factor of a circumjacent wall. This principle of the city state, governed by an elective magistracy, was later imitated in European Greece. When over-population made expansion imperative, this organization of the *polis*—already tried and tested in the wars against the surrounding highlanders—showed itself altogether superior to the challenge of the native tribes of 'Graeca Magna', Sicily, Cyrenaica and Chalcidice. The decisive phase occurred when, after two centuries, the process of expansion was brought to a halt, for the growth in population continued, thus making necessary economic and social adjustments of a far-reaching kind. By its success in solving these problems and replacing the old pattern of kinship relations with a franchise based on property, Athens made room for new social classes to emerge; and thus this city became the leading *polis* and 'the instructor of Hellas'. In the struggle with the Achaemenid Empire during the sixth century B.C. the *polis* organization of Athens became the bulwark of freedom against the 'barbarian despotism' of the Persian state. Here is one root of that contrast which has since come to be recognized as the distinguishing factor between 'East' and 'West'.

We now turn to the fourth aspect of all this: Greek philosophy. That too originated in Ionia, at about the end of the seventh century B.C., and from there was transplanted to 'Graeca Magna' (Lower Italy); but it was only later on that in the motherland of Greece it reached a maturity hitherto undreamt of. The 'freshness, acumen and ingenuous confidence' which Zeller discovered in Greek philosophy first appear in the Ionian philosophers. Boldly indifferent to the most sacred traditions, they reflected on fundamental questions concerning the relationship between man and the world, and of man with himself, endeavouring to make the human reason their only court of appeal. Thus from the Milesian thinkers to Plato and Aristotle, Greek philosophy took its own distinctive and peculiar way. 'Whatever Greeks acquire from foreigners,' says one of Plato's disciples, 'is finally turned by them into something nobler.'[8]

This distinctive cultural genius grew, flourished and decayed. Gilbert Murray has pronounced that despite its great achievements the Olympian religion proved ultimately a failure.[9] The old rites were purged, morally, and refined; but this in itself contributed to a process of moral degradation, in that the behaviour of sacral powers, lying wholly outside the moral sphere, was now ascribed to anthropomorphous gods. Through its intellectual failure to rise to a strict monotheism the religion of Olympus finally tottered into the confusion of later antiquity which identified every new god with some facet or other of the old ones, or else took refuge in unbridled mysticism. And in the end, even the attempt to make Olympianism a religion of the *polis* was also doomed to failure.

The real religion of the fifth century B.C. was a devotion to the city herself, in her personal yet eternal aspect. This idolization of the *polis*, cold-shouldered but not conquered by Olympian religion, set Greek society on the road which led to disintegration and eventually to fusion with oriental cultures and religions in the great melting-pot of Hellenism. Within this setting Greek philosophy—dominated during the first half of the third century B.C. by the Stoa—developed into a cosmopolitan wisdom in which ancient Olympian religion was sublimated. Thus a breach was made for the influx of oriental mysticism and occultism. It was these which, elevating Greek philosophy into neo-Platonic mysticism, finally reduced it to the forms of a polytheistic syncretism.

The contrast between Hellene and barbarian evolved in a way which reflects the same development. Already at the outset of the seventh century B.C. Hesiod is found using the term 'Panhellenes' to express a nationalistic sentiment of long standing.[10] According to him the Hellenes were set apart by their language and by their culture, based upon and moulded by it: also by their political organization in the *polis*, their attention to physical fitness, and above all by their *paideia*, their 'conditioning' in rhetoric, philosophy and the things of the spirit. So it was that in the classical period Athens established her position as *the polis*, at the very centre of the whole *oikoumenē*. The Hippocratian school declared that the temperate zone was bound to be the most favourable to the development of the human race. They conferred on their own Hellenic culture the status of an absolute norm; between Hellenes and barbarians therefore there existed a perpetual state of war.[11] Along with criminals, the barbarians were excluded from the mysteries. Aristotle put them on the same level with the animals.[12] In contrast to the ideal type of the Hellene, the barbarian was depicted as embodying all the vices: as uncivilized, stupid, evilly disposed, lawless, servile, cowardly, miserly, cruel, deceitful and gluttonous. This ideology came to a head in the war against the Persians in the fifth century B.C., when the latter became, as it were, a prototype of the barbarian.

The same century, however, witnessed the growth of a more objective point of view. Herodotus makes a study of oriental countries, familiarizes himself with the wisdom of Persian scholars, learns to respect the ordered structure of the state, the art and the science he found to be flourishing there. He sees oriental influences at work on Hellas and here and there even admits the meritoriousness of the oriental civilizations—a failing which was later to earn him a rebuke from Plutarch, who calls him *philobarbaros*, a lover of barbarians. The broadening of his horizon forced Herodotus to understand the notion of 'barbarian' in a relative sense. He discovered that the Egyptians too called all non-Egyptian speaking peoples 'barbarians', and he concluded that every nation has its own *nomos* or traditional way of ordering things—an opinion exploited in the Sophistics of a later time. Yet for him the gulf is not bridged; it is there by virtue of blood-relationship, language, shared *mores* and shared divinities. Indeed his whole way of writing history is based on the contrast with the barbarians. It was Thucydides who first broke through the 'horizontal' contrast and substituted the idea of a 'cultural lag'. Barbarians were simply people at a lower stage of development. In many respects the Greeks of prehistory resembled the barbarians of the present day; and there were still Greek tribes even now who carried on like barbarians. Thucydides in fact introduced the idea of evolution and supported it with the climatological theory of the Hippocratian medical school, whereby a geographical contrast takes the place of a racial one.

Sophistics drew from these relativizing ideas the conclusion that all men are alike by nature. The doctrine of natural law makes its *début*. 'God has created all men free; none has the nature of a slave.' The like physical constitution of all human beings is testimony to this; and thus *physis* stands over against *nomos* (tradition or custom). This cosmopolitan attitude, however, was confined to a small group of Sophists; and the feeling of national superiority continued undisturbed and was further strengthened by the tragic drama itself. In one of Aeschylus' tragedies Queen Atossa sees her son, the Persian king,

Xerxes, in an allegorical dream, standing in his chariot with two women straining at the bit. The Persian woman submits willingly to her reins, but the Greek woman smashes the cross-beam, thus hurling the king out of the vehicle. Even Euripides was obsessed by this contrast: 'It befits Hellenes to rule over barbarians, not vice versa; for the latter are slaves, the former free men.'

Ideas of this sort were rife among the classical philosophers. Plato's Utopia is a Greek state, hostile towards the barbarians. Aristotle is more conservative still. He sees men as being created unequal; there is a difference of 'degree' between the free man and the slave like that between male and female, soul and body, human kind and the animals. Nevertheless, his scientific approach forced him into an illogical position. He admits differences between the peoples which are determined by geographical factors; and although they are barbarians, he calls the northern peoples—such as the Thracians and Scythians—'free', whilst on the other hand among the Asian peoples whom he called 'servile' there were in fact Greeks.

The great change came first of all with the arrival of Alexander the Great and of Hellenism, which was its outcome. Being of semi-barbarian (Macedonian) origin he was able to pass for a Greek only because of his education at the hands of Aristotle. His mentor counselled him to be a leader to the Hellenes, but towards the barbarians a despot. Alexander proceeded to govern in a manner completely contrary to that classical Greek advice, and within the *oikoumenē* which he had conquered purposely implemented a policy of racial fusion. The ethnical contrast between Hellenes and barbarians was pushed into the background, and the ideal of *paideia*, the education of all men in conformity with the Greek norms, took its place. In the religious sphere Alexander prepared a way for the development of Hellenistic syncretism by having himself included among the Greek gods of the state, after having first been raised to the dignity of son of Zeus—Ammon in Egypt. This turn of events even led the Cynic philosophers to glorify a barbarian uncouthness as true *physis*, in contrast to the artificial *nomos* of humane traditions and institutions. Not unconnected with this was the idealization of the barbarian, the idea—already present in Homer—of the moral rectitude and bliss of peoples 'in the state of nature', for already of old Paradise lost had been looked for in that quarter. In proportion as the *oikoumenē* expanded, so the edge of the civilized world was pushed ever farther and farther afield.

Whereas in Homer the frontiers were formed by the Scythians in the north and the Ethiopians in the south, we find their place taken at a later date by the Hyperboreans and Antipodeans respectively; to the east it was the Indians and then the Chinese. Xenophon transferred the politico-educational ideal to Persia. Thus mythological phantasy, ethnographical studies and philosophical speculation combined to bring about a total change of view regarding barbarians. It was to the oriental barbarians that Greek philosophy turned in its search for the sources of wisdom. Following in the steps of Jewish authors, later schools of philosophy, such as the neo-Pythagoreans and neo-Platonists, tried to refer the entire culture of other peoples to a Jewish source; and their example was copied by various Christian apologists.

On one side therefore the development of Hellenic civilization resulted in the spread of Hellenic—that is to say 'Western'—manners, religion and thought into the Orient, a process enormously facilitated by the increasing dissemination of the Greek language itself. On the other side it was a case of the oriental cults and religions flowing in and thereby setting in motion the 'orientalizing' of the West.

3. ROME AND HELLAS

It was Rome which introduced a new element into the process by which contrasting traditions were being fused together in cosmopolitan fashion, and provided a counter-movement against the orientalizing trends. This movement proved to be one of the chief factors in accentuating the contrast between 'Occident' and 'Orient'. The Roman Republic emerged in an outer region of Hellenic civilization and rose to importance as a semi-barbarian state; but unlike Macedonia after the time of Alexander, Rome was neither absorbed by Hellenistic orientalism nor infused with it. Even when the expanding Roman Empire itself developed a cosmopolitan civilization, a structural difference persisted between Rome on the one side and the East Mediterranean lands on the other. The point of reference at first was Hellenic culture and the difference at that time showed itself in a cultural backwardness; but it developed more and more obviously into a sharp divergence. One motive in Julius Caesar's Gaulish expedition was the desire to provide some counterpoise to Pompey's conquests in the oriental countries to the east of the Mediterranean basin. The victory won by his successor, Augustus, at the battle of Actium (31 B.C.) against the Alexandrian monarchy of Antony was seen as a repetition of the victory of Hellas over the Persians, four and a half centuries before. Augustus' victory meant a fresh period of expansion for Hellenic culture in the Orient, whereas in central and western Europe Caesar's work proved fully effective.

However, the Roman Empire was unable to prevent the steady increase of oriental influences. Having itself arisen out of a confederacy of city states which were carrying on the Hellenic tradition in a latinized form, the empire in its oriental dominions succumbed entirely in the end to the heritage of the great Hellenistic monarchs, who in turn kept alive the traditions of Persia, Babylonia and the ancient Near East. In Egypt the Roman emperors simply stepped into the shoes of the Ptolemies and the Pharaohs. Rostovtzeff maintains that the absolute state socialism of the Egyptian economy was the exact opposite of the structure of Greek economic life.[13] These political, social and economic traditions of the Orient slowly but surely prevailed over the western part of the empire and transformed the imperial rule into a pure military dictatorship in republican guise. Christopher Dawson sees in the social and economic history of the later centuries of the empire the history of the Egypto-Hellenistic system, in its principal features, only being applied in the other provinces as well. The empire of Diocletian and Constantine the Great was a semi-oriental state, having more in common with the Persian monarchies than with the Roman Republic.[14]

We must bear in mind, however, that these oriental traditions in the western part of the Roman Empire never succeeded in getting a really firm foothold; this was true not only of the politico-theocratic ideology, but also of the literature and its development. During the first two centuries under the empire the Latin language continued to carry the onus of a general revival of the classical tradition through the Greek world as a whole. Rome would appear to have been the centre of a counter-movement, within the empire, which carried on —albeit with certain limitations—the struggle of classical Hellenic culture against oriental 'barbarism'.

The growth of an Hellenic consciousness among the Romans is yet another indication of this. The Romans fairly soon forgot about their barbaric origin. The term 'Hellene', which at one time had signified a racial distinction, by now had reference to a cultural norm; and the Stoic philosophy in consequence explained the contrast with barbarism as the difference between *humanitas* and *inhumanitas*—

humanitas being measured in terms of ideals which were latinized, no doubt, but were still essentially Greek. As against an orientalized Greece, Rome intended to champion and protect the original traditions of Hellas.

4. WESTERN AND EASTERN CHRISTIANITY

The course of the Church's history during the first four centuries was tied very closely to the political evolution of the Roman Empire. In the fourth century A.D., as a result of the 'orientalizing' process, the gravitational centre of the empire shifted to the Hellenistic Orient. After the empire had been reorganized under Diocletian, the emperors no longer resided in Rome; and the founding of Constantinople in A.D. 330 contributed more than anything else to the speedy decline in importance of the old capital. The beginning for the Church of the 'Constantinian era' was connected directly with that event, in that the acceptance of Christianity as the state religion coincided with the removal of the imperial centre to the Orient. From the third century onwards Rome and the Church of Rome were gradually latinized, and that threatened to estrange them from the eastern part of the empire. From the time of Constantine the imperial palace at Constantinople was the focus of ecclesiastical unity much more than the Apostolic Chair of Rome. Constantine's successor paved the way for the Caesaropapism of a later time when he made the Church of the Eastern Provinces a state church, answerable to the imperial government.

The Byzantine Empire is not to be regarded as simply the continuation of the East Roman Empire after the decline of Rome.[15] In the sixth century the Emperor Justinian made a tremendous effort to restore the empire to its ancient frontiers; but first the Arab invasions and then the loss of large parts of Italy to the Lombards threw back Byzantium for good and all on to Asia Minor and the Balkans; and when the Syrian and Macedonian emperors undertook a reconsolidation it was on this narrower front. Byzantium and its civilization are therefore not to be measured by the yardstick of classical Greece or Rome. It is rather to be seen as part of the oriental world, a parallel perhaps to the Sassanian monarchy of Persia and the Caliphates of Damascus and Baghdad.

Many people even today continue to regard Byzantine history as an extension, in a decadent form, of that of the Roman

Empire. In fact, Byzantium very early and quickly became an oriental monarchy.[16]

As early as the third century the Emperor Aurelian, on returning from his Syrian expedition, had introduced the oriental ideal of a sacral monarchy in the guise of a solar monotheism, and this prepared the way for Constantine's conversion to Christianity. All this found its fulfilment in Byzantium, under the powerful influence of the Zoroastrian kingdom which the Sassanian monarchs had maintained in Persia from the third century.

Yet this strong oriental influence was not the only factor. Admittedly the bureaucratic system did continue the traditions of Persia and Egypt, yet it sprang from the civil service of the Roman Republic and from the organization of the Hellenistic monarchies. Beneath the trappings of Caesaropapism there lay hidden an ancient Roman Caesarism, depending upon the acclamation of the army and the people. It is to Byzantium that Western Europe owes the preservation and perfecting of Roman law. Whenever Byzantine civilization enjoyed a period of renaissance, there was a revival of classical learning too. Its study of mathematics inspired the pursuit of knowledge within Islamic civilization and thereby also the rise of science in the Europe of the Middle Ages.

Ever since the eighth century—by which time Byzantium had become an overwhelmingly Asiatic state—there had persisted a conflict between the oriental and Hellenistic elements, which came to the surface in the controversy over images between iconoclasts and iconodules. Whatever part was played in this struggle by an aversion to the growing power of the monasteries and the advances of idolatry, it was also an oriental hostility towards Hellenic culture that impelled the emperor and the army of the eastern provinces to give their support to the iconoclasts. The victory of the iconodules therefore issued in a general revival of Hellenic culture.

Byzantium then in some sense forms a bridge with the Orient, and that is certainly true of her distinctive achievement in the arts. In that field Byzantium developed a style peculiarly her own, fusing together into an organic unity elements of both East and West. The tension with the Western Church was bound, however, in the long run to reach a breaking-point. What in particular lay behind the disputes over dogma was the struggle of the Western Church for ecclesiastical self-government. This and the quarrels about images caused a breach made irreparable by the papal action in turning for support to the youthful Carolongian Empire. The decline of the West Roman Empire conferred on the Church of Rome a freedom of manoeuvre to which the Byzantine Church could not aspire. Although Byzantium outlived the Western Empire by a thousand years, the Church of Rome set about its missionary task among the barbarians of western Europe and made over the imperial crown to the barbarian king, Charlemagne. Byzantium on the other hand, determined to impose its theocratic imperialism upon the Slavs by force, slowly but surely spent its strength in an unending war which indeed brought victory, in a military sense, but at the same time spelt defeat in the spheres of culture and religion. Because of her theocratic imperialism Byzantium failed to impart her culture to the barbarian peoples of eastern Europe whom Orthodox Christianity had counted within its fold. The Slav peoples acquired only the artistic and religious elements of Byzantine culture, whilst the classical aspects of the tradition remained confined to court circles within the capital. The extreme spirituality or other-worldliness of the monks could in no way offer to defend the Church against domination by the state; it had no part or interest in the cultural and social activities or the work of reform which had their centre in the monasteries of western Europe.

Besides the various internal causes, powerful external factors helped to bring down the Byzantine Empire. The fourth crusade (A.D. 1202), which was directed against Byzantium, deprived her for half a century of her emperor and irreparably damaged the prestige of the empire. Above all, it was exposed to continuous pressure from the Muslim armies, under which it eventually collapsed. Nevertheless, because it lasted for a thousand years, the Byzantine Empire has been of enormous importance in the development of Western civilization; for it confronted this twin brother with a culture over against which it could recognize its own distinctively 'Western' trend and character.

5. THE REACTION OF THE ORIENTAL CHURCHES AND THE SPREAD OF
CHRISTIANITY IN THE EAST

Hellenistic civilization always encountered resistance in the eastern provinces. Within the bosom of Christianity itself the resulting tensions led to the separation of the oriental Churches from Rome and Constantinople. For a considerable time, the chief centre for the growing self-consciousness of 'Syriac-speaking' Christianity was

Edessa, a town east of the Euphrates, on the dividing-line between the Roman and Persian Empires.[17] Long before the conversion of the Roman Empire, in fact by the beginning of the third century A.D., Osroene—with its capital at Edessa—had become a Christian state; and from there Christianity spread eastwards to Persia and northwards into Armenia. In Syrian literature there was expressed an intense national pride which went so far as to claim for Edessa the status of God's 'elect', in the place of the Jewish people, who had rejected Christ. Another centre of national self-consciousness was Egypt. In Alexandria Christianity was predominantly Greek; but as early as the third century it was making its way among the indigenous population, which had remained untouched by Hellenic civilization, and there the Greek language was gradually ousted by the Coptic. The Church took over from the ancient state religion and became the instrument of an Egyptian nationalism which found its rallying-point in the unconditional authority of the Patriarch of Alexandria. At the time of the Arian controversy in the first half of the fourth century, there was as yet no question of any separatist tendency, so far as Egyptian Christianity was concerned. Athanasius, the Alexandrian Patriarch, did not set himself to champion any specifically Egyptian interest, but with the unreserved support of Rome defended the doctrinal integrity and freedom of the Church against the imperial policy of Constantinople, which was backed by the bishops and leading theologians of the East. However, towards the end of the fourth century, these doctrinal dissensions became increasingly a trial of strength between the Patriarchates; the weakening of the Empire after the death of Theodosius the Great (A.D. 395) contributed not a little to this. In the condemnation of Origen's ideas by the Patriarch of Alexandria, under concerted pressure from the Egyptian monks (A.D. 399), one can see already at work the tendency to drive out those Hellenistic influences which had been so strong among the School of Catechists.

The conflict between Alexandria and Constantinople came to a head in the Christological disputes during the first half of the fifth century. In the West, the year of the Council of Chalcedon (A.D. 451) saw the decisive battle in which an alliance of Catholic Romans and Arian Germans overthrew the pagan Mongols under Attila. Four years later Rome was plundered by the Vandals. Through all these menacing events the prestige of the Pope of Rome increased out of measure. In the doctrinal struggle he stood firm for the integrity of dogma, not merely, as in the past, against the purely opportunist *Reichseinheitspolitik* of the imperial court in Constantinople, but this time also against Alexandria, and in particular against the excesses of Alexandrian theology, violently enforced by the solid mass of Egyptian monks at the 'Robber Council' of 449. In the struggle for power, aspects of Alexandrian theology which were quite justifiable in themselves were converted into a national ideology of 'Monophysitism'; and this in turn became the slogan of a long-standing hostility towards all things Hellenistic and the impact which they made. The conflict with Rome was fundamentally doctrinal in character; it certainly revealed an opposition between 'western' and 'eastern' theology—it was the former that emphasized the full reality of Christ's manhood. On the other hand the battle with Constantinople was fought primarily on the politico-ecclesiastical front. There was no question of any clash of principles at the level of doctrine, because imperial policy was extremely fluid, concerned only with the problem of unity with the western part of the empire, now threatened by the barbarians, and always prepared for any form of compromise with Alexandria likely to be to its own advantage. It was precisely in opposition to this *Reichseinheitspolitik* that the Egyptian Church entrenched herself in her ideological Monophysite position, for it gave her an impregnable doctrinal bulwark against the intrusive Hellenism of the Imperial Church. It was an inevitable effect of Byzantine Caesaropapism that the Hellenized peoples of the Near East should break away into heretical nationalistic movements.

Why was it that the nationalism of the separated oriental Churches had such a slight effect on the future course of Christianity? In a certain sense, of course, one may regard Egypt and Syria as the counterpart of the Germanic peoples of Europe. In both cases these were nations subdued by the Roman *imperium* and incorporated into the empire. Why then did Christianity not take a similar course in West Asia and Africa and in western and northern Europe? The disparity is a profound one; in large measure the reasons for it are to be found in the history of the East Roman Empire and its Church, and the way in which that history diverges from the course taken by church-state relationships in the Western Empire. The dissolution of the empire in the West conferred upon the Church of Rome a freedom tending to obscure the fact that the Germans had been converted by the general threat of domination on the part of a foreign state. Byzantine Caesaropapism, on the other hand, stultified the free development of the Churches in the Near East and drove them, by way of reaction, into a sterile nationalism. All the same, there were in those Churches signs of vitality which held out real prospects of missionary expansion to the south and east. The vitality, however, was drained away and the missionary enterprise overtaken by the rise of the Islamic power, which offered to anti-Byzantine sentiment a far more effective ideology than anything that heretical Christianity was able to provide.

It is of some importance therefore to sketch, in outline at least, the picture presented by Christianity's expansion to the south and east. It came into Abyssinia from Egypt, winning its way to the royal court as early as the first half of the fourth century and it took deep root in that country. From the very start the Orthodox Church of Ethiopia was associated with the Coptic Church; and after the Christian kingdom of Axum had been almost completely isolated by the Islamic subjugation of Arabia, this relationship was the Ethiopian Church's only connection with the rest of Christendom. 'Encompassed on all sides by the enemies of their religion,' wrote Gibbon, 'the Ethiopians slept near a thousand years, forgetful of the world by whom they were forgotten.'[18] During that 'dark age', Christianity became thoroughly assimilated to the environment; it was 'naturalized' by the Agao tribes who adapted it to their own tribal heritage. In the thirteenth century the struggle between the Christian and Muslim kingdoms for political ascendancy stimulated a racial and cultural nationalism which advanced still further the conversion of Abyssinia to the Christian faith. Christianity there owed its survival to this patriotic spirit and to the circumstance that the highland fastnesses of the country were virtually impregnable.

Christianity reached Nubia, probably, in the sixth century. There the Christian kingdoms, whose ecclesiastical connection was with the Coptic Church, held out against Islam for about eight hundred years. According to Trimingham, it was weaknesses within the Christian communities themselves which ultimately accounted for the success of Islam. By far the greater part of the clergy were Egyptians. Christianity, as the state religion, was restricted to the principal towns and larger villages. In fact the mass of the rural population was never converted. Consequently, when the rulers became Muslim, the whole structure collapsed. If that is what happened in that region, it is scarcely surprising that in Arabia the Christian communities brought into existence through the impact of various centres in Mesopotamia, Abyssinia and Persia were slowly eliminated by the victorious advance of Islam.[19]

Great Armenia was the first country of any size in which Christianity became the official religion, probably in order to counterbalance the pressure exerted by Persia and the state religion of that country, Zoroastrianism. The Armenian king had just then freed his land from the Persian yoke, in the second half of the third century A.D. Most of his people, although superficially converted *en masse* and baptized, regarded the Church simply as a prop to their nationalism. From A.D. 363 onwards, when Persia regained control, Christianity was suppressed as being the religion of the Roman enemy. Yet it was the Church itself that sanctioned its isolation by going over to Monophysitism at the beginning of the sixth century A.D. It obstinately entrenched itself in this position and showed no missionary zeal or desire to enlarge its frontiers. With the Georgian Church things were very much the same.

Thus although the spread of Christianity northwards was halted in Armenia and Georgia, there were still plenty of opportunities for it in Asia. Edessa was not only the focal point of Syrian Christian nationalism; it was also a starting-point for penetration into Mesopotamia and the borders of Persia. In spite of this widespread dissemination of the faith, however, the Christian communities were a small minority; and so they remained. The reasons why they failed to emulate the success of the Church within the Roman Empire lie partly, as Latourette suggests,[20] with the religious policy of the Sassanids, who ruled Persia from A.D. 226 and patronized Zoroastrianism. This religion, run by a powerful hierarchy and supported by the monarchy, was able to offer a more united and energetic resistance than any of its Hellenistic competitors. But above all, Christianity had become—since its adoption by Constantine—the official religion of Persia's traditional enemy. Only the formation of a national church organization, which by the beginning of the fifth century A.D. had cut itself off completely from the Roman Empire, served to lighten the heavy load, at the same time saving the Church from a repetition of the harsh and prolonged persecution under which it had suffered during the previous century. To cap this achievement of autonomy, the Mesopotamian-Persian Church went over to Nestorianism. Its motives for so doing were in no way doctrinal, for this Church had taken no hand in the doctrinal controversies of the West. In a far more obvious and direct way than in Egypt and Syria the turning to an heretical faith was in this instance meant to give a doctrinal backing to isolationism and feelings of aversion towards the Byzantine Church. Nestorian Christianity then was the only kind to which the Sassanian monarchy accorded official recognition.

The fact that Christianity remained the religion of a small minority in Persia was of decisive importance, so far as its future in Asia was concerned. It leaned heavily on Syrian culture and was taken along with them by Syriac-speaking peoples; but this gave it nothing like the prestige in Asia that the cultural heritage of Rome possessed for the Germanic races of Northern Europe. 'It is one of the inviting but futile pastimes of the historian to conjecture what might have been the future had the Persian Empire, like the Roman, become Christian,' says Latourette. But it was precisely because of its success in the Roman Empire that Christianity found no access to Persia. The future lay with the great opponent of Christianity. Significantly enough, Latourette adds, on second thought, that the conversion of Persia would probably not have made all that difference since Persian Christianity, like Zoroastrianism, would presumably have been blotted out by Islam.[21]

Anyone who considers the history of missions in Asia will rightly conclude that Persia was of exceptional strategic importance. Christian evangelism had to pay very dearly for its success in the Roman Empire; it meant the Church became heir to that radical antithesis between itself and the Persian Empire, which Greece bequeathed to Rome and to Byzantium; and thereby she spoiled her own chance of entering upon a victorious course in Asia, as she had done in the West. In central Asia to the north of Persia, eastward of the Caspian and west of the Oxus river, Christianity enjoyed a widespread influence for a thousand years or more; and between the ninth and eleventh centuries it had, to all appearances, a splendid chance of becoming the dominant faith throughout those regions. But after the Muslim conquest of Persia, which ousted the Zoroastrian state religion as a religious and political bulwark against Byzantium, central Asia lay open to Islam. A mass conversion to Islam of the

Turks east of the Oxus seems to have taken place in the eleventh century A.D. The dominant position of Islam eventually constrained the Mongols in Persia to embrace that religion at the end of the thirteenth century; for after vacillating for a time between Islam and Christianity, the Il-khans and their successors naturally opted for the religion of the majority of their subjects. Even before that, the Byzantine Empire had been harassed by a wave of Muslim Turks from central Asia, followed later by a fresh wave of Ottoman Turks who were likewise ardent Muslims. Such Christian communities as still remained in central Asia were annihilated in the fantastic slaughter which accompanied the conquests of Timur, or Tamerlane, in the second half of the fourteenth century. He too had chosen Islam.

Any attempt to explain the failure of Christianity to expand in Asia must also, no doubt, take into account various factors within mediaeval Christendom itself. The choice made by the Mongols of Persia in favour of Islam coincided with the final bankruptcy of the Crusades and with a manifest decline of Christianity in Western Europe at about the end of the thirteenth century. European Christianity had first to undergo a regeneration and to realize that Islam had blocked the continental approaches to Asia, before it was able to achieve, in the modern period, an entirely new approach to the Asian peoples, this time not along the land routes but across the oceans.

Yet even if Christianity had been able to set itself up in Persia on a permanent basis—and also among the primitive peoples of central Asia—that would still not have opened any door to India or China. Islam itself, in spite of its established position in central Asia, has made only a very limited impression on China; and although in North India it managed to forge an empire, even that has never constituted a real danger for Hinduism. Granted that Christianity has penetrated into China to some extent, it has none the less remained the religion of an urban and foreign minority there. For a time—but then only during the period of Mongol domination—it did seem to stand some chance of spreading; but the fall of the Mongol Empire definitely put an end to that. In India the Christians never got beyond being a minority group which managed to keep going as a separate caste, using foreign languages—Syriac or Pahlavi—and relying upon its connections with Nestorian Christianity in Mesopotamia and Persia, which were increasingly threatened after the rise of Islam and eventually severed from their base. Here is further testimony that the

Christian triumph in the Roman Empire contributed a good deal to its failure in Asia. In the Middle Ages, any profound encounter between Christianity and the major civilizations of Asia was out of the question. At the time there was a much more critical problem to be resolved: the encounter with Islam.

6. THE CHALLENGE OF ISLAM

(a) The Origin of Islam related to Christianity

Christopher Dawson pronounced on the rise of Islam in a pithy aphorism when he said that Muhammad was the Orient's answer to the challenge of Alexander the Great. This would reduce Islam to a sort of protest movement, with its roots striking back a thousand years before Muhammad into the period which saw the rise and triumph of Hellenism. In this way of describing it there is contained an important truth which could apply just as well to the view that Islam arose as a reaction to Christianity; for we have already established that the victory of Christianity in the Roman Empire was bound up with the fact that it had inherited the deep contrast between Hellenistic civilization and its competitors. One might see, therefore, in the rise of Islam the culmination of a counter-movement directed against the dominating influences of Hellenism.

By the seventh century A.D. Christianity had already found its way into Arabia from various directions. In the land of Saba—the modern Yemen—once the hub of Arabian civilization, it had arrived from Abyssinia and for a time during the preceding century had been the religion of the state, until the country was overrun by the Persians. In the north, Arabia felt the impact of Syrian and Mesopotamian civilization. When Muhammad was making his appearance in Mecca, Syria and Mesopotamia fell under Persian domination; but even before he died, these regions were reconquered by Byzantium and made the object of a policy of compromise on the emperor's part, with the aim of getting the Monophysite Churches back into the Church of the Empire. Arabia was in a typical position for a borderland country, exposed to all kinds of vague and elusive repercussions permeating through from the more advanced Christian civilization. One might compare it with the way in which various Christian ideas filtered through into Scandinavia, during the period when Europe itself was being Christianized.[22] The Indians of North America and the Negroes in Africa found themselves in a similar situation during the early stages of Western missionary impact. At any rate it was a situation that threw Arabian society into a state of ferment and in the sixth century seems to have brought about a progressive change from a matrilineal system to one wholly or largely patrilineal. This change was bound up with the growth of individualism.[23]

It is most instructive to compare the history of the Christianizing process in Abyssinia with the situation of Arabia during the earliest Islamic period. There are several good reasons for making this particular comparison: the links between the kingdom of Axum and South Arabia, the Arabian (Semitic) colonization in Abyssinia, the spread of Judaism in both territories, the initial sympathy of Muhammad for Abyssinian Christianity and the manner in which Christianity was disseminated among the Agao tribes of Abyssinia. This parallel gives us some idea of what might have happened in Arabia had the circumstances not been what they were; and it gives support to the view that in Arabia Islam played, as it were, a substitutionary rôle which in Abyssinia was undertaken by Christianity. Abyssinian Christianity was based in fact on what the independent Agao tribes of the mountain districts had inherited, at one remove, from the Monophysite Church of Syria via the Christianized kingdom of Axum. This derivative tradition became fused with a mixture of pagan and Judaic tribal mythology. It gave rise to a thoroughly indigenized cult, literature and ecclesiastical organization, which conserved many ancient practices such as polygamy and the 'trial marriage' custom. There was a close bond between the Church and the divinely ordained monarchy.[24]

Axumite Christianity had a direct part to play in the early years of Muhammad's career. When his followers were being persecuted in Mecca by Quraish, the prophet bethought himself of seeking asylum in Abyssinia which had sent such effective help to the persecuted Christian Arabs of Yemen. In the fifth year of his Call (A.D. 615) refugees began to cross the straits in small parties. This event is referred to by Muslim writers as the first *Hijrah*, or 'flight'. The story goes[25] that the Ethiopian king asked the refugees: 'What is this religion for which you have abandoned your people and yet have neither adopted mine nor any other known religion?'; whereupon their leader explained that they were:

> . . . a barbarous nation, worshipping idols, eating carrion, committing shameful deeds, killing our blood-relations, forgetting

our duty towards our neighbours, the strong among us devouring the weak. Such was our state until God sent us an apostle, from amongst ourselves, with whose lineage, integrity, trustworthiness and purity of life we were acquainted. He summoned us to God, to believe in His unity, to worship Him and abandon the stones and idols . . . He commanded us to speak the truth, to be faithful in our trusts, to observe our duties to our kinsfolk and neighbours, to refrain from forbidden things and bloodshed, . . . from consuming the property of orphans and from slandering virtuous women. He ordered us to worship God and associate no other with Him, to offer prayer, give alms and fast . . . So we trusted in his word and followed the teachings he brought us from God. . . . Wherefore our countrymen turned against us and persecuted us to try and seduce us from our faith, that we might abandon the worship of God and return to the worship of idols.

The leader also quoted appropriate texts from the Qur'an, which made it appear that Islam was a form of Christianity, and after hearing his defence the king gave protection to the refugees. Some of them became Christians and therefore the first converts from Islam to Christianity. Sir William Muir remarked, in connection with this story, that:

> If an Arab asylum had not at last offered itself at Medina, the Prophet might haply himself have emigrated to Abyssinia, and Mohammadanism have dwindled, like Montanism, into an ephemeral Christian heresy.[26]

This last comment seems rather wide of the mark; for the strictures upon Christianity which one finds in the Qur'an would seem to be aimed at precisely that form of it which, in Muhammad's day, flourished in the Axumite kingdom. The story is instructive in that it reflects the moral revolution in the pagan way of life, brought about by Islam. In that initial period the affinity with Christianity was still felt to be so close that the conversion of a number of refugees did in fact take place.

To a certain extent Islam does seem to have filled a vacuum in Arabia, created between them by, on the one hand, a paganism plunged into a social crisis and already crumbling at the roots and, on the other, a Christianity which had up to that time made no convincing appeal to the tribes of central Arabia, because its impact remained confusing and uncertain. It is possible that Muhammad's monotheistic message found a point of contact in the vague notion of a 'high god'—the deposit of Jewish-Christian ideas which had already wormed their way into the tribal polytheism.

The truth is that when Islam was still in the initial stages of its development there was nothing likely to prevent the new movement from being accepted as a peculiar version of Arabian Christianity. In fact the Christianity of some of the Abyssinian tribes, when once they had adapted it to their ancient traditions, differed much more drastically in many respects from what we understand by Christianity than did Islam. But more cogent still is the argument from Muhammad's own conviction that he was in the direct line of the Jewish-Christian prophets and books of revelation. The one difference between him and the earlier apostles (rusul) was that he was an Arab, sent to a people who had never before received an apostolic visitation, in order that they too might hear the time-honoured message.

In itself there was nothing strange about this idea and it bears out an ancient tradition according to which the Twelve Apostles parcelled out the known world between them. Parthia was assigned to Thomas; to Bartholomew, part of India; to Matthew, Ethiopia; to Philip, Asia Minor; to Mark and Barnabas, Alexandria—and so forth.[27] Quite possibly, by 'India' in this tradition is meant Southern Arabia. However, in the tradition of Arabian Christianity there is no person playing a significant rôle comparable in importance with that of Frumentius vis-à-vis the Abyssinian Church, or having the missionary pre-eminence which the traditions of the Russian Church, the Syrian Church in India and the Coptic Church ascribe respectively to Andrew, Thomas and Mark. Thus the spread of Christianity in Arabia cannot be said to have thrown up any remarkable personality on its own ground; and there never has been in central Arabia any question of a calculated missionary enterprise. It was in this vacuum that Muhammad emerged as the Apostle to the Arabs.

Muhammad himself neatly characterized the rôle allotted him by the divine call, when he gave himself the title: al-nabî al-ummî (S. VII: 156/8). As nabî, prophet, he ranged himself in the succession of the prophets of the ahl al-kitâb (Jews and Christians) whose task it was to deliver the revelation in written form.[28] The term ummî can be interpreted in a variety of senses. The version most in keeping with the contexts in which the term occurs is: 'the prophet who is risen up among the Gentiles'.[29] If that is so, then the term is taken from the Hebrew ummoth ha-'olam: that is, 'the nations of the world.' By this expression the Jews designated the Gentiles, thereby acknowledging that even out of the 'nations' prophets had come forth, as for example Balaam and Job. This Jewish expression turns up in the Qur'an in the form *al-ummíyûn* (S. LXII:2; III:19, 69), which is the counterpart of the *ahl al-kitâb* (People of the Book) (S. III:19). When one finds *ummíyûn min ahl al-kitâb*—literally: 'Gentiles among the people of the Book' (S. II:73)—this must be taken to mean Arabs, originally pagan, but now converted to Judaism: i.e. proselytes.[30] The probability of the term *ummí* being in fact borrowed from Hebrew spoken idiom is strengthened by the fact that it occurs first in Medinan verses—first, that is, during the period when Muhammad was in frequent contact with Jewish communities. The context is always some passage of polemic aimed at the Jews; and on one occasion the Jews are made to employ the term to signify the pagan Arabs (S. III:69).

As *al-nabî al-ummî* Muhammad had a double function. As an Arabian prophet, arisen from among the Gentiles, he was called to be an Apostle of God to the Gentiles (S. LXII:2): in this respect his authority was that of the Taurât (Torah)[31] and Injîl (The Gospel) (S. VII:156). But that involved his second function as the one sent as an Apostle also to the People of the Book. 'Say to those who have received the Book, and to the Gentiles, Do ye surrender to God? If they become Muslims, then are they guided aright; but if they turn away—thy duty is only preaching,' (S. III:19).

This twofold function reminds one of the apostleship of Paul, who as Apostle to the Gentiles preaches the Gospel 'to the Jew first and also to the Greek' (Rom. 1:16). By the same token that he proclaims himself Apostle to the Gentiles Muhammad lays a sharp accusation at the door of the Jews who, though professing to be the friends of God, will not bear the burden of the Taurât, which was laid upon them; but they behave like an ass beneath a load of books (S. LXII:2, 5 ff.). This accusation constitutes a remarkable parallel to Paul's (Rom. 2:17–24; 3:29 ff.).

From about the middle of the third century *anno Hegiae* Muslim apologists began to collect proof-texts for Muhammad's apostleship from the Old Testament, chiefly such as had to do with the promise to Ishmael and his descendants. The New Testament proof-texts were above all concerned with the promise of the 'Counselor' (Jn. 16:7). Lay the New Testament promise upon that of the Old, and you get some idea of Muhammad's function. Thus the term *al-nabi al-ummi* signifies both the Arab prophet raised up to the Arabs and the prophet to the Gentiles from among the Gentiles. Arab particularism and Muslim universalism are both implied in the term.

This means that Muhammad is a counterpart of Paul. In the New Testament the Greeks have a double function: as opposed to the Jews they are a paradigm of the Gentiles; but they are also, vis-à-vis the barbarians, the representatives of Hellenic civilization. Although the Greek word *ethnē* does of course signify 'Gentiles' in the New Testament, in classical Greek usage it carries the connotation of 'barbarians'. In his evangelistic mission Paul accepted the challenge, as it were, on a double front, knowing himself to be under an obligation to both Greeks and barbarians, to preach the Gospel to the Jew first and also to the Greek. Now just as Paul was an 'apostle to the Greeks', so Muhammad is an apostle to the Arabs. In that rôle he reacted against the one-sided addiction of Christianity to the Hellenistic *oikoumenē* and the conversion of the Roman Empire. Against the Hellenistic *oikoumenē*, the extension on a world scale of the *polis* of the Greeks, there rose up Islam, the equally universal extension of the Arab *ummah*.

However, from the standpoint of Hellenistic civilization, the semi-nomadic Arabs are nothing more than 'barbarians', and this implication is present in the term *ummi*. Just as the Greek *ethnē* originally meant 'barbarians', so something of the same depreciative sense clings to the word *ummi*, implying 'under-developed, ignorant, uncouth'. Muslim tradition has frankly preferred this interpretation, since it provides evidence for the divine origin of the Qur'an which came from the mouth of an 'illiterate prophet'. Quite apart from any doctrinal interest, there are very good grounds for the rendering 'illiterate' here;[32] for Muhammad regarded those who possessed *Taurât* and *Injíl*—Holy Books written in languages beyond his compass— as representatives, certainly, of a much higher stage of civilization, in comparison with which the Arab was indeed illiterate. Somewhere between the senses of 'pagan' and 'uncivilized' stands the interpretation which would relate *ummi* to the Hebrew 'am ha-'areṣ, the people of the land, 'the people who know not the Law' and are therefore half heathen, half barbarian.[33] Muhammad then is 'the leader of the masses against privileged minorities of wealth and sophistication',[34] champion of the native Arab proletariat, and destined to become the leader also of the half native, half foreign Syrian proletariat within the Byzantine Empire.

Within the context of this range of meanings the term 'Gentile' stands over against not only the Jew but the Christian too. 'Gentile' in the New Testament is invariably opposed to 'Jew', so that Paul often addresses the Christians as 'Gentiles'; but where 'Gentile' stands in contrast with the Church, the latter is being thought of as the New Israel, the people of the New Covenant. Still, in so far as 'Christianity' sprang from and merged itself with Hellenic civilization, the evangelization of the Gentiles was at the same time a process of disseminating this Christianized Hellenism among the barbarian peoples. It was against this dual aspiration that Muhammad reacted, in his rôle as *al-nabî al-ummî*. Over against Hellenistic Christianity he set an Arabian version, no less universalistic, but on an opposed footing. Whereas the Holy Spirit had led Paul to Greece and Rome and Spain, he was the Apostle who was to start out on a universal mission from Arabia.

The combination of Arab particularism and universalism can be taken to illustrate yet another aspect of the expression *al-nabî al-ummî*. Just as the word *ummî* corresponds to the Hebrew plural *ummôt* (that is, 'nations', 'Gentiles'), so the noun *'ummah'* (meaning the Muslim 'people' or 'congregation') belongs with the Hebrew singular *ummah* (Aramaic: *'ummetha*). Muhammad is the prophet of the chosen and victorious 'congregation', 'the best people that has been raised up unto mankind' (S. III:106). This process of remoulding the Arab community into a universal congregation can be understood only when one takes account of the relationship between Islam and Judaism.

(b) The Origin of Islam related to Judaism

In the parts which they had to play Paul and Muhammad also had in common the fact that both were directly confronted with the Jews, and furthermore the activity of both had been prepared for to a certain extent by that same Judaism, which had penetrated into both the Graeco-Roman world and the Arabian peninsula. Through Christianity Israel had stepped outside its own boundaries and had arrived among the Greeks. In the same way one might describe Islam as the form which Judaism took when, stepping outside itself once more, it broke into the Arab world.

The parallel breaks down, of course, and at that on two points of fundamental importance. Christianity did not, like Islam, spring into existence in the heathen world, but arose out of the Gospel of Jesus, the Messiah of Israel. Paul and all the disciples were Jews, whereas Muhammad was a Gentile. Whilst in the Hellenistic world Judaism merely paved the way for the Gospel to spread, Islam itself was a result of Judaism's penetration into the Arab world; and in the Hellenistic world no real parallel to Islam can be said to exist. A second difference is that, strictly speaking, Christianity did not derive from Judaism, but from Israel, whereas behind the rise of Islam there lay an 'Arabicized' Judaism that had already undergone a lengthy Talmudic development.

Although in the New Testament itself there is no opposition between Jewish and pagan converts to Christianity, seeing that the dividing wall between Jew and Gentile has been broken down (Eph. 2:11 ff.), nevertheless there were in the early Church strong tensions which at times led to passionate argument and strife. The question whether circumcision was necessary was never settled in the early Church. The decree of the so-called council of the Apostles (Acts 15) was indeed the salvation of the mission to the Gentiles as well as of that to the Jews. It was ordained that of 'those of the Gentiles who turn to God' nothing more should be required than to keep the so-called 'Noachian commandments'; yet this tallied very closely with the conditions which the rules of the Jewish synagogue imposed on the uncircumcised who wanted to become converts to Judaism (Acts 15:19 ff., 29). For that reason, the 'believers who belonged to the party of the Pharisees' could do no other than resign themselves to this compromise. For all that, Paul's victory at the council of the Apostles was more apparent than real. The counter-mission of extremist Judaizers in Paul's territory still went on, while James and Peter continued to waver in their attitude over various matters, for fear of the circumcision party (Gal. 2:12). They were afraid that if they sat down to eat with the uncircumcised, it might prejudice the mission to the Jews with which Peter had been expressly charged (Gal. 2:8).

The compromise decided upon by the council of the Apostles did nothing to remove the sharp antagonism between the mission to the Gentiles on the one hand and the aims of the circumcision party on the other. An unbridgeable gulf separated these two points of view;

and between them, as between the Gospel and the 'perverted gospel' (Gal. 1:6), Jewish Christianity remained in a state of suspense. With the collapse of the Jews as a nation, Jewish Christianity also went to rack and ruin. The uprising in A.D. 67–70 presented the Jewish Christians with the impossible choice between declaring their solidarity with Jewish nationalism or becoming a 'fifth column'. The only possibility was to emigrate to East Jordan. After the fall of Jerusalem they lost all contact with non-Jewish Christians in the Graeco-Roman world; and at about A.D. 100 the Jews pronounced an anathema upon them. Thus they slowly disintegrated or were absorbed by Gentile Christianity. Of course Jewish Christian influences remained at work, finding their way into the various currents of Gnosticism. Some of these filtered through into Arabia, where they perhaps played a part in forming the traditional legends concerning ʿĪsā (Jesus), which one comes across in the Qur'an.[35]

Through this turn of events the fundamental significance of Jewish Christianity was completely obscured. I am not now referring to the extreme importance of the Jewish Christians as witnessing to the fact that the Gospel 'is to the Jew first'. What concerns us here is the missionary rôle which Jewish Christianity could have discharged by way of complement to the evangelization of the Gentiles. In the resistance which the people of Israel, as a nation, put up against Roman imperialism, circumcision was treated as a kind of test case. Imperial decrees dealt with it as a perversion on a par with castration, to be punished therefore as a capital crime; whereas for the Jews it was the visible token of their election, for which they were ready to suffer martyrdom. The monotheism and ethics of the Jews had a magnetic attraction for the Hellenistic world, which turned thousands into 'worshippers of God'; yet the number of proselytes remained very small, because for the Hellenistic non-Jew circumcision was a well-nigh insuperable barrier. It was precisely on that score that Jewish Christianity might have become such a powerful recruiting force among peoples who had long been accustomed to the use of circumcision. These included—in historical times at any rate—more especially the Semito-Hamitic peoples, the Malays and the Polynesians.[36] The people of Israel realized at the time that the circumcision was something they shared with many others (cf. Jer. 9:25; Josh. 5:9; Ezek. 3:18; 32:19 ff.; Gen. 17:23 ff.). Certainly, the entry of Judaism into countries such as Ethiopia, Egypt and Arabia was facilitated by the circumstance that the would-be proselyte in those places found circumcision no problem. The two oriental peoples for whom Christianity became part of their national heritage—the Copts and the Ethiopians—had long been familiar with the custom.

Thus there could have been, for Jewish Christianity, an opportunity for missionary expansion among the circumcised, which would have counterbalanced the non-Jewish apostolate towards 'the uncircumcision'. As happened with Israel itself, a primitive tabu-cum-initiation rite might have become for these peoples a sign of the Covenant, and the Covenant with Israel, on the other hand, have become a Covenant embracing every nation. As a counterpoise to Pauline theology both Old and New Testaments could certainly offer points relevant to this view. From the demand for a 'circumcision of the heart' Jeremiah had not yet drawn the ultimate conclusion that the circumcision of the flesh was now pointless (Jer. 9:25 f.; 31:31 ff.; cf. 1 Cor. 1:31; 2 Cor. 10:17). In the Gospels the chief bone of contention is the commandment concerning the Sabbath day, whilst the circumcision is taken completely for granted (Lk. 2:21; Jn. 7:23 f.).

For a variety of reasons, the compromise reached by the council of the Apostles amounted to nothing more than a face-saving solution. To start with, Palestinian Jewry, whose ruling with regard to the 'worshippers of God' had been taken over, never recognized the 'worshippers' as fully fledged Jews; whereas the Hellenized Jew did not split hairs over the value of becoming an official 'proselyte'.[37] But above all Paul's message was not, like that of Hellenistic Judaism, an ethic made up of spiritualized extracts from the Torah; it proclaimed 'the circumcision of Christ', which had come to replace the 'circumcision of the flesh' (Col. 2:11 f.; Phil. 3:1 ff.; Rom. 10:4; 3:30). The fundamental question raised at the council of the Apostles was this: whether Paul's Gospel was valid for the Jews also. It was never explicitly accepted by the Jerusalem community as being so; and the issue was never fully clarified, since Jewish Christianity was hopelessly outstripped by its Gentile counterpart and pretty well liquidated under persecution. As a result the relations between Gentile and Jewish Christianity were bedevilled by those prevailing between Palestinian and Hellenistic Judaism; and they went awry. The course of history showed just how calamitous this was. Whilst Paul broke the bounds of Judaism and became 'to the Greeks a Greek', no missionary enterprise of equal intensity developed in the other direction. Jewish Christianity could only have survived if it had managed to spread effectively throughout the 'Syrian society'. In that case, an extensive missionary movement might have materialized, bringing the peoples of the 'Syrian' area and of Africa into the Christian fold, and so matching the success of Hellenistic Christianity among the Germanic nations of the north. Such a 'Syrian' Christianity, being the fruits of a Jewish–Christian apostolate, would then have attained a social and religious pattern of its own, clothing with a Christian ethos the traditions of the Torah and itself contributing the ancient native customs and ritual conceptions, just as the Christian pattern of life in the West welded together Gentile-Christian, Graeco-Roman and Germanic traditions and ideas. That missionary expansion, however, did not take place. Jewish Christianity gave no proof of its ability even to set up a spiritual centre of its own, like Rabbinic Judaism in Babylonia and in Palestine.

So it was that Islam came to fill the gap left by the one-sided expansion of Christianity within the Hellenistic world on one hand and the weakness of Jewish Christianity on the other. Islam met the great missionary challenge of the Syrian areas, and its expansion there effectively matched that of Gentile Christianity under Hellenism. The extent to which Islam in this respect exploited the function which Jewish Christianity had neglected is plain from the importance attached to circumcision in the Muslim religion.[38] Muslim traditions acknowledge that circumcision had been a universal or common custom in ancient Arabia.[39] The background to circumcision in both Israel and Arabia is a primitive initiation-rite (*khitân*, the Arabic word for 'circumcision' corresponds with the terms for 'son-in-law' and 'daughter-in-law' and for 'marriage' (cf. Gen. 4:24 ff.) and the Hebrew words for 'son-in-law' and 'father-in-law': *hathan* and *hothen*). The transfer of the custom from ancient Arabia to Islam was taken for granted. It is therefore all the more remarkable that it is nowhere mentioned in the Qur'an. This in itself would suggest that circumcision does not have the same significance in Islam as in Israel, though it came none the less to be of fundamental importance there. According to a Muslim tradition handed down by Bukhârî, the Byzantine emperor Heraclius, a contemporary of Muhammad, read in the stars a portent of 'the king of the circumcised'; whereupon a messenger, sent by the king of the North Arabian state of Ghassân, came in to him with the intelligence that Muhammad was proclaiming

Islam. The envoy, who was himself circumcised, informed the emperor that circumcision was a prevailing custom among the Arabs. It is a tradition which quite explicitly represents Muhammad in the rôle of 'opposite number' to Byzantium, and Islam as the religion for the circumcised, as over against Hellenistic Christianity. Muhammad thereby assumed the historic rôle of the Jewish people.

Although Muslim law (*fiqh*) hedges over circumcision as an obligatory practice, it has in fact become a matter of exceptional importance for the great mass of Muslims. To some extent, the custom has come to be treated as the criterion for membership of the Muslim *ummah*, as well for Muslims as for others. The explanation for this is that the Muslim *ummah* has gathered up into itself an ancient tribal consciousness. In the Indonesian archipelago this association is so strong that the Achehnese of Northern Sumatra, for example, regard the act of circumcision in itself as admitting to membership of the Muslim community; and in Java the verb 'to circumcise' means literally to make into a Muslim (*njelamaké*).[40] Thus the part played by circumcision in Islam is not unlike that of the sacrament of baptism among the Christian peoples of Europe, who have been received, more or less *en masse*, into the Church.

The Jewish communities living in Arabia during the seventh century A.D. belonged to an exotic branch of Judaism. Two of the three Jewish tribes in Medina most likely consisted of Arab proselytes; but the third branch—Qurayzah—which lived, not like the other two by husbandry, but by industry and trade, included, by all accounts, a core of Jews from Palestine itself. In the Qur'an the Medinan Jews are referred to as *Banû Isrâ'îl*—the very term used for the Old Testament People of Israel (S. II:38 ff.; 207). For the rest, the Jews kept themselves distinct from their Arab environment by maintaining a number of their own customs.[41] In all probability Jews had already settled at Jathrib (Medina) prior to A.D. 450, that is, before the revision of the Babylonian Talmud had been concluded. Moreover, since a large majority of the Jewish communities consisted of proselytes, a specifically Arab type of Judaism must have developed in this case, which none the less preserved its own life in distinction from its pagan surroundings. Between themselves, however, the Jewish tribes of Medina preserved very little unity, and in political affairs they behaved much like Arab clans. Economic, political, social and religious considerations governed, at least in part, their relationship with the Arab tribes. They had a very positive influence on their pagan environment. Monotheistic ideas had pushed the local gods right into the background and had helped to bring about a widespread acceptance of Allah as a sort of 'high god'. As the people of a sacred Book they were a civilizing influence, so that the art of reading and writing was fairly widespread in Medina.

It was a mixture of political and religious motives that prompted the Arab inhabitants of Medina to invite Muhammad to join them. Muslim tradition has it that the Medinan Jews entertained strong Messianic expectations. That must certainly have been one factor in the hopes of the Arab population that Muhammad would be able to act as peacemaker between the various tribes with their interminable feuds. Muhammad himself, in so far as his departure from Mecca meant his abandoning his family possessions, was very much inclined to compare the *Hijrah* with the experiences of earlier prophets. 'Verily, we have sent you an Apostle to witness against you, even as we sent an Apostle to Pharaoh: but Pharaoh rebelled against the Apostle, and we therefore laid hold on him with a severe chastisement,' (S. LXXIII:15). He expected that the Jews of Medina above all would hail him as a second Moses.

Before the *Hijrah* itself, and more especially when it seemed likely that he would go to Medina, Muhammad apparently tried to model Islam on the Jewish religion. His supporters in Medina had already brought in the Friday observances, linking them with the Jewish preparation for the Sabbath. After his arrival Muhammad instituted a fast on the Jewish Day of Atonement, the fast of *'Ashûrâ*; and even the Muslim word for a fast, *saum*, is derived from the Hebrew. He took over other Jewish customs too, such as the Monday and Thursday fasts which he personally observed, whilst the Jewish practice of noontide worship was added to the morning and evening worship already much in use at Mecca. Thus in the last Meccan period and for a time after the *Hijrah*, Muhammad tended to develop his religion along the lines of the Jewish cultic observances. His method of adaptation is strikingly illustrated by his concessions regarding the food of the People of the Book and marriage with their women (S. V:5 ff.). The list of forbidden things, given in the aforementioned verses (namely: blood, pork and animals that had died a natural death or had been strangled or sacrificed to idols) has a curious similarity (apart from the mention of pork) to the 'Noachian commandments' agreed upon by the early Christian Church at the council of the Apostles, where the practice of Hellenistic Jewry was taken as a precedent (Acts 15:19 f., 28 f.). These verses of the Qur'an apparently reflect a similar practice.

So far as one can see, the Jewish communities in Arabia recognized only one way for the pagan Arab to embrace Judaism: and that was by becoming a proselyte. Nothing is heard of the possibility—such as Hellenistic Judaism freely allowed—of becoming a 'worshipper of God'. Muhammad's attitude shortly after the *Hijrah* must lead one to suppose that for himself and for the pagan Arabs he saw a way into the fold of Judaism very much like that which had earlier been made for the Greek 'worshippers of God'. In Arabia it was not the necessity for circumcision which constituted the barrier, but rather the total observance of the Jewish Law; and to that extent the issue on which Muhammad parted company with the Jews was analogous to that which divided Hellenistic Judaism from the Judaism of the Pharisees. Muhammad, so to say, confronted the Jews with the same peculiarly personal pretension as Paul had presented to the Pharasaic party of the early congregation in Jerusalem; but whereas at the council of the Apostles there appeared at least to be some basis for an agreement, between Muhammad and the Jews there was from the very outset no common ground. Muhammad's initial expectations, where the Jews were concerned, rested on ignorance and *naïveté*: hence his vehement indignation when he very quickly came to realize that the Jews were sticking to every detail of their prolix system of rabbinical commandments and prohibitions (S. IV:158; VI:147; X:60; XVI:119). The relevant verses of the Qur'an read remarkably like the New Testament. Muhammad argues that God has laid the burden of the commandments concerning food upon the Jews as a punishment for their wickedness (cf. Gal. 3:19). Their restrictions are of their own invention: '. . . Of what God has sent down to you for food, have ye made unlawful and lawful? Say: Has God permitted you? or invent ye on the part of God?' (S. X:59 f.; cf. Acts 10:15; 11:9).

Closely connected with this idea of an agreement based on the Noachian commandments is Muhammad's appeal for reconciliation with Jews and Christians on no other basis than that of a common monotheism: 'Say: O People of the Book, come to a word (which is) fair between us and you, (to wit) that we serve no one but God, that we associate nothing with Him, and that none of us take us

Lords beside God,' (S. III:57). Monotheism and the Noachian commandments were likewise common ground between Palestinian Judaism and Hellenistic 'worshippers of God'. In this connection it is much to the point that in Sura XVI the argument that God has laid down only the Noachian injunctions, and the attack on the Jewish regulations about food, are followed immediately by a pericope concerning Ibrâhîm (Abraham) 'who was a hanif and who was not of those who take other gods beside God' (S. XVI:115–120, 121–124).

Muhammad's ideas about Ibrâhîm form one of the main pillars of what he has to say regarding Judaism. Even in the Meccan verses Ibrâhîm appears in the line of prophets, from among whom he is selected for a special rôle, in that he is called hanif. The word stands in opposition to mushrik (polytheist). In the account of his conversion Ibrâhîm says: 'I turn my face to Him who has created the Heavens and the Earth, as hanif; I am not one of the mushrikin,' (Sura VI:79). A hanif is one who professes the natural monotheistic religion; and it is to this that Muhammad summons us to be converted. 'Then set your face toward the religion as hanif, (to wit) the fitra of God wherein He was created (fatara) man; there is no change in God's creation,' (S. XXX:29). The word fitra means the original, natural knowledge of God. So runs a Muslim tradition: 'Every child is born according to the fitra; it is only the parents who make it a Jew or a Christian or a Magian.'[42] The fitra is the religion of the hanif. Muhammad very probably borrowed the word hanif from current usage, in which it denoted those who, though influenced by Christianity and Judaism, yet held to a simple, universalistic monotheism, without committing themselves to either religion. It seems that the term had previously been used by Jews and Christians to mean either 'pagan' or a follower of the 'partially Hellenized Syro-Arabian religion'.[43]

Muhammad made this word the corner-stone of his monotheistic message, which he centred more and more on the figure of Ibrâhîm. In later Muslim usage the word hanif has often been employed in the sense of 'the pure, orthodox religion'; and the term Hanîfíya means the religion of Ibrâhîm, identified with pure Islam. Particularly during the Medinan period Muhammad focused his preaching on the proclamation of the 'religion of Ibrâhîm': the true Muslim is hanif.

It was thus that Muhammad stepped into the arena between the contending parties of Judaism and Christianity, both of which lay claim to Ibrâhîm. 'They say: Become Jews or Christians that you may have the true guidance. Say: Nay! the religion of Ibrâhîm as *hanîf*, and not of the *mushrikîn*,' (S. II:129). 'O people of the Book! Why dispute about Ibrâhîm, when the Taurât and the Injîl were not sent down till after him? Ibrâhîm was neither Jew nor Christian, and not of the *mushrikîn*. They among men who are nearest of kin to Ibrâhîm are surely those who follow him and this prophet, and they who believe,' (S. III:58 ff.). The argument against the Jewish regulations concerning food comes in at this point. 'All food was allowed to the children of Isrâ'îl, except what Isrâ'îl forbade himself (cf. Gen. 32:32), ere the Taurât was sent down. Say: Bring you then the Taurât and read it, if you be men of truth. And whosoever after this invents the lie about God: These are evildoers. Say: God speaks truth. Follow, therefore, the religion of Ibrâhîm, *hanîf*, who was not of the *mushrikîn*,' (S. III:87 ff.).

This argument is strongly reminiscent of that which Paul advances in his letters. Although in attacking the Torah the two men concentrate on different points—on the food regulations in the one case and circumcision in the other—their methods are analogous. Both appeal to the religion—or faith in Paul's case—of Abraham, which was very much older than the Torah ('which came four hundred and thirty years afterward': Gal. 3:17). Both proclaim that those who follow Abraham are 'nearest of kin' (or are 'the sons' of Abraham: Gal. 3:7 ff.). Just as Muhammad's argument leads up to his own prophetic status, so Paul's culminates in the Gospel of Jesus as Lord (Rom. 4:23 f.). Both start from the premise that Abraham was no 'Jew': according to Muhammad he was *hanîf*, and according to Paul, 'the father of all who believe' (Rom. 4:9 ff.). Their starting-point, in other words, is the promise that Abraham 'shall become a great and mighty nation (Hebrew *goy*; LXX: *ethnos*), and all the nations (Hebr. *goyim*; LXX and N.T. *ethnē*) of the earth shall bless themselves by him,' (Gen. 18:18; Gal. 3:8; cf. Rom. 4:17). It serves to remind one directly of this text, when Muhammad proclaims: 'Verily, Ibrâhîm was an *ummah*, obedient to God, *hanîf*, and he was not of the *mushrikîn*. Grateful was he for His favours: God chose him and guided him into the straight way. And we bestowed on him good things in this world, and in the the world to come he shall be among the just. Then we revealed to you, that you should follow the religion of Ibrâhîm, *hanîf*. He was not of the *mushrikîn*,' (S. XVI:121 ff.). Muhammad, the *nabî al-ummî*, the prophet among the '*ummot hâ-ôlâm*, the nations of the earth, fulfils the promise made to Abraham: so that now the '*ummot hâ-ôlâm* (Gen. 18:18: *goye ha-'areṣ*), if they follow the religion of Ibrâhîm, partake of the blessing bestowed on Ibrâhîm's *ummah* (Gen. 18:18: *goy*).

It is possible to go even a step further. The word *goy*, as used in Genesis 18:18, makes no distinction between the people of Israel and the Gentiles; in fact *goy* (plur. *goyim*) denoted both. In that respect the word *hanîf* is similar, in that the original meaning of the term implied both 'Muslim' and 'Gentile'. In the Old Testament, *goyim* came more and more to signify 'Gentiles' as opposed to the people of Israel, which was known as '*am*. But Abraham, who received the promise that he should become a mighty *goy* and a blessing also to the *goyim*, was prior to that division and was therefore the father of all *goyim*, Jews and Gentiles. In regarding him as 'worshipper of God', *hanîf*, Muhammad is in line with those rabbinic utterances which likewise include the 'worshippers of God' within the scope of general salvation. One such saying runs: 'Among the *goyim* there are righteous men who have their part in the world to come.' One might think there is a direct connection here with the Qur'anic verse about Ibrâhîm already referred to: '. . . and in the world to come he shall be among the just,' (S. XVI:123). Another rabbinic saying has it that '*a goy*, who keeps the Torah, is as precious in God's sight as the High Priest himself'.[44] If for *goy* we substitute *hanîf*, we get exactly what Muhammad wants to say about Ibrâhîm: and parallel with this is Paul's argument about the Gentiles who do by nature what the Law requires —an idea to which he gives point by referring to Abraham who, as being uncircumcised, long before the Law was given had righteousness imputed to him by faith (Rom. 2:14; 4:9 ff.).

On two points of fundamental importance Muhammad's thinking parts company with Paul's. First, Muhammad envisages no radical break with Judaism. He treats Ibrâhîm as an (Arab) 'worshipper of God' and thus remains inside the fold of Judaism in the way that the Greek 'worshippers of God' stood within Hellenistic Judaism. Muhammad clings to the position which, by the decision of the Apostles' council, was accorded to the Gentiles within the earliest Christian community. We have seen that this was a settlement in appearances only, since Paul did not claim a relative status for the 'worshippers of God' alongside, or next to, the circumcised Jewish

Christians, but was proclaiming that both uncircumcised and circumcised, the Greek and the Jew, are justified by God's grace as a gift, through the redemption which is in Christ Jesus. In the nature of the case a compromise between Paul and the Pharisaic party of Christians was not possible. In Muhammad's preaching too there was essentially no room for agreement with the Jews, but for another reason: to wit, his claim that every prerogative lay with the 'worshippers of God', that is, with the Muslims. Whilst Paul proclaimed that the Gospel had been preached beforehand to Abraham (Gal. 3:8), Muhammad saw the patriarch as a 'worshipper of God'.

The second point of difference follows from the first. Paul makes Abraham, as it were, a Christian before Jesus, by taking the promise to Abraham up into the Gospel. Muhammad makes Ibrâhîm a Muslim before Islam, by conceiving of Ibrâhîm's religion as the original monotheistic worship of God, i.e. as Islam. Therein lies the force of Muhammad's contention that Ibrâhîm's religion existed already before the Law and before the Injîl too, so that Paul is caught napping by his own arguments and outmanoeuvred. If the Gospel precedes the Torah, Islam precedes both Torah and Injîl!

The controversy touched upon here, both as it involved Paul and as it concerned Muhammad, in fact went hand in hand with an already open conflict with the Jews. However fundamentally different, therefore, might be the substance and the causes of the conflict in either case, its character was to a remarkable degree the same. There are two reasons for that. The first is that in both instances the opposing party were the Jews, who clung obstinately to the Torah. The second is that, from both an active and a passive point of view, Muhammad followed most of the way in the footsteps of his Christian counterpart: passively, in so far as the Jews rejected his message just as emphatically as they did the Gospel, thus forcing Christianity and Islam to look for support beyond the frontiers of Jewry—that is to say, among the Gentiles: actively, in that because he was up against the selfsame antagonist, the Christian pattern of controversy offered Muhammad, directly or indirectly, a model for his own.

Muhammad's appeal to Ibrâhîm first became an extraordinarily deadly weapon against the Jews soon after the *Hijrah*, when his preaching underwent its baptism of fire from the Jewish opposition. For the most part, the Jewish arguments have to be deduced from Muhammad's own polemic. Muslim tradition has handed down some of the powerful

Jewish broadsides: 'There comes forth no prophet from among the Arabs.' They found warrant for this assertion in Muhammad's behaviour: 'He is just a king.' A real prophet does not strive for power nor after the lusts of the flesh. There must be a good deal of truth in these reports; for Muslim tradition has on the whole been very careful to paint the picture as much in Muhammad's favour as possible. It is eager to make out that the Jews quite deliberately rejected their Messiah, since they saw only too well the resemblance between Muhammad's character and that of the 'servant of the Lord' (Is. 42) and the Messianic king (Zech. 9). Other traditions depict the Jewish expectation of a governor (in accordance with Genesis 49:10-12), which Muhammad obviously fulfils.[45] Such traditions were undoubtedly formulated on the model of Christian polemic against Judaism; but they find no confirmation in the Qur'an.

The assault on Judaism figures prominently in the Medinan verses of the Qur'an. Here, evidently, was the target of Muhammad's main attack. The excruciating enigma that he—the seal of the Old Testament prophets and spokesman for the religion of Ibrâhîm—had yet been unconditionally rejected by the Jews became an obsession with him. He hit upon a solution in line with that of the New Testament: it would seem that throughout their history the Jews had always rejected their prophets, up to, and including, 'Isā (Jesus) (S. II:58, 81, 85 f.; III:177, 181; IV:154; V:74 f.). Yes indeed; the Torah affords evidence in plenty that they have broken God's covenant (S. II:25, 38, 77; IV:153 f.; V:15 f.). That the Jews saw at once how well Muhammad's censure of their obduracy advanced his claim to be in line with the New Testament appears from their biting irony: 'And they (i.e. the Jews) say: Uncircumcised are our hearts,' (S. II:82). Muhammad has no answer to this except to declare that God has cursed them in their infidelity (S. II:82). The preceding verse traces the course of their unbelief up to the rejection of 'Isā. We have here a kind of denunciatory preaching much in the style of Jeremiah (Jer. 9:25; cf. Lev. 26:41) and highly reminiscent of Stephen's address (Acts 7:51-53 is closely paralleled by Sura II:81-83).

To this is joined the accusation that the Jews are 'twisting words from their proper meanings' (S. IV:48; V:16; cf. V:45; II:70); in other words, they are committing *tahrif*. This theme too is familiar from the controversies between the Christians and Jews. Compare Paul's accusation (2 Cor. 3:14 f.: 'But their minds were hardened. . . .

Yes, to this day whenever Moses is read a veil lies over their minds . . .')
with Muhammad's: 'Then after that your hearts become hard like
rocks, or harder still. . . . A part of them heard the word of God,
and then, after they had understood it, perverted it, and knew that
they did so,' (S. II:69 f.).

The crucial difference between Paul's position and Muhammad's
was that in the Torah Paul shared common ground with the Jews,
whereas Muhammad did not know the Torah and therefore had to
rely entirely on what the Jews chose to tell him about it: hence the
suspicion that they were concealing parts of the Torah and distorting
it so as to get rid of texts that had a bearing on his prophethood
(S. VII:156; LXI:6). He was probably borrowing from Christian
polemic directed against the Mishna and Talmud when he alleged that
the Jews 'with their own hands transcribe the Book corruptly, and
then say: this is from God,' (S. II:73), though he himself, copying
the Jews, by the 'Taurât' probably implied the Talmud (cf. S. III:72).

The fact is that Muhammad took over the charge which the
Christians had levelled against the Jews—that they had spurned their
own prophet, Jesus—only now he applied it to himself (S. LXI:6, 14;
V:82, 110; III:44, 45); and the very fact that he saw himself heir to
the prophetic status of Jesus obliged him to resist indignantly what
he regarded as the deification of Jesus by the Christians (S. V:19).
For him the exaltation of Jesus as Son of God is on the same plane
with the presumption alike of Christian and of Jew in aspiring to be
'the sons of God' (S. V:21; cf. Hos. 11:1; Ex. 4:22; Mt. 2:15; Rom.
8:14, 17). These Jewish and Christian pretensions, being mutually
exclusive, cancel each other out (S. II:105/7/14; XXI:93; XXIII:55;
XXX:31). They both 'assign partners to God' (S. IX:33; LXI:9).

In its violence and bitterness Muhammad's quarrel with Judaism
recalls the antagonism towards the Jews maintained in the New Testament. Like the Christian Church, Islam considered itself the legitimate
offshoot of Judaism. Muhammad found himself in a peculiar situation
in that the Jews, besides being an obstinate and extremely dangerous
adversary in religious matters, constituted a political hazard too.
In that respect his position was essentially different from that of Jesus
and even from Paul's. It could be compared only to a later stage of
the struggle between Christianity and Judaism, after the destruction
of Jerusalem in A.D. 70, when the Jews as a nation were immersed in
the struggle for self-preservation and Christianity, having lost contact

with Palestine, had come to lie wholly on the Roman side of the dividing line. Since Muhammad was expected, in his political capacity, to be able to pacify the feuding tribes, and this had been one reason for his coming to Medina, his conflict with the Jews was bound to take on a political colouring. However it was the religious quarrel that proved decisive in bringing about the final rupture. Muhammad's theocratic claims to be a prophet, once they had been scorned by the Jews, brazenly and in public, could not just be left in the air. Some other basis for them must be found.

A definite break with the Jews came in the second year A.H. (*Anno Hegirae*). The front of battle was drawn up on both sides. Muhammad now for the first time addressed them as *Yâhûdi*, whereas previously he had called them simply *Banû Isrâ'îl*, the People of the Taurât.[46] Conversely, there was a hardening of the term 'Muslim'; instead of denoting simply 'monotheist', one who 'is surrendered (*muslim*) to God', it tended more and more to become the name for group, and *Islâm* came to mean the religion and the exclusve community of which Muhammad was the acknowledged leader (S. III:80 f.; XXII:78).

One manifest result of the rupture was an alteration of the *qiblah* or 'direction for prayer'. Perhaps even in Mecca, and certainly in the early Medinan period, Muhammad followed Jewish-Christian practice in facing towards Jerusalem for worship.[47] Because of the Jews' hostility and on the strength of a revelation, he was moved in the second year A.H. to turn and face the Ka'bah instead. The spot on which, according to tradition, this took place became the site of the *masjid al-qiblatain* (the mosque of the two *qiblahs*). As a matter of fact, there may have been some interval between Muhammad's dropping the Jerusalem *qiblah* and adopting the Meccan one—in the verses referring to the change there are several strands.[48] One Muslim tradition suggests that Muhammad was probably driven to make the change by the taunts of the Jews about his having to resort to their *qiblah*.[49] At any rate, they took no pains—according to the Qur'an—to hide their defiant and critical feelings (S. II:136).

Muhammad found that there was warrant even for the new *qiblah* in the Book (of the Christians and Jews)—a fact which the people of the Book would have preferred to conceal (S. II:139). Indeed both Qur'an and tradition maintain that Muhammad's intention was to restore the original *qiblah*, just as he had recovered the original religion. In some traditions the new *qiblah* is called the '*qiblah* of Ibrâhîm'.[50] Possibly even in Mecca Muhammad had attested a connection between the Ka'bah and Ibrâhîm as the progenitor of the Meccan people (S. XIV:38–41; cf. S. XI:76; XLIII:25–29).[51] At any rate he based the change of *qiblah* in Medina on the story of Ibrâhîm, who with Ismâ'îl was commanded to 'purify the House (i.e. the Ka'bah)' or 'to raise its foundations' (S. II:119, 121). That is why the Ka'bah became the sanctuary of the original monotheistic religion of Ibrâhîm, who was *hanîf, muslim*. In directing the *qiblah* in Medina towards the Ka'bah Muhammad anticipated the 'purification' which he was to carry out after his victorious entry into Mecca. God had already allotted to Ibrâhîm the site for the House and had bidden him proclaim a *hajj* to the people who come as worshippers of God (plural of *hanîf*), associating no other god with him (S. XXII:27 ff.).

It would be unfair to regard the introduction of the Ka'bah into the religion of Ibrâhîm and the change of the *qiblah* as a political stratagem. On the contrary, they were a necessary outcome of Muhammad's mission to recover the original monotheism from which both Jews and Christians had defected. The turning away from Jerusalem and towards Mecca was of crucial importance, and—in that respect—not unlike Jesus' judgment upon Jerusalem (Mt. 23:37 ff.). Jesus, as the risen Lord, sends out his own from Jerusalem to the ends of the earth (Acts 1:8). The Gospel passes from the Jews to the Gentiles. Muhammad's change of *qiblah* implies the same kind of decision. Mecca takes the place of Jerusalem; and at the same time Mecca becomes complementary, as it were, to Rome and Constantinople. Obedient to his Lord's command, the Apostle Paul journeyed to the ends of the earth and preached the Gospel also at Rome. The Roman Catholic Church has in fact turned her *qiblah* away from Jerusalem to Rome itself; and after the conversion of Constantine the claims of Rome had to compete with those of Constantinople. Later still Moscow was to become a 'third Rome'. Thus Jerusalem has had quite a string of competitors; yet neither Rome nor Constantinople nor Moscow has ever been able to play a hand as strong as Muhammad's when he declared the Ka'bah to be the House which had once already been the centre of Ibrâhîm's religion.

Muhammad's assertion is easier to understand when one remembers how important the Ka'bah was as a Semitic sanctuary. Even before his time the Ka'bah had been associated with the vaguely mono-theistic idea of the 'high god', interpenetrated by Jewish-Christian influences. The pagan, pre-Islamic poet of Medina, Qais, never refers in his poems to the local Meccan deities, but instead speaks of Allah, the Creator, whom he extols as 'Lord of the House' (that is, of the Ka'bah).[52] The people of Mecca knew Allah as Creator and Preserver (S. XIII:17; XXIX:61, etc.), upon whom they called in times of especial danger (S. X:23, etc.) and to whom they assigned his own special part of the sacrifice (S. VI:137), yet only in conjunction with their worship of other local deities (S. VI: 109 ff.).[53]

The Ka'bah was a characteristically Semitic sanctuary or sacred relic. As the ancient Arab religion was first and foremost a 'stone cult', the Ka'bah was considered holy probably because of the black stone embedded in the eastern corner: and the *maqâm Ibrâhîm* (Station of Abraham)—the stone on which he stood when he 'raised the foundation of the Ka'bah' (S. II:121)—was sacred too. The sacredness of the Ka'bah makes the whole city and its environs *Haram*, a place of Godly peace and refuge. The cubic form of the Ka'bah reminds one of the apse of the Temple at Jerusalem; whilst the parti-coloured tapestry which covered it—known in Islamic times as *kiswa*—recalls a common Semitic custom by which the tabernacle of Israel, the Canaanite high places (cf. Ezek. 16:16), the throne of Solomon and the sacred tents of ancient Arabia were hung with coloured tapestries.[54] The procession around the Ka'bah (*tawâf*), which Muslim tradition itself associated with the dancing and singing of the angels about the throne of God, is one of several features that point to astral symbolism. The Meccan cult was nothing if not syncretistic.

The Qur'an says that the Ka'bah was 'the first House that was founded for mankind' (S. III:90). Indeed, the idea that Ibrâhîm was to 'raise' the foundations of the Ka'bah suggests that it was already in existence (S. II:121). The Muslim legend elaborates upon these verses of the Qur'an. With Hâgar and Ismâ'îl, Ibrâhîm journeyed to Arabia, guided by the *sakîna* (Hebr. *shekhinah*, the presence of God) in the form of a whirlwind with a serpent's head. It circled about the foundations of the Ka'bah and said: 'Build on me!' Gabriel brought to Ibrâhîm the black stone, which had been preserved since the Flood. When the building was finished, he took up his place on the *maqâm*

Ibrâhîm, which then rose high above all mountains, and called upon all mankind to perform the *hajj*. Other legends go back as far as Adam who, after the Fall and the expulsion from Paradise, came to Mecca, followed by the Paradisal tent which had been his dwelling; and round this he moves in procession (*tawâf*), in imitation of the angels. The black stone served him for a seat. Taking the tent of Paradise as their prototype, his descendants make the Ka'bah; but this in turn is swept away by the Flood, so that Ibrâhîm finds only a reddish mould.

It is not difficult to trace in these legends the familiar cosmogonic motives of the cosmic serpent, the cosmic mountain, the world-tree and the navel of the world, which were the common property of the Near East, and in Jewish and Christian legends were applied even to the Temple of Jerusalem. The Qur'an calls Mecca *umm al-qurâ*, mother of the cities (S. VI:92; XLII:5); and in popular Muslim literature it is described as 'the navel of the earth'.[55] Before creation the Ka'bah was an alluvion within the cosmic ocean, the nucleus from which heaven and earth were formed. As the earth's highest point the Ka'bah corresponds to the pole-star, the highest point in the heavens; as cosmic mountain and navel it also represents the nether world and is, in that capacity, the tomb of a number of prophets. Even the so-called 'actual grave' of Muhammad is situated at Mecca.

The legends then were elaborations of primeval ideas; and once Muhammad had put the Ka'bah in place of the Jerusalem Temple, he had established a link with them. At the same time Jerusalem was still in an honoured position as 'the holy city' (*al-quds*). It was above all the sacred rock which became the centre of devotion, ranking next the Ka'bah in order of dignity.[56] Muslim tradition could without any trouble fall in with the Jewish-Christian conception of the sacred rock as navel of the earth, and with various legends in the Talmud and Targums, according to which Melchizedek had set up his altar there, Abraham had brought his sacrifice, and so forth. It was a theme exploited by Islam again and again, a rich vein of cosmogonic motives. God charged Moses to regard the rock as *qiblah*: and it was Muhammad's wish to do the same, until he received the divine commandment to turn to the Ka'bah.

Furthermore Muslim tradition established a connection between Muhammad's 'night journey' and the Temple rock at Jerusalem.

The 'remote place of worship' (al-masjid al-aqsâ) in the relevant verse of the Qur'an probably means the seventh heaven, to which Muhammad was taken up in a nocturnal vision (cf. Paul's vision in 2 Cor. 12:1 ff.) on the occasion of his initiation into the prophetic status (cf. S. LXXXI:19 ff.; LIII:1 ff.). Later tradition, however, takes the remote place of worship to be the Temple rock at Jerusalem, on which indeed, in Jewish-Christian legend, all prophets are said to have done their worshipping.[57] Other themes which certainly come in here are the transfiguration (Mt. 18:1 ff.), the heavenly Jerusalem and the legend about Jesus' ascension from the Temple rock.

Although the political ends of the Caliphate of Damascus had a lot to do with promoting the religious importance of Jerusalem, these Muslim traditions show how closely Mecca and Jerusalem were associated in the consciousness of Islam. Just as, in the Old Testament, ancient pagan sanctuaries like Hebron, Shechem and Bethel were 'historicized' as places where the patriarchs had worshipped, Muhammad in a similar way 'islamized' the Ka'bah. In opposing ancient Arab paganism he adopted the Jewish-Christian method, but at the same time went one better by putting Mecca in the place of Jerusalem.

The Hijrah achieved therefore a double purpose: it represented Muhammad's breaking with Meccan paganism, whilst making inevitable a rupture with Judaism as well. This is trenchantly expressed by the title of 'the seal of the prophets' which Muhammad assumed (S. XXXIII:40). He took his prophetic message from the prophets of the 'people of the Book', but at the same time beat them at their own game. It was with good reason that the Hijrah was taken to mark the inception of the Islamic era; for that twofold break—with paganism and with Judaism (and Christianity)—is the key to Islam's existence as a religion in its own right. Once again Judaism had evinced its mysterious power to implant something of its own genius within the soul of paganism. One might say that Muhammad, at the time of his removal to Medina, was halfway to becoming a Jew; but as has so frequently happened throughout the history of the Diaspora among the nations, this Jewish influence upon him had the effect of an inoculation. A minor dose of the Jewish spirit immunized him against the full impact of Judaism. The same might be said of the influence of (Hellenistic) Christianity, which had powerfully affected his mind at an early stage.

As he replaced Jerusalem with Mecca and as he proclaimed the religion of Ibrâhîm, so also did Muhammad follow in the footsteps of Moses. Careful scrutiny will show that the Qur'an provides a whole number of illustrations of this point; and of these the most important can be briefly indicated. When he broke with the Jews in the second year A.H. Muhammad felt prompted to replace the Jewish fast of 'Ashûrâ by a new custom of fasting during the month Ramadân. What occasioned this was probably Muhammad's victory over the Meccans at Badr, which took place in that very month and year. Muslim tradition has it that originally Muhammad connected the day of 'Ashûrâ and its fasting with the deliverance of Moses at the Red Sea.[58] Just as Moses' break with the Pharaoh was followed by the destruction of that ruler's chariots and horses, so the victory at Badr followed upon the Hijrah. The event placed the seal of divine intervention upon his prophetic mission, as against the scepticism of the Jews. Moreover, in the same year, as a substitute for the Hajj to Mecca which was not as yet practicable, Muhammad instituted in Medina, on the tenth of the month Dhu 'l-Hijja (i.e. the day of the Hajj) a ritual in which two rams were slaughtered, 'for my people' and 'for Muhammad and his household' respectively—an obvious reminiscence of the High Priest in the Old Testament and of his rôle in the Temple worship at Jerusalem on the Day of Atonement.[59] In that way, apparently, he intended also to provide a substitute for the Jewish Aseru, which was in fact a fast commemorating the Day of Atonement. This idea is supported by the fact that the fast of 'Ashûrâ is still a custom among Muslims, as a voluntary undertaking on the tenth of the month Muharram, the first month of the Muslim year. It is also the month when, in Muhammad's own day, the Hajj was probably observed ('the sacred month', S. II:190, 214; S. V:2, 98).[60] Thus Muhammad appears to have instituted the high-priestly slaughter ritual on the day when the Hajj took place in Mecca, thereby taking over into Islam and superseding not only the Jerusalem Temple but the sacrifices of the Day of Atonement.[61]

There is yet another striking parallel between the month Ramadân and the Jewish Aseru in that both are connected with the coming down of divine revelation.[62] According to Jewish tradition, it was on the Day of Atonement, aseru, that the second tablets of the Law were handed over to Moses (Ex. 34); whilst according to the Qur'an, the Qur'an itself was sent down in the month Ramadân (S. II:181), or in the 'night of power' (*lailat al-qadr*, S. XCVII:1). That night falls in the second half of the month Ramadân, and Muslim ideas about it agree in a good many respects with Jewish ideas about the Day of Atonement.[63] Here again is a pointer to Muhammad's rôle as a new Moses, receiving a new Law, the Qur'an.

Something else that confirms this is the mention of *furqân*, which is as much tied up with the descent of the Qur'an as with the giving of 'the Book' to Moses (S. II:181, 50). The word *furqân* could be rendered as 'salvation' (Aram. *purqan*; Syr. *purqana*) or 'distinction, separation' (Arab. vb. *faraqa*).[64] In the Qur'an it evidently signifies a Book of Revelation. The reference to 'the Book and the *furqân*' looks like a reminiscence of the two tables of stone (Ex. 24:12; cf. S. II:50). The 'forty nights' during which God was conferring with Moses (S. II:48) recall on the one hand the 'forty days and forty nights' mentioned in Exodus, and on the other the descent of the Qur'an in 'the night of power'; whilst the establishment of the entire month Ramadân as a month of fasting reproduces the continuity of the 'forty days and forty nights' (N.B. S. VII:138 talks about 'thirty nights' which God completed with ten other nights). The Muslim idea that the 'night of power' falls within the last part of the month Ramadân likewise reminds one of the account in Exodus, according to which God gave Moses the two tables of the testimony when 'he had made an end of speaking with him upon Mount Sinai' (Ex. 31:18).

In this connection, the Muhammad-Moses parallel can be taken even further. Like Moses, Muhammad has to go through the experience of seeing the God-given *furqân* rejected and answered with idolatry (S. XXV:1–4; cf. S. II:48–51). Then again, the Qur'an speaks of 'the day of the *furqân*', by which is meant the battle of Badr (S. VIII:42), when the final 'separation' and 'salvation' from the power of the Meccan pagans took place,[65] as also from the Jews. The Qur'an itself is called *furqân*, as being the successor to the Taurât and the Injîl. Thus the word refers to both the giving of a book and the divine sanctioning of Muhammad's prophethood, manifested in the victory at Badr. Similarly, the Qur'an links up the deliverance from Pharaoh in the closest possible way with the giving of the two tables to Moses ('the Book and the *furqân*', S. II:48 ff.; VII:132 ff.).

Moses confesses the sin of his people, who had worshipped the golden calf, in the words '*hudnâ ilaika*', that is, 'we have behaved like yahûdî'—the very term for Jews which Muhammad uses after he had broken with them in Medina (S. VII:155). God's answer is that there is mercy for those who follow the '*nabî al-ummî*', him who is described in Taurât and Injîl (v. 156; cf. S. VIII:29; XXI:49). We remember the Jewish view that the 'Ashûrâ relates to Moses' receiving the second tables of the Law, after he had smashed in pieces the original tables out of indignation over the setting up of the golden calf. Now Muhammad, in considering the giving of the *furqân* to Moses, seems to have had in mind particularly the giving of the second tables (S. VII:142 ff.; cf. S. II:48 ff.; XXI:49).

Muhammad did indeed therefore follow in Moses' footsteps. There was the *Hijrah* (cf. Exodus from Egypt) and consequently the battle of Badr (cf. deliverance from the hosts of Pharaoh): the giving of the Qur'an (cf. the giving of the first tables): the consequent disillusion at the unbelief of the Medinan Jews (cf. the worship of the golden calf), followed by the descent of the *furqân* (cf. the giving of the second tables) signified by the revelation of God's decision in the victory at Badr, which is the Jews' last chance of being converted (cf. Moses' pleadings with God to show mercy on his people). Like Moses in the desert, Muhammad stood in Medina face to face with the stiff-necked people of Israel who disclaimed their own election (S. II:38, 44, 116). On him there rested—as upon Moses—the task of carrying out God's punishment on his people. The manner in which he did so, when compared with Moses' conduct (cf. Ex. 32:25 ff.), was remarkable both for its political expertise and for its moderation (cf. S. XXXIII:25–27).

Before leaving this subject I propose to add something about the characteristic evolution of the idea of *ummah*, which throws an interesting light on the rise of Islam in relation to Judaism. The word *ummah* derives from the Hebrew '*ummah* (Aram. '*ummetha*'). In the Old Testament the plural form, '*ummoth*, occurs three times: twice in a context associated with Arabia (sons of Ishmael, and a Midianite: Gen. 25:16; Num. 25:15) and once as a synonym for *goyim*, nations or Gentiles (Ps. 117:1). The word may well have made its way early into the Arabic; at any rate it acquired a special significance in the Qur'an[66] where, generally speaking, it denotes some specified group, whether racial, social, linguistic or religious, which falls within the divine plan of salvation.[67] Bound up with the question of ethnical and religious diversity is the question of what distinguishes believers from unbelievers. Noah was given blessings for *'ummoth*; yet the next we hear is that grievous punishment awaits other *'ummoth* (S. XI:50; VII:167). The *'ummoth* are involved in the history of belief and unbelief in this way. To each *ummah* God has sent an apostle (*rasûl*) or admonisher (*nadhîr*) (S. VI:42; X:48, etc.; S. XXXV: 22, 40). Thus each *ummah* has its appointed time (*ajal*), after which it falls into a decline through its lack of belief in the apostle sent to it (S. VII:32; X:50, etc.): then it awaits God's judgment (S. VII:32 ff.). At the Last Judgment each apostle will be called to witness against the *ummah* which had rejected him (S. IV:45, etc.; XLI:24; XLVI:17).

This idea of *ummah* agrees closely with what the Old Testament calls *mishpâhâ*, that is, everything that forms a complete and homogeneous community with characteristics of its own, which is under either God's blessing (Gen. 12:3: 'families' of the earth; cf. Amos 3:2) or his judgment (Mic. 2:3; Jer. 8:3). The word for this idea in the New Testament is 'generation' (*genea*, the Greek equivalent of *mishpahah*, cf. LXX; Jer. 8:3; cf. Lk. 11:29; Mt. 24:34) or sometimes 'tribe' (Mt. 24:30; cf. Rev. 1:7). In the Qur'an too *ummah* means in some places the 'time appointed' for the judgment (synonym. *ajal*), where it comes even closer to the New Testament term 'generation'.

Muhammad now joins the succession of earlier apostles and stands amidst his *ummah*, against whom he too will witness at the Last Day (S. XXVIII:46, etc.). The Arabic-speaking peoples are now provided with their own admonisher, addressing them in their own language, just as *'ummoth* of former days were each addressed by their apostle in their own tongue (S. XIV:4). The sacred books of the Jews and Christians were written, of course, in a strange language (*a'jami*); but the Qur'an is in plain Arabic (S. XVI:105; LXVIII:37; XII:2; XX:112; XXXIX:29; XLIII:2) and does not need first to be interpreted (S. XLI:44; XXVI:192 ff.; XLIV:58; XIX:95).

Muhammad has been sent to the *ummîyûn* as an apostle from among themselves (S. LXII:2)—and indeed to an *ummah* which had never before received an apostle or a book of revelation in their own language, the Arabic being, in other words, the language of the *ummîyûn*, the Gentiles. There turned, as it were, upon these ideas of *ummî* and *ummah* a change of direction which in the Meccan period of Muhammad's life was potential only, but in Medina was brought out into the open. When a book of revelation was given in Arabic, that meant to the Arabs something very much like what the

Septuagint meant for the Hellenistic 'worshippers of God' (is not the legend about the verbal inspiration of the Septuagint rather on a par with the similar doctrine regarding the Qur'an?) and what the Greek New Testament came to mean for Greek-speaking Christians. After the break with the Jews in Medina there occurred a shift of accent as with the Christian Church after the destruction of Jerusalem, when her Jewish centre was lost and she looked more and more earnestly for support to the Greek-speaking world.

In Mecca Muhammad had often proclaimed that 'men were one *ummah*: then they became at variance; and had not a decree previously gone forth from thy Lord, their differences had surely been decided between them!' (S. X:20, etc.). The passage reminds one very much of the story of the tower of Babel. 'Had God pleased He could have made you one '*ummah*': but He causes whom He will to err, and whom He will He guides,' (S. XVI:95; XLII:11 ff.; II:209). Now comes Muhammad with the Arabic Qur'an to recall mankind to the one, true, original *ummah* (S. XLI:44 f.; XLII:5 f.). This one *ummah* is the *ummah* of all preceding prophets and apostles, the *ummah* of Ibrâhîm. It is the People of the Book, the Jews and Christians, who have become divided through their unbelief and jealousy towards each other (S. XLII:11 ff.). Muhammad's *ummah* is the one universal and original *ummah*, standing over against the pernicious feuds and schisms of the People of the Book (S. III:17).

It is in Medina then that the lines of attack are mapped out. The Jews and Christians together form an *ummah* which has passed away: they have the reward of their deeds (S. II:128, 135). They belong already to the past; and upon their *ummah* the judgment has already been executed. Now is the age of the *ummah* of Muhammad. Their refusal to believe in Muhammad's prophethood proves that they have already cast away their own apostles, Mûsâ and 'Isâ.

Whilst Ibrâhîm, together with Ismâ'îl, was raising the foundations of the Ka'bah, he prayed: 'O Lord, make us Muslims, and our posterity a Muslim *ummah*,' (S. II:122). Now, through the turning of the *qiblah* to Mecca, God constitutes the Muslims an '*ummah* in the midst' (S. I:137), that is to say, the true and original *ummah* of Ibrâhîm, who was neither Jew nor Christian, but '*hanîf, muslim*'. The climax comes in the declaration to the Muslims: 'You are the best *ummah* that has been raised up unto mankind,' (S. III:106).

In this way the idea of *ummah* is narrowed down to the exclusive community of Muslims. The *Hijrah* had been the first and crucial phase in the process. Generally, the *Hijrah* was the usual departure of the apostles from the *ummah* which had rejected them. They washed their hands of their *ummah* and gave it over to perdition, at the same time themselves receiving the divine promise that after judgment has been fully carried out, they shall dwell 'in the land' or 'on earth' (*fi 'l-ard* could mean either, like the Hebrew *ha-'ares*) (S. XIV:16). The apostle will set up a new *ummah* in place of the old one which has been destroyed. Now that is precisely what Muhammad had in fact done. The eventual conquest of Mecca was a necessary consequence of his apostleship; he inherited 'the land' of the Meccan *ummah* upon which God's judgment had fallen, and with it he inherited also 'the earth', as once Noah, after the Flood, had brought forth a new *ummah* which was to fill the earth.

The story of Ibrâhîm and Lût (Abraham and Lot), as told in the Qur'an, follows the pattern of the Flood story. Ibrâhîm warned his people of the coming fire; but only Lût believed in him saying: 'I am *muhâjir* (i.e. betake me) to my Lord'. The word *muhâjir* means literally: I do *Hijrah*. In the Medinan verses of the Qur'an this is invariably a group term signifying those who have performed the *Hijrah*. Thus the apostle's *Hijrah* is his decisive act of turning away and so leaving his unbelieving *ummah* to the deluge or the fire (cf. S. XIX: 49 f.) in order to found a new *ummah*. The break with the Jews shows that, like the calf-worshippers in the desert, they do not belong to the true *ummah*. Yet there were some Jews converted to Islam, just as among the people of Mûsâ there had been 'a certain *ummah* who guide with truth' (S. VII:159). The true *ummah* of Ibrâhîm and Mûsâ and Muhammad directed the *qiblah* towards the true Jerusalem, towards Mecca. As after the *Hijrah* of earlier prophets—into the Ark, out of Mesopotamia, out of Egypt—so now was it given to the true *ummah* under Muhammad to inherit the earth.

In the way things worked out one can see three separate and distinct factors. First: the Meccans are Gentiles (*ummî*), who as yet had had no Book and no apostle. Secondly: the Meccans are the descendants of Ibrâhîm; the Ka'bah is the oldest and earliest sanctuary on earth; Mecca is 'the mother of the cities'; their *ummah* is the original, universal *ummah* of Ibrâhîm, which had relapsed into paganism but is destined, none the less, in the present age to constitute the one, true *ummah* under the *nabî al-ummî*, the apostle with an Arabic revelation to the Arabic-speaking *ummah*. The translation from the first to the second of these aspects can only be brought about through the *Hijrah*, whereby the old *ummah* is given up to destruction and the new *ummah* is born. Out of Medina comes the 'reformation' of the Meccan *ummah*.

There exists a document of the second year A.H., known as the 'Constitution of Medina', which throws a remarkable light on the potency of the *ummah* idea. This constitution was promulgated by Muhammad when the final separation from the Jews already seemed inevitable, but he was not yet able to do without their political co-operation: that is to say, before the battle of Badr. The document dates therefore from the crucial period when, politically speaking, Islam was coming to maturity as an 'independent' religion. Muhammad's biographer, Ibn Ishâq, says in his introduction: The Apostle of God wrote a writing between the Emigrants (*muhâjirûn*) and the Helpers (*ansâr*: the Muslim inhabitants of Medina who welcomed Muhammad), in which he made a treaty with the Jews, confirmed them in their religion and possessions, and gave them certain duties and rights.

The first article affirms that the three parties to the agreement 'are a single *ummah* distinct from other people'. The Jews are thus expressly included in the one *ummah* of Medina, which is here a purely political conception, embracing all the inhabitants of Medina, whether Muslim, pagan Arab or Jew. The Jews are described as 'one only *ummah* along with the believers', though the difference in religion is not thereby resolved: 'To the Jews their religion and to the Muslims their religion,' (Art. 25). There seems to be a sharp distinction drawn here between religion (*dîn*) and *ummah*, the latter being an entirely neutral local community within which equality and freedom of religion is to be the rule. Against this must be set several clauses pledging the Jews to support Muhammad's policies and never to conclude separate treaties or go to war merely on their own account.

All that reduces the *ummah* to the minimum. In Mecca, Muhammad's prophetic mission miscarried because he insisted on going the whole way—he wanted to convert the whole community there into the *ummah*. In Medina his approach was extremely tactful and politic. Closer scrutiny reveals, however, that in this document of *Realpolitik* the theocratic basis of the *ummah* idea has not disappeared but been kept in the background. The Constitution is an edict of 'Muhammad the prophet'. All disputes must be referred 'to God and to Muhammad' (Art. 23). This provision sounds rather like the verse in the Qur'an: 'Wherever there is anything about which you differ, with God does the decision rest,' (S. XLII:10); but there is a very significant difference here. The reference in the Qur'an is to the judgment of the apostle in dividing as between believers and unbelievers (S. X:48), whereas the Constitution is referring to non-religious disputes. All the same, Muhammad's political authority did rest on his status as a prophet, which was taken as an unquestionable basis for it and promulgated as such. There was freedom of religion: yes—for those who conceded the prophet's position as leader of the Medinan community! And therein lies the essential ambiguity of this Constitution. The Jews are to enjoy freedom . . . except to do the one thing by which their existence as Jews stands or falls: to reject Muhammad's claim to prophethood. Of course, it is not said in so many words. To all appearance it is Muhammad's political authority alone which is being proclaimed.

Thus a latent virus of theocracy is seen to lie at the back of the 'neutral ummah' idea. The valley of Jathrib (Medina) is declared to be 'sacred for the people of this document' (Art. 39), an affirmation which can only make sense if Medina, like Mecca, is thought of as being potentially a Muslim centre. Muhammad is already creating a basis here for the expression al-haramaini (the two sacred cities), identified with Mecca and Medina. The religious orientation of the ummah idea is apparent above all in the stress laid on the unity of all believers, of the Muslims, for whom all traditional obligations towards other inhabitants of Medina are overridden by an unconditional loyalty towards the brethren in the Muslim faith (Arts. 19, 22, 47). It is also laid down that the Constitution 'does not protect a wrongdoer or traitor' (Art. 47). It is easy enough to see that what may properly be understood here by 'wrong' and 'treachery' is to be decided, in the last resort, by Muhammad and the Muslim ummah solidly united behind him—that ummah which now replaces the traditional community and its loyalties to clan or tribe. The Jews, who until then had fitted nicely into the scheme of tribal relationships, could no longer count on the Muslims to honour any of the traditional obligations.

In fact this Constitution puts Muhammad into the position of a traditional tribal chief. He proclaims himself leader of the 'super-tribe' of Medina[68]; so that the *ummah*—to outward appearance neutral, but at its centre Muslim—is firmly grounded upon the ancient conception of the tribe. In the month following the battle of Badr it was decreed that one fifth of all the spoils taken on a Muslim expedition should go to Muhammad (S. VIII:42).[69] During the next few years the Muslim *ummah* established positive relations with various Arab tribes in much the same way as any powerful tribe might do.

For the Jews there was no place in this *ummah* at all—either in its initial and seemingly neutral manifestation, in its development as a tribe or in any circumstances in its religious aspect. On the contrary, as the one party offering unqualified resistance to Muhammad on the ground of religious principle, they were a deadly danger; and as a 'fifth column' they could not—in the long run—be tolerated. The drama was played out in three acts, starting with the defeat and expulsion of Qaynuqâ in the year after Muhammad had broken with them. The second act came a year later with the expulsion of an-Nâdir; and finally, in A.D. 627, all men of Qurayzah were put to death and their women and children sold as slaves. That solved the Jewish question in Medina. The next year the Jewish colony at Khaybar was defeated, but was allowed to continue cultivating the land on condition that half the produce were handed over to the Muslim owners. Similar treaties were imposed on the three other Jewish colonies which remained. The Caliph 'Umar was the first to order the expulsion of all Jews from the Hijâz, appealing to the tradition concerning Muhammad's verdict that 'there cannot be two religions in Arabia'.

Consequently, the position of the Jews (and Christians) was regulated on the pattern of the pre-Islamic system of 'security', in which weak tribes or settled communities were made to pay for the protection (*dhimmah*) afforded by the strong nomadic tribes (cf. S. IX:29).[70] The status of *dhimmî* gave the Jews and Christians outside the Hijâz the possibility of continued existence, even if it was, in principle, only as outcasts. At different periods and in various regions under Muslim domination they have in practice enjoyed a large measure of freedom, occupied positions of importance, taken part in industry and commerce and made brilliant contributions to Arabic science, art and literature. Jewish scholars of modern times maintain that in the hey-day of Islam the Jews felt themselves completely at one with the Muslim peoples. The coming of Islam to Spain set them free from the tyranny of the West Goths; and under the Umayyad Caliphate of Cordova they played a full part in the efflorescence of culture.[71] The collapse of Spanish Islam in face of the Berber invaders marked the beginning of periodical persecution of the Jews. Their agony, however, began as soon as Islam was driven out by Western Christendom; for that confronted the Jews with the choice between expulsion, conversion and extermination. Generally speaking, their treatment at the hands of Islam depended very much on changing political circumstances. At all events, the record of Islam compares not unfavourably with that of mediaeval European Christianity. It might even be said that they tended in opposite directions. Christianity started off with a Messiah who had been crucified by Jews and Gentiles; but once it had found a home in the pagan world, it gave the Jews a taste of its power. Islam began with a prophet revenging himself on the Jews for having rejected him; but, once it was in a position of unassailable strength, Islam gave to the Jews a legal protection which in fact often ensured for them a considerable degree of freedom.

Abraham Geiger has probably put his finger on the real reasons for this difference when he says that Islam was content to live quietly side by side with Judaism. There was no need for fighting. Confident in its own strength, Islam looked proudly down on Judaism. Akin by reason of their monotheism, their eastern origin and language, each held to their own foundation: the Muslims to their Qur'an, the Jews to their Tenach and Talmud. They had no intimate knowledge of each other's sacred books. On the other hand, the relation of the Church to the Jews was something entirely different. To the mighty Church the continued existence of Judaism was a thorn in the flesh. Its very existence was insupportable, an insult to the Church; and every Jew was a living denial of her truth. Church and Synagogue took their stand on the same Scripture. The Church regarded herself as the true Israel. That is why the position of Judaism and of the Jews was of necessity far less happy within Christendom than within Islam.

Then again, Christianity has never been able to detach itself so decisively from Judaism as Islam was able to do. In Medina Muhammad superseded Judaism completely with Islam and put Mecca in the place of Jerusalem. When once he had settled accounts with the Medinan Jews, the Jewish problem was solved. Since that time Islam has never again been disturbed by Judaism, never felt the Synagogue to be a spiritual competitor. Christianity, however, though it may have travelled far from its point of departure, has never quite been able to pull this thorn out of its flesh. That would have meant disowning its own Jewish Messiah and putting away the Jewish New Testament. Even in the ghettos of mediaeval Europe the Jews still represented the troubled conscience of Christendom.

For the Synagogue, however, Islam and Christendom are the great persecutors, for the most part without distinction. Listen for a moment to the gifted Jewish poet of twelfth century Spain:

> Babylon oppresses me, up to her fall: Then Persians, Greeks, and Edom's People all, So that from land to land I needs must flee. And Ismaël now for 461 years already has held me in his claw: Is there no end that we shall ever see? [72]

Edom (Christianity) and Ishmael (Islam) are equally the oppressors of Israel. Between Church and Mosque lies the Synagogue:

> always hated and despised by both, apostle of a religion of peace, such as brooks no discord, waiting for that day when the God of Sinai shall have established His throne in the hearts of all men and nations. [73]

To Judaism Christianity and Islam have always seemed to be a compromise with paganism. [74] Christians are 'proselytes of the gate' (*gere ha-sha'ar*). [75] Muhammad is on a par with Paul: both were masters of the art of coming to terms with more ancient religious customs and attitudes, to the greater glory of their own creed. [76]

It we set aside the ultimate theological question, we have to admit that this Jewish indictment contains an important truth. Judaism was taken by both Paul and Muhammad out of its own confines and brought within the pagan world; it became 'to the Greeks a Greek' and 'to the Arabs an Arab'. The Arab universal *ummah* is the counterpart of the Greek universal *ekklēsia*, and the Arab Qur'an a pendant to the Greek New Testament. Christianity and Islam therefore are the contrasting forms in which Judaism passed into Hellenistic and Syrian civilization. Rome and Byzantium on the one side, Medina and Mecca on the other have aspired both to replace and to represent Jerusalem. Christianity came to be the religion of that Roman Empire which had destroyed Jerusalem, blotted out the existence of Jewry as a nation and forbidden the Jews to set foot in their holy city. Islam became the religion of the Arab Empire hatched out among the Jews of Medina; it drove the Jews out of Arabia and made Jerusalem the holy city of Islam. Christianity, becoming the religion of Western civilization, was destined to spread throughout the world. Islam, the religion of Syrian civilization, was likewise destined for a world mission. Through the door of both religions Judaism has made its entry among the nations.

(c) *The Expansion of Islam*

The expansion of Islam after the death of Muhammad compares in a number of ways with the Germanic invasions in the West. Both movements were, in their own manner, part of a *Völkerwanderung* consequent upon the decline of Hellenistic civilization. Yet a further resemblance between them is that they both adopted a 'heretical' religion. The earliest German kingdoms were all Arian: Burgundians and Visigoths in Gaul, Ostrogoths in Italy, Visigoths and Suevians in Spain and the Vandals in Africa. In view of their power, their importance as a missionary force and their cultural vigour, there still seemed at the close of the fifth century to be a great future in store for these kingdoms, and thus also for Arianism. Moreover the Arian form of church organization was that which fitted in best of all with ancient Germanic tradition.

Nevertheless Arianism was evidently no match for Catholic Christianity. It lacked just the great prophetic leader who might have been able to fashion it into the dynamic and victorious faith of the Germanic peoples. Then also the Arian kingdoms—with the one striking exception of the Vandals in Africa—lacked the capacity to develop an imperial and cultural ideology of their own to counter the enormous prestige of the Roman Empire and of Hellenistic civilization. Unlike Islam Arianism could not act the rôle of heir to the anti-Hellenistic civilizations, but went on living in the shadow of Rome. So it was that in the German kingdoms the Catholic Church, with its strong organization and its interests centred in Rome, survived; whereas the Christianity encountered by Islam was Monophysite and Nestorian and violently anti-Byzantine. In the end the conversion of the Franks to Catholicism proved as decisive a factor in the West as did the Muslim conquest of Persia in the East. In the seventh century A.D., whilst the Byzantine Empire was vainly trying to win back the schismatic Eastern churches, in Western Europe was laid the foundation for a new civilization under Catholic patronage.

If Arianism lacked a prophetic personality of genius, another influential religious movement certainly possessed one in the person of its founder, Mani. Manicheism anticipated in some respects what was to be the rôle of Islam, and of Sh'itism in particular. In his attitude to Christianity and in his prophetic self-consciousness Mani was curiously like Muhammad. During the fourth century and the earlier part of the fifth Manicheism was a serious rival to Catholic Christianity and was engaged in vigorous missionary activity in Persia and Central Asia. Mani wrote extensively in both Persian and Syriac. In China his religious system lasted until the seventeenth century. It seemed able to command all that was needed for the conquest of Asia; but it failed—probably for the same reason as Nestorianism. The crucial point was that in Persia, under pressure from the Zoroastrian state religion, it was never able to attract more than a persecuted minority. Within the Roman Empire it came too late; and then it collapsed under persecution by Christianity, itself already promoted to the rank of a state religion. Had it come upon the scene a few centuries earlier, Manicheism—and not Christianity— might very well have become the religion of the Roman Empire and of Europe. Had it turned up in Arabia—and not in Persia— Manicheism might possibly have fulfilled the rôle in history which fell to the lot of Islam, and Muhammad might have achieved nothing more than to become the founder of a persecuted sect.

The expansion of Islam beyond the borders of Arabia after the death of Muhammad did not rest on the conversion of individuals. It went forward at high pressure, as it were, carried along by the success of Muhammad's new 'protection' system, which was super-tribal and was applied in the political, social and economic spheres. Of that system his *ummah* was the corner-stone. The triumphant entry into Mecca finally established the authority of Islam in Arabia; and as the warring tribes were pacified, it became necessary to go looking for fresh spoils in more fertile regions. There is an important truth contained in Caetani's thesis—supported by Becker and other modern scholars—that the growth of Islam represents the last major Semitic migration, in that it marks the final stage in an age-long process of gradual infiltration from the barren desert to the adjacent

Fertile Crescent.[77] To that migration Islam gave an impetus which enabled it to become a mighty movement in cultural history.

It has been said that it was in the first place 'Arabianism' and not Islam that triumphed.[78] It is true that not until the second and third centuries A.H. did the bulk of the peoples of Mesopotamia, Syria and Persia go over to Islam; and even then it was primarily in order to avoid paying tribute and to gain entry to the ruling class. Yet there is no opposition or contrast between Arabianism and Islam. The status of *dhimmī* which was given to the conquered populations was fully compatible with the Muslim *sharī'a*. Again, an Arabian foundation was indispensable to Islam, resting as it did on an Arab Qur'an, and with Arabian holy cities as its centres. The orthodox theory of the Caliphate insists that the Caliph must be descended from 'Quraish'. When the distinctive properties of Israel and Jerusalem were transferred to Arabia and Mecca, Islam emerged as an independent religion.

That is why there is nothing elsewhere really comparable to the function discharged by Arabianism in Islam. It united in itself all those features which in the rise of Western civilization were contributed by Israel, by the Germanic tribes and by Rome. Like the Hebrew Exodus before it, the Arabian migration brought within the orbit of ancient civilization in the Near East the fermenting influence of a monotheistic message and religion. Arabianism was allied to the Germanic *Völkerwanderung* in this respect: that it shows us primitive tribes taking over the heritage of a higher cosmopolitan culture and with it the political concept of 'empire'. The initiative which the Arabs displayed in thus taking over an ancient civilization has its parallel among the Romans, who in a similar way adopted the Greek tradition. In a sense, the rôle of the Arabic language too might be said to parallel that of the Latin. Still, Mecca was no Rome. The Caliphate was very soon transferred to Damascus; and the creation of Baghdad by the Abbasids put an end to the genuinely Arab phase of Islam. The fact that the cultural and political centre shifted to the area of ancient Mesopotamian civilization shows clearly enough that the Arabs neither could nor would resist the magnetic influence and cultural prestige of the Fertile Crescent. Baghdad became another sort of Byzantium. The gulf which separates the history of Western Europe from Byzantine civilization likewise separates it from the history of Islam. Through the decline of the West Roman Empire and after a long period of incubation, commonly known as the

'Dark Ages', the Germanic *Völkerwanderung* led to a cultural re-orientation of the barbarian peoples of Europe, who learned to stand on their own feet, establish their own centres and handle the Graeco-Roman tradition from their own distinctive viewpoint. Islamic civilization, on the other hand, shot up like a gourd in a fertile soil which had already for centuries past yielded a rich cultural harvest. In this respect the Arabs showed themselves as ready pupils as the succession of nomadic conquerors who during the course of Chinese history have poured into the Hwang Ho valley. Arab civilization was Arabian neither in its origin, its fundamental structure nor its main ethnical elements. It comprised, as has been remarked,

> . . . the Hellenized Aramaic and the Iranian civilizations as de-veloped under the aegis of the caliphate and expressed through the medium of the Arab tongue. In another sense it was the logical continuation of the early Semitic civilization of the Fertile Crescent originated and developed by the Assyro-Babylonians, Phoenicians, Aramaeans and Hebrews. In it the unity of the Mediterranean civilization of Western Asia found its culmination.[79]

It was then a truly cosmopolitan civilization which grew up under the Abbasid Caliphate. It spread indeed as Hellenism had once spread; and one could compare the part played in the time of its full maturity by the Abbasids with the career of Alexander the Great, for that emperor too had been of semi-barbarian stock. He too had carried the day against the Persians, with consequences of no less importance in the strategic, political and cultural spheres. It was only his premature death at the time of his sojourn in Babylon that forestalled his intention of shifting the centre of his empire to Mesopotamia and raising there a yet more glorious tower of Babylon. Before him too lay the prospect of advancing into Central Asia and India.

It is chiefly through the labours of C. H. Becker that proper attention has at last been paid to the important Hellenistic strain in Islamic civilization.[80] Others who have interested themselves in the subject have put forward the thesis that Islam, even to the very banks of the Ganges, is still part and parcel of our Mediterranean civilization.[81] There are a number of arguments that support such a conclusion: one relates to the important fact that the scientific and philosophical heritage of Graeco-Roman antiquity was revived and carried on in Islamic civilization and was eventually passed on to mediaeval Europe. So far one would be justified in regarding Islam along with Byzantium and Western Christianity as equally entitled to be called heir to the Graeco-Roman legacy. But then at the same time due stress must be laid on the particular way in which Islamic civilization treated its inheritance. The fact is of paramount importance that the centres of this civilization during its prime—if we set aside for the moment Spanish Islam—lay in Mesopotamia, Iran and the borderlands of Central Asia. As regards Islamic mysticism, medicine, astrology and the esoteric sciences, Iranian influences were overwhelming there. Above all the form of government, political ideology and social structure were to a very large extent modelled on the examples of centralized bureaucracy in ancient Mesopotamia and Iran; whilst in contrast to the Hellenistic empire and its successors, Islam never permitted the tradition of the Greek *polis* the slightest influence on its own political concepts.[82] Moreover the Greek genius for rational and speculative thought was never really able to germinate, since orthodox Islam, with its essentially legalistic and conservative religiosity, could never come to grips at a fundamental level with the Greek intellect. On the contrary Muslim orthodoxy took care to confine that sort of mentality to a very narrow field of dogmatic speculation, and beyond that left it to dangerous heretics and suspect philosophers. The writings of Averrhoes were well-nigh forgotten in the Islamic world until the interest of Europeans during the last century drew attention to them once more. Again it is true to say of the elements of Roman law which Islamic law has incorporated that the distinctive spirit of Roman law, so deeply impressed upon Byzantine and Western jurisprudence and legislation, had no chance to shed its influence over the comprehensive sanctity of the Muslim *sharī'a*. It has been part of the mysterious power of Islam to impose upon the civilization that flourished under its patronage its own outwardly sovereign forms, without itself being materially affected by or fundamentally transforming the content.

It is worth noticing that the rise of Islam ultimately transformed the Mediterranean from what it had been in ancient times and in the Graeco-Roman world—an inland sea—into the frontier between the Islamic and European worlds. In the end Islam was driven back out of Spain, and the Christian Church of North Africa amounted to no more than an episode—albeit a most important one—of Roman Christianity, in which the indigenous Berber population had no share of any consequence.

So far as the 'legacy' of antiquity is concerned, it makes better sense to speak of a partitioning or dividing up of the estate between Islam and the Christian world than of executors administering a joint inheritance. In the rise and expansion of Islamic civilization the anti-Hellenistic reaction was always a predominant feature.

Probably that aspect of Islamic expansion which is of greatest moment and is in any case of far-reaching significance for the course of world history is the fact that, as opposed to Christianity, Islam succeeded in winning itself a permanent foothold in Asia. The Oxus and Jaxartes—the traditional, geographical, political and racial frontier between Iranians and Turks—were crossed as early as the beginning of the eighth century. It was the first immediate challenge to the Mongoloid peoples and to Buddhism. Bukhara, together with Samarkand and the province of Khwârizm, was quickly to become a centre of Muslim civilization. In the same period a movement southwards reduced Baluchistan and Sind and reached as far as the southern Punjab. Transoxiana and North India marked the limits of Arab expansion and also, in two respects, a crucial turning-point. First it became clear at this juncture that Islam could not, by military conquest, push forward any further into the domains of the great oriental religions. China as such—excluding Turkestan—has never been brought within the orbit of Islam. In India neither the Arab invasion in the eighth century nor the Turkish conquests of three centuries later ever enabled Islam to become a serious rival to Hinduism, even if it did manage to build a great empire in the north, with an impressive display of power and culture. Unlike Zoroastrian Persia and Christendom of the Near East, both the 'primary' civilizations of Asia remained impregnable to Islam.

In respect of race too this borderland between the Persians and the Turks implies a turning-point, in that Turkish peoples now make their appearance in Islamic history for the first time, and also for good. The rise of the Ghaznevid empire of Afghanistan and Punjab (A.D. 962–1186) represents the first victory of the Turkish element in its struggle with the Iranian element for ultimate mastery in Islam. Bâbur, founder of the North Indian Mogul dynasty, was of mixed Turkish and Mongol descent. The Turks, as members of the body-guard, worked their way into the Abbasid administration; and in the tenth century Turkish dynasties rose to power in Egypt and Syria. The nomadic Saljûq Turks, coming from the steppes of Turkestan, overran Baghdad in the middle of the eleventh century. In Asia Minor they were superseded by the Ottoman Turks, who gave the *coup de grâce* to the Byzantine Empire, penetrated into Europe as far as Vienna and extended their sway over Western Asia. Right up to the present century their Sultans usurped the title of Caliph; and they represented to modern Europe the strength and civilization of Islam.

It was Asian peoples—the Mongols and the Turks—who set back irrevocably the growth of Christianity in Asia. The Mongol maelstrom more or less obliterated all traces of Christian penetration; and when the Mongol rulers of Persia were converted to Islam in the closing decades of the thirteenth century, the quarrel between the two religions was settled in favour of Islamic expansion into Asia. However, these peoples did not have it in them to make a really positive contribution to the progress of Islamic civilization. The Mongols went beyond all bounds in carnage and destruction and ended up by accepting the traditional religious, political and social pattern of Islam. The Turks in practice maintained the existing structure of Byzantine society, replaced the ruling class with their own aristocracy, utilized the existing bureaucracy and its apparatus and, in so far as it seemed practicable and desirable to do so, adapted the cultural heritage to their own rigid Muslim orthodoxy. In the history of Islamic civilization the 'Turkish period' meant stagnation and decline. Completely absent here were all those forces of revolution and reform which in the history of Christianity made the coming of the Germans on to the scene the prelude to a new civilization.

7. EUROPE, OCCIDENT, ORIENT

From the earliest stages of its rise to power up to the past few centuries of Western expansion Islam was always the chief competitor of the European Christian world. The initial period of Muslim conquest also points to the caesura which divides Christian antiquity from Western Christian civilization. Henri Pirenne epitomizes this in his well-known thesis that 'without Muhammad there would not have been Charlemagne'.[83] The Germans did not destroy that Mediterranean unity which was the distinctive feature of the ancient world; but the Occident was to some extent 'Byzantinized', and the Mediterranean spirit dominated European civilization as a whole from the fifth to the seventh century. What caused the break with the tradition of antiquity was the rapid advance of Islam, as a result of which East and West were finally separated. When the continental Occident parted company with the Mediterranean—which in its western part had become a Muslim lake—the two main consequences were a severing of connections with the old Roman Empire, which continued to exist in Constantinople, and the constitution of a new Roman Empire under Charlemagne. Islam, of course, was not the occasion of the break between East and West, which dates—as we shall see in the next chapter—from an earlier time; but it was the pressure of Muslim conquest which pushed the Occident further along that road and, finally, out of the Mediterranean association of peoples.

The concept of *Occidens* had already acquired a missionary con-notation in the fifth century. It was applied to those western areas which lay outside the sphere of influence and the authority of the Roman emperor, but still under the missionary mandate of the *ecclesia Romana*. The Pope vigorously resisted the attempt by the emperor at Constantinople to lay claim—because of his title *imperator Christianorum*—to these missionary territories in the West.[84]

Exposition of the Latin Bible, the Vulgate, was used to point this politico-ecclesiastical antithesis. Out of the *Oriens* comes forth re-demption (Mt. 24:27); a star shall arise (*orietur*) out of Jacob (Num. 24:17; cf. Mt. 2:2; Is. 41:2; 60:1 ff.); the coming Messiah is the *oriens ex alto* (the day shall dawn from on high, Lk. 1:78; cf. Zech. 6:12). Set over against this is the *Occidens*: darkness, evil and doom. Thus the missionary movement of the Church towards the West and North acquired a cosmic significance: salvation had come to the heathen places, to the seat of darkness, evil and death.[85] As early as the sixth century, the high altar in the churches was built facing towards the East; whilst at the west end the 'Michael's tower' was situated, as a protection against the demons—for the archangel Michael was regarded as overlord of the occidental nations.

This low view of the *Occidens* as the home of the Gentiles, of barbarians and slaves,[86] still taken as a matter of course by the Roman Church and Empire of the sixth century, was felt by the Christian empire of Charlemagne to be intolerable. The term *Europa* replaced the outworn *Occidens* to denote the Carolingian Empire. Latin Christianity had already provided *Europa*—the appellation of a Roman province—with a saint of her own, Martin of Tours; and that gave this territory, no less than Christian 'Asia' and 'Africa' which teemed with saints, a proper dignity. *Europa* as a distinct and independent idea first came into being through the *Völkerwanderung*; and it was claimed by the missionary Pope Gregory the Great as the barbarian region within his jurisdiction (as opposed to that of the Byzantine Empire). A new contrast—between Europe and Byzantium—was now added to the traditional contrast between *Romani* and *Graeci* or between *Occidens* and *Oriens*.[87] The idea received still sharper definition from the Arab invasion, at which time the chronicle of the battles of Tours and Poitiers spoke of the Arabs' opponents as the *Europenses*. That, of course, was in A.D. 732.

The idea of *Europa* was charged with rich meaning by Scriptural commentators who linked it up with Japheth, because his posterity, according to Genesis 10, inhabited the North and West. The early Church Fathers, Ambrose and Augustine, in their exegesis, had already established a connection between the promise that Japheth would be enlarged and would dwell in the tents of Shem (Gen. 9:27) and the inclusion of the Gentiles in the Church now effected in Christ (since he has arisen out of Shem's posterity). In the seventh century this interpretation was applied explicitly to Europe, the land of Japheth and the Gentiles, as opposed to the land of Ham (Africa) and of Shem (Asia).[88] It was thus that in the political sphere the limitations of the ancient Roman Empire were transcended and on the religious front there was a break-through on the part of Roman Christianity with its mission to the Gentiles. Those two factors were fused together into the idea of *Europa*. The term was eminently suitable therefore as a description of the Carolingian Empire. Out of the old *orbis Romanus* there grew the *orbis Europae*; and the Popes became the metropolitans of Europe and its emperor.[89]

However the grand idea perished with the Carolingian Empire, and did not revive until a very much later time. In its stead came the *Renovatio Imperii Romanorum*, an idea full of inner contradictions, because the continental East Frankish Empire which since 962 had been carrying on the Carolingian tradition could not possibly represent the Mediterranean unity of the ancient Roman Empire: so that the 'Renovation' rested entirely on the twin supports of the liaison with the Roman Pope and an obstinate yearning to retrieve the unity of the Mediterranean area.

This contradiction which the mediaeval empire contained within itself and the compelling allure which the Mediterranean exercised as a result form part of the ideological background to the Crusades, which were in fact an attempt to force the Muslims out of their dominant position in the Mediterranean. Although the Crusades were on the whole a miserable failure, in that respect they were indeed successful; for their one permanent achievement was to recover the Mediterranean as a trade-route for the Occident. To this Venice owed her increasing prosperity; and it gave impetus to those forces which later on were to render so dynamic the social and economic structures of European society.

At the back of all this—and even more far-reaching in its implications—lay the idea that the unity of Christian antiquity, which men were now determined to restore, had had its centre and its focus in Jerusalem, itself the centre of the universe. The Crusades were a struggle between the two inheritors of the legacy of Judaism for possession of Jerusalem, the Holy City. It is true that holding on to Jerusalem was scarcely a matter of life and death for Islam; but whether from a religious or a political point of view, it was considered one of her inalienable rights. What Mecca meant to the Muslims, however, the Christian Occident found in Jerusalem: the goal of her pilgrimage and the spiritual lodestar in her firmament, the centre of that invisible unity which she could find neither upon the continent of Europe nor in the hopeless cause of the 'Mediterranean idea'. There was in the Crusades an unworldly longing after the unattainable; in them the faith of the West was expressing its sense of 'orientation' towards Jerusalem, towards the tomb of Jesus, the historical *locus* of the Cross and Resurrection, Messiah, *Oriens*, the source of the Light. To see that as the primary fact is not to overlook the barbarous lust for conquest, the wild hunt after fortune, glory and material advantage, the savage bigotry and gross superstition which marked the course of the Crusades. They were a thoroughly mediaeval phenomenon; but then without the Crusades the Middle Ages, as the West knew them, would be inconceivable. Their end presaged the dawn of modern history.

The Renaissance once more paved a way for the idea of *Europa*; but unlike the mediaeval *Renovatio Imperii Romanorum Christiani*, it nourished itself upon pagan antiquity. The changed direction of outlook—turned now towards the Atlantic—was in its effects and implications of like importance to Islam's turning the *qiblah* towards

Mecca. Jerusalem, the Mediterranean and Islam were no longer the first preoccupation; for the Occident began to reach out to the discovery of new continents and to spread itself around the globe. Politically this emancipation expressed itself in the alliance between the French king, Francis I, and the Turks against the Emperor Charles V, when the latter proposed to continue the Crusades with an expedition against North Africa. The Reformation set its seal on the transition into a new epoch by rejecting outright and on principle the 'Crusading idea'.

That opened a fresh chapter in the relations between Occident and Orient. The expansion of Europe was embarked upon as a final Crusade. One might say that the *volte-face* in the direction of the Atlantic bore the stamp of an eschatological consciousness. The Western Ocean was 'the end of the earth', to which the apostle Paul had already brought the Gospel from Jerusalem, from the Orient, the source of salvation. Mediaeval maps depicted the terrestrial paradise as being in the eastern part of the world.[90] Dante's *Inferno* had its axis exactly underneath Jerusalem, which was the navel of the earth. In the early Middle Ages it was generally accepted that civilization flows from East to West and that mankind would meet its final doom when that movement reached the uttermost limits of the Occident. Hugh of St Victor declared that:

> the course of events has gradually been moving westward, until now it has reached the end of the earth and we must face the fact that we are approaching the end of the ages.[91]

The Middle Ages then were obsessed with a strong eschatological conviction that the Occident was drawing near the end of the ages. With the crossing of the Atlantic comes a leap into the 'beyond'— a leap beyond the end of the world and the end of time.

There has been a remarkable give and take in the encounter between the Occident and Islam. The German invasions and the adoption of Christianity by the Germanic peoples, followed by the Arab conquest and the rejection of Christianity by Islam, mark the beginning of the Middle Ages—an interlude of nearly five hundred years during which the Christian and Muslim worlds seem to have settled into a position of stalemate. The close of the Middle Ages saw yet another redisposal of fronts. The Mongol invasions put paid to the centre of Islamic civilization in the Near East; but their conversion ensured the victory of Islam in Asia at the expense of Christianity. The intrusion of the Turks spelt the doom of Byzantium and carried Islam right into Central Europe. Yet in Western Europe Columbus set out on his explorations across the Atlantic in the very year when the capture of Granada made the final *reconquista* and the expulsion of Islam a certainty. The emancipation of modern Europe meant primarily emancipation from the menace of Islam.

8. THE EXPANSION OF THE WEST

The author of the voluminous *History of the Expansion of Christianity* has likened the course taken by Christianity in the history of the human race to the fluctuations of an incoming tide.[92] Viewed in the context of mankind as a whole and in the light of three major criteria—geographical expansion, inner vitality and total effect—Christianity is seen to have had periods alternately of advance and regression. Yet each larger wave has carried the waters a little further and a little higher than the one before. To begin with, there was progress during five centuries. The first and longest recession, from roughly A.D. 500 to 950, was succeeded by a forward thrust, lasting from about 950 to 1350. Then came another setback, briefer and more limited than the previous one, persisting from 1350 to 1500, or thereabouts. The next surge of the tide, sweeping on to about the middle of the eighteenth century, petered out in a lull which permitted a rallying of resources for the major advance that occurred between 1815 and 1914—the 'great century' during which Christianity became for the first time a world-wide faith.

The similitude no doubt has some illustrative value; but it raises the question whether it is legitimate to describe this irresistible, incoming tide as the course of 'Christianity'. At any rate one must add that this 'Christianity' underwent not a few profound transformations before it eventually managed to spread itself around the globe. It forsook its starting-point in Judaism and went over to Hellenistic civilization. It survived the collapse of the West Roman Empire and was then appropriated by the Germanic peoples; and when the mediaeval *Corpus Christianum* disintegrated, yet a new upsurge thrust it into the arena of modern history. What is more, it is a very particular and one-sided course which Christianity has pursued in order finally to achieve its extension over the whole world, as we see and know it today. The initial expansion in Africa and Asia was brought to a standstill in every direction and in the end was cancelled out by the rising counter-tide of Islam, sweeping away even the Byzantine civilization in which Christianity had been firmly planted during so many centuries. In all conscience, it is impossible to detect in 'Christianity' any peculiar property which would guarantee its spreading over the entire world as a matter of necessity. The injunction to preach the Gospel 'unto the uttermost parts of the earth' was with Christianity from the very beginning; but neither in the period of antiquity nor during the Middle Ages did the possibility exist of actually carrying out such a command. It was with this in mind that when dealing with the process of world-wide expansion which modern history has effected we have preferred to speak of the expansion of 'the West'; for that describes most adequately what the process has really entailed. Indeed, the term is a far less comprehensive one than 'Christianity', since the latter is older and much more various in its meaning. During the last few decades of the fifteenth century it even looked as though Western Christianity, hemmed in between the Turkish Empire and the Atlantic, had no prospect whatever of further expansion, was doomed in fact to wither slowly away. On the other hand it was precisely the course taken by Christianity in the West that from the outset contributed in a special and exceptional way to the propagation of the Gospel; so that one is fully justified in saying that 'the West' is not simply a recent phase in the long evolution of Christianity, but has itself contributed an original *penchant* for growth. Christianity in its Western course so transcended itself as to reach out and embrace the world. The cause of this does not lie in Graeco-Roman civilization, nor is it to be accounted for as a prolongation or resumption of the Germanic *Völkerwanderung*; for neither of these ever showed the slightest capacity for such expansion. What we have here is a unique passage of history in which an interplay of various factors has been at work.

The expansion of the West is a very special instance and manifestation of the driving force which carried the Gospel from Jew to Greek and then from Greek to barbarian. At the same time this helped to produce and to release, in Greek and barbarian alike, dynamic impulses which were thereby multiplied in countless new ways. The remarkable, pluriform symbiosis which has come about within the history of Christianity—a symbiosis of the characteristics of Israel with those of Graeco-Roman civilization and of the converted barbarians—has proved to be a tremendously prolific factor in the process of Western expansion across the world.

The attitude towards Asian peoples and cultures which Europeans so often adopted during the earliest period of modern colonial expansion—and which they fairly often have even today—is in several respects similar to that of the Greeks towards the *barbaroi* in the classical era of Hellas; and the change which came over the self-conscious awareness of 'being Greek', as Hellenism developed through the fusion with non-Greek civilizations and a cosmopolitan spirit and outlook steadily increased, has a parallel in the contemporary growth of a world culture as a result of the Western impact on the non-Western world. On the one hand one can see how Western colonialism has given full rein to a cultural, racial, political and social 'superiority complex', strongly reminiscent of the aloofness and *hauteur* which Hellas displayed towards all non-Greek peoples. Yet on the other hand there is the growing sense of responsibility for the 'education' of the Asian and African peoples and of the duty to disseminate the best that is in Western civilization; and all this very properly reflects a great tradition of Greece: the ideal of *paideia*.

But that is only a part of it. If Western colonial dominance proved irresistible as it thrust onwards into the remotest corners of the non-Western world, that is because there lay behind it an urge other than that which actuated the Greek and Roman colonists and inspired the conquests of Alexander the Great. The non-Western world needed not only to be civilized; above all else it had also to be Christianized. Its peoples were regarded not only as barbarians but as 'Gentiles' too. Thus it was not in the first place the Hellenic tradition that the European attitude reflected, but the Israelitic background. The global outlook which came in the wake of colonial expansion drew its deepest inspiration from the Bible. Where Israelitic notions of exclusiveness and election became fused with the superiority complex of Hellas, the stage was set for outbursts of colonial fanaticism under the guise of various motives of a religious, nationalistic, racial, social or economic character and accompanied at times by repulsive manifestations of hypocrisy. Over against this must be set the genuine concern for lifting the 'natives' and 'uncivilized peoples' up to the level of Western civilization. The high seriousness of this concern was owing largely to the stirrings of a missionary enthusiasm, sure of its task and of its call to spread the Light amid the darkness of heathendom. The assault on social evils, the use of medicine to relieve physical distress, the lifting of men out of their backward state, out of their poverty and ignorance, their liberation from the bonds of social tyranny and pagan custom, the introduction of an enlightened, democratic idealism—all these things have found their deepest inspiration, consciously or unconsciously, directly or indirectly, in the biblical promise of salvation for all the Gentiles. Of course in the history of Christianity the Greek—and for that matter the barbarian too—holds indispensable place with the Jew. The Western peoples, whose boast it is that they have spread the light of civilization and salvation around the world, were in origin themselves barbarians— only caught up in the progress of the Gospel from Jew to Greek, from Greek to barbarian, and thus Christianized. The Chinese—to mention no others—were perfectly justified in looking down from the heights of their age-old and illustrious culture upon the 'Red Barbarians' who forced a way into their coastal territories and in dismissing them as uncivilized upstarts. So too with the Europeans: as their initial contacts turned through the long years of colonial domination into something more permanent and more profound, there slowly dawned upon them what had already been remarked by the Greek historian Herodotus: that other 'civilized' peoples do apparently exist beyond the boundaries of one's own culture. It was this discovery that did so much to precipitate the crisis within the European consciousness of cultural superiority. No wonder then that in view of the outburst of twentieth century barbarism which sprang from the very heart of Europe in the shape of National Socialism, men cast a hypercritical eye over the history of Western colonialism. The West today is faced not only with the question wherein the advantages and peculiar merits of its own civilization consist vis-à-vis other civilizations, but with the far more excruciating question whether it is not precisely in the West that the 'barbarian' and the 'Gentile' have made their appearance in an exceptionally obnoxious form.

It has been justly observed that European penetration of the East began as a crusade[93]—as the last of the Crusades. The pioneers of Portuguese aggrandizement certainly regarded themselves as genuine crusaders for Christendom. At the start of its modern career of expansion Europe was fired, as it had been in the Crusades, with a strange missionary enthusiasm; and the extent to which this was so is illustrated best of all, perhaps, in the person of Christopher Columbus. It agrees well with his name that what most spurred him on to his enterprise—as he wrote in his diary under 27th November, 1492, when having reached the Bahamas he imagined himself on the threshold of China—was an earnest longing 'that it should lead to the growth and glory of the Christian religion'. With the bullion which he planned to obtain he intended to finance a new Crusade and so eventually to free Jerusalem. His journal attests a faith truly worthy of Abraham—a faith in that God of Israel who fulfils and goes beyond all his promises. Columbus set sail just one day after the enforced exodus of his fellow Jews from Spain, determined to scale undreamt of heights of fame and thus to atone for their humiliation.[94] There is then in that vision of his a unique and symbolic amalgam of contradictory motives which have all had an active part to play in Western expansion. The inner dynamic which had brought the West into being was also a force driving it on towards self-transcendence.

Admittedly it was the *last*, the final crusade; and long before already crusades had shown themselves to be an inherently impracticable proposition. Columbus discovered America and Vasco da Gama found the sea-route to India; and although there was a further encounter with Islam in Asia, those events portended none the less the end of a period in which the *Corpus Christianum* was confronted with the *Corpus Islamicum* as its principal opponent. When the West turned towards the Atlantic, it was in effect bidding farewell to the Mediterranean *oikoumenē* and setting out on its world-embracing course.

Alongside that outward movement, and related to it in the closest possible way, went the succession of internal revolutions which Western civilization has undergone. Yet right up to the end of the eighteenth century colonial relations were so much a matter of purely commercial interest, had been consistently so superficial and had so little affected the internal life of Asian peoples that if at that time the colonial powers had withdrawn from the non-Western world for good and all, hardly a trace of European influence would have remained. It was the Industrial Revolution which first gave to European influence its really penetrative force, in such measure as not only to draw the Asian societies slowly but surely into the ever-expanding web of Western economic imperialism, but to subject them also to a gradual transformation calculated to affect every aspect of their total structure. Besides being the climax to a number of earlier revolutions within Western civilization, the Industrial Revolution operated as a lever by which other features in the development of the West could be made over to the civilizations of Asia.

One may take that caesura in the history of Western expansion as a convenient point at which to embark on some consideration of the place of Christian missions within the process as a whole. Up to the second half of the eighteenth century missionary enterprise was the concern of governments or of commercial companies. This was true, of course, first and foremost of the two Roman Catholic powers of the Iberian peninsula, which had taken the lead during the earlier centuries of discovery and conquest overseas; but the East India Companies of the Protestant English and Dutch were scarcely less autocratic in their direction of the Church. Then with the missionary activities of eighteenth-century Pietism began a new trend which the next century was to see developed to the full. The major change came in the nineteenth century, when for the first time in its history Christianity was propagated very largely without the patronage of governments and princes or even of colonizing agencies. The subject is a complicated one; and to do it any justice at all, one would have to deal with it at considerable length. French Roman Catholic missions were not alone in serving as a major channel for the imperialistic aspirations of their government. The protection afforded by the military and naval authorities and the diplomatic representatives of Great Britain and the United States to missionaries along with other of their nationals—especially in China—may not always, or even often, have been a cover for political ends; but in any event it gave rise to grave misunderstandings where the independence of missionary activity was in question. Although governmental assistance to Christian institutions such as schools and hospitals in the colonies was fully justified in the context of a general educational and social policy, the fact remained that it was a Western strategy that was facilitating, indirectly at least, the spread of the Christian religion. The Church sometimes followed in the wake of colonial penetration; and there might just possibly have been some question of collusive planning in those circumstances. In the vast majority of cases, however, even this was inconceivable, as the arrival of the Christian missionary preceded the establishment of white supremacy. However that may be, the two things were seen to be interdependent aspects of the encroachment of Western civilization. Generally speaking, missionaries have set their face against the exploitation of Asian and African peoples by white colonizers; and one can even point to the support which colonial governments have extended to missionary activities with a view to counteracting the bad effects of the Western impact.

All these arguments—to which a great many others could be added—fail however to take hold of the fundamental point at issue: namely, that the nineteenth century, which was the 'great century' of missionary enterprise, was at the same time the 'great century' of industrialism, capitalism and colonialism too. It was no mere coincidence that the two large Protestant countries which took the lead in the Industrial Revolution—Great Britain and the United States—also had the lion's share of Protestant missions or that the countries to shoulder responsibility for Roman Catholic missions in the nineteenth century were France, Belgium, Germany and Northern Italy—those Roman Catholic countries or areas, in fact, which adopted mechanization first and profited by it most. 'The new life which expressed itself in learning, industry, commerce, and territorial expansion also showed itself in the propagation of the Christian faith,'—so Latourette concludes; and he adds the tentative suggestion that 'this was probably because that new life had in part (although by no means fully) Christian origins.'[95] It would be better perhaps to put it rather differently and say that if it was from the side of the West that the world-wide propagation of the Gospel came about during the nineteenth century, what that really means is that the revolutionizing forces perpetually at work within Western civilization—spreading it at last, during that century, around the entire world—ultimately derive their impetus from that particular history which reaches out from Zion to the very ends of the earth.

A distinguished Indian critic and historian, Panikkar, has characterized the 'Vasco da Gama' period of Western dominance as a climacteric in Asian history, involving: 'a qualitative break with the past which justly entitles the changes to be described as revolutionary.' At the same time he gives it as his settled opinion that Christian missions in Asia have proved to be a failure.[96] The main reason for this, as he sees it, is that the missionaries 'not only preached the exclusive truth of the Christian religion, but made claims for the

uniqueness of European culture.' The former, he says, is altogether
alien to the mind of Asia and the latter has been dismissed by Asians
as 'Western cultural aggression'.

Now this contention of his really contains a contradiction. If the
West has indeed succeeded in bringing about a 'qualitative break' in
the history of the Asian peoples—one which has affected 'their
religious and philosophical systems, the material set-up of their
lives and their mental outlook . . . to an extent which it is not possible
for anyone to estimate now'—then that surely amounts to a 'cultural
aggression' witnessing to the uniqueness of the culture that has proved
itself capable of engendering such revolutionary changes. It is not
exactly easy to see therefore why propagating the doctrine of a
monopoly of truth must be doomed to failure because it is alien to
'the Asian mind'; and however much one may wish to express one's
gratification at 'the most complete collapse' of Christian missions in
China, one must at any rate allow that the ideology which has dealt
this fatal blow is one that violates 'the Asian mind' with a ruthless
fanaticism that makes the goings-on of the Christian missions look
like a parlour game.

Yet this talk of 'the failure of the Christian missions' is not
completely without foundation, even though the real point at issue
is not what Panikkar supposes it to be. There are in fact three points
that should be made.

The first is that whilst Western civilization has made its way
in the non-Western world as an irresistible and all-pervasive influence,
it is only among primitive peoples that the direct effects of missionary
enterprise have given incontestable proof of their importance. Amid
the major cultures and religions, on the other hand, the Church
stands as a small and dwindling, albeit qualitatively significant,
minority. Before Islam in particular the Christian missions find
themselves just as powerless today as during the Middle Ages; and
even the 'last Crusade'—the expansion of Western civilization—has
done nothing to alter that.

In the second place, although indigenous Churches have been
implanted and in the course of the present century, especially since
the end of the Second World War, have come to have a life of their
own with a considerable measure of independence, in respect of both
quantity and quality Christianity is still something overwhelmingly
Western in character.

Thirdly, Western missions during the past one hundred and fifty years have had their roots in the rank and file of the Western Churches. That has been the background; and it has meant that the home base was formed very largely by a Christianity of a markedly bourgeois stamp. That same Industrial Revolution which ushered in the 'great century' also produced the European proletariat and the anti-Christian ideology of Marxism, with the consequent exodus of the working class from the Church. Whereas the countries of Western Europe have met the challenge of Marxism with a steady rise in the general standard of living, the challenge which in an intensified and multiplied form faces the Christian Church today is that of the poverty of those hundreds of millions in the non-Western world who belong to the 'external proletariat'. It is a challenge which a Western bourgeois type of Christianity is in no position to answer.

Six

The Revolutionary West

I. THE ROMAN EMPIRE AND THE WEST

FOR several centuries after Christianity had made its appearance in the Roman Empire there was really nothing to indicate that a Western civilization could emerge as a peculiar and thoroughly distinctive phenomenon. On the contrary, the tendency was in the reverse direction—to move further and further away from those traditions that were to awake to new life in the West only at a later date. Although the process of Hellenization which had gone on since the time of Alexander the Great had not been able to do away with the traditions of the Greek city state, it did mean that they were progressively submerged in the bureaucratic type of society prevalent throughout the ancient Near East. Nor was the Roman expansion towards the East proof in the long run against this influence. Its encroachment began in fact as early as the end of the third century B.C., when after the conquest of Sicily the Roman Republic took over from that island an absolutist, agrarian state system, in origin both Egyptian and Hellenistic. Thus the Roman Empire was the hybrid product of Hellenistic monarchy on the one hand and Italic confederation on the other. However earnestly Augustus might champion the patriotic ideals of ancient Rome against the Alexandrian monarchy of Antony and Cleopatra, and however loyal he might claim to be to the traditions of the Republic and its cultural forms, his real model was the Hellenistic Orient, not early Rome or classical Greece. The Romanizing of Western and Central Europe admittedly had the very great merit of bringing those regions within the orbit of Mediterranean civilization and thus of providing for several centuries a bulwark against barbarian invasion; but with the empire being so quickly orientalized, even in the western provinces the old municipal traditions were swamped under the forms of imperial absolutism. At the very same time as a centralized bureaucracy was unifying the empire and so making it possible for the privileges of Roman citizenship to be extended throughout the provinces as well and just when the great jurists of the third century were elaborating the principles of civil rights and liberty as fundamental elements of Roman law, the basis of all these ideas was being steadily undermined.

The state religion of Rome was far too weak to constitute an effective barrier against the various oriental cults and philosophies; and from the reign of Augustus onwards oriental forms of emperor-worship forced their way year by year further into the western regions of the empire. By the beginning of the fourth century A.D. the cult of *Sol Invictus* (the invincible sun) as supreme deity of the empire, and of the emperor himself as being its earthly manifestation, was firmly entrenched as the official religion. It is difficult to imagine how the barbarian invaders who engineered the collapse of the West Roman Empire could have proved the exception to the general rule and have escaped being drawn into this ancient pattern of divine kingship, which would have thrust itself upon them by way of Hellenism and of Rome from its home in the ancient Near East. The infiltration of oriental religions and patterns of society was something which neither the city-state traditions of classical Greece nor the municipal principles of early Rome were in the long run able to withstand. That events did take a different turn in the West is owing to the intervention of Christianity; but at the same time it must be recognized that Christianity did not contrive to do this entirely in its own strength. It had the backing of ancient Roman traditions which it had itself rescued from the tidal wave of oriental religions that threatened to engulf them.

Adolf Harnack has rightly said that the ancient Roman Empire, its order and its culture, lived on to some extent in the Catholic Church of the West.[1] So far as Roman religion is concerned, that had nothing worth while to offer Christianity; but its formal concepts—of tradition, continuity, legality and discipline—which were general and essential elements in Roman culture, did become important.[2] Christianity's real competitor was not the oriental cults—not even when they were as popular as the Isis-cult or as Mithraism—nor was it Graeco-Roman philosophy in general. It was neo-Platonism which came more and more to constitute the real danger to the Church, representing, as it did, the ultimate phase of Hellenism. In the East Roman Empire Christian theology was mesmerized, up to a point, by the powerful attractions of neo-Platonist thought and of whatever tended in that direction. The Church of Rome was able to put up an effective resistance, partly because it had these early Roman traditions to hold on to.

Originally the Roman cult of the state was centred in the king, who united in his person all political and sacral functions. When kingship was abolished and a republican form of government took its place, the political function of the king naturally disappeared, but his sacral function could hardly be dispensed with. Something very much like what had happened in Greece then happened to Rome. In Greece, after kingship had made way for republicanism, the king (*basileus*) retained his status as supreme priest. In the Roman Republic the private deities of the royal house were adopted into the public cult—a fact which accounts for the peculiar character of Roman state religion. On the one hand abolishing the political function of kingship introduced a type of government which differed essentially from the oriental systems. The republican system, which centred upon the Roman Senate and was based on the citizen-class of Italy and the provincial municipalities, became the breeding-ground of those civil rights and the equality in law which Rome has bequeathed to the West. On the other hand the Republic preserved intact the sacral foundation of the state as a divine guarantee of the common welfare. Concern for the maintenance of the republican tradition was bound up, therefore, with a concern for the ancient religion of Rome. Augustus combined the function of Princeps of the Senate with the office of Pontifex Maximus, the latter being the supreme priest of the state who carried out the sacral functions of the ancient king. The palace and private temple of the emperor once more became the centre of the state, as in ancient times the royal house with its private cults had been. It was the fatal weakness of the republican form of government that it remained dependent on sacral foundations rooted in the ancient concept of divine kingship. When the emperor-cult emerged, it formed a link with this unbroken tradition.

That is why the Roman aristocracy, in attempting to preserve the republican tradition, lacked any deeper spiritual incentive and clung jealously to the ancestral ceremonies, though these had long been ossified and lifeless. The famous petition presented by the senator Symmachus in A.D. 384 to the Christian emperor Valentinian II, which urged him to restore to its former place of honour the altar of Victoria —removed from the session-room of the Senate by the previous emperor—was in fact a detailed apology for the ancient cult which had been the glory of Rome for so many centuries, a bulwark of the public welfare and the sanctions of the law.[3] Rome had no ideal which

was at once religious and political and was strong enough to compete
seriously with Christianity or absorb it; and for the future development
of Roman Christianity this was to prove of far-reaching importance.
In the East Roman Empire the case was very different. There the
Church was woven into the texture of the orientalized state, which
drew its strength from the magnificent system of neo-Platonic
philosophy.

2. CHURCH AND EMPEROR IN THE FOURTH CENTURY

In the fourth century two things happened which were to
determine the course of Church history: they were the conversion
of Constantine the Great and the formation of a body of Christian
dogma.

The political ideology already elaborated during the third century
put the Supreme God (*Summus Deus*) in the centre of the state
religion, at the summit of a syncretistic pantheon. It breathed much
the same spirit as the neo-Platonic philosophy of Plotinus. Both were
modelled on the ontocratic pattern which—as we saw in Chapter Four
—underlay the oriental civilizations. Plotinus envisaged the whole of
reality as emanating from the highest Essence, which is purely spiritual,
and proceeding through the progressively more material spheres of
pluralistic existence. Within this hierarchy the gods were intermediate
between the spiritual One and the material world in which mankind
is obliged to live.

The Christian parallel to neo-Platonism appears to some extent in
the theology of Origen, who had been a pupil in the philosophical
school of Alexandria, probably at the same time as Plotinus. Origen
set God the Father, the Son and the Holy Spirit in a hierarchical scheme
of mediation between Creator and creation, which bears a close likeness
to the emanation theory of Plotinus. The historical fact of the Incarnation was actually subsumed into an idealistic concept of excarnation.
Whereas Origen regarded the Son as 'the second God', Arius went
still further and conceived of the Son as only the supreme creature.
These were the predominant modes of thought in the Church of the
eastern part of the empire. So far as the Church in the West was
concerned, theology was still inchoate during the third century and
subsisted mainly on a vague monotheism, addicted—rather naïvely—
to the pagan term *Summus Deus* (supreme deity). This does not mean,
of course, that all dividing lines between Christian theology and pagan

philosophy were obliterated. The exclusive character of the Christian message, which refused to admit of inferior deities and insisted upon the scandalous facts of Incarnation and Crucifixion, formed a solid barrier. But the atmosphere was monotheistic generally and sharp distinctions tended to become blurred.[4]

The general mood of the times very greatly influenced the ideology which was to guide the policies of Constantine the Great and his successors. The *Summus Deus* was held to be the supreme power, to be adored by Christians and pagans alike; and this left both groups free to put whatever construction upon it they preferred. That Constantine's conversion was genuine there is no doubt; but he regarded the *Summus Deus* or *Summa Divinitas* of the Christians in the same light as the gods of Rome: that is, as a divine power guaranteeing the prosperity of the empire. Attempts to suppress the Church by persecution had been completely futile; and it was this that convinced Constantine that the real power lay with the God of the Christians and not the gods of the pagans.

Although Constantine prohibited emperor worship and did away with the offerings at official ceremonies and grew more and more outspokenly contemptuous of the pagan religion, he never resorted to coercion.[5] In the reign of his son Constantius, however, events took a different turn; the climax to this came in A.D. 380, when in the eastern part of the empire Theodosius the Great made the orthodox faith obligatory for all his subjects. Paganism was identified with heresy and must therefore expect to suffer not only the divine wrath but also public retribution at the hands of God's earthly executor, the state. In the subsequent decades all temples were officially ordered to be destroyed; and this was the policy thereafter consistently pursued. The Civil Code of Justinian, in A.D. 529, begins with Theodosius' law of A.D. 380. Christianity had stepped into the shoes of the Roman state religion.

One other factor which had a great deal to do with promoting the growth of a Christian state cult and accelerating its development was the attitude of the Christian emperors toward the doctrinal controversy which divided the Church in the fourth century. Their chief, in fact their only concern was to maintain the unity of the public cult as the basis and guarantee of the unity of the empire. After the Council of Nicaea in A.D. 325—an innovation made by Constantine with a view to unifying and centralizing authority within the Church—imperial policy was to interfere more and more with ecclesiastical affairs. Constantius forced the doctrines of Arius and Origen upon the Church; but after his death there was a *volte-face* in imperial policy. It then switched its support to the anti-Arian doctrines of Athanasius, and these were adopted by the majority in the Church. Thus it was that in A.D. 380 the 'orthodox faith' became the religion of the state.

The course of events seemed therefore to be leading inevitably to Byzantinism. We have the conflicts over dogma which were fought out within the Church during the fourth century to thank for the fact that the Church in the western part of the empire was not carried away on that particular current, but followed an independent course of its own, the result of which was that Western and Eastern Christianity went their separate ways. That is not to say that from then on the Western course has always been consistent or clear. On the contrary, the Western Church has to a great extent shared in a general idea of Christianity as a compulsory religion, officially prohibiting all private pagan cults as well as the Jewish and heretical faiths. Ecclesiastical leaders in the West may have protested against imperial pressure applied to the Church; but if they did so, they were not defending any principle of religious liberty, but only attacking the imposition of false doctrines.

In the Eastern Church the general atmosphere was pervaded by a mode of thinking which finds a striking expression in the theology of Eusebius, one of the leaders of the Origenist party. The closing chapters of his *Historia Ecclesiastica* and his 'Life of Constantine' (*Vita Constantini*), which he wrote after the death of the emperor, make the latter out to be the fulfilment of certain biblical predictions. Constantine ushered in the age of salvation; his reign had a messianic quality. He had brought about the victory over the demonic powers which had continued to thwart the saving effects of Christ's appearing. Therefore he was the image of the Logos, the image of 'the Great Emperor'.[6] In this manner Eusebius, the fore-runner of Byzantinism, translated the pagan cult of the emperor into Christian terms. Admittedly his eulogy only referred to the person of Constantine, not to the imperial authority as such; but his theology became the model for the attitude of the Byzantine Church towards the emperor.

It was through the conflict over dogma that the Western Church came to reject such a theology as a matter of principle, and that, with her insight whetted and tempered in the struggle, she was compelled to a fresh view of the relationship between church and state. The first milestone on this road was the unyielding opposition of Athanasius, bishop of Alexandria from A.D. 328, to the doctrines of Arius, which the opportunism of imperial policy would have forced upon the Church. In A.D. 339 Athanasius felt imperial pressure obliged him to take refuge in Rome. His arrival made that city the centre of opposition to Arianism and occasioned the first outbreak of an open conflict between the Western Church on one side and the emperor and Eastern Church on the other. The Western Church, not split by speculative arguments, came down unanimously on the side of Athanasius in confessing the real incarnation of the Word. The break became an open one at the Council of Sardica (Sofia) in A.D. 343, when the Western Church declined to recognize the deposition of Athanasius, proceeded with the meeting after the Eastern delegates had left, solemnly anathematized the Arian and Origenist doctrines and drafted a petition to the emperors of both parts of the empire, earnestly requesting them to put a stop to all public interference with the internal affairs of the Church. The conflict became more acute; and ten years or so later the emperor was admonished by the Western bishops 'not to confuse the Roman government with the order of the Church, nor to import the Arian heresy into the Church of God.'[7] This statement distinguished clearly between church and state and based the freedom of the Church upon its calling to obey the Truth. In the years that followed, the first martyrs in the struggle of the Church with a Christian emperor went into exile. Bishop Hosius of Cordova, one of the leaders of the opposition, in a powerful protest referred the emperor to Matthew 22:21: 'Therefore we are not entitled to govern on earth, and you, Emperor, are not entitled to sacrifice. I write to you thus out of a care for your salvation!' Athanasius even went so far as to brand Constantius as the Antichrist, because he transferred the prerogatives of the Church to the palace, usurped her authority and tyrannized over her.[8]

The Western Church of the fourth century found the greatest champion of the Church's freedom in Ambrose of Milan. In A.D. 385 he refused to set aside a church building for the empress, where she and her court could listen to preaching of the Arian doctrines she found so agreeable, arguing that: 'To the Emperor belong the palaces, to the priest the churches'. In a famous sermon, delivered in the heat of the fight, he represented to the emperor that he could have no greater honour than to be called a son of the Church: 'For the Emperor's place is inside, not above the Church.'⁹ When Ambrose goes on to identify the Church with the bishops, declaring that 'in matters of faith the bishops use to judge the Emperors, not the Emperors the bishops', we can already see the first signs of the struggle for power which in the mediaeval struggle between Pope and emperor gave rise to so much disorder and confusion. In the fourth century, however, there could be no question of anything like that. Five years afterwards, in prophetic and pastoral mood, the bishop was so bold— as Nathan had been with David—as to demand penance of the emperor for a gruesome massacre which he had ordered his soldiers to carry out in Thessalonica. This bearing of the Western Church towards the emperor was in the true prophetic tradition; it was also the primary cause and earliest manifestation of a deep-seated rupture with Eastern Christianity.

No doubt these events were eloquent too of a difference between the mentality of Latin and Greek. The outlook of the Roman Church had always been extremely pragmatic and concentrated on juridical questions of church order, episcopal authority and discipline; it put little store by discussions of a speculative kind. This Latin spirit has imprinted itself heavily upon the later development of Roman Catholicism. Yet in itself this does not really explain fundamentally the attitudes of the Western Church. Ambrose had an intimate knowledge of Greek literature and was infinitely more indebted to the Greek Fathers than to Tertullian and Cyprian, whom he completely ignores. The ultimate source of the conflict was the clash between a strongly biblical kind of thinking which turned on the dynamic realities of sin and grace in the personal realm and the idealistic bent of Greek thinking in terms of mortality and immortality. Over against the speculative theologies of the Eastern Church—governed, in the last analysis, by the ontocratic pattern which had always formed the basis of imperial absolutism in the great civilizations of Asia—the Western Church stood guard over the dogma of the Incarnation. It was this which inspired her prophetic resistance to the emperor. As a man among men and a member of the Church he was subject— as the Church well knew—to the same commandments and to the same judgment as all other believers.

3. AUGUSTINE'S *DE CIVITATE DEI*

Whilst the East Roman Empire kept itself inviolate and was approaching a period of great cultural splendour, the Western Church, amid the waves of barbarian invasion, was faced with the task of building anew for the future of the mission fields of continental Europe. In that hour of crisis a noble vision of her calling and of what it meant in terms of world history was given her in Augustine's great work, *De Civitate Dei*. The vision was brought to birth and to its full stature in Augustine's mind by the deep impression which Alaric's capture of Rome in A.D. 410 had made upon him. He worked at the book until the year 426. The spear-head of his apologetic was aimed at those pagan circles which—faithful to the ancient Roman idea of the public cult as guarantee and bulwark of the welfare of the state— wanted to make Christianity and the neglect of the gods responsible for the fall of Rome.[10]

Augustine's work proved to be the very opposite of Eusebius' theology of the Christian empire, although there was no intention on Augustine's part of attacking it. Just as Eusebius prescribed the course of the Byzantine Church, so Augustine's vision laid a foundation for the future of Western Christianity. He totally discarded the ancient Roman patriotism which, despite his prophetic attitude, had been an active influence on Ambrose. A contemporary of Augustine's, the Christian poet Prudentius, regarded the Roman Republic as an unwitting instrument of God's providence and put the soldiers who gave their lives for Rome in the same category as the Christian martyrs. Even Augustine's devoted pupil Orosius took the nativity story in Luke 2 as proof that it had pleased God not only to become man, but to become a Roman citizen as well.[11] Orosius' *Historia adversus Paganos*, written at Augustine's request, is apologetic, designed to show God's providence at work in the Christianizing of the Roman Empire, the peace and order of which permitted him to be 'a Roman among Romans, a Christian among Christians, a man among men'. He pinned all his hopes on the continued existence of *Romania*, that is, the cultural, linguistic, social and juridical unity which Rome had conferred upon the nations.[12]

Considered against the background of the general tendency in Christian circles to call attention to the providential benefits of the Roman Empire in its Christianized form, Augustine's vision is all the

more astonishing. He rejects the idea that a fusion might be possible
between the 'city of God' (*civitas Dei*) and the earthly city (*civitas
terrena*). Neither the *pax Romana* under Augustus nor the notion of
a providential purpose attaching to the Constantinian era plays any
part in his thought. On the contrary, the history of Rome since the
Carthaginian War is a story of uninterrupted moral decay.[13] The
unification of the empire, so far from being a blessing, had simply
resulted in the oppression of small nations. Rome had always been
the city of pride and inordinate longing for power. The worship of
its gods had never protected it from calamity; but then the Christianizing of the empire had not averted the impending catastrophe either.
Although he gives the *Christiana tempora* their due and sincerely admits
that the conversion of the emperor and the abolition of the pagan
state cult were both important events,[14] he never speaks of a Christian
empire. He merely recognizes Christian emperors, whose personal
piety in a general way ensured the welfare of the state.

Augustine returns to the eschatological outlook of the Bible, which
during the second and third centuries had certainly been obscured but
had been brought to life again in times of persecution and handed on
through Hippolytus' commentary on 'Daniel' and Victorinus' first
Latin commentary on the 'Revelation of John'.[15] Augustine takes up
this tradition; he sees Rome as the *civitas terrena* whence arise the
enemies of the *civitas Dei*. During the twelve centuries of her history
Rome had been obsessed by the lust for glory (*cupiditas gloriae*). Like
the Pharisees, she 'has her reward' and has therefore no reason to
complain if the true virtue of the saints of the city of God is withheld
from her. As Babel was the first Rome, so Rome is the second Babel;
and Roman history has been nothing but a more splendid repetition
of the twelve centuries of the Assyrian Empire (identified with Babel).
Eastern dominance has made way for Western dominance, which has
united the world. 'What are states but gangs of robbers on a large
scale, if justice is lacking in them? Conversely, what are gangs of
robbers but miniature states?' Rome started as an asylum for criminals,
and Romulus slew his brother. The archetype of Rome, as of Babel,
is the city which Cain built (Gen. 4:17). Romulus too built a city,
'which was to be the capital of this *civitas terrena*, which is the matter
of this book'.[16]

Just as the *civitas terrena* is a community of men and gods (i.e. of
demons or fallen angels), so its counterpart, the *civitas Dei*, consists of

the *civitas coelestis* of the angels and the *ecclesia* of the elect, which here on earth pursues its pilgrimage. The *civitas Dei* is the 'city of God', the heavenly Jerusalem, of which the elect already enjoy that citizenship which makes them strangers and sojourners on earth. The Latin word *civitas* was taken over from the Vulgate, where it is invariably a rendering of *polis*. It means 'citizenship' as well. Thus the Latin term sets the heavenly city in a political context much more emphatically even than the Greek terminology of the New Testament, which has already been discussed in Chapter Three. For that reason it would be a grave mistake to interpret the contrast between the heavenly and the earthly *civitas* as a contrast between church and state. It is in an apocalyptic light that Augustine's work views the impending fall of the Roman Empire, although he resists the Judaistic fondness for nice calculations: 'Who knows in these things the will of God?' He who understands these things, however, has only to make comparison with the 1,240 years of Assyrian history to see clearly enough what the Roman Empire's twelve centuries portend. The Church Father's view—which is entirely in line with the New Testament— is that the fall of Rome is a sign of the last days preceding the descent of the heavenly city.

De Civitate Dei was not, therefore, constitutive for the subsequent history of the Western Church in the same way as Eusebius' theology proved to be for Byzantinism; for again and again in the later centuries Augustine's work has been too strong an intellectual meat, it seems, for the tender stomach of Western Christianity. The Middle Ages seized upon it eagerly—misunderstanding it lamentably and diminishing its stature in the process—in order to vindicate the Roman Catholic Church as an organization bidding for power in competition with the state. In his biblical and eschatological thinking Luther rediscovered Augustine; but at the same time he reduced Augustine's apocalyptic evaluation of the state to a mere dualistic partitioning of functions between state and church. Calvinism put plenty of stress on the civic implications of the *civitas Dei*, but has failed to do justice to the eschatological tension. The apocalyptic expectations which the sects have kept alive represent an element in Augustine's vision which had been pushed on one side; but this now becomes an obsession with them, making them blind to the light of God's grace and patience, which in the *De Civitate Dei* is shed upon the Christian emperor. Augustine's vision, brought to birth at a moment of change and crisis in the history of the world, has continued to lie like a charge of dynamite beneath all the theologies and ecclesiastical concepts of the Western Church.

One cannot deny, of course, that Augustine's work, splendid as it is, gives some occasion for confusing the heavenly city with the Church on earth as an historical organization and that his doctrine of double predestination has obscured the eschatological picture. Then too his appealing to the emperor to use his power in order to suppress the Donatist schismatics became an example and justification for mediaeval intolerance. His lucid awareness of the demonic background to the earthly state and its lust for power and glory lets him down completely over his naïve separation of the emperor's Christian faith from that person's function as head of the state. However reluctantly, one has to admit that Augustine's mistakes and shortcomings have often been much more influential in the history of the Western Church than has the magnificent and fundamentally biblical grasp he displays in his eschatological insights. Even so, if the Caesaropapism of Byzantium kept itself in being by drawing strength from the Origenist tradition of Eusebius, it is no less true that Augustine's thought has moulded the restless and dynamic factors at work in Western history.

4. POPE AND EMPEROR

The break-down of the West Roman Empire gave a new turn to the conflict between the Western Church and the emperor. The Church of Rome became sole champion and patron of the people and city of Rome; and the Pope came to stand for the Latinity of the original Roman Empire, over against Hellenized Constantinople.[17] This in turn affected the character of the quarrel between church and state. The original issue had been the freedom of the Church; but in the latter part of the fifth century it became more and more a trial of strength, with the apostolic chair of Rome on one side and the Church and emperor of Constantinople on the other. That the Roman Church was monarchical in structure gave colour to the suggestion that the Pope was claiming an authority comparable to that of the emperor.

What inevitably gave added force to this idea was the encounter with the German invaders of Europe, who were converts to the Catholic Church. Where the barbarians were concerned, the Roman

Church was sole heir and representative of classical antiquity. The Roman liturgy spoke in one and the same breath of 'the enemies of the Roman name and the enemies of Catholic faith'. Despite the troubled relations with Constantinople, even Rome took it for granted that the emperor was still the focal point of the state; and the missal asked 'that God may subject to our Emperor all barbarian nations'. The Germans inherited the Catholic faith along with the idea of the Roman Empire; they had had no part in the Church's struggle for freedom, and for them Byzantine Caesaropapism was the classic example of what the relationship between Christian Church and Christian state should be. The fresh ties which the Pope established with the Frankish kingdom were bound to bring with them the same sort of tensions as had formerly existed between Rome and Constantinople; but in this case there could be no prospect of a solution. The Roman Church had itself equipped the Germans with the idea of a Christian Roman Empire. In the struggle it maintained throughout the Middle Ages against the claims of the Imperium, the task of the Sacerdotium was to lay the spirits it had itself invoked. The conflict was of an extremely complex kind. Both parties to it swung to and fro between Byzantinism on the one hand and the vision of Augustine's De Civitate Dei on the other. On both sides truth and falsehood were inextricably confused. It was necessary and right for the state to set its face against Papocaesarism; but then, its case was obscured by the Caesaropapist pretensions of the emperor, which the Church quite justifiably opposed.

The full import of the struggle becomes apparent as soon as one remembers how very often, in the course of the centuries, Western Christianity has been tempted to conform to the Byzantine pattern. Byzantine iconography had transferred the symbolism of the Caesar myth to the image of Christ. He is depicted, like the Sassanid kings and Roman emperors, as the 'Cosmocrator', in his hand the cosmic ball (the later 'imperial orb'), standing upon the clipeus or cosmic ring, the nimbus or aureole of Sol Invictus about his head, clothed with the imperial mantle of triumph, the celestial mantle embroidered with stars. The churches display his image standing at the centre of the dome. Even the ceremonial candles and candelabra are borrowed from the imperial ritual. Enthronization and imperial apotheosis provide the ritual models for the iconography of Christ's transfiguration and ascension and of the last judgment. In this transfer of the symbolism of Caesar worship to Christ no doubt the original purpose was to express hostility towards the pagan state; and this is reflected in the imperial titles accorded to Christ in the New Testament.[18] The very fact that this symbolism was carried over greatly assisted the Christianizing of the state; but in Byzantium at least it did not lead to a clash of interests. On the contrary it came to express the idea that Caesar is a mirror of Christ, and Christ of Caesar.

The Byzantine cult of the emperor maintained the ancient pattern of divine kingship in a Christianized version. The court ceremonial involved rites of a sacral character in which the emperor was accorded the honours due to a deity bodily present, in his own palace and seated upon a throne which did duty in every respect for an altar. This was the cult which in many particulars served as a prototype for the monarchical ideology of the Christianized Germanic and Slavonic peoples. Throughout the Middle Ages in the West the king was held to be *vicarius Christi et Dei*; and his person, being the visible representation of Christ, was numinous and sacred. By virtue of holy unction, the central act in the rite of consecration by the Church, the king, like his counterparts in the Old Testament, was 'the anointed of the Lord'. The similarity between the consecration of king and of bishop made it clear that the king was regarded as a priest, after the Old Testament example of Melchizedek. In general terms the theology of the earlier Middle Ages took a broad view of the sacramental; and within that context it took the anointing of monarchs to be a sacrament which conferred, among other things, the charismatic power to heal the sick.[19] All this applied in still greater measure to the consecration of emperors in the Middle Ages. Though the deification of the Byzantine emperor had already aroused criticism at the court of Charlemagne, that did not prevent the Western emperors from aping Byzantium in the matter of the royal apparel, insignia and ceremonial. 'We have to go back as far as the ancient Orient and Mesopotamia,' observes Eichmann, 'if we want to get at the roots of our mediaeval rite of coronation, regal investiture and insignia.'[20]

The conflict between Pope and emperor in the West made a deep intrusion then into the very ritual of coronation. The Byzantine *autocrator* carried his divine authority in his own person. He was head of the Church and himself nominated the Patriarch. True, it became customary in the fifth century A.D. for the Patriarch to crown the emperor, probably in imitation of the Sassanid coronations, where the king was crowned by the high priest; but this custom was of secondary importance in Byzantium. In Western Europe, however, the coronation was a major weapon in the hands of the Church when it had to contend with the state's pretensions to authority. From the ninth century onwards, more and more use was made of the argument that since the coming of Christ no man can be both priest and king and that the bishop has *per se* an authority higher than the king's, since the bishop carries out the anointing, the king merely receives it.[21] Those who opposed this and championed the essential autonomy of the royal function relied on the Byzantine conception of the royal authority as divinely ordained and constituted through the choice and acclamation of the people. The priestly blessing was just an additional confirmation of the fact. In order to divest the royal authority of any priestly character, the Church made drastic changes in the coronation ritual, so that the emperor was first given something like the status of a deacon in the Church and then the status of a layman, and nothing more. Along with this devaluation on the Church's part went a development in the constitutional sphere, which more and more subordinated the royal authority to the law of heredity and election.[22] From this we can see how the conflict of church and state, through the activity of both, ended by depriving the state of its sacral character. What testifies more than anything else perhaps to the irresistible power of the ontocratic ideology is that even in more recent times the West has only with great difficulty contrived to escape its binding spell. From Lutheranism and Romanticism in Germany, absolutism in France—and British monarchism too—it has exacted its full dues.[23]

It is in fact hardly adequate to talk about a mediaeval conflict between church and state. The real antagonists in this drama were the two opposed realities of *civitas Dei* and *civitas terrena*; and the polarity between them, in an eschatological context, far transcends the conflict on the historical plane between ecclesiastical and political claims. The Church no more stood for the *civitas Dei* than the state represented the *civitas terrena*. There was not so much a clash of incompatible ideas—and still less a struggle between belief and unbelief —as a contest between opposing powers disputing with each other for supreme authority over an order of life which both conceived to a very large extent in identical terms as a comprehensive *Corpus Christianum*. If the Byzantine pattern provided a model for the imperial claims, that was very largely true of the papal claims as well. Of course the conflict would have issued in an acceptable compromise, had the Pope been satisfied with a position like that of the Byzantine Patriarch. Two irreconcilable factors stood in his way, however. Against Frankish and German Byzantinism the Roman Church held the pass for the great tradition of the freedom of the Gospel, which Athanasius and Ambrose had defended against the East Roman emperors. Yet at the same time the Pope was determined to be the one and only successor to the authority of the Christian emperors within the West Roman Empire. The title *Vicarius Christi* was taken over by the Pope from the emperors, to whom it had originally belonged. Through his endeavours to strip the king of all priestly authority the high priest in the papal chair arrogated more and more of royal power to himself. The celebrated *Donatio Constantini*—probably a grant by the Frankish king Pepin of certain Italian territories, which laid a foundation for the Papal State as a protection for the Pope against the Langobards—was used in later centuries to justify the papal claim to political dominance over the Occident. The doctrine of the 'two swords'—of spiritual and of secular power—in a *single* hand, called in to support the papal claims when they reached a climax at the beginning of the fourteenth century, had in fact already been formulated five centuries earlier by theologians at the Frankish court to bolster up Charlemagne's authority; over against the Roman Empire—last manifestation of the *civitas terrena*—the Frankish king was a new David leading the people of God, bearing the twin swords of secular and spiritual power, commissioned by Christ to be the ruler of the *Imperium Christianum*.

In the thirteenth century the powerful Hohenstaufen emperor, Frederick II, who was very much under the influence of Islamic civilization, revived Charlemagne's claims. He pronounced himself to be the priest-king, under the call of God and having an authority derived directly from him, not mediated by the Pope. As *Vicarius Christi*, the emperor was not only above all kings, but also above the Pope himself. It was his Messianic mission to restore the divine order among men and to revive the universal dominion of Augustus as lord and saviour of the world. Frederick's dream ended in the complete collapse of his empire, just as half a century later hubris of a similar kind on the Pope's part led to a most wretched disaster. In the long run, Caesaropapism and Papocaesarism turned out to be not merely incompatible, but even mutually destructive.

So it was that during the Middle Ages those forces which were to shatter the edifice of the *Corpus Christianum Romanum* and were destined to open the way through to modern civilization were gathering their strength. The mediaeval order had to give way, because it proved impossible to build a truly Christian order to an ontocratic pattern. It would be an unfair and one-sided judgment of the mediaeval West simply to say that it set out to reproduce, in the realm of ecclesiastical and political affairs, the sacral pattern of the Roman Empire. If that were the case, the Middle Ages in the West would have done no more than prolong, under a new guise, the ancient ontocratic pattern of the great primary civilizations. What was really unique about its history during this period was the dramatic fashion in which the ontocratic order disintegrated—not under pressure of external forces nor through any inherent principle of senile decay; it was exploded from within by an intolerable pressure, by the force of the collision between the two powers, each of which claimed the sole authority over it. In other cultures the rival aspirations of kings and priests had created tensions; but these had always been a normal phenomenon which found its proper place within the traditional framework of society. Only in the history of the West have those forces been at work which proved able to demolish the foundations of mediaevalism. It is therefore utterly wrong to try and push the mediaeval West into the same category with the oriental cultures or to call the latter 'mediaeval'. Furthermore the term 'Middle Ages' in itself precludes such a comparison, if only because it was invented to denote precisely that period which the West has put behind it—a period therefore which did not share the permanent character of the oriental cultures. It is of the greatest significance that the theocratic model offered by the Old Testament made such a strong impression on Western Europe in mediaeval times; for the Davidic kingdom carried within itself the seeds of its own decay. The key to the extraordinarily dynamic nature of mediaeval Western history is not the struggle between king and priest; it lies rather with the judgment that falls alike on throne and altar. Beneath the surface of things rages the conflict between heaven and earth, theocracy and ontocracy, the kingdom of the Lord and the power of men, the Spirit and the flesh.

To conclude then with an account in summary outline of this dynamic process: the first period (A.D. 600–900) begins with Pope Gregory the Great, who founds the territorial power of the Papacy in Italy, mightily defends the primacy of Rome against the ambition of Byzantium and by his missionary vision moulds the history of Western Christianity. After Boniface has reorganized the Church of the Frankish Empire so that harmony prevails between Pope and king, the climax comes with Charlemagne's Byzantinism. The dissolution of the Frankish Empire under his successors puts the Church in a position of independence and makes her the main pillar of political unity. The end of this period finds both church and state in a situation of extreme decadence.

In the second period (A.D. 900–1300), on the one hand the Carolingian tradition is recovered in the East Frankish Empire, and on the other the Papacy reaches the zenith of its power. The first phase (910–1050) is marked by a reformation of the Papacy under the combined influence of church and state. In the second phase (1050–1122), however, the Pope takes over leadership of the reform movement from the emperor, challenges the latter's claim to authority over the Church and finally arrogates to himself political supremacy over the entire world. The Concordat of Worms is a kind of armistice. A third phase (1122–1300) starts with a sharp reaction against the political aims of the Papacy in the shape of the Cistercian reform movement; but once Bernard is dead, the Pope's worldly power becomes greater even than it was before. The collapse of the German Empire represents no more than a Pyrrhic victory, however; for the Papacy, now exhausted, falls at last under the control of France.

The third period (1300–1517) is for the Papacy one of rapid decline. It sees the rise both of various independent reforming movements and of national states. The mediaeval order disintegrates and gives place to those novel forces which it has itself brought into being.

5. FEUDALISM

During the Middle Ages the tensions existing between Church and state prevented an absolutist or centralized order of society from emerging in the West; but there developed instead a distinctively feudal structure. In the feudal system the ancient Aryan aristocratic pattern was preserved.[24] After the collapse of the West Roman Empire the Germanic tribes who then invaded Western Europe re-established the institution of the noble and his household, who both protected and exploited the peasantry living on his estate. This institution was embodied in the feudal system, which also imposed a more comprehensive arrangement whereby the support of stronger families was ensured to relatively weaker ones in return for their allegiance in time of war. The French *menes* of the Dark Ages—hence the term *demesnes*—was in essence the old Aryan household. Mediaeval kings adhered to the Aryan tribal custom by which the chieftain, as head of the wealthiest and most important family, was expected to defray the entire costs of his various establishments out of the revenue from his own estates.

It appears that the Germanic invaders took over such of the contractual institutions of the later Roman Empire as were of use to them in their efforts to reconstruct, on a pyramidal basis, something of what they had destroyed. In so doing, they merely completed a process set in motion when the bureaucratic organization of the empire had started to disintegrate.

Mediaeval European society is by no means the only instance of a feudal order; but the system acquired there a special character which one does not come across anywhere else at all. The feudal order prevailing in China during the greater part of the second millennium B.C. never recovered from the *coup de grâce* it received in 221 B.C. Japan alone offers a close parallel with mediaeval Europe; for Japanese society was likewise ruled by a sovereign, but next him and below him were numerous overlords who rendered only limited and conditional services and were not part of any bureaucratic apparatus. At a rairly early date the rulers of the politically dominant centre did establish political unification of a loose kind, but then the tasks confronting them did not call for the co-ordinated use of forced labour on a big scale. Nor were thy oevercome by the forces of an oriental despotic state.[25] In both Japan and mediaeval Europe the feudal system successfully withstood all attempts to impose a centralized and bureaucratic despotism. The Taikwa reform of A.D. 646 was not able to achieve its end of absolute rule without making radical concessions to the powerful feudal interest, in particular, by assigning tax-free land to important officials who had set themselves up as hereditary landowners and, like their European counterparts, had introduced a 'sole heir' system of inheritan e. Wittfogel asserts that although many elements of Chinese culture were certainly present, the decentralized society of the Japanese Middle Ages, with its property-owning basis, bore a much closer resemblance to the feudal order of the remote European world than to the hydraulic pattern of neighbouring China. The absolutist Tokugawa régime was similarly powerless to enforce its acquisitive demands throughout the empire as a whole. The major part of the revenue remained in the hands of great feudal vassals.[26]

Once the Shogunate had been established in A.D. 1184, the situation in Japan was rather like that which had prevailed in Western Europe at about A.D. 800. Charlemagne reorganized his empire on the pattern of the East Roman Empire and that was itself essentially a continuation, in modified form, of the West Asiatic empires. Imperial inquisitors, the *missi dominici*, periodically traversed the empire and looked into the conduct of the emperor's officials in the provinces and sub-provinces. In the same way, Yoritomo reproduced the archaic Japanese pattern. Both Charlemagne's 'Holy Roman Empire' and Yoritomo's Bakufu system were forms of bureaucracy superimposed on a feudal pyramid—but beyond that point important differences appear between them. The 'Holy Roman Empire' very soon became a purely nominal affair, whereas the Bakufu (Shogun) in Japan grew in power, conferring political unity upon the country as a whole through a bureaucratic system which overlay and dominated the 'pyramidal' elements in the state and filled the place occupied in the late seventh and early eighth centuries by the former imperial organization. The position of the emperor and his organization during the period of Bakufu dominance in Japan has been compared with that of the Pope and the papal machinery in mediaeval Europe.[27] The papal establishment was from one point of view a part survival of the West Roman Empire; and the imperial establishment in the Japan of the Bakufu—where the emperor was high priest of the nation—was in a sense a survival of the pre-Bakufu empire. The comparison is a useful one to make, if only because it helps one to see how striking the differences are; for whilst the Japanese emperor was deprived of his former authority as political head of the state and became a mere puppet figure, the Papacy reached a position of power from which it was able eventually to lay down the law to the emperor. In Japan there was no room for genuine competition between two rival powers. The Middle Ages in Europe on the other hand owe their intensely rhythmic character to the tensive relations between church and state.

Even when Japanese feudalism was in the forefront, the ideology of divine kingship continued in the background and was never really interrupted. The ruling group was deeply imbued with Confucianism, modified more or less to suit the circumstances. At the humbler, local level there was no growth of opposition to the absolutist rule of the feudal lords, which required complete submission. Prostration was the gesture symbolizing this; and it has persisted into modern times. In mediaeval Europe the ambitions of those political rulers who aimed at a centralized absolutism were frustrated most effectively by the Church, which eventually assumed a unified control over society. The Church allied itself with the feudal gentry whose interest as landowners demanded that there should exist in perpetuity organs of political power which were independent of the state. A good example of this is the signing of Magna Carta by the King of England in A.D. 1215. The bishops and feudal lords, acting in concert, forced him thereby to give legal recognition to a form of balanced, constitutional government. The charter was primarily a concession made 'to God' in favour of the English Church, granting it full liberties, and in particular the right to free elections. Freedom to leave the kingdom at will meant that the clergy could go to Rome without permission from the king.[28] The Church, in the struggle for the right to govern itself as a religious body, also strengthened the secular nobility as a property-owning and organizing force. An essentially independent body within mediaeval agrarian society, the Church encouraged the growth of a balanced feudal order; and that eventually gave birth to the modern society which we have in the West. After A.D. 962 the renovated 'Roman Empire' comprised a number of feudal states so loosely federated that it has been justly described as 'a confusion roughly organized'. The nature of feudal contracts was such that any additional monies which might be required of his vassals by a king or by some inferior nobleman could only be had as a grant, expressly and voluntarily made, by the vassals themselves. In later practice this meant simply that taxes could not be raised without consent of the taxed; and still later there grew out of this the principle of 'no taxation without representation'. In this way feudal Europe created the fiscal basis of the popular control of government. Besides the independent forces which clergy and nobility represented, there was yet another factor which increased steadily in importance: the cities of mediaeval Europe with their various forms of burgher associations. Thus there evolved in Western Europe a multi-centred structure of society for which Japan, although it maintained its feudal order, affords no parallel.

6. CITIES

The idea of the Roman Empire is not the only thing which the Church transferred to the Occident. It also took particular care that the tradition of the Roman cities should not be swallowed up in the barbarian flood. From the beginning of the sixth century the word *civitas*—the Latin equivalent of the Greek *polis*—had the special meaning of 'episcopal city'. The Church carried on the pattern of the Roman administrative districts by turning them into religious ones, of which the episcopal cities formed the centres. The commercial development of these cities had as a basis the economic activity of the Roman Empire; but it was not able to survive the effects of Islamic invasion, which isolated the Occident from the Mediterranean. Yet when trade declined generally and the Carolingian Empire went over to a closed domestic economy, it was the Church which saved the old Roman cities which now came entirely under episcopal direction.[29] When Islam was obliged to surrender control over the sea-routes in the eleventh century and the Occident once again had access to distant markets, the cities prospered, developing their economic life and status on a scale undreamt of in the ancient world. It was the growth of commerce which brought about the new vitality of city life in Italy and the Netherlands.

Henri Pirenne gives an invaluable account of how over-population of the land led in the course of the eleventh century to the formation of merchant colonies, which established themselves in the episcopal cities or in the shelter of fortified military stations created by princes. The legal status acquired by these new mercantile groups, who went under the name of 'burghers', gave them a position of signal advantage, since they had slipped the reins of demesnial and seigneurial authority to which agrarian society was subject. Like the cleric and the noble, they enjoyed a law of privilege. The unique character which this rising middle class gave to the cities of the Occident cannot be accounted for simply in terms of their commercial and industrial activity, for that is an indispensable condition for the growth of city life in every civilization. What was without precedent in the growth of the occidental cities was their concentrating *exclusively* on commerce and industry—for in antiquity and in other civilizations these have always been intimately connected with and dependent on a rural economy.

> At no era in history is there so marked a contrast as that which their social and economic organization presented to the social and economic organization of the country. Never before had there existed, it seems, a class of men so specifically and strictly urban as was the mediaeval bourgeoisie.[30]

We saw earlier on how in the civilizations of Asia the towns were never able to emerge as independent entities and how they were always constrained to function within the bureaucratic system. Although as regards their structure the Greek and Roman cities were an exceptional phenomenon, compared with the towns of the primary civilizations, they too failed to produce a type of men like the mediaeval bourgeoisie of the Occident. The ancient cities were originally confederations of tribes, drawn together by the bond of a common worship. In ancient Rome the *civitas* was the political and religious association of tribes, to cater for the needs of which the city had been built. Every member of that association, whether living within the walls or outside, was equally a citizen of it. The city was the religious, political and administrative centre for the whole territory of the tribe after which it was customarily named. The association of citizens was founded on the cult of the city gods and had a sacred character. The *plebs* was something outside the organization of the cult; as such, it had no rights either of property or of citizenship. When general democracy had been established through a series of revolutions, economic conditions were such as to make still wider the gap between the wealthy and the poor. Even the liberal professions were more or less closed to the citizen. He was taught simply to despise labour and in consequence lacked the ethos without which there could be no urge to change conditions for the labouring poor. In the end the municipal system declined in the wake of the ancient religion. It could not survive the advance of individualism and was absorbed into the empire.[31]

The mediaeval cities of the Occident have a quite different origin. When the 'burghers' came to the episcopal cities and military strongholds and settled down in them, an entirely new element entered the existing social order. In striking contrast to the plebeians whose revolt touched off a process of political and economic decay among the cities of antiquity, the nascent middle class of the Middle Ages actually created occidental city life. Behind this movement in the spheres of industry and commerce there was a spirit at work which one can also see reflected in the zeal of the Crusades—that venture which so greatly contributed to the renewed prosperity of the Mediterranean trade-routes. It is more than a coincidence that the campaign within the episcopal cities for the rights and liberties of the emerging middle class went hand in hand with papal opposition to the emperor. In northern Italy, where the movement began, this new class formed a united front with the clergy, both religious and secular, against the régime of the bishops nominated by the emperor; and they joined in a common protest against interference by the 'lay' authority in the government of the Church. It was likewise within the walls of the episcopal cities that the earliest communes were formed. The oldest of them—that of Cambrai in northern France—was proclaimed in 1077 as the outcome of an uprising among the inhabitants of the commercial suburb against their 'Simoniac' bishop. He was on his way at the time to receive the investiture at the hands of the emperor. Only two years before, the *Dictatus Papae* had affirmed the Pope's exclusive right of investiture.

From a simple social group given to the pursuit of commerce and industry, the corps or *communio* of burghers was gradually transformed into a legally constituted body with an independent status and a legal organization of its own. The city law which was evolved in the course of the twelfth century guaranteed the common rights of the burghers and a general freedom, admitting by implication the absence of serfdom or slavery. Instead of the contempt for labour which had permeated the ethos of the ancient cities, the artisan was accorded a positive dignity in that he shared to the full the privileges and duties of citizenship. The mediaeval cathedrals were built by free citizens, who carried out their work in the service of God, the Maker of all things. In relation to the traditional feudal structure of the surrounding rural society, the freedom enjoyed by the city made definite and permanent inroads on the seigneurial rights of the landowning classes. Therein lies the key—as Max Weber has pointed out—to their novel and revolutionary character, when one compares them with all non-occidental cities.[32] If the universal Church had not deliberately employed its authority to do away with the tribal traditions, a revolution of this kind would have been impossible.

Gradually emancipation spread from the cities to the rural classes. Whilst that was happening, the rôle of liquid capital became steadily more important, whereas the advantages of landownership—on which rested the privileged status of the clergy and the nobility—lost something of their significance. Very early in the thirteenth century armed contingents of citizens in France put power in the hands of the monarchy, which then set itself up as the protector of civic liberties. Once the cities had won a place in the Estates next the clergy and the nobility, which they did in the fourteenth century, the way was opened for a steady progress towards that position of decisive influence which they have occupied in the formation of the modern state and of modern society.

One is bound to see in the emancipation of city life a positively 'lay' spirit at work, which was to come fully into its own during the Renaissance period. The elementary schools for the burghers' children, founded by the municipal councils in the first half of the twelfth century, were the first lay schools of post-antiquity. As the clergy were not subject to municipal jurisdiction, to deal with official correspondence and accounts the cities used the services of laymen only, the 'clerks' being drawn from the clerical establishments. From the beginning of the thirteenth century national idioms were gradually adopted; and the cities took the initiative in introducing the vulgar tongue as the language of municipal administration. These innovations were of far-reaching importance in the process of laicizing Western civilization. This lay spirit, so far from being secular, was animated at first by an intensely ascetic and mystical temper; it was what made the cities support with enthusiasm the Papal protest against simony and imperial investiture in the eleventh century. But to the extent that the Gregorian movement became a struggle for worldly power, the lay spirit displayed increasingly anti-clerical tendencies. That explains the ardour with which the city populations in the thirteenth century received the Franciscan and Dominican preachers. The mendicant orders were a new feature of society. Unlike the monastic orders of earlier periods, the mendicants of the thirteenth century did not depend on agriculture or landownership, but were associated with the money economy of the cities. Shepherding the urban masses and preaching to them in the common tongue, they checked the growing anti-clericalism of the city population and bridged the gulf between papal ideology and urban emancipation. At the same time they did a very great deal to prepare the ground for the Italian Renaissance. Through the institution of a Third Order and through their daily wanderings and preaching in many places the mendicants gave impetus to a spiritual reawakening which in turn broadened the outlook of the fanatically particularist cities and helped them to settle their differences. That mystical love which Francis had for the beauty of God's creation moved men to rediscover the Italian landscape through art; and as background to the portraiture of the saints this found its way into the Church.

The Pope's struggle for the freedom of the Church came to mean defending the freedom of the papal state and of Italy from the dominant power of the German emperor. One result was that the Italian city states, which had emancipated themselves from both imperial and clerical patronage, developed a secular conception of politics. The Church itself, by its total rejection of the emperor's priestly claims and by drawing such a rigid distinction between ecclesiastical and worldly authority, was the real inventor of this novel idea. The Pope obliged Frederick II to detach his ideology of divine emperorship from his title to his Italian possession, which he therefore had to govern as a purely secular territory. Thus the Sicilian kingdom became the fore-runner of the modern secular state.

7. RENAISSANCE

In his book, *Out of Revolution*, Eugen Rosenstock-Huessy makes European history out to be a series of revolutions which have determined, through a dialectical sequence, the character of the European nations. He sees the Pope as the oldest revolutionary in Europe. The revolutionary element in papal resistance to imperial absolutism lay in the intervention of the spiritual shepherd in the purely territorial questions of the Apennine peninsula.[33] Indeed the efflorescence of the Italian city states is very closely connected with the 'papal revolution'. They had extricated themselves from the feudal system and in the fourteenth century rated the German emperor at the most as reinforcing the power which they already in fact possessed. The rise of a unified monarchical state, such as replaced the feudal order in France, in England and in Spain, was prevented in Italy by the Papacy, which was itself too weak to engineer a political unification.

The despotism and unbounded lust for power which ran riot in many an Italian city and princely court quite frequently threw up a new factor which became a characteristic of the political spirit of the Renaissance and a constitutive element in the modern European conception of the state. It was the idea of the state as a consciously contrived human invention. The modern term, 'state', comes from the name given to the Italian tyrants and their courts, *lo stato*—a reference to their actual power, which came to be used to denote the territory ruled by them. The example of Frederick II's secular state in Lower Italy and Sicily—rigorously and most rationally governed and exploited by 'the first modern man to sit on a throne'[34]—found its imitators among both major and minor Italian tyrants of the fourteenth century. Sicily has had a notable rôle to play as the connecting-link between the Mediterranean world and the empires of the ancient Near East. At the close of the third century B.C. the Sicilian kingdom of Syracuse was the critical spot where the process began which was to orientalize the Roman Republic. There the Romans encountered an organized example of Hellenistic statecraft which declared that the state has absolute power and owns all land. Under Byzantine domination this system was continued; and then came the Muslims, who combined Arab and Byzantine techniques of absolutist rule. There would appear to be some connection between the introduction of the centralized administration of the Domesday Book in England—commanded in 1085 by the Norman king, William the Conqueror, and representing a radical break with the feudal system —and the Norman ascendancy in Sicily, where they learned familiarity with the 'magnificent exploit' of an oriental despotic tradition.[35] Frederick II, who became King of Sicily in 1198 and later rose to be King of Germany and Roman Emperor, took over the Norman heritage. Measured against the feudal society of the Occident, his oriental system of government—which he also attempted to apply in Italy—was something fundamentally new. One can see here a striking demonstration of how deeply the conflict between church and empire had set its mark on occidental history. Unlike the earlier Roman encounter with Sicily, Frederick's example did not touch off any orientalizing process; but it did give an initial fillip to the political ideas of the Renaissance and make the first breach in the structure of feudal society through which there was to emerge the modern territorial state. The idea of the sacred empire had come to nothing, frustrated by the papal revolution. It was not Frederick's 'Mediaeval Caesar' mythology, but his rational principles of legislation based on the theory of natural law, his tolerance resting upon an attitude of scepticism and his interest in the sciences of mathematics, astronomy and physics, then being promoted by Arab civilization, which have been of importance for the creation of modern Europe.

Whilst the example of Sicily formed a bridge from imperial absolutism to the modern territorial state, the Venetian Republic preserved the ancient tradition of the city state and passed it on to the renascent cities of the twelfth century. Venice was the only city, geographically part of the West, which maintained an unbroken independence and had a continuous political development. The re-organized constitution which this city adopted in 1172 kept its form essentially unchanged until the republic was conquered and terminated by Napoleon. Its pattern and its spirit were much like those of Athens in her prime. The north Italian city states, beginning a new lease of life in the twelfth century, looked to this model for their political principles and thus reproduced, in a mediaeval context, an image of classical Hellas.[36] In Florence, equal status for every free citizen, without any automatic admission of hereditary privilege, produced a flourishing civic culture, unrivalled by anything the Renaissance has to show. The peculiar restlessness which takes possession of the emancipated human being is typified in the tumultuous history of this city state. Machiavelli's objective political realism was derived from 'a long acquaintance with modern life'. His scientific and experimental mind was in quest of the most rational principles for constructing a state. In one of his later writings he argues for the democratic form of a republic and thinks the people more perspicacious in the choice of political leaders than the prince.[37]

What part the rediscovery of ancient culture had in the Renaissance is a vexed question. Burckhardt observes that the birth of the modern consciousness could have happened without help from the culture of antiquity, but that on the other hand one cannot understand why the Renaissance has been of such paramount importance in the history of Western culture if one disregards its intimate connection with the Italian national genius, into which so much of ancient culture had been absorbed. A renaissance of that tradition only became possible, however, because it had first been relinquished and made remote by a twofold interruption: once by the Christianization of the empire and the downfall of the pagan state religion, and a second time by the transfer of this Christian *imperium* to the Occident. The Renaissance flowered in the northern part of Italy, which had taken the full strain of the whole process: in the clash between Roman Pope and German emperor, in the medley of Germano-Lombardic constitutions, in its ties with European chivalry in general and through ecclesiastical and cultural influences coming from the north. That double interruption created the sense of distance and the psychic tension which must be there before a spiritual 'rediscovery' becomes possible.

The revival of ancient culture was in form, and partly also in substance, the apprehending afresh of a tradition handed down by the Church itself. To that extent the Renaissance belongs to the late Middle Ages; only there now shows itself for the first time—and just here the originality lies—an inner contradiction which in fact the blending of Christian belief with pagan culture had always contained. Dante, in the *Divine Comedy*, holds the biblical story and the story of antiquity in a sustained parallel. With Petrarch and Boccaccio this equipoise gives way to an open admiration for the ancient tradition, without their being conscious of any opposition.

It is the glory and the blessing of that heritage from the ancient world that through it a certain amount of secular culture was handed on. Yet the pagan motives, however watered down or overlaid with Christian ideas they might be, were bound sooner or later to reassert their power. The Renaissance was also a reaction against the worldliness of the Church, from which the most sensitive natures were the very ones to suffer most. Machiavelli complained that the Italians were more irreligious and immoral than any other people, because the Church and its ministers set the worst example. Men gave themselves up enthusiastically to the cult of fame and were only too ready, out of a feeling of disillusion and resentment, to exchange the worship of the saints for a cult of the tombs of the great and famous.

But they did not go quite as far as a genuine revival of ancient paganism. The pagan gods stayed dead. Humanism brought a mighty reawakening in literature and philosophy, but no return to a defeated religion. On the other hand Renaissance man was much too firmly tied to the churchly tradition of the Middle Ages to be able to press on with a real reformation of the Church itself. At rock bottom, the Renaissance was an inner rebirth of mediaeval man, in which Franciscan mysticism, apocalypticism and the urban lay spirit were conjoined in a remarkable way. Cola di Rienzo's attempt—typical of the Renaissance—to bring ancient Rome back to life received a strong mystical impulsion from the extremist 'Fraticelli', in whom the original Franciscan nonconformity was still very much alive. The whole Renaissance period was shot through with violent religious reactions of contrition and penitence, such as that which put Florence, at the very zenith of her prosperity, beneath the theocratic authority of a Savonarola.

The Italians crossed the horizon, not only of the ancient world, but of the Middle Ages too. In the thirteenth century we find them taking part in voyages of discovery in Atlantic waters. In 1291, the year of the fall of Ptolemais—last stronghold of the Christian orders in the Near East—the Genoese made the earliest known attempt to find the sea-route to the East Indies. This urge to exploration went hand in hand with a lively concern for matters of geography, statistics and history. It was all the outcome of a spirit of experimentation, directed also towards mathematics and astronomy and in conjunction therewith to various practical ends. Thus the Italian cities, through their connection with the Mediterranean world, were destined to become pioneers in unlocking the doors of the mediaeval Occident.

8. GERMANY AND THE REFORMATION

From the start of the sixteenth century a divergence begins to occur, and then to become more and more clearly discernible, between the culture of Southern and Central Europe on the one hand and that of Western Europe on the other. Whilst Italian autonomy was destroyed under foreign domination, Germany too—after her trading towns had enjoyed a period of prosperity under early capitalism—reverted slowly but surely to her original feudal, agrarian structure. The shift of the trade-routes brought economic decay to the Hanseatic towns and the great cities to the north of the Alpine pass, all of which consequently lost their importance. In Germany the empire held its position at the top of the hierarchy within a feudal structure. Even German humanism remained addicted to mediaeval categories of thought; and there is an enormous divide between Machiavelli's secular rationalism and the emotional Renaissance nationalism of his German contemporary—and one of the last knights of the epoch—Ulrich von Hutten.

Luther too in many respects belongs to the later Middle Ages.

One cannot regard the Reformation as a break, pure and simple, with mediaeval Christianity. As a spiritual upheaval it meant something much more than the inception of a new period of European history. The struggle to affirm the sovereignty of the Word of God and to liberate it from the constraint of the Church, the struggle for the recognition of God's grace, and not human merit, as the sole ground of redemption—this was not delimited by the particular situation of the Roman Catholic Church at the time; rather is it of the prophetic core of the Bible itself. To that extent the Reformation must be seen as carrying on the papal revolution of the eleventh century. The radical quality of Luther's sixty-second thesis: 'The Church's true treasure is the holy Gospel of the greatness and the grace of God' sets it on a par with the first deposition of the Gregorian *Dictatus Papae* of 1075: 'The Roman Church is instituted of God alone'. Just as the Pope, in reliance upon that foundation, declared himself the true emperor and claimed the right to depose other emperors (articles 8 and 12), so in 1520 Luther made it his warrant for burning publicly 'the accursed bull of the Antichrist' and the *corpus iuris canonici*. There is moreover a similarity in the historical circumstances which inevitably surrounded both these revolutions. The Pope's resistance to the emperor's exercise of authority over the Church—at bottom a prophetic assertion of the Church's freedom— turned more and more into a bid for power and more especially into a struggle for the independence of the papal state and for papal influence in Italian politics versus the German emperor. Just as the freedom of the Italian city states would have been inconceivable apart from the papal revolution, so, conversely, the Reformation gave the chief impetus to the formation of the German nation and its emancipation from the commanding influence of Italy.

It did so, however, in a sense quite different from that which the German humanists had in mind. Luther threw over the theory that the existing empire was a continuation of the Roman Empire. In his 'Address to the Christian Nobility of the German Nation' he stressed the fact that the Roman Empire had long before been destroyed by the Muslims, that the Donation of Constantine had been exposed as a fraud and that the Pope had no power, therefore, to transfer the empire from the Romans and Greeks to the Germans. By turning against the Pope Luther dealt a fatal blow to the idea of the Holy Roman Empire. Although his opposition was not directed towards the emperor, he had in fact taken the decisive step which was to lead to the creation of a German nation. The German princes had helped already to prepare the way for this when they intensified their patronage of the churches and monastic houses within their territories in order to protect them from financial exploitation by the Papacy. Furthermore, the Council of Constance in the middle of the fifteenth century had already treated the German *natio* as a single unit alongside the Italian, French and English *nationes*. The nations of Europe took shape within the walls of the Church.

The expression, 'Holy Roman Empire of the German nation', which became current at that time and designated the German part of the empire, epitomizes in its self-contradictoriness the conflict between the 'regiment of princes' and imperial centralism. Side by side with this there raged the conflict between curialism and the conciliar principle, which preoccupied the Councils of Reform in the fifteenth century. The Reformation established the German nation as a republic ruled by princes on an ecclesiastical basis. As opposed to the mediaeval situation, in which the bishops had been the military rulers, the lay princes now became civil regents of the territorial churches. This Lutheran system substituted the princes for the bishops, but dropped the mediaeval hierarchy. In place of the universal order of Pope and emperor was put a civil republic of competing territories. Each of these had its own university, with faculties of theology and jurisprudence which offered authoritative interpretations of the Bible and of Roman law.

The revolutionary proclamation of the priesthood of all believers and the far-reaching educational reform which was to equip the whole people of Christ to read the holy Scriptures and the catechism for themselves did not work out as might have been expected. The freedom brought by the Reformation remained strictly confined to the personal realm and was progressively overshadowed, in the Church as in the affairs of society, by patronage on the part of the princes. The eschatological spirit of the Bible which, in Luther's dynamic and dialectical thinking, had informed his distinction between the kingdom of this world and the kingdom of God hardened into a static dualism which separated, along parallel lines, the temporal from the spiritual life.[38] The ethics of 'inner-worldly asceticism', as Troeltsch calls it, was a radical departure from the Roman Catholic dualism of the *homo religiosus* and *homo laicus*; but it shifted the duality to the individual Christian soul.[39] The antithesis between the precinct of the cloister and the world became an antithesis between the inner and the outward life. Monasticism was repudiated and worldly toil raised to the level of a divine vocation; yet Lutheranism was unable to stomach the full consequences of such a radically new ethics. The prince kept a watch on church and society in order to ensure that the faith of his subjects should come to no harm; and thus he exercised a patriarchal tutelage which simply took the place of the monastery walls. The mediaeval *Corpus Christianum* was carried on in fact, but in a territorial form.

The course of social development in central Europe during the sixteenth century strongly favoured this conservatism. The city councils, which next to the princes formed the chief pillar of the Reformation, might have proved a powerful antidote to the patriarchal system, if a steady decline in the fortunes of the urban communities had not set in after the sea passage to India had been discovered and the trade-routes had altered in consequence. From about the middle of the sixteenth century, although capitalism had already begun to develop, the older feudal structure once again went into the lead. Labour was surrounded now by a new ethos; but it was an ethos still imprisoned within a mediaeval view of society, which continued to uphold the existing order of things, based as it was on an agrarian consumer economy. The Scholastic doctrine of the unproductiveness of money and the mediaeval prohibition of interest were maintained, whilst the traditional doctrine of the 'estates' or 'degrees' formed a positive barrier against any social complications that might have ensued as a result of increasing commercial activity. Even serfdom, which actually grew worse towards the end of the sixteenth century, was accepted as one of the 'estates' and a condition not at all incompatible with the freedom of the faith. It was the ruling authority which, as the agent responsible for social and economic organization, profited by the increased mobility and improved prosperity resulting from the intensified efforts of the working population and from the general raising of the intellectual level. It was that authority which little by little introduced the change-over to West European methods of production. The advance from a feudal and primitive capitalist economy to a modern economy was the work of the state; and it was the Lutheran doctrine of the state which assisted it—indirectly—to centralize and to augment its power. In the process of economic and social renewal Lutheran ethics and social theory failed to play a creative rôle. For that there was needed a spirit of another kind.

9. WESTERN EUROPE AND CALVINISM

Whilst in the social and economic field Central Europe maintained the late mediaeval pattern, the West European peoples pressed on with the development of urban life which had begun already in the Middle Ages but was now to be implemented in a more fundamental way; and it was they who, stepping over the threshold, entered upon the *modus vivendi* of the modern world. They took control of the situation, they brought the civilization of Europe to the Americas, and it was owing to them that Central Europe itself was obliged in the end to adjust its life to the course of West European evolution. Our particular concern in this section will be to consider briefly a factor which has played such a predominant part in the history of Western Europe: the rise of constitutional democracy.

That Central Europe and Western Europe went different ways is only partly to be explained in terms of social and economic factors; for the process had begun to be evident when the discovery of the sea-route to the East, which shifted the chief centre of trade to the seafaring nations of Western Europe, had scarcely had time to make its influence felt. Again, differences of temper between Lutheranism and Calvinism had a great deal to do with the divergence; but they do not explain it either, since it was non-theological factors which chiefly determined the separate courses taken by the two main branches of the Reformation. The interplay which there was between spiritual motives and social and economic circumstances is reflected in the contrasting personalities of the two reformers. Even Luther the professor remained a man of the people, poetic, mystical, the victim of sudden impulse and sudden temptation, ready to compromise outwardly, so long as inwardly the integrity of his faith was not impaired. Calvin never disclaimed his origin as a French lawyer, was a typical West European townsman, his personality formed in an atmosphere of aristocratic intellectuality permeated by humanism, rational and of a Latin lucidity, his emotions controlled and methodically disciplined, logical in the extreme. Luther, in his outlook always a German, whose thinking was in territorial and patriarchal terms, never broke free from the agrarian pattern. Calvin, even as the leader of tiny Geneva, had an international outlook and a broad ecumenical vision. Whereas Luther had a deep-rooted mistrust of the ability of the Christian congregation, when left to itself, to carry out any reform, and put the whole burden of responsibility upon the nobility and the civic councils, Calvin employed the strictest discipline to organize a church which was independent, conscious of its purpose and capable of pressing for radical reforms.

Yet there was nothing sectarian about the way in which Calvin methodically set about organizing a holy society. Above anything else what shaped the aspect of primitive Calvinism was the leadership of Calvin himself in carrying through the Genevan programme of reformation. In Geneva he was able to apply the theocratic idea of a new relationship between church and government and to put it to a practical test. As against the Lutheran notion of the guardian-state, the Roman Catholic subjection of the state to the Church and the sectarianism which rejected the state altogether, Calvin proposed a theocracy in which church and government had each its proper task, without either being subordinated to or mixed up with the other, but both being joined in a closely reciprocal relationship through a common allegiance to the Word of God. The church order which he proposed on the one hand guaranteed a strictly independent status to both church and government and on the other kept the firm hand of ecclesiastical discipline over the civil power. In strict justice one must admit that Calvin's theocratic conception overreached itself; for it had all the drawbacks of an aggressive sectarian ideal and was certain to lead to an organized tyranny on the part of the Church over society. Its most serious weakness was that it could only be made to work properly under the conditions of the *Corpus Christianum*, which Calvin took for granted as part of the heritage of the Middle Ages. As those conditions weakened, the theocratic ideal necessarily took on a different complexion. All the same, the basic principles of Calvin's régime in Geneva came to be of great historical importance.

Calvin combined the ideas of the confessing church and the 'nation-church' with fruitful results. His theocratic outlook conformed very closely to the norm of the Old Testament, where God's covenant with his people governs the whole of life and where the critical voice of prophecy guides the state and keeps it in contact with revelation.[40] That is why, in assessing the merits of a constitution, he does not look at it merely from the point of view of authority like Luther, but above all having regard to the general well-being. The crux of the matter is that the ruling authority must not misuse the charge laid upon it by God. On this point judgment is to be propounded from two sides, as it were: from above and from below. It is not the only act of God's providence that he appoints 'authorities'; but pre-eminently his will and his work are fulfilled 'in that he has broken in pieces the bloody sceptres of overweening kings and has overthrown lordly empires such as were not to be endured', just as by his servant Moses he rescued the people of Israel from the tyranny of Egypt. Subjects are pledged to obedience even to tyrants; but Calvin expressly ascribes the right to resist to the *magistrats inférieurs*, whose office it is 'to restrain the evil passion of kings'.[41] He cites a number of examples from the history of the Greek and Roman republics where the tribunes of the people have opposed themselves to the Roman consuls and the *demarchi* to the Athenian senate. The job of a government, he says, is to act as *tutor populi libertatis*; and he considers the most desirable form of government to be that which allows to a people the choice of its own governors.[42]

The kind of democracy which has sprung up on the soil of Calvinism bears a character all its own. It is of a constitutional type and based on a recognition of God's law and its claims as binding upon all. God's law is the same thing as the 'natural law' and constitutes the norm of the civil as well as the ecclesiastical order. It assumes the closest co-operation between church and government and a recognition, on both sides, of their respective rights and duties. It combines a full acknowledgment of the equality of all men before God with an equally thoroughgoing recognition of the powers conferred upon men by God and of the necessity for obedience. This conservative kind of democracy is of an essentially different origin and inspiration from the egalitarian democracy based on the Stoic doctrine that men are equal by virtue of the primal law of nature, and anchored in human rationality. As opposed to this Hellenic type of democracy, the type bred by Calvinism bears a markedly Old Testament character.

Calvin's own thought has several points of contact with democratic theory of the egalitarian type, in its recognition of the general good, the right of a people to freedom, a potential harmony between positive justice and the law of God (identified with natural justice) and, speaking generally, a rational approximation of society and the state. This was the more so because during the Middle Ages the Stoic tradition had likewise struck up a firm connection with Christian thinking. Calvin's younger contemporary and collaborator, Beza, upon whom the events of St Bartholomew's Day, 1572, had made a deep impression, defended as *ultima ratio* the principle of 'the sovereignty of the people' as positive cause for abrogating the duty of obedience to the ruling authority. A further step was taken by John Knox and the Scottish school in their resolute opposition to the principle of hereditary monarchy. Knox went so far as to call upon the people, in their capacity as private persons, to execute reforms in the religious sphere and, if need be, to intervene by force in the arena of power politics by forming 'covenants' for the defence of the Gospel. All this continued to be on a strictly biblical foundation. Cromwell too was no devotee of a republican theory—but the course of events left him no option. A more pronounced tendency, however, was towards a rationalistic conception of natural law. The strict Calvinist, Althusius, developed from the theory of the people's sovereignty a rational construct of the state and of society, based on a view of equality which was both Stoic and humanistic. With Grotius, the pioneer of international law, one enters the entirely humanistic atmosphere that one associates with Erasmus. The theoretical emancipation of natural law from theology is succinctly expressed in Grotius' thesis that the law of reason would still be operative, even if—as indeed is impossible—there should be no God. In practice, of course, the line of division was not always sharply drawn. William the Silent, the Calvinistic leader of the Dutch in their revolt against the Spanish power, was an advocate of toleration; and the state-church idea was considerably modified as a result.

The Genevan theocratic ideal could not be taken just as it stood and transplanted to states which consisted, not of a single town with its handful of citizens, but of entire peoples. Although Calvinism in the seventeenth century did not lose sight of the principle of the nation-church, it moved in the course of its development a long way in the direction of the sectarian ideal of the holy congregation. Side by side with this Puritan and Pietist strain there emerged yet another in the form of Independency. It totally rejected the idea of the *Corpus Christianum* and at the same time took leave of the theocratic idea characteristic of the Old Testament and of early Calvinism. Independency was akin to the modern understanding of democracy as resting on the separation of Church and state. The Pilgrim Fathers, the products of that original Congregationalism which became the seed-bed of Independency, emigrated to New England with the missionary purpose of finding a place where they might demonstrate the value to mankind 'of a pure and democratic church'. In another direction Independency sowed the seeds of the English Revolution, which in turn was to set its mark on the growth of modern democracy. Even the original Calvinism adjusted itself to this development, so that neo-Calvinism has taken up into its theory the practice of toleration within the 'inter-confessional' state, and the binding link between Calvinism and democracy is set down as a self-evident principle.[43] Although modern democracy is to a very considerable extent the outcome of political movements and of economic theories and influences based on an egalitarian idea of 'natural law', Calvinism did create a climate of civic freedom in which these ideas were able to shake themselves free of the theological bond. On the other hand the emphasis laid by Calvinism on the God-given powers of the ruling authority has put a strong check on the process of emancipation. English democracy bears the mark of Calvinism most obviously, whilst democracy in France, though it bears traces of Calvinistic influence through its connections with the American Revolution, is in fact almost entirely the product of an egalitarian and rationalistic ideal. American democracy in its original form offers a bridge between the two types.

10. CAPITALISM

If the connection between Calvinism and the growth of modern democracy is far from being simple or direct, no more so is the relation between Calvinism and the rise of modern capitalism. However, there are several pointers in this case. They indicate that from the very start the Calvinist spirit has had a strong affinity with the urban atmosphere: that it engaged itself very much with the interests of the middle class in Western Europe (that class which was moving in the direction of modern capitalism) and that it encouraged a mentality congenial to the capitalist ethos and one within which that ethos was able to flourish. Max Weber's well-known essays on *The Protestant Ethic and the Spirit of Capitalism* have been intensively criticized and have met with a great deal of misunderstanding.[44] The point generally overlooked is that Weber's articles are preliminary to a comprehensive study of 'the economic ethos of the world religions' (*Die Wirtschafts-*

ethik der Weltreligionen). He was fascinated by the question: by what combination of circumstances it has come about that in the West—and nowhere else but in the West—'cultural phenomena have appeared which (as we like to think) lie in a line of development to having *universal* significance and value.' Only in the Occident has science reached a stage of development that we can accept as 'legitimate'. The same is true of the typically pragmatic way of writing history which the Occident inherited from the Greeks, and of the highly rationalized systems of occidental law, of which Roman law is the native soil. The evolution of occidental music, architecture, sculpture and painting is unique. A kind of literature which relies completely on the art of printing, and likewise the whole area of specialization—in particular, the specialist official who is the main pillar of the modern state and its economy—are something known only to the Occident. The state as a political system, with a rational 'constitution', law and administration carried on by expert officials, is peculiar to the Occident. 'And the same is true of the most fateful force in our modern life, capitalism.'[45]

Capitalism as such is by no means confined to the Occident. On the contrary, it is to be found in every civilization where a 'barter economy' is superseded by a money economy.[46] But alongside these common forms of capitalism one particular kind has been developed in the Occident, which has no parallel elsewhere: namely, 'the rational capitalistic organization of (formally) free labour', not run according to some coercive policy or on the basis of irrational speculation but in an adjustable relationship to marketing-prospects. The techniques of exact calculation which are pre-requisite for the rational organization of trade have been developed only by the Occident; for they are bound up with progress in the modern natural sciences, which in their turn have reaped considerable advantage from the fact of their usefulness in the economic sphere. This usefulness of the sciences is of a piece with the characteristic structure of occidental law and administration. Behind it all lies the rise of the occidental bourgeoisie and of modern rational socialism which opposes the free wage earner to the big industrial entrepreneur. The peculiar form of occidental 'rationalism' has determined the course of economic development. This economic rationalism has likewise been moulded by the influence of purely economic relations; but it has nevertheless made a decisive contribution to the growth of modern capitalism.

Where did this economic rationalism come from? It originated in a particular disposition of the human psyche which opposed itself to and surmounted certain traditional barriers which in other civilizations have simply persisted. This has absolutely nothing to do with 'the temper of single-minded concentration on pecuniary gain'.[47] The significant thing about modern capitalism, as the dominant feature of present-day occidental culture, is that for the world as a whole it depends upon a special ethos—an ethos which the non-Christian cultures are to all appearances incapable of generating. One certainly cannot say of Christendom in general that it was bound to produce or promote such an ethos. On the matter of the 'capitalist spirit' in fifteenth century Venice and Florence—or in South Germany and Flanders—and of the economic ethos of various Renaissance personalities, Weber has shown that there is a complete absence, in these instances, of precisely the essential elements of the modern capitalist ethos. Commerce in Babylon, Greece and Rome and in Muslim civilization reached a quite highly developed stage of proto-capitalism, but never got beyond that. The further step was left to Western Europe. As for the explorations undertaken by Portugal and Spain—and any consequences which their discoveries may have had[48]—they certainly give no sufficient ground for explaining what happened in Western Europe; for in that special type of capitalism which evolved in countries strongly influenced by Protestantism neither Spain nor Portugal had any part. As Calvinism appeared and flourished in those very countries which were also the first to be affected by the ethos of modern capitalism, and as that ethos and Calvinism itself both emerged during the same period, the question naturally arises as to what connection there may be between the two movements and how they may have influenced each other. A relevant point here is that in the process by which the original Calvinism became the Puritanism of the seventeenth century changes in the structure of society played a crucial rôle and that these changes were brought about partly by economic factors.

The fundamental reason why Calvinism was so important to the rise of modern capitalism is that it concerned itself in a positive way with the implications of an urban money economy. It was possibly 'the first systematic body of religious teaching which can be said to recognize and applaud the economic virtues'. The social ethic of Calvinism was constructed on the practical basis of urban industry and commercial enterprise. Calvin's doctrine of usury, although a very conservative one, dealt with the rights and wrongs of money-lending in the light of existing circumstances. He dismissed the oft-quoted passages from the Old Testament and the Fathers as irrelevant, because they were designed for conditions which no longer existed; and he regarded credit as a normal and indeed inevitable part of the life of society, leaving it to the individual conscience to ensure that neither credit nor interest went beyond the requirements of natural justice and the golden rule.[49]

It was above all the seventeenth century Puritan version of Calvinism, set amidst a rising middle class whose commercial and industrial activities were steadily increasing, that created an economic ethos decisive in its effects on the growth of the modern spirit of capitalism. Unremitting hard work on the part of the individual, submitted to a strictly ascetic, methodical self-discipline and to an unconditional faith in God's election and calling, was made the means to sanctification of the believer and the instrument of victory in the fight against temptation. Faith is not merely to find expression *in vocatione*, as Luther taught, but more especially *per vocationem*. In labour vocation is fulfilled; it is an instrument *ad majorem Dei gloriam*; it is the token by which a man may recognize his own election. In the works of Baxter, whose pastoral and practical influence was very considerable during the second half of the seventeenth century, one can see this ethos changing in the direction of eighteenth century utilitarianism. To be industrious becomes an end in itself. The struggle to get rich, if it means having an appetite for pleasure and luxury, is utterly reprehensible; but regarded as a sustained struggle on the part of God's stewards to use his gifts properly, productively and profitably to the maximum degree, it becomes an absolute command. He therefore put a high value on the specialized division of labour, because that enhanced the labourer's skill and improved productivity from the point of view of both quantity and quality. Already present here are those tendencies which led eventually to Adam Smith's apotheosis of the division of labour. The specialist on one side and the 'man of affairs' become the ethical ideal; hence there arise the ethos of rational bourgeois commercialism and the equally calculated organization of labour.

> The Puritan wanted to be the man with a calling. We have to be; for when asceticism was transferred from the monastic cell to

the world of business and began to dominate the 'innerworldly morality', it added another stone to the building of the mighty cosmos of modern men, to the technical and economic pre-suppositions of the economic order tied to automatic machine-production, which now imposes upon all who are born into it a style of living. But now that spirit has left the body—whether for good, who can tell? Capitalism has triumphed; and since in any case its foundation is the machine, it no longer needs that support.[50]

II. THE ENGLISH REVOLUTION

In the political revolution which had such a profound effect on the life of the English nation in the seventeenth century and has permanently set its stamp upon the character of that nation, Calvinism entered the course of world history for the first time as a significant political force. Together with Holland—which suffered a period of retrogression, however, after her 'golden age'—England became the first modern nation. Just as Italy was shaped by the papal revolution and Germany by the Reformation under Luther, so has England been cast in the mould of the Puritan revolution. It is wrong to depict the history of modern Europe as a decline into nationalist particularism and to contrast that with the 'universalism' of the Middle Ages. The revolutions which have given their distinctive forms to the European nations are significant precisely because of their universal claims and ideals. They were no more 'particularist' than, say, the 'Davidic empire' of Charlemagne or the papal insistence on the independence of the papal state. The European idea of the 'nation' is not a modern reversion to some form of tribalism. It represents rather the universal-istic consciousness of the biblical 'chosen people' and the citizenship of the ancient *polis* breaking through the restrictive claims of the *Corpus Christianum Romanum*, the inner contradictions of which were laid bare by the very struggle between the two powerful claimants, each successfully engaged in breaking the back of its rival's uni-versalism. The mythical universalism of the pagan divine kingship is timeless. Christian universalism is historical; and that is why it has been propagated in occidental history through a series of revolutions.

'. . . in the England of the seventeenth century the conscious deliberate resolve to be itself the master of its fate takes complete possession of the nation.'[51] Cromwell has been described as 'the most typical Englishman of all time'.

> All the incongruities of human nature are to be traced somewhere
> or other in Cromwell's career. What is more remarkable is that
> this union of apparently contradictory forces is precisely that
> which is to be found in the English people, and which has made
> England what she is at the present day.[52]

In their rebellion against royal absolutism during the seventeenth
century the English people made their voice heard for the first time.
The mediaeval *Natio Anglicana*, consisting of King, Lords spiritual
and temporal and Commons, was thenceforth to be spoken of only
as 'the people of this Nation', as the Parliamentary resolution of 1649
on Charles I puts it. What then took sovereign place was the idea of
the *Populus Christianus*, deriving its structure from the Church—and
indeed from the congregation—just as the *Natio* takes its structure
from the Church as a whole. In the line of European revolutions,
this was the last gift by the Church and by Christianity to secular
politics.[53]

At the very root of this idea that 'the people' constitute the 'nation'
lies an identification with the people of Israel. 'Hebraic nationalism'
is something essentially different from the 'Renaissance nationalism'
which both on the continent and in England was always the preserve
of a small educated class. God's covenant with his chosen people was
the school in which the whole people learned to see themselves as the
elected instrument for reaching the goal of universal freedom. When
Henry VIII set up the 'national church', it meant snapping the
universal link which bound Christendom together. The Puritan
revolution on the other hand, like the Reformation itself, had a
universal and international aim and outlook; it aroused the people to
a sense of mission, of their mission to be 'a light to the nations'.
Cromwell has been of consequence upon the wider stage of history
because he made 'the true freedom of the Christian man' the foundation
of polity. 'Liberty of conscience, and liberty of the subjects—two as
glorious things to be contended for, as any God hath given us.'
The national consciousness which he awakened was therefore
essentially a consciousness of civil liberty, and that was identical with
'the interest of the nation' and 'the interest of Christians'.[54] That
national consciousness went hand in hand with a triumphant sense of
international responsibility for the cause of freedom. For Cromwell
the struggle of the Protestant Alliance against Spain really did mean
fighting the Lord's battles with 'the Roman Babylon'. Even in the

nineteenth century British imperialism could still thrive on the belief in 'an unseen superintending Providence controlling the development of the Anglo-Saxon race'.[55] The 'Hebraic' stamp of this imperialism must answer for the not inconsiderable amount of Pharisaism which has been one of its persistent features; but on the other hand, just because it has had that Old Testament background, it has been saved from sinking into naked, pagan self-adulation and the glorification of power, which is the mark of Fascist imperialism.

Something of the effect of the English revolution may be gathered from the remarkable variety of uses to which the word 'common' has been put in different kinds of compound expressions.[56] The 'common law', which Parliament championed against the arbitrary rule of the Stuarts by appealing to the ancient Magna Carta, was merged by Cromwell with the divine Law which it is for the Chosen People to obey. The Glorious Revolution of 1688 was felt to be a restoration of the common law. The reformation of the Church involved the substitution of a 'Book of Common Prayer', which gave the congregation an audible part in worship, for the 'Divine Office' of the Roman Mass. A parallel development was the increasing use of the term 'Commonwealth', signifying the community and the common interest of Christian people. Thus Baxter, in his *Christian Directory*, could say that 'everybody as a member of the Church or the Commonwealth' is to make his utmost endeavour to strive 'for the weal of the Church or the Commonwealth', of which the true representative is 'the House of Commons'. 'For religion, grex and king!' was the watchword of those who started the revolt against the royal absolutism in 1642. What was at issue was the reformation of the Church through a recovery of the rights of the people, the congregation (*grex*) and the 'Commons'; and behind all this lay the example of the Scottish reformation, which had brought with it the setting up of an independent Presbyterian church and revolution on the part of the *magistrats inférieurs*. The German reformation had been accompanied by a revolution of the princes; and the Genevan reformation of Calvin was essentially urban in character. In England, however, it was the landed gentry who ranged themselves against the higher aristocracy, the bishops and the king, and as 'the Commons', took 'lawful authority' into their own hands. It is to this above all that English democracy owes its conservative character—a character which it has maintained through every change in the political and industrial spheres, and in spite of the typically bourgeois ethos of Puritanism.

It was Milton who gave classic expression to the genius of the English revolution; and with him—much more than with Cromwell —the belief in a universal vocation to freedom was founded on a belief in Reason.[57] He was convinced that the English people were to reproduce the theocracy of ancient Israel and were to bring the message of universal liberty to all nations. In support of this he laid an individualistic stress on the autonomy of man, somewhat akin to that of the Renaissance. His writings reflect a strong sympathy with the egalitarian doctrine of the sovereignty of the people. John Locke went still further in that direction. Although he would derive the historic growth of government from the initial action of God's providence, he makes little or nothing of the religious basis of the state. The state does not exist to the glory of God, but only for the welfare of the individual—which he interprets in the sense of a utilitarian empiricism. His *Letters on Toleration* reduce the Churches to the status of free associations which in all moral and political affairs are to accommodate themselves to the ordinances of the state. The Toleration Act of 1689 did indeed uphold the state Church; but it also recognized the dissenters as 'denominations' and allowed them religious liberty. The theocratic relationship between state and church which Calvin—and in a different form Cromwell also— had envisaged finally made way for a point of view which set a new course towards the Enlightenment.

12. THE INDUSTRIAL REVOLUTION

The Puritan ethos, which from the very beginning had found expression particularly in a political consciousness, came little by little to exert an increasingly powerful economic influence. The landed gentry and the rising urban middle class made common cause during the Rebellion and were actuated by a common spirit which eased social tensions and gave the gentry a more open-minded attitude towards business and trade. The agrarian revolution, which preceded the industrial revolution in England, had important consequences. Agricultural methods were rationalized on an economic basis; this released a considerable labour force which found itself obliged to look for work in the towns. In the last quarter of the eighteenth century the structural development of England's primitive capitalist economy reached a stage of impasse. The ruthless exploitation of land and people in the colonial possessions had reached its furthest limit and a lack of raw materials was hindering the growth of the export trade.[58] This kind of situation, in which a limit had been reached, was, of course, not unique: it can be found in the history of other cultures based on primitive capitalism. The rise of the mediaeval city, the growth of an economic rationalism and the proclamation of religious and civil liberties had certainly given a distinctive turn and direction to occidental civilization; but none of this had as yet thrown up an economic structure with the capacity to reveal just how important that particular trend of events was to prove to the future course of history in the world as a whole.

It was in conjunction with advances in the field of technics that an economy of this kind first began to emerge. The story of technical progress in Western Europe shows a sharp increase, from the thirteenth century onwards, in the number of inventions, keeping pace with developments in science and with the growth of the urban middle classes. The crux lay not in the inventions as such—for other cultures could boast similar inventions of their own—but in the use to which these things were put. Thus it was cultural and social conditions, together with the particular stage of economic structure reached at the time, which were to be of such universal significance; for these factors enabled the technical inventions, which from the middle of the eighteenth century were so drastically transforming the textile industries of England, to usher in the Industrial Revolution. These inventions in fact crystallized the situation for primitive capitalism, enabling it to pass through the barrier of economic satiety into the phase of capitalism and industrialism as we know them today. From England the Industrial Revolution spread across Europe, first to the southern Netherlands, then to France and the Rhineland, the north Netherlands and Austria. During the last quarter of the nineteenth century the rest of Germany was industrialized; and at about 1900 the process began in Russia. The Meiji revolution of 1868 opened the door to industrialization in Japan, whose example was followed during the First World War—although with less determination—by colonial territories such as India and Indonesia, whilst even Egypt and Turkey tried to make a beginning. Only since the Second World War has industrialization been expressly included in the development programmes of the now independent states of Asia.

The Industrial Revolution has become a kind of irresistible bull-dozer, forcing a way for Western civilization into the non-Western areas of the world.

Just as the religious and political revolution in seventeenth century England created a type of the free citizen, so the Industrial Revolution gave that same citizen unquestioned supremacy in the economic sphere. Cromwell had given a political construction to religious liberty. During the eighteenth century the basis of that liberty became more and more preponderantly an economic one. The middle classes were for tolerance and civil liberty for the reason—and to the degree—that these were likely to enhance the prosperity of industry and commerce. The philosopher with the greatest influence among the bourgeoisie was Locke, not only as a champion of toleration, but above all because he came to the defence of property as the corner-stone of their way of life: 'to be enjoyed in safety and security, based not upon conquest but upon man's labour and toil'. In this justification of property in so far as it is the fruit of 'labour and toil' the spirit of Puritanism lives on, but it is no longer the religious view of property as a hallowed instrument, dedicated to the greater glory of God. The end proposed —enjoyment 'in safety and security'—already leans hard in the direction of a purely individualistic hedonism. Even there the citizen could know that he was on firm ground. Adam Smith, the founder of classical economics, in his *Inquiry into the Nature and Causes of the Wealth of Nations* (1776), declared economic liberty to be an axiomatic principle of the natural order, regulating economic life; and behind it he saw at work the invisible hand which through economic self-interest fulfils a providential plan. His theory of economics was an appendage to moral philosophy, which he taught. The bourgeoisie then needed no moral justification for their endeavours in the economic sphere above what those same endeavours, the increase that accrued to the wealth of the nation and their own safety and security could provide.

The Industrial Revolution had turned 'labour and toil' from a moral asset into an unremitting necessity, for the entrepreneur could not otherwise hope to stay in competition or keep pace with the continual changes resulting from technical progress. The religious and moral content which the concept of the 'natural law' still held for Locke and Adam Smith was more and more drained out of it, and the natural law of economic life grew to be more and more a biological struggle for survival. 'The bourgeoisie'—so runs Karl Marx's biting criticism in a famous passage of the Communist Manifesto—'wherever it has got the upper hand, has put an end to all feudal, patriarchal, idyllic relations. It has pitilessly torn asunder the motley feudal ties that bound man to his "natural superiors," and has left no other nexus between man and man than naked self-interest, than callous "cash payment".'[59]

13. THE AMERICAN REVOLUTION

The revolution which called into being the independent United States of America forms a link between the English Revolution of the seventeenth century and the French Revolution. It stands between the two, not merely in a chronological sense, but also by reason of its peculiar character. As a rebellion on the part of English colonists against their motherland it was activated by a Puritan spirit, closely akin to that which had inspired Cromwell's rebellion. But the leaders of the American Revolution were deeply imbued with the spirit of the Enlightenment—not only Jefferson, but also Benjamin Franklin, who represented the revolutionaries officially in Paris and obtained a ready hearing among those circles who were preparing for the French Revolution. Lafayette fought with the American convoys. The type of democracy which arose out of the American Revolution exhibits certain traits therefore which link it essentially with the English type, but on the other side with the French type as well. More than that, the American Revolution paved the way for industrial development on an unimagined scale, which has left that of the parent country far behind.

In the chain of European revolutions the American Revolution is, however, particularly distinctive. In this case, there was no age-old tradition to be surmounted. The burden of which men were seeking to be free was not one which the structure of their own society had imposed. Yet it was a genuine revolution, and not simply a colonial war of liberation. The seeds of this revolution had been sown and had germinated in Europe and then had been transplanted to the New World. The United States took their specifically Protestant character from their origins; and it is one which in spite of the flood of Roman Catholic immigration during the past hundred years or so they continue to preserve. It is the radical wing of Protestantism that has set its mark permanently on the structure of American society. Latourette has raised the question of why the radical Protestantism of the older American stock remained such a powerful force throughout the nineteenth century and has carried this influence into the twentieth. In the colonial period only a small minority of the population was actively committed to it; and at the start of the present century it comprised a mere sixth of the total population. Yet in the influence which Christianity has exerted that minority has played a leading rôle and to a large extent has formed the idealism of the nation.[60] Why should this have been so? It may have been owing to the prestige which priority of arrival conferred, to a greater share of courage and initiative, to a more imaginative social vision and stronger incentive to change. These factors, however, hardly get to the root of the matter. For that one has to go back to the European 'prehistory' of the United States; for what has lent the American Revolution its peculiar vitality and at the same time has made it a link in the chain of European history is the spirit of the radical Protestantism which originated in Britain, but which was, of course, an outcome of the Reformation.

Whereas in England itself the Independency of the Commonwealth period, although it has had a lasting effect on the English nation through its rôle in the Revolution, proved as an ecclesiastical movement to be no more than an interlude, in America it was able to come to full bloom and thus in large measure to shape the destinies of the country as a whole. The Mayflower Compact, which the Pilgrim Fathers concluded whilst they were still *en route* for New England in 1620, took the idea of the Church covenant as the basis for a civil and political constitution. That rigorously Puritan and democratic spirit profoundly influenced later arrivals as well. Although the Congregationalist Church was in fact originally a state church, so thoroughly was any kind of pressure from the state repudiated that from its consequent position the Church became an important factor in achieving that separation of church and state which the United States came to regard as a fundamental principle. The principle did not in this case arise—as it did in the case of the French Revolution —out of a move to secularize the state or from any aversion to ecclesiastical tyranny, but was deeply permeated by the Congregationalist idea of the autonomous congregation and the utilitarian view of the state which flows from it. Just because this democratic idea animated from the very beginning not only the Church but the body politic as well, the separation of church and state was able to become a positive principle by which the relationship between them was made to depend not on any formal bond of obligation but on the free concurrence and co-operation of the citizen, who learned to make his Christian profession and to live it out both in the Church and in the varied circumstances of civil life.

Through its emphasis on personal conversion and the added strength which it gave to those radical Protestant groups which took their stand on the priesthood of all believers, the Great Awakening also acted as a stimulus to the movement for democratic self-government and produced a heightened consciousness of the inalienability of human rights and of the freedom to which by their origin men are entitled. The growth of religious liberty was closely associated with the urge to political independence, of which religious toleration was one of the essential supports. The principle of religious liberty as an incontrovertible human right was guaranteed by the Declaration of Rights of 1776 and was written into the Constitution in 1791. In Jefferson, who played so momentous a part in bringing about the Constitution, one can trace the American conception of democratic freedom to its twofold source. There was first the idea of the Chosen People, which the dangerous migration to New England had served to invigorate and inspire, and of which Jefferson was an earnest advocate. The New World was a new Canaan in his eyes, a land of promise, and destined to be 'the signal of arousing men to burst the chains under which monkish ignorance and superstition had persuaded them to bind themselves, and to assume the blessings and security of self-government.'[61] Yet at the same time he was a typical representative of the liberal and humanitarian nationalism of the eighteenth century. The 'second Revolution', of which he was the pioneer, drew much of its inspiration from the French Revolution. In France this revolution might seem to have failed; but it was the vocation of the New World to bring to pass the universal ideas of the French Enlightenment. Thus the 'Chosen People' idea was:

> secularized and democratized under the impact of the natural rights concept of eighteenth century Enlightenment, it was broadened by the growth in space and wealth and numbers, by the visible blessings of Providence, and it became one of the elements out of which an American national consciousness arose at the beginning of the nineteenth century.[62]

That nineteenth century nationalism hardened under the impact of the movement which pushed the frontier farther and farther to the West. It felt the influence of a rising political and economic imperialism; yet it never lost its original conviction of a universal responsibility for the liberation of the world.

14. THE FRENCH REVOLUTION

In spite of the direct links which undoubtedly exist between the American and French Revolutions, the passage from the one to the other involves a leap into a different spiritual climate. The background to the French Revolution contains nothing of the Old Testament theocratic outlook of Puritanism on the relation between church and state, where political renovation goes hand in hand with religious renewal, of which it is in fact the product. The forces of the Reformation which in seventeenth century England broke the supreme power of royal absolutism, in France had suffered an eclipse, politically speaking, and had remained confined to a small religious minority. The dominant church had remained to the very end firmly wedded to the *ancien régime*. For the French philosophers in the eighteenth century the source of their political ideas was the Enlightenment. In the United States, the Declaration of Independence of 1776 regarded the rights which all men equally possess as the gift of the Creator. The *Déclaration des droits de l'homme* of 1789, however, waters the theological notion down to a vague reference to a 'Supreme Being' and takes as a basis of democratic government the radical doctrine of the people's sovereignty.

How far removed the French Revolution stands from its predecessors may be estimated from the work of two thinkers whose political and social theories made such an important contribution to it. The theory that the prince derives his authority, not from God, but from the will of the people had already been enunciated by Hobbes in the seventeenth century, was taken over by the *philosophes* and by them was disseminated throughout Europe. The sheet on which the *Déclaration des droits de l'homme* was distributed in Paris displayed above the title-heading itself the radiant eye of God within the triangle which, though suggestive perhaps of the Trinity, was explained as 'the supreme eye of Reason'. Beneath the heading appeared the symbol of the serpent biting its own tail. Although no explanation is offered, this symbol is scarcely difficult to understand. It is the age-old cosmological idea of the Primeval Serpent, the mythical representation of the waters of chaos which surround the universe, sometimes referred to in the Old Testament as leviathan. In Chapter Two we examined the relationship between the primeval chaos, out of which—according to ancient mythology—all things have come into being, and the pagan ontocratic state, which derived its divine and absolute power from its being identified with the cosmic totality of the universe. Even more remarkable is it that to his principal work, in which he elaborates his ideas about the nature, origin and purpose of the state, Hobbes gave the title of *Leviathan* (1651). On the title-page of the first edition there stand the words from the Book of Job about the monster's matchless power: '*Non est potestas Super Terram quae Comparetur ei.*'[63] Hobbes did not interpret this mythical monster as being the pagan state. He was writing at the time of the Civil War in England; and he took 'Leviathan' just as a symbol of the 'Christian Commonwealth' which he expected would be the outcome of the struggle. His theory is, of course, a secularized version of Puritan ideas of theocracy.[64] He uses the Old Testament to show that the kingdom of God is meant to be understood as a commonwealth, constituted by the consent of the people, which as a 'holy nation' brings into being a new kind of divinity, a collective organism or 'Leviathan', a body politic (*civitas*) which Hobbes calls a 'mortal god': hence the absolute power of the government of such a commonwealth, no matter whether it take the form of a monarchy, an aristocracy or a democracy. A theory of this kind still moves in a climate of Calvinistic thought; it rests on a penetrating analysis of the biblical concept of theocracy, employs a biblical terminology and is intended to provide the foundation for a Christian government. Here one can see quite clearly the link between the theocratic covenant idea which actuated Cromwell and the purely rational, egalitarian concept of the 'social contract' which underlay the French Revolution. The features of this state—all-powerful and yet vested in the sovereign will of the people—are ambivalent indeed; for they are those on the one hand of the pagan state and on the other of a conception of democracy Christian in its origins.

Even in the case of Rousseau a century later, the structure of his political ideas still bore unmistakable traces of Calvinist influence. His 'Anglomania' sprang from the close association in his own mind of the England of the seventeenth century with Geneva, the town of his birth, from which he had been exiled. He knew very well that the ideas he had developed in the *Du Contrat social* could never be applied in a modern state of any size. Calvin he revered as a great legislator and political leader, the creator of a republican community imbued with a theocratic awareness, derived from the Old Testament, of being a holy nation. In a Geneva which his nostalgic longings had idealized he found an example of those civil liberties and that true patriotism which were lacking in the France of his own day, and this image became the inspiration for his project of an ideal state. With Rousseau, however, the Calvinist spirit had been thoroughly secularized, natural religion had now completely taken the place of the Christian faith and the values of liberty and equality—the twin props of Rousseau's utopia—were rooted in an ethical rationalism in which a strong Stoic influence can be detected. At the same time he pleaded with such fervour and strength of feeling for the unity of all citizens in a devotion to the national community that patriotism can truly be said to have become a religion with him.

The rising bourgeoisie did as much as royal absolutism to set the stage for the French Revolution. In the conflict which took place in 1787 between the parliament and the king and formed an immediate prelude to the outbreak of revolution, ancient liberties were resuscitated which dated back to the Middle Ages. From the outset of the fourteenth century the 'third estate' had been represented in the States General, which the king convened in order to strengthen his monarchical claims against the imperial universalism of the Pope. To some extent the towns grew in importance as the territorial state achieved its emancipation; power was centralized through the absolute authority of the monarch, backed up by the ideas of sovereignty to be found in Roman law. Yet the third estate formed at the same time a counter-weight to the monarchy; and since any exceptional expenditure on the king's part required the consent of the States General, they were sometimes able to coerce him into doing what they wanted. Whereas in England the seventeenth century saw the Commons established as the ruling power, in France the omnipotence of the royal administration reached its climax during that period. Bossuet expressed the position in his dictum that 'the royal throne is not the throne of a man, but the throne of God himself.' As the bourgeoisie became politically self-conscious in the eighteenth century, they were bound to come into conflict with this absolutism in the long run, not simply out of anti-monarchism, but because the theory of the *droit divin* had a religious foundation which crumbled inevitably before the onslaught of secularist rationalism. By the time Montesquieu could venture the remark that even if God did not exist men ought still to love justice, sentence had already been passed, in principle, on the myth of royal omnipotence.

That is why the French Revolution is of such general historical consequence. It gave political form to a new image of man and of the world—an image based essentially on the sovereignty of reason and one which in fact dispensed with the hypothesis of God's existence. The laws which govern the universe and human society within it are—as Montesquieu put it in the preface to his *De l'Esprit des Lois*— 'derived from the nature of things'. Philosophically speaking this was a way of apprehending the world which released modern scientific rationalism from the trammels of religious tradition. In the political, social and economic spheres it was to ensure the supremacy of the 'victorious bourgeoisie', which saw itself as the embodiment of the new type of man. It therefore insisted on identifying 'liberty, equality and fraternity' with its own interests, which were founded on that fourth great prop: the right to 'property'.

15. THE SCIENTIFIC AND TECHNOLOGICAL REVOLUTION

There is no other single aspect of Western civilization which so clearly exemplifies the radical break the West has made with non-Western patterns as the rise of modern science and technology. So predominant a feature has this become that it looks as though the whole peculiar course of Western history has been leading towards this climax and fulfilment. It is also the melting-pot in which Western influence bursts through its historical confines to spread itself across the world.

> Modern science was born in Europe, but its home is the whole world . . More and more it is becoming evident that what the West can most readily give to the East is its science and its scientific outlook.[65]

It is certainly not wide of the mark to see in the development of modern science and technology the continuation of something started by the Greeks. Admittedly the primary civilizations afford examples of a pre-scientific rationalism—but it lies always under the interdict of magical and mythical ways of thinking. It was Greek science which, for the first time in history, proffered a wholly naturalistic interpretation of the universe *in toto*. 'Logos' began to drive out myth. Thales, the earliest of the Milesian philosophers, made use of knowledge which Babylonian astronomy and Egyptian geometry had accumulated; but the crucial point of novelty was that his cosmology left 'no room for Marduk at all'.[66] What were the implications of this approach? They become fully apparent when one remembers that it involved the practice of experimental research. The Atomists, for example, through a process of observation were able to demonstrate the existence of a physical reality which was extra-sensible. Along with that, in the period of the Ionian philosophers, the conviction grew that nature could be 'reproduced' by technical processes which must bring its workings within the grasp of man's intelligence and—potentially at least—under his control. A further matter of great consequence was the study of mathematics, which the Pythagorean School, in particular, pursued as a method of ascetic contemplation, believing that so pure a science must offer a key to the riddle of the universe.

Seeing that these beginnings were so full of promise, it seems all the more remarkable that Greek science never transcended its limitations by crossing the threshold that divides it from modern science. The Pythagorean doctrine—which Plato restated and refined —that numbers form the basis of the real world remained imprisoned in a current of *a priori* mathematical reasoning directed to the religious purpose of purifying the soul; and so it was never related to an exact observation of nature—the essential step to which modern physics owes its amazing advances. The mechanical arts carried a social stigma and the contempt in which they were held hindered technological progress. Archimedes designed his machines as mere geometrical *jeux d'esprit*. Through the influence of Plato mechanics became detached from geometry and, being neglected by philosophers, took its place as a part of 'military science'. Physics and chemistry were held in disrespect. The philosopher was a free citizen who left the practical sciences to his slaves, just as the soul left to the body all contact with the material world.[67] Thus technology was characterized by ever improving standards of manual dexterity and an almost complete absence of new basic inventions and even of borrowings which might have altered the existing technical pattern. The lack of instruments of exact measurement and of any technique of chemical analysis made fundamental progress in science impossible.

The naturalistic interpretation of the universe too did not go beyond a certain point. Although Greek cosmology did manage to overcome the mythological way of apprehending the world, it remained, as Whitehead puts it, essentially 'dramatic'. Nature was a drama in which each thing played its part, but in order to exemplify general ideas, converging to an end.[68] The Greeks believed the world to be finite because it is ordered 'cosmically', as a cosmos. Aristotle deduced the finitude of the world from his conviction that the world was comprehensible.[69] At the root of this view there lay the concept of the eternal and immutable Essence which is identical with God and with nature.

The Europe of the Middle Ages took over the heritage of Greek science; yet there emerged, slowly but surely, a new mentality which was fundamentally alien to Greek civilization. The growth of modern medical science is a striking example of this. For fifteen centuries—up to the seventeenth century in fact—the generally accepted view regarding the circulation of the blood and the functions of the heart was that of the Roman physician, Galen (second century A.D.). Galen holds a place in the history of medicine like that of Ptolemy in the history of astronomy and geography. Early in the fourteenth century appeared the first treatise on anatomy to rely on experimental knowledge obtained by opening up the human body: Mundinus' *Anathomia*. Never before had a corpse been dissected for the purpose of studying how the human body looks from inside. It is certainly not a coincidence that a beginning was made with Western anatomy at a period when the papal power was declining and the destruction of the mediaeval universal order was already under way. It was another three centuries before William Harvey, on the evidence of his observations in anatomy, demonstrated once for all by his own discovery of the circulation of the blood that what Galen had taught was wrong. This pioneer in modern physiology has justly been described as 'the Columbus of the blood' and 'the Galileo of medicine'.[70] The threshold of modern science had been crossed.

It has been said of Harvey that the secret of his success consisted 'in the acquisition of the gift of patient observation'.[71] That is true, of course; but we do well to remember the really astonishing fact: that only in modern Europe—and nowhere else—has this 'gift' been acquired. It would seem desirable at this point to indicate, very briefly, what the major pre-conditions and assumptions are which underlie the rise of modern science.

The roots of modern science must be looked for in the Middle Ages. Whitehead makes the point that for Western Europe the Middle Ages were one long training of the intellect, of schooling in the sense of order—and not merely in a general sense, but in the form of an inexpugnable belief that every detailed occurrence can be correlated with its antecedents in a quite definite manner, so as to exemplify general principles. It is this instinctive conviction which provides the motive power of research: that there is a secret—and a secret which can be unveiled.

> When we compare this tone of thought in Europe with the attitude of other civilisations when left to themselves, there seems but one source for its origin. It must come from the medieval insistence on the rationality of God, conceived as with the personal energy of Jehovah and with the rationality of a Greek philosopher. Every detail was supervised and ordered: the search into nature could only result in the vindication of the faith in rationality . . . In Asia, the conceptions of God were of a being who was either too arbitrary or too impersonal for such ideas to have much effect on instinctive habits of mind. Any definite occurrence might be due to the fiat of an irrational despot, or might issue from some impersonal, inscrutable origin of things . . . the faith in the possibility of science, generated antecedently to the development of modern scientific theory, is an unconscious derivative from medieval theology.[72]

Northrop too recognizes that the 'theoretical' character of Western science, in contrast to the 'aesthetic' apprehension of reality in Asian civilizations, must ultimately be derived from a decision of faith. He reminds us that the traditional ideal knowledge in Asia is not metaphysical at all, in the Western sense of the term. It is, on the contrary, extremely positivist, since it assumes that no reality exists except that which is immediately apprehended. Max Planck quite rightly maintained that positivism, if conceived as a complete philosophy of science, would paralyse the progress of science. This consequence of positivism has been difficult to demonstrate in the West, because few creative scientists have been positivists and because the positivists always in practice smuggle in theoretically formulated meanings for the terms they use. Western science is based on an inferred and postulated type of knowledge, 'designating unobserved electrons, electromagnetic propagations, or the unseen God the Father. . . .'[73]

In view of all this it is a serious mistake to conceive the rise of modern science as a rationalist movement. The Middle Ages did take over the Ptolemaic cosmology of antiquity; but the Greek apperception of an eternal, unchanging Essence, manifesting itself in the unending but finite universe, was at bottom irreconcilable with faith in a personal Creator. With Nicholas of Cusa, in the fifteenth century, a new approach begins to emerge. According to Nicholas, the world shares in God's infinity, but is at every juncture distinguishable from him. God is infinite 'absolutely', but the world is infinite 'concretely': that is to say, the world is a spatially unlimited multiplicity of concrete, finite objects. The mediaeval mystic, Eckhart, had already used the symbol of the unending circle to represent God's infinitude. Nicholas of Cusa proceeded to apply this symbol to the world itself, which he conceived as an 'unending circle' in the strictly mathematical sense of the phrase. This mathematical reasoning picks up the threads of Pythagorean and Platonic thinking, which had been ousted during the Middle Ages by Aristotelian philosophy; but it takes a turn which Plato's thought was unable to take. The mathematical symbol is applied to the human consciousness; but not only this—the mathematical attributes of concrete objects are taken to be the symbols of their divine origin. It was this way of thinking that gave men access to the mathematical physics of modern times.[74] Kepler took this line of approach, but went further still. In his *Harmonices mundi* he starts from the conviction—confirmed by experience—that the laws of mathematics are to be met with in nature, so that man discovers himself in nature and in studying nature is able to reflect upon God's ideas in creation. In the seventeenth and eighteenth centuries mathematics, whilse it retreated more and more into the realm of abstract thought, established the paradox that the most recondite abstractions offer the best means of checking what we think, and the way we think, about concrete facts. For Kepler this paradox was still an expression of the divine harmony in creation; but to a greater and greater extent the method of procedure itself predominated over the symbolic interpretation. Bacon had laid a foundation for the modern inductive, observational method; and it was by precision of method that Descartes set out to establish a new basis for philosophy. Newton's God was simply a principle which could account for the origin of our planetary system; as for the laws which regulate it, he deduced them from a basic principle of mechanics. Laplace drew the inescapable conclusion that such a system does not require the hypothesis of God's existence. No less destructive was Hume's argument that the God required as the author of the mechanism of nature is the sort of God who makes that mechanism.

The rise of modern science is inextricably bound up with the triumphant progress of modern technology. History offers many examples of the results of human whimsicality in the technical field; yet for thousands of years there was scarcely a change in the number or character of tools available to the manual worker. Even Greek civilization made no progress in that respect. What more than anything else brought about the technological revolution in Europe was a valuation of free labour which had no earlier parallel. From the eleventh century on, there was a rapid replacement of human by non-human energy. 'The chief glory of the later Middle Ages was . . . the building for the first time in history of a complex civilization which rested not on the backs of sweating slaves or coolies but primarily on non-human power.'[75] The manual worker in Europe became not only his own master, but sometimes even the agent of cultural progress. Chemistry, 'ostracized' in the ancient world, became more and more an honoured science. The mechanical conception of the universe engendered by modern physics brought in its train the idea that nature can not only be understood by the human reason, but may also be imitated by human hands. The nineteenth century—which can be said to have invented the systematic method of invention—brought the exultant affirmation that knowledge is power.

In our own century, both science and technology are in the throes of a crisis. There is a growing uncertainty regarding meaning and purpose and an acute awareness of the limitations of human knowledge and capability. We move amidst a technological revolution, the full significance of which can only be grasped in the context of the overall development which goes by the name of 'secularization'. The discoveries of atomic science have shattered the deterministic and mechanistic world picture and have raised in a fundamentally new way the question of the nature of human knowledge.

Thus modern man is thrown back, by the very progress of science and technology, on to the primordial riddle: 'What is man?' That question does not make its appearance as something alien or strange, but in fact as the motive which lies concealed beneath the rise of modern science. It is from within that the crisis comes. Jaspers suggests —not without justification—that modern science could not conceivably have arisen apart from a spirit and a driving force which have their roots in biblical religion.[76] Modern science is impelled by an indefatigable interest in everything empirically real. The task confronting it can never be finished—not only because the cosmos of the sciences has no limits, but also because of the need to keep on re-examining the first principles and very foundations, and to begin again afresh. In its ceaseless advance science treads the brink of the abyss of inanity. By the radical nature of its quest it finds itself involved in the paradox that as a matter of principle it mistrusts the evidence of the senses, and yet can only rely upon empirical facts. Behind this scientific attitude there lies the biblical belief that the world is God's creation. Yet nothing can be further removed from it than this interest in the concrete world; for it contemplates the mind of God in creation, without ever recognizing God himself. In the give and take between theoretical construction and experimental experience the logos is for ever entering into the crisis and through it rising again to renewed and richer insight. The Bible proclaims the Logos incarnate, crucified and resurrected, the firstfruits of a new creation. The cosmos is not the in itself perfect form which the Greeks imagined it to be, but rather the creation in travail, reaching out towards redemption. There is a biblical ethos of truth; and it comes into being through the tensions proper to the personal relationship of faith—a reaching out which never comes to perfect knowing, but is man's self-offering to the Lord. The ultimate compelling motive of modern science is an irresistible pressing towards that truth to which Job required all theological constructions to be subjected, so that in the end he might encounter the reality of the Lord's self-revelation.

Modern science has now entered an awe-inspiring and hazardous region. Once ontocracy has been destroyed, there is left only the Creator to countermand chaos. Yet faith is not the obvious or inevitable consequence. On the contrary, modern science and technology seem to make 'God' a superfluous hypothesis. Perhaps it is precisely in that fact itself that there lies the most cogent indication of their origin in the religion of the Bible.

16. SECULARIZATION

The revolutionary history of the West up to the present time is rightly held to have been a continuous, ongoing process of secularization which nothing has been able to halt, let alone reverse. When we say this, of course, we say nothing new; but this movement, this trend, is like a distinctive thread running through the pattern of Western history as it is outlined in this chapter. The process cannot be rightly and properly weighed unless one realizes that the vital impulse behind it comes from the biblical message and that the course it has taken has its beginning in biblical history.

The term 'secularization' derives from the word *seculum*, the Latin equivalent of the Greek word *aiōn*, which itself is the accepted term in the New Testament for 'age, period, era'. Consequently the term also came to mean 'world'. Whereas in the 'primary' religions 'the world' is a mythical concept and whereas the Greeks always conceived of the 'Cosmos' in exclusively spatial terms, the Bible at once —from the very first verse of the Book of Genesis—sets the world in the dimension of time and history. Right from the start the primary reference of the Hebrew expression *'olam* is to time and history— within which the Lord moves with his people towards his Kingdom.

It is the German theologian Friedrich Gogarten who has defined secularization most adequately as '*Vergeschichtlichung der menschlichen Existenz*' (human existence comes to be determined by the dimension of time and history).[77] This takes its beginning in Israel. Here is raised the protest against the religion of cosmic totality, against the 'sacralizing' of all being, against the supremacy of fate, against the divinizing of kings and kingdoms. Here a break is made with the everlasting cycle of nature and the timeless presentness of myth. Here history is discovered, where the Covenant between Creator and creation, between the Lord and his people, bursts open the solid oneness of the universe. Here there is proper room for man and here the taste of freedom. The world is now radically secularized, becomes creation moving forward to regeneration, is made the arena of history, is in much pain and travail, waiting for the redemption and consummation of all things.

In the Bible this secularization is dialectical in character. It is opposed to the power of the ontocratic pattern of the ancient religions of the Near East and offers total emancipation from it. Abraham sets forth from Mesopotamia and Moses leads the Exodus out of Egypt. Yet in the course of its history the nation which had raised the sword of secularization against its enemies finds that same weapon directed against itself. It is within Israel that the sacred kingship is destroyed, the holy temple brought down and the holy people scattered among the nations. In the New Testament this history reaches its ultimate climax at the Cross of Golgotha where God's judgment is passed upon the Messiah of Israel, upon God's own appointed Son.

An analogous dialectic governs the history of Christianity. It starts with the Church, freed from the tyranny of the Hellenistic deification of the state, Christianizing part of the pagan world; but in the end the *Corpus Christianum* which the Church has built up collapses from within, under the impact of forces which the Church herself had stirred into active life. 'Christianization' is a process bound sooner or later to be turned against itself; for the Word of God 'is sharper than any two-edged sword' (Heb. 4:12) and the judgment begins 'with the household of God' (1 Pet. 4:17).

Christianization and secularization are thus involved together in a dialectical relation. There is the closest connection between this fact and all the cross purposes and misunderstanding which inevitably go hand in hand with both these terms.

The term 'secularization' is often employed in the sense of 'being conformed to this world' (Rom. 12:2). Israel, it is said, was subject to a secularizing process in adapting herself to the cultural, social, economic and religious pattern of the surrounding civilizations.[78] Again, the mediaeval Church or Islam is judged to be a form of 'secularized theocracy'. Clearly the term 'secularization' here means precisely the opposite of what we have just broadly described as the creative and liberating activity of the Word of God. It is a curious thing about the history of Christianization that these two contrary processes of secularization are simultaneously at work within it. That same Church which rescues the world from being dominated by pagan sacral powers is itself tempted to domination, this time in a 'Christian' form. Yet this is something which provokes not only the censure, the prophetic judgment, of the Word of God, as that is proclaimed by the Church itself, but equally the protest of a world set free by the Church from the tyranny of pagan gods and refusing to wear another yoke of slavery, even if the label it carries is now a Christian one.

The paradoxical dynamic of the course taken by history in this respect is strikingly summed up in yet a third sense of the term 'secularization'. This refers to the fact that in a 'Christianized' world Christian ideas of one sort or another, Christian values and ways of living and thinking acquire a life of their own, like ripened fruit, like children fully grown or like the ever-widening circles a stone makes when it is thrown into the water. In the course of modern history this process has given rise to a bewildering variety of phenomena. The ideas and values thus liberated may remain in greater or lesser degree associated with their Christian origin; but such emancipation may also lead to a radical cleavage or even to open enmity.

Not only modern nationalism, democracy, liberalism, capitalism and socialism, the concepts of modern science and the rise of modern technology, but also various philosophies of history as mutually irreconcilable as those of Comte, Hegel, Marx and Nietzsche—they are all, in this sense, the 'secularized' products of Christian civilization.

In holding that this complex process of 'secularization' is essentially historical in character at every point, what we are really saying is that it is irreversible. Once the ontocratic pattern of the pagan religions has been disrupted fundamentally, there can be no returning to a pre-Christian situation. That is why modern science and technology tread the very brink of nihilism. The National Socialist 'revolution of nihilism' brought right out into the open what had been already foreshadowed in Nietzschean philosophy: that there insinuates itself into modern nihilism a powerful nostalgia for that way of life grounded in pagan religion, which disintegrated upon the arrival of the Christian Church. The fanaticism and destructive violence which marked the revolt were so immeasurably extreme because it was an attempt to do the impossible. The fact that it failed shows that the way back to the pre-Christian religious pattern had become impassable.

The impact of the West within the non-Western world begins a new chapter in the history of secularization. For the first time in human history the great 'primary' civilizations of Asia, as well as the Muslim world, are faced with a civilization that has made a radical break with the religious pattern. This is an unprecedented event even in Christian history; for never in the past has there been such an encounter as this between on the one hand the great pre-Christian societies and the post-Christian Muslim world and on the other Christianity in such a thoroughly secularized phase as modern Western civilization is. We do not know what may happen as a result of this.

When a technocratic ideology is grafted on to a society in which the traditional religious way of life has scarcely been disturbed and where the great mass of people continue to practise it, the deep-rooted affinity between religion and nihilism stands exposed.

It is helpful to make a clear distinction between secularization and secularism.[79] The first is a continuing historical process, the second a fixed and absolutized ideology with a tendency towards pagan or nihilistic totalitarianism. The relation of the Christian Church to the advancing history of secularization is in any event a positive one; it carries responsibility for it and is intimately concerned and involved with what that process brings in its train, with all that it so richly promises and with its appalling threats and dangers.

> Today secularized modern civilization is subduing the non-Christian world which missions have not been able to subdue. Apparently the step to its secularized and therefore isolated content is easier than the complete transfer to Christianity. Yet the two go together; and the consequences of secularism confront us forcibly with the Christian question.[80]

17. THE COMMUNIST REVOLUTION

(a) Marxism: a Western Doctrine

With the rise of Marxism the secularizing process which has marked the course of Western civilization enters a new and critical phase, giving particularly virulent expression to the full and contradictory dynamism enshrined in the variety of meanings attached to the term 'secularization'. Although there has been no fully fledged Communist revolution in Western Europe, Marxism is in origin an entirely Western phenomenon. At the same time, the fact that 'the first socialist country in the world' lies outside Western Europe—and even more the spread of Communism in Asia—serves to indicate quite clearly that in Marxism the tendency of Western civilization to transcend itself assumes a form and proportion without precedent.

Marxism arose in the Western Europe of the nineteenth century and is to be understood entirely within the context of that period. The growth of capitalism, the French Revolution and the Industrial Revolution had produced a society in which a self-conscious bourgeoisie had taken control of cultural, social, political and economic affairs. Marx himself came from the bourgeoisie and grew up in an atmosphere permeated by the ideals of the Enlightenment, a confidence in human reason and the unassailable truth of modern science.

This was the society which found itself confronted, willynilly, with a formidable problem in the tumultuous upsurge of an urban proletariat, itself the product of those very triumphs of industrialization and technology which had served to emancipate the middle classes. The really significant thing about Marxism was that it responded to the challenge of the proletarian revolution, pronouncing it to be a necessary stage in the evolution of Western society. It was principally Hegel and Feuerbach who furnished Marx with the philosophical method and philosophical presuppositions he needed for constructing his ideology of revolution. From Hegel he acquired the dialectical view of world history which regards it as a continuous, rational, comprehensible movement, proceeding from thesis through antithesis to synthesis, towards the goal of ultimate freedom. Using such a dialectical methodology, he turned Hegel's historical idealism inside out and transformed it into historical materialism. Thus he took German idealism, which had been the first line of defence or at any rate of self-justification for the bourgeoisie and the Prussian state, and forged it into a powerful weapon in the hand of their enemy, the proletariat:

> Just as philosophy finds her material arsenal in the proletariat, so the proletariat finds its spiritual arsenal in philosophy.[81]

It was Feuerbach who helped to give this radically new turn to his thought. He it was who, as Marx himself testified, 'used the Hegelian method in order to criticize and to complete Hegel, by reducing the metaphysical absolute Spirit, to Man.'[82] He exposed theology and metaphysics as concealed anthropology and went over to a radically atheistic humanism. 'God was my first belief, Reason (*die Vernunft*) my second and Man my third and last.' Yet Feuerbach did not go far enough, because he settled for an abstract conception of man. Marx unmasked religion as not only a projection of man but also the product of social relationships. With him 'the exercise of critical judgment shifted from heaven to earth, from religion to natural right, from theology to politics.'[83]

This philosophical genealogy—from Hegel by way of Feuerbach to Marx—epitomizes the close connection between the history of

Christian civilization in the West and the secularizing process; and it enables one to see how inextricably interwoven they are. Hegel's speculative metaphysics was really a secularized Christian theology. Feuerbach started off as a theologian, turned in his disappointment to Hegelian philosophy, which he proceeded to expose as a form of theology in disguise, and ended up by discovering that the 'God' of theology is nothing other than the deified being of man. His atheism was profoundly anti-theological, arising as it did out of a theologian's frustration and disappointment over a theology unable to vindicate its own pretensions.

If therefore we are to understand the radical character of Marx's critical approach against the background of secularization as a typically Christian phenomenon, we must take particular note of that strain of passionate feeling which blazes within and behind it—the passion indeed of the biblical prophet. Born of Jewish stock—his grandfather on his mother's side had been a rabbi—Marx did not belie his origins in either thought or conduct. Truth for him was quite inseparable from praxis, from its consequences in action. 'The philosophers have only interpreted the world in one way or another; the thing now is to change it.' The political revolution which he foresaw and wanted to prepare for was for him the expression of an overture to total revolution which would give rise to a new type of men. By this means the proletariat, within which man becomes a complete slave to wrong and, as it were, loses himself, announces the dissolution of the existing world order and ushers in the new. Within this new order the dehumanizing process is brought to an end and man fully recovers his identity. This is a secularized biblical eschatology in which the proletariat has assumed the broad features of the Servant of the Lord, whose vicarious suffering for the whole creation inaugurates the new age.

The tendency in Western Europe has been for Marxism, and for social relations generally, to develop along evolutionary rather than revolutionary lines. That is partly to be accounted for by the fact that the critical Marxist view of society as it then was arose out of, and was inherent in, that revolutionary dialectical process which has been the constant stimulus of Western civilization. Here the Industrial Revolution went hand in hand with those very forces of renewal and innovation which gave it birth; as a result society was transformed and the working class came gradually to share in the increasing prosperity and steady advance towards democratization. That is not, however, the only reason why a Communist revolution failed to materialize in Western Europe. We have to remember too that the success of the Industrial Revolution in Western Europe was fostered to a considerable extent by the well-nigh unlimited possibilities that existed for economic expansion in the non-Western world. The labouring masses of Western Europe enjoyed their share of benefit from this; and so the centre of gravity of the 'class struggle' was shifted from the 'internal proletariat' to the 'external proletariat', the illiterate millions of Asia and Africa.

(b) Russian Communism

The fermenting process which heralded and set the scene for the triumph of the Communist revolution in Russia took place among the intelligentsia of that country during the nineteenth century.[84] The leaven at work in it was a 'nihilism' that sprang up on the soil of Russian Orthodox Christianity and was the negative expression of a Christian ascetic spirit and of Russian apocalypticism. In this Western influences played a particular and active part; for in Belinsky's revolutionary, atheistic socialism, with its burning—and Christlike— love for suffering humanity, at the close of the 'forties in Russia the same thing was happening as had occurred in Germany through the extreme 'leftist' Hegelianism of Feuerbach and Marx. Belinsky was the spiritual and intellectual father of Russian Communism. Bakunin took some part as an emigrant in the West European revolutions and influenced Marx's doctrine regarding the messianic mission of the proletariat, although his anarchism made him an enemy of Marx's ideas about the state. Bakunin's militant atheism foreshadowed the atheistic propaganda of modern Soviet Russia. Tkachev, the first Russian to talk about Marx, opposed the view that the development of industry under capitalism was something which applied in Russia as elsewhere. He was the fore-runner of Lenin.

Even in the nineteenth century therefore the distinctive line to be taken by the Russian Revolution was marked out—a line which ran parallel to that of West European Marxism, but was nevertheless independent of it in the way it adapted Western influences to suit the Russian mentality and the conditions of Russian society. To begin with, Marxism in Russia was of an entirely Western cast; but that particular line of development came to a dead end with the defeat of the Mensheviks. It was Leninism that set forward Marxism in its Russian form, amalgamating it with the traditions of the old revolutionary intelligentsia. Lenin, accepting the fact that there was no capitalistic middle class, pursued the consequences to their logical conclusion and simply 'skipped' the period of capitalism which according to Marx's doctrine must of necessity precede the revolution. The Russian people, a nation of labourers and peasants, were identified with the proletariat; Russian messianism was merged with the messianism of the proletariat. If this meant that the classical version of Marxism was both 'Russianized' and orientalized, one must remember on the other hand that Russian messianism too had been formed under Christian influences and that, as Berdyaev observes, it was closely akin to Jewish messianism.[85]

This leap straight from a pre-capitalistic phase—or at most from one of merely incipient capitalism—to large-scale industrialization was made possible only by a religious and messianic faith in the power of technics and of modern science to redeem and save. In the new Marxist-Leninist philosophy, which with its totalitarian claim to all-embracing absolute truth took the place of the vanquished orthodoxy of the Russian Church, dialectical materialism was used to support and vindicate this messianic Marxism.

As it develops, Russian Communism exhibits two tendencies which would appear to be mutually opposed. On the one hand it is a sure consequence of the growth of a technocratic society that as modern scientific thinking is brought into play the secularizing forces unleashed by it are bound in the long run to undermine the absolute authority of Communist dogma. In so far as the socialist experiment succeeds, precisely to that extent does it engender a new bourgeoisie among those few deputed to exercise, on behalf of the rest, 'the dictatorship of the proletariat'. This minority then finds itself beset by very much the same kind of symptoms of an inner malaise as the bourgeoisie in Western countries—but with this fundamental difference: that those spiritual forces which in the West led to the rise of the bourgeoisie are not present in this case to offset a dangerous nihilism. There is not even the Church's proclamation of the eschatological message of hope to answer its challenge. On the contrary, as the strength of messianic expectancy in the Communist faith diminishes, so its latent nihilism will more and more assert itself. The problem is indeed a fearsome one; and it is rooted ultimately in the fact that the history of Christian apocalyptic is reflected, albeit in a debased form, in the history of Marxist apocalyptic. As Martin Wight says:

> The Russian Revolution was the parallel to the Incarnation, the realisation of meaning within history, with an implicit judgment on the world at large. There followed an exaggerated expectation of the world revolution, which would be the final and explicit judgment. When the world revolution did not happen, the Communist movement turned its attention to the tactics of an indefinitely prolonged epilogue. The fundamental difference between the two apocalyptics is that Marxism denies the extra-historical category and therefore forces the fulfilment of history within the historical process itself.[86]

All this points at the same time to something else, to an opposite tendency which in Russian Communism to date has been much to the fore: namely the necessity for the totalitarian state. What led up to this was a twofold course of events, stemming partly from Western and partly from Russian history. To the 'Right', Hegel's 'pan-logism' leads directly to the reactionary glorification of the Prussian state, which finds its place in his metaphysical system as the realization of the absolute *Geist*; whilst to the 'Left' it follows a course through Feuerbach and Nietzsche to National Socialist totalitarianism. Classical Marxism exposed the state as 'organized power' dedicated to the service of the ruling class and its interests. The state remains indispensable during the period of transition from Socialism to Communism; but under the 'dictatorship of the proletariat'—that is, under the sway of the great labouring majority—it will gradually die away; and in the classless society the state will have ceased to exist. Although this theory has never been repudiated in Russian Communism—not even under Stalin—the prospect which it holds rorth is relegated to the fairly remote future, not least because of the need to defend Communism against still existing non-Communist states. In point of fact, what we have seen is the growth of a totalitarian and technocratic state, administered by a bureaucratic machine under party dictatorship. In contrast to Marx, Lenin concentrated from the very start on the problem of how to capture and keep a hold over the power of the state. He maintained that it is easier to bring about the dictatorship of the proletariat in an absolute monarchy than, say, in the Western democracies. The political and

economic backwardness of Russia was the very thing which made
it ripe for social revolution.

Here one can see how Lenin quite consciously ties up with Russian
history and disassociates himself from the history of the West, which
provides the basic model for Marx's historical determinism. This it
is which lends strength to the idea of Bolshevism as the third phase
of the Russian world empire, the continuation in a new form of the
imperium of Peter the Great, itself a transformation of the Moscow
Tsardom.[87]

One has to bear in mind in this connection that Russian history
has itself been constantly exposed to the tensions resulting from the
East-West problem. Throughout the nineteenth century this subject
was the occasion of impassioned argument between 'Slavophiles' and
'Westernizers'. Whereas the latter looked towards the future and
contended that Russia had lagged behind in her development and had
somehow to catch up with a Europe which they had in fact idealized,
the Slavophiles dreamed about a no less idealized past which had
assumed its characteristic form in the Muscovite Empire of the 'pre-
Petrine' era. Danilevsky prophesied that the downfall of the 'degenerate West' would be followed by the rise of Slavonic culture—
a turn of events not unlike the *Völkerwanderung*, when Roman
civilization collapsed and the European civilization of the Romano-
German peoples was born.[88] Yet a third school of thought, the
Eurasian, put the emphasis on Eurasian unity, which found its political
expression in the empire of Jenghiz Khan and his successors and later
in Tsarist Russia. This ideology, although far from homogeneous,
would seem to correspond more closely than any other to that
maintained by the Soviet Union.[89]

The standpoints of those who have attempted a critical assessment
of Russia's history are likewise various. Berdyaev envisages Russia as
a Christianized Orient which for two centuries past has been laid bare
to strong influences from the West. The Muscovite kingdom possessed
an oriental culture—that of the Christianized Tartar Empire—shaped
in lasting contrast to the 'Latin' west. After the fall of the Byzantine
Empire the messianic doctrine of Moscow as the third Rome became
the ideological basis of the Muscovite Tsardom; and closely bound
up with it was the struggle for a national church. Peter the Great
secularized the Orthodox Russian Empire; but this Western influence
was and remained something alien to the people. Other historians

defer to the idea that it was Asiatic influences that first estranged Russia from Europe.[90] They compare the Mongol invasion in the thirteenth century, which was the decisive factor in the separation, with the Ottoman conquest of the Balkans. Though freed from her own Asiatic conquerors, Moscow none the less continued to develop along lines basically similar to the trends within the Ottoman Empire.[91] When the empire was 'Westernized' under Peter the Great, the effect was to stimulate a nationalistic effort, and as a result of that the advance of a Eurasian empire under Russian control—at the expense of the historic European community. The Soviet Union has always been non-European, if not anti-European.[92]

(c) Communism and the Non-Western World

This sketch of various cross-currents and ideas with a bearing on the historical growth of Russia's situation between Asia and the West should give some impression of the internal tensions and of the ambivalence which would seem to be inherent in an intermediate rôle of that kind. It exemplifies the way in which a non-Western society feels the increasing pressure of a Western civilization in process of rapid development. Russia under Peter the Great, when confronted with the modern West, drew the logical conclusion, in part at any rate, and she did this before the primary civilizations of Asia and before the Muslim world. Two centuries later she was again first in adopting a revolutionary Western ideology; and so she has been able to take the lead in spreading this revolutionary doctrine throughout the non-Western world. The manner in which Russia has herself accommodated this Western infiltration is a touchstone for the answer which other non-Western societies may give to the challenge of Marxism. The crucial question, surely, is whether the introduction of Western technocracy occasions a fundamental rift in the traditional ontocratic pattern of the state. If it is true that Bolshevism is a technocratic extension of the Tsarist régime, then where the Asian societies are concerned the prospect of an affirmative answer to our crucial question would appear to be even less likely, since the Tsarist régime, for its part, was the Russian successor—still further orientalized under Asiatic influences—of a Byzantine Empire in which, as we have seen, the ontocratic pattern of the primary civilizations of the Near East was carried forward in a Hellenized and Christianized form. How much more strongly therefore must a Communist régime in China feel the enormous attraction of the traditional pattern—a pattern which, under the sway of the Confucianist ideology, has held the Chinese Empire in thrall right up to and into the twentieth century.

It says quite a lot that Marxist doctrine gets itself tied up in uncertainties and contradictions as soon as it comes to deal with the transition from an Asiatic society to socialism. In broad outline, Marx singled out four successive modes of production as representing the periods of advance in the economic forms of society: Asiatic, ancient, feudal and modern-bourgeois.[93] Needless to say, this theory was completely determined by the situation of nineteenth-century Western civilization. Is it applicable, though, to any non-Western society? It is so only when modern capitalism encounters and makes its impact upon such a society in a state of feudalism. Yet that is in conflict, surely, with the express admission which one finds, not only in many of the utterances of Marx and Engels, but initially also in the writings of Lenin, that the Asian societies—up to and including Tsarist Russia— are one and all typical of 'oriental despotism'.[94] One must set side by side with that, however, the embarrassment and confusion in which Marxism and most certainly Leninism find themselves placed on this score: a dilemma from which they escape only by attributing a 'feudal' character to the Asiatic and Tsarist societies. In wanting to take a revolution which was determined entirely by the unique development of Western civilization and to apply it to non-Western societies quite innocent of that development, Marxism creates for itself an insoluble problem. Just here lies the crux of the Western impact on the non-Western world—one which the West has so far proved unable to resolve. Communism has cut the Gordian knot by proclaiming and expediting the technocratic revolution among civilizations at bottom still regulated by the ontocratic pattern of oriental despotism. Yet this solution, drastic though it is, has not even touched, let alone answered, the root problem of how the non-Western civilizations are going to be able to break away from their basic pattern, unless by virtue of those profound and powerful spiritual factors which have steered Western history forward on its unique course.

(d) The Islam of the Technocratic Era

Communism has been aptly described as the Islam of the twentieth century.[95] The description is apt, not merely because it brings out the strategic importance of Islam in the relation of the West towards the non-Western world, but because it affords opportunity to sum up—sketchily, of course, but under a few convenient heads—the rôle of Communism.

1. Communism is a 'post-Christian' phenomenon. The Christian civilization of the West begat it and brought it into being as a reaction to and derivate of Christian theological cogitation about God, man, the world and history. The dialectical fashion in which the Communist Revolution sets itself over against Christian history is a pseudo-theological reiteration of the contrast which Christianity sees between the 'Old' Covenant and the 'New'.

Similarly Islam is a 'post-Christian' religion, offshoot of a Christian stem, a product of that process by which Christian theology, formulation of dogma and contention over it grew and developed within the early Christian Church from the second to the seventh century A.D. By a kind of dialectical recapitulation the Muslim creed—that Muhammad is 'the seal of the prophets'—turns the Christian creed concerning Jesus' prophetic-Messianic status against Christianity.

By the yardstick of a fundamental and critical analysis based on a biblical and thus prophetic viewpoint, Islam and Communism are both poor in spiritual content, unoriginal and lacking independence. That their growth has been colossal and has assumed something of a universal stature suggests the giantlike proportions of the dwarf who seems even bigger than the giant on whose shoulders he has elected to stand.

2. In Communism the spirit of Israel has reaped what might be called a second harvest, of more rapid growth than the first yield, Christianity, which prepared and fertilized the soil. Once liberated from its mediaeval ghetto, where the Talmudic tradition had been kept alive, Judaism quickly brought to the surface, in the form of Marxism, an explosive force aimed at that Western Christianity which had stunted its growth.

Equally astounding had been the rapid upsurge in the seventh century A.D. of that other 'second outcrop' of Judaism which likewise took advantage of the 'firstfruits'. Denied all room to expand within the Hellenistic Christian world and forced into isolation within Arabia, the Jewish Diaspora fed upon the tenacity and strength of its rabbinic spirit until it had shown the world through the triumph of Muhammad's prophetic claims the full force of its opposition to Hellenistic Christianity. It seems that only in a dialectical conjunction with

Christianity is it possible for Judaism to give real scope among the Gentiles to its bent for universality; for the rest, whether in the Near East, North Africa or in Asia, the Diaspora is locked in a visionless isolation.

3. Communism is a Christian 'heresy' which has achieved independence and stands, as it were, on its own authority. It is a counter-church; and its typically heretical character consists in its having fastened, with fanatical single-mindedness and in necessary and fully justified protest against a prevalent bourgeois version of Christianity, upon a *partial* truth which it exalts into the one complete, exclusive and infallible dogma at the expense of all other aspects and points of view. This fixation stifles—or gravely hinders at any rate—the free play of the revolutionizing powers secreted in God's proclaimed Word, like a charge of dynamite, time and again blasting away the barriers which human prejudice and pride throw around the fullness of truth. At the same time, this heresy holds a challenge for Christianity. It calls upon Christianity to mend its ways and to turn from its own heretical one-sidedness and emasculation of the truth in its fullness. When Christianity stoops to a sterile anti-Communism, at once defensive and aggressive, it does indeed show itself to be that very caricature of the prophetic, biblical message—as rigid a heresy as any —which Communism has rejected with justifiable indignation.

Islam too, in the first instance, was fully admitted by Christian theologians to be an (Arian) heresy. Only when it evolved into a complete *Corpus Islamicum*, a counter-image to the *Corpus Christianum*, was it transformed into a self-supporting and comprehensive religion. As soon as the original protest against a dominant type of Christianity —a wholly justifiable reaction to Hellenizing and paganizing influences —became a fixed and autocratic system of dogma, a dam had been flung across the irresistible current, which in Western Christianity then broke away through mediaeval scholasticism. Right down to the present time, however, Islam has invariably held a mirror up to Christianity. Although the Crusades are of course a thing of the past, Christianity has never yet been able to answer the vital question which Islam sets before it: whether it is not itself a Hellenistic 'heresy' of the primitive Church, which has unfolded in the form of Western civilization.

4. Marxism emerged as the messianic ideology of the 'internal proletariat', which had been produced by a 'dominant minority'

owing its peculiar genius and authority to the dynamic evolution of Western civilization.

Islam owed its triumph to the 'external proletariat' of Arabia, North Africa and the Near East, which was dominated by Hellenistic and Byzantine Christianity and rose up against it.

5. The way was paved for Russian Communism by the radical, ascetical and apocalyptic strains in Russian Christianity and by the leavening process which had taken place under Western influence among the nineteenth century intelligentsia. Originally a Western phenomenon, Marxism underwent a transformation in 'the first socialist country of the world', when it came to be grafted on to the traditional pattern of 'oriental despotism' inherited from Byzantium. That despotic pattern, centred in Moscow as 'the third Rome' and furnished by Peter the Great with a certain Western allure, had for centuries past formed the basis of the Russian state and of Russian society.

In the case of Islam, the soil was prepared and fertilized by Monophysite and Nestorian Christianity and by the ascetic Christianity which had already made its influence felt in primitive Arabia. The original message of Muhammad, partly Christian and partly Judaistic, fused with the primitive tribal consciousness to become the messianic ideology of the Arabian people as the 'elect' and of Mecca as the true Jerusalem. Through the caliphate of Baghdad Islam came to be modelled on the age-old pattern of the ancient civilizations of the Near East; and this later became, in its Byzantine form, the model for the Turkish Empire on the one hand and Tsarist Russia on the other.

6. The estrangement between Roman and Byzantine Christianity became a decisive rupture in the schism of A.D. 1054; and the antithesis between the Christian West and Tsarist Russia was a continuation of it. Thus the rivalry which exists today between 'the West', championed by the United States, and 'the East', led by the Soviet Union, is the most recent phase of that antithesis.

The rupture between the Christian and Muslim worlds too is by way of being a 'schism' between rivals who are heir to a common cultural and religious heritage. There persists to this very day an unresolved antithesis between the West with its 'modern crusade' of colonial and economic domination and the Muslim world, protecting itself against that with the 'modern jihad' of Muslim renaissance and Arab nationalism.

7. The orientalizing process which Marxism has undergone in the
Soviet Union has been reinforced to an uncommon degree by the
Eurasian character which Russia had earlier acquired both through
the Mongol invasions and by reason of her enormous continental
expansion beyond the Caucasus, over Central Asia and into the Far
East. She owes the tremendous power of attraction which she exercises
to that orientalized form in which Marxist ideology has embarked
upon its course throughout the non-Western world. In the Bolshevik
Revolution the most westerly outpost of Asia has discovered a highly
effective defence against the threat of Western domination, because it
pursues a Western ideology in an orientalized style; and this is the
ground of its claim to be the champion of the 'awakening' non-
Western peoples.

In the same way one can regard Islam as an 'orientalized'
Christianity, the decisive reply of the 'marginal' peoples of Arabia,
North Africa, the Near East and Persia to the pressure which
Hellenized Christian imperialism exerted upon them. The closing
decades of the thirteenth century, when the last bulwark of the
Crusaders fell to the Muslims and the die was cast which settled the
choice of the invading Mongols in favour of Islam and against the
Christian faith, also decided the future of Christianity among the
great primary civilizations of Asia. The dramatic character of that
period and its crucial importance suggest a comparison with the
advance of Communism in Asia during the past few decades, in the
final phase of Western colonial ascendancy.

There is none the less one radical difference. The contest in Asia,
which was decided in favour of Islam, was over the conversion of
primitive Central Asian tribes. In Africa today there is an analogous
struggle, again among primitive peoples who must yield before a
higher, universal religion; and again this time Islam as a non-Western
religion holds the trump cards. The Communist success in China has
achieved what neither Islam nor Christianity could manage: that is,
the unprecedented conquest of one of the great primary civilizations
of Asia. Along the great continental routes of communication
Christianity did at one time reach as far as China, from Persia and the
Near East. At a subsequent period the control of such means of
communication passed to Islam. Then in the nineteenth century
Western Christian civilization gained entry into inland China, by the
seaward approaches this time, thus outflanking Islam's domination of

the continental routes and with all the further advantages which the modern development of the West conferred. The winning trick however was played in the middle of the twentieth century by an ideology which in common with mediaeval Islam already had the advantage of dominating the Eurasian continent and to that could now add a victorious faith in modern technocracy, taken over from the West.

8. One more point of similarity Communism shares with Islam: it is that they are alike impervious to Christian missionary influence. The dialectical relation to Christianity, to which both these 'post-Christian' phenomena owe their origin, makes them both apparently immune from conversion. Faced with Communism, Western Christianity displays for the most part a combination of missionary impotence and a half aggressive, half defensive 'crusading' spirit, which bears a striking resemblance to the spiritual deadlock of mediaeval Christianity when faced with Islam.

9. This brings us to the final and crucial point in respect of which Communism, considered in relation to Islam, denotes a phase in the history of mankind totally without precedent and a challenge to Christianity which is entirely new: it is that Communism is the Islam *of the technocratic era*. The Muslim world, although as adamantine in its resistance to conversion as ever, had grudgingly to recognize in the nineteenth century the superiority of modern Western civilization. Now however Christianity finds itself up against an ideological power armed with a messianic consciousness of infallible and universal truth and proclaiming its belief in the victory of atheistic technocratic society. On the final showing, it transpires that Christianity has lost the winning trump—namely the superiority of the industrialized West—to this new Islam. Christianity is now thrown back upon the naked weakness of the Gospel or on the naked force of its own latent but extremely virulent technocratic atheism. In any event, a modern 'Crusade' must inevitably be as godless as the Communist 'jihad' it is intended to combat.

It is no kind of pedantic gesture to insist with the greatest emphasis upon the atheistic-technocratic character of the basis of Communism. In fact there is every apparent reason for calling this new Islam a new 'religion'. Its messianic ideology, which has taken over the functions of Russian Orthodoxy and of Christian Tsarism, has a wholly religious structure. The great memorial monument in East

Berlin which honours the soldiers who fell during the Second World War is built to a design which reminds one very much of the ancient Hindu sanctuaries with their reliefs and texts from the Mahābhārata, but replaced of course in this instance by reliefs depicting the epic story of the Russian army and people in the Second World War and by the words of Stalin. These stand on both sides of the broad avenue which leads up to the central dome-shaped shrine, erected on top of a mound fulfilling in every respect the function of the 'cosmic mountain'. The shrine is surmounted on the inside by a representation of the Kremlin in miniature, at the very place where an image of the *Christos Pantokrator* stands within the apse of Greek Orthodox churches and where in the Church of St Sophia, confiscated by Islam, the apse is crowned by the calligraphic 'Allah'. Here one finds flanking the model, in place of the holy apostles—or of the first four caliphs—the 'icons' of the new saints, the Soviet workers. That is just one striking instance, which could be multiplied many times over, of the 'religious' nature of Communist ideology.

Nevertheless, to ascribe to Communism the character of a new 'religion' is seriously to misunderstand it. Rather, what we now see before us is the full consequence of what the Christian theologian Feuerbach, father of Communist atheism, did by his 'unmasking' of Christian theology; for this Communist 'theology' is indeed nothing other than anthropology—and that not in any veiled form, but in the open guise of a titanic creed, promulgating the triumph of the new technocratic man. The forms which that creed can assume are at the most only *pseudo*-religious. To call it a 'religion' looks suspiciously like running away from the confrontation which Communism is forcing upon Christianity in facing it with the atheist character of modern science and technology, twin-brothers of the Christian faith and nurtured in the womb of Christian civilization.

Seven

The Western Impact and the 'Awakening' of the Non-Western World

I. THE VIRUS AND THE DISEASE

IT is easier to describe in detail and at some length how the encounter between the West and the non-Western world has developed during the past few centuries than it is to plumb those influences which, though they lie deep beneath the surface of events, have been decisive in their effects. It is also difficult to account for the real nature of the various motivating factors in concise and conclusive terms. Perhaps the worst handicap is that we ourselves are in the thick of what is taking place and most probably are at the end of only the very earliest, initial phase. The transformation is so radical and the turn of events more often than not so unpredictable that only the most provisional soundings are possible. Certain factors in this process are indeed known; but a great many others continue to elude us. There is no settled observation post, nor any touchstone by which to form an objective judgment. Our situation is rather like that of a ship which is adrift in a powerful current, its course no longer either controllable or precisely known. Moreover there is no 'metereological institute' for observing and forecasting cultural developments, and no basis solid enough to make such a thing conceivable. It is now widely realized that 'the unchanging East' is a fiction and an hallucination which has sorely afflicted the Western mind and outlook. A further misunderstanding, no less disastrous, now threatens, however; it is to suppose that the tumultuous changes within the non-Western world are mainly the result of forcing the pace in an attempt to overtake the West, as it were, in seven league boots: as though 'the West' were not itself caught up in a process of transculturation even more far-reaching, if that were possible, and as though it were still quite legitimate to view this process without any regard to its global dimensions and consequences.

When it comes to a situation as dramatic as this—one which

moreover is unamenable to an objective, strictly 'scientific' approach
—one is naturally inclined to fall back on certain figures of speech.
Thus we hear of the 'revolt' of Asia and of the 'storm over Asia'.
Expressions such as 'Africa emergent' and, especially, 'the awakening
of the non-Western peoples' are much in vogue. Somewhat less
spectacular but equally figurative terms relate to the as yet unverified
thesis of a 'renaissance', 'resurgence' and 'reformation' with which
the non-Western world is currently engaged. On the Asiatic side,
naturally enough, there are those who cherish the idea of a 'recovery
of Asia', consequent upon the 'retreat of Europe' from the position
of 'Western dominance'. One way or another there is no end to the
procession of metaphors and abundance of talk about birth and
birth-pangs, awakening out of sleep or narcosis, revolt against fatal
pressure or the pressure of fate, emerging from the ocean of sub-
conscious passivity, a boxer recovering from the temporary effects
of a knock-out.

There are, of course, other types of comparison which yield a
more adequate picture of the particular rôle the West is playing as
a factor in this process. One might say that the Western influence has
acted as a 'catalysator', which precipitates rapid change and fresh
combinations within a stable chemical structure.

But perhaps it is biological processes which offer the closest
parallel. The impact of the West reminds one very strongly of a
virus penetrating a biological organism. The virus produces a certain
disorder in the tissue, which can prove either noxious or beneficial.
If the organism is not able to withstand the disease, then it is destroyed;
but if on the other hand the organism holds its own, by being subjected to the course of the disease it can acquire an enormously
enhanced resistance and become immune from any further attack by
the same virus. An apparently harmless virus can also undergo a
transmutation which causes it to act upon a given organism with
devastatingly powerful effect. Thus there is a high degree of reciprocity between the nature of the virus, the organism and the course
taken by the disease. Furthermore, a virus-laden person, although
himself immune through having successfully resisted a disease, can
spread the virus among others in his vicinity with pernicious effect.
Finally, there is the possibility of calculated prevention by the use of
inoculation.

This complex of facts relating to virus infection and its consequences offers some striking analogies with a whole set of phenomena connected with the encounter between the West and the non-Western world. We have had occasion already to make use of this figure of speech in connection with the rise of Islam and with our account of what occurred at that time. Indeed the early history of Islam bears a unique resemblance to present-day cultural developments; and that is one of the main reasons why we paid so much attention to it. The Muslim world became the first great competitor of the Western Christian world and can be said to have anticipated, in both an active and a passive sense, the upsurge of the non-Western peoples in recent times. In the course of its history the European Christian world has also thrown up a number of secondary phenomena with a marked 'immunity' from the prevailing Christian religion; but broadly speaking the Germanic peoples have remained prone to the 'disease' known as 'Christianity'. In the Arab regions, however, the Jewish-Christian-Hellenistic virus has penetrated the social organism in such fashion as to render it—after a period of not particularly dangerous infection and of highly successful resistance—thoroughly immune where Christianity is concerned. Islam is the product of this process; and wherever it has spread, it has proved able to maintain its identity in face of the existing cultural patterns—yet nowhere has it made a really shattering or revolutionary impact upon them.

The crucial question which the transformation of the non-Western world presents today has therefore been raised earlier by the meeting of Christianity with Islam: will the penetration of the Western 'virus' produce a permanent 'disease' in the non-Western world, or will the result be a condition of 'immunity' from further attack by the Western virus? Factors which were operative in the rise of Islam are present on both sides of the modern encounter—but their force is incomparably greater today. The Western virus is a fresh mutation of that which generated Islam in the seventh century; it has split up into a large number of viruses possessed, whether separately or together, of an enormously intensified power of penetration. Then too the simple tribal society from which Muhammad sprang was a mere pigmy in comparison with the Asian civilizations now feeling the impact of the West.

Moreover, between the extremes of Islamic and of Western civilization there is a wide range of varying possibilities. In the past the civilizations of India and China have shown a remarkable capacity for absorbing the nomadic invader; but to what extent they will prove capable of absorbing the Western impact it is impossible to say. It may well be that the storm passing through Asia now will prove, like the Mongol storm, to be violent but shortlived, and that the intrusion of Western ways of life will at the most enrich and stimulate, without cutting at all deeply into the traditions of Asia. It is also feasible that Asian civilizations will follow in the wake of Byzantine civilization, which took the Christian virus permanently into its system to be sure, but without allowing itself to be radically affected and transformed thereby.

It is a fact—and one of considerable importance—that so far Christianity has given no proof of its power radically to regenerate and transform the traditional patterns of the ancient Eurasian civilizations. If anything, the evidence suggests quite the reverse. The history of Byzantine and Russian civilizations shows that what happens when a society is 'Christianized' may not be very different from what occurs when a society is 'Islamized'. In the organism of the East Roman Empire, with its unbroken continuity, the Christian virus was not a radical or a dynamic factor at all. Any disturbing influence it might have had was stultified by the astounding tenacity and resilience shown by the ancient pattern and structure of society. It is extremely doubtful whether the history of Western civilization would have taken such a revolutionary course either, if the fall of the West Roman Empire had not provided just the circumstances that were requisite.

Today, for the first time in history, Christianity faces a real test of its resources in its encounter with the 'primary' Asian civilizations. They are in the grip of violent, even convulsive, reactions—a sure sign that the Western virus has succeeded in penetrating the Asian organism. After an exhaustive study of the period of Western dominance in Asia, Panikkar has concluded that it marks a dividing line in the history of the Asian peoples. The massive nature of the changes that have already taken place, the upheavals which have radically transformed their ancient societies and the ideas which have modified their outlook involve 'a qualitative break with the past which justly entitles the changes to be described as revolutionary'.[1]

One can fully admit this as a fact and still offer an interpretation which would seek to explain it, not as a consequence of the strength of the Western impact, but as the normal working of a specific 'law' of history, to which the Asian civilizations are subject along with the rest. Toynbee, in *A Study of History*, attempts an interpretation on these very lines. The universal 'law' or principle which he claims he is able to discover in the history of all civilizations in reality boils down to this: that the course of Hellenic and then of Western civilization can be comprehended in a scheme applicable to all other civilizations as well. It would take too long to show how this theory is bound to land itself in unresolvable contradictions and distortions and in point of fact gets itself tied up in all directions. It does not take into account the crucial fact that in the history of Western civilization there is a demonstrable break with the previous Hellenic civilization —a departure from the characteristic pattern which has no parallel elsewhere. The 'universal state' which according to Toynbee's theory marks the beginning of the end for every civilization, in the history of Hellenic civilization had this fatal effect only in the case of the West Roman Empire; and even then it was by virtue of the unique fact that Western civilization was breaking away from that pattern. In the Byzantine, Islamic and Asian civilizations on the other hand the 'universal state' is a normal, periodically recurrent phenomenon, in which the pattern of the 'ontocratic state' manifests itself over and over again through a succession of ups and downs. For that matter, the late Roman Empire itself was really nothing more or less than a reabsorption of Graeco-Roman society into the ancient Near Eastern cultural pattern. In the case of Islamic civilization—and in flagrant contradiction of his own theory—Toynbee admits this uninterrupted continuity, when he describes the Arab Caliphate as a reproduction of the Achaemenid Empire a thousand years earlier.

Once this *vitium originis* of Toynbee's thesis has been recognized, his theory regarding the modern period of world history becomes easy enough to understand. He assigns to the Western impact on the history of civilization in Asia the same sort of rôle that the German barbarians had once fulfilled within the Roman Empire. Thus Chinese, Japanese and Indian society must, in each case, have experienced a 'universal state' fairly recently—in the form of the Mongol and Manchu Empires, the dictatorship of Hideyoshi and the Tokugawa Shogunate, and—in India—the Mogul Empire. The theory breaks down because in one sense it makes far too little, and in another sense far too much, of the Western impact and its significance. The so-called 'universal states' of Chinese and Indian society (the case of Japan is a somewhat different issue) are in fact just new editions of earlier empires and can therefore only pass for evidence of decay because, exactly as with the West Roman Empire, continuity has been interrupted by the Western impact. It is that invasion by the civilization of the West and not any hypothesized immanent principle that has made such a deep incision in Asian history. At the same time the theory asserts far too much, in so far as it ascribes to Western civilization on a world scale the same dominant and revolutionary rôle it has played in the Europe of the past. No historian, however authoritative he may be, has any right to jump to any conclusions on this point; for no one can say at this juncture whether the present crisis points to anything beyond a passing disorder.

There are quite a number of signs that the transformation which the non-Western world is undergoing is not a movement in just one particular direction, but is more like a large-scale process of fermentation in which various extremely diverse and contradictory tendencies are involved. We see the non-Western religions parading as the champions of world peace, and yet providing an ideological foundation in the struggle for political power—hampered in the race to acquire strong military resources only by the limited material potential. We see the growth of modern forms of nationalism of a markedly progressive type, bent on uplifting and caring for the mass of the people; and side by side with all that—or sometimes cutting right across it—the emergence of violently reactionary modes of nationalism, inspired by an intense yearning to revive the religious patterns of the past. Everywhere modern parliamentary systems are springing up, most of them on such weak foundations and so sadly lacking a social structure which might effectively support them, that their collapse would in many cases appear inevitable. Where there is a new rising middle class, it is usually unable to withstand the tremendous pressure and attraction exerted by the bureaucratic system; and its economic ethos and organization are nearly always of a traditional kind. The need to avoid the disastrous mistakes made in the past by Western capitalism and to tie everything neatly to a planned economy leaves little enough room for independent economic forces to grow strong and thus to provide an influence which might permanently counterbalance traditional tendencies towards monopolistic centralism. When there is a deliberate attempt made to construct a secular state, a theoretical basis for assessing politico-religious ideologies radically and critically is very often wanting; and sometimes the 'secular spirit' is just an offshoot of the same tree that bears the branches of religion. The ancient religious heritage can wear the disguise of a modern humanism or agnosticism; and beneath the surface of rationalistic philosophies there may well lurk a mentality addicted to magic and superstition. It is by no means unusual to find an intensified consciousness of historical mission and calling grafted on to an unsuperseded mythical outlook. That is the kind of total impression one gets over and over again from situations which may differ one from another quite widely in some respects. It will become more apparent, however, if we now proceed to concentrate our attention on the principal areas affected by the encounter with the West.

2. THE GROWTH OF INDIAN NATIONALISM AND RENASCENT HINDUISM

Because of the 'colonization' of India the entry of Western civilization into that country and its eventual penetration have in practice been identified with the consequences of the British ascendancy there. However far-reaching the political and cultural effects of this on Indian life have been, the foreign régime would never have made such a revolutionary impact on all levels of Indian society, had it not been for the overwhelming influence of the capitalist economic system. It was this, first and foremost, which so thoroughly transformed the structure of society—even in the villages—that the conditions were created for the rise of a national state and culture. In pre-British India the conditions necessary for this, whether objective or subjective, were entirely lacking. The conquests of earlier invaders had given them a political ascendancy which simply took the old social structures for granted and did nothing to change their economic foundations. British capitalism was the first invader to turn India into an economic colony, more and more closely geared to the interests of a rapidly expanding British industrial system. Marx had already offered the diagnosis that 'England had a double mission in India: one destructive, the other regenerating—the annihilation of the old Asiatic society, and the laying of the material foundations of Western society in Asia.'[2] The situation was not the same, however, as with the break-up of the traditional economy of the European countries; for there the transformation occurred from within and at the instance of the indigenous rising bourgeoisie, whereas with India

it was a matter of foreign interests, not centred in the rule of a
conquest-régime—as had been the case with previous invasions—but
governed almost entirely by the economy of Great Britain. The
consequence was that those very forces which served to free Indian
society from the grip of an obdurate traditionalism at the same time
made her the slave of foreign imperialism. If therefore the rise of
Indian nationalism has been tumultuous and full of inner contradictions, the ambivalent rôle of British capitalism in its day of power
must be held very largely accountable for that, since the growth of a
national consciousness began under the very influence which impeded
and sometimes even stifled its free development. The British colonial
régime swept away the traditional system of land tenure, because it
was completely unsuited to the requirements of a capitalist economy.
Proprietary rights in the soil had always belonged to the tribe or
its subdivisions—the village community or clan or fraternity settled
in the village; but these were gradually replaced by a system of private
ownership.[3] In some parts of the country the class of tax collectors
were made landlords (*zemindari*), paying fixed rents to the East India
Company. Elsewhere ownership on the part of the individual peasant
was introduced (*ryotwari*); and where that happened the existing
system of tax assessment according to the actual amount of produce
was dropped and fixed payments in cash were levied instead. When
times were bad and the harvest poor, the fixed charges still had to be
met; and there was much mortgaging, selling and purchasing of
land as a result. The communal character of the village was undermined, since the various essential functions relating to village life
were in course of time taken over by the state. Agriculture was
commercialized and specialized to satisfy the market and also for the
production of raw materials needed by industry in Britain. The influx
of British manufactured goods and the growth of urban industry in
India itself brought about the decay of the village industries; and this
in turn disrupted village autarchy. The transforming of the villages
into administrative units of a centralized state, dependent on the
total economy of the country, did more than anything else to encroach upon the tenacious inertia and passivity which had always
been there at the base of the social pyramid. It has also opened a way
for more advanced forms of co-operation on a nationwide scale.[4]

New social classes began to emerge as a part of the same process.
Whilst the landlord class was on the whole conservative politically

and economically, the peasant proprietors gradually acquired a national consciousness, as they more and more felt the pressure of a centralized state. A fair proportion of farmers, both owners and tenants, joined the ranks of the landless labourers. Out of the mass of impoverished peasants and artisans the modern working-class was formed. It was illiterate; and not until after the First World War did it awaken to national and class consciousness. It was the new intelligentsia and the rising bourgeoisie who became the spear-head of the nationalist movement.

As village autarchy slowly disintegrated, great cities sprang up which felt the impact of the new dynamic economy and of India's increasing participation in world trade. These cities bred an independent attitude and outlook, the like of which the traditional townships—always tied to the apron strings of a bureaucratic centralism—had never known. The growth of an urban middle class was greatly facilitated when in 1835 a scheme for providing an 'English education' was introduced. Its original purpose was chiefly to promote 'European literature and science among the natives of India'; but in the latter part of the nineteenth century it was extended to include the training of native administrators, indispensable to the proper functioning of a modern state. In addition to this there was later on a relatively small but qualitatively important number of Indians who received their education in Western countries. Thus the spread of English education proved to be one of the main factors in breaking down the numerous linguistic, communal, social and religious barriers and in the creation of a uniformly trained middle class with direct access to the sources of modern Western civilization and to Western ideas.

It is very true, as Lord Cromer of Egypt has said, that colonial rule is necessarily conservative. It is equally true however that Western colonialism inevitably revolutionizes. If it was impossible for even the East India Company to imitate without modification the ways of the Mogul government, with the change-over to direct rule under the British Crown after the middle of the nineteenth century it was simply not practicable to balk the introduction of modern political ideas any longer. The title *Kaiser-i-Hind* which Queen Victoria assumed was quite useless as a substitute for the ancient idea of the sacral kingship; nor could the colonial administration, however partial it might be and however hard it might struggle, as a system, to make itself as independent as possible of the motherland, push the British constitutional tradition and control by the British parliament to one side. The Mogul rulers had established Islam as the dominant religion, and for the rest had confined themselves, like their predecessors, to maintaining an agro-managerial and tax-collecting bureaucracy. British colonialism interfered as little as possible with the indigenous religious and social traditions and had not the least intention of putting Christianity in the place of Islam. Its arrival was nevertheless incomparably more disruptive than Muslim control, which had had rather a stagnating effect on Hinduism. The British method of indirect rule left the existing princely courts alone, so far as was possible, but at the same time deprived them of their real power and prestige. Through the persisting communal barriers the British legal system edged its way in, not only in matters relating to the penal code—where the fundamental principle was equality before the law—but also in the sphere of civil law, still very largely left intact. As the range of modern technology rapidly expanded and the whole Indian peninsula was opened up to modern traffic, trade and industry, the British administration found itself compelled to interfere ever more drastically with wider and wider areas of Indian life.

In all this one fact, which overshadowed all the rest, remained perfectly clear: the system was insuperably 'foreign'. It was this which concealed the real sting, inflicted the deepest wounds and must be held to account, primarily at any rate, for the transformation which has come upon Indian civilization. Since time immemorial India had known 'foreign' invaders. She had long been inured to them; and she had in the end absorbed them all. The Muslim conquerors had imposed a religion which could scarcely be assimilated, because of its Jewish-Christian origins; but it had also become immune from any further penetration by that virus and so itself held no danger for the main body of Hinduism. The two religions took up defensive positions towards each other; and in other respects the Mogul rule was basically so traditional that it functioned as an indigenous régime. But the British Râj was so incontrovertibly 'foreign' in its very being, in its whole spirit and activity, that Indian civilization found itself for the first time at a loss for any effective means of resistance. The key to this 'foreignness' was not the British attitude of racial superiority, for in a caste-ridden society that fitted in perfectly well; nor was the fact of colonial dependence on a remote country overseas, unpalatable though it was, in itself all that difficult to digest. India could quite well have accommodated herself to being dominated by what must always have been a relatively small group of white people, biding her time until the régime either disappeared of its own accord or was forced out. What made the 'foreignness' such a thorn in the flesh was an imponderable and yet highly effectual dynamic spirit which, as the Indians intuitively realized, was the arch-enemy of the deepest urges and aspirations from which in the past had flowed the very life-blood of their civilization. Fundamentally what the British intervention had disturbed was the 'ontocratic pattern'. Thus the clearest light falls upon the enigma of transformation in India during the last one and a half centuries, not from any reactionary bid for self-preservation or any attempt on the part of Indian civilization to shield itself from the foreign impact, but where it has tried in one way or another to make something of that foreign spirit its own. Just there lies the critical issue on which battle has been joined. The struggle is an obstinate one and the final outcome unlikely to be declared for some time to come. Some of the signs are that the Indian organism is putting up a successful fight against the disease, is producing antidotal substances and is busily acquiring immunity. Yet there are other indications, no less positive, which suggest that further crises of decisive importance are still to be expected and that the well-tried measures of the past—to absorb or to contain the foreign impact—will prove quite inadequate in this encounter with the West.

There can be no question that the activities of Christian missions have been of incalculable importance in this struggle; but the growth of modern India offers no exception to the general rule that missionary expansion and its consequences are caught up in the whole complex of Western penetration. The ancient Syrian Orthodox Church of South India exemplifies the fate that the Christian Church can expect within the continuum of Indian society: it can only continue to exist by becoming part of the caste system. The Jesuit embassy to the court of Akbar, Xavier's efforts at evangelization, they were scarcely perceptible ripples on the surface; and even the Protestant missions of the eighteenth century would have left hardly a trace behind them, had it not been for what has happened since, over the past one hundred and fifty years. The reactions of modern India to the Western impact are to be understood only against the background of the Christian missions and their influence. The reverse is equally true.

This interaction was already apparent at the start of the nineteenth century in the earliest attempts to reform Hinduism, which were embodied in the Brahmo Samāj. The author of that society, Ram Mohan Roy (1772–1833), adopted enthusiastically the ideas of the European Enlightenment; and it was in that light that he interpreted Christianity, welcoming it above all for its social message and its emphasis on the value of the human being. With a plea for English education he combined a passionate call for social reform. He rejected the caste system, championed the rights of women, challenged the authority of Brahman religion and took issue with superstitious customs and beliefs. As a reforming sect, the Brahmo Samāj came as something in which the growing class of educated Hindus, who saw the need for Westernization, could take refuge against the claims made by the Christian missionaries. Its social activities are nowadays an accepted part of the modern Indian scene; but its weak spot was its religious basis. In the long run it has not proved so easy to maintain a complete harmony between imported Western ideas and the religious philosophy of the Vedānta. Under the leadership of Keshab Chandra Sen (1838–84) the Brahmo Samāj was refashioned as a syncretistic sect in which the Christian and Western elements were submerged in various forms of ecstatic Bhakti religion.[5]

The setting up of the Arya Samāj in 1875 was an unmistakable sign that the Western impact was making itself yet more deeply felt. The tremendous attraction of English education, Christian and neutral, as well as the mass conversions of outcastes to Christianity were a challenge to orthodox Brahmanism. The leader of this militant organization, Dayanand Saraswati, found a firm basis for the defence of Hinduism in the plenary authority of the Vedas. A strict monotheist, he found there the sanction he required for a forceful campaign against idolatry, animal sacrifice, sacerdotal rule and various social evils such as untouchability and child marriage. He was convinced that the contents of the Vedas agreed completely with the teachings of modern science, and that gave him a spring-board for his attacks on the inconsistent and anti-rational texts of the Bible. The Arya Samāj established an Anglo-Vedic College in Lahore with the avowed aim of combining the study of Hindu literature and Sanskrit with the study of English and modern science. The movement's influence however remained limited owing to its rigid exclusivism, which ignored the post-Vedic development of Hinduism and entered the lists against the characteristic tradition of complete tolerance.

Hopes then centred upon an All-India movement, to give expression to the Westernized ideas of the educated classes and to revive the great religious and philosophical traditions of Hinduism. The way for this was prepared partly by theosophical propaganda for a reformed universal Hinduism and partly through the message of Ramakrishna Paramahamsa (1836–86), which comprehended all religions in a single creed of the ultimate mystical unity of all reality. It was Swamī Vivekananda (1863–1902) who proclaimed this message, founded on the philosophy of the Vedānta and conjoined with a call for the renewal of Hindu society, as the ultimate basis of Hinduism. With this in view he set out to arouse the national consciousness; and he became the prophet of this message in Western countries too.

In the meantime the nationalist movement for political independence had gathered strength. It was a nationalism which in the very nature of the case bore an ambivalent character. In many respects it was a recognizable product of the Western impact which had broken through the traditional social structures and brought into being a new middle class equipped with the education, the sense of cultural unity and the civic outlook which enabled the Western idea of the national state to take root in its midst. On the other hand, as it was driven to adopt more and more positively antagonistic attitudes and courses of action—and especially when it began to involve broader sections of the population—the nationalist struggle was thrown back on the religious and cultural resources of traditional Hinduism. In the personality, vision, activity and historic rôle of Mahātma Gandhi the tension pent up in that ambivalence was unleashed with extreme force, and in his whole life and thought the man was an incarnation of the Hindu ontocratic pattern. That was certainly the secret of his appeal for the masses in the villages. It is not to be wondered at that the Bhagavadgītā became for him increasingly the source of his religious inspiration, for this Song is one of the most vital sections of the Mahābhārata Epic, which is itself the quintessence of Hinduism in symbolic form, as was pointed out in Chapter Four. The Song is a catechetical instruction regarding the place of man in the universe around him and the true purport of all human action. The scene of the battle, for which the instruction is meant to prepare us, is a place of strife in the sacred world, where Arjuna, the initiate, ignorant as yet of the cosmic significance of the conflict, is to be released by his initiator, Krishna, from the bandages blindfolding him and given a sight of the cosmic order.[6] Gandhi's campaigning for a sacred Hindu society, his ideal of 'Ramrajya' and his Swadeshi philosophy, as well as his insistence on the caste system and his call for a return to a simple economy centred on the 'charkha', the spinning-wheel, must be seen against that background. This religious nationalism was grounded in a cosmic theory, in a belief in the mystical unity of all existence. This was the source and goal of all religions; and Hinduism was the comprehensive expression of it. From this belief arose his deeply felt repugnance towards Western technocratic society, which he condemned as 'satanic'.

At the same time the phenomenon of Gandhi reveals something of the depth and the strength which the impact of both Western civilization and the Christian message has acquired in India during the course of this century. Apart from this he is hardly to be understood. His conception of an independent national state—and his indefatigable struggle for it—only became possible because they formed part of a counter-phase to British colonialism. His political action had about it a dynamic realism which transmuted Hindu ascetic ideals of mystical self-deliverance into a force capable of rousing the masses of the people. His fight against untouchability, although its aim was to assert the full cohesion of the Hindu community, showed all the same a prophetic and passionate concern for the lot of the outcastes which had a Christian inspiration and would have been unthinkable without it. He read the Bhagavadgītā as a 'gospel', coloured by his interpretation of the Sermon on the Mount. It is not just a coincidence that countless numbers of Hindus have interpreted the life—and more especially, the death—of Gandhi in accordance with their idea of the sacrifice of Jesus Christ.

Mahātma Gandhi is venerated by the people of India as the father of the fatherland; yet the outcome of his struggle for independence is far from being what he had hoped and imagined it would be. In India, as elsewhere, the impingement of the West has pursued a logic of its own. What in the end set its seal upon the political structure of independent India was not Gandhi's ideal of a sacred country, but the left-wing and agnostic humanism of Nehru. India has proclaimed itself a sovereign democratic republic, based on a socialist pattern of society. The declared intention of the government that this pattern should be casteless—already put into practice through various legislative measures of social reform—has laid the axe to the roots of the whole caste system. Although discrimination against the outcaste, so called, may still persist in the villages, untouchability as such is no longer countenanced.[7] The 'joint family' is fast disappearing. The Hindu Marriage Bill has legalized inter-caste marriages, set up monogamy as a standard and given the right of divorce to women. Through the explosive effects of the principle of universal suffrage the masses are learning to think in terms of human rights. The ideal of the Welfare State, which found expression in the First and Second Five Year Plans, is based on the assumption that it is possible for democracy to engineer drastic changes in society without destroying freedom. As Pandit Nehru has pointed out, 'there are no examples in history where this kind of experiment has been tried in any country'.

The main nerve of the experiment on which independent India has now embarked is located in the idea of the secular state. The validity of the principle is denied by the Hindu communal organizations; and the working out of the idea in practice faces a tough obstacle in the traditional structure of society. But the really fundamental problem is the difficulty of getting such a conception firmly implanted in a soil so ill prepared and also of giving it a clear and positive content. Panikkar argues convincingly[8] that the joint family and the sub-caste groups have amounted to a total denial of the idea of the social whole, of community in fact. For the first time in India, the community projects have been using the term 'community' to denote the quality of relationship within a whole society, transcending communal, caste and other sectional interests. This notion of community—as distinct from religion on the one hand and the state on the other—is new to India, where in the cultural pattern of the past religion, community and state have never been distinguished from one another in that way.[9] Even today the Hindu objection to the principle of the secular state is based on the classical theory that the state's proper task is to administer the 'sanātana dharma', the eternal cosmo-social law.[10] Thus the most stubborn features of resistance derive from the ontocratic pattern of Hindu society.

What really threatens the new idea of the secular state however is not that orthodox Hindu opinion which rejects it outright, but a fresh atmosphere of thought in modern Hinduism which accepts the idea—and even actively supports it—whilst interpreting it in such a way that it is absorbed into Hinduism itself. Dr Radhakrishnan's modern Hindu apologetics are infused with this new ethos.

> Hinduism is more a way of life than a form of thought. While it gives absolute liberty in the world of thought it enjoins a strict code of practice. The theist and the atheist, the sceptic and the agnostic may all be Hindus if they accept the Hindu system of culture and life. Hinduism insists not on religious conformity, but on a spiritual and ethical outlook in life.[11]

To a certain extent this view accords well with the classical position of Hinduism, which has always found a place for agnostic and even 'atheist' philosophies which accept the axiom of 'karma-saṁsāra' as a sufficient explanation of life's vicissitudes, though they might question the existence of an ultimate reality. The only stipulation was that they should conform to the recognized practices of Hinduism as prescribed by the caste-dharma. In modern Hinduism that classical stipulation is replaced by a demand for conformity to 'the Hindu system of culture and life'. This vague and somewhat elusive formula leaves room in fact for a modern form of Hindu secularism, differing— as Dr Devanandan explains—from other forms of secularism. The Hindu secularist of today is no philosophical secularist with an organized system of thought which seeks to explain life without reference to God; he is ready to accept and carry out Hindu religious rites, whether he believes in them or not. He defends Hinduism when it is attacked, and he maintains that his chief concern is with the realities of the immediate present, as being of more importance than the possibilities of a remote future which at best can only be matter for speculation.[12] All the same we have to realize that this modern Hindu secularism is concerned to give a meaning to Hinduism which will enable it to function as the spiritual basis for the modern Welfare State. It is not simply that some of the major tenets, such as belief in karma-fatalism, are pushed into the background; there is also an active interest in building up a just order of society in the here and now, a demand for social legislation which will ensure freedom from the tyranny of religious custom, besides a critical attitude towards religions in general and traditional Hinduism in particular.[13]

The point at issue is what exactly does Hinduism continue to represent, if this modern secularism is indeed a part of it? It looks as though this secularism, whilst it means on the one hand a thorough revision of the pattern of society and the modes of Hindu thinking, is on the other hand the prime factor in making Hinduism the national ideology of India. The very unity created by the modern Welfare State is transforming Hinduism from a composite religion of various 'samayas' and 'mārgas' into a 'sanātana dharma', a comprehensive religion universally applicable to mankind everywhere and at all times. The basic principle of religious relativism, made popular chiefly by Gandhi, acts as the cement so vitally necessary to building up a unified nation. In the Basic Education Scheme it was this principle which supplied a foundation for the secular state.[14]

In view of all this it is clear that the struggle for religious liberty, now being waged by the Indian Church, is one of the most profound consequence, since its effect must be to clarify the conception of the secular state. It has rightly been said that religious freedom is the pre-condition and the guardian of all other freedoms. It is the corner-stone of democracy. Leading Christians in India are well aware of their Christian responsibility in this respect.

> History bears testimony to the fact that the growth and development of democratic political institutions and democratic social values depended in great measure on the religious convictions of Christian citizens in the Western countries of the 17th and 18th centuries where democracy as we know it, first took root. It may well be claimed that in countries which have adopted a democratic constitution and where the majority of people are convinced believers in other religions, Christian citizens have a special responsibility, not only to help to work effectively the democratic structure of Government, but also to translate the democratic values of life in terms of social action . . . their religious faith places unique emphasis upon just those convictions about the nature and destiny of man which furnish the foundations for what has been described as the democratic view of life.[15]

3. CHINESE REVOLUTIONS FROM THE T'AI-P'ING REBELLION TO COMMUNISM

As the nineteenth century proceeded, the Chinese Empire was compelled slowly but surely to yield to the increasing pressure of Western expansion. It is quite understandable that the Chinese were prepared to resist to the last ditch in that struggle; for the Western intrusion was something completely alien to the traditional structure of their civilization. China has known many barbarian invasions and conquests in the course of her history; and these have been in some degree essential to its characteristic rhythm. Again and again the conquering invaders had learned to adapt themselves to the age-old pattern of Chinese society, which as a result preserved a fundamentally unbroken continuity. The Europeans however did not come in the first place as conquerors but as traders. As far back as the sixteenth and seventeenth centuries the Portuguese found themselves up against almost impenetrable barriers. The T'ang and Sung dynasties in earlier centuries had opened the empire freely to foreigners, who traded not only in the ports but in the chief cities of the interior and particularly in the capital. But the Europeans, it seems, were not willing to submit to the conditions which Arab and Persian traders had come to accept. Once they had gained a footing as traders on the coasts of Persia, India and the East Indies, the Portuguese tried to set themselves up as the controlling authority; and their violent, ruthless behaviour was well known to the Chinese. The consequence was that under the Ming and Manchu emperors the Europeans were carefully restricted to a single city and its immediate environs.[16] The motives however lay deeper than this might suggest. Whereas Europeans thought in terms of the right to trade, the Chinese regarded it as a gracious concession on the part of the celestial court, granted to foreign visitors who were no more than barbarians bringing tribute. China simply did not recognize the existence of independent foreign states; and her view of the world had no place in it for the idea of sovereign states to be treated with on an equal footing. In theory the Ming government forbade Chinese nationals either to emigrate to, or trade with, foreign countries. In fact a policy of seclusion was implemented from early in the sixteenth century onwards. That Europeans were known as *yang-kwei*, or 'ocean devils', was more than whimsicality. As a land-ward-looking people, the Chinese were inclined to view with suspicion all strangers arriving off their shores, which had no military defences.[17]

The major economic problem was that European countries were anxious to pursue trade with a country that did not really need European products, since its economy was self-supporting. It wanted foreign trade only in order to obtain treasure and certain luxury commodities. What eventually broke open this closed economy was the making available of cheap manufactured goods; yet even in the first half of the nineteenth century it was still not possible for British manufacturers to establish markets in China. The need to redress the adverse balance of British trade with China led to the sale of opium. The impossibility of any normal commercial relationships was bound to produce a crisis. The 'Opium War' was the first and inevitable result. By the treaties concluded during the twenty years or so after 1840 China gave formal assent to the equality in law of other nations with herself; but this principle was directly at variance with the Chinese view of the world and it threatened the very foundations of the empire. The treaties did more than introduce the new principle of equality. They robbed China of the freedom to lay down her own conditions of trade and established the principle of extra-territorial rights for European citizens. Extremely important too were the provisions by which the Chinese government undertook to protect Christian missionaries—and other articles which went still further, in placing Chinese Christians to some extent under the protection of foreign powers.

Thus was created a direct link between European trade, naval power and Christian missions. It would be hard to deny that the open dislike shown by China towards all three aspects of the Western intrusion was a pretty well inevitable consequence of that connection. Up to 1842 traders and missionaries alike had been confined to the foreign 'factories' on the riverside at Canton. It was natural enough that when the restrictions were lifted, it should be in respect of both categories. However that may be, the historical connection referred to above sealed the fate of Christian missions, which for the first time in Chinese history now had the chance to spread and develop to the full. In one vital respect they were at a disadvantage as compared with the Jesuit mission begun in the last quarter of the sixteenth century. The Jesuits had been quite unconnected with foreign traders; and their mission was not associated in the minds of Chinese officials with any particular foreign authority. The Jesuits based their approach on two principal supports: they sought to impress the educated Chinese with their scientific knowledge and they sought an intellectual basis for harmonizing Christian doctrine with Confucianism. Despite their influence at the imperial court and the spread of Christianity during the seventeenth century, which seemed so full of promise, the end result was very small. Latourette shows that by the start of the nineteenth century Christianity had made almost no impression on China. If after 1835 missionaries had gradually stopped arriving, within a few years the Church in China would probably have ceased to exist and would have disappeared without trace.

It is within this setting that the T'ai-p'ing Rebellion, which about the middle of the nineteenth century rocked the empire to its foundations, appears in all its historic significance. The Rebellion—one of the biggest in world history—involved the whole of Central China and parts of North and South China, with a population of at least a hundred million. The number of victims alone amounted to twenty million. The Rebellion was a bridge between the peasant revolts which had so often ravaged China down the years of her history and the revolutions of the twentieth century.

The Chinese term for 'revolution'—namely, *ko-ming*—is rooted in the traditional idea of the renewal of the mandate of heaven. Chinese historiography views the comings and goings of past dynasties on these lines: heaven can revoke the mandate given to an emperor, should that accord with the will of the people.[18] Generally speaking peasant revolts have had the effect of weakening whatever dynasty might be in power at the time, although the *coup de grâce* was usually administered either by a rival section of the nobility or by foreign invaders. The uprisings owed their origin to economic depression, which drove hordes of peasants to the mountains or to outlying areas where they formed themselves into companies of bandits. As a band grew and took to overrunning whole towns, it would clash directly with the government. The final stage was when turncoat officials who had joined the bandits civilized them; and then their leader became a general—or on one occasion actually emperor.[19] In this religious factors were as important as social and economic ones. The fourteenth century peasant revolt which put an end to the Mongol dynasty was led by a mendicant monk, a member of the secret society of the 'White Lotus', which found its support in Buddhist-Taoist popular religion, mixed with strands of Manicheism. When with the backing of the nobility he had founded the Ming dynasty at Nanking and had conquered Peking itself, the leader switched over from being the proletarian revolutionary and became instead a champion of the traditional political and social order on Confucian lines. Although land was redistributed and rents and taxes were reduced so that the lot of the peasants was improved, no fundamental change was made in the existing order.

Even though the T'ai-p'ing Rebellion did not fully succeed, it is possible to detect in it the familiar outlines of the peasant uprisings. Since the end of the seventeenth century the population had more than doubled under a strong government, without there having been, however, a proportionate increase in the area of habitable land. The Manchu government, by the nineteenth century decadent and corrupt, was less capable than ever of carrying out the needed agrarian reform. It lapsed into a retrograde absolutism which favoured everything conventional and orthodox in Chinese culture. All that was bound up with the fact that the Manchus were, by origin, of a foreign race and governed China as a select ruling caste. Right from the start it was Southern China which became the rallying-ground of resistance. The coastal region had been the stronghold of the last Ming pretenders and partisans in the final struggle with the Manchus during the first half of the seventeenth century. Their close contact with Europeans and the backing they received from the Portuguese made the inhabitants of this southern region particularly suspect with the government. In 1673 there had been the great uprising of the south, which it took nine years to suppress. That the region could not be relied on was the reason why the Manchus recruited only a quarter of the Chinese representation in the civil service from among southerners. Because it was exceptional for them to be selected for the examinations, the southerners entering the civil service were very capable and keen. All the same, they were not given the more senior posts. This discrimination served to feed their resentment, added to which there was the frustration of the large number of southerners failed in the examinations, though very many of them had a good deal more acumen than the average Manchu candidate.

Along with agrarian unrest and with these sentiments of rebellion and hostility towards the Manchus there was increasing pressure from the Europeans. The T'ai-p'ing Rebellion broke out soon after the Opium War and reached its climax amid the renewed fighting between the British and the Manchu forces, brought to an end by the treaties of 1858. The awakened spirit of nationalism vented itself upon the Manchus, whose utter impotence became only too apparent when they were defeated twice in succession.

Considerable as was the part played by these social and political factors, they were not in themselves the heart of the matter. The surprising thing about the T'ai-p'ing Rebellion was that it started as a revival of Chinese Protestant Christianity. The Christian origin of the movement is beyond question.[20] A set of tracts, the work of a Canton printer who had been the first Chinese convert of a certain Scottish missionary, came into the possession of one, Hung Hsiu-ch'üan. He obtained them in 1834 from the author, who was distributing them near the Examination Halls in Canton, where Hung, a village school-teacher, was sitting the examination for the second time —and again without success. When nine years later he failed for the fourth time, a cousin called his attention to the tracts, long since forgotten. To Hung's amazement they seemed to confirm some visions he had had during a delirium in 1837, when his third failure had brought on a nervous breakdown. In his ecstasy he felt himself caught up into heaven, where he was charged by the Almighty with destroying idolatry. He was now firmly convinced that the God who had appeared to him was the Shang-ti of the Christian tracts. In 1846, having had two months' instruction from an American Baptist missionary in Canton and having received the whole Bible in Morrison's Chinese version, Hung came in contact with a community of some two thousand believers in Kwangsi, gathered together by one of his cousins. This man had been converted by Hung and had immediately become a most fervent preacher of the new faith. The community carried on regular worship of Shang-ti, was full of zeal against idolatry and firmly believed in Hung's divine commission.

Hung's sense of mission was fired by a prophetic indignation with idolatry and with corrupt princes, which he caught from the biblical quotations that made up such a considerable part of the tracts he had been given. With this prophetic summons came the conviction that he was predestined to restore the empire and establish the true theocracy. In 1851 he raised the standard of revolt and proclaimed the new dynasty, calling it 'The Kingdom of Heaven of Great Peace' (*T'ai P'ing T'ien Kuo*). He himself was the *T'ien Wang* or *T'ai P'ing Wang* (Heavenly or Peaceful King). In 1853 the T'ai-p'ing army captured Nanking, which was to become the capital of the new dynasty.

The T'ai-p'ing creed was essentially Christian and Protestant. The complete Bible, printed extensively in Nanking, was distributed free to supporters and converts. The creed, in a classical 'trimetric' style, taught converts and children belief in God the Creator and in Jesus, his Son; and it continued with an account of the history of China down to the revelation received by Hung. It was an account which bore the marks of Hung's Confucian upbringing. It described the prehistoric sage-kings' as 'honouring God' and attributed the decline of true religion to Ch'in Shih Huang Ti, the first emperor to confer on himself the divine title *Ti*, and to the Han and Sung emperors, because they had introduced Buddhism and had patronized Taoism.

Hung was known as the 'younger Brother of Jesus'; but this did not mean that he was held to be divine. He assiduously avoided including in his royal title the usual term for 'emperor', since it contained the character *ti*, applied in the phrase *Shang-ti* to God. Again the influence of ancient Chinese ideals was reflected in the organization of the T'ai-p'ing government. The king, whom his followers referred to as 'Celestial Virtue' (*T'ien Tê*), wore the five-clawed imperial dragon robe. Government departments and officials were given names taken from the classical *Chou li*, a work of the fourth century B.C. which describes how the state was organized under the Chou dynasty (1050–244 B.C.). The reform put through by the T'ai-p'ing government involved in many respects a radical break with Chinese traditions; for it was based on Christian ideas of equality, strongly tinged with ancient Chinese and especially Taoist notions of a primeval ideal condition of society. A drastic programme of land reform was proposed, to be based on the principle of communal ownership, but it was implemented only to a very limited extent. Women were given equal rights with men and were admitted to the government examinations and the army. Battle was joined against foot-binding, prostitution and trafficking in girls, and rape was made punishable by death. Monogamy became a prescribed practice. The Ten Commandments were accepted as law and considered to be absolutely binding. The use of opium, alcohol and tobacco was strictly prohibited. Idolatry came under fanatical attack and iconoclasm was reckoned to be a sacred duty. The reform extended even to the literature, which it was thought desirable to adapt to the usage of the spoken language.

The principle that all men are equal also found expression in a new attitude towards foreigners, who were now treated as qualifying for equal rights and privileges. They were held to be under Chinese jurisdiction however. The extra-territorial rights which the Manchu government had conceded to Europeans the T'ai-p'ing government now rescinded, since they conflicted with the principle of equality between the European and the Chinese. Protestant missionaries were favoured; but they had no freedom of movement in the interior, because it was the responsibility of the T'ai-p'ing believers themselves to spread the true faith.[21]

The T'ai-p'ing movement is thoroughly typical—as much so in its initial successes as in its ultimate failure. Complete dedication to a theocratic ideal forged the community into a highly disciplined army, led by generals who were past masters in the arts of guerilla warfare and fifth column tactics. Yet not even this movement was able to escape the moral decline and growing corruption of the ruling *élite*, which in the end have vitiated all dynasties and revolutionary movements in China. As soon as Nanking had been taken, a luxurious court was established there. Internal dissension arose which had a fatally debilitating effect. The army, composed of southerners, got no recruits on its expedition to the north; and its iconoclasm aroused hostility among the masses. By failing to capture Peking it gave the Manchus opportunity to retrieve their position, retake Nanking and destroy the T'ai-p'ing state.

European intervention contributed a good deal to the final *débâcle*. In 1860 the British occupied Peking and then forced the Manchus to sign treaties opening more ports to trade, permitting foreign merchantmen to ply the Yangtze River and securing terms of customs revenue favourable to the European. They no longer set any store therefore by such advantages as the T'ai-p'ing government could offer. On the contrary, the Rebellion was a nuisance to commerce. The British despatched a force against the T'ai-p'ing army and lent General Gordon to organize the Manchu troops. One has heard tell of the bitter ironies of history.

> . . . Gordon, who was to die in Khartum in 1885 at the hands of the soldiers of the Mahdi, a Muslim Messiah, won his fame and the title 'Chinese Gordon' by helping to put down a comparable movement of religious fanaticism allied to revolutionary politics. But in China the religion concerned was Christianity. One of the most pious soldiers in British history thus assisted in destroying a mass movement of the greatest nation of the world towards Christianity.[22]

Another more essential historical parallel suggests itself here as having a greater claim to attention: the rise of Islam and the emergence of Muhammad. If the T'ai-p'ing movement had succeeded and had overthrown the Manchu government, it would in all probability have done for China what Islam did in another context: that is, to remould a non-Western civilization to the pattern of a non-Western type of Christianity. But whereas Islam developed right from the start as an independent religion, based on its own charter of revealed truth, T'ai-p'ing Christianity was grounded firmly in the Bible. One cannot help wondering whether this would not have been a case of the Bible functioning as a sort of Qur'an. The T'ai-p'ing government did seriously contemplate substituting the Bible for the Sacred Books of Confucianism as the textbook in the Public Service examinations. A contemporary European observer foresaw that if this proposal were carried out, it would constitute a revolution 'as unparalleled in the world for rapidity, completeness and extent, as is the Chinese people for its antiquity, unity and numbers.'[23] A revolution it most certainly would have been; but it is not at all clear what course Chinese Christianity would have taken as a result. T'ai-p'ing Christianity had this essential feature too in common with Islam, that it recognized no distinction between church and state. Brief as its career was, the T'ai-p'ing state had already moved a long way in the direction of the traditional ontocratic pattern of the centralized bureaucratic state; and it is hard to see how in the long run it could have escaped being swallowed up in the powerful vortex of the Chinese tradition.

One thing is certain: the action of the British in intervening to save the Manchu dynasty can be justified only from the standpoint of an appallingly short-sighted and small-minded commercial interest. The prevarication of Western missionaries at the time has come in for some fairly devastating criticism too. Max Weber comes to the conclusion that, when allowance has been made for everything that might be argued against it, the T'ai-p'ing movement did nevertheless:

> . . . on many important heads involve a break with Confucian orthodoxy and offer incomparably better prospects of the growth of an indigenous religion relatively close to Christianity than the hopeless missionary experiments of the occidental confessions. It may well prove to have been the last chance for such a religion to emerge in China.[24]

Fifteen years later, in 1935, another critic capped a still more scathing verdict with the comment:

> The Chinese masses, today, if they accept a western ideology, are more inclined to turn to the doctrines of Marx and Lenin than to those of Luther.[25]

That is true enough; but it is highly questionable whether T'ai-p'ing Caesaropapism would have proved any more effective as a bulwark against the rising tide of Marxism than Russian Byzantinism has done.

A study of the T'ai-p'ing movement is none the less rewarding in that it helps uncover the root of those fundamental problems with which China has to contend in the modern period. Anyone is free to imagine what the prospects and outcome of an unsuccessful experiment might have been; but it is sheer foolishness to base one's judgment of the course which events in modern China have in fact taken on speculations of that sort. Whatever one might think about the growth of an indigenous Chinese Christianity and its likely effects, the truth is that over a longer period the 'hopeless missionary experiments of Western confessions' have made an impact on the traditional structure of Chinese civilization not a whit less revolutionary than the drastic and violent assaults of the T'ai-p'ing rebels. The Western missionary enterprise in China has proved to be one of the main channels of entry for Western civilization, especially since 1858, when the treaties were signed, permitting Christian missionaries to travel and preach in any part of the empire. Protestant missionaries were the chief pioneers in introducing Western medicine and surgery. They founded schools which offered a Western tradition of education and thus became, as Latourette affirms, 'the main forerunners of the educational revolution which was to come.'[26] The efforts of missionaries to relieve famine and disease and to improve living standards were reinforced by the use of Western scientific methods. The scientific study of Chinese religion and civilization, and of the language, to which a number of missionaries devoted themselves, did much to encourage a critical outlook. One way or another the preaching of Christianity, in however diluted a version it was presented and received, served to weaken the Confucian traditions.

It would be beside the point here to go into the question of how China, although ostensibly retaining her sovereignty, was subjected from 1860 onwards to mounting pressure on the part of foreign governments so that she entered the twentieth century virtually an 'occupied country'. It is just worth recalling the triple rôle played by Japan. In the first place, that country burgeoned forth in the last quarter of the nineteenth century as one of the principal candidates for imperialist expansion at China's expense. Secondly, this expansionist policy was a direct result of the Westernization of Japan, which the Meiji reform had set in motion. The major threat to China's independence apart, this made Japan the outpost and pioneer in Asia of Western civilization. She became the chief centre for Chinese students going abroad in order to get a Western education. Thirdly, in the Russo-Japanese War, which ended in 1905, Japan proved for the first time that an Asian country could carry the day over a Western power, provided it took full advantage of Western science and technology. In this three-sided rôle, Japan came to represent for China all the paradoxical tensions which the Western impact brings in its train.

As it turned out however, the Chinese Empire was in no position to follow the example set by Japan. The measures taken in 1898 during the 'hundred days of reform' were undone by the empress dowager and any trace of them that remained was wiped out by the Boxer Revolt. From 1905 a series of imperial edicts promised the introduction of constitutional government by gradual stages; but they remained a dead letter and were overtaken by the revolutionary course of events. The Civil Service examinations were abolished in 1905; and that knocked away the corner-stone of the Confucian edifice or—to put it better—accepted it as a *fait accompli* that Western education had already supplanted the traditional system. The attempts made to salvage Confucianism as a sort of universal religion of human reason and even to build round the person of Confucius a kind of Confucian Church were without any solid foundation. Then when the monarchy fell in 1912 the last prop was knocked from under the entire system.

This does not mean, of course, that the Confucian tradition has been obliterated. It does mean that both its ontocratic foundation and the social structure of which it had come to be the classical expression have been irreparably undermined by the impact of the West. Hinduism may be metamorphosed into the universal religion of a casteless society; and Buddhism may eventually lose its monastic character and become the paramount philosophy of modern humanism and nihilism—and both religions may be revitalized as nationalist ideologies. For Confucianism no such transformation is even possible. It has become too much the ideology of a bureaucratic privileged class ever to be a vehicle for nationalistic revival, and it is much too closely bound up with a classical ideal of education to be capable of adjustment to the dynamic spirit of Western civilization. It has also grown too much accustomed to leave the satisfaction of any deeper mystical aspirations the individual may have to popular religions such as Buddhism and Taoism to offer a spiritual refuge on its own account in a time of chaos, confusion and the break-down of accepted values. What will probably survive is a Confucian standard of ethics, a principle of human self-respect and of an aristocracy of the spirit, a conception of fixed social norms and of responsibility in the various relations between men. A 'Confucian mentality', in this sense, could be a leavening influence within a wide variety of social systems and ideologies.

The revolution of 1911 involved a good deal more than just the setting up of a republic. It meant the falling to pieces of an ancient order which had stood through storm and stress for more than two thousand years and had shown itself possessed of a unifying and stabilizing power without parallel. The Western impact had demonstrated its strange power to uproot great primary civilizations; but it was by no means certain that Western values would be relevant to the making of a new society. Within this ideological vacuum a number of experiments took place which set their mark on four successive phases.

The first few years of the Republic saw the attempt of Yuan Shih-k'ai to preserve the unity of the empire, threatened by the defection of various territories; but that ended in failure, with his trying to declare himself the first emperor of a new dynasty. The years after the First World War witnessed the rising tide of nationalism, which was anti-Japanese, anti-Western and anti-Christian and was especially strong amongst students, who had imbibed modern ideas, not only abroad but also in Chinese colleges and schools of a Western type. The centre of intellectual and political ferment was the University of Peking. Wu Yü reinterpreted Chinese history from an anti-Confucian standpoint; and Lu Hsün in his *Diary of a Madman* pilloried the hollowness of traditional Chinese society and depicted Confucianism as cloaking the grossest barbarity. Ch'en Tu-hsiu and his circle expressed themselves unreservedly in favour of Western democracy and science, rejecting traditional Chinese culture root and branch. Hu Shih on the other hand, starting from typically Chinese premises, set out to discover modern thought in Chinese history, which he again interpreted from an anti-Confucian point of view.

The literary revolution which he began spread a single form of the vernacular throughout China, thus bridging a gulf between the masses and the *élite* and tending to promote national unity. Along with an emancipation from the old patterns, the 'New Thought' movement propagated the idea of a cultural renaissance.

In 1926, after a decade of turmoil and disintegration, the armies of the Kuomintang or Nationalist Party, led by Chiang Kai-shek, began to get most of the country under their control. Three factors shaped the history of the Kuomintang and of the Nationalist Government which it established. The first was the intervention of Japan, which began in 1931 and was reinforced in 1937 by a full-scale invasion of the whole country. That decimating struggle with the Japanese made it impossible to construct anything like a normal state and had a good deal to do with the ultimate failure to defeat the Communists. A second factor was the ideological weakness of the Kuomintang. Sun Yat-sen, the founder and 'the father of the Chinese revolution', had died in 1926. Of his 'Three People's Leading Principles' (*San Min Chu I*) the first—nationalism—was straightforward enough; but the principles of democracy and socialism were open to a variety of diverse, and even opposing, interpretations. Sun admired Marx, but rejected the materialistic view of history and the doctrine of class warfare. His theory that liberty is not for the individual but for the state certainly smacks of totalitarianism; and his doctrine of the 'five powers' pointed in that direction too. This doctrine added to the familiar triad of Western democracy two traditional elements of the Chinese bureaucratic system: one 'power' for examinations through which all officials were to be screened and one for censorship or control. After the break with the Communists in 1927 the Kuomintang became more and more conservative and reactionary. The attempt to revive the traditional Confucian virtues, which gave its character to the 'New Life Movement', simply exposed the ideological void in which the party was floundering. The only purpose which it served in fact was to maintain the existing social structure. To fight shy of any fundamental social and economic reform meant being forced back into the grip of a bureaucratic capitalism sponsored by a military dictatorship, which in the struggle against the Communists—the third factor which determined the history of the Nationalist Government— lost the backing of even the liberal intelligentsia.

So the turbulent course of China's modern history has issued, for the present at least, in a full-blooded Communist régime. It now remains to comment briefly on this, to try and throw a little light on some of its main aspects and implications and thereby to suggest what its real significance may be.

First, the principles of democracy and socialism, on which the Chinese Republic as conceived by Sun Yat-sen was founded, could not possibly have worked out in China along the lines of occidental history. Whatever the future of modern India may be, there at any rate the experiment has had a proper chance. Colonial dominance over a long period on the part of a Western people whose own history has clothed the idea of democracy in flesh and blood has been a stabilizing factor in India's progress towards the status of a sovereign democratic state; and it has proved to be of decisive importance for the political and cultural training of the governing class. China on the other hand has been exposed, under a moribund imperial régime, to a gradual process of disintegration, dismemberment and undermining of her civilization, a prey to imperialist powers on every side, tossed to and fro between confusing ideological extremes, a vessel adrift in the maelstrom of world history. It is not surprising that the intelligentsia, frustrated in its search for a settled point amid the general decay of traditional values and despairing of the various experiments intended to revitalize a dying civilization, should more and more lean towards an uncompromising radicalism.

It was at Peking University, amidst the intellectual excitement and questing of the years round about 1920, that this radicalizing process took place. There it was that Ch'en Tu-hsiu abandoned his early faith in a version of British liberalism; there too Mao Tse-tung gave up his original belief in democratic reformism and Utopian socialism along with his admiration for Hu Shih's ideas of a Chinese renaissance and turned to the conviction that only the doctrine of Marx and Lenin held out any prospect of a complete transformation of Chinese society. As in Russia, the Communist movement was set going not by workers or peasants but through the initiative of a radicalized intelligentsia.

Secondly, it is not irrelevant to remember that the Communist doctrine is of Western origin and is at the opposite extreme to the whole tradition of Chinese culture. The Communist victory should serve to explode once for all the fallacy that the Christian message would never stand a chance of winning the heart of the Chinese people because it runs counter to Chinese traditions. Marxist-Leninist doctrine is something so completely foreign to China's civilization and tramples so ruthlessly on all her most cherished values that even the most intolerant behaviour on the part of Western missionaries can still be called mild in comparison. Again, any objection to Western missions' introducing a Western system of education must surely seem trivial when one thinks of the adamant inflexibility of Communist indoctrination and training in the dogmatics of Marxism.

In the third place, the Communist victory inevitably confronts us with the challenge which the T'ai-p'ing Rebellion had in fact already created. Where the T'ai-p'ings failed, there—just a century later—the disciples of Marx and Lenin have succeeded. Mao Tse-tung and his coterie are known to have made a particular study of the T'ai-p'ing Rebellion and to have drawn a number of important conclusions from it. The blindness of the Western powers and the sterile hesitancy of the missionaries with regard to T'ai-p'ing Christianity point to certain limitations and a peculiar one-sidedness which by virtue of its distinctive history would seem to be inherent in Western Christian civilization as such. Whilst the British government had no more sense than to keep the Manchus in the saddle, and whilst Western missions since the time of the Jesuit mission in the seventeenth century onwards have been hunting repeatedly for points of contact between Christianity and Confucianism, T'ai-p'ing Christianity found a spontaneous and living answer in its proclamation of a message involving a radical and violent repudiation of deep-seated Chinese religious traditions; at the same time it gave expression to a burning desire for political and social liberation. Mao Tse-tung went entirely against the whole Marxist theory, as that was spelled out to him from Moscow, when he started the Communist revolution by organizing a peasants' revolt in his native province of Hunan, where the T'ai-p'ing Rebellion also had met with considerable success. From the initiative of T'ai-p'ing Christianity, the implications of which have been totally ignored by such baptized Christians as Sun Yat-sen and Chiang Kai-shek, this anti-Christian Chinese has drawn the basic and creative conclusion.

The remarkable thing is that this heretical adaptation of Communist tactics to the fundamentally agrarian structure of Chinese society has proved to be possible without any essential deviation from orthodox Marxism. The writings of Mao Tse-tung are basically orthodox. Despite the fact that the Russian leaders and their Chinese adherents took exception to Mao's method from the very start, Communism has evinced a dynamic openness to the essential needs of Chinese society, as Western Christianity in general has obviously failed to do.

The fourth point is this: that contrary to the Marxist theory of dialectical materialism Communism in general—and Chinese Communism in particular—proceeds on the assumption that spiritual and mental transformation come before material improvement. Its whole activity is directed to the collective creation of a radically new type of human being; and its massive use of indoctrination, pursued by every available means, has the one aim of producing total conversion. Such a system of collective revivalism does not affect merely the individual person, however; it sets out to recreate the whole structure of society as well. It is an approach which, so far as China is concerned, really completes a process touched off by the impact of the West and of Christian missions. Their uprooting influence has made a thorough renovation of Chinese society quite inevitable, although they themselves were in no position to assume responsibility for the task. In this respect too T'ai-p'ing Christianity was a straw in the wind. The message it received was Protestant, individualistic and pietistic; but from this it lost no time in drawing 'theocratic' conclusions and it resolutely set about tackling the basic social and economic problems.

In connection with our fifth point it is worth recalling that at the end of Chapter Six the historical rôle of the Communist Revolution in Russia was brought up as a parallel to the rise of Islam. The Communist victory in China strongly invites comparison with the expansion of Islam in Asia. Just as the latter confronts us with the failure of Christianity to win the Asian peoples, so Chinese Communism denotes the bankruptcy of European-American civilization in that country. In both cases it was a 'heresy' which ultimately prevailed. But as an expanding force Communism is incomparably more effective than Islam. Islam has never managed to penetrate to the heart of China. Furthermore Islam lies bound and shackled in the fetters of pre-industrial society, whereas Communism appears in the rôle of a saviour with a universal message for the technocratic era.

What then is the upshot of all this? It is surely to be comprehended —and this is the sixth point at issue—in one crucial fact: that for the non-Western civilizations the Communist ideology can hold out no genuine prospect of re-creation or of fundamental renewal, because it is itself the prolongation of what we have been calling the 'ontocratic pattern' of the state. We must refer back to our analysis of the T'ai-p'ing Rebellion, from which we concluded that the theocratic system of the T'ai-p'ing state was based essentially on a Caesaropapist structure and that if it had overthrown the Manchu government, it would have continued—and eventually have strengthened and solidified—the pattern of the ontocratic state; for that pattern, though falling slowly into decay, would have acquired a fresh sanction in the form of the Christian religion. Between the Communist revolutions in Russia and in China there is a close parallel resemblance in this respect: that in both cases a pre-industrial society is transformed into a technocratic one, yet without any revolutionary change in the basic pattern of 'oriental despotism'. Indeed all the signs are that in a technocratic era its scope is immeasurably widened and its potentialities increased. However, that is not all there is to be said on the question. The historical course of the technocratic era has its own logic, which is by no means the same thing as the logic of the historical and dialectical materialistic theories.

Lastly, a comment on the 'débâcle of missions' in China.[27] The scorching criticism levelled against Christian missions, not only on the part of the Communists but on that of many Chinese Christians as well, is aimed at their connection with Western civilization and Western imperialism in particular and also at their inability to foster the growth of a really dynamic, self-governing, self-supporting and expanding Chinese Church. The fact that in a Communist civilization an independent 'missionary' activity, by whatever private organ or agency it might be carried on, is simply out of the question and the unconditional support which Communist doctrine gives to a politics of total power make it just about as hard to take this criticism seriously as it is to credit the Chinese Christian 'Three Self Movement'. There one has an ideology which, objectively speaking, can only end with the Christian faith's being swallowed up in the 'Self' of the Communist state. Nothing in all this, however, excuses Christian missions from profound and heart-searching self-examination; on the contrary it must surely drive them to it. But no amount of self-examination and self-criticism will be of use unless it takes into account the relationship between Christian missions and Western civilization, along with the total context of that relationship. One of the aims of this book is to contribute to that end.

4. THE MUSLIM WORLD UNDER THE WESTERN IMPACT

Since Islam is a world religion which has spread over three continents in the course of its history, the expression 'Muslim world' embraces a wide variety of cultural developments and structures, extending from West Africa to the Indonesian archipelago. Moreover, the expansion of the modern West has impinged upon each of these Muslim areas and peoples in ways so diverse, and reaction to it has correspondingly varied so much from one case to another, that it would be quite impossible to range such an oddly assorted conglomeration under a single denominator. However, a detailed survey of the nicer distinctions is no part of our business in this brief sketch, which is concerned rather with certain basic features plainly recognizable amid the mass of confusing and conflicting data.

One has to remember first of all that for Islam—unlike the Asian civilizations—this intrusion on the part of the modern West was not some new and strange phenomenon, coming straight out of the blue, so to speak; it meant simply that the Christian civilization with which Islam had been fiercely at loggerheads from the very outset was now turning up again in a fresh guise. However, Western Christianity had undergone far-reaching changes since the mediaeval period, whereas Islam itself had, generally speaking, continued to live from the thirteenth century onwards on the great religious and cultural heritage of the past. We pointed out in Chapter Five the main reasons why its encounter with the rational thinking of Greece never had and never could have a dynamic effect upon Islam. Those reasons are to be found in the basic structure of Muslim theology as much as in the thoroughly orientalized Hellenistic tradition which shaped the climactic years of Muslim civilization. The decline of the West Roman Empire gave the Christian Church opportunity to rediscover the scientific, philosophical and political heritage of classical Greece and thus to allow all that to leaven the secularizing process within the onward movement of Western history; whereas Islam, like Byzantium, remained steeped in the unbroken tradition of the ancient pattern of the Near East. It was therefore inevitable that when in the nineteenth century the Muslim world began to feel the unsettling impact of secularizing influences from the West it should remain both outwardly and inwardly ill at ease with their motives and unable to gauge their real significance and dimensions.

Because the encounter between Islam and the modern West took place primarily at the political and social level, it has naturally enough been taken as putting to the proof what has come to be known as the Muslim 'theocratic' system. As it is admittedly difficult to find a really adequate term for this, one might as well accept that designation, provided it is clearly understood that whatever cohesion and staying power the system may have, these have only been acquired through the deliberate stifling of all those explosive forces that imparted to the *biblical* theocracy its quality of restlessness—unique, paradoxical and revolutionary.

The *sharīʿa*—the Canonical Law of Islam—is a comprehensive system of regulations covering every aspect of life, whether religious, political, social, domestic or individual. The first part contains injunctions regarding religious duties and matters of ritual. The second corresponds closely to the first but confines itself to the juridical and political sphere; and then there is a host of equally precise injunctions having to do with manners and customs—in short, with the social and cultural aspects. The primary and essential function of the *sharīʿa* is to exert a theocratic domination over the whole of life and only in the second place to provide a determinative body of law in a purely juridical sense.

When this system came up against modern, secular civilization it was by no means the first time that its inner cohesion had been put to the test. Such totalitarian religious claims were bound to fall foul of sheer human obstinacy and wilfulness and to clash with the tenacious cultural traditions of the converted peoples. The whole doctrine met with strong resistance, even in the hey-day of Muslim history.[28] It was opposed on three scores, the first of which has to do with the external character of the *sharīʿa* and the other two with its all-inclusiveness as a system. Mysticism, even in its orthodox form, was an intrusive element which seriously compromised the absolute character of the *sharīʿa*. Religiousness of a mystical kind is really a way of avoiding strict acceptance of the Law, because it regards the outward precepts as only a first step on the mystical path which eventually leads the religious seeker on to the lonely heights of ineffable communion with God. There is not necessarily any hypocrisy involved here; but it does mean that the ordinary Muslim has acquired—and accepts without question—the habit of mental reservation. Then too this mysticism has been very much mixed, in practice, with popular magical ideas of various kinds. The second type of opposition began early and has deeply affected the development of the *sharī'a*: it was the reaction inevitably aroused by its totalitarian claims. The Qur'an does not contain a legal system among its revelations, but it does resolve a number of problems that arose incidentally in the course of Muhammad's career. However, after the initial period, when the centre of government shifted to Damascus, the jurists lost their influence over the real conduct of the political community and started to build up a legal system based on the Qur'an and the tradition, but hardly at all in touch with the realities of political life. That ideal legal system was impracticable; and the jurists admitted as much themselves when they pessimistically declared that the *sharī'a* could only be realized in the golden age of the first four caliphs and in the eschatological period of the coming Mahdi. Still, its observance was, theoretically at any rate, the duty of every Muslim. The political authorities were ready enough to pay lip-service; but in practice they enacted whatever ordinances they wished and established civil courts alongside those of the *sharī'a*. In the end the powers of the latter were restricted to ritual and family matters which were closely bound up with the religious conscience of the people. Political and administrative institutions, a great part of the penal law and of large-scale commercial enterprise came under the authority of the secular government. In so far as it relates to constitutional and international law and the law of war, the *sharī'a* has never been in force. The glaring contradiction between religious theory and secular practice is above all reflected in the history of the Caliphate. According to all the rules laid down by the theologians, the Caliphate should have taken over the rôle of the Prophet in government, jurisdiction and conduct of the holy war. In point of fact, after rapidly becoming secularized it gradually lost its power until it was no more than a puppet in the hands of rival governments. Soon after the end of the fourteenth century it was supplanted by the Turkish Sultanate, so that even the Arab prerogatives of the Caliphate no longer remained intact.

Quite apart from the political factor, another thing which constitutes a challenge to the exclusive authority of the *sharī'a* is the law of custom ('*ādat*; '*urf*). Although legal theory has never accepted this as one of the foundations of the *sharī'a*, it is a factor of tremendous importance; and throughout the Muslim world, whether those legal ordinances which have a practical bearing (i.e. on ritual duties and personal relationships) are actually observed or not has to a great extent depended on whether they are consistent with the traditional law of custom.

Whilst there is this undeniable discrepancy between the ideal pretensions of the *sharī'a* and its real status, one thing of inestimable importance has remained true, right through the course of Islamic history. It is that the theory, as such, has never been impugned. This is where the Western impact introduces a genuinely new element into the situation which now confronts Islam: it has exploded the 'myth' of the *sharī'a*.

The effect of the Western impact was an inevitable one; and that Turkey should be the place where its more extreme consequences have been taken to heart is no accident. The French Revolution had begun to make its influence felt in that country through the Sultan's legal and social reforms, even before the beginning of the nineteenth century. A middle class appeared, imbued with the ideals of *watan* (fatherland), *hurriyet* (liberty), *khalkdjilik* (democracy) and *meshrutuyet* (constitutionalism). Growing opposition to the reactionary and tyrannical régime of Sultan Abdul Hamid II on the part of this new bourgeoisie erupted into the Young Turk Revolution of 1908. However, the Ottoman Empire remained a Muslim state. The Young Turks had three ends in view: nationalist Turkism, conservation of the decaying empire under the banner of Islam and parliamentary constitutionalism; but as those three aims were incompatible, they were really attempting the impossible. Turkey's defeat in the First World War spelled the end of an unrealizable project.

The dilemma of Islam when confronted with the imported Western ideals of nationalism and liberalism is apparent in the teachings of one of the most interesting intellectuals of that period, Kemal Atatürk's predecessor, Ziya Gökalp, who based his bold plans for reform on his interpretation of Islam as a purely ethical religion.[29] Gökalp proclaimed the Islamic law of custom—which Muslim jurists have never accepted as a fifth fundamental principle of the *sharī'a*—to be a 'divine revelation'. On this basis he advocated far-reaching religious reforms. First, religion and state were to be separated, in order to ensure that Islam would cease to dominate over the political and social life of the Turkish nation; and then religion was to be something quite distinct from oriental civilization so that the essential values of Islam could be preserved side by side with European civilization and Turkish national culture. This programme, which has contributed a great deal to the formation of modern Turkey, was summed up in his threefold aim of *Türkleshmek, Islāmlashmak, Muasirlashmak*: 'Turkification', Islamization, Modernization.

At the end of the First World War, however, total calamity had befallen the Ottoman Empire; and in such an emergency the Turkish nation was not to be saved by theories, but by the political genius of Kemal Atatürk alone. He was the least romantic of men and a convinced atheist. He dispensed entirely with Islam and with the Ottoman myth and with all quixotic dreams of unifying the Turkish race. Thus of the triple programme of Gökalp and the Young Turks there remained only the one goal of modernization (or Westernization). For Turkey, her territories reduced after the war, no other way held the possibility of continued independence. 'Our religion is extremely rational and natural. A natural religion has to conform to the laws of reason, science and logic,' declared Atatürk, a year before he did away with the Caliphate. His decision to do that was more far-reaching in its consequences than the thoroughgoing secularization of the new Turkish state; for it demolished one of the sacred pillars of the Muslim conception of government.

At the end of the fourteenth century the Caliphate had been usurped by the Ottoman Sultan. It was a situation not without parallel in the Holy Roman Empire of the German nation and in the claim of the Russian Tsars to have inherited the sacred privileges of the Byzantine emperors after the Turkish conquest of Constantinople. Ziya Gökalp had proposed leaving the caliph in a position of spiritual leadership rather like that of the Pope in the Western world. The comparison was a specious one, however, because it left out of account the very essence of *sharī'a*, which allows of no separation between religion and the state. Once the Sultan had been deposed, Atatürk drew the only logical conclusion and two years later abolished the Caliphate, at the same time reducing Islam in effect to the status of a private religion. Although not in the manner of the Communist Revolution in Russia some years previously, modern Turkey thus declared for a thoroughly secularist state.

All this made it evident that one effect of the Western impact was to lift the veil of sacral theory and force Islam to face the hard fact which that theory had served to conceal. What no Muslim had ever had the courage to admit openly was now brought into the open by the simple decision of an atheistic Turkish president, imbued with the ideas of the French Revolution: namely, that the Caliphate had long been nothing but a mere cipher. This sacred institution had been grounded in the third source of the *shari'a*, the infallible consensus of the Muslim community (*ijma*). Naturally enough, its abolition provoked sharp reactions throughout the Muslim world and gave rise to considerable confusion. A congress was convened at Mecca; but all it revealed was that at this juncture a consensus of the community was non-existent, let alone infallible.

It seemed wisest to admit the impracticability of restoring the Caliphate and make theory conform with the logic of the facts; and that was what the great Muslim poet and philosopher, Sir Mohammad Iqbal, actually did. He recognized that the Caliphate had long since lost all the real power and concluded that for the time being each Muslim nation would have to withdraw more deeply into itself, focusing its vision upon itself alone until all should be strong and powerful enough to form a living family of republics. What might it be, though, this 'deeper self'? Iqbal confesses to a great admiration for modern Turkey, 'which alone has shaken off its dogmatic slumber and attained to self-consciousness. She alone has claimed her right of intellectual freedom; she alone has passed from the ideal to the real . . .' Yet this same intellectual freedom led not only to the abolition of the Caliphate—which Iqbal accepts calmly enough—but also to the separation of religion from the state right along the line—a divorce which he rejects because, as he rightly says, it implies a dualism completely alien to Islam. Although he warmly welcomes the liberal movement in modern Islam, he also points out that liberalism tends to be a disintegrative force. He compares the crisis within modern Islam to the Protestant revolution in Europe, the effect of which was gradually to displace the universal ethics of Christianity with systems of national ethics—a tendency resulting in the First World War. 'It is the duty of the leaders of the world of Islam to-day,' Iqbal concludes, 'to understand the real meaning of what has happened in Europe, and then to move forward with self-control and a clear insight into the ultimate aims of Islam as a social polity.'[30]

Mohammad Iqbal has become the spiritual father and national hero of what is nowadays the largest Muslim state: Pakistan. The function of his philosophical speculation resembles to some extent that of Hegel's philosophy in nineteenth century Germany. Iqbal's dynamic idealism was, like Hegel's, just the kind of philosophy needed for the purpose of creating a new state. Again as with Hegel, there are two opposed tendencies in Iqbal: a progressive idealism and a reactionary theory of the state. A secular state he held to be an impossibility; for all that is called secular is, at the roots of its being, sacred.

> There is no such thing as a profane world. All this immensity of matter constitutes a scope for the self-realization of spirit. All is holy ground. As the Prophet so beautifully puts it: 'The whole of this earth is a mosque.' The state according to Islam is only an effort to realize the spiritual in a human organization. But in this sense all state, not based on mere domination and aiming at the realization of ideal principles, is theocratic.[31]

The case of Pakistan should indeed show whether or not Islam is in a position to adopt the principles of the French Revolution whilst at the same time keeping the *sharī'a* as the foundation of the state and of society. The country's constitution was drafted to form the basis of a sovereign, independent state wherein:

> . . . the principles of democracy, freedom, equality, tolerance and social justice as enunciated by Islam, shall be fully observed; wherein the Muslims of Pakistan shall be enabled individually and collectively to order their lives in accordance with the teachings and requirements of Islam, as set out in the Holy Qur'an and Sunnah.

One thing the as yet brief career of Pakistan has already shown: what a tremendous liability is taken on by any state which adopts its political principles from modern Western civilization and then tries to make them take root in the soil of a religion which has not itself evolved those principles, because they form no part either of its structure or of its inner disposition. Just as to secularize the Turkish state without any compromise was the only way of salvaging the remains of Anatolia from the ashes of the Ottoman Empire, so the proclamation of an Islamic state was for Pakistan the only means of justifying her separate existence. For Islam the latter course is obviously far and away the more intriguing in that it involves her in the whole business of squaring the circle, engendered by the need for Westernization. From the point of view of sheer governmental expediency, however, it is more tempting to take up the secularist sword and hack boldly through the Gordian knot than take the infinite pains required by the attempt to unravel it, at the risk of a whole run of disasters. Even so, the history of modern Turkey proves that a secular state cannot dodge the problem of Islam either.

In Egypt too impassioned argument arose over the abolition of the Caliphate. In 1925—before a year was out—a book was published in Arabic with the title: *Islam and the Fundamentals of Authority*. The author, Shaikh 'Ali 'Abd Al Râziq, had been among the first students to receive a secular Western education at the new university in Cairo, founded on the initiative of certain Egyptian nationalists in 1908. Upon his return from Oxford, where he read economics and political science, he was appointed a judge of the *sharī'a* courts. The main thesis of his provocative book was precisely that the Muslim world did not need the Caliphate. Muhammad's authority was spiritual only and not political. He did not even try to found a state. The *sharī'a* which he mediated was concerned only with religious, and not with civil affairs.[32]

The book came under heavy fire from religious leaders. The Azhar court condemned the author and deprived him of membership of the *'ulama* (the corporate body of religious authorities). It was all too clear that what he was advocating—separation of religion and state and the end of the *sharī'a* as a civil code—flagrantly contradicted orthodox Muslim theory. Râziq's was the unhappy plight of the intellectual *déraciné*, at home neither among his co-religionists nor with the West. However much he might sympathize with this courageous shaikh, no Western Islamist could possibly support his views on the history of Islam or accept the arbitrary, 'scientific' method by which he reaches his conclusions.

Still, it was one thing to dismiss a heretical shaikh and quite another to dispose of the issue he had raised. His censurers ignored entirely the equivocal position of Islam within their own country; for the Constitution adopted by Egypt when she achieved independent status in 1922 recognized Islam as the official religion, but in other respects only served to demonstrate just how impossible it is to apply the *sharī'a* to the circumstances of a modern state. In framing the constitution common law was largely ignored.

It is not every Muslim, however, who can turn a blind eye to the plain discrepancy between sacred theory and the realities of civil life. The subversive movement known as the *Ikhwān-al-Muslimūn*, the Muslim Brotherhood, points home the fact that where Western civilization infiltrates a great deal of bewilderment is bound to result. The Brotherhood has a big following throughout the Near East; and this it owes in part to the general malaise—social, cultural, political and economic—of the urban intellectual and quasi-intellectual sections of society in particular. Perhaps this accounts for the extremism of its ideology, which makes it an enemy of the government, as also for its ardent xenophobia. At bottom, though, the movement is a passionate protest on the part of men who cannot reconcile a modern constitution with the totalitarian demands of Muslim canon law. It cherishes a nostalgic image of the time of the Prophet as the golden age, representing this as the only perfect model for all real progress; and that age it aims to restore by substituting for the current heretical régimes a genuinely orthodox government which would accept the *sharī'a* as the one basis of civil life in all its aspects. The Muslim Brotherhood, with its 'theocratic' extremism, offers a much needed outlet for the thought and feelings stirred up in those orthodox Muslims who regard themselves as the victims of an intrusive foreign influence for which they have the deepest aversion, because although they detest its spirit and its aims they cannot help admiring its power. Several times the movement has been outlawed and obliged to 'go underground'; but whether it can be suppressed or no, this kind of zealotic orthodoxy represents a considerable under-current throughout the Muslim world and remains a problem there for every national government which tries to combine allegiance to Islam with modern statecraft and the vital need to build an effectively conducted welfare state on Western lines.

Since achieving her independence Indonesia has tried to meet the difficulty by adopting a sort of middle way. The Indonesian Republic is neither a secular nor a Muslim state. Its draft constitution has for its ideological basis the fivefold principle of the *Pantjashila* (an old Javanese Sanskrit term meaning 'five principles') only remotely resembling the 'six arrows' of Kemalist Turkey (republican, nationalist, populist, *étatiste*, secular, revolutionary), the secularist character of which it emphatically rejects. Four of these principles are quite 'normal' to a modern state. They are: respect for human values, democracy, social justice and nationalism. The crux lies in the first principle: *Ketuhanan Jang Maha Esa*, meaning 'Almighty and One Godhead'. This rather vague term (*ketuhanan* is a neuter derived from *Tuhan* = God) was purposely chosen so that a connection between the state and religion could be maintained without the proclamation of an Islamic state. What a hybrid affair this vaguely religious provision is appears evident enough from the Ministry of Religious Affairs, which represents a compromise in the relation of religion to the state between the theory of complete separation and the theory of union.

The evolution of Islamic law under Western influences reflects the irresistible progress of secularization in the Muslim world.[33] Although, as we have seen, there have been from the eighth century onwards large sectors to which the *shari'a* has never been made to apply, nominally it has always reigned supreme over every sphere of life. The really novel consequence of legal reform on the Western pattern has been to set a civil code as a rival alongside the *shari'a*. Under the Ottoman Empire in the second half of the nineteenth century a complete dichotomy between the secular and *shari'a* courts was established; and the latter were reserved for cases involving personal status and family law. This almost entirely put an end to the authority of the *shari'a* over a wide field, including commercial and criminal law and much of civil law as well, substituting for it various codes of a mainly Western complexion. Yet to the average Muslim of the more conservative type this move seemed vastly preferable to any attempt at tampering with the *shari'a*; for it allowed the possibility of preserving intact the sacred precepts as the perfect law for the golden age. Then after the First World War it became evident that even this stand could no longer be taken in face of the need to reform the law still further—even that part which was specifically Islamic. Since the only alternative was to abandon it altogether, the religious jurists in several Near Eastern countries reluctantly agreed to co-operate in reforming the *shari'a*; and so even the *shari'a* itself is nowadays being adulterated with concepts of law deriving largely from the West. In Egypt the revolutionary régime which came to power in the early 'fifties took the next step by abolishing the *shari'a* courts. It is now only a question of time before cases of personal status too are conducted in the national courts, exclusively by men with a modern background and training, as lawyers and legislators come to be drawn more and more from among the ranks of those who have enjoyed a Western and secular education. The military dictatorship in Pakistan has taken a still more drastic step by suspending the constitution and bringing to an abrupt end the work of the Law Reform Commission, charged with making the constitution conformable to 'Qur'an and Sunnah'.

It is against the background of this advancing secularization, which is certainly not stopping short even at what have been the entrenched positions of Islamic law, that one has to assess the growth of 'Muslim modernism', as it is called. The phrase refers not so much to any clearly definable movement as to a gradual change in the spiritual climate of living, of thinking, feeling, acting and reacting, in those circles and centres which have made contact with the West and to a greater or less degree have felt its influence. Unco-ordinated, ambiguous, full of inner tensions and contradictions, the 'modernist' mentality is more at ease on the emotional, intuitive level and fights shy of rational self-clarification. In so far as it achieves formulated expression at all, it is generally accessible in a host of pamphlets and booklets; and even in more voluminous writings it seldom aspires to the level of systematic thinking.

In India Muslim modernism put in an appearance during the latter part of the nineteenth century, when the new middle class needed to fashion a liberal Islam in terms compatible with the contemporary West.[34] By the end of the century, when this Muslim middle class had become less of a dependant on and much more of a rival to its British counterpart, its self-reliance had taken a more aggressive form. It was even alleged that the amenities of modern civilization were a direct product of the splendid Muslim culture of the past. Amīr 'Alī's The Spirit of Islam became pretty well the classical example of the approach and set the tone for the apologetics of the succeeding decadess As the Muslim bourgeoisie grew more and more frustrated during the period between the wars, so they tended to repudiate the Western influence. Liberalism too was superseded by a fresh, creative vision of shaping the future. Under the spell of Nietzsche and Bergson, Mohammad Iqbal returned from Europe with a resounding message which was to transform Islam into a type of mystical humanism. His championship of political collectivism as a means of self-preservation led eventually to the creation of Pakistan.

A striking feature of this avant-garde modernism on the Indian continent is that it is championed by laymen, principally officials of various kinds, lawyers, men of property and university teachers—a fact which perhaps accounts for its often daring freedom of thought. There is, however, a serious flaw in the situation. Gibb has pointed to a marked difference between thé Christian West and the Muslim world.[35] Whereas in the West it is very largely the theologians themselves who are reshaping religious thinking in terms of the prevailing philosophical and historical ideas, the vast majority of orthodox Muslim theologians cling to an unremitting conservatism; they defend Islam without knowing the modern world which they are defending it against. On the other hand the average middle-class apologist upholds a speculative reconstruction of Islam on liberal lines, which has no real foundation in the orthodox structure. Gibb assumes too much, though, when he concludes that this modernism is 'primarily a function of Western liberalism'. The sad thing is that it is neither orthodox nor liberal; rather is it a reaction set up by the intrusion of various bits and pieces of Western civilization. Whilst Western liberalism is a specific phase in the development of a whole culture, Muslim modernism is rootless and lacking any real spiritual background. Unlike nineteenth century liberalism, with its growing historical and critical sense and its uncompromising attack on the very foundations of Christian doctrine, Muslim modernism is without any really scientific basis for its apologetic interpretation of Muslim history; and for all its critical attitude towards the authority of tradition, it continues to treat the divine infallibility of the Qur'an and the Prophet's authority and person as though it had never heard of the possibility even of intellectual and religious doubt. The signs of an awakening in this direction are very few and far between.

In Egypt a type of modernism has arisen which is rather different from the 'advanced' modernism of India. The initiative in this case came from among the orthodox theologians themselves, centred in the ancient Azhar University in Cairo. These men styled their movement *Salafiyyah*, because they wanted to restore the original Islam of the *Salaf*, that is, the first generation.

Muhammad 'Abduh and his pupil, Rashīd Riḍā, published a voluminous commentary on the Qur'an, in which they set out to reinterpret the Holy Book in the light of modern thought. Because they were themselves a 'shoot' of orthodoxy, in the course of time their ideas have gradually permeated the orthodox ethos. As compared with the *avant-gardisme* of Indian modernism, this Egyptian movement was highly conservative; for these men had hardly any real understanding of—or more than superficial contact with—Western civilization and their mental climate was that of the traditional Muslim culture and theology. Actually the movement has by now pretty well exhausted its usefulness. In one direction it has done good, in making the average Muslim feel confident that his religion can pass muster with the modern West in every respect and that it was quite ready for a 'reformation' and a 'renaissance'. On the other hand the movement has never managed to face the challenge of secularism; and to that extent it has accentuated still further, if anything, the trend towards a conservative isolationism, by furnishing its apologists with fresh weapons of defence and attack. It is significant that this particular movement has given no new or telling impetus to anything coming after it. Secular and religious education have grown so far apart that no efforts to reinterpret or remould the orthodox position can any longer bridge the gulf between them.

The Western impact also brought about a changed attitude towards Christianity. The encroachments of Western civilization were extremely painful to the Muslim consciousness, because bound up with them was the incomparable and intolerable cultural superiority of Christendom. Christian missions were a much more effective influence as a vanguard of modern cultural ideals than as the purveyors of Christian doctrine. Evangelization, whether by word or deed, was felt by Muslims to be a standing criticism of their civilization in its backwardness and decay. The inevitable reaction set in. Amīr 'Alī presented Muslim history in such a way as to give Indian modernism a glittering and exciting picture of its own superiority to Christianity at every turn. His book, written in English for an 'advanced' middle class, had its Arabic counterpart in Muhammad 'Abduh's *Islam and Christianity in their Attitudes to Learning and Civilization.* 'Abduh contrasted Islam—rational, tolerant, the champion of equality and liberty as well as of scientific investigation—with a wretchedly antiquated Christianity—a faith addicted to the monastic and the miraculous, rejecting rational processes of thought and suppressing spiritual and social freedom by the machinations of a fanatical and priestly hierarchy.[36]

Thus it has become the generally accepted thing to envisage Christianity as an individualistic, isolating and negative faith, without bearing or influence on practical affairs and so not really a force to be reckoned with in the struggle against the new materialistic philosophies. As a religion of ascetic renunciation it is unsuited to the genius of the West.[37] A favourite theme is the notion of Islam as the true mean between Communism and capitalism. One writer, who until a few years ago was a leading economist and politician in Indonesia,[38] has made an interesting study of the development of capitalism, in which he explains it as following inevitably from Jesus' teaching about total self-denial—a doctrine which in practice gave tyrants and profiteers a free hand to exploit their fellow-men. Marxism went to the other extreme and became a message of implacable hatred. Between those two opposites Islam is the golden mean, teaching neither impractical love nor a devastating hatred, but a combination of respect for one's neighbour with a manly defence of one's proper interests. Islam then is reasserting today what it originally proclaimed: that as the successor to Judaism and to Christianity it is the final religion for the whole of mankind. Whereas the end product of Christianity is the capitalist system, the opposite of that—Communism —is the product of Judaism. Thus history repeats itself, and Islam is once again to save this world. In promulgating a middle way between the extremes represented by its predecessors—Judaism (now Communism) and Christianity (now capitalism)—Islam will mediate and proclaim peace to the world.

The book *City of Oppression*[39] by Muhammad Kāmil Husain a member of the medical profession in Egypt, is a rare and rather surprising example of a sympathetic attempt to interpret Christianity by going direct to the New Testament itself. It is an imaginative reconstruction of the tensions and bigotries and fears at work within the desire to crucify Christ—a deed which Hussein describes as humanity's crucifixion of its own conscience.

There are signs therefore of a changed attitude towards Christianity, perhaps no less apologetical and polemical than the traditional controversies, generally speaking, yet indicating a shift of emphasis resulting from the need to justify Islam at the bar of modern civilization.

The time has not yet come, it seems, for a more radical self-examination on the part of Islam, which would involve subjecting its very foundations, the historical revelation embodied in the Qur'an and the conception of an all-embracing religious and social system, to frank and possibly devastating criticism. No one can say when that time will arrive—or whether it will come at all. The crucial question, which the Muslim people themselves will have to answer, is still whether Islam is capable of responding in that way to the unprecedented challenge of Western secularization.

5. A NOTE ON MODERN JAPAN

We have had to restrict ourselves in this chapter to considering the effects of the West's impact on the two great 'primary' civilizations of Asia and on the Muslim world, which from its inception has been the chief antagonist of Western civilization. Even so, one cannot pass over in complete silence the story of Japan's Westernization, at least so far as two of its principal aspects are concerned.

The first thing to be said has to do with what is sometimes described as Japan's 'Western fever'. The expression suits very well with the comparison we have already made between the Western impact upon the non-Western world and the symptoms engendered in the human body as a result of a virus infection. Thanks to a number of inter-related factors thrown up in the course of her history and to her peculiar geographical situation as an archipelago at some distance from continental Asia, Japan was indeed prepared, up to a point, for the Western intrusion in face of which she was obliged to open her doors after the middle of the nineteenth century. Her society presented a feudal structure which even the Confucian tradition, when it was introduced, was never able to invest with the solidity and enduring strength of Chinese civilization. Japan owed the raising of her culture above the level of a tribal religion to the influence of Asian continental civilization, and leading circles there have always shown themselves restless, much inclined to experiment and markedly interested by foreign influences. As early as the eighteenth century a prosperous middle class had sprung up in certain large towns, and before the middle of the nineteenth century there were already signs of a transition from an agrarian to a mercantile economy and, in embryonic form, of various elements of modern capitalism. The country was thus not altogether unprepared when in 1868 her doors were flung open to full-scale industrialization; but on the other hand it is clear that the strongest pressure was needed—something in the nature of an occidental invasion—in order to force an entry and that industrialization cannot possibly be regarded as a natural stage in the internal development of Japan. Japan's condition in that momentous year should be compared, not with the state of Britain's economy on the eve of her Industrial Revolution, but rather with the still predominantly agricultural scene of Tudor times, when manufacture depended chiefly on domestic handicrafts.[40]

Even that comparison is misleading, as it might give the impression that Japan took a 'cramming-course' in Western history and went through, as it were, in double quick time. In fact neither the Meiji revolution nor what preceded it at all resembles anything in Western history. It was pointed out in Chapter Six what a crucial difference there was between Japanese feudalism and that of the mediaeval West. The West made a fundamental break with the feudal structure and did so under the influence of those very forces which during the feudal period had inhibited the growth of a centralized despotism; whereas Japan, even in its modern period, never took leave of the feudal tradition or abandoned the myth of oriental monarchism. What the Meiji Restoration did was to perpetuate time-honoured notions regarding the ontocratic pattern of the imperial state. It was itself the work of a self-perpetuating Samurai oligarchy. There certainly was industrialization; but this was directed and controlled, not by an independent middle class, but by already existing feudal clans who now vested their power in industry, banking and trade, within the framework of a centralized, bureaucratic and militaristic state. Their aim was national self-defence and imperialistic expansion.

The parallel, in certain respects, between the growth of modern Japan and that of modern Germany is too obvious to be altogether ignored. In both cases the rapid development of a bureaucratic, militaristic, industrialized state combined with fervent nationalism and a mediaeval mythology of 'Holy Empire' to produce the pernicious self-idolization that had its climax and suffered its catastrophe in the Second World War. In both cases modern technocracy touched off the nihilism latent at the heart of religion. There is this affinity; and yet it should not blind us to the qualitative difference in each case. The myth of the Third Reich was no more—or less—arbitrary and artificial than the state Shinto cult, but it was much more dangerous. Zen Buddhist nihilism too, though not unconnected with the suicidal heroics of the Samurai, was fairly harmless, compared with National Socialist nihilism. Westernizing a pagan civilization no doubt has its risks; but measured against the explosive forces released when a Western civilization is paganized, such risks are about as great as those of conventional, as opposed to atomic, warfare. In the past Japan has from time to time persecuted Christianity—but chiefly from fear of its political uses as a 'tool' of Western imperialism. The anti-Christian genius of German nihilism, on the other hand, opened up satanic depths of inhumanity which only a Christian civilization making a desperate stand against the Messiah of Israel can disclose.

Our second point concerns the position of Japan in the modern world. The past hundred years of Japanese history are proof of how greatly Western civilization has enhanced its power to expand since the Industrial Revolution. It has shown itself capable of transforming a country which for many centuries had led a life of total seclusion and of turning it within a generation or so into one of the major imperialist powers in the world—and that, during the very period when Western imperialism was at the height of its influence throughout the non-Western world. Japanese imperialist aggrandizement has had as much to do as Western imperialism with the rise of revolutionary movements in non-Western countries. One has only to point to three significant dates. In China Sun Yat-sen's first attempt at revolution coincided with the aggression committed by Japan against that country in 1894–5. Japan's victory over Russia in 1905 triggered off the uprising of the proletariat in Moscow. Japanese imperialism reached its highest pitch in the Second World War, with incalculable repercussions. In the event Communism triumphed in China; and in Indonesia the stage was set for revolution. One can only speak of 'Western dominance' in the twentieth century therefore in a qualified sense which implies not so much imperialist activity on the part of Western countries as the further outreach of forces already Westernized. Japan's recent history is convincing proof that 'Westernization' does not so much hustle the non-Western world through an abbreviated course of modern Western history as open a door to participation in the history of that 'one world' which Western expansion has made possible.

Eight

Christianity in a Planetary World

I. THE END OF AN ERA

THE tremendous changes which are taking place in the modern world have made more and more people conscious of the fact that we have come to the end of an epoch. That is not a novel idea in itself; indeed it is part of that sense of time and history which runs in the very blood-stream of Western civilization. It springs from the paradoxical conviction that the 'fullness of time' refers to the end of the ages and yet has made its appearance in the midst of history so that it is 'between the times' that we now live, looking back to the fullness which is yet to come, expecting the coming of him whom we proclaim to be the historical man of Nazareth. The apostle Paul was sure that he had 'fulfilled' the Gospel and had carried it to the ends of the earth at the close of the ages. The Revelation of John sees the approaching collapse of the Roman Empire as a sign of the impending judgment of God and descent of the New Jerusalem. It was several centuries before Augustine's prophecy that the time of this 'second Babylon' was running out looked like being fulfilled. The Middle Ages never learned to emerge from the shadow of the Roman Empire. In the end church and state each accused the other of representing antichrist; and the 'Occident' remained subject to the belief, which blazed up from time to time, that it lived 'at the ends of the earth' and the end of the ages. At the Reformation Rome and Islam were still seen in an apocalyptic light. Our modern age, however, seemed bent on emancipating itself from the power of the eschatological expectation: that is, until the present century—anticipated by a few lonely prophetic voices in the century preceding—announced once more the 'decline of the West'.

It goes without saying that modern man would not listen to a prophecy of this sort, if it were not presented to him in 'scientific' dress. Moreover Spengler's fatalism has now been transposed for us into a major key in Toynbee's thesis that as yet Western civilization does not seem to have entered the phase of the 'universal state' and that we hold our future partly at any rate within our own hands. That does not alter the fact that neither in the temporal nor the spacial dimension is there left a really hopeful prospect for modern man. The growth of knowledge and of power brought us face to face with historical boundaries which could not be denied; and it was precisely through our determination to free ourselves finally from these that we came to replace the apocalyptic end of the ages with the concept of temporal infinity. Extending our knowledge and power over the whole natural world certainly exploded the pathetic fallacy that Jerusalem must be the centre and the West the 'end' of the earth; but at the same time it swept away all delusions about looking to the East for an imagined paradise or a better future. We live in a planetary world without centre or confines, yet for that very reason limited and finite. In broadening its perspective our world is at the same time swallowed up in astronomical space; for after all in that context a planetary world is nothing more than a planet. The space travel of today can no longer arouse even an echo of the music once made by the discovery of new continents and peoples at the close of the Middle Ages. The threat of global war hangs over every advance in knowledge and in power, and we grow more conscious than ever before of being imprisoned on this insignificant planet.

The remarkable thing is that it is precisely the manner in which a distinctively Western civilization is reaching its final consummation —and the way in which it is being experienced—that bears out its claim to 'universality'. It is in the West that a human society has been transformed into *the* society *par excellence*; and it is an expansion of the West that has made our world a planetary world, whilst it is again the West which has achieved the demotion of the earth to the status of a paltry planet. It is in the West that a civilization liberates itself—and with itself all other civilizations—from provincialism and self-perpetuation and comes to grips with the question of the future of mankind.

The size and true significance of the historical changes which are now happening to our world become apparent as soon as one compares the end of the present era with earlier times of crisis inaugurating change and entry upon a new period of history.

The technological revolution of our times has been likened, it is true, to the Neolithic revolution which introduced the primitive phases of agriculture and thus laid the foundations of all civilization, first in the Old World and later—though independently—in the New. Until the invention of the machine, mankind had built upon the foundations of agricultural society and been confined within the limitations belonging to this mode of production. It is also true that the Neolithic revolution was world-wide in character. There is however a radical difference here in that the Neolithic revolution is a part of prehistory. When our researches in Magdalenian and Mesolithic archaeology—that is to say into those phases which preceded the Neolithic revolution—have reached a more advanced stage, it may well be possible to answer the question, not yet resolved, as to why certain areas rather than others in both the Old and New Worlds were first to attain the advanced technical levels and social structures necessary to the development of agriculture. Even so we can never hope to do more than establish what were the particular conditions and circumstances which proved more favourable in certain regions than elsewhere. The rise and progress of Western civilization, on the other hand, lie entirely within the framework of history; and it is by analysing its own past that through its researches the West has been able to give some account of its development. The modern technological revolution is not the result of circumstances beyond the reach of more detailed clarification, but is the outcome of a unique course of civilization in the West, in which clearly discernible spiritual motives and a particular view of God, man and the world have played a decisive part.

None the less it looks as though we do indeed stand at the end of an era—an era which started with the Neolithic revolution. Then the foundation was laid for the rise of various civilizations in various regions. Now it is the technological revolution—accomplished by one particular civilization, namely, that of the West—which promises to assume a world-wide character. Nobody can yet say whether regional types of clearly distinguishable civilizations will be produced once again in specific centres by the conditions prevailing under modern technology, as was formerly the case on the world-wide Neolithic basis; but a possibility of this kind is difficult to reconcile with the apparently irreversible trend of modern history towards a planetary world. What is far more important, we seem now to be witnessing the arrival of a new type of man. The era of the 'third man' is probably coming to an end; and the future would appear to lie with a new type, appropriately described as the 'fourth man'. The 'newness' does not merely consist in a new mode of technology, but in the fact that the modern technological revolution is part only of a larger revolutionary process which seems likely to uproot and destroy the corner-stone of all human society as we have known it hitherto, from its most primitive to its most civilized forms. That corner-stone is religion.

In all civilizations up to the present religion has had an absolutely indispensable and predominant part. Christian civilization, of course, has always been religious; and Christianity has fulfilled a function within it which other religions have discharged in other civilizations. It was first of all the Industrial Revolution which ousted the Christian faith from its pre-eminent position, putting modern science and technology there in its place. It is extraordinarily difficult to say what the significance of this turn of events really is, since we ourselves are caught up in it and its unprecedented character prevents us from drawing any useful inferences from analogous historical circumstances. It seems legitimate—and necessary even—to wonder whether the present technological revolution does not confront Christianity for the first time in its history with the crucial question whether the 'fullness of time', which makes all things new, does not involve a revolution in man's outlook and relation to his fellow men and to the world, in so far as that can be said to fall within the technological dimension. For the first time in the history of mankind, that is to say, the ontocratic pattern has been broken through and superseded by the technocratic pattern. To what extent are we entitled to see in this breakthrough at the technological level a working out of that fundamental, radical indictment of the ontocratic pattern which is expressed in the early chapters—and especially in the eleventh chapter —of Genesis and forms the burden of the whole biblical message?

We have seen how Israel's life and culture were conformed to the pattern of the ancient Near Eastern civilizations and how Israel clothed her unique message in the garb of that ontocratic pattern. Throne and altar, kingship and temple—all were modelled according to a common standard. The New Testament proclaims that in Jesus Christ, the crucified Lord, the Temple is done away. By the New Covenant the Temple at Jerusalem comes under the judgment already fallen upon the tower of Babel and has no continued existence. In the centuries that followed, however, Christianity once more made herself temples, so that she was in no position to give fitting expression to her message that through the Cross the Temple is done away. Christianity simply continued to build—like the people of Israel before her—upon the technological, artistic, cultural and religious forms which the ancient ontocratic civilizations had already brought to a well-nigh unsurpassable degree of perfection. At last, in the rise of modern technology, the way is opened for a new pattern to break through with irresistible power, thrusting the Temple once and for all from its place at the centre. Now an expendable element, it is relegated to a position of, at the most, secondary importance as an ornament to society.

That technological revolution was nurtured in the bosom of Christian civilization and indeed is one of its 'children'. Through it a radical change in the very structure of Christianity is now making itself felt, is working itself out at those points in the structure wherein Christianity has hitherto most closely resembled the other religions. All religions—Christianity included—have had a structural affinity to the Neolithic era; and by that is meant the era of agricultural-cum-pastoral societies, for which the Neolithic revolution provided a basis and the major primary civilizations the characteristic patterns. The Neolithic era was that in which societies were—and were bound to be—unconditionally religious. It is that form of society which the modern technological revolution has transformed, quintessentially and for the first time. The position of Christianity in respect to this revolution is an extraordinary one, precisely because Christianity was responsible for bringing it about. As the revolution spreads to other societies, so there—just as in the West—it augurs the beginning of the end for the Neolithic era. Yet despite all similarities there is still a profound difference here, which consists in the unique relationship of Christianity to the revolution, like that of a father to a son who has reached adulthood. The son may rebel against his father's authority; and yet the father can see in the rebellion his own spirit reflected. If the son should be illegitimate, then the father must recognize that his own extraction is not all that unimpeachable. In all kinds of ways he can discover himself in the encounter with his own image and likeness. Christianity is faced in the technological revolution with one particular question of the utmost urgency: what are we to make of the fact that the 'fullness of time' has come upon us—and that, not merely in history, but in mid course of the Neolithic era?

The non-Western societies and religions, on the other hand, encounter the modern technological revolution as a stranger. It may be that they are finding what they have taken in to be something of a Trojan horse. It is also possible that they are discovering too late the extremely useful character of this immigrant against whom their doors had once been closed. For the most part the technological revolution comes in as an intruder and makes itself at home, suspect, feared, and yet admired for its astounding proficiency. The more this revolution is able to do its work and the more deeply it penetrates, the more does the structure of a society change. Where the predominant religion is able to accommodate itself to such structural modification and after a time even take a leading part in the process itself, it is able not only to undergo a metamorphosis and survive, but eventually even to strengthen its position. Yet such a religion will inevitably find the new type of 'the fourth man' springing up in its midst; and in that situation it is, *qua* religion, totally at a loss. It is bound to discover that in so far as it comes to terms with the technological revolution it is being carried along with ever increasing momentum upon a current the direction of which no longer lies under its own control. It will learn by experience that this revolution conserves within itself the lethal property of destroying, in the long run, the very roots of religion. Perhaps too this discovery is in store for it because it must pay the heavy price of its own lethargy and conservatism and make way for a fully fledged technocratic ideology which can no longer find an excuse for any religion at all.

Karl Jaspers wonders whether we are not just on the eve of passing through another 'time of axis'; but the suggestion demonstrates once again the inadequacy of that philosopher's idea of a first 'time of axis', which is supposed to have occurred in the Eurasian world of the first millennium B.C. We argued in Chapter Four that this theory attempts to refer what are in fact disparate entities to a common denominator and that only in the case of Israel and of classical Hellas was it possible to speak of a radical breakaway of that sort. The present 'time of axis' has indeed begun in that civilization which Israel and Hellas produced between them.

In his book *From the Stone Age to Christianity*, Albright describes our situation today as:

> . . . strangely like the Graeco-Roman world of the first century B.C. . . . the civilized world had achieved unity and prosperity under Graeco-Roman culture and Roman domination, only to discover that its material and intellectual life was so far ahead of

its development that the lack of integration became too great to permit of further progress on the old lines. Jesus Christ appeared on the scene just when occidental civilization had reached a fatal impasse.[1]

This argument, however, ignores a number of fundamental differences. The Gospel entered the Hellenistic *oikoumenē* as one among many oriental religions; and the early Church really had nothing to do with bringing about a unified Hellenism or the Roman Empire. It was, on the other hand, precisely the impact and outreach of Western Christian civilization, and its guiding influence, that brought into being the planetary world of our time. It is *within* the Christian world that the lack of integration is becoming so very acute; and Western influences, so far from bringing with them a new harmony, are disturbing and destructive. Of course the Gospel did not enter the Graeco-Roman *oikoumenē* claiming to be an 'integrating factor' or a panacea for its social and cultural malaise. On the contrary, Jesus declared that when the Gospel of the Kingdom was preached, it would be as a sign of the approaching end of the age, mounting to a climax with wars and tribulations.

It would be more true to say that what we are witnessing now is the end of an era begun when Christianity spread throughout the Graeco-Roman *oikoumenē*. The conviction grows upon one that it is at the close of the 'Constantinian era' that we stand. No doubt the expression 'Constantinian era' is in itself scarcely adequate to characterize the peculiar course of Western history. It does not take into account those profound differences which since the time of Constantine the Great have developed between Eastern and Western Christianity, driving them ever farther and farther apart; and it ignores the fact that the Western Church first became aware of her peculiar calling and destiny in resisting the ecclesiastical policies of Constantinople. One might indeed with justice refer to the history of Byzantium as a 'Constantinian era'; but in applying the term to the history of the West, it is essential to bear in mind that from the time of the struggle between Pope and emperor onwards so many opposing currents and forces have met within the *Corpus Christianum* that again and again attempts to achieve integration have foundered upon the rock of their own inner contradiction. We must emphatically reject the suggestion that Christianity today either should or could return to a situation like that which prevailed during the first three centuries after Christ. The early Church lived in a pagan world, the Church of today in a world unsettled and uprooted within and without, but a Christian world. The dangers of modern technocracy confront the Church with a far more exacting task than did ever the emperor-worship of antiquity—for the Church bore no responsibility for that. The dimensions of our planetary world bring us into infinitely closer vicinity to the global perspective of the Gospel-proclamation 'to all the nations', and likewise to that world-wide power which Satan proposed giving to Jesus, than the relatively provincial boundaries of the Graeco-Roman *oikoumenē*.

One can therefore only speak of the end of the 'Constantinian era' in the qualified sense of an era in which throne and altar constituted, as it were, the two focal points of the ellipse of Christian society, which at times came very close to assuming the form of a circle with a single centre: an era in which Christianity was the official and dominant religion. It is legitimate, in that sense, to talk about a 'post-Christian' civilization. Yet one must bear in mind that the Constantinian era covers the same period as the revolutionary history of the West and that from the very start the proclamation of the Gospel and the life of the Church have been accompanied by the ambiguous phenomenon of 'Christianity'. In view of that it would be nearer the truth to assert that the Constantinian era is exhibiting —just now especially—a power and virulence without precedent; and that so far from living in a 'post-Christian' world we are going through a period in which those forces which took root and sprang up in the very soil of Christianity itself are displaying and deploying themselves to the full.

This holds true particularly of the spread of Western civilization throughout the world. Panikkar bases his book, *Asia and Western Dominance*, on the thesis that we have now arrived at the close of the 'Vasco da Gama era'; and this leads him straight on to his second thesis—not likely to work itself out in full until we enter the next historical epoch—that in no circumstances will the non-Western world ever again be able to revert to the pre-colonial period. The Western impact has brought about 'a qualitative break' among the non-Western civilizations. They have been caught up irretrievably into the drama enacted first of all by the West, but now in process of spreading on to the stage of world history.

It seems likely enough that, if we want to give some account of this present period of history and of what it signifies, that can still be done most adequately from a biblical viewpoint as outlined at the end of the third chapter. Old Testament history could not repeat itself, of course; but it has had its analogies in the subsequent history of 'Christianity'; and that history has meant also the realization of many potentialities merely latent in the New Testament. The transition to the third phase, which we are seeing now, does bear a certain resemblance to the end of Old Testament history and the passing of Israel into the *oikoumenē*; but even this has picked up in its career the Greek and barbarian features of Christian history, just as the course of that history has itself helped to determine the planetary dimensions of the present *oikoumenē*. History does not repeat itself; it is cumulative. As the seeds grow, so the seeds of Satan grow among the rest. The kingdom of Christ and the kingdom of antichrist both have the ends of the earth and all the nations as their final goal.

2. THE GOSPEL IN A PLANETARY WORLD

The present trend towards global unification by means of modern technology is incomparably more intensive than anything to which the Roman Empire under Augustus could possibly have aspired; and yet the ancient *oikoumenē* was something very much more homogeneous than the world of the twentieth century. The gap between the cultural and technological standard of life, say, in the capital city and that of primitive society at the barbarian fringes of the empire was negligible compared with the contrasts prevailing in our own time. Whilst atomic science busies itself with bringing about yet another revolution in modern technology, among the islands of South-east Asia there are tribes still living in the stone age. Nowadays however there are, in principle, no more 'fringes' or outposts; and should military or economic interests so require, any primitive society may be plunged, without warning or apology, into the atomic age.

Technological progress has always borne the mark of Cain; but this atomic age confronts us with the unprecedented fact that atomic war can only mean atomic suicide. Obviously the technological revolution has reached a stage of total impasse, even though nothing can now bring it to a halt. It is absolutely unrealistic to speculate about the rise of a world civilization without facing up to this crucial fact. All technocratic ideologies which proceed on the assumption that opportunities of unifying mankind and raising the general standard of living are now unlimited simply ignore the suicidal implications of future technological progress. In face of all this the messages of universal peace which modern Buddhism, Hinduism and Islam propound with a variety of voices fall to the ground, being no more than a misguided attempt to cure the ills of the technocratic era with the medicines of the Neolithic one.

Amidst these apocalyptic forebodings, these false Christs and false prophets, the Gospel of the Kingdom is being proclaimed throughout the world (Mt. 24). The Church faces the task of rethinking her missionary obligation through her encounter with the dangers and the expectations of the time.

First of all it behoves the Church to get clear in her own mind what it means, fundamentally, to be living in the technocratic era. The International Missionary Council, which met at Jerusalem in 1928, took note of the rapidly increasing secularism and materialism engulfing the modern world. Along with that went the suggestion that in order to join issue with these things Christianity should form a common front with the other religions. There are still a lot of people ready to champion any proposal of this sort; and it colours a good many of the approaches made from the Christian side to the phenomena of 'secularism'. It will be necessary to deal with this suggestion very firmly indeed; and this book is intended as a contribution to that end. That is its overall purpose. Here therefore we can only touch by way of summary on a few of the principal arguments. In Chapter Six it was pointed out how confusing and contradictory the terms 'secularism' and 'materialism' are. In so far as they refer to the modern mentality, which goes hand in hand with the rise of technocracy, that is an historical phenomenon thrown up by Christian civilization itself—a recent phase in the continuous process of structural modification which Christianity has undergone in the course of its history, particularly in the West. The Gospel is neither 'secular' nor 'religious', but it declares the fullness of time to be within human history and is therefore as an eschatological message essentially historical too. The technological revolution is the evident and inescapable form in which the whole world is now confronted with the most recent phase of Christian history. In and through this form Christian history becomes world history. The technocratic era, though it is not the Kingdom of God, is not the kingdom of Satan either; it is a phase of history in which the Lord and Satan are both at work. A timeless Gospel and a timeless Church are a will-o'-the-wisp. All mankind, whether living at the most primitive level or in the centres of modern civilization, is faced with a process which nothing can either reverse or hold in check—a process of transformation and of the interpenetration of cultures, propelled by the sheer force and forward thrust of the technological revolution. Einstein has no advantage in the kingdom of God over primitive man in the hinterlands of New Guinea; but in the march of history the former heads the column and the latter must follow; it cannot be otherwise. Christianity is essentially historical. The Gospel that takes away every privilege from the Jew, the Greek and the barbarian is nevertheless preached in history— beginning at Jerusalem—to Athens, to Rome, to the barbarian and to the ends of the world. Whilst the Gospel cannot be identified with Christian history—for it proclaims the close of the ages—no more is it to be divorced from history; for wherever the Gospel is preached and believed, there one will of necessity find 'Christianity'. Whether they like it or not, the non-Western civilizations are confronted now with a full scale invasion by technocracy; and it is not possible for them—even should they wish to do so—to dodge the impact of that intrusion or the relentless transformation it involves. The event in itself presents them neither with Jesus Christ nor with Satan. What they do encounter in it, through a process of torrential change, is the full power of Western civilization, ambiguous, dangerous, emancipating and enslaving, renewing and destroying, welcomed and yet feared, good and evil. In the midst of this encounter the Church has to stand and 'interpret', until this invading history is no longer suffered as a blind process, a glorious or a pernicious fatality, but men come at last to understand what the voices which speak to them through that history are saying and they learn to distinguish between the voice of Christ and those of his counterfeits.

Where the voice of Christ is understood, the technological revolution is conceived as history and not as process: as a series of continual human decisions and not as happening inevitably 'in the course of nature': in the light and the dark of the 'latter days' and not as the final phase or the ultimate goal: under God's judgment and grace and not in bondage to biological or sociological laws. Where the Gospel is believed, there is the truth accepted that there can be no returning to the age of 'religion'. This demolishing of the mediaeval *Corpus Christianum* represents—as it also anticipates—the doing away with every *corpus religiosum*, just as the destruction of the Temple at Jerusalem signifies that all our temples are, in principle, abolished. There is no way back, but there is a way ahead. Just as again and again in the course of Western civilization the proclamation of the Gospel has dynamited the entrenched positions of religion, so the Gospel carries on with its revolutionary task in assailing the positions of the technocracy. We saw in Chapter Six how very often the instigators of a revolution have ensconced themselves within their vested interest, have raised their purposes to the status of an absolute and final purpose and have mistaken their own work for the new creation. That is why each revolution contains within itself the germ of the next one, as the tree disseminates the seed from which itself has sprung. The impasse in which our technological revolution now finds itself confronts us with issues of such urgency, and the mortal danger which threatens our atomic age is so overwhelming, that only another revolution can save us—a revolution which will release here and now, in our planetary and technocratic world, re-creative forces like those which burst their way through the religious world of the West in the Renaissance, the Reformation and the subsequent movements.

One thing is certain: in no circumstances whatever could this new revolution mean returning to the age of 'religion'—and that applies as much to Christianity as to the other religions. We must rid ourselves once and for all of the idea that somehow or other Western civilization has got to be or can be 're-Christianized' through some restoration, in a new guise, of the *Corpus Christianum*. That civilization today is not less Christian than it was in the Middle Ages; it simply represents a new phase of Christian history. It is therefore not the case that the non-Western world can be or ought to be 'Christianized' in the sense that the traditional non-Western religions would in the long run give place to Christianity in some version or other of the *Corpus Christianum*. It is quite conceivable, of course, that officially at any rate Hinduism, Buddhism and Islam may disappear from the scene in certain areas. For this the recent history of China is a writing on the wall. The non-Christian religions may be unseated by a technocratic ideology, but not by a *Corpus Christianum* which quite definitely belongs to a bygone age. So long as the Church clings fundamentally to that conception of what Christianity is, she will never in her approach to the non-Western world be able to shake off the idea that proclaiming the Gospel there primarily and necessarily entails a meeting with the non-Christian religions. The discussions at the International Missionary Council conference at Madras and afterwards, occasioned by Kraemer's *The Christian Message in a Non-Christian World*, illustrated clearly to what a great extent the Church has confined her outlook on the missionary task to the 'religious' dimension. One of the leading Chinese Christians opposed to the thesis of the book argued that the great sages of China, such as Confucius, Mencius and Moti, had been 'truly inspired by the spirit of our God, the God of our Lord Jesus Christ'.[2] So long as the Church remains under the spell of that kind of thinking, she will not meet the onslaught of modern 'secularist' forces with the Gospel of a new heaven and a new earth, but will go on clinging to obsolete positions which the course of Christian history has already reduced to rubble and which cannot survive the judgment of God. That is why she is defenceless from the outset in face of the 'materialism' which she reckons to combat.

3. ' CHRISTIANIZATION ' AND SECULARIZATION

The grave fallacy of thinking that Christianity should form a common front with other religions against the threat of modern secularism and atheist materialism makes a tremendous appeal in Western countries. It mesmerizes thousands of honest Christian people, both Roman Catholic and Protestant, and is one of the most seductive ideas of the Moral Rearmament Movement. The idea is made all the more attractive by the welcome it receives among the devotees of other religions.

One suggestion in particular which is always being brought up is that of an alliance between Christianity and Islam. Very considerable confusion threatens on this point. It is matter for rejoicing that thanks to closer cultural and economic relations with Islamic peoples and a growing sense of interdependence among the nations Western jurists are coming more and more to realize how important it is to get better acquainted with the teachings of the Divine Law of Islam; but it is not so commendable when such studies are encouraged and applauded because of a conviction that:

> today the anxious countries of the West find in the Islamic world some of their most bold and uncompromising allies in resisting the drive for world supremacy by those whose Prophet is Marx.

This commendation on the Western side is answered on the side of Islam with a declaration to the effect that:

> . . . Islam is one of the three great monotheistic religions now engaged in the fight for the souls and minds of free men against the rising tide of atheistic historical materialism.

Saudi Arabia's Minister of Finance likewise asserted that:

> The United States can have confidence in our mutually beneficial dealings, because our religion and our law are strongly opposed to communism and because our word is our bond.[3]

It goes without saying that so far as Saudi Arabia is concerned the Aramco Concession Agreement is interpreted as agreeing fully with the *sharī'a*, which still constitutes the basis of all jurisprudence in that country. It is equally plain, not only that the Americans, as the second party, reject that basis as heartily as Saudi Arabia must surely and hotly repudiate the secularized background of modern Western law, but that the oil concession at which the contract is aimed must itself be totally inimical to any such sacred foundation. Here then are Christian and Muslim clasping hands across the bridge of a common hypocrisy. Probably neither partner is fully conscious of the pretence on its own side or on that of the other contracting party; but it is too much to ask us to see this as a case of perfect innocence. Neither the American oil experts nor the Saudi Arabian government can shut their eyes to the tragic and apparently inescapable process of secularization which, with the intrusion of Western oil interests and the outbreak among the Saudi Arabians of a pernicious 'gold-lust' going hand in hand with it, has taken hold of a country until recently wellnigh hermetically sealed off from the outer world. Yet we are asked to believe that these allies are called and chosen for the task of building a dam against 'the rising tide of atheist materialism'!

If one may speak of this as an instance of hypocrisy—and in the sphere of commercial and economic interests it is perhaps understandable enough and only to be expected—the root of the thing is an obstinate failure to apprehend, which in a most damaging way likewise continues to afflict Christian theology and the Christian Church. It is no exaggeration to say that even in the middle of this twentieth century the Church has pretty well no suspicion of the degree of revolution which the rise of modern science and technology implies for her faith and order, her life and work and her position within, and approach to, the modern world. True, there are signs of an awakening, thanks especially to the profound renewal of our theological thinking, set in motion by Karl Barth. In various countries of the European continent, in Great Britain and in the United States as well as in some of the Asian Churches, there are voices—lonely voices still, it is true—with the courage to state the problem in sharp terms. Above all in Germany, owing to the complete breaking up of her cultural traditions which has confronted that country within a few decades, first with the National Socialist revolution and then with the catastrophic effects of the Second World War and the Communist occupation of East Germany, the lead has been taken in reasoned appraisal of this question. Bonhoeffer's *Letters and Papers from Prison*, in which he utters his prophecy of a 'religionless Christianity', do influence current ecumenical discussion. Among those associated with the Evangelical Academies in Germany the thought of the young Marx is being considered afresh; whilst the situation of the Church in East Germany is leading to a fundamental re-thinking of what the Gospel means in face of Communist atheism.

Yet however gratifying such signs of a deep re-orientation of the Church and its theology may be, these swallows still do not make a summer. One point of real significance is that all this heart-searching is not confined to theologians; there are also eminent physicists intensively involved with it—among them the German atomic physicist and philosopher, Carl Friedrich von Weizsäcker. In his various writings he explains in his brilliant fashion how modern science and technology have come to assume the place previously occupied by religion and the Church; and furthermore he witnesses impressively to the dire straits, spiritually speaking, in which the Christian physicist finds himself caught by the complex of ethical and theological questions that his subject involves. This might not be so bad, were it not that, as von Weizsäcker is obliged to admit, the Churches and theology leave the modern physicist most deplorably in the lurch—despite the fact that Christian theology is itself responsible for the rise of modern science.

> The pathos of endless progress which drives modern physics and technology on transfers a predicate of God to the world and turns towards time as no pagan has ever done, but as the Christian turns to that eternity which has appeared in the midst of history.

He then ventures to ask whether the 'wonders of modern technics' are not part of those works to which Christ alluded when he said that we should also do the works that he did and greater works than these. This reference to John 14:12 he himself describes as blasphemous; yet the fact that the secularization of Christianity—which is in accordance with God's will—has led to unprecedented power over the world forces him to propound this question.[4] It is the same physicist who is driven to this conclusion, who yet at the same time perceives with devastating clarity the nihilistic tendency of modern science.

The Christian faith in the modern world will lose more and more of its redeeming power and will become more and more evidently a salt which has lost its savour, unless it can summon up the courage —'blasphemous' or no—to risk facing the hazardous encounter with the very 'atheism' and 'nihilism' which the preaching of the Gospel has itself produced. That is the 'needle's eye' through which the theology of the twentieth century must pass if it is to enter the kingdom of God. To decide thus—and the decision will certainly mean leaving behind many of the 'treasures' of religion and many traditional postures—is the only thing that will enable the Church to answer at all adequately the question which modern, thoroughly secularized man sees set before him. Only then, instead of falling back on hopelessly antiquated and untenable religious propositions, will she have the nerve to meet the challenge of Communism with open eyes; and only then will her judgment upon it be truly redemptive.

At first sight it looks as though it is primarily the Church in the West which has to deal with these so very exacting and complicated problems. Is not the setting of the Asian and African Churches a world in which the religious pattern is still overwhelmingly predominant; and is it not therefore their primary task to enter into a fruitful dialogue with that religious environment? Has it not been cause for dismay that the missionary enterprise has so often failed to take any profound or serious interest in the religions amid which the Gospel has been proclaimed, and is that not one reason why some Churches planted in the mission field have found themselves living in a cramping isolation? One could of course argue elaborately and with passion as to why Church and missions should bestir themselves, should have an intense concern for, and make a systematic study of, the growth and life of religion in Asia and Africa. Yet I would myself say most emphatically that for the Churches of the non-Western world no less than for the Churches in the West what has first priority here and now is this business of secularization and of our encounter with it. The lesson of China's recent history certainly lends weight to this argument. As yet, the missionary movement can scarcely be said to know its ABC in this matter, let alone to understand the full extent of what it implies. If it did, then the Communist revolution in China would have been sufficient in itself to bring about a spiritual revolution in missionary thinking. Except for a few sharply critical voices, however, one notices little or nothing of that kind—unless the emotional shock administered to the home base and the need to look around for other mission fields are to be confused with genuine re-orientation. As regards the priority, there is another powerful consideration which forces one to the same conclusion: namely, the fact that the really strategic points for the Church in the discharge of her apostolic obligation lie in the processes of 'rapid social change' in the non-Western world and not in those areas where the traditions still maintain an uninterrupted life. Whether secretly or plainly for all to see, it is precisely within those torrents of change that the energies and impulses making for secularization are at work. There is a real danger that the Churches in Asia and Africa might continue to lead an existence, so to speak, on the side-lines of this strategic highway; and for this there are two reasons. A chief means of incursion into the 'great society' is the way of political emancipation and of economic and social change-overs leading to a modern 'welfare state'; but nearly everywhere in the non-Western countries the Christian Churches form tiny minorities with little part in the business. Secondly, these Churches—with the exception of the Church in Japan—generally speaking have their roots in a rural society and show little awareness of how vitally important are those tumultuous processes of urbanization and industrialization which within a matter of years can uproot settled traditions and consign them to the scrap-heap. Even if these Churches were on very much more familiar terms with their religious environment than they are and even if they were to be in much closer contact with it, there would still be no guarantee whatever that they would be likely to deploy their modest forces in a really justifiable and proper way.

There is another point which lends even more weight to the contention that the non-Western Churches too ought to focus their theological reflection on the encounter with secularization. These

Churches are an outcome of the Western missionary movement, which spread across the world during the same period and to a great extent by the very same paths as the expanding capitalism and technology of the West. Oriental nationalism has not stinted itself in exposing that coincidence and putting it under the spotlight of its criticism, yet seldom in a manner which touches the core of the problem involved. The Christian missions too have in general evaded the problem; and when the attacks of nationalism have simply forced it upon them, they have in most instances left the Churches in the mission field without a sufficient and radical answer to it. The matter needs to be stated boldly and squarely dealt with; and it is high time that this were done. Take for an example the remarkable development of Pietism. That movement played a most influential part in the growth and spread of missionary work during not only the eighteenth but also the nineteenth century. At the same time German Pietism was a vital factor in the genesis of romanticism and vehement nationalism, which in their turn were the fore-runners of irrational racism and the crypto-pagan 'myth of the twentieth century'. Side by side with that there is a line running from Pietism to the origins of Marxism itself. Friedrich Engels, co-founder with Marx of that ideology, came from a Pietist family and himself underwent a genuine conversion to atheistic materialism. Naturally enough, the missionaries who took the Gospel overseas were not themselves aware of these various connections—still less the people in Asia and Africa who were converted under their influence. Today, however, a Church which fails to take serious account of the fact that in non-Western countries as elsewhere the modern secularist ideologies often derive from the Christian faith stands blind to their challenge and impotent to meet it.

Here we come at last to the heart of the matter. A confrontation with the non-Christian religions will not touch the root of the problem unless it be preceded and prepared for by thoroughgoing, theological consideration of the nature of religion—that is, in the revealing light of the Word of God. We return once more to the biblical analysis essayed in the second and third chapters. The creative activity of God's Word exposes the religion of the Gentiles as *nihil*, 'nothingness'. The tower of Babel, apotheosis of the religion of cosmic totality, is not completed, because the Lord intervenes. This is the merciful judgment proclaimed through the preaching of the Gospel to the ends of the earth, among the peoples scattered over the face of the earth. They learn that from the very outset their religion has been doomed to failure. The 'Christianized' Gentiles and barbarians of the West have taken this lesson thoroughly to heart, have applied the disclosure to all religion. That is not to say that in so doing the West has surrendered the resolve 'to build ourselves a city and a tower. . . .' But a change of crucial importance has none the less been made; for the second part of that phrase has been relinquished. Men have seen through the illusion, have given up the pretension of primeval religion that this could still be a tower 'with its top in the heavens'. It is a reductive move without parallel and one which gives to the activity of building a city and a tower—dispossessed now of its ultimate religious purpose and meaning—a kind of obsessive intensity springing from the conviction that man is engaged here in an impracticable enterprise, unfinishing and unfinishable—but which for that very reason is for ever exacting the toll of an impossible, unfinishing and unfinishable effort on his part. That is the glory and the desperation, the greatness and the wretchedness too, of the technocracy which has ousted ontocracy. The spell of a divine universe is broken; upon every temple there falls the devastating judgment that it has been 'made by man'. Even modern science has to do simply with a 'man-made' universe. It moves among the stars and probes the inmost secrets of the atom; and in all this man comes face to face with himself.

A Christian theology which has not yet taken to heart the full implications of this turn of events will all the time be approaching the non-Christian religions from precisely the wrong angle. So long as Western Christian civilization itself continued to be modelled partly on a religious pattern, the religious approach was inevitable and there was some point in it; but in the secularized situation of the twentieth-century West we need to clear away, once and for all, any false idea of the Gospel of the crucified and risen Lord as having the character of a religious message. The tower of Babel has *no* top; and it is not the business of Christian theology to fill that vacuum, either by providing the unfinished tower with a Christian top or by showing that the top which the non-Christian religions are trying to build in fact largely resembles the Christian one, so that the most it could require would be a Christian 'finishing touch'.

No: the point of encounter between the Christian faith and the non-Christian religions does not lie at the top, but at the base; or rather, it lies in co-operation of Christians with non-Christians in a concerted effort to 'build ourselves a city and a tower. . . .' Time was when the people of Israel had to do this, and wanted to do it, entirely by themselves; they had to try and construct an order of life which would not be a reproduction of the city and tower of Babel, but one in which they alone among all the nations of the world— chosen, it is true, only to act for the moment on behalf of the rest— were to bear the full consequences of God's intervention, as a result of which mankind 'left off building the city'. Israel's way of life was to be a 'torso', the unfinished experiment of a people bound for the city and the tower which they could not build for themselves, but which they were to receive as a gift from the Lord. They conjoined in one eclectic whole all manner of stones for the building, fragments hauled out of Babel, wrenched out of the harmonious perfection, the divine totality, of the ontocratic pattern by which men had set out to build in Babel. This edifice of theirs, exuberantly haphazard and impossible to classify, knocked together out of an astonishing variety of bits and pieces, was the Torah—not an end in itself, but an object-lesson to the nations of the world in building a city and a tower *without* a top in the heavens. The Torah was fulfilled in Jesus Christ; and this fulfilled Torah was proclaimed among the Gentiles. Greek, Roman and barbarian alike ceased to build their city and their tower and from loose stones and broken fragments started to piece together a new whole—a structure so disjointed, so provisional and so completely lacking the final authority of a blue print, of a single architect and master builder, that it had to be subjected again and again to radical revision, as parts tumbled in upon one another or were deliberately broken off.

Now the non-Western civilizations have begun to learn this lesson too; they too have left off building their city. For them too the myth of the top in heaven is exploded—the myth of the heavenly emperor and of the sacred cosmo-social order: the myth of the *sanātana dharma*, of the divine Veda and the sacred caste system: the myth of the all-embracing authority of the *sharī'a* and the absolute necessity of the Caliphate. Here too, of course, much energy is from time to time expended in efforts to 'achieve the top'; and new ideologies, new myths, will essay to fill the vacuum. Nevertheless they will be no more than attempts which carry the seed of their own failure within them, simply because there is no going back on the break with the past which has already occurred. Here too technocracy is taking the place of ontocracy; and, just as in the West, so here technocratic man will try to 'achieve the top' with new and incomparably more efficient resources. All the same, modern technocracy—unlike ontocracy—bears about with it, like a shadow, the knowledge that in acting thus it is attempting the impossible; for the very 'heaven' which the top is required to reach is 'man-made' too.

Yet building in this way gives opportunity for the Christians to join with the non-Christians in getting down to work together. It means that in genuine solidarity the Christian can help to bring up stones for the building, prised from the structure of the non-Christian religions: that once the religious myth has been blown away, there is room for the traditions of the non-Christian cultures to bring forth their treasures: that there can take place a new and noble and creative work of reinterpreting the past: that free and proper use can be made of the rich stores of wisdom and experience deposited within the history of African and Asian cultures. Here are opportunities in inexhaustible abundance for the Christians to steep themselves no less completely than their non-Christian fellows and compatriots in the values, spiritual and material, social and individual, philosophical and psychological, political and economic, of the non-Western civilizations. In that way a Christian can make as vital a contribution to the renewal of Islamic or of Indian civilization as any Muslim or Hindu.

Of course such possibilities can only be turned to good account where the impact of secularizing factors has already made a breach in the totalitarian authority of the sacred tradition. Yet even that is not enough. It is at least equally important that the Christian Church has a sound theology of secularization, enabling it to take the fullest advantage of such scope as may in fact exist. The struggle for 'religious liberty', however necessary that may be, is being fought on the wrong front if it is simply and solely a campaign for guarantees of freedom for the Christian 'religion'. That only serves to keep alive in the minds of adherents of the other religions—as well as among the Church's own members—the fatal notion that what Christianity must be after is the setting up of a religious community. The best guarantee of real 'religious liberty' is in the readiness of Christians to make common cause with all those movements and individuals who wish to promote liberty as such—liberation, that is to say, from the fetters of 'sacred' tradition, together with the renewal of society in the direction of a truly secular and man-made order of life.

In this age of ours 'Christianization' can only mean that peoples become involved in the onward movement of Christian history. The preaching of the Gospel takes place in the context of that expanding history and at the same time supplies the freedom of decision and the eschatological outlook which drive it onward and deliver it from the curse of ideologies. That is the setting for a Christian encounter with the non-Western world. The Church belongs to the present and the future, not to the past; and so it is not from the past that she can ever hope to capture the non-Western world. It just is an indisputable fact that the non-Christian religions at the present time are subject to drastic change and find themselves faced with the necessity for drastic re-orientation. No matter whether that inner ferment expresses itself in pro-Western or anti-Western sentiments, it is in any case a sure sign that the revolutionary history of the West has begun to permeate these non-Western organisms. Modernist movements within the various non-Western religions express this mostly by their current determination to put 'the Middle Ages' behind them. That is a striking example of reinterpreting the past in terms of Western history. The criteria by which these shocks and tremors now happening to the non-Christian religions are appraised derive very largely from our Christian perspective and our own interpretation of Christian history. The missionary, Alexander Duff, when he introduced the English system of Christian education at about the middle of the last century, hoped and firmly expected that this was planting 'a mine under the rock of Hinduism'. It has recently—and quite rightly—been said that the mine has indeed exploded, but the rock has turned out to be a sandbag. The crucial question which Duff failed to answer is: granted that you can pulverize the rock of Hinduism, what is to take its place? Not only were his expectations unfulfilled; they were based on false premises. What, in fact, is 'Hinduism'? India is now a secular, democratic state, with the triad of the French Revolution written into her constitution; but there is not the ghost of a chance that this state will become a 'Christian' one; on the contrary, its whole atmosphere is pervaded by the spirit of Hinduism. Certainly one may speak of 'missionary failure', if one conceives the ultimate purpose of the mission to be replacing Hinduism with Christianity. The notion in itself, however, is an impossible one; for Christianity just is no longer in a position to fulfil such a rôle, even supposing some miracle were to tumble Hinduism in ruins tomorrow. The one and only thing that Christianity could offer to India, should such a miracle occur, would be a fully fledged, but secular, democratic state; and that is precisely what India has created already of her own initiative. 'Hinduism' is not a timeless entity; it is much more like a river the current of which has now reached a state of tremendous acceleration, bringing the Hindu pattern of life into the dynamic onrush of Christian history. It is possible, of course, that Hinduism will be swept away by a technocratic ideology. It is also possible that India will remain Hindu for the rest of time. That might be a matter of life and death to the Hindus, but it is certainly not so for the Church. In preaching the Gospel she is not concerned with the question whether—or for how long—such and such a 'religion' may survive, but simply with the future of man, no matter if he be Hindu, agnostic, Communist or nihilist. In any case this question of the future of man cannot by-pass the questions of life and death which our atomic age presents to the world of today. A religion which seeks to avoid that confrontation may be filled to the brim with religious values and experiences, but it is doomed beyond reprieve to belong to a bygone age.

This view of the non-Christian religions as timeless entities is exemplified again in Lord Cromer's famous dictum that 'Islam cannot be reformed . . . reformed Islam is Islam no longer, it is something else.'[5] This thesis would tie Islam, a priori, to an immutable pattern. Yet nobody can prevent the Muslims from radically revising their social and religious system and calling this creation of theirs the true Islam. It may well be that the Turkish revolution will have its imitators; but it is just as likely that Islam will prove able and willing to adapt itself, however drastically, to the requirements of modern society. Through the impact of the West Islam is already involved in modern history. The mysterious thing about Christian history is precisely this: that when an alien civilization is drawn into this 'sphere of influence', it becomes liable to a process of transmutation which Christianity itself has undergone and which is apparently foreign to its original structure. Somewhat after the manner of the Reformation, modern Islamic thought is seeking to reinterpret Islamic history by going behind the Muslim 'Middle Ages' and getting to grips with 'original Islam'. The need to justify Islam at the bar of modern civilization is forcing it to re-orientate itself by the example of Christian history and along the same lines.

4. FAVOURITE CONCEPTS TESTED

The Church proclaims the Gospel in the context of this historical meeting between a Christianity in its phase of twentieth century Western civilization and the non-Western civilizations and religions. Whether they will or no, these are entering upon an epoch in which 'religion'—in the traditional sense of a dominating social pattern— can no longer sustain itself, or at least can only do so at the cost of existing in a perpetual state of crisis. In a dynamic situation of that sort, what is to be the criterion of a truly 'indigenous Church'? From the very beginning, the Churches which the missionary outreach of Western Christianity has planted in the non-Western world have had to endure the odium of their foreignness. For this the Western missions are very much to blame because, generally speaking, they have been all too easily satisfied with exporting duplicate versions of their own particular type of Christianity. Furthermore, they have been so intensely patriarchal in their solicitude and such dutiful organizers that they have left very little room indeed—again, generally speaking—for the duplicate Churches to develop a pattern of their own or to follow their own inspiration freely. Above all, there has been, on the part of Western missions as a whole, a serious failure to grasp the paramount significance of Western domination on the one hand and of the rising tide of oriental nationalism on the other. However one would have to go very thoroughly into all the circumstances in order to do justice to this question. We must let it rest at that and confine ourselves to asking what qualifications the Church should possess at the present time if it is to deserve the epithet 'truly indigenous'. Is our norm to be the position occupied for centuries past by, say, the Anglican Church and the Free Churches in Great Britain or by the Evangelical Church in Germany? It would be difficult, as anyone must admit, to find better examples of Churches which have come to be part of the national life. In both missionary circles and among those of the non-Western Churches which have severely criticized Western missionary policy, the position of the Western Churches within their own countries has been taken, though for the most part implicitly, to be the rule and guide for all. The ideally 'indigenous' Indian Church is a church as deeply rooted in Indian life as are the British Churches in the life of Great Britain.

To apply this measuring-rod is justifiable enough, so far as it goes; and one cannot get round it by pointing to the fact that it is precisely this excessive identification of the Western Churches with Western society that now threatens to deprive the salt of its savour, or even by asking us to remember the tragedy of Germanized Christianity under the Nazi régime. The risks and temptations that we run by indigenizing the Church may be enormous; but they can never be an excuse for making it into something foreign or alien. A Church of India which is truly indigenous will be exposed to the dangers of syncretism, nationalism, racialism and cultural absorption to a very much greater degree than one which continues to bear the heavy stamp of its foreign origin. The fact remains that the Church of India can properly fulfil her calling only when she meets the challenge and the risk in the freedom of her faith and not under the shelter of any Western defences.

Yet none of these considerations gets to the heart of the matter, because they overlook the fact that 'an indigenous Church' is a category of Christian history. The Church, having its citizenship in heaven, is stranger and sojourner upon the earth. But the Church has not miraculously fallen down from heaven either; it comes into being in the course of 'Church history' and 'world history', through the proclamation of the Gospel from Jerusalem even to the ends of the earth and in the midst of an expanding 'Christianity'. The Western Churches themselves are all foreign in origin, seeing that Church history was a movement from Jew to Greek and from Greek to barbarian. It is not simply that the Church has been 'indigenized' among the Western nations; for it would be nearer the truth to say that they have been formed and transformed by that Christian history in which they have played their part and out of which even the most determined outbursts of modern nihilism are unable to draw them back into a pre-Christian paganism. During the last two centuries missionary expansion and the spread of Western civilization have gone together. Because the non-Western nations are now taking their share in Christian history therefore, the criterion for what constitutes a truly indigenous Church in the non-Western world can only be settled in relation to the present phase of Christian history. The Church herself stands within the process of cultural interchange and indeed is actively contributing to it. Obviously the tremendous efforts which a lot of Western missionaries now make to see the Church thoroughly rooted in indigenous cultures are frequently crossed by the impact of the 'great society' and the rise of national states, in which many local communities find themselves jerked out of their isolation and tossed into the melting-pot of modern civilization. It is a radical operation for which the indigenous Churches as a whole were ill-prepared. Whilst Western missions are blamed on the one hand for having introduced a 'foreign style', they have on the other hand been guilty of failing to realize how rapidly the non-Western world needs to develop in order to catch up with the West. The contradictory nature of these accusations illustrates a contradiction in the character of the Western impact and its consequences. Generally speaking, the non-Western world has not been at all bothered about the 'foreignness' of Western civilization, so long as it was simply a question of taking over those elements of it thought to be desirable. Many of the most vital factors which have disrupted the non-Western world from the beginning of the nineteenth century have been foreign, although without them the rise of independent national states in Asia and Africa would have been simply inconceivable. There is a real danger that a Church beset with too tender a conscience about her foreign origin and character may waste her energies in adapting herself to aspects of an indigenous culture already consigned to the past and doomed to become out of date. The critical question that in our time faces the world-wide Church is whether she is able and ready to serve her Lord amidst the needs of such a rapidly changing world as ours. The problems which the Church has to face in Tokyo or Hong Kong are vastly different from, say, the concerns of a village congregation in South India or the question of what missionary approach should be adopted towards a recently discovered Papuan tribe in the interior of New Guinea. But whatever the circumstances, the Church and her missions cannot hope to serve the interests of a village or tribal community unless they make full allowance for the fact that in principle the twentieth century no longer countenances the isolated community and that therefore one of the most urgent lines of Christian service is to make ready, materially and spiritually, for the arrival of modern civilization.

Closely bound up with this is the question whether there is a need for an 'Eastern theology'. It is obvious enough that the Asian and African Churches have been theologically educated so far by a more or less straightforward transference of Western theological ways of thought. No doubt there is an urgent need for creative work on the part of Asian and African theologians—and laymen could surely be prominent among them—in which they would squarely face up to their environment with its various cultural and religious currents and would think out the great questions of doctrine and ethics in a fresh and appropriate way. If this were to happen at a really profound level, there would naturally come to the fore some aspects of the biblical message which have been much neglected in the West; and some new heresies would be formulated too. The idea of an 'Eastern theology' suggests a number of possibilities. The Eastern Orthodox Churches have guarded and maintained the tradition of the ancient Church in a manner quite foreign to the development of theology in the West. It may very well be that through ecumenical contacts with them the Asian and African Churches will find the Eastern Orthodox tradition amazingly relevant to their own particular problems—and discover too that Syrian Orthodox theology in India, or even the Ethiopian Orthodox Church, can make a fruitful contribution in the meeting with the non-Christian world. One might recall, in another direction, the tremendous conflict which raged in the early Church over the powerful and seductive attraction of syncretism, Gnosticism, neo-Platonism and Manicheism. The present-day situation of the Church vis-à-vis modern Hinduism and Buddhism shows a good many points of similarity to that early Christian period. Here then is a highly promising field of investigation for Indian, or Japanese, theology.

Yet none of these considerations really constitutes a sufficient argument for pleading the necessity of a distinctive type of 'Eastern theology', as it were, in its own right. The Eastern Orthodox Churches have long been forcibly isolated within the Hindu and Islamic worlds —and for some decades past in the Communist world too. Their dogmatic traditions have been conserved in such fixed and static forms that only the most dynamic reinterpretation of their heritage could turn it into a seminal and vital means of encounter with the non-Christian world of today. So far as the challenge of modern Gnosticism is concerned, no answer made to that is likely to be feasible which fails to take into account the solid exchanges of Western theology with German idealism and its twentieth-century successors.

It would seem on the whole wiser to let go the idea of a specifically 'Eastern' theology. As ecumenical discussion grows amid this planetary world, what we need rather is a broad variety of cross-fertilization. Even now it is no longer possible to hold satisfactory dialogue with modern nihilist and existentialist philosophies without taking into consideration their affinity to Buddhist philosophical systems—an affinity readily acknowledged in those quarters—or without taking heed of the growing influence of Buddhist literature and Buddhist missions in Western countries. What is indeed possible is that a clear exposition of views by a Japanese theologian, with modern Zen Buddhism in mind, could prove extremely helpful to Western Christianity; just as Japanese theology in its turn might well hail Karl Barth's dogmatics, not least as an outstanding contribution to its own dialogue with a non-Christian environment. If opportunities for mutual contact should open up, the Churches of China and East Germany could be of excellent service to one another in the theological confrontation with atheistic Communism; and the Russian Orthodox Church could learn some crucial lessons from them both.

It is time the missionary encounter were set firmly at the centre of our theological concern. That—and not some independent kind of 'Eastern' theology—offers the real way of escape from the narrow limitations of a one-sided 'Western' theological tradition. A shift of that sort, which for the theology of the twentieth century will be tantamount to another Reformation, is urgently needed and will require a concerted ecumenical effort. In particular 'the history of religions', which has so far remained a marginal extra to the corpus of general theological studies, will have to undergo some far-reaching structural alterations. It will have to concentrate on first studying and then learning to face up to the entirely new situation into which the Western impact has precipitated the non-Western world; and from that vantage-point it must look out in two directions. First it must contribute to the effort which the non-Western world is now making at a new self-evaluation; it must enter into this discussion and must help rethink the past, present and future of the non-Christian religions; it must play both a critical and a prophetic rôle, stepping into the breach in order to ask the basic questions which those religions themselves either suppress or ignore. Then, on the other side, it could prove a powerful stimulus to Christian theology by insistently relating its every aspect to the questions thrown up by the non-Christian world.

In this planetary world the encounter with non-Christian ways of life and thought belongs at the very heart of Christian theology. Now that the unity of mankind is something actually within our purview, we simply must be up to date enough to bring the *whole* world into *all* our thinking, whether it be in the field of dogmatics or of ethics or in matters pastoral and liturgical—just as the Apostle Paul had in mind the whole compass of the world, as it was known in his day, when he envisaged the *whole* creation 'groaning in travail together until now' (Rom. 8:22). This is not merely a question of a wider horizon, geographically speaking. In our time anyone can see for himself what Paul divined by the searching light of revelation: that this is a world full of 'a-theists' (Eph. 2:12). The effect of secularization has been to make the 'groaning in travail' of the non-Christian world dramatically audible. If 'the history of religions' as an academic discipline should remain deaf to that, it will not only become sterile and useless to theology and to the Church, but will very quickly end up as a quaint museum-piece and nothing more.

One must also set against that background the undertaking urged upon the Church and her missions above all in the writings of J. Merle Davis: that is to say, the 'comprehensive approach'.

> Under this approach, evangelization is cure of sick bodies, of broken-down, inefficient, and eroded farms, of illiteracy, of insufficient and unbalanced diet, unsanitary homes, impure drinking water, of a subsistence level of existence, of filthy villages, of the moral, mental and spiritual stagnation of corrupt practices and conditions. Every effort upon this wide and comprehensive front of Christian service is a part of the Evangel and is required to enable the individual to reach the fulness of the stature which is in Christ.[6]

The task here laid upon evangelism is so fundamental and the vision unfolded so direct a consequence of biblical prophecy concerning the *shalom* and the *pleroma*—the fullness of living of the New Jerusalem—that for this if for no other reason we are in duty bound to realize what it involves for the present course of Christianity in a planetary world.

What we need in particular to ask is whether that kind of vision can be preserved intact beyond the limited dimensions within which the distinguished authority mentioned above has developed it. What I have in mind here is not the justifiable emphasis which this programme lays on rural communities, but a particular slant it gives to rural reconstruction as a bulwark against 'secularization'.

> In view of the rapidly growing secularization of all modern life which is defeating the religious interpretations of non-Christian as well as Christian cultures, the comprehensive program of the Church takes on an enormous significance. . . .
> There is no greater issue facing Christians in the modern world than the question, 'How can we bring under the aegis of the Church education, health, recreation, livelihood and the other areas of life which are now being left to the secularizing influence of government and private agencies?' To abandon these areas to the domination of irreligious forces and to fail to make them vehicles of the Christian witness amounts to a betrayal of God as Creator of all and In-dweller in all of life.[7]

Within the restricted circle of a relatively isolated and as yet only superficially disturbed village community, this approach might seem to be not only the obvious way for the Church to demonstrate that she is the body of Christ but also—up to a point—a practicable one. Much more, however, is being claimed than this. The comprehensive approach is to throw up a defensive wall against the secularist threat to the whole of modern life and against domination by the forces of irreligion—and that in the name of God, the Creator. The whole of life must be kept—or brought back—under the aegis of the Church. Thus the Church is put into the position of being the guardian or patron of religion vis-à-vis the secular power of government or of private agencies.

The idea of the comprehensive approach is sound in itself and is, of course, a genuinely biblical idea; but one cannot help thinking that if it is based on the sort of claim described above, it is bound not only to degenerate into a fine sounding, empty slogan, but to give rise to a distorted view of the Church's calling in modern history. It may not be intended or have even been contemplated; but the strict implication here is surely that if the world is currently being secularized, that must be a satanically inspired error from which we must, if possible, retreat into a kind of mediaevalism, with the Church patronizing every sphere of life. The crucial fact which seems to be completely overlooked here is that the comprehensive approach cannot hope to accomplish anything at all, unless it comprehensively and intensively resorts to every modern means available, and that these not only owe their existence to the 'secularization' but effectively promote it. The 'cure of sick bodies' makes a backward village community absolutely dependent on the resources of modern medical science, which are among the greatest achievements of our secularized world; it brings down the death-rate and upsets the traditional stability of social life; it creates fresh needs and fresh wants; it lays the village open to a money economy and the world market—the sole agencies through which a 'cured body' can go on providing itself with the means of enjoying in the future the same standard—or, if possible, even a better standard—of physical security. The fight against illiteracy opens the door to the immensely powerful influence of the modern press, to education, to every form of secular propaganda, which grows all the more fascinating and desirable when the 'aegis of the Church' is employed to keep it at a safe distance. These few examples must suffice. Why do we suddenly launch our criticism when the modern welfare state and all sorts of private agencies make use of exactly the same means? What mysterious religious powers does the Church possess that alone beneath her aegis can a penicillin injection and the alphabet become the instrument of God the Creator, whilst in other hands they would appear to be deadly poison? Or does the Church shuffle off responsibility for all the harmful though accidental consequences that her 'approach' may unexpectedly produce on to the secular agencies who then, with their planning and welfare programmes, just have to do their best to organize the improved standard of living, migration to the cities, addiction to a money economy and so forth, in such a way that they can still retain some measure of control over the accelerating processes of modern life?

It would be most unfair just to use these objections as a stick to beat the idea of the comprehensive approach. If my remarks are critical, they are only meant to spare the concept of this approach the frustration which must inevitably arise as its basic weakness is exposed by its contradictory results. Obviously we have here a good illustration of the muddle and obtuseness inherent in a great deal of our missionary thinking. Of course we are in dire need of a comprehensive approach to the enormous problems confronting us in this technocratic era. All the more reason therefore why we should resist at any price the temptation to rest content with solutions that point, not towards the future, but towards a past which can never return.

The truly comprehensive task of the Church was admirably expressed in ecumenical discussion some years ago now, in the proposition that the whole Church must bring the whole Gospel to the whole world. That provides a genuinely eschatological perspective; for the 'wholeness' spoken of here is the 'wholeness' which goes hand in hand with the 'end of the ages'. At the same time it is a fully historical perspective. The Church is raised up and increased down the centuries; the preaching of the Gospel does not begin with us, in the here and now, but it goes on in a world already deeply affected by Christian history. Truly ecumenical thinking will of necessity be truly historical thinking too; and thinking that is truly historical is bound to view the past and the present in the light of the future. The period of Western missionary activity overseas is drawing to a close; but that can only mean that now the 'whole Church' throughout the world takes over full responsibility for the vision, the dynamic initiative and the historical vocation which up to now the Western missions have been implementing. As for the terms 'Western' and 'missions', they are due for a thorough re-examination. It may well be that they will not survive this scrutiny and must be thrown out in favour of other terms which can better express the commitments of the world Church in this present age. Already the organization, methods and outlook of Western missions are being subjected to intense criticism; and it seems very likely that within the context of ecumenical discussion and a growing experience of ecumenical co-operation we shall get a fundamental rethinking and indeed trans-formation of the Western missionary enterprise in all its aspects. If, as a result, we can succeed in detaching the categories 'Western' and 'missions' from the emotional atmosphere of personal and national prestige which threatens to engulf them, there should be no objection to the continued use of these terms. As a matter of fact, it may well turn out that all attempts to replace them amount to no more than playing about with words and thus dodging the real problem; for whatever we do, we shall still be faced with the inescapable reality of the fact that the Lord goes on working in history. The Gospel is preached from Jerusalem to the ends of the earth; world history is *en route* from Stone Age to Atomic Era; in and through that history Christianity moves on.

5. ECUMENICAL THEOLOGY OF HISTORY

The sober truth is that ecumenical thinking has so far hardly even begun to move in this direction. Indeed the age in which we live would appear to be particularly ill-fitted for seeing clearly and steadily what the historical implications are. In Asia and Africa the Churches have all their work cut out to steer a course of their own amid the surging currents of anti-Western nationalism and the struggle to be rid of all the fetters of colonialism and crypto-colonialism. Great Britain and continental Europe are still in the throes of the change-over to a post-colonial era, whilst the United States is taken up with the demand made upon her by her new-found global responsibilities, embracing 'West' and 'East' alike. It does seem a highly inopportune moment for asking Christian theology anywhere to risk tackling here and now such a delicate issue as the logical connection between 'Westernization' and the new planetary mode of human existence on the one hand and evangelization on the other. It is perhaps much like pushing one's fist into a nest of hornets!

Yet one must maintain with the utmost emphasis that the time for such an enterprise is precisely now; and that it demands a united, ecumenical effort to think theologically and thus to be thoroughly prepared and fully equipped for the task, whatever the hazards may be. If in our theological reflection we ignore this, if we fight shy of the risks involved or try to leave it over for another generation to settle, then the problems will simply overtake our theology and find it unprepared, naked and defenceless. But that is not all; for an evasion of that sort means that Christian theology would be running away from a responsibility which the period of world history on which we have now entered lays upon it ineluctably. The realms of the human spirit have their own law of a *horror vacui*; and should theology permit a vacuum here, other ideologies will possess and fill it— ideologies which have borrowed their apparatus from Christian theology itself and now use it to compete with the Christian Church or to express their fierce hostility towards it. It is evident enough, surely, that every ideology, be it secular or religious, which aims to proselytize the world nowadays works to an explicit or implicit philosophy of history, with itself as the fulfilment of the historical world-process, conducting mankind to the final goal of global unity and peace. Even modern Buddhism, although it alleges the total vacuity and meaninglessness of all earthly events, can only recommend itself to modern nations and to modern man by thoroughly historicizing its message. It is equally evident however that these philosophies of history derive from the biblical, prophetic way of thinking and yet for that very reason are powerless to implement their claims to give human history an ultimate meaning.

Consequently there is desperate need for a truly ecumenical theology of history. The Christian Church has to do for our age what at a turning-point in world history Augustine did for his own and for succeeding generations: namely, to interpret past and present, discerning the signs of the times in the prophetic light of the dawning Day of the Lord. This the Church can only do—as Augustine did in his own day—with the intellectual and philosophical equipment which the twentieth century affords and with the historical and scientific knowledge now placed at her disposal. That means that the best theological approach to history must inevitably be a 'Christian philosophy of history' which is 'contemporary' in the sense of being highly provisional and relative. All genuine theology shows a full awareness of this, but addresses itself notwithstanding to the task now set before it, in faith and hope.

A sound theology of history is no merely theoretical business, something 'all right for theologians'. It has an extremely practical relevance and urgency, above all to two of the most thorny problems facing this and future generations: the struggle for world peace and the struggle for world-wide prosperity—two things which belong inseparably together.

One indispensable condition for ensuring peace in the world is that there should be developed an international law applicable to, and accepted by, mankind as a whole. What exactly is international law?

> Public international law in its historical evolution is essentially the product of European Christian civilization, and for the greater part of western civilization at that.[8]

Thus it is an undeniable fact that the existing body of international law as it stands today:

> is not only the product of the conscious activity of the European mind, but has also drawn its vital essence from a common source of European beliefs, and in both of these aspects it is mainly of western European origin.[9]

No nation outside Europe made any essential contribution to this development. The new nations, as they joined the international community, readily adopted the rules which they found already governing inter-state relationships. 'In this respect all nations of the world are linked by a common body of law, which originated in the West, but which has been adopted by the East,' says that distinguished expert, Verzijl; 'and in those common legal ties I see one of the outstanding proofs of the ultimate unity of the human race.'[10]

Obviously this is something more than a scientific statement; it expresses a faith based on a Christian philosophy of history, as that has developed in the West. All the same, it is doubtful whether such a philosophy of history possesses that creative vision which marks its source—marks, that is to say, the really prophetic theology of history; for on two vital points it exhibits a grave weakness. First, the present structure of international law does not enable it to bridge the gulf between the Western countries and Soviet Russia. The United Nations Charter dates from before the atomic era and has already become dangerously obsolete. There is a telling historical analogy which serves to illustrate the dilemma. The Second Lateran Council of A.D. 1139 anathematized the use by Christian knights of the cross-bow *adversus Christianos et Catholicos*; but Christian standards did not apply to heathen or heretic.[11] This new lethal weapon was therefore employed in the Crusades against both Muslim and Byzantine. Toynbee has likened the mediaeval West's invention of the cross-bow to the invention of the atom bomb.[12] Indeed in 1945 the Japanese 'heathen'—like the Muslims before them—discovered by experience that the Christian standards did not apply to them; and the 'heretics' of Communist Russia would presumably suffer the fate of their mediaeval Byzantine predecessors, were it not for the fact that they happen to have mastered the secret of the twentieth century 'cross-bow' for themselves. The consequence is the complete stalemate of the cold war; and neither International Law nor the United Nations Organization, though both spring from the universal perspective of Christianity, is able to break down the curtain of iron.

In the second place, the present structure of International Law is no longer adequate, now that the peoples of Asia and Africa are included within the United Nations. International Law emanated from the 'Christian nations'; but when Turkey was invited to join the

Concert of Europe in the middle of the nineteenth century, 'civiliza-tion' became the new common factor. Since the two world wars this criterion of 'civilized nation' as a basis for membership of the now virtually universal 'family of nations' has been abandoned and replaced, in the United Nations Charter, by the formula 'peace-loving nations'. Seeing that most of the members are poor, technologically backward countries—former colonies, generally speaking—their love for 'peace' naturally entails a strong determination to press for a change in the *status quo* of international relations.

> . . . the new majority demands an international law that will promote the welfare of all and will thus guarantee the possibility of a decent standard of living. The international community is not merely one of peace; it must needs be a welfare community, concerned with the welfare of any one of its members. The world community is bound to become a welfare community, just as the nation state became a welfare state.[13]

There is then a direct link between the question of peace and that other crucial issue, the struggle for universal welfare.

> The French Revolution was the consequence of refusing to adjust existing law to the reasonable requirements of the rising middle classes. Western Europe has learned its lesson since then. When the working class presented itself for admission, this was granted and the law was changed to meet the new needs. In Russia the refusal to change the task of the state and the function of the law to comply with the needs of the working people led to the Soviet Revolution and the 'dictatorship of the proletariat'.
> In a way, class struggle is also waged among the nations. The 'Christian Nations' succeeded in gradually widening their circle to admit others so that the transition to the group of 'Civilized Nations' could take place without any great shocks. Will the 'Civilized Nations' find the courage really to open their 'charmed circle' to those formerly excluded, and to accept graciously the consequences of admitting the larger group of the 'Peace-loving Nations'? That is the fundamental . . . prerequisite for the existence of 'one world', which should be both a welfare com-munity and a community of peace.[14]

Röling, who is here quoted, considers this to be 'an almost super-human task'. We prefer to put the same thing in a different way by saying that at this moment of decisive change in the world's history the Christian conception of the unity of mankind, which has given birth to International Law and to the idea of the United Nations, demands a prophetic reinterpretation of the ideas of 'Law' and 'Peace'. The Church, which subsists on the *torah* (law) and *shalom* (peace) revealed in biblical history, has access to that genuinely revolutionary theology of history which is the fundamental answer to the need of our century.

There is yet another aspect to this question, closely connected with the struggle for a higher standard of living. It is foolish to go on using offensive terms when there is no necessity to do so; but also it is unrealistic to wrap hard facts up in soft words. 'Assistance to under-developed countries' is a hard fact for which we should be well advised to find, if not a milder, at least a more adequate expression. Both the idea of 'assistance' and the value-judgment implied in 'under-developed' arouse the strongest antipathy on the part of those countries which are at the receiving end of all this solicitude. It carries far too many associations with the detestable ideology of 'the white man's burden'. Not unnaturally, neo-colonial 'assistance' is much harder still to put up with, since the free and reciprocal consent upon which it rests brings out into the open, directly and for the first time, the harsh realities of economic weakness and dependence. To be in a state of subordination is not necessarily humiliating in itself; but to have to turn for help to the master from whom one has just obtained one's freedom is adding insult to injury. Indeed it is not unlikely that the rich man, as he dispenses his charity, will experience a strong sense of self-satisfaction, when he recognizes his former slave in the wretched Lazarus at his door.

The fact is that the expression, 'assistance to under-developed countries', was a most unhappy choice. The thing, surely, is this: that in this planetary world of ours such fantastic inequalities of welfare as between different peoples and nations constitute a persistent source of danger to world peace, as any country where economic contrasts of this sort obtain must live perpetually on the verge of revolution. It is not so much a matter of helping as of a collective and gigantic effort on the part of mankind as a whole to achieve a world-wide economic democracy, in which the potential sources of welfare are exploited to the maximum degree and used to benefit as much of mankind as possible. Therefore a slogan like 'economic democracy for the world' would much better describe what the aim of the nations should be in this twentieth century. However it is extremely doubtful whether any slogan, however splendid it may sound, would remain uncontaminated for very long, since it is bad deeds that give a bad name, and not vice versa. The heart of this problem does not in fact lie in the 'under-developed countries'; they have always been there, and the world has never lost very much sleep over them before. A low standard of living was just one of the facts of life, no more to be avoided—so far as the great mass of human beings were concerned, at any rate—than the facts of disease and death. It is the 'highly developed countries' that during the modern period have crossed that threshold, that supposedly impassable barrier, for the first time in the world's history; and they have won for themselves a lasting and rapidly rising standard of prosperity which has put them streets ahead of the rest of mankind. This 'high development' of theirs did not come out of the blue; it is a product of Western Christian civilization, brought about through the complexities of history in which a whole range of factors, such as the rise of democracy, modern capitalism, the technological revolution, a high valuation of labour and socialist and liberal movements, have been at work.[15] This achievement of the West has become a standard and gauge for levels of material well-being in other parts of the world. It is a standard beyond the reach of the traditional structure of society: it requires a social transformation, a society organized on a technocratic pattern. Just how far-reaching does this transformation have to be? According to the Communist ideology, only a radical break with the traditional pattern, in which religion was the dominant factor, offers a way out of the bondage of 'under-development'. On this point the Western countries are highly uncertain and ambiguous. Their 'assistance' is restricted, as far as possible, to the technical aspects and, generally speaking, holds off from any ideological implications. That makes all the more urgent the challenge to the Church to take much more seriously than she has done hitherto the tremendous responsibility which the West has assumed towards the rest of the world in leaving behind the old levels of prosperity and entering upon the technocratic era.[16] It is a Christian civilization which has unlocked the door to this Aladdin's cave. It is nonsense, of course, for the non-Western peoples to accuse the West of 'materialism', whilst themselves making every effort to reach the same standard of living within as short a time as possible. Yet it serves only to show how morally confused and theologically blind the Christian Church is, if she is content to proclaim that 'man shall not live by bread alone', when in point of fact Christianity itself has come perilously close to toying with the miracle that commands the stones to become bread. The Old Testament promises an earthly *shalom*—that life in the good land where 'you shall eat and be full' (Deut. 8:10). In the New Jerusalem the leaves of the tree of life shall be for the healing of the nations (Rev. 22:2). Next to our concern to banish the possibility of a global atomic war comes this struggle for a higher standard of living; it is this which will more and more predominate in the history of the present century. It is a prime duty of the whole Church to think out afresh the perils and the promises which this involves, so that amidst the false Christs and false prophets there may go forth an unequivocal proclamation of the Risen Lord. What we now most desperately need is a clear theology of 'materialism', a theology of wealth.

6. ISRAEL AMID THE NATIONS

Here, in conclusion, let me add a brief note on the subject of Israel. In our journey through mankind's history we began with the birth of 'Israel amid the nations'; and we conclude with the present situation of 'Christianity in a planetary world'. That 'one world' —and first and foremost Christianity within it—stands today confronted with the unsolved enigma of Israel's existence amid the nations. The same year, 1917, saw the entry of the United States into the First World War, the Communist Revolution in Russia and the establishment in Palestine, with British support under the Balfour Declaration, of a national home for the Jewish people.

The end of the Second World War, which rang the knell of colonialism and spelled victory for Asian and African nationalism, also brought with it the creation of the state of Israel. This is a century teeming with dramatic events; but among them all that one is *simpliciter sui generis*. It looks as though all the insoluble problems that torment this century meet at this point. How are we to understand the setting up of the state of Israel? Is it a climax to the long annals of Western Christian anti-semitism, culminating in the hell of German Hitlerism? Is it the final stage in the liberation of the Jew from his ghetto? Is it the birth of a new and independent nation in a land which has been in fact the cradle of nationalism? Is it a resurgence of the former antagonism between Judaism and Islam? Is it the extreme outcome of the conflict between Islam and the West

—an intrusive spear-head in the form of a Westernized state? Or does it perhaps set the seal upon the indestructible bond linking the history of Israel with that of the West?

Who is in a position to disentangle all this? If the fact of the state of Israel is a riddle, it is also true that every ideological or over-simplified approach to a solution overrides the complexity of the question.

> . . . the passions aroused by Palestine have done so much to obscure the truth that the facts have become enveloped in a mist of sentiment, legend and propaganda, which acts as a smoke-screen of almost impenetrable density.[17]

Here the Christian Church is at last brought face to face with a challenge which for nineteen centuries past—ever since the destruction of Jerusalem by the Romans in A.D. 70—it has been able to evade. Israel has continued to exist; but the Church's sole encounter with it has been by way of the synagogue and the Diaspora. In the process of becoming 'Christianized' the West of course took full account of the logical conclusion to be drawn from Paul's apostolic mission to the Romans and his Roman citizenship; but it never took to its own heart what Paul felt so deeply in his—an anguish that nothing could appease and which drove him to wish himself accursed and cut off from Christ for the sake of his kinsmen according to the flesh (Rom. 9). That is why the Church has never come to grips with the elusive meaning of the earthly promises given in the Old Testament regarding the land and people of Israel and the city of Zion. The Church's own exegesis has been that in Christ these promises had already been fulfilled; but the Church itself never worked this out in practice. On the contrary, Rome, Constantinople and Moscow have all been eager to lay claim to Zion's inheritance for themselves. Howbeit, the Lord of history is not mocked. Jerusalem might be destroyed, but then Mecca appears—to inherit her universal claims and her blessings upon earth and, when the Jewish people no longer have a country of their own or any existence as a nation, to become a stumbling block and unrelenting enemy towards Graeco-Roman Christianity. As a rival power Islam might be thrust aside by the modern West; but then the nemesis of world history takes good care that a new Islam shall arise, summoning all the peoples of the earth to turn their *qiblah* towards Moscow—new heir to Zion's universal claims and earthly blessings.

Of course Israel is not the Messiah; and the state of Israel is by no means the eschatological fulfilment of the Old Testament promises for Zion. But Rome, Mecca and Moscow, New York and Peking—none of these is the new Zion either. The unyielding riddle of the Jewish nation in its earthly, concrete existence mirrors a universal world-embracing riddle in prototype. What nation has a claim, a *right*, to existence upon this earth, unless by grace and favour of the Lord of history, whose judgments are unsearchable and his ways past finding out?

We live in a time of crisis: and *krisis* is a biblical word. In the Bible it signifies 'judgment', but along with that, 'justice' and 'salvation'. The Servant of the Lord 'will not fail or be discouraged till he has established justice (*krisis*) in the earth; and the coastlands wait for his *torah*,' (Is. 42:1 ff.; Mt. 12:18 ff.).

Bibliography and List of Sources

We are grateful to all the publishers and authors concerned who have given us permission to use extracts from their works. Every effort has been made to trace the owners of copyright works, but if any have been omitted we trust they will accept this expression of our thanks. Where direct quotations have been used, the note is marked with an asterisk.

Except where otherwise stated the Bible quotations are taken from *The Revised Standard Version of the Bible*, published by Thomas Nelson and Sons Ltd., copyrighted 1946 and 1952.

The quotations from the Qur'an are in many places Dr A.Th. van Leeuwen's own translations, but he acknowledges his indebtedness at various points to J. M. Rodwell's translation, *The Koran*, published by J. M. Dent and Sons Ltd., and in one instance, Sura III:57, to Dr Richard Bell's translation, *The Qur'an*, published by T. and T. Clark. The Qur'anic references are numbered according to the Editio Fluegel.

Chapter One
*1. C. C. West and D. M. Paton (ed.), *The Missionary Church in East and West* (S.C.M. Press, London, 1959), p. 83.
*2. Randwijck, S. C. Graaf van, 'Some Reflections of a Mission Board Secretary' in *The Ghana Assembly of the International Missionary Council, 1957/8* (Edinburgh House Press, London, 1958).
3. Albright, W. F., *From the Stone Age to Christianity* (New York, 2nd edn., 1946), p. 51.
4. Jaspers, Karl, *Vom Ursprung und Ziel der Geschichte* (Munich, 1955), p. 31.
5. Jaspers, op. cit., p. 78.
*6. Kroeber, A. L., *Anthropology* (Geo. G. Harrap, London, rev. ed., 1948 and Harcourt, Brace & World Inc., New York), p. 260 f.
7. Linton, Ralph, *The Tree of Culture* (New York, 1955), p. v.
8. Heimann, Betty, *Studien zur Eigenart indischen Denkens* (Tübingen, 1930), p. III ff.
*9. Kroeber, A. L., and Kluckhorn, Clyde, 'Culture. A Critical Review of Concepts and Definitions'. Papers of the Peabody Museum, Vol. XLVII (i) (Cambridge, Mass., 1952).
*10. Kroeber, *Anthropology*, pp. 252–3.
11. Kroeber and Kluckhorn, op. cit., p. 145.
12. Niedermann, Joseph, *Kultur, Werden und Wandlungen des Begriffs und seine Ersatzbegriffe von Cicero bis Herder* (Florence, 1941), pp. 170, 223 ff. cf. Fabre, Lucien, *et al.* 'Civilization, le mot et l'idée exposés' (*Première Semaine internationale de synthèse*, Vol. II, Paris, 1930, pp. 61, 79). Locher, G. W., *De Sociologie en cultuurkunde van Zuidoost-Azië en het*

Zuidzeegebied in haar betrekking tot de algemene cultuurwetenschap (Groningen, 1955), p. 5.

13. Locher, op. cit., p. 6.
14. Kroeber, A. L., 'The Ancient Oikoumene as an Historic Culture Aggregate' (*Journal of the Royal Anthropological Institute of Great Britain and Ireland*, Vol. LXXV, p. 9).
    Locher, G. W., 'Culturele anthropologie en Oecumene' (*De Heerbaan, Algemeen Zendingstijdschrift*, Vol. 10, Sept./Oct., 1957, p. 183).
*15. Benedict, Ruth F., *Patterns of Culture* (Routledge & Kegan Paul, London, 1935), p. 4 f.
16. Malinowski, Bronislaw, *The Dynamics of Culture Change*, ed. by Phyllis M. Kaberry (New Haven and London, 1945), Introduction; pp. 1 ff., 26 f.
17. Kodanda Rao, P., *East versus West. A Denial of Contrast* (London, 1939), p. 155 ff.
*18. Kohn, Hans, *Orient and Occident* (John Day, New York, 1934), p. 76.
19. Toynbee, Arnold J., *A Study of History*, Vol. I (London, 1934), pp. 51, 30.
20. Marvin, Francis S., *The Unity of Western Civilization* (London, 4th edn., 1936).
*21. Sarton, George, *Introduction to the History of Science*, Vol. I (Williams & Wilkins, Baltimore, for Carnegie Institution, 1927), p. 29.
22. Hu Shih, *The Chinese Renaissance*, The Haskell Lectures, 1933 (Chicago, 1934), p. 65 f.
23. Speer, Robert E., *Race and Race Relations* (New York/Chicago, 1924), p. 126.
24. Northrop, F. S. C., *The Meeting of East and West* (New York, 1946), p. 375.
25. Radhakrishnan, S., *Eastern Religions and Western Thought* (London, 2nd edn., 1940).
    Radhakrishnan, S., *East and West in Religion* (London, 1933).
26. Kat Angelino, A. D. A. de, *Colonial Policy*, Vol. I (The Hague, 1931).
27. Rougemont, Denis de, *Man's Western Quest* (Allen & Unwin, London, 1957 and Harper & Row, New York), p. 28.
*28. Rougemont, op. cit., p. 146.

Chapter Two

1. Boman, Thorleif, *Das hebräische Denken im Vergleich mit dem Griechischen* (Göttingen, 2. durchgesehene Aufl., 1954), p. 19.
2. Barth, Karl, *Kirchliche Dogmatik*, III/1 (Zürich, 1945), p. 147 ff.
3. *biblos geneseōs*, Mt. 1:1, is a literal quotation of Gen. 5:1 in the Septuagint.
4. Pedersen, J. P. E., *Israel. Its Life and Culture* (London/Copenhagen, 1926).
5. Leeuw, G. van der, *De primitieve mensch en de religie* (Groningen/Batavia, 1937), p. 23.
*6. Leeuw, G. van der, *Religion in Essence and Manifestation* (Allen & Unwin, London, 1938), p. 30, quoting from Saintyves, *La Force Magique*, p. 46.
7. Kraemer, H., *The Christian Message in a Non-Christian World* (London, 1938), p. 154.
*8. Groot, J. J. M. de, *Religion in China* (Putnam, New York/London, 1912), p. 2.

*9. Volz, Paul, *Das Dämonische in Jahve* (Tübingen, 1924), pp. 9, 31.

10. Köhler, Ludwig, *Theologie des Alten Testaments* (Tübingen, 1936), p. 26 ff.

11. Held, G. J., *Magie, Hekserij en Toverij* (Groningen, 1950), p. 75.
    Lowie, R. H., *Primitive Religion* (New York, 1924), p. 151.

12. Mowinckel, S., *Psalmenstudien I, Awân und die individuellen Klage-psalmen* (Kristiana, 1921), p. 39 ff.
    Pedersen, op. cit., p. 448.

13. Cassirer, Ernst, *Die Begriffsform im mythischen Denken* (*Stud. der Bibl. Warburg*, I, Leipzig/Berlin, 1922).
    Cassirer, Ernst, *Philosophie der symbolischen Formen*, II, *Das mythische Denken* (Berlin, 1925).

14. Rosenzweig, Franz, *Der Stern der Erlösung* (Frankfurt, 1945), p. 47 ff.

15. Pedersen, op. cit., p. 57.

16. cf. Leeuw, *De primitieve mensch en de religie*.

17. Jeremias, D. F., 'Semitische Völker in Vorderasien' in *Lehrbuch der Religionsgeschichte* (Tübingen, 4th imp., 1925), p. 496.
    Toynbee, Arnold J., *A Study of History*, Abridgment by D. C. Somervell (London, 8th edn., 1948), pp. 19 f., 92 ff.

18. Böhl, F. M. Th., *De Babylonisch-Assyrische godsdienst* (Sumer en Akkad) in *De Godsdiensten der wereld*, ed. by G. van der Leeuw (Amsterdam, 2nd imp., 1948), p. 122 ff.

19. Gunkel, H., *Genesis* (Göttingen, 3rd edn., 1910).
    Gunkel, H., *Schöpfung und Chaos in Urzeit und Endzeit, Eine religions-geschichtliche Untersuchung über Genesis 1 und Apok. 12* (Göttingen, 1895).

20. Frankfort, H. and H. A. *et al., The Intellectual Adventure of Ancient Man* (Chicago, 1946), p. 168 f.

21. Brongers, H. A., *De Scheppingstradities bij de profeten* (Amsterdam, 1945), p. 56 ff.

22. cf. Gunkel, *Schöpfung* etc., p. 30 ff.

23. cf. Frankfort, H., *Kingship and the Gods* (copyright 1948 by University of Chicago Press), pp. 57 f., 194 f.

24. cf. Hos. 2:14; 9:10; 11:1; 12:10, 14; 13:4; Amos 2:10; 3:1; Is. 4:5; 9:16; 43:16; 48:21; 50:2; 51:10; Jer. 2:6; 7:22 ff.; 9:3 ff.; 14:14; 23:7; 31:32; 34:13; Ezek. 20:5 ff.; Mic. 6:4; 7:15; Hag. 2:6.
    cf. Brongers, op. cit., p. 94 ff.

25. Rad, G. von, 'Das theologische Problem des alttestamentischen Schöp-fungsglaubens', *Werden und Wesen des Alten Testament*, Beihefte zur Zeitschrift für die alttestamentische Wissenschaft, 66 (Berlin, 1936), p. 138 ff.
    cf. Rad, G. von, *Theologie des Alten Testaments* (Munich, 1957), p. 143

26. Gunkel, *Genesis*, op. cit., p. XIII f.

27. Barth, *Kirchliche Dogmatik* III/1, pp. 88–95.

28. Bentzen, Aage, *Messias-Moses redivivus-Menschensohn* (Zürich, 1948).
    cf. Wright, G. Ernest, *The Old Testament against its Environment* (London, 1950), pp. 27 f., 65 f., 94 ff.

*29. Frankfort, *Kingship* etc., p. 313

30. Wright, op. cit., p. 97 ff.

31. Gunkel, op. cit., p. 46.
    Wensinck, A. J., 'The Ocean in the Literature of the Western Semites'
    (Verh. d. Kon. Akad. v. Wet. te Amsterdam. afd. letterk., nieuwe
    reeks, XIX, nr 2), p. 21 f.
    Pedersen, op. cit., p. 527.
32. Dürr, L., *Die Wertung des göttlichen Wortes im Alten Testament und im
    Antiken Orient* (mitteil. d. *Vorderasiat.-ägypt.* Gesellschaft, 42. Band,
    Leipzig, 1938).
    Albright, W. F., *From the Stone Age to Christianity* (New York, 1946),
    pp. 145, 285.
    Boman, op. cit., p. 45 ff.
    Frankfort *et al., The Intellectual Adventure* etc., p. 178.
    Jeremias, A., *Das Alte Testament im Lichte des alten Orients* (Leipzig,
    4th edn., 1930), p. 42.
33. cf. Boman, op. cit., p. 49.
34. Vriezen, Th. C., *Onderzoek naar de paradijsvoorstellingen bij de oude
    Semietische volken* (Wageningen, 1937), pp. 22–119.
35. Gilgamesh Epic XI, 9 f.
    cf. Heidel, A., *The Gilgamesh Epic and Old Testament Parallels* (Chicago,
    2nd edn. 1949,), p. 45.
36. Kristensen, W. B., 'De plaats van het zondvloedverhaal in het Gilgames-
    epos' (Versl. en med. Kon. Ak. v. Wet., afd. Lett., V, 2, Amsterdam,
    1917), p. 54 ff.
37. Langdon, S. H., *Sumerian Liturgical Texts* (Philadelphia, 1917), Plates
    XIX:11 and XXI:16-17 (cf. S. N. Kramer in the Bulletin of the
    American Schools of Oriental Research, No. 94 (April, 1944), p. 6).
38. Kristensen, W. B., *Het leven uit de dood* (Haarlem, 2nd edn., 1949),
    p. 34 ff.
39. Gilgamesh Epic, X, II, 5; cf. Heidel, op. cit., p. 73.
40. Bergema, H., *De Boom des levens in schrift en historie* (Hilversum, 1938),
    p. 323 ff.
    cf. Baudissin, W. W. Graf, *Adonis und Esmun. Eine Untersuchung zur
    Geschichte des Glaubens an Auferstehungsgötter und an Heilgötter* (Leipzig,
    1911), pp. 104, footnote 1; 373, footnote 1.
41. Meissner, Bruno, *Babylonien und Assyrien*, II (Heidelberg, 1925), p. 139 f.
42. Wünsche, August, 'Die Sagen vom Lebensbaum und Lebenswasser',
    Altorientalische Mythen (*Ex Oriente Lux*, Vol. I, Heft 2/3, Leipzig, 1905).
    Holmberg, U., 'Der Baum des Lebens' (Annales, Academiae Scientiarum
    Fennicae, Ser. B, Vol. XVI, no. 3, Helsinki, 1922-3).
    Nötscher, Friedrich, *Altorientalischer und altestamentlicher Auferstehungs-
    glauben* (Würzburg, 1926).
    Bergema, op. cit.
43. Vriezen, op. cit., pp. 56 f., 145 ff.
44. Virolleaud, Charles, *La légende Phénicienne de Danel* (Paris, 1936), p. 121.
45. Heidel, op. cit., p. 267.
46. Oppenheim, A. L., in *The Biblical Archæologist* (American Schools of
    Oriental Research), Vol. VII, no. 3.
47. Ravn, O. E., *Zeitschrift der Deutschen Morgenländischen Gesellschaft*
    (1937), p. 352.

48. Ebeling, E., *Keilschrifttexte aus Assur religiösen Inhalts*, I (Berlin, 1915), no. 8.
Harper, R. F., *Assyrian and Babylonian Letters*, Vol. IX (London, 1892–1914), no. 878, vs. 8.

49. Böhl, F. M. Th., *Archiv für Orientforschung*, Vol. XI, 1936, no. 7, p. 207.

50. Böhl, F. M. Th., 'Babylon, de heilige stad' (*Ex Oriente Lux*, Vol. III, no. 10, p. 513 f.). This scholar refutes the suggestion of W. F. Albright (*From the Stone Age to Christianity*, p. 113) that the Genesis story should refer to an earlier period, the destruction of Babel by the Hittite King Mursilis (*c.* 1600 B.C.).

51. Böhl, op. cit., pp. 491–525.
Gunkel, *Genesis*, pp. 95–9.
Busink, Th. A., *De Toren van Babel* (Batavia, 1938).
Wetzel, Friedrich and Weissbach, F. H., 'Das Hauptheiligtum des Marduk in Babylon, Esagila und Etemenanki' (*Wissenschaftliche Veröffentlichungen der Deutsche Orientgesellschaft*, 59, Leipzig, 1938).

52. Buck, A. de, *De Egyptische voorstellingen betreffende den oerheuvel* (Leiden, 1922).

53. Busink, op. cit., p. 48 f.
Lenzen, H. J., *Die Entwicklung der Zikkurat von ihren Anfängen bis zur Zeit der III, Dynastie von Ur* (Leipzig, 1941).
Wright, G. Ernest, 'The Significance of the Temple in the Ancient Near East' (*The Biblical Archæologist*, Dec. 1944, p. 74).

54. Wright, op. cit., p. 74 ff.
Albright, W. F., *Archæology and the Religion of Israel* (Baltimore, 1942), p. 148 ff.

55. Ezekiel 43:15: the word *har'el* is translated by the Revised Standard Version as 'the altar hearth'. It denotes the upper stage of the altar. The term 'bosom of the earth' (Ezek. 43:14) is misunderstood by the Revised Standard Version as 'the base on the ground'.

56. *The Biblical Archæologist*, IV, 2; I, 1.
Gunkel, *Schöpfung* etc., p. 122 ff.
Oppenheim, A. L., 'The Mesopotamian Temple' (*The Biblical Archæologist*, VII, 3, p. 56).
Nelson, H. H., *The Biblical Archæologist*, VII, 3, p. 48 f.

57. Virolleaud, op. cit., p. 121.

58. The very uncertain text can only be interpreted according to ancient translations. In the Septuagint the construction of the sentences deviates considerably.
Cf. Vriezen, op. cit., p. 219.
Jahn, Gustav, *Das Buch Ezechiel* (Leipzig, 1905).
Hölscher, G., *Hesekiel* (Giessen, 1924).
Herntrich, V., *Ezechielprobleme* (Giessen, 1932).
Gressmann, Hugo, *Archiv für Religionswissenschaft* (Leipzig, 1907), p. 365.
Eissfeldt, Otto, *Baäl Zaphon* (Halle, 1932), p. 20 ff.
Virolleaud, Charles, 'La Révolte de Košer contre Baäl' (*Syria*, XVI, 1935, p. 30 ff.).

59. Bergema, op. cit., passim.

60. Meissner, Bruno, *Babylonien und Assyrien* (Heidelberg, 1925), II, p. 17; Gunkel, *Genesis*, p. 36.

*61. Frankfort, *Kingship*, etc., p. 341.

62. Wright, G. Ernest, *The Old Testament against its Environment*, p. 64, note 36.
    Boer, P. A. H. de, *Het Koningschap in Oud-Israël* (Amsterdam, 1938), p. 12.

63. Buber, Martin, 'Königtum Göttes' (*Das Kommende* I, Berlin, 2nd edn., 1936).
    Buber, Martin, 'Biblisches Führertum' in *Kampf um Israel* (Berlin, 1933).
    Buber, Martin, 'Het geloof van Israël' in *De Godsdiensten der wereld*, ed. G. van der Leeuw (Amsterdam, 1948).

*64. Frankfort, *Kingship*, etc., p. 52 f.

65. Balscheit, Bruno, *Gottesbund und Staat* (Zürich, 1940), p. 10 ff.

66. Miskotte, K. H., *Als de goden zwijgen* (Amsterdam, 1956), p. 181.
    Buber, Martin, *Uber die Wortwahl in einer Verdeutschung der Schrift* (Berlin, 1930).
    Alt, A., *Die Ursprünge des Israelitischen Rechts* (Leipzig, 1934), p. 33 ff.
    Dussaud, R., *Les origines cananéennes du sacrifice israélite* (Paris, 1921).

67. Hempel, Johannes, *Das Ethos des Alten Testaments* (Berlin, 1938), Ch. V.

68. Bertholet, Alfred, *Histoire de la civilisation d'Israël* (Paris, 1929), p. 306.

Chapter Three

1. Kittel, Gerhard, Art. '*barbaros*', *Theologisches Wörterbuch des Neuen Testament*, Vol. 1, B and A 3 (Stuttgart, 1933-).

2. Meyer, E., *Blüte und Niedergang des Hellenismus in Asien* (Berlin, 1925).

3. Kittel, Gerhard, *Die Religionsgeschichte und das Urchristentum* (Gütersloh, 1932), p. 42 ff.

4. Kittel, Art. '*hellèn*', *Th. W.N.T.*, Vol. 2, C 4.

5. The translation of the Revised Standard Version: '. . . and since I have longed for many years to come to you, I hope to see you in passing as I go to Spain' does not acknowledge the meaning of the original Greek text.

*6. Clement, *First Epistle to the Corinthians*, 5:6-7, cf. *A New Eusebius*, ed. J. Stevenson (S.P.C.K., London, 1957), p. 4.

7. Cullmann, Oscar, *Christus und die Zeit* (Zürich, 1946), p. 169 ff.
    Barth, Karl, *Rechtfertigung und Recht* (Zürich, 1944).

8. Kaerst, J., *Die antike Idee der Oikoumene in ihrer politischen und kulturellen Bedeutung* (Leipzig, 1903), p. 18.
    Vogt, Joseph, *Orbis Romanus. Zur Terminologie des römischen Imperialismus* (Tübingen, 1929), p. 10.

9. Cf. Septuagint, Ps. 17:16; 18:5; 24:1; 32:8; 48:2; 49:12 etc.; Is. 10:14, 23; 13:5, 9, 11; 14:17, 26 etc.

10. Baumgarten, F., Poland, F., Wagner, R , *Die Hellenisch-Römische Kultur* (Leipzig and Berlin, 1913), p. 13 f.

11. Strathmann, H., Art. '*polis*', *Th.W.N.T.*, VI, p. 520 ff.
    Wilamowitz-Moellendorff, Ulrich von, 'Staat und Gesellschaft der Griechen' (in *Die Kultur der Gegenwart*, II, 4, 1², Leipzig, 1923, p. 25).

12. Schlier, Heinrich, Art. '*eleutheros*', *Th. W.N.T.*, II, p. 484.

13. Kleinknecht, Hermann, Art. '*nomos*', *Th.W.N.T.*, IV, p. 1016 ff.

Chapter Four

1. Kroeber, A. L., *Anthropology* (London, 1948), p. 785.
2. Kroeber, op. cit., p. 772.
3. Cf. Linton, Ralph, *The Tree of Culture* (New York, 1955), p. 139 ff.
4. Jacobs, M., and Stern, B. J., *Outline of Anthropology* (Cambridge, 1948), p. 27.
5. Weber, Alfred, *Kulturgeschichte als Kultursoziologie* (Leiden, 1935), p. 13 ff.
6. Schmidt, W., and Koppers, W., 'Gesellschaft und Wirtschaft der Völker' in *Der Mensch aller Zeiten*, Vol. III, *Völker und Kulturen*, Part I (Regensburg, 1924), p. 104.
7. Linton, op. cit., p. 257 ff.
8. Wittfogel, Karl A., *Oriental Despotism. A Comparative Study of Total Power* (New York/London, 1957).
9. Jaspers, Karl, *Vom Ursprung und Ziel der Geschichte* (Munich, 1949). Cf. his discussion with Alfred Weber, op. cit., p. 264 ff.
10. Gaerte, W., 'Kosmische Vorstellungen im Bilde prehistorischen Zeit: Erdberg, Himmelsberg, Erdnabel und Weltströme' (*Anthropos*, Vol. IX, 1914, pp. 956–979).
11. Wales, H. G. Quaritch, *The Mountain of God. A Study in Early Religion and Kingship* (London, 1953).
    Schebesta, P., *Les Pygmées du Congo belge* (Namur, 1957), p. 156.
    Schaerer, H., *Die Gottesidee der Ngadju Dajak in Süd-Borneo* (Leiden, 1946), p. 19.
12. Eliade, Mircea, *Traité d'histoire des religions* (Paris, 1953), p. 321.
13. Karlgren, B. J., 'Some Fecundity Symbols in Ancient China', *Bulletin of the Museum for Far Eastern Antiquities* (Stockholm, 1930), No. 2.
14. Mus, Paul, 'Cultes Indiens et Indigènes au Champa' (*Bulletin de l'école française d'Extrême Orient*, XXXIII, p. 406 ff.).
    Stutterheim, W. F., *Indian Influences in Old Balinese Art* (India Society, 1935).
    Akkeren, Philippus van, *A Monster. Yet the Perfect Man* (The Hague, 1951), p. 12 ff.
15. Eliade, Mircea, op. cit., p. 234 ff.
16. Bosch, F. D. K., *De Gouden kiem* (Amsterdam, 1948), p. 49 ff.
17. Bosch, op. cit., p. 99 f.
    Kielhorn, F., 'Deopara Inscription of Vijayasena', *Epigraphia Indica*, I, p. 310 ff.
    Dupont (*Journal of the American Oriental Society*, 53, 1933, p. 329).
    Mus, Paul, 'Barabudur' (*Bulletin de l'école française d'Extrême Orient*, XXXII, 1932, pp. 412, 423 ff.).
18. Bosch, op. cit., p. 224 ff.
19. Eliade, op. cit., p. 323.
20. Parva, Ashvameda, quoted by Coomaraswamy (*The Inverted Tree*, Quarterly Journal of the Mythic Society, XXIX, p. 20) according to the version utilized by Sankara in his commentary on the *Bhavagad Gîtâ*, XV, 1.
21. Bosch, op. cit., p. 191 f
22. Auboyer, J., 'Le caractère royal et divin du trône dans l'Inde ancienne'

in *The Sacral Kingship, Contributions to the Central Theme of the VIIIth International Congress for the History of Religions*, Rome, April, 1955 (Leiden, 1959), p. 181 ff.

23. Auboyer, op. cit., p. 188.
24. Snellgrove, D. L., 'The Notion of Divine Kingship in Tantric Buddhism' in *The Sacral Kingship*, p. 204 ff.
25. Basu, A., 'Hindu Doctrine of Divine Kingship' in *The Sacral Kingship*, p. 167 ff.
    Aurobindo, Sri, *The Spirit and Form of Indian Polity* (1947), p. 11 ff. (now reprinted in *The Foundations of Indian Culture*, published by Sri Aurobindo Library, New York, 1953, p. 372 f.).
26. Gonda, J., 'The Sacred Character of Ancient Indian Kingship' in *The Sacral Kingship*, p. 172 ff.
27. Gonda, op. cit., p. 179 f.
28. Wales, op. cit., p. 38.
*29. Mo tzu, Chinese text. Sun Yi Jang's ed. in the *Wan Yu Wen K'u*, Vol. 2, p. 151.
    Cf. D. H. Smith, 'Divine Kingship in Ancient China' (*Numen*, International Review for the History of Religions, Vol. IV, Fasc. 3, E. J. Brill, Leiden, September, 1957, p. 180).
30. Groot, J. J. M. de, *Religion in China* (New York, 1912), p. 194 f.
31. Bredon, J., *Peking. A Historical and Intimate Description of its Chief Places of Interest* (Shanghai, 1920), p. 141.
    Cf. Fitzgerald, C. P., *China. A Short Cultural History* (London, 1935), p. 33.
32. Groot, de, op. cit., p. 117 f.
33. Widengren, Geo, 'The Sacral Kingship of Iran' in *The Sacral Kingship*, p. 242 ff.
34. Widengren, op. cit., p. 249 ff.
35. L'Orange, H. P., 'Expressions of Cosmic Kingship in the Ancient World' in *The Sacral Kingship*, p. 481 ff.
36. L'Orange, H. P., 'Domus Aurea—Der Sonnenpalast' (in *Serta Eitremiana*, 1942).
    Cf. L'Orange, H. P., *Studies on the Iconography of Cosmic Kingship in the Ancient World* (Oslo, 1953), p. 18 ff.
37. L'Orange, *Studies* etc., p. 35 ff.
38. L'Orange, op. cit., p. 85 ff.
39. Shelvankar, K. S., *The Problem of India* (1940), p. 102.
*40. Marx, Karl, *Articles on India*, introd. by R. P. Dutt (People's Publishing House, Bombay, 1951), p. 75 f.
41. Frazer, J. G., *Totemism and Exogamy* (London, 1910), p. 329.
42. Held, G. J., *The Mahābhārata. An Ethnological Study* (London/Amsterdam, 1935), pp. 42 ff., 82 ff.
43. Sarkar, Benoy Kumar, *The Positive Background of Hindu Sociology*, Book I, *Introduction to Hindu Positivism* (Panini Office, Allahabad, 1937).
    Sarkar, Benoy Kumar, *The Political Institution and Theories of the Hindus. A Study in Comparative Politics* (Leipzig, 1922).
44. Panikkar, K. M., *The State and the Citizen* (Bombay, 1956).
*45. Sarkar, *The Positive Background* etc., p. 6.

46. Sankaranarayanam, P., 'Human Person, Society and State. The Classical Hindu Approach' in *Human Person, Society and State. A Collection of Essays*, ed. by Committee for Literature on Social Concerns (Bangalore, 1957), p. 56 ff.

47. Dubois, J. A., *Hindu Manners, Customs and Ceremonies*, transl. Henri K. Beauchamp (Oxford, 1897), p. 290.

48. Aiyangar, K. V. Rangaswami, *Considerations on Some Aspects of Ancient Indian Polity* (Madras, 2nd edn., 1935), p. 69.

49. Panikkar, op. cit., p. 118 f.

50. Desai, A. R., *Social Background of Indian Nationalism* (Bombay, 1948), p. 8 ff.

51. Rhys Davids, Mrs C. A. F., 'Economic Conditions according to Early Buddhist Literature' (in *Cambridge History of India*, I, Cambridge, 1922), p. 200 ff.

52. Fick, R., *The Social Organization in N.E. India in Buddha's Time* (Calcutta, 1920), p. 137 ff.
Rhys Davids, T. W., *Buddhist India* (Calcutta, 1st Indian edn., 1950), p. 13 ff.

53. Heimann, Betty, *Indian and Western Philosophy. A Study in Contrasts* (London, 1937).

54. Heimann, Betty, *Studien zur Eigenart Indischen Denkens* (Tübingen, 1930), p. 9 ff.

55. Heimann, *Indian and Western Philosophy*, p. 118.

56. Fitzgerald, op. cit., Ch. XI.

*57. Linton, Ralph, *The Tree of Culture* (Alfred A. Knopf, New York, 1956), Ch. XXXVII, p. 552.

58. Fitzgerald, op. cit., p. 169 ff.

59. Weber, Max, *Gesammelte Aufsätze zur Religionssoziologie*, I (Tübingen, 1920), pp. 276–536.

60. Shryock, J. K., *The Origin and Development of the State Cult of Confucius* (New York, 1932), p. 15 ff.

61. Duyvendak, J. J. L., *The Book of Lord Shang* (London, 1928), p. 66 f.

*62. Groot, de, op. cit., pp. 1 ff., 189.

63. Fitzgerald, op. cit., p. 269.

Chapter Five

1. Toynbee, Arnold J., *A Study of History* (Abridgment by D. C. Somervell, London, 8th edn., 1948), pp. 68 ff., 76.

2. Toynbee, op. cit., p. 27.

3. Art. 'Antike und Orient', *Religion in Geschichte und Gegenwart*[3], I (Tübingen, 1957 ff.).
Art. 'Griechische Religion', *R.G.G.*[3], II, 1.

*4. Herodotus, 1, 60. (Trans. J. Enoch Powell, Clarendon Press, Oxford, 1949, p. 27 f.)

5. Chadwick, H. M., *The Heroic Age* (Cambridge, 1912).

6. Murray, Gilbert, *Five Stages of Greek Religion* (New York, 3rd edn., 1955), p. 56 ff.
Chadwick, op. cit., Ch. XVIII.

*7. Herodotus, 2, 53. (Op. cit., p. 135.)

*8. *Epinomis, Plato,* Vol. VIII (trans. W. R. M. Lamb), Loeb Classical Library (Heinemann, London, 1927 and Harvard University Press), p. 473. Cf. Art. 'Antike und Orient', *R.G.G.*³.

9. Murray, op. cit., p. 65 ff.

10. Cf. Jüthner, Julius, *Hellenen und Barbaren* (Leipzig, 1923), p. 5 f.

11. Livius, 31:29, 15: 'Cum alienigenis, cum barbaris aeternum omnibus Graecis bellum est eritque.' Cf. Art. *'barbaros'*, A 3, *Th.W.N.T.*

12. Aristoteles, Eth. Nicom., VII, I, 1145ᵃ, 30.

13. Rostovtzeff, M. I., *The Social and Economic History of the Roman Empire* (Oxford, 1926), Chs. X & XI.

14. Dawson, C. H., *The Making of Europe* (London, 1932), Ch. I.

15. Dawson, op. cit., Ch. VI.

*16. Diehl, Charles, *Byzance. Grandeur et décadence* (Bibliothèque de Philosophie Scientifique, Paris, 1919), p. 1.

17. Dawson, op. cit., Ch. VII. Latourette, K. S., *A History of the Expansion of Christianity* (Eyre & Spottiswoode, London, 1938–45, and Harper & Row Inc., New York), I, pp. 91 ff., 171 ff., 356 ff.; II, 10–13, 229 ff., 263 ff.

18. Quoted in Trimingham, J. Spencer, *Islam in Ethiopia* (Oxford University Press, London, 1952), p. 43 ff.

19. Trimingham, J. Spencer, *Islam in the Sudan* (London, 1949), p. 76 ff.

20. Latourette, op. cit., I, pp. 104 f., 173, 225 ff.

21. Latourette, op. cit., I, pp. 107, 231; II, 280.

22. Latourette, op. cit., II, p. 293.

23. Watt, W. Montgomery, *Muhammad at Medina* (Oxford, 1956), p. 387.

24. Trimingham, *Islam in Ethiopia,* Chs. 1 and 2, passim.

*25. Trimingham, op. cit., p. 44 f.

*26. Muir, Sir William, *The Life of Mohammad* (Grant, Edinburgh, 1923), p. 70.

27. Socrates, *Historia Ecclesiastica,* Book I, Ch. 19. Eusebius, *Historia Ecclesiastica,* Book III, Ch. 1.

28. Horovitz, J., *Koranische Untersuchungen* (Berlin/Leipzig, 1926), p. 47 f. Horovitz, J., Art. *'Nabî', Encyclopedia of Islam* (Leiden/London, 1934).

29. Horovitz, Art. *'Nabî',* and Paret, R., Art. *'ummî', Enc. of Islam.* Fischer, H. L., *Kleinere Schriften,* II (Leipzig, 1888), p. 115–7. Blachère, R., *Le Coran. Traduction selon un essai de reclassement des sourates,* Vol. I (Paris, 1947–51), p. 655. Moubarac, Y., *Abraham dans le Coran. L'histoire d'Abraham dans le Coran et la naissance de l'Islam* (Paris, 1958), p. 144. Bijlefeld, W. A., *De Islam als na-christelijke religie* (The Hague, 1959), pp. 148, 295.

30. Wellhausen, J., *Skizzen und Vorarbeiten* (Berlin, 1884–99), IV, p. 13, footnote 2. The translation (Bell, R., *The Qur'an,* 2 vols., Edinburgh, 1927–39) 'common people' is, certainly with regard to this text, Sura II:73, too weak. The translation 'illiterates' (*The Koran,* J. M. Rodwell's translation, London, 1909) does not fit in with the accusation that they 'transcribe the Book'.

31. Sura VII:156–8 is a Medinese addition, cf. Nöldeke, T., with Schwally, F., *Geschichte des Qorāns* (Leipzig, 1909), I, p. 159 f.
Bell, R., *The Qur'an*, Sura VII:156–8.
Blachère, R., *Le Coran*, Sura VII:156–8.
Horovitz, J., Art. '*Tawrāt*', *Enc. of Islam*, Vol. IV, p. 706.

32. Buhl, Frants, Art. 'Muhammad', *Enc. of Islam*, Vol. III, p. 641.
Buhl, Frants, *Das Leben Muhammeds* (Leipzig, 1930), p. 131.

33. Cf. the translations of Sura II:73: 'common people' (R. Bell), and of Sura VII:156, 158: 'The prophet of the common folk' (Arberry, A. J., *The Koran Interpreted*, 2 vols., London/New York, 1955–56).

34. Reissner, H. G., 'The Ummî Prophet and the Banu Israil' (*The Moslem World*, 39, 1949, p. 278).

35. Vaux, B. Carra de, Art. '*al-Sâbi'a*', *Enc. of Islam*, Vol. IV, p. 21.
Vaux, B. Carra de, Art. '*Indjil*', *Enc. of Islam*, Vol. II, p. 501.

36. Galling, K., Art. '*Beschneidung*' I, *R.G.G.*[3].
Meissner, B., *Babylonien und Assyrien* I (Heidelberg, 1920), p. 390.

37. Kuhn, K. G., Art. '*prosèlutos*', *Th.W.N.T.*, VI, p. 730 ff.
Kuhn, K. G., 'Ursprung und Wesen der talmudischen Einstellung zum Nichtjuden', *Forschungen zur Judenfrage*, 3 (1939), p. 220.

38. Wensinck, A. J., Art. '*Khitān*', *Enc. of Islam*, Vol. II, p. 956.

39. Wellhausen, J., *Reste arabischen Heidentums* (Berlin, 1897), p. 174 f.
Cf. Ranke, H., *et al.*, Art. '*Beschneidung*', *Reallexikon der Vorgeschichte* I (Berlin, 1924–32), p. 445 (see Art. '*peritomè*', *Th.W.N.T.*, p. 75, footnote 17).

40. Hurgronje, C. Snouck, *The Achehnese*, I (Leiden/London, 1906), p. 398.
Hurgronje, C. Snouck, *Verspreide Geschriften*, I (Bonn, 1923), p. 402.

41. Learsi, Rufus, *Israel. A History of the Jewish people* (Cleveland, 1949), p. 12 ff.
Wensinck, A. J., *Mohammed en de Joden te Medina* (Leiden, 1928), p. 41 ff.
Watt, op. cit., p. 192, n. 1 and 2.

42. Macdonald, D. B., *The Religious Attitude and Life in Islam* (Chicago, 1908), p. 243.

43. Buhl, Frants, Art. '*hanîf*', *Enc. of Islam*, Vol. II, p. 258.
Moubarac, op. cit., pp. 151–61.
* Watt, W. Montgomery, *Muhammad at Mecca* (Clarendon Press, Oxford, 1926), p. 162 ff.
Watt, *Muhammad at Medina*, p. 205.

44. See Art. '*prosèlutos*', *Th.W.N.T.*, VI, p. 741.
Strack, H. L., and Billerbeck, P., *Kommentar zum Neuen Testament aus Talmud und Midrasch*, II (2nd edn., 1956), pp. 719–721.
Kuhn, *Ursprung* etc., p. 219 f.

45. Wensinck, op. cit., p. 54 ff.
Blachère, op. cit., annot. on Sura IX:30.
Casanova, P., Art. '*Idrîs et 'Ouzair*' (*Journal Asiatique*, Vol. 205, 1924, pp. 356–60).

46. Speyer, H., Art. '*Yāhūd(i)*', *Enc. of Islam*, Vol. IV, p. 1146.
Blachère, op. cit., Index, *sub voce* 'Fils d'Israël'.

47. Schwally, F., *Geschichte des Qorāns*, I (Leipzig, 1909), p. 175, footnote K.
Andreae, Tor, *Der Ursprung des Islams und das Christentum* (Upsala/

Stockholm, 1926), p. 4, supposes the *qiblah* in Mecca to have been faced towards the East.

48. Bell, op. cit., Sura II:136–47.

49. Goeje, M. J. de, (ed.), *Annales quot scripsit Abu Djafar Mohammed ibu Djarir at-Tabarī*, Vol. I, (Leiden, 1879–1901), p. 1280.
Cf. Schoy, C., Art. '*kibla*', *Enc of Islam*, Vol. II, p. 985.

50. Tabarī, I:378; II:13.

51. Beck, E., 'Die Gestalt des Abraham am Wendepunkt der Entwicklung Muhammads'. Analysis of S. II:118 (124)–135 (140) (*Le Muséon*, 65, 1952, pp. 73–94).
Bijlefeld, op. cit., p. 126 ff.

52. Goldziher, I., *Zeitschr. Deutschen Morgenl. Gesellsch.*, 57, 398.

53. Macdonald, D. B., Art. 'Allāh', *Enc. of Islam*, Vol. I, p. 302.

54. Wensinck, A. J., Art. '*Ka'ba*', *Enc. of Islam*, Vol. II, p. 584.

55. Wensinck, A. J., 'The Navel of the Earth' (Verh. Kon. Akad. v. Wetensch. Afd. Letterk., Nieuwe Reeks, XVII, No. 1, p. 60 ff.).
Wensinck, Art. '*Ka'ba*', IVth part, *Enc. of Islam*, Vol. II, p. 584 ff.

56. Walker, J., Art. '*Kubba al-Sakhra*', *Enc. of Islam*.

57. Schrieke, B., Art. '*Isrā*'', *Enc. of Islam*, Vol. II, p. 553.
Horovitz, J., Art. '*Mi'rādj*', *Enc. of Islam*, Vol. III, p. 505.
Buhl, Frants, Art. '*al-Kuds*', *Enc. of Islam*, Vol. II, p. 1094.

58. Bell, R., *The Origin of Islam in its Christian Environment* (London, 1926), p. 124 f.
Watt, *Muhammad at Medina*, p. 203.

59. Wensinck, *Mohammed en de Joden* etc., p. 138 ff.
Muir, W., *The Life of Mahomet and History of Islam* (London, 1858–61), Vol. III, p. 51 ff.

60. Wellhausen, *Reste arabische Heidentums*, etc., pp. 94–101.

61. Caetani (*Annali dell'Islam*, Vol. I (Milan, 1905), Introduction, p. 431 *et seq.*), calculating the date of 'Ashûrâ, rejects the probability that this day originally, during the period of conterminating with the Jewish day 10th Tishri, should have been celebrated at 10th Muharram. Therefore we are forced, *a fortiori*, to look for an explanation of the reason why 'Ashûrâ was put at 10th Muharram.

62. Gotein, F., *Zur Entstehung des Ramaḍān* (*Der Islam*, XVIII, 1929, p. 189 ff.).

63. Plessner, M., Art. '*Ramaḍān*', *Enc. of Islam*, Vol. III, p. 1111.

64. Jeffery, Arthur, *The Foreign Vocabulary of the Qur'ān* (Baroda, 1938), p. 225 ff.

65. Bell, R., *Introduction to the Qur'ān* (Edinburgh, 1953), p. 137 f.

66. Horovitz, J., *Koranische Untersuchungen* (Berlin/Leipzig, 1926), p. 52.

67. Paret, R., Art. '*Umma*', *Enc. of Islam*, Vol. IV, p. 1015.

68. Thomas, Bertram, *The Arabs* (London, 1937), p. 125.

69. Watt, op. cit., p. 232.

70. Watt, op. cit., p. 245 f.

71. Geiger, Abraham, *Das Judenthum und seine Geschichte* (Breslau, 1865–71), p. 150.

*72. Geiger, op. cit., p. 109.

*73. Köhler, Kaufman, *Systematischen Theologie des Judentums* (Leipzig, 1910), p. 325.

74. Jocz, Jacob, *The Jewish People and Jesus Christ* (London, 1949), p. 12.
Judah, ha-Levi, *Kitab al Khazari*, IV, 10 and 11.
Maimonides, *Mishneh Torah*, Kings 11:4; *Responsa* (edn. Leipzig) § 58.
Cf. *Judaism and Christianity*, Essays presented to P. P. Levertoff, ed.
L. Gillet (London, 1940), p. 233.
Cf. Montefiore, C. G., *Rabbinic Literature and Gospel Teachings* (In Spirit and Truth) (London, 1930), p. 330.

75. Jocz, op. cit., p. 13 f.
Cf. Bloch, Joseph, *Israel und die Völker* (Berlin, 1922), pp. 50–64.

76. Learsi, op. cit., p. 53.

77. Caetani, *Annali dell'Islam*, Vol. II, pp. 831–61.
Becker, C. H., *Cambridge Medieval History* (Cambridge, 1911–), Vol. II, Ch. 9.

78. Hitti, Philip K., *History of the Arabs* (Macmillan, London, 1946), p. 145 f.

*79. Hitti, op. cit., p. 174 f.

80. Becker, C. H., 'Der Islam im Rahmen einer allgemeinen Kultur-geschichte', *Zeitschr. Deutschen Morgenl. Gesellsch.*, 76, 1922, 23 = *Islamstudien*, I (Leipzig, 1924).

81. Grousset, R., *Orient und Okzident im geistigen Austausch* (Stuttgart, 1955), p. 30.

82. Kraemer, Jörg, *Das Problem der islamischen Kulturgeschichte* (Tübingen, 1959), p. 36.

83. Pirenne, Henri, *Mohammed and Charlemagne* (London, 1939), pp. 140 ff., 284 f.
Cf. Dennett, Daniel C., 'Pirenne and Muhammad' (*Speculum*, XIII, 1948, p. 165 f., with bibliography).

84. Fischer, Jürgen, *Oriens-Occidens-Europa, Begriff und Gedanke 'Europa' in der späten Antike und in frühen Mittelalter* (Wiesbaden, 1957), p. 35 f.

85. Fischer, op. cit., pp. 60–74.

86. Pirenne, op. cit., p. 144.

87. Pirenne, H., *Histoire de l'Europe des invasions au XVIᵉ siècle* (Paris/Brussels, 1936), p. 2 (*A History of Europe from the Invasions to the Sixteenth Century*, New York, 1939).
Fischer, op. cit., p. 47 ff.

88. *De Civitate Dei*, XVI, 2, 17.
Kamlah, W., *Apokalypse und Geschichtstheologie* (Göttingen, 1935), p. 10.
Vogt, J., 'Orbis Romanus—Zur Terminologie des römischen Im-perialismus' (*Philosophie und Geschichte*, 22, Tübingen, 1929), p. 29.
Fischer, op. cit., pp. 10–19.

89. Rosenstock, E., 'Die Furt der Franken und das Schisma' in *Das Alter der Kirche*, ed. by E. Rosenstock and J. Wittig, I (Berlin, 1927), p. 513 ff.

90. Grunebaum, G. E. von, *Medieval Islam. A Study in Cultural Orientation* (Chicago, 1946), p. 60.

*91. Wright, J. K., *The Geographical Lore of the Time of the Crusades* (American Geographical Society, New York, 1925), pp. 260, 234.

92. Latourette, Kenneth Scott, *A History of the Expansion of Christianity*, Vol. VII (Eyre & Spottiswoode, London, 1941, and Harper & Row, Inc., New York, 1945), p. 418.

93. Panikkar, K. M., *Asia and Western Dominance* (Allen & Unwin, London, 1953), p. 480.

94. Rougemont, Denis de, *Man's Western Quest* (London, 1957), p. 105 ff.

*95. Latourette, op. cit., Vol. IV, p. 19.

*96. Panikkar, op. cit., pp. 479, 454 ff.

Chapter Six

1. Harnack, Adolf, *Lehrbuch der Dogmengeschichte*, I (Tübingen, 1909), p. 147.

2. Harnack, op. cit., pp. 147, 151.

3. Latte, Kurt, *Die Religion der Römer und der Synkretismus der Kaiserzeit. Religiongeschichtliches Lesebuch*, ed. by A. Bertholet (Tübingen, 2nd edn., 1927), pp. 89–92.

4. Berkhof, H., *De Kerk en de Keizer* (Amsterdam, 1946).

5. Lietzmann, H., 'Der Glaube Konstantins der Grossen' (Sitzungsberichte der Preussischen Akademie der Wissenschaften zu Berlin, 1937, Phil.-hist. Klasse, pp. 263-75); and *Geschichte der Alten Kirche*, Vol. III (Berlin, 1938), pp. 141–53.

6. Berkhof, op. cit., p. 76 ff.

*7. Athanasius, 'Historia Arianorum' in *Athanasius, Werke*, 1, ed. H.-G. Opitz (Berlin, 1940), 34, 1.
Cf. Berkhof, op. cit., p. 98.

*8. Athanasius, op. cit., 76, 1.

*9. Ambrosius, 'Sermo contra Auxentium de basilicis tradentis' (*Migne*, P. L., Vol. XVI, col. 1007–1018).

10. This purpose is explicitly stated by Augustine at the beginning of his *Retractiones*.

11. Cf. Peterson, *Der Monotheismus als politisches Problem. Ein Beitrag zur Geschichte der politischen Theologie im Imperium Romanum* (Leipzig, 1935), p. 90 ff.

12. Boissier, Gaston, *La fin du Paganisme* (Paris, 1891), VI, 4, 2.

13. Augustine, *De Civitate Dei*, I, 30 f., 1; II, 18, 1; II, 21, 1.
Cf. Kamlah, Wilhelm, *Christentum und Geschichtlichkeit. Untersuchung zur Enstehung des Christentums und zu Augustins 'Bürgerschaft Gottes'* (Cologne, 1951), p. 178.

14. *De Civitate Dei*, I, 1, 1; I, 7, 1, 15, 1; III, 31, 1; V, 23, 1 etc.; V, 25.

15. Neumann, K. J., *Hippolytus vom Rom in seiner Stellung zu Staat und Welt* (Leipzig, 1902), pp. 26 f., 34 f., 58.

16. *De Civitate Dei*, XV, 5, 2.

17. Ehrenberg, Victor, *Ost und West: Studien zur geschichtlichen Problematik der Antike* (Brünn, 1935).

18. Goldammer, Kurt, 'Die Welt des Heiligen im Bilde des Gottherrschers', in *The Sacral Kingship* (Leiden, 1959), p. 513 ff.

19. Bloch, Marc, *Les rois thaumaturges. Etude sur le caractère surnaturel attribué à la puissance royale particulièrement en France et en Angleterre* (Publications de la Faculté des Lettres de l'Univ. de Strasbourg, 19, Paris/Strasbourg 1924), p. 55 ff.

*20. Eichmann, Eduard, 'Von Kaisergewandung im Mittelalter' (*Historisches Jahrbuch*, 58, 1938, p. 268 ff.).

21. Lilienfein, H., *Die Anschauung von Staat und Kirche im Reich der Karolinger* (Heidelberg, 1902), pp. 96, 109, 146.

22. Kern, Fritz, *Gottesgnadentum und Widerstandsrecht im früheren Mittelalter. Zur Entwicklungsgeschichte der Monarchie* (Leipzig, 1914), p. 115.

23. Heiler, Friedrich, 'Fortleben und Wandlungen des Antiken Gottkönigtums im Christentum' in *The Sacral Kingship*, pp. 543, 578 ff.

24. Linton, Ralph, *The Tree of Culture* (New York, 1955), p. 360 ff.

25. Wittfogel, K., *Oriental Despotism. A Comparative Study of Total Power* (New Haven, 1957), p. 197.

26. Wittfogel, op. cit., p. 199.

27. MacLeod, W. C., *The Origin and History of Politics* (New York, 1931), p. 194.

28. Petit-Dutaillis, Ch., *The Feudal Monarchy in France and England*, trans. E. O. Hunt (London, 1936), p. 92.

29. Pirenne, Henri, *Mohammed and Charlemagne* (New York, 1957), p. 147 ff.

*30. Pirenne, Henri, *Medieval Cities* (University Press, Princeton, 1925), p. 136 f.

31. Coulanges, Fustel de, *The Ancient City* (New York, 1956), pp. 134 ff., 219 ff.

32. Weber, Max, *Wirtschaft und Gesellschaft, Grundriss der Sozialokonomik* III (Tübingen, 1925), p. 529.

33. Rosenstock-Huessy, E., *Die Europäischen Revolutionen und der Charakter der Nationen* (Stuttgart/Cologne, 1951), p. 11 f.; American edition *Out of Revolution* (New York, 1938).

34. Burckhardt, J., *Die Kultur der Renaissance in Italien* (Berlin, 1928), p. 2 f.

35. Haskins, C. H., 'England and Sicily in the Twelfth Century' (*English Historical Review*, XXVI, London, 1911, pp. 435 ff, 664 ff.).

36. MacLeod, op. cit., p. 341 ff.

37. Burckhardt, op. cit., p. 87 f.

38. Cf. Niebuhr, H. Richard, *Christ and Culture* (London, 1952), p. 181.

39. Cf. Troeltsch, Ernst, *Die Soziallehren des christlichen Kirchen und Gruppen* (Tübingen, 1919), p. 444.

40. Troeltsch, op. cit., p. 642.
    Cf. Choisy, J. E., *L'état chrétien calviniste à Genève aux temps de Théodore de Bèze* (Geneva, 1902), p. 516 f.

41. Calvin, J., *Christianae Religionis Institutio*, IV, Ch. 20, § 30 f.

42. Troeltsch, op. cit., p. 666.
    Beyerhaus, G., *Studien zur Staatsanschauung Calvins* (Neue Beiträge, Herausgegeben von Bonwetsch und Seeberg, VII, 1910), p. 108 ff.

43. Kuyper, Abraham, *Calvinism* (Stone Lectures) (London, 1932).
    Choisy, op. cit.

44. Weber, Max, *Gesammelte Aufsätze zur Religionssoziologie*, I (Tübingen, 1920), pp. 17–206; English translation *The Protestant Ethic and the Spirit of Capitalism* (Allen & Unwin, London, 1930).
    For criticism on Weber's thesis see:
    Weber, op. cit., p. 17, note 1;
    Troeltsch, op. cit., p. 704, note 381;
    Tawney, R. H., *Religion and the Rise of Capitalism* (John Murray, London, 1926), p. VII ff.; Ch. IV, note 32.

*45. Weber, op. cit., p. 17 (English translation).

46. Weber, op. cit., p. 46 (English translation).

*47. Tawney, op. cit., Ch. IV, note 32.

48. Robertson, H. M., *Aspects of the Rise of Economic Individualism* (Cambridge, 1933), p. 57 ff.

49. Tawney, op. cit., p. 116.

*50. Weber, op. cit., p. 203 f.

*51. Cramb, J. A., *The Origins and Destiny of Imperial Britain* (John Murray, London, 1915), p. 7 f.

*52. Gardiner, Samuel Rawson, *Cromwell's Place in History* (Longmans, Green, London, 1897), pp. 114, 116.

53. Rosenstock-Huessy, op. cit., p. 300.

*54. Kohn, Hans, *The Idea of Nationalism, A Study in its Origins and Background* (Macmillan Co., New York, 1945), p. 174 ff.
Cf. *The Letters and Speeches of Oliver Cromwell, with elucidations by Thomas Carlyle*, ed. Sophia Lomas (London, 1904), Vol. II, pp. 290 f., 340 f.; Vol. III, pp. 11–13.

*55. Egerton, Hugh E., *A Short History of British Colonial Policy* (Methuen, London, 1897), p. 476.

56. Rosenstock-Huessy, op. cit., p. 270 ff.

57. Kohn, op. cit., p. 174.

58. Sombart, W., *Der Moderne Kapitalismus*, Vol. II, 2 (Leipzig, 1902), p. 1137 ff.

*59. Laski, H. D., *Communist Manifesto: Socialist Landmark* (Allen & Unwin, London, 1951), pp. 122–3. (Here quoted from 1921 imprint.)

60. Latourette, Kenneth Scott, *A History of the Expansion of Christianity*, Vol. IV (5th edn., 1941), p. 382 f.

*61. Jefferson, Thomas, *The Writings of*, ed. H. A. Washington, Vol. VII (Riker, Thorne & Co., Washington, 1853–4), p. 450.
Cf. Kohn, op. cit., p. 311.

*62. Kohn, op. cit., p. 270.

63. Kohn, op. cit., p. 180.

64. Schneider, Herbert W., 'Christian Theocracy and Hobbes's "Mortal God" ' in *The Sacral Kingship*, p. 627.

*65. Whitehead, A. N., *Science and the Modern World* (University Press, Cambridge, 1926), p. 4.

*66. Farrington, B., *Greek Science. Its Meaning for Us*, Vol. I (Penguin, London, 1949), p. 32 f.

67. Farrington, op. cit., II, pp. 130, 142.

68. Whitehead, op. cit., p. 18.

69. Weizsäcker, C. F. von, *Zum Weltbild der Physik* (Stuttgart, 6th edn., 1954), p. 125.

70. Berg, J. H. van den, *Het menselijk lichaam* (Nijkerk, 1959), p. 31.

*71. Farrington, op. cit., II, p. 68.

*72. Whitehead, op. cit., pp. 17–18.

*73. Northrop, F. S. C., *The Meeting of East and West* (Macmillan Co., New York, 1946), p. 366.

74. Weizsäcker, op. cit., p. 129 ff.

*75. Farrington, op. cit., II, p. 169.
76. Jaspers, Karl, *Vom Ursprung und Ziel der Geschichte* (Munich, 1949), p. 90 ff.
77. Gogarten, Friedrich, *Verhängnis und Hoffnung der Neuzeit. Die Säkularisierung als theologisches Problem* (Stuttgart, 1953).
78. Wendel, Adolf, *Säkularisierung in Israels Kultur* (Gütersloh, 1934).
79. Gogarten, op. cit., p. 138 ff.
*80. Weizsäcker, op. cit., p. 265.
*81. Marx, Karl, 'Die Frühschriften', ed. by Landshut and Mayer, *Der historische Materialismus*, I (Leipzig, 1932), p. 279.
*82. Rühle, Otto, *Karl Marx, Leben und Werk* (Avalun, Hellerau, 1928), p. 42. Banning, W., *Karl Marx* (Utrecht, 1960), p. 60.
*83. Feuerbach, L., *Sämmtliche Werke*, Vol. 2 (Wigand, Leipzig, 1846), p. 410. Marx, op. cit., p. 265.
84. Berdiajew, Nikolai, *Beteekenis en oorsprong van het Russische communisme* (Amsterdam, 1948); N. Berdyaev, *The Russian Idea* (London, 1947).
85. Berdiajew, op. cit., p. 125.
*86. Wight, Martin, 'The Church, Russia and the West' (*The Ecumenical Review*, Vol. I, No. 1, 1948, p. 42).
87. Berdiajew, op. cit., p. 130.
88. Danilevsky, N. Y., *Russland und Europa* (1867, German trans. by Karl Nötzel, Stuttgart/Berlin, 1920).
Cf. Locher, Th. J. G., 'Een Russische voorloper van Spengler' (*Verslag van het vierde congres van nederlandse historici. 1938*, pp. 23–7).
89. Halecki, Oskar, *The Limits and Divisions of European History* (London/ New York, 1950), p. 88.
90. Halecki, op. cit., p. 91 ff.
91. Ranke, L. von, *Geschichten der romanischen und germanischen Völker von 1494 bis 1514* (Berlin, 1825); Engl. trans. by P. A. Ashworth (London, 1887), p. 1 ff.
Pirenne, Henri, *A History of Europe from the Invasions to the Sixteenth Century* (New York, 1939), p. 466.
Vernadsky, G., 'On some parallel trends in Russian and Turkish history' (Transactions of the Connecticut Academy of Arts and Sciences, 36, 1945, p. 25 ff.).
Vernadsky, G., *Political and Diplomatic History of Russia* (Boston, 1936), p. 170 ff.
92. Halecki, op. cit., p. 98 f.
93. Many passages in *Das Kapital*, *Theorien über den Mehrwert* and *Zur Kritik der politischen Ökonomie*.
94. Wittfogel, op. cit., p. 376 ff.
95. Monnerot, Jules, *Sociologie du Communisme* (Paris, 1949).

Chapter Seven

*1. Panikkar, K. M., *Asia and Western Dominance* (Allen & Unwin, London, 1953), p. 479.
*2. Marx, Karl, *Articles on India*, introd. by R. P. Dutt (People's Publishing House, Bombay, 1951), p. 12.
3. Mukerjee, R., *Land Problems in India* (London, 1933), pp. 16, 36.

4. Desai, A. R., *Social Background of Indian Nationalism* (Bombay, 1948), Ch. III.

5. Farquhar, J. N., *Modern Religious Movements in India* (London, 1929), p. 52 ff.
   Sarma, D. S., *Studies in the Renaissance of Hinduism in the Nineteenth and Twentieth Centuries* (Benares, 1944), p. 112 ff.
   Krämer, Adelheid, *Christus und Christentum im Denken des modernen Hinduismus* (Bonn, 1958), p. 33 ff.

6. Held, G. J., *The Mahābhārata. An Ethnological Study* (London/Amsterdam, 1935), p. 335.

7. Devanandan, P. D., 'Caste, the Christian and the Nation in India Today' (*The Ecumenical Review*, Vol. XI, No. 3, p. 273).

8. Panikkar, K. M., *Hindu Society at the Crossroads* (Bombay/Calcutta, 1955).

9. *Revolution and Reconstruction* (The Federal Council of the S.C.M. of India, Pakistan and Ceylon, Bangalore, 1957), p. 77.

10. Sankaranaryanan, P., 'Human Person, Society and State. The Classical Hindu Approach' in *Human Person, Society and State* (Bangalore, 1957), p. 56 ff.
    Panikkar, K. M., *The State and the Citizen* (Bombay, 1956), p. 119.

*11. Radhakrishnan, S., *The Hindu View of Life* (Allen & Unwin, London, 1927, and Macmillan Co., New York), p. 77.

12. Devanandan, P. D., 'The Religious and Spiritual Climate of India Today' (*The Ecumenical Review*, Vol. VIII, No. 3, p. 308 f.).

13. Devanandan, P. D., 'The Renaissance of Hinduism in India' (*The Ecumenical Review*, Vol. XI, No. 1, p. 55).

14. Devanandan, P. D., *The Gospel and Renascent Hinduism*, I.M.C. Research Pamphlet, No. 8 (London, 1959), p. 14.

*15. Devanandan, P. D., and Thomas, M. M., *India's Quest for Democracy* (Y.M.C.A. Publishing House, Calcutta, 1955), pp. 52–3.

16. Fitzgerald, C. P., *China. A Short Cultural History* (Cresset Press, London, 1935), p. 470.

17. Sansom, G. B., *The Western World and Japan* (London, 1950), pp. 108, 150 ff.

18. Legge, J., *The Chinese Classics* (Hong Kong/London, 1865), III, Pt. II, p. 292.
    Franke, O., *Geschichte des Chinesischen Reiches* (Berlin/Leipzig, 1930–52), II, p. 4 f.

19. Eberhardt, W., *Conquerors and Rulers* (Leiden, 1952), Ch. I, III.

20. Foster, John, 'The Christian Origins of the Taiping Rebellion' (*The International Review of Missions*, Vol. XL, No. 158, April, 1951, p. 156 ff.).
    Boardman, E. P., *Christian Influence upon the Ideology of the T'ai-p'ing Rebellion, 1851–1864* (Madison, Wisc., 1952).

21. Franke, W., *Das Jahrhundert der Chinesischen Revolution* (Munich, 1958), Ch. II, 1.

*22. Foster, op. cit., p. 157.

*23. Cf. Meadows, T. T., *The Chinese and their Rebellions* (London, 1856), p. 446.
    Cf. Foster, op. cit., p. 167.

*24. Weber, Max, *Gesammelte Aufsätze zur Religionssoziologie*, I (Tübingen, 1920), p. 509.

*25. Fitzgerald, op. cit., p. 578.

*26. Latourette, Kenneth Scott, *A History of Modern China* (Penguin, London, 1954), p. 79.

 27. 'First Thoughts on the Débâcle of Christian Missions in China' in *The International Review of Missions*, Vol. XL, No. 160, p. 411 ff.
Paton, David M., *Christian Missions and the Judgment of God* (London, 1953).

 28. Leeuwen, A. Th. van, 'The Response of Islam to the Impact of the West' in *The Missionary Church in East and West*, ed. by C. C. West and D. M. Paton (London, 1959).

 29. Heyd, Uriel, *Foundation of Turkish Nationalism. The Life and Teachings of Ziya Gökalp* (London, 1950).

*30. Iqbal, Mohammad, *The Reconstruction of Religious Thought in Islam* (Clarendon Press, Oxford, 1934), pp. 151–5.

*31. Iqbal, op. cit., p. 147.

 32. Adams, C. C., *Islam and Modernism in Egypt* (London, 1933), p. 259 ff.

 33. Anderson, J. N. D., *Islamic Law in the Modern World* (London, 1959).

 34. Smith, William Cantwell, *Modern Islam in India* (London, 1946).

 35. Gibb, H. A. R., *Modern Trends in Islam* (Chicago, 1945), p. 47.

 36. Dorman, H. G., *Toward Understanding Islam* (New York, 1948), p. 71 ff.

 37. Sayyid Qutb, *Al- 'adálat al- Ijtimá'iyyah fî-l-Islâm* (*Social Justice in Islam*) (Cairo, 1945), trans. from the Arabic by John B. Hardie (Washington, 1953), p. 278 f.
Haykal, Muhammad Hussain, *Life of Muhammad* (Cairo, 1935).
Cragg, Kenneth, *The Call of the Minaret* (New York, 1956), pp. 247, 253.

 38. Prawiranegara, Sjafruddin, *Islam dalam pergolakan dunia* (*Islam amid the Tribulations of the World*) (Bandung, 1949).

 39. Husain Muhammad Kāmil, *Qaryah Zālimah* (*City of Oppression*) (Cairo, 1954) (trans. by Kenneth Cragg).

 40. Sansom, op. cit., p. 527.

Chapter Eight

*1. Albright, W. F., *From the Stone Age to Christianity* (John Hopkins Press, Baltimore, 1946), p. 311.

*2. *The Authority of the Faith*, International Missionary Council, Madras Series, Vol. I (New York, 1939), p. 43.

*3. Introduction by Dr Saba Habachy to *Islamic Law in the Modern World*, by J. N. D. Anderson (Stevens, London, 1959, and New York University Press).

 4. Weizsäcker, C. F. von, *Zum Weltbild der Physik* (Stuttgart, 6th edn., 1954), p. 264 f.

*5. Cromer, Earl of, *Modern Egypt*, Vol. II (Macmillan, London, 1908), p. 229.

*6. Davis, J. Merle, *New Buildings on Old Foundations* (International Missionary Council, New York/London, 1947), p. 233.

 7. Davis, op. cit., p. 232 f.

*8. Rosenne, S., 'The Influence of Judaism on the Development of International Law' (in *Netherlands International Law Review*, Sijthoff, Leiden, 1958, pp. 119–149, 120).

*9. Verzijl, J. H. W., 'Western European Influence on the Foundation of International Law' (in *International Relations*, I, 1955, pp. 137–146, 137). Cf. Röling, B.V.A., *International Law in an Expanded World* (Djambatan, Amsterdam, 1960), p. 10.

10. Verzijl, op. cit., p. 146.

11. Schwarzenberger, G., 'The Standard of Civilisation in International Law' (in *Current Legal Problems*, Vol. 8, London, 1955, pp. 212–234, 221). Cf. Röling, op. cit., p. 18.

12. Toynbee, Arnold J., *Civilization on Trial* (New York, 1948), Ch. IX.

*13. Röling, op. cit., p. 83.

*14. Röling, op. cit., pp. 122, 124 f.

15. Brand, W., *The Struggle for a Higher Standard of Living. The Problem of the Undeveloped Countries* (The Hague, 1958), p. 332 ff.

16. Myrdal, Gunnar Karl, *An International Economy* (New York, 1956), p. 165 f.

*17. Antonius, George, *The Arab Awakening* (Hamish Hamilton, London, 1938), p. 386.

Bible References

Index